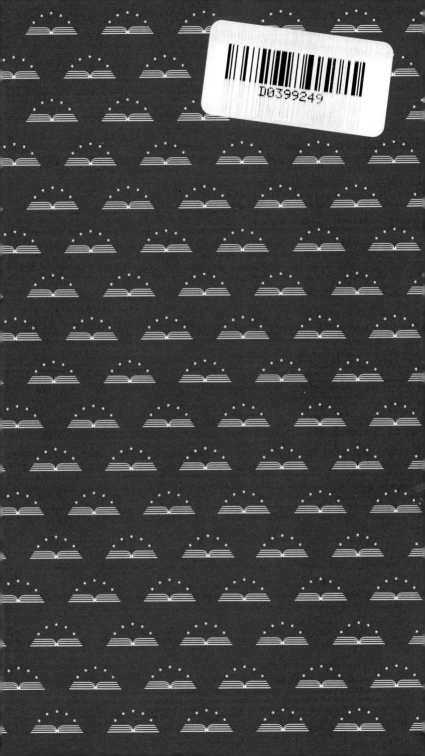

REPORTING WORLD WAR II
PART TWO

# REPORTING WORLD WAR II

PART TWO

AMERICAN JOURNALISM 1944–1946

THE LIBRARY OF AMERICA

Some of the material in this volume is reprinted with permission of the
holders of copyright and publications rights. Acknowledgments can be
found on page 931. Cartography on pages 895–911 © Richard Natkiel, 1995.

The paper used in this publication meets the
minimum requirements of the American National Standard for
Information Sciences—Permanence of Paper for Printed
Library Materials, ANSI Z39.48—1984.

Distributed to the trade in the United States
by Penguin Books USA Inc
and in Canada by Penguin Books Canada Ltd.

Library of Congress Catalog Number: 94–45463
For cataloging information, see end of Index.
ISBN: 1–883011–05–1

First Printing
The Library of America–78

Manufactured in the United States of America

Advisory Board for *Reporting World War II*

# Contents

# The Italian Campaign: "Waiting for the Next Attack"

by Ernie Pyle

### "Those Lulls That Sometimes Come in War"

IN ITALY, Feb. 16 — (by wireless) — When I joined "X" company it was in one of those lulls that sometimes come in war. The company was still "in the lines," as you say, but not actually fighting.

They had taken a town a few days before, and since then had been merely waiting for the next attack. We moved forward twice while I was with them, always in night marches, and on the last move the company went into battle again.

These intervals give the soldiers time to restore their gear and recuperate their spirits. Usually they come weeks apart.

A regiment will be bivouacked over an area a mile or more square, with the men in foxholes under olive trees, and the company, battalion and regimental command posts set up in farmhouses.

\*     \*     \*

In areas recently passed over by battles the towns have been largely evacuated — in fact practically all of them are mere heaps of rubble from bombing and shelling — and no stores are open. There is little chance of buying wine.

But this regiment had gone sniffing into cellars in a depopulated town and turned up with all kinds of exotic liquors which they dug out of the rubble.

The result was that you could make a tour on foot of a dozen company and battalion command posts around the perimeter of the town and in nearly every one discover a shelf full of the finest stuff imaginable.

It was ironic to walk into a half-demolished building and find a command post set up in the remaining rooms, with soldiers sitting in front of a crackling fireplace, and at 10 o'clock in the morning, with enemy shell bursts making the old building tremble, be offered your choice of cherry, peach, apricot and half a dozen other varieties of fine brandy out of fancy bottles. But I must say a windfall like that doesn't come often.

*     *     *

Our company command post consisted of one table, one chair and one telephone, in a second-story room of a stone farmhouse. In most of these two-story farmhouses the stairway goes up the outside. You hang blankets at the door for blackout, and burn candles.

Five platoons of the company were bivouacked in olive orchards in a circle around the farmhouse, the farthest foxhole being not more than 200 yards away. Some soldiers just dug regular foxholes and put their blankets at the bottom. During the day they would sit at the edge of the hole cleaning guns, writing letters or just talking, and at night they would sleep at the bottom of the foxhole. Others dug more elaborate places.

I've always been struck by the work some men will put into a home as temporary as a foxhole. I've been with men in this company who would arrive at a new bivouac at midnight, dig a hole just big enough to sleep in the rest of the night, then work all the next day on a deep, elaborate, roofed-over foxhole, even though they knew they had to leave the same evening and never see that hole again.

In the olive groves throughout this bitter Cassino area there are pitiful testimonials to close-up warfare. In our grove I don't believe there was a single one of the thousands of old trees that hadn't at least one bullet scar in it. Knocked-off branches littered the ground. Some trees were cut clear down by shells. The stone walls had shell gaps every so often, and every standing thing was bullet-pocked.

You couldn't walk 50 feet without hitting a shell or bomb crater. Every house and shed had at least a corner knocked off.

*     *     *

Some soldiers were sleeping in the haymow of a stone barn. They had to get up into it via a stepladder they had pieced together, because the steps had been blown away. Between the house and the barn ran a footpath on a sort of ledge. Our men had been caught there that first night by a tank in the valley below firing at them point-blank. One soldier had been instantly killed, and as we walked along the path a few days later his steel helmet was still lying there, bloody and riddled with holes. Another soldier had a leg blown off, but lived.

The men were telling me of a replacement—a green soldier—who joined the company the day after, when this soldier's leg was still lying in the path. The new soldier stopped and stared at it and kept on staring.

The other boys watched him from a distance. They said that when anyone came along the path the new man would move off to one side so as not to be seen. But as soon as they would pass, he would come back and stare, sort of hypnotized. He never said anything about it afterwards, and nobody said anything to him. Somebody buried the leg the next day.

Scripps-Howard wire copy, February 16, 1944

### "The Night Was Full of Distant Warfare"

IN ITALY, Feb. 23—(by wireless)—Our company was alerted for its night march just before suppertime. We got the word about 4 in the afternoon, and we ate at 4:30. Word was passed around to collect 24 hours' field rations at suppertime and a full supply of ammunition.

At chow time the soldiers all held their tin hats crooked in their left arms while holding their mess kits in their right. At the end of the mess line the soldiers put five "C" ration cans into each man's hat and one bar of "D" ration.

After supper, the men rolled their one blanket inside their one shelter half while there was still light. Early darkness had come before 5:30. It was chilly. A misty rain began to fall. The men just lay or sat in their foxholes under the doubtful shelter of the olive trees.

Full darkness came over the olive grove, the artillery raged and flashed around half the horizon, and the concussion crashed and ran across the sky along the sounding board of the low clouds. We of our little company were swallowed in a great blackness.

We were connected to the war by one field telephone which ran to the battalion command post a quarter mile away. Nobody knew when the marching order would come. We just had to sit there and wait.

*     *     *

There were only two places to get out of the rain. Both were pig sheds dug into the side of a bank by an Italian farmer and stacked over with straw.

Lieut. Jack Sheehy, the company commander, and four enlisted men and I crawled into one and dragged the phone in after us. A few sergeants went into the other.

We lay down on the ground there in the pig shed. We had on our heavy coats but the chill came through like anything. The lieutenant had an extra blanket which he carried unrolled when not actually in battle, so he spread it out and he and I both sat under it. We huddled against each other and became a little warmer.

The lieutenant said, "I used to read your column back home, and I never supposed we'd ever meet. Imagine us lying together here on the ground in Italy."

Then we talked a little while in low tones, but pretty soon somebody started to snore and before long all of us were asleep although it still was only 7 o'clock.

Every now and then the lieutenant would phone battalion to see if any orders had come yet. Finally he was told the line to regiment was out.

Linemen were out in the darkness feeling with their hands, tracing the entire length of the line trying to find the break. Around 9 o'clock it was open again. Still no marching orders came.

A dark form appeared fairly silhouetted in the open end of the shed and asked if Lieutenant Sheehy was there. The lieutenant answered yes.

"Can the men unroll their blankets?" the form asked. "They're wet and cold."

The lieutenant thought a moment and then he said, "No, better not. We should get the word to go any minute now, certainly within half an hour. They better keep them rolled." The form said, "Yes, sir," and merged back into the darkness.

By 10 everybody in the shed had awakened from their nap. Our grove was deathly still, as though no one existed in it, for the night was full of distant warfare.

Now and then we'd get clear under the blanket and light a cigarette and hide it under the blanket when we puffed it. Over on the far hillside where the Germans were we could see a distant light. We finally decided it was probably a lamp in some unwitting Italian farmhouse.

*      *      *

For a little while there was a sudden splurge of flares in the distance. The first was orange and then came some in green, and then a white and then some more orange ones. Our soldiers couldn't tell whether they were German or ours.

Between flashes of artillery we could hear quite loud blasts of machine guns. Even I can distinguish between a German machine gun and ours for theirs is much faster.

Machine guns are rarely fired except in flashes, so the barrel won't get too hot, but once some jerry just held the trigger down and let her roll for about fifteen seconds. "Boy, he'll have to put on a new barrel after that one," a soldier said.

The time dragged on and we grew colder and stiffer. At last, nearly at midnight, the phone rang in the stillness of our pigshed. It was the order to go.

One of the boys said, "It's going to be a bitch of a thing to move. The ground is slick and you can't see your hand in front of you."

One sergeant went out to start the word for the company to assemble. Another disconnected the field telephone and carried it under his arm. Everybody wrestled into the harness of his heavy packs.

"Assemble down by the kitchen tent," the lieutenant told the first sergeant. "Platoons will form in this order—headquarters, third, first, second, and heavy weapons. Let's go."

The first sergeant moved off. I moved after him. The first two steps were fine. On the third step I went down into a ditch and said a bad word. That's the way it was with everybody all the rest of the night.

Scripps-Howard wire copy, February 23, 1944

*"A Certain Fundamental Appreciation for the Ridiculous"*

IN ITALY, Feb. 24—(by wireless)—After the marching order came it took our company about 15 minutes to get itself together, with the head of the line assembled at the appointed place in front of the kitchen tent at the edge of the olive grove.

It was midnight. The night was utterly black. It was the dark of the moon, and thick, low clouds further darkened the sky. "In two years overseas, this is the blackest night we've ever moved," one soldier said.

With a couple of others, I felt my way from our pig shed down to where we thought the kitchen tent was. We knew we were near it, but we couldn't see it.

"It's up ahead about 50 feet," one soldier said.

I butted in and said, "No, it's over to the right about 30 feet."

Just at that moment a flash of fire from one of our nearby cannon brightened the countryside for a split second, and we saw the tent. It was six feet in front of us. That's how dark it was.

\*        \*        \*

One by one the platoon leaders felt their way up to the head of the column, reported their platoons ready in line, and felt their way back. Finally the lieutenant said, "Let's go."

There's no military formality about a night movement of infantry. You don't try to keep step. Nobody says "Forward march," or any of that parade-ground stuff. After a rest the lieutenant says, "All right, let's get along." And everybody gets up and starts.

In trying to get out of the orchard we lost our various places. Finally everybody stopped and called each other's name in order to get reassembled. The lieutenant and the sergeant would call for me occasionally to make sure I was still along.

When we fell in again, I was marching behind Sergt. Vincent Conners of Imogene, Ia. His nickname is "Pete." We hadn't gone far before I realized that the place behind Pete was the best spot in the column for me, for I had found a little secret.

He had a rolled-up map about two feet long stuck horizontally through the pack harness on his back. By keeping close to it, I could just barely make out the vague white shape of this map. And that was my beacon throughout the night.

It was amazing how you could read the terrain ahead of you by the movement of that thin white line. If it went down a couple of inches, I knew Pete had stepped into a hole.

If it went down fast, I knew he had struck a slope. If it went down sideways, I knew his feet were sliding on a slippery slope.

In that split second before my own step followed his, I could correct for whatever had happened to him. As a result I was down only once the whole night.

*   *   *

We were startled to hear some magnificent cussing down at one side, and recognized the company commander's voice. He had stepped right off into a narrow ditch about two feet deep and gone down on his back. Bundled as he was with pack-sacks, he couldn't get out of the ditch. He finally made it on about the third try.

The thing that always amazes me about these inhuman night movements of troops in war areas is how good-natured the men are about it. A certain fundamental appreciation for the ridiculous carries them through. As we slogged along, slipping and crawling and getting muddier and muddier, the soldier behind me said:

"I'm going to write my Congressman about this."

Another soldier answered:

"Hell, I don't even know who my Congressman is. I did three years ago, but I don't now."

The first voice was that of Pfc. Eddie Young, of Pontiac, Mich., the company's runner and message carrier. You get to know voices very quickly. Even though I was a newcomer to the company, there were a dozen men I could name in the blackness by their voices.

Eddie Young's voice especially haunted me. It was fast, and there was a tolerant and gentle humor in it. It was a perfect duplicate of the voice of my friend Ben Robertson, the correspondent who was killed in the Clipper crash at Lisbon a year ago. Whenever Eddie spoke, I could not help feeling that Ben was marching behind me.

The company's first sergeant is Bill Wood of Council Bluffs, Ia., a tall man who carried a heavy pack, and when he fell there was a lot of him to go down. Whenever Bill would fall we'd hear him and stop. And then we could hear him clawing with his feet and getting part way up and then hitting the mud again, and cussing more eloquently with each attempt.

It really was so funny we all had to laugh. When Bill finally got back in line he was good and mad, and he said he couldn't see anything funny about it.

It took us half an hour to feel our way out of the big orchard and down a few feet onto the so-called road, which was actually not much more than a furrow worn by Italian mule carts. There were knee-deep ruts and bucket-sized rocks.

Once on the road, the column halted to let a train of pack mules pass. As we stood there, the thought occurred to all of us:

"It's bad enough to be floundering around on the ground and mud, but now it'll be like groveling in a barnyard."

Scripps-Howard wire copy, February 24, 1944

## "The Trail Was Never Straight"

IN ITALY, Feb. 25 — (by wireless) — At long last our company was really under way on its night movement up into the line. It was just past midnight, and very black. The trail was never straight. It went up and down, across streams, and almost constantly around trees.

How the leaders ever followed it is beyond me. The trees on each side had been marked previously with white tape or toilet paper, but even so we did get lost a couple of times and had to backtrack.

Our pace was miserably slow. The rain had stopped, but the mud was thick. You literally felt each step out with the toes of your boots. Every half hour or so we'd stop and send runners back to see how the tail end of the column was doing. Word came back that they were doing fine, and that we could step up the pace if we wanted to.

Somewhere in the night, both ahead of us and strung out behind us in files, was the rest of our battalion. In fact, the whole regiment of more than 3000 men was moving that night. But we knew nothing about the rest.

Throughout the night the artillery of both sides kept up a steady pounding. When we started, our own guns were loud in our ears. Gradually we drew away from them, and finally the explosion of their shells on German soil was louder than the blast of the guns.

The German shells traveled off at a tangent from us, and we were in no danger. The machine-gun and rifle fire grew louder as our slow procession came nearer the lines. Now and then a front-line flare would light up the sky, and we could see red bullets ricocheting.

The gun blasts made a continuous crashing in the night, yet they were always so brief they didn't give you a revealing view of the trail ahead.

The nagging of artillery eventually gets plain aggravating. It's always worse on a cloudy night, for the sounds crash and reverberate against the low ceiling. One gun blast alone can set off a continuous rebounding of sound against clouds and rocky slopes that will keep going for ten seconds and more.

And on cloudy nights you can hear shells tearing above your head more loudly than on a clear night. In fact, that night the rustle was so magnified that when we stopped to rest and tried to talk you couldn't hear what the other fellow said if a shell was passing overhead. And they were passing almost constantly.

\*     \*     \*

At last we passed through a village and stopped on the far edge to rest while the column leader went into a house for further directions. We had caught up with the mules and drawn alongside them.

One of the muleskinners out in the darkness kept up a long monologue on the subject of the mules being completely done up. Nobody would answer him, and he would go on:

"They're plumb done in. They can't go another foot. If we try to go on, they'll fall down and die."

Finally, some soldier in the darkness told him to shut up. We all privately endorsed his suggestion. But the monologist got huffy and wanted to know who that was. The voice said it wasn't anybody, just a new replacement soldier.

Then the muleskinner waxed sarcastic and louder. He had an objectionable manner, even in the dark.

"Oh, oh!" he said. "So we've got a baby right from the States telling me how to run mules! A tenderfoot, huh? Trying to talk to us veterans! A hero right from the States, huh?"

Whereupon one of the real veterans in our company called out to the gabby skinner:

"Aw, shut up! You probably haven't been overseas two months yourself."

He must have hit the nail on the head, or else his voice carried command, for that's the last we heard of the muleskinner.

\* \* \*

It was almost midnight when the company reached its bivouac area and dug its foxholes into the mud. Always that's the first thing to do. It becomes pure instinct. The drippy, misty dawn found our men dispersed and hidden in the bottom of shallow, muddy depressions of their own digging, eating cold hash from C-ration cans.

They attacked just after dawn. The Germans were only a short distance away. I stayed behind when the company went forward.

In the continuously circulating nature of my job, I may never again see the men in this outfit. But to me they will always be "my" company.

Scripps-Howard wire copy, February 25, 1944

# "Wide Awake on an Island Beachhead"

by Vincent Tubbs

### No Picturesque Battle Scenes in SWP War

WITH MARINES AT CAPE GLOUCESTER—(Via Air Mail)—You can't see much of the battle because this war isn't being fought like battles of old such as Washington crossing the Delaware, the Crossing of the Marne or the charge up San Juan Hill.

There will be no painting of the general standing in the bow of the boat, long line of advancing and defending troops or fiery steeds charging up a hill to come out of this war—not unless the artist has a terrific imagination or is a whale of a liar.

Most of the news about a battle comes from the injured returning from the front, from a soldier being relieved or from an officer who is in on the planning and execution.

You can't see much of a battle even if it's just up the road from you and you go to it yourself. I know because I've just returned from Hill 660, the final objective of marines who established the beachhead in this sector.

Hill 660 is ours. We took it last night after some of the meanest fighting the marines have ever experienced—including the struggle for Guadalcanal. Jap casualties exceeded 3,000; ours were not meagre.

I started to the war, in company with Enoc Waters of the Defender, aboard a GI truck. We walked a while, grabbed another truck, walked some more—traveling thusly over disgustingly bumpy and muddy roads, to the regimental command post of the unit that assaulted the Hill. Here I saw my first Jap—a live one.

We had started away when my brain registered "that's a Jap

you're about to pass." I jerked back to look at him; stopped almost in front of him. He smiled wryly, knowing my thoughts.

We stumbled on toward the war—over tree stumps, mud bogs and debris of every description. A terrific barrage had been laid on this area by our heavy field guns.

"Hello there," a voice to our left called. "Where y'all going?" a marine drawled from beneath a shelter half under which was built an uncovered pallet of small tree limbs.

"Up the hill to the war, if we can make it. What's cooking around here?"

"Oh, nothing much now. We hear they took the hill last night. The fighting was right here yesterday, y'know."

"Yep, looks like it. What sort of outfit is this?"

"We're a mortar platoon—did a little work yesterday. Laid down a barrage up yonder," one of the muddy men said. "There were lots of Japs in here then. Y'all been over by Hill 150?"

"Naw, where's that?"

"Right there," he said, pointing to a small hump behind us. "There's a lot of Jap bodies over there. Seen any?"

"Yeah, we saw one back there at headquarters alive. Next one we see we want him to be dead."

"Well, come on over here; we'll show you some."

What they exhibited defies description, but there was, among other revolting sights, remnants of a Jap machine gunner who had knocked off nearly 20 marines before they got him and they didn't leave much.

On the verge of vomiting, we debated whether we should go further. The marines pointed out a trail, said there was a wire to guide us, conjected the journey little short of 660 yards; so we pushed on.

Before we left, a tiny marine returning from sick bay where he was treated for combat fatigue said there was scuttlebutt about 30 Japs who escaped during last night's action and who were reported headed toward the tank trail which we must ultimately cross.

Nevertheless, we went along bravely, with warnings about snipers ringing in our ears.

One hundred steps along the muddy, mosquito-infested

trail we got a scare. The top of a tree split by shell from one of our 105-mm. guns teetered in the sultry breeze; then toppled to earth with a resounding crash.

We, like veteran bush fighters, dropped to the ground, submerged ourselves in mud a foot deep; then abused everything that grows out of the ground when we discovered we weren't being attacked by the 30 stray Japs.

Plowing along, holding to the wire for both guidance and support, we reached the tank trail, forded a small stream and came upon two marines sitting on boxes beneath a shelter half. Before them was a switchboard. Here we waited for a tank to take us to the Advanced CP. The communications post is as interesting a spot as can be found in a battle area. All information is transmitted through the switchboard; so this correspondent just sat there and listened to operations going on at the crest of the hill a few hundred yards away.

Here sat two fellows, the operator and his troubleshooter, who listened last night, just as you listened to your radio, to the battle up the hill. They told the story:

The Japs were dug into the side of the hill in pillboxes and machine gun nests that stair-stepped up the incline. Our first assault was an attempt to storm these positions, but the Japs sat in their little caves and mowed down our men.

The attack was repulsed so we drew back to lick our wounds and work out new strategy.

It turned out that 105-mm. guns, 75-mm. howitzers and 50-cal. machine guns joined mortar platoons in blasting into the hillside.

In the meantime, the weapons company of the marine division circled the foot of the hill, set up gun positions on the Japs' north flank and began to blast away with the same type of artillery.

Detachments from two companies stole around the opposite side of the hill to attack from the south and east. Other elements of these companies, along with another company, attacked up the hill's west side.

The Japs were almost completely encircled and, like in other such instances, found it impossible to get out of the pocket so dug in to fight it out.

General Sherman tanks joined the assault, some rumbling

as far as 300 yards up the steep hillside. When a stubborn pillbox was encountered, the tank rolled up, stuck the muzzle of its 75-mm. gun into the bunker and blasted away. There was silence.

In other instances the Sherman would run atop such a pillbox and wriggle itself there until the bunker caved in, bringing both bunker and tank crashing down on the occupants. There was silence.

Troops leaving the regimental command post were brought up aboard other tanks which themselves could advance only about half way up the hill.

Men climbing the hill from this point crawled along like babies—on all fours, their muddy hands grasping vines and digging into the earth where the heel of the preceding man had left a dent.

All the time the enemy fought back from caves, nests and pillboxes that had survived the barrage. The marines fought for almost every inch of ground.

"I don't see how we ever did it," the operator said. "It was hell just to have to climb up—to say nothing about fighting while you climbed."

A crack of bush broke the conversation and brought our heads about with a start. Out walked two heavily armed soldiers and one big, strong-looking man who carried no arms.

He looked at me, asked: "What are you doing up here?"

When I showed my insignia which was being worn on the underside of my collar because shining metal makes a good target, he said something about correspondents getting into the thick of things like saps and, after a few other questions, signed my identification card.

"Go on up the hill," he added as he went off, his protectors before and after him. My card now bore the signature of a colonel in the U.S.M.C.

Back at the switchboard calls were now coming through rapidly. One conversation was that a Jap carrying one of our 30-cal. carbines had just been killed.

During a lull, the fellows pulled out a Jap's belt of a thousand stitches (supposed to protect the wearer from harm), gave me bills of Jap Government Philippine and Australian invasion money.

Then—the rains came.

Our 105's opened up on Jap positions along Borgen Bay, just beyond the hill's crest. The concussions sent gusts of wind around us that rocked the broken treetops above our heads. We watched them closely.

Then came the grinding sound of an approaching tank. Soon it was in the ravine there below us. Thumbs went up and the driver yelled out we'd have to wait until he reached a spot with better traction before we could board.

We pulled along beside the tank to a spot some twenty yards distant and climbed aboard. We were frightful sights of mud and muck.

When the tank ended its run we were at what is called Advance Command Post. The mud came above our knees.

Things were surprisingly casual here. One marine yelled:

"Souvenir hunters right up the hill there. You can find all you want. Chow will be served right here." And he began to take the warm food containers off the tank.

The marine with me said they had been living in the mud for twenty-one days—no change of clothing, no water for washing, the food C Ration until the day before, but there had been hot coffee last night . . . right in the midst of the battle, when someone made a fire and a brew.

We moved off to climb to the top of the hill. We had to crawl hand over foot. Half the time we were prone in the mud, scrambling for a firm footing.

From the hilltop we could look down into Borgen Bay, across its expanse and into what we were told was the Jap bivouac area into which the 105's were firing.

Things were so quiet, so disinteresting (we couldn't even see the Japs that were being knocked off) that we turned and slid back down the hill to the CP.

Our tank was about to take off so we climbed aboard, found there was standing room only.

A few hundred feet down the track we came upon a group of men trudging along in the muck. The tank stopped. A marine behind me nudged and said, "That's General Rupertus." The general climbed aboard. Back at the regimental command post the tank stopped to let the general off. We then climbed on trucks that took us to the site of our original landing on this island. We walked an additional two miles to our campsite.

The little actual shooting we saw is called "mopping up." We couldn't see much of that.

### Homesick Joe in Pacific

CAPE GLOUCESTER (Via Air Mail)—"It's gone and started raining. I'm lonesome as a man can be-e-e. It's gone and started raining . . ."

The rain was beating a tattoo on the tent top. We were tired, wet, miserable, heart sick. We didn't know where the singing was coming from and we didn't care but we did know that it sounded good and the guy was singing right out of the depths of his heart.

"If you read my letter, baby . . . you sho musta read my mind. . . ."

We just lay there in the mid-afternoon heat and listened to the rain and the singing. The rain and the heat are perpetually with us here. The singing—especially this kind—isn't. It comes very rarely—only when a man gets full . . . very full.

"Y'know, I love my wife," a soldier said. "I really love my wife and I've never known how much I love her until right this minute."

Nobody answered the soldier. It wasn't necessary. We all knew what was going on inside of that man. We all knew what he was thinking; we were all thinking the same thing, so we just sat there and thought.

Then the soldier got up and walked out of the tent into the rain. As he moved away we could hear his voice rising in song:

"Take me back, baby. Try me one more time-e. Take me back, baby. Try me one more ti-ime."

Those of us left in the tent looked at each other; then went back to our individual thoughts. The rain kept beating on the tent top.

### Men Can't Sleep; They Talk, Dream of Home

CAPE GLOUCESTER—(Via Air Mail—Censored)—Nobody sleeps at night in the camp area of the quartermaster truck unit with which this correspondent is making home on this beachhead.

When dusk comes the men saunter into their tents and bed down. There's an awful lot of time between dusk and daybreak, a fact that you can appreciate, in case you never knew it before, if you will just try lying on a canvas cot those 12 hours, while the rain beats down outside, and any side you may lie on jabs into the hard canvas and gets sore after a spell.

Anyhow, we all bed down at dusk . . . but some don't sleep . . . for several reasons. First, we sort of "sweat out" an air raid; secondly, we don't want to be asleep if a Jap decides to run up into our camp, starts throwing grenades and generally raises hell.

Sometimes we talk but not much. However, what we talk about—when we do talk—should warm up some hearts and writing pens back there in the States.

This correspondent can find no better way to put these conversation pieces down than in the form in which they appear in my notebook. These are the voices of the men who are keeping war from American shores and the talk might go like this:

"Wonder how things are going back there? Wonder whether the folks are in this thing with us—up to the hilt? Do you think we'll find things better when we get back?" begins Voice No. 1.

*"They had damned well better be. I suspect if I hailed a cab and the driver tried to hand me some stuff, I'd pull him out by the collar and peel his head like it was a banana," will go a second voice.*

"What do I want?" is the third voice. "Oh, I don't know exactly, but I guess it's something like a good job—no charity—just the privilege of a free man's place in a free man's world and the opportunity to build the kind of life I want to live."

Here there might come a lull in the conversation while ears

prick up at the sound of movement outside the tent. A long interval of silence; then a voice from a dark corner:

"Gee, I'm going to be glad to see my sister. This guy she married is supposed to be the perfect man. I want to see the bloke—sort of size him up."

"And man, am I gonna have a time raiding the ice box. I can see it all now—those glistening hardwood floors, the clean walls, that knee-deep bed with clean sheets and my slippers beside it."

"I can see mine, too," another voice whose owner is also hidden by the night, will put in.

"It ain't nothing like that, but it's mine—a sort of tumble-down shack, you might say. Holes in the roof and a bucket always handy to catch the rain.

"Some pasteboard boxes I'm saving in a corner so I could use them for inner soles when my shoes got thin . . . that old, creaking rocking chair, a couple of missing boards in the porch and the rickety steps I planned to fix. Still it's mine."

"Hacienda or hovel, it's home just the same," sympathizes Voice No. 1.

Silence again—another long interval of it. Then the sound of soft snoring in one corner and movement in another as a soldier sits up under his mosquito net, beginning to talk again.

"That guy had better be nice to my sister. I'll twist his neck if he don't."

"I wonder how my old man is getting along," another reminiscent voice will sing out, almost as if the owner had been jabbed with a hat-pin.

*"He's getting kinda old now. They don't go into detail in the letters; just say he's okay. Guess he's still going squirrel hunting, though. Boy, he sure can shoot not to be able to see any better than he can. Can't read a paper without his glasses but he's hell on a squirrel."*

"I hope my dog ain't dead. He was getting a little weak in the hind legs and couldn't hear very well," the voice with the married sister interrupts.

"Whatahell you mean bringing up your dog when I'm talking about my old man?"

"Cut it," an impatient sergeant's voice will say. "Let me see whether I can think out what home means to me.

". . . That cafe next to the show with the fried fish in the window smelling up the whole neighborhood . . . that drug store where they never had enough ice-cream to last until after 9 o'clock . . . that scale outside the door where I used to stand and watch the female chassis go by.

"That church down the street where Mom used to go every Sunday and where I always cropped up when there was a Sunday school picnic . . . that straw hat and those white trousers I used to sport on Easter Sunday.

"That sharp black Alpaca overcoat I got just before I was drafted . . . that number I've got scratched on the wall beside the telephone and the girl who answers when I call it.

"Man, that's home to me—and I'm going to sleep tonight and dream about it. Hell, if they get us, we're just got—then we won't have to worry about ANYTHING anymore.

"Break it off, Jack, break it off," an irritated voice from another tent will howl out—and the howl will bring a hundred more requests for silence, some of which will be annotated with plain and fancy swearing; others with threats of untold physical violence.

These are the dreams of men wide awake on an island beachhead. They are dreams that tantalize—even torture, but they come nocturnally with the surety and quickness of Pacific nightfall, repeating themselves and adding embellishments as the weeks wear on.

Nostalgia is perpetually with us over here, expressing itself in hundreds of ways, but never more vividly to this correspondent than from the lips of the young marine returning from the battle for Hill 660.

When climbing onto the muddy, bumping truck, he banged his knee against the steel bed, then sprawled around the feet of a dozen tired men to find himself staring in the face of a dead buddy lying on a litter square.

He picked himself up and threw a hurt glance in the direction of a jovial marine who said: "Didn't your mother warn you there'd be days like this?"

The little fellow looked over the truck's side at the feet of a dead Jap jutting out of the mud in which rain had almost buried him and said to the jungle toward which he lifted his eyes:

"Gee, I'll be glad when I get back home."

*Baltimore Afro-American*, March 18, 1944

# Search for a Battle

by Walter Bernstein

THE ATTACK was to jump off at nine in the morning. The objective of my infantry regiment was a long, steep ridge that stood like a door at the head of the valley we occupied. The pattern of attack was familiar and orthodox: first an hour of dive-bombing to soften the objective, then a half hour of artillery, and finally the infantry to do the dirty work. It was a pattern that had been followed ever since we had landed in Italy. Everyone was getting tired of it. Our regiment had fought through Sicily and all the way up from Salerno, and the men were particularly tired of walking. They were not tired of fighting, if fighting meant that they would get home sooner, but they were very weary of long night marches and then hours of fancy mountain climbing in the face of enemy fire. This struck them as a hell of a way to fight a war that was supposed to be so mechanized and motorized, and they frequently said so. My job in this operation was going to be with the headquarters of one of the attacking battalions. I was now on duty at regimental headquarters, which was in a one-room farmhouse by the side of a dirt road, and the plan was for me to join the battalion as it marched past the regimental command post during the night on its way to the jump-off point. The battalion was scheduled to come by at two in the morning, and someone was supposed to wake me. No one did. When the guard was changed at midnight, the old guard forgot to tell the new guard. At four-thirty the regimental C.P. moved out, leaving me behind. I was asleep in a haystack and they could have moved the whole Fifth Army without my hearing them. A horse nibbling at the hay was what finally woke me. It was six o'clock.

There was no one around the place when I slid out of the hay, and the road was deserted. It was just getting light. Fog lay like chalk over the valley, twisting at the bottom as it began to rise. The air was cold and damp. The only living thing in sight seemed to be the horse, and he was no bargain. I dressed, put on my helmet and pistol belt, then went up to the farmhouse and looked in. There was nothing inside but guttered candles, torn and empty K-ration boxes, and piles of straw on which the officers had slept. I returned to the hay-stack and made up my bedding roll. Most of the line troops carried only a raincoat and half a blanket. At night they wrapped the half blanket around their head and shoulders, put the raincoat over that, and lay on the ground. I had a whole blanket and a shelter half, a combination which, by comparison, was equal to an inner-spring mattress. After mak-ing up the roll, I ate a bar of K-ration chocolate. As the fog lifted, it revealed the mountains along the valley. At the end of the valley was the ridge we were going to take, looming black and forbidding through the mist. I finished the choco-late, slung the bedding roll over one shoulder, and started along the road toward the front.

There was no activity at all on the road, which seemed strange, considering that an attack was coming off. The valley was completely quiet. There were not even the ordinary morning-in-the-country noises. I walked for about a mile without seeing anyone and then passed an artillery battery dug in beside the road. The guns were camouflaged with nets. The men sat beside them, eating out of C-ration cans. No one looked up as I passed. Ahead of me, growing larger, was the high ridge. Before it were a few small hills. Between these hills and the ridge was another, smaller valley, running at right angles to the one I was following. Our men would have to cross it under fire. It was seven o'clock now, and there was still no sound of gunfire.

I had gone half a mile past the artillery when I heard a car behind me. A jeep was coming up the road. It stopped when I thumbed it. A colonel was sitting next to the driver, and he said, "Hop in." I climbed into the back and sat on my bedding roll. "We're going to the regimental C.P.," the colonel said. That suited me; I could find out there where my battalion was. The colonel must have been important, because the driver, a staff sergeant, drove very carefully, as if he were driving a sedan instead of a jeep. The road was full of holes, and he actually went into second for some of them, which is a rare thing to do with a jeep. I kept my eye out for planes. The ceiling was still very low, but you never could tell. The road curved to the right, when we came to the first of the little hills, and then headed straight for the ridge. The colonel told the driver to slow down. We caught up to a young lieutenant walking along the road, and the colonel leaned out and asked him where the regimental C.P. was. "Damned if I know," the lieutenant said. He needed a shave and looked tired. "Well, what outfit are you?" the colonel asked. "Support battalion," the lieutenant said. He turned off the road and started across a field toward some vehicles parked under a tree. The colonel looked as though he were going to call him back, but finally he ordered the driver to go ahead. A hundred yards beyond, we came to a crossroads, and there was an M.P. here. The colonel shouted his question about the regimental C.P. at him and the M.P. waved us to the left. We took the road he had indicated, but it soon turned into a cow path and finally petered out altogether in front of an old farmhouse. Another M.P. was standing there, scratching his head. We stopped beside him and the colonel asked directions again. The M.P. kept scratching his head, but he pointed across a field to a wooded hill. The driver started off again. The M.P. called, "Hey!" We stopped, and the M.P. said mildly, "You better be careful crossing that field. It's supposed to be mined." None of us said anything for a moment; then the colonel sighed and told the driver to go ahead.

The driver went slowly across the field, following what he probably hoped were wheel tracks. I shifted around so that I was sitting on the side of the jeep with my feet on the back seat. I wondered briefly whether I shouldn't sit on my helmet, but decided that it wasn't really necessary. We didn't hit any mines, but we thought about them and it seemed like a long time before we got across that field. There was a dirt road on the other side and we followed it as we ascended the hill. Halfway up the hill we reached the C.P., which was in a grove of trees. I saw the regimental commander and his executive officer standing in a large excavation; the C.O. was talking over a telephone. The drivers and other headquarters-company men were digging foxholes and putting up a black-out tent. We parked under a tree. I thanked the colonel for the lift and went off to see if I could find someone I knew. I finally found the sergeant in charge of the intelligence platoon, a New Yorker named Vrana, whom I had been with in Sicily. He was sitting in a ditch by the side of the road, fooling around with a hand radio. I asked him where the battle was and he said it hadn't started yet. "We got observation on top of this hill," he said. "I was just talking to them. They said they couldn't see a damned thing." Vrana thought that the best way to find the battalion was to go up to the observation post and try to spot it from there. I could climb to the crest of the hill and walk along it until I found the post. He thought it was safe. He said that there had been only a little shelling, and that the enemy had settled down to throwing one shell into the C.P. every twenty minutes. "But on the nose," Vrana said. "You can set your watch by those bastards."

I said goodbye and started up the hill. It was easy climbing and I got to the top without much trouble. I came across a telephone wire there and followed it along the crest. The hill dipped into a saddle. I went down into it and was halfway up the other side when I heard the sound of men descending above me. They turned out to be two infantrymen, looking very dirty and completely bushed. One carried a rifle and the other had the base plate of a mortar. The rifleman said wearily, "How do you get out of this damned place?" I told them to follow the wire.

"You know where C Company is?" the mortar man asked me.

I asked him what outfit.

"Second battalion," he said.

"We just got relieved," the rifleman said. "Only nobody knows where we're supposed to go."

"I ain't even sure we been relieved," the mortar man said.

"I'm sure," the rifleman said. "The lieutenant come by and said we were relieved. That's good enough for me."

"The lieutenant got killed," the other man said.

"So what?" the rifleman said. "He relieved us before he got killed."

I said that I didn't know where C Company was but that they could probably find out at the C.P., and then it developed that they weren't even from our regiment. Their outfit had been in the line for eight days, and had held the hill we were on against four counterattacks; they had been spread all over the place and when our regiment had moved through, the night before, they had got mixed up. Now all they wanted was some hot chow and a place to sleep for a few days. Finally they decided to go down to the C.P., and moved off, cursing with the mechanical passion that everyone picks up in the Army.

I continued to follow the wire. It led up the slope to the top of the hill, which I suddenly realized was now flat and grassy. I felt very conspicuous. I ducked low and was creeping along beside the wire when a voice called my name. In a hollow between some rocks were three members of our regiment's intelligence platoon. The man who had called me was a private named Caruso, a small, dark man whom I had also known in Sicily. I crawled down to them. They said that they were the observation post. The two others were a lieutenant named Bixby and a private named Rich. You couldn't see anything from the hollow, but they said it was more comfortable there. "It's also healthier," Caruso explained. At that moment we heard the whine of a shell, growing steadily louder, and then a great swish, as though someone were cutting the tops of the trees with a giant scythe.

"See what I mean?" Caruso said.

"They throw one like that every twenty minutes," Lieutenant Bixby said. "You can set a clock by it."

I said I had heard about that before; the shells were landing below, in the C.P.

Caruso laughed. "I bet they're sweating down there," he said.

The fact that the shells were aimed at the C.P. and not at them seemed to make them happy. Caruso reached behind a rock and drew out a cardboard box full of rations. "How about something to eat?" he said.

"You just finished breakfast," Rich said.

"I got something better to do?" Caruso asked. He rummaged around in the box and came up with a can of meat balls and spaghetti. He opened it with a trench knife and ate the whole can, using the knife as a spoon.

While Caruso was eating, the lieutenant kept looking at his watch. Finally he said, "Listen." Very far away there was the faint cough of a gun, and then a rising whine and a sudden heavy rush of air as another shell passed over our heads. "See?" the lieutenant said, looking very pleased with himself. "Twenty minutes on the nose."

When Caruso had finished his meal, we climbed out of the hollow and up to the crest of the hill, where we lay on our stomachs, looking across the smaller valley toward the ridge. The lieutenant had a pair of field glasses. He looked through them and said, "There's fighting on the side of the ridge." He handed me the glasses. Through them I could see faint puffs of smoke halfway up the ridge and movement among the trees and rocks. "That's for me," I said. I was greatly tempted just to stay at the observation post. Sitting in the hollow was safe and secret, and no shell in the world would find me there. The air was getting warmer and the grass was soft and only a little wet. I could sleep. But I had to find the battalion, so I stood up, shouldered my roll, said goodbye, and started off again.

Lieutenant Bixby had said to follow the wire, which he thought led to the ridge. There was not even a suggestion of a path, and if you didn't know regimental wire teams you wouldn't think the wire could possibly lead anywhere. Finally, halfway down the hill, the wire brought me onto a muddy path that ran diagonally down the hill. The path was screened by trees and seemed insulated from the rest of the world. The air was cold down there. The only sound was the squish of my shoes in the mud, and even that was a cold, clammy sound. It was easy going, but there was nothing pleasant about it. It was like walking in a cold jungle. But I soon lost myself in the rhythm of walking. It wasn't until I was almost at the foot of the hill that I discovered that I had also lost the wire. I walked back a few yards, then decided that it wasn't worth going all the way back up the hill. I had no idea where the path led, but if the fighting was halfway up the ridge the valley was probably safe. If it wasn't safe, I was just out of luck. I started to descend again, only slower. It was very quiet. The path straightened out near the bottom of the hill and the trees became sparser. Then it dipped suddenly and I began to walk fast.

The path turned abruptly. Ahead of me was a group of men. I went for the ground, but it was unnecessary—they were Americans. There were four of them, carrying a blanket stretched out between them. Lying on the blanket was another soldier. His feet were drawn up and his face was buried in his arms. He lay very still. The men came slowly toward me, carrying the blanket with great care. They all had rifles slung over their shoulders; their faces were drawn and their eyes were deep in their sockets. They stopped when they reached me and one of the two front men said, "You know where the medics are?" His voice was too tired to have any expression; it seemed to come from a great distance. I said I didn't know. "We got to find the medics," the soldier said. "We got a man hurt bad." I said they would have to climb the hill and then maybe they could send down from the observation post for one of the first-aid men at the C.P. The soldier was silent for a while, then he said again, "We got to find the medics." The three other men stood silent, looking at the one who was talking. The blanket was stiff with caked blood. The wounded man was scarcely breathing. Once in a while his fingers twitched and tapped weakly on the blanket. I said that they would pick up a wire further along and that it would take them to the observation post. "Thank you," the man who had spoken to me said. He shifted his feet, moving very gently so as not to disturb the wounded man. "All right," he said to the others. "Left foot." They began to walk again, synchronizing their steps so that they wouldn't shake the blanket. As they passed, I stepped aside, but not quickly enough to avoid brushing against one of the rear men. He said, "Excuse me." They moved up the path slowly, like sleepwalkers, and I watched until they turned the corner and were out of sight. Then I went on along the path, following the tiny trail of blood they had left.

The path broadened at the foot of the hill and before I knew it I was in the valley. It was wider than I had thought, looking at it from above; the ridge seemed a couple of miles away. The path ended at a dirt road running through the valley, but I decided to cut straight across and head for the ridge. The ground was soft and grassy; it felt good to be walking on the level again. There was a lovely tranquillity in the valley, and the ridge was quiet again. I had walked about two hundred yards from the foot of the hill when there was a rush of air and a clap of thunder, and I fell flat on my face. When the ground had settled down, I lifted my head and looked around. A thin cloud of smoke and dust hung peacefully in the air a hundred feet to my left. There was nothing else to be seen. I lay there until I began to feel a little foolish, then stood up and began walking toward the ridge again. This time I got about twenty yards before there was the flat wham of something going very fast and another thunder clap. This time the smoke was closer. Then, while I was still lying on the ground, another shell hit only thirty feet away, throwing dirt all over the place. I stood up, bent low, and ran like hell. Another shell landed somewhere behind me, but I didn't stop until I got back to the foot of the hill. The first thing I saw was a ditch, and I hopped into that. It was full of water, but it was deep. It could have been full of hydrochloric acid as long as it was deep.

I lay in the ditch perhaps twenty minutes. There was no more shelling. The echoes still rang in my ears, but the valley was quiet again. Finally I climbed out of the ditch and started along the base of the hill, keeping under cover as much as I could. The road through the valley curved toward me, and I found myself walking on it. I went slowly, trying to look all around me at once. My clothes were wet and I began to shiver. The valley was deathly quiet. I couldn't stop shivering, and then I felt afraid. I wasn't afraid of snipers, or even of mines, which can irritate you so much that eventually you say the hell with them, just to be able to walk freely and with dignity again. But there is something about heavy artillery that is inhuman and terribly frightening. You never know whether you are running away from it or into it. It is like the finger of God. I felt cowardly and small at the base of this tremendous hill, walking alone on the floor of this enormous valley. I felt like a fly about to be swatted. It was a lousy feeling. I was very angry until I realized that there was nothing I could do about it. Then I began to wish I were somewhere else.

The road hugged the base of the hill and then swung out into the valley again. I stayed on it, partly from inertia and partly to assert myself. All of a sudden I heard an automobile horn. I looked up and down the road, but nothing was in sight. The horn blew again. It was a nice, raucous city horn; I thought I was imagining things. The horn blew again and a voice called out, "You dumb son of a bitch, where do you think *you're* going?" The voice came from the hill. I looked over and saw a soldier standing above me near some bushes, waving. "Come back here!" he yelled. "You want your goddam head blown off?" I started toward him. I had almost reached him when he yelled "Run!" and jumped in among the bushes. I started to run, and then there was the whistle of a shell and a loud crack and a piece of the hill flew into the air. I hit the ground, digging with my nose, and the soldier stuck his head out of the bushes and yelled, "Here! In here!" I got up and ran toward him and he pulled me through the bushes. There was a shallow cleft in the hill, hidden by foliage, and parked in the cleft was a jeep. In the jeep was another soldier and on the back was a reel of telephone wire. "I hope you got insurance," the soldier in the jeep said, "because the way you travel around this country you're sure going to need it." As soon as I got my breath, I asked him what he meant, and the first soldier took me by the arm and pulled me back to the bushes. He held them apart and asked me what I saw. I couldn't see anything. "Over there by the foot of the ridge," he said. I looked again. "You see it?" he said. I saw it. A German tank was sitting in a field below the ridge. It was far away, but you could see that it was a heavy tank and you could see the black cross on the side. "Get a load of that kraut bastard," the soldier said. "He nearly blew us off the road."

We went back to the jeep and he explained that they and another man had come around the other side of the hill along a wide trail, stringing wire for the battalion, and the tank had opened fire, forcing them to take cover in the cleft. The tank was apparently afraid to come down into the valley, since we had covering fire on it, but it would fire on anything that moved. The one who had yelled to me was short and red-faced; his name was Jenkins. The other was tall, with a long, sad face and huge hands, and Jenkins called him Tex. "He really comes from Oklahoma," Jenkins said, "but he served two years at Fort Sam Houston, so everyone calls him Tex." I asked if they had done anything about the tank. Jenkins said they had sent the third man up to the artillery observation post to put some fire on it. He said we had men working their way up the ridge; he didn't think they were meeting much opposition, since all the firing he had heard had been light and sporadic. There seemed to be nothing to do but wait, so I sat down in the jeep and relaxed. The two other men went into what was apparently a running argument about the relative attractions of French women in Algiers and Italian women in Italy. Jenkins was upholding the French.

"They got more class," he kept saying to Tex.

"Maybe so," Tex said, unimpressed, "but what good is it if you can't get anywhere?"

"That's just what I mean," Jenkins said triumphantly. "That's *class.*"

Just then there was the crackle of a shell overhead. "That's it!" Jenkins said. He rushed to the bushes and held them apart so that he could look across the valley. Tex and I followed him. "It's our goddam artillery," Tex said. "They finally realized there's a war on." The shell had hit a hundred yards or so from the tank. The tank began to move, obviously trying to retreat, but something must have been wrong, because it turned only part way around. Another shell landed closer, and Jenkins whispered, "You kraut bastard, stay there, stay there!" The tank looked like a huge bug, twitching as it strained to get away. Another shell came over, but this one was farther off, and then two more, closer.

"How can you hit a tank from that distance?" Tex asked. "It'd be a miracle."

"Shut your face!" Jenkins said, without looking at him. He was whispering to the artillery, "Hit the bastard, hit him, *hit* him!"

But the next shell was off the target and the two after that were even farther off, and then the tank spun around, wobbled for a second, and lumbered out of sight. Two more shells went over, but it was too late. The tank was hidden now.

"God *damn!*" Jenkins said, turning back to us. He looked as if he were going to cry.

"Listen," Tex said. "Them guns have been firing since Salerno. I bet right now they got bores as smooth as a baby's bottom. You're lucky they get as close as two hundred yards to what they're aiming at."

Jenkins got into the driver's seat of the jeep and started the motor. "That tank ain't going to stick his nose out no more," he said. "We might as well get this wire laid." Tex went around behind the jeep, so that he could follow it and see that the wire didn't get tangled as it was reeled out, and I got into the front seat. We drove out through the bushes and headed across the valley toward the ridge but bearing away from the part of the ridge where the tank had disappeared. "He ain't going to bother us," Jenkins said, "but there ain't no sense giving him the chance." We drove across the valley in second, Tex walking behind, paying out the wire. Once we heard the crackle of a shell going over. Jenkins slammed on the brakes and we both spilled out, but the shell kept going and we heard it hit on the other side of the ridge. When we got to the base of the ridge, Jenkins parked the car and said he'd be damned if he was going to lug that wire up a mountain; he was going to wait for the man they had sent to the artillery observation post. I offered to help them, but he said they'd better wait for him. I said I thought I'd be on my way then. I got my bedding roll and thanked them for saving my life. "Hell," Tex said. "He might have missed you." Jenkins warned me to watch out for trip wires on the way up; while they had been pinned down by the tank, they had heard some explosions on the ridge that sounded like mines, and trip wires were the favorite German method of mining a mountain. I thanked them again and started off.

There was no path up the ridge here, so I went straight up. It wasn't hard going at first; the ground was soft and I had to fight my way through bushes, but they weren't too thick. Then the soft ground ended and rocks began. They were big rocks, with thickets growing between them, and I had to hop from one to another. Even this wasn't too bad, but then the rocks ended and there was nothing but thickets, which I had to claw my way through. They were full of thistles, and after a few minutes my hands and face were bleeding. Finally I stopped and looked back. The valley was just the same, calm and green and peaceful. In the distance I could see dust on the road, which meant that trucks were moving up. Then I heard the sharp sounds of small-arms fire above me and to the right, so I headed that way. The sounds grew louder and distinguishable: the crack of a rifle and the riveting-machine burst of a German machine pistol, and then the slower, measured answer of our machine guns. I stopped to get my breath, and when I started again my legs felt very heavy. My pistol dragged at my side and the bedding roll felt as heavy as a sack of flour. But as I approached the firing, I began to feel life-size. The valley fear and sense of insignificance disappeared and I felt human, and very important. I didn't know how close I was to the top of the ridge, but that didn't matter now.

The ridge grew steeper; the rocks appeared again, and then the bushes. I ripped my way through. My uniform was soaked with sweat and my helmet bounced up and down on my head and slid over my eyes. At last I got on a trail which went uphill. The firing was very near now, but it had slackened. Alongside the path, I saw, ahead of me, three soldiers with red crosses on their arms, standing over another soldier on the ground. They paid no attention to me. When I got closer, I saw that two of them were working on the man on the ground, cutting away his uniform around a lumpy brown stain on his side. The third man was standing a little apart. He was a medical captain. I asked him where the battalion C.P. was and he pointed up the trail without speaking. I kept on the trail and began to encounter signs that there had been a fight. There was a German machine-gun emplacement dug in between two trees, the gun still pointing down the mountain, and two dead Germans lying beside the gun. Farther up, cases of German ammunition were scattered around. The trail widened. It mounted a little further and then ran for a while along the side of the ridge, hidden from the top by an overhanging cliff. I came upon the mouth of a cave in the cliff.

Two officers were sitting before it, looking at a map. One was the battalion commander, a young, tough colonel with a mustache. The other was the regimental intelligence officer, a child lieutenant who looked about eighteen when he was shaved. He was one of the people I was supposed to have gone with. When he saw me, all he said was, "You're a little late, aren't you?" I told him what had happened. "You missed all the fun," he said. "We've already chased the krauts off the hill." I asked what the shooting was, and he said it was just some isolated snipers the boys were cleaning up. "You can go on up to the top of the hill if you want," he said. "Just keep your head down."

I said I'd take a quick look and continued up the trail. There were infantrymen scattered along it, opening packages of K ration or sleeping or just sitting and smoking. None of them were talking. There were also several men lying on the ground with blankets over their faces. The path grew steeper and then dribbled out among some rocks. I started to climb up over the rocks and a voice said, "Keep your head down." A soldier was sitting behind a large rock at the top. I kept low and climbed up to him. "This is the end of the line," he said. "Unless you want your head handed to you." I dropped my bedding roll, climbed the rock, and looked over. Everything was exactly the same. There was the other side of the ridge dropping off beneath me and at the bottom was a green little valley, and then another ridge. Beyond that were more ridges, rising and falling in the same pattern. There seemed to be no end; it was like being in an airplane over a sea of clouds that stretched forever into space. It was very quiet on top of the ridge. There was no more firing and the air was warm and motionless. Then there was the sound of planes and two of our dive-bombers appeared, flying very high and fast, heading for the next ridge. When they were over it, they gunned their motors and then heeled over and went down with terrible directness in a long, plummeting dive, the motor sound lost in the screaming of the wings; and when it seemed that they would never pull out, they pulled out, and from the bottom of the planes, like droppings from a bird, the bombs fell beautifully down and hit and exploded. Then the planes flattened out and climbed and sped swiftly back toward their field.

I lay there for a while longer and then climbed down to the soldier behind the rock. "How does it look?" he asked.

"It looks familiar," I said.

*The New Yorker*, September 23, 1944

# The Italian Campaign:
## "Perpetual Astonishments of a War Life"

by Ernie Pyle

### "A Life of Flying in Combat"

IN ITALY, March 14—(by wireless)—As I got to know the A-20 gunners better and better, they gradually began to tell me their inner feelings about a life of flying in combat.

Several had just about completed their missions, yet they said they were willing to stay if needed and fly extra missions.

In any squadron you'll find many men willing to fly beyond the stated missions if it's put up to them, but you'll average only about one who is actually eager to go on. In our squadron I found such a gunner in Sergt. John D. Baker, of (839 Park Ave.) Indianapolis.

Sergeant Baker is 21. He has flown more missions than anybody in the squadron, men or officers. He says it is his ambition to fly a hundred.

Many in our squadron have gone beyond the required goal. Some are still flying, and others have gone on to the breaking point and had to be grounded. The flight surgeons try to sense when the strain is beginning to get a man.

Some of them seem to have nerves that are untouchable. One of my pilot friends told me that on a mission earlier in the day, when the flak was breaking all around, he didn't think much of the danger but kept thinking that if a fragment should break the plexiglass globe, and let the below-zero air rush through the plane, he would be one mad pilot.

Another one told of the funny reflexes you have up there. For example, every combat airman knows you needn't worry about the flak you see, for if you see it the danger is over and you haven't been hit. Yet this pilot, after a harmless puff of smoke appears ahead of him, goes around it.

\*     \*     \*

One of the gunners—a man with a fine record—told me he had not only become terrified of combat but had actually become afraid to fly at all.

He said that when the generators came on that morning, and the radio in their tent started crackling, it made him dream they were being attacked in the air. He dreamed that a bullet came up through the fuselage and hit him in the throat.

Another one told me he felt he just couldn't go on. He had completed his allotted missions, and nobody could doubt his courage. He wanted to go and ask to be grounded, but just couldn't bring himself to do it.

So I urged him to go ahead. Afterwards I got both sides of the story.

The officers told me later that they were kicking themselves for not noticing the gunner's nervousness in time and for letting it go until he had to hurt his pride by asking to be grounded.

But those are men's innermost feelings. They don't express them very often. They don't spend much time sitting around glooming to each other about their chances.

Their outlook and conversation is just as normal as that of a man in no danger at all. They play jokes, and write letters, and listen to the radio, and send gifts home, and drink a little vino and carry on just like anybody else.

It's only when a man "has had it"—the combat expression for anyone who has had more than he can take—that he sits alone and doesn't say much, and begins to stare.

\* \* \*

Sergt. Alban J. Petchal of Steubenville, O., and Charles Ramseur of Gold Hill, N.C., both have flown their allotted missions, both have been wounded, both are true veterans, quiet and kind and efficient.

Sergeant Petchal, although an Easterner, is in a way something of the same kind of man as my cowboy friend Sergt. Buck Eversole. He doesn't like any part of war, but he has done his job and done it well.

Sergeant Petchal never heard of Buck Eversole, and yet the morning I left he spoke about his place in the war with the same sort of sadly restrained philosophy and even in almost the same words that Buck Eversole had used at the front. He said, "The job has to be done, and somebody has to do it, and we happen to be the ones that were picked to do it, so we'll go on doing it the best we can."

And Sergeant Ramseur said, "I don't ever want to fly again, but if they tell me to keep on flying then I'll just keep on flying, that's all. You can't do anything else."

Scripps-Howard wire copy, March 14, 1944

### "Their Hunger Most Surely Was Genuine"

WITH THE ALLIED BEACHHEAD FORCES IN ITALY, March 22 —(by wireless)—We were due to sail for the Anzio beachhead a few hours after I got aboard our LST.

But at the last minute came a warning of a storm of gale force brewing in the Mediterranean, so we laid over for 24 hours.

Some of the sailors took the opportunity next day to go ashore, and asked if I didn't want to go along. But I said, "What for? I've been ashore for three months already." So I stayed aboard, and just killed a full day with doing nothing.

We were tied up along the waterfront street of a small port city near Naples. All day long the dock was a riot of Italians grouped down below to catch cookies and chocolates and knick-knacks the sailors and soldiers would throw down to them.

There must have been 200 people on the dock, either participating in the long-shot chance of actually catching something, or there just to look on.

Most of them were children, boys and girls both. Mostly they were ragged and dirty. Yet they were good-natured.

Every time a package of crackers went down from above, humanity fought and stamped up over it like a bunch of football players. Now and then some youngster would get hurt, and make a terrible face and cry. But mostly they'd laugh and look a little sheepish, and dash back in again after the next one.

All Italian children call all American soldiers "Hey, Joe,"

and all along the dock was a chicken-yard bedlam of "Hey, Joe, bis-ueet." Each one crying at the top of his lungs to call attention to himself, and holding up his hands.

\* \* \*

The soldier's favorite was a stocky little fellow of about 8, with coal-black hair and a constant good humor. He was about the only one of them who wasn't ragged, the reason being that he was entirely clad in military garb.

He had on a blue Navy sweater. Then for pants he had the biggest pair of British tropical shorts you ever saw, which came clear below his knees.

His legs were bare. He had on gray Army socks rolled down to his shoetops. And on his feet were a pair of brand-new American GI shoes, which must have been at least size 8. To top it all off, he had a beguiling grin with a tooth out in the middle of it.

This youngster was adept at walking on his hands. He spent hours walking around the muddy stone street on his hands, with his feet sticking straight up in the air.

The soldiers and sailors were crazy about him, and every time he finished his little performance he'd get a flood of crackers. I finally figured out that he was walking on his hands so much because it was easier than walking in those gigantic shoes.

Pretty teen-age Italian girls in red sweaters would come and stand at the edge of the throng watching the fun. But the sailors and soldiers at the rail would soon spot them, and the play for them would start. Reluctant and timid at first, they would finally obey the sailors' demand that they try to catch something too, and pretty soon would be in there battling for broken crackers.

Most Americans are touched by the raggedness and apparent hunger of the children over here. But it was hard to feel sorry for these kids, for although maybe some of them really were hungry, the rest of them were just having a wonderful mob-scene sort of good time.

It was the old women in the crowd that I could hardly bear to look at. Throughout the day there must have been a couple of dozen who came, tried for half an hour to catch something, and finally went dejectedly away.

They were horrible specimens of poverty and insanitation. They were old and pitiful, and repulsive. But their hunger most surely was genuine.

*        *        *

One elderly woman, dressed in tattered black and carrying a thin old shopping bag on her arm, stood at the far edge of the crowd, vainly beseeching a toss in her direction. Finally one sailor, who had just started on a large box of nabiscos piece by piece, changed his mind and threw the entire box toward the old woman.

It was a good throw and a good catch. She got it like an outfielder. But no sooner did she have it in her arms than the crowd was upon her. Kids and adults both tore at the box, scratched and yelled and grabbed, and in five seconds the box was empty and torn.

The poor old woman never let go. She clung to it as though it were something human. And when the last cracker was gone she walked sort of blindly away, her head back and her eyes toward the sky, weeping with a hideous face just like that of a heartbroken child, still gripping the empty box.

It was a lot of fun watching this foreign riot of childish emotions and adult greed that day. But some of it was too real—greed born of too great a necessity—and I was glad when word came that we would sail that night.

Scripps-Howard wire copy, March 22, 1944

### "Nobody Is Wholly Safe"

WITH THE ALLIED BEACHHEAD FORCES IN ITALY, March 28 —(by wireless)—When you get to Anzio you waste no time getting off the boat, for you have been feeling pretty much like a clay pigeon in a shooting gallery. But after a few hours in Anzio you wish you were back on the boat, for you could hardly describe being ashore as any haven of peacefulness.

As we came into the harbor, shells skipped the water within a hundred yards of us.

In our first day ashore, a bomb exploded so close to the

place where I was sitting that a fragment came through the window of the room next to mine.

On our second evening ashore a screamer slammed into the hill so suddenly that it almost knocked us down with fright. It smacked into the trees a short distance away.

And on the third day ashore, an 88 went off within 20 yards of us.

I wished I was in New York.

*     *     *

When I write about my own occasional association with shells and bombs, there is one thing I want you folks at home to be sure to get straight. And that is that the other correspondents are in the same boat—many of them much more so. You know about my own small experiences, because it's my job to write about how these things sound and feel. But you don't know what the other reporters go through, because it usually isn't their job to write about themselves.

There are correspondents here on the beachhead, and on the Cassino front also, who have had dozens of close shaves. I know of one correspondent who was knocked down four times by near misses on his first day here.

Two correspondents, Reynolds Packard of the United Press and Homer Bigart of the New York Herald-Tribune, have been on the beachhead since D-day without a moment's respite. They've become so veteran that they don't even mention a shell striking 20 yards away.

*     *     *

On this beachhead every inch of our territory is under German artillery fire. There is no rear area that is immune, as in most battle zones. They can reach us with their 88s, and they use everything from that on up.

I don't mean to suggest that they keep every foot of our territory drenched with shells all the time, for they certainly don't. They are short of ammunition, for one thing. But they can reach us, and you never know where they'll shoot next. You're just as liable to get hit standing in the doorway of the villa where you sleep at night, as you are in a command post five miles out in the field.

Some days they shell us hard, and some days hours will go

by without a single shell coming over. Yet nobody is wholly safe, and anybody who says he has been around Anzio two days without having a shell hit within a hundred yards of him is just bragging.

*    *    *

People who know the sounds of warfare intimately are puzzled and irritated by the sounds up here. For some reason, you can't tell anything about anything.

The Germans shoot shells of half a dozen sizes, each of which makes a different sound of explosion. You can't gauge distance at all. One shell may land within your block and sound not much louder than a shotgun. Another landing a quarter mile away makes the earth tremble as in an earthquake, and starts your heart to pounding.

You can't gauge direction, either. The 88 that hit within 20 yards of us didn't make so much noise. I would have sworn it was 200 yards away and in the opposite direction.

Sometimes you hear them coming, and sometimes you don't. Sometimes you hear the shell whine after you've heard it explode. Sometimes you hear it whine and it never explodes. Sometimes the house trembles and shakes and you hear no explosion at all.

But I've found one thing here that's just the same as anywhere else—and that's that old weakness in the joints when they get to landing close. I've been weak all over Tunisia and Sicily, and in parts of Italy, and I get weaker than ever up here.

When the German raiders come over at night, and the sky lights up bright as day with flares, and ack-ack guns set up a turmoil and pretty soon you hear and feel the terrible power of exploding bombs—well, your elbows get flabby and you breathe in little short jerks, and your chest feels empty, and you're too excited to do anything but hope.

Scripps-Howard wire copy, March 28, 1944

### "You Just Lie in Your Foxhole"

WITH FIFTH ARMY BEACHHEAD FORCES IN ITALY, April 1 —(by wireless)—The American infantry fighters on the

Fifth Army beachhead were having a welcome breathing spell when I dropped around to leave my calling card.

There's nothing that suits me better than a breathing spell, so I stayed and passed the time of day. My hosts were a company of the 179th infantry. They had just come out of the lines that morning, and had dug in on a little slope three miles back of the perimeter. The sun shone for a change, and we lay around on the ground talking and soaking up the warmth.

Every few minutes a shell would smack a few hundred yards away. Our own heavy artillery made such a booming that once in a while we had to wait a few seconds in order to be heard. Planes were high overhead constantly, and now and then you could hear the ratta-ta-tat-tat of machine-gunning up there out of sight in the blue, and see thin white vapor trails from the planes.

That scene may sound very warlike to you, but so great is the contrast between the actual lines and even a little way back, that it was actually a setting of great calm.

*         *         *

This company had been in the front lines for more than a week. They were back to rest for a few days. There hadn't been any real attacks from either side during their latest stay in the lines, and yet there wasn't a moment of the day or night when they were not in great danger.

Up there in the front our men lie in shallow foxholes. The Germans are a few hundred yards on beyond them, also dug into foxholes, and buttressed in every farmhouse with machine-gun nests. The ground on the perimeter line slopes slightly down toward us—just enough to give the Germans the advantage of observation.

There are no trees or hillocks or anything up there for protection. You just lie in your foxhole from dawn till dark. If you raise your head a few feet, you get a rain of machine-gun bullets.

During these periods of comparative quiet on the front, it's mostly a matter of watchful waiting on both sides. That doesn't mean that nothing happens, for at night we send out patrols to feel out the German positions, and the Germans try to get behind our lines. And day and night the men on both sides are splattered with artillery, although we splatter a great deal more of it nowadays than the Germans do.

Back on the lines, where the ground is a little higher, men can dig deep into the ground and make comfortable dugouts which also give protection from shell fragments. But on the perimeter line the ground is so marshy that water rises in the bottom of a hole only 18 inches deep. Hence there are many artillery wounds.

When a man is wounded, he just has to lie there and suffer till dark. Occasionally, when one is wounded badly, he'll call out and the word is passed back and the medics will make a dash for him. But usually he just has to treat himself and wait till dark.

For more than a week these boys lay in water in their foxholes, able to move or stretch themselves only at night. In addition to water seeping up from below, it rained from above all the time. It was cold, too, and of a morning new snow would glisten on the hills ahead.

Dry socks were sent up about every other day, but that didn't mean much. Dry socks are wet in five minutes after you put them on.

Wet feet and cold feet together eventually result in that hideous wartime occupational disease known as trench-foot. Both sides have it up here, as well as in the mountains around Cassino.

The boys have learned to change their socks very quickly, and get their shoes back on, because once your feet are freed of shoes they swell so much in five minutes you can't get the shoes back on.

Extreme cases were evacuated at night. But only the worst ones. When the company came out of the lines some of the men could barely walk, but they had stayed it out.

\*      \*      \*

Living like this, it is almost impossible to sleep. You finally get to the point where you can't stay awake, and yet you can't sleep lying in cold water. It's like the irresistible force meeting the immovable object.

I heard of one boy who tried to sleep sitting up in his foxhole, but kept falling over into the water and waking up. He finally solved his dilemma. There was a fallen tree alongside his foxhole, so he tied some rope around his chest and tied the other end to the tree trunk, so that it held him up while he slept.

Living as these boys do, it seems to me they should all be down with pneumonia inside of a week. But cases of serious illness are fairly rare.

Maybe the answer lies in mind over matter. I asked one sergeant if a lot of men didn't get sick from exposure up there and have to be sent back. I'll always remember his answer.

He said, "No, not many. You just don't get sick—that's all."

Scripps-Howard wire copy, April 1, 1944

### "A Look I Dread To See"

WITH FIFTH ARMY BEACHHEAD FORCES IN ITALY, April 5 —(by wireless)—One day I was driving on a muddy lane alongside a woods, with an officer friend of mine who has been wounded twice and who has been at war a long time.

On both sides of the lane were soldiers walking, returning to the rear. It was the typical movement of troops being relieved after a siege in the front line. Their clothes were muddy, and they were heavily laden. They looked rough, and any parade ground officer would have been shocked by their appearance. And yet I said:

"I'll bet those troops haven't been in the line three days."

My friend thought a minute, looked more closely as they passed, and then said:

"I'll bet they haven't been in the line at all. I'll bet they've just been up in reserve and weren't used, and now they're being pulled back for a while."

How can you tell things like that? Well, I made my deduction on the fact that their beards weren't very long, and although they were tired and dirty, they didn't look tired and dirty enough.

My friend based his on that, too, but more so on the look in their eyes.

"They don't have that stare," he said.

A soldier who has been a long time in the line does have a "look" in his eyes that any one with practice can discern.

It's a look of dullness, eyes that look without seeing, eyes that see without transferring any response to the mind. It's a look that is the display room for the thoughts that lie behind it—exhaustion, lack of sleep, tension for too long, weariness that is too great, fear beyond fear, misery to the point of numbness, a look of surpassing indifference to anything anybody can do to you. It's a look I dread to see on men.

*      *      *

And yet it's one of the perpetual astonishments of a war life to me, that humans recover as quickly as they do. You can take a unit that is pretty well exhausted, and if they are lucky enough to be blessed with some sunshine and warmth, they'll begin to be normal after two days out of the line. The human spirit is just like a cork.

When companies like this are pulled out for a rest, they spend the first day getting dug into their new position, for safety against occasional shellings or bombings. Usually they've slept little during their time in the line, so on their first night they're asleep early and boy, how they sleep.

Next day they get themselves cleaned up as best they can. They shave, and wash, and get on some fresh clothes if their barracks bags have been brought up. They get mail and they write letters, and they just loaf around most of the day.

On both the second and third days, they take on replacements and begin getting acquainted with them. All over the bushy slope where they're bivouacked, you see little groups of men squatting in tight circles. These are machine-gun classes. The classes are for the new men, to make sure they haven't forgotten what they learned in training, and to get them accustomed to the great necessity of knowing their guns and depending on them.

Replacements arrive in many different stages of warfare. The best method is for replacements to come when a whole regiment is out of the line for a long rest. Then the new men can get acquainted with the older ones, they can form their natural friendships, and go into their first battle with a feeling of comradeship.

Others arrive during these very short rest periods, and have only a day or so to fit themselves into the unit before going on into the great adventure.

The worst of all is when men have to join an outfit while it's right in the line. That has happened here on the Fifth Army beachhead.

*     *     *

There have been cases here where a company had to have replacements immediately. It was in circumstances where no front-line movement whatever in daytime was possible. Hence the new men would have to be guided up at night, establish themselves in their foxholes in darkness, and inhabit that foxhole until it was all over.

I feel sorry for men who have to do that. All of us who have had any association at all with the possibility of death know that the main thing you want is not to be alone. You want company, and preferably somebody you know.

It must be an awful thing to go up to the brink of possible death in the nighttime in a far-away land, puzzled and afraid, knowing no one and facing the worst moment of your life totally alone. That takes strength.

Scripps-Howard wire copy, April 5, 1944

# *Issei, Nisei, Kibei*

by The Editors of *Fortune*
drawings by Miné Okubo

WHEN the facts about Japanese brutality to the soldier prisoners from Bataan were made known, Americans were more
outraged than they had been since December 7, 1941. Instinctively they contrasted that frightfulness with our treatment of
Japanese held in this country; and, without being told,
Americans knew that prisoners in the U.S. were fed three
meals a day and had not been clubbed or kicked or otherwise
brutalized. Too few, however, realize what persistent and
effective use Japan has been able to make, throughout the
entire Far East, of U.S. imprisonment of persons of Japanese
descent. This propaganda concerns itself less with *how* the
U.S. treats the people imprisoned than *who* was imprisoned.
By pointing out, again and again, that the U.S. put behind
fences well over 100,000 people of Japanese blood, the majority of them citizens of the U.S., Japan describes to her Far
Eastern radio audiences one more instance of American racial
discrimination. To convince all Orientals that the war in the
Pacific is a crusade against the white man's racial oppression,
the enemy shrewdly notes every occurrence in the U.S. that
suggests injustice to racial minorities, from the Negroes to the
Mexicans and Japanese.

The enemy, of course, deliberately refrains from making
distinctions among the various kinds of detention we have
worked out for those of Japanese blood in this country. Unfortunately, Americans themselves are almost as confused as
the Japanese radio about what has happened to the Japanese
minority in this country—one-tenth of 1 per cent of the
nation's total population. There are three different types of
barbed-wire enclosures for persons of Japanese ancestry. First
there are the Department of Justice camps, which hold 3,000
Japanese aliens considered by the F.B.I. potentially dangerous

47

to the U.S. These and these alone are true internment camps.

Second, there are ten other barbed-wire enclosed centers in the U.S., into which, in 1942, the government put 110,000 persons of Japanese descent (out of a total population in continental U.S. of 127,000). Two-thirds of them were citizens, born in the U.S.; one-third aliens, forbidden by law to be citizens. No charges were brought against them. When the war broke out, all these 110,000 were resident in the Pacific Coast states—the majority in California. They were put behind fences when the Army decided that for "military necessity" all people of Japanese ancestry, citizen or alien, must be removed from the West Coast military zone.

Within the last year the 110,000 people evicted from the West Coast have been subdivided into two separate groups. Those who have professed loyalty to Japan or an unwillingness to defend the U.S. have been placed, with their children, in one of the ten camps called a "segregation center" (the third type of imprisonment). Of the remainder in the nine "loyal camps," 17,000 have moved to eastern states to take jobs. The rest wait behind the fence, an awkward problem for the U.S. if for no other reason than that the Constitution and the Bill of Rights were severely stretched if not breached when U.S. citizens were put in prison.

Back in December, 1941, there was understandable nervousness over the tight little Japanese communities scattered along the West Coast. The long coast line seemed naked and undefended. There were colonies of Japanese fishermen in the port areas, farmlands operated by Japanese close to war plants, and little Tokyos in the heart of the big coastal cities. There were suspected spies among the Japanese concentrations and there was fear of sabotage. Californians were urged to keep calm and let the authorities take care of the problem. In the first two weeks the Department of Justice scooped up about 1,500 suspects. A few weeks later all enemy aliens and citizens alike were removed from certain strategic areas such as Terminal Island in Los Angeles harbor, and spots near war plants, power stations, and bridges. But Californians did not completely trust the authorities. While the F.B.I. was picking up its suspects, civilian authorities were besieged with tele-

Citizens and Aliens, all people of Japanese blood on the West Coast were carted off to custody.

The Tanforan Race Track, near San Francisco, was one of fifteen Army assembly centers.

phone calls from citizens reporting suspicious behavior of their Oriental neighbors. Although California's Attorney General Warren (now governor) stated on February 21, 1942, that "we have had no sabotage and no fifth-column activity since the beginning of the war," hysteria by then had begun to spread all along the coast. Every rumor of Japanese air and naval operations offshore, and every tale of fifth-column activity in Hawaii, helped to raise to panic proportions California's ancient and deep antagonism toward the Japanese-Americans.

For decades the Hearst press had campaigned against the Yellow Peril within the state (1 per cent of the population) as well as the Yellow Peril across the seas that would one day make war. When that war prophecy came true, the newspapers'

Horse Stalls had to be cleaned, for human use, but the smell of manure persisted for months.

For their food handout, the *évacués* waited in long queues at the central mess hall.

campaign of hate and fear broke all bounds. And, when Hearst called for the removal of all people of Japanese ancestry, he had as allies many pressure groups who had for years resented the presence of Japanese in this country.

The American Legion, since its founding in 1919, has never once failed to pass an annual resolution against the Japanese-Americans. The Associated Farmers in California had competitive reasons for wanting to get rid of the Japanese-Americans who grew vegetables at low cost on $70 million worth of California land. California's land laws could not prevent the citizen-son of the Japanese alien from buying or renting the land. In the cities, as the little Tokyos grew, a sizable commercial business came into Japanese-American hands—vegetable commission houses, retail and wholesale enterprises of all kinds. It did not require a war to make the farmers, the Legion, the Native Sons and Daughters of the Golden West, and the politicians resent and hate the Japanese-Americans. The records of legislation and press for many years indicate that the antagonism was there and growing. War turned the antagonism into fear, and made possible what California had clearly wanted for decades—to get rid of its minority.

By early February both the Hearst press and the pressure groups were loudly demanding the eviction of all people of Japanese blood—to protect the state from the enemy, and to protect the minority from violence at the hands of Filipinos and other neighbors. A few cases of violence had, indeed, occurred, and spy talk ran up and down the coast. On February 13, a group of Pacific Coast Congressmen urged President Roosevelt to permit an evacuation; a week later the President gave that authority to the Army. On February 23, a Japanese submarine shelled the coast near Santa Barbara. Lieutenant General John L. DeWitt, on March 2, issued the order that all persons of Japanese descent, aliens and citizens, old and young, women and children, be removed from most of California, western Oregon and Washington, and southern Arizona. The greatest forced migration in U.S. history resulted.

At first the movement inland of the 110,000 people living within the prohibited zone was to be voluntary. The

Regimentation for men, women, and children made these little Tokyos more ingrown than ever.

Privacy was gained only by hanging curtains between crowded beds. There was too much idle time.

Japanese-Americans were merely told to get out. Within three weeks 8,000 people had packed up, hastily closed out their business affairs, sold their possessions or left them with neighbors, and set forth obediently toward the east. But Arizona remembered all too well how California had turned back the Okies in the past, and many Japanese-Americans were intercepted at this border. Kansas patrolmen stopped them. Nevada and Wyoming protested that they did not want to receive people found too dangerous for California. About 4,000 got as far as Colorado and Utah. It became apparent that the random migration of so many unwanted people could result only in spreading chaos. By March 29 voluntary evacuation was forbidden, and the Army made its own plans to control the movement.

They packed up again, after six months, and were all herded out of the Army centers.

Jammed into trains, they were sent farther inland into new soldier-guarded camps.

The *évacués* reported to local control stations where they registered and were given a number and instructions on what they could take (hand luggage only) and when they should proceed to the first camps, called assembly centers. Although they were offered government help in straightening out their property problems, many thousands, in their haste and confusion, and in their understandable distrust of government, quickly did what they could for themselves. They sold, leased, stored, or lent their homes, lands, personal belongings, tractors, and cars. Their financial losses are incalculable.

The Army, in twenty-eight days, rigged up primitive barracks in fifteen assembly centers to provide temporary quarters for 110,000. Each *évacué* made his own mattress of straw, took his place in the crowded barracks, and tried to adjust to his new life. By August 10 everyone of Japanese descent (except those confined to insane asylums and other safe institutions) was behind a fence, in "protective custody." They were held here (still within the forbidden military zone) until a newly created civilian agency, the War Relocation Authority, could establish other refuges farther inland. WRA's job was to hold the people until they could be resettled in orderly fashion.

WRA appealed to the governors of ten nearby western states. With one exception, Colorado's Governor Carr, they protested that they did not want the Japanese-Americans to settle in their domain, nor did they want any relocation center erected within their borders unless it was well guarded by the Army. Finally nine remote inland sites were found, all of them on federally owned land. (One assembly center in eastern California became a relocation camp.) Most of them were located, for lack of better acreage, on desolate but irrigable desert tracts. More tar-papered barracks were thrown up, more wire fences built, and once more the people moved. By November, 1942, all the *évacués* had packed up their miserably few possessions, had been herded onto trains, and deposited behind WRA's soldier-guarded fences, in crowded barracks villages of between 7,000 and 18,000 people.

They felt bitterness and anger over their loss of land and home and money and freedom. They knew that German and

Deposited in a desert camp, whipped by sandstorms, they were put in new barracks.

Crowded into a single room, this family managed to improvise a Christmas celebration.

Italian aliens—and indeed, Japanese aliens in other parts of the U.S.—had been interned only when the F.B.I. had reason to suspect them. Second-generation citizens of German and Italian origin were not evacuated from California; nor were the second-generation citizens of Japanese descent elsewhere in the U.S. put behind fences.

Although the *évacués'* resentment at regimentation within WRA's little Tokyos is deep, it is seldom expressed violently. Considering the emotional strains, the uprooting, and the crowding, no one can deny that the record of restraint has been remarkable. Only twice have the soldiers been asked to come within a WRA fence to restore order.

But WRA and its director, Dillon Myer, have been under almost continual attack by congressional committees in Wash-

Victory gardens are planted even though minimum food is given to everyone.

Public showers and latrines are provided but the Japanese tradition of tub bathing persists.

ington, and by a whole long list of badgering groups and individuals on the West Coast. The Dies Committee goes after WRA* and the Japanese minority at frequent intervals. Even Hedda Hopper, the movie gossip, prattles innuendoes. Not wishing to "imply anything," she noted last December that "we've had more than our share of explosions, train wrecks, fires, and serious accidents" since WRA has released so many of the *évacués*. Actually, not one of the 17,000 has been convicted of anti-American activity.

WRA has usually been criticized for the wrong reasons. It has been accused of turning loose, for resettlement, "dangerous Japs." The implication usually is that no Japanese-American should be released, although from the very beginning WRA's prescribed purpose was to help the *évacués* to find some place to live outside the prohibited zone. Again and again, the pressure groups and California Congressmen have urged that WRA's ten centers be turned over to the Army. (In February the President, instead, dropped WRA intact, with its Director Dillon Myer, into the Department of Interior.) Most frequently Mr. Myer has been charged with pampering the Japanese-Americans. Almost every day the Hearst papers fling the word "coddling," with the clear implication that all persons of Japanese descent, citizen or no, women and infants, should be treated strictly as prisoners of war, which of course they are not.

No one who has visited a relocation center and seen the living space, eaten the food, or merely kept his eyes open could honestly apply the word "coddling" to WRA's administration of the camps. The people are jammed together in frame barracks. A family of six or seven is customarily allotted an "apartment" measuring about twenty by twenty-five feet. It is a bare room, without partitions. The only privacy possible is achieved by hanging flimsy cotton curtains between the crowded beds.

Furniture is improvised from bits of scrap lumber: a box for a table, three short ends of board made into a backless chair.

*Herman P. Eberharter, a member of the Dies Committee, has said of its September, 1943, findings, ". . . the report . . . is prejudiced, and most of its statements are not proven." The committee wound up by suggesting three policies, all of which the WRA had already adopted.

The rabble rouser spreads disaffection among the *évacués*, distrusted and discarded by society.

At Americanization classes the old people learn the three R's and some history of the U.S.

The family's clothing and few personal possessions are somehow stuffed neatly away — on shelves if scrap lumber, a priceless commodity in all camps, is available. Otherwise, they are stuffed away under the beds. The quarters are usually neat. There are no cooking facilities and no running water in the barracks, unless the *évacué* has brought his own electric plate or had a friend "on the outside" send one in. As in Army camps, each block of twelve or fourteen barracks (250 to 300 people) has its central mess hall, laundry building, public latrines, and showers.

With faithful regularity, irresponsible yarns are circulated that the *évacués* are getting more and better food than other Americans. Actually, the food cost per day is held below 45

The loyal *évacué*, who has courage to face race prejudice "outside," can go east for a job.

cents per person. For 15 cents a meal the food is possibly adequate, but close to the edge of decent nutrition. In most camps, located far from dairy districts, milk is provided only for small children, nursing and expectant mothers, and special dietary cases. There are two meatless days a week and a heavy emphasis on starches. Nearly a third of the food requirements are grown on the irrigated fields of the camp itself. This reduces the actual cash outlay for food to 31 cents per person.

Practically everyone who wants a job can work, and most of the able bodied do. They plant and till the camp's vegetable acreage, prepare the food in the mess halls, do stenographic work for the Caucasian staff, work in the cooperative store.* In some centers they make furniture for the administration building or cotton mattresses to take the place of the hard straw pallets. Some are barbers and cobblers for the community, doctors in the hospital, scrubwomen in the latrines, garbage collectors. The maximum wage (a doctor, for instance) is $19 a month; the minimum, $12; the average, $16. In addition, those who work get a clothing allowance for themselves and their dependents—at the most, $3.75 a month for an adult in the northernmost center.

Individual enterprise is forbidden. To set up one's own dressmaking service within the community, or to sell shell jewelry or anything else to the outside is prohibited. In order to keep the center wage uniform, all economic activities must be conducted through the community cooperative, which pays its barbers and other workers the standard stipend. With their small monthly wage, and by dipping into their prewar savings, most *évacués* buy extras to eat, but they can get only nonrationed food, since they possess no ration books. They send to the mail-order houses for some of their clothes, buy shoes, yard goods, and clothing at the cooperative store. Their children go to school in the barracks village, and when they are sick, to the center hospital.

Thus the pampering and thus the humiliation. A doctor distinguished in his profession, who lived with grace and

---

*WRA has a lexicon of its own: Caucasian is the term for appointed administrative personnel, to distinguish them from the *"évacués,"* sometimes called "colonists"; beyond the gate is "the outside."

charm in a decently comfortable home before the war, is to day huddled in a small room with all his family. He practices his profession for $19 a month at the center hospital, serving under a Caucasian of lesser accomplishments, hired for considerably more money. A man who spent twenty years building up his own florist business or commission house, or who operated a large vegetable farm in one of California's valleys, is merely "stoop labor" on the center's acreage.

The record of Japanese-Americans during the depression indicated that they did not take to public relief. They were too proud. They stuck together, helped each other, and almost never appeared on WPA or home-relief lists. To virtually all of them it is now galling to be distrusted wards of the nation, their meager lodging and food a scanty handout, the payment for their labor somewhat the same.

They have always been an isolated, discarded, and therefore ingrown people. Today this is more true than ever. The barracks village as a rule is literally isolated. At Manzanar, California, for example, the center is but a tiny square in a vast and lonely desert valley, between two great mountain ranges. Spiritually the people are just as isolated as that. Thrown together in a compact racial island of their own frustrated people, they grow in upon themselves and each other; they become almost completely detached from American life, the war, the world. Their small children speak more Japanese than they would if they competed daily with other American school children. The teen-age boys and girls are ostentatiously American in clothes, slang, and behavior. It is as if they were trying too hard to convince themselves that they *are* Americans. They know that they must and will go out the gate soon.

The adults think about themselves, and about the past they left. With time and distance, California's farm valleys, towns, and cities become more golden-hued than ever to the *évacués*. They brood vaguely and fearfully on the future; the war, sometimes, seems like a vague abstraction, the cause of their troubles. And they think about rumors—which they often trust more than they do printed, official announcements. It may be a rumor that the Army will take over. Or that the *évacués* in this center will all be transported to another. This is the most nightmarish rumor of all to people who have moved so much in the past two years.

They think, too, about the endless details of their camp life. Each group of 250 or so *évacués* has a block manager who gets $16 a month for listening to their complaints and, if possible, straightening out innumerable daily problems. The food in the mess hall is badly prepared; there is no toilet paper in the ladies' latrine; the neighbors play the radio too late and too loud; the roof of No. 29 barracks has a small leak.

Finally, there are gossip and politics. The Japanese-Americans back in California went their way without much participation in politics as most American citizens know it. In the barracks village of WRA there is little real self-government. Most of the centers have a Council made up of block representatives or managers. But there is only a slight area within which such a congress can make community decisions. Usually at the meeting of the Council the members do little more than listen to new rules, new plans of WRA, handed down from Washington or the local director. The block representatives are expected to pass on this information to all the people.

Originally WRA ruled that citizens alone could hold office in the centers, but this proved to be unwise. Two-thirds of the *évacués* are citizens, but most of these American-born Nisei are from eighteen to twenty-eight years of age—too young to take on such responsible jobs as the block manager's. Besides, among the Japanese-Americans born here are hundreds of Kibei—young men who were sent to Japan for part of their education. Not all—but a large percentage of them—are pro-Japan, particularly those who gained the latter part of their education in Japan. Disliked by the Nisei majority, outnumbered and maladjusted, the Kibei often have become a nuisance, creating little areas of disaffection in the center.

Thus it turned out that the Issei—the aliens, parents of the Nisei and Kibei—could best provide the authority, stability, and seasoned wisdom needed in a block manager. They possessed a tradition of family and community leadership, and had commanded respect in the past. Above all they usually have an earnest desire to make the block of 250 or more people in which they live function in an orderly and quiet fashion. They are aliens primarily because U.S. law forbade them to become citizens. Many of them have a real loyalty to the U.S., not because the U.S. has invited their loyalty but because they look to their children's American future for their own security.

Politics in the centers has nothing to do with office or votes or *apparent* power. But it *is* power—the power of demagoguery, of spreading the infection of bitterness, exaggerating an instance or affront into an issue that may even get to the point of a small strike against WRA. The leaders have not invariably been pro-Japan. Some, both aliens and citizens, who had been good Americans became indignant at their loss of freedom and their right to participate in the life of the nation.

It may be that the administration was not willing to permit a big funeral for a man accidentally killed when a work truck overturned; it may be that three or four of the Caucasian staff displayed signs of race discrimination; it may be a rumor more plausible than fact. The "politicians" take any one of these, or a series, and worry it into a big camp issue. How great an issue it becomes depends most of all on the degree of confidence the center as a whole has in its director and the coolness and fairness with which he customarily handles his people. Too often the administration is out of touch with the main issues and grievances within the camp. WRA suffers, like every other agency, from the manpower shortage. Competent center directors and minor personnel are scarce. Often enough the director finds his Caucasian staff more of a problem than the *évacués*.

The two so-called "riots," which brought the Army over the fence, arose from the accumulation of small grievances, whipped up to a crisis by groups struggling for power and eager to put the administration on the spot. There was, in each instance, a strike. Actually a strike in a relocation center is self-defeating since almost all labor in the community works to provide goods and services for the *évacués* themselves; no morethan a handful work in the staff mess and office building.

Only when violence occurred, and the director thought he needed help in maintaining order, was the Army invited in.

But trouble rarely reaches either the strike stage or violence. The people in the Pacific Coast's little Tokyos rarely appeared on police blotters in the past, and now the crime record of WRA centers compares favorably with that of any small cities of their size, or, indeed, with any Army camp. Most of the policing is done by the *évacués* themselves, appointed to the "internal security" staff of each center.

Policing should be simpler than ever from now on. The ideological air has been cleared; the pro-Japan people have been moved out. The process of sifting the communities, separating the loyal and the disloyal, is virtually complete. The "disloyal" have been sent to a segregation center in northeastern California, leaving the other nine centers populated only by the loyal.

To all the *évacués* the two words, registration and segregation, are almost as charged with emotion as that disturbing term, evacuation. Quite simply the two nouns mean that a questionnaire was submitted to all adults in the centers to determine their loyalty or disloyalty. On the basis of this, plus F.B.I. records and in some instances special hearings, WRA granted or denied the *évacués* "leave clearance," the right to go East and find a job. The same information was used as a basis for segregating the "disloyal" in a separate center. About 18,000 (the "disloyal" and all their dependents) will sit out the war at Tule Lake, within a high, manproof, barbed-wire enclosure, unless Japan shows more enthusiasm than she has to date for their repatriation. (These 18,000 must not be confused with the few thousand interned by the Department of Justice.)

But separating the loyal and the disloyal is not so simple a job as it might seem. Loyalty is difficult to measure accurately on any scales, and the sifting of the *évacués* was clumsily handled. The process began in February, 1943, when the Army decided to recruit a combat unit of Japanese-Americans. A registration form was printed containing twenty-eight questions to determine loyalty and willingness to fight.

It was to be filled out by all men of military age. Someone realized that it would be well to have just such records on all adults in the centers. Plans were suddenly changed and everyone from seventeen years of age up was given the twenty-eight questions.

Nothing is more disastrous in a rumor-ridden, distrustful, neurotic community like a relocation center than to make one explanation of purpose today and a quite different one tomorrow. The people, newly arrived in the WRA centers, were still stunned by their evacuation, loss of property and freedom, and were acutely conscious of their stigma as "enemy." There was misunderstanding about the purpose of registration at most of the centers. The questionnaire was so carelessly framed its wording had to be changed during the process of registration. A few thousand refused to fill out the form at all. Others, remembering that they had lost business, home, and their civil rights, wrote angry ("disloyal") answers. They had no enthusiasm for defending a democratic America that had imprisoned them for no crime and without trial.

WRA, in an effort to be fair, has granted hearings in recent months for those who wished to explain the answers they made in anger or confusion. Pride made a few people stick to what they first wrote. There is little question that the majority of adults sent to Tule Lake feel loyalty to Japan, but there are also behind Tule's fences a few thousand who are not disloyal.

Most of the Issei who chose Tule Lake are there because of firm ties of loyalty to Japan, or strong ties of family relationships. Some Issei were afraid of bringing reprisals upon their relatives in Japan by affirming loyalty to the U.S. The parents who chose Tule Lake usually have taken all their children with them. Only a few sons and daughters over seventeen, who had the right to choose for themselves, could resist strong family pressure. It is ironic and revealing that at the high school at Tule Lake, civics and American history are popular elected courses.

Japan, however, makes no legal claims of protective interest in the Nisei or Kibei. When the Spanish consul visits Tule to report conditions to Japan, he is legally concerned only with the welfare of the Issei, the nationals of Japan. And, under U.S. law, the Nisei and Kibei cannot abrogate their American citizenship during wartime, even if they want to. Their expatriation, and even the repatriation of most of the Issei to Japan, during the war, is unlikely. Negotiations for the exchange of civilian war prisoners have been slow, and the delay is due to Japan, not to the U.S. State Department.

To a minority living at Tule Lake, Japan's unwillingness to arrange frequent exchange of prisoners is not disheartening. This minority does not want to set sail for Japan; it wants to stay in the U.S. People are at Tule Lake for many complicated reasons besides "disloyalty" and family relationships. There is evidence, for example, that some chose this kind of imprisonment for reasons of security and weariness. This is indicated

by the percentages of people in the various centers who said they wanted to be segregated. When the decision was made last fall to turn the Tule Lake camp into a segregation center, nearly 6,000 out of 13,000 residents of that center decided to stay put. This high percentage of "disloyal," the highest in any center, is explained in part by unwillingness to be uprooted and moved again. In the Minidoka relocation center, in Idaho, only 225 people out of 7,000 chose to go to Tule.

There are a few tired and discouraged people from other WRA centers who went to Tule Lake because they knew that the barbed-wire fences in that camp would stand permanently throughout the war. They reasoned that they would have certain refuge for the duration, while the other centers, according to *évacué* rumor, might be abruptly closed, and everyone turned loose without resources.

Some chose Tule Lake imprisonment as a gesture against what they consider the broken promises of democracy. For example, there is a young Nisei who enlisted in California early in 1941 because he felt strongly about fascism. He was abruptly thrown out of his country's army after Japan attacked the U.S. and put behind the fences along with all the other *évacués*. In February, 1943, when he was handed a questionnaire on loyalty and his willingness to defend the U.S., he was too angry to prove his "loyalty" that way; he had already amply demonstrated it. He is at Tule Lake, not because of his love for Japan, but as a protest to the government he honestly wanted to serve back in 1941.

There is the Japanese-American who fought in the last war in the U.S. Army, and is a member of the American Legion. When the Japanese struck Pearl Harbor, he offered his services to the Army and to industry in California. He was turned down. Sent to a relocation center he became a "troublemaker," with the slogan, "If you think you are an American, try walking out the gate." He was packed off to an "isolation center," and finally wound up at Tule Lake. Last year the U.S. Treasury received a check from him, mailed from behind Tule's barbed wire. It was a sum in excess of $100 and represented his income tax for the calendar year, 1942, when he had received belated payment for his 1941 services as navigator on a Portuguese ship. He insisted on paying his tax, as usual. He has, of course, no wish to go to Japan. He too sits out the war at Tule Lake in protest against the failure of democracy.

The minority who are in Tule for reasons of weariness or protest are not important numerically. But they show what can happen to people who are confused, discouraged, or justifiably angry. They reveal some ugly scars inflicted by our society. It is too early to speculate about what will happen to these 18,000 prisoners. A few thousand, at the most, may get aboard the *Gripsholm*. Will all the rest be shipped finally to a defeated Japan? Or will they be a postwar U.S. problem?

Where the Tule Lake prisoners will end their days is less important to consider than what is to become of those "loyal" *évacués* who are still in the nine other centers. Everyone deemed loyal, by the sifting process of registration and hearings, has been granted "leave clearance." Fortified with a handful of official papers, a numbered identification card bearing his picture and fingerprints, an *évacué* can set forth to the East. He gets his railroad fare, $3 a day travel money, and if he has no savings, $25 in cash.

During the last twelve months, 17,000 *évacués* have had the courage to go "outside." They are, with rare exceptions, young and single, or married but childless. A Nisei has to muster considerable courage to go out into the society that rejected him two years ago. From behind the fence "the outside" has become vague, enormous, and fearful. The huddling together, which is resented, is nonetheless a cohesive, protective force, hard to overcome. As he leaves the soldier-guarded gate, the young Nisei is about as lonely as any human being could be; he faces even more prejudice than his father did as immigrant contract labor.

The most powerful magnets to draw him out are letters from friends who have already gone east. Those who have made the plunge usually report back to their friends enthusiastically. The people who have started a new life—most of them from eighteen to thirty years old—are the pioneers. In the factories and in the restaurants and hotels, in the offices and in the kitchens where they work, they are building a future not merely for themselves, but for those who may follow. When they write back, "We can eat in *any* restaurant in New York," they spread a little hope. Or, "I attracted very little attention on the train." Or, "In Chicago, nobody seems to care that I have a Japanese face." They tell of the church groups who are almost alone in providing some kind of organized social protection for those who relocate in cities like Chicago.

They are being sent "outside" wherever a not-too-prejudiced community provides opportunity. Seven WRA regional officers have staffs scouting for job prospects, talking to employers of farm and industrial labor, sounding out public opinion, and, in general, smoothing the way. Illinois has taken more relocated American Japanese than any other state—4,000. Most of these have found jobs in and around Chicago. Winnetka housewives compete for Nisei servants, and even the Chicago *Tribune* has been calm. Only Hearst howls.

Ohio's industrial cities have taken about 1,500 from the relocation centers. Although special clearances have been needed for the eastern defense area, a few hundred have already gone to New York City, and the stream to the northeastern states will increase steadily. Scattered throughout midwestern states like Wisconsin, Montana, and Iowa are hundreds more.

There are, of course, areas of resistance. Antagonism to WRA's *évacués* is apt to increase not diminish when the European war ends and the casualty lists come only from the Pacific. Utah has taken about 2,000 *évacués*—mostly in Ogden and Salt Lake City where at first they were quietly absorbed. But last month the state A.F. of L. petitioned Salt Lake City authorities to deny business licenses to people of Japanese ancestry. Two thousand have gone to Colorado, but recent campaigns like Hearst's in the Denver *Post* and proposed new discriminatory legislation keep the state aroused. Wayne W. Hill, a state representative in Colorado, wearing the uniform of a sergeant in the U.S. Army, got emergency leave from his camp last month to beg the Colorado Legislature not to pass a bill barring Japanese aliens from owning land. About to be discharged from the Army, he said, "I am just as willing to die a political death as I am to die in battle to preserve American freedom." He was warmly applauded, but the House passed the bill; the Senate turned it down fifteen to twelve.

Arizona has had such a spree of race hating in the last year that WRA does not try to place people of Japanese ancestry there. A year ago the governor signed a bill making it impossible to sell anything—even a pack of cigarettes—to a person of Japanese descent without first publishing in the newspaper, days in advance, one's intention to do so, and filing documents with the governor. The law was declared unconstitutional after a few months' operation. It was not aimed merely at the new WRA settlers who number fifty-seven. It was intended to strangle Arizona's prewar Japanese-American population (632), many of whom make a good living in the highly competitive business of vegetable farming.

With only 17,000 young, unencumbered, and fairly bold Nisei out on their own, the biggest and hardest job of resettlement remains. The supply of young people without dependents is not unlimited. Early this year the Army, which had previously accepted only volunteers,* decided to draft the Nisei, like Negroes, for segregated units. This new turn of events will draw off a few thousand *évacués*. But the most difficult problems are obviously the large families and the older people. Depending heavily on the well-known tightness of the family unit of its *évacués*, WRA believes that many of the young men and women already relocated will soon bring their parents and small sisters and brothers out. Perhaps these Nisei who are so aggressively American themselves will not want their families held behind the fences.

However, in WRA centers there are hundreds of families with several young children, none old enough to leave alone. He is a courageous father who dares to start a new life with these responsibilities when, at the center, food, shelter, education, medical care, $16 a month, and clothing are provided. Farm families are often afraid to go to the Midwest to try a totally new kind of agriculture. And many feel that they are too old to start again as day laborers. There are the men who had retail, export, import, wholesale, commission businesses. The concentrated little Tokyos in California made possible a whole commercial structure in which the Japanese provided goods and services for each other. Presumably there will be no more little Tokyos to serve.

Even if the *évacués* were allowed back on the Pacific Coast tomorrow, they could not readily establish themselves in the old pattern. Quite apart from race prejudice, the gap they left has closed in two years. Except for the few who own land, they would have to build in California as patiently as they

---

*No less than 1,200 Nisei have already volunteered from behind the wire fences of the centers. Including Hawaiian Nisei, the total in the armed forces in January was close to 10,000. Some are doing intelligence work in the South Pacific. An all-Japanese-American battalion did distinguished service in Italy, with heavy losses.

now do in the East. They have been more thoroughly dislocated than they realize as they think nostalgically about California.

No one can gauge how soon the prewar unwillingness to accept charity or government relief deteriorates into a not-unpleasant habit of security. It is too much to expect of any people that their pride be unbreakable. Some of the old farm women who were "stoop labor" all their lives, even after their Nisei sons' landholdings or leased acres became sizable, have had the first rest in their history. Most of the old bachelors who had always been day laborers frankly enjoy the security of the centers.

If the war lasts two more years, and if WRA has succeeded in finding places for 25,000 more Japanese-Americans in the next twenty-four months (and WRA hopes to better that figure), it will be a job well done. That would leave some 45,000 in the relocation centers, as continuing public wards, not to mention over 20,000 at Tule Lake and the Department of Justice internment camps. Whatever the final residue, 25,000 or 45,000, it is certain that the "protective custody" of 1942 and 1943 cannot end otherwise than in a kind of Indian reservation, to plague the conscience of Americans for many years to come.

Meanwhile in the coming months, and perhaps years, a series of cases testing the constitutionality of evacuation and detention, even suits for recovery of property will come before the higher courts. Verdicts of "unconstitutional," or even eventual settlement of property claims cannot undo the record. It is written not only in military orders, in American Legion resolutions, Hearst headlines, and Supreme Court archives. It is written into the lives of thousands of human beings, most of them citizens of the U.S.

When future historians review the record, they may have difficulty reconciling the Army's policy in California with that pursued in Hawaii. People of Japanese blood make up more than one-third of the Hawaiian Islands' population, yet no large-scale evacuation was ordered after Pearl Harbor and Hickam Field became a shambles. Martial law was declared; certain important constitutional rights of *everyone* were suspended. The Department of Justice and the military authorities went about their business, rounded up a few thousand suspects. In Hawaii, unlike California, there was no strong political or economic pressure demanding evacuation of the Japanese-Americans. Indeed, had they been removed, the very foundation of peacetime Hawaiian life, sugar and pineapple growing, would have been wrecked. General Delos C. Emmons, who commanded the Hawaiian district in 1942, has said of the Japanese-Americans there: "They added materially to the strength of the area."

For two full years the West Coast "military necessity" order of March, 1942, has remained in force—an unprecedented *quasi*-martial law, suspending a small minority's constitutional rights of personal liberty and freedom of action. Those loyal *évacués* who can take jobs in war plants in the East have reason to ask why they are forbidden to return to California to plant cabbages. Mr. Stimson and Mr. Knox have assured the nation that the Japanese enemy is *not* coming to our shores. The Pacific Coast is now a "defense command," no longer "a theatre of operations," in the Army's own terminology. Each month the March, 1942, order seems more unreasonable.

Perhaps the Army forbids the *évacués* to return home less for military reasons than because of strong California pressures and threats. The Hearst papers on the Pacific Coast promise pogroms if any Japanese citizen or alien is permitted to come home. New groups like the Home Front Commandos of Sacramento have risen to cry: "They must stay out—or else." The Associated Farmers and the California Grange, the American Legion and the Sons and Daughters of the Golden West reiterate the theme of *or else*. Politicians listen and publicly urge that the despised minority be kept out of California for the duration.

There are Californians who care about civil liberties and human justice and see the grave danger of continued *quasi*-martial law but they have difficulty getting their side heard. The California C.I.O., the League of Women Voters, and segments of the church are all putting up a fight against continued "protective security." They work side by side with the Committee on American Principles and Fair Play, a group that includes such distinguished Californians as President Robert G. Sproul of the University of California, Ray Lyman Wilbur, and Maurice E. Harrison.

Lieutenant General John L. DeWitt, who ordered the evacuation in 1942, encouraged California's racist pressure groups when he said, "I don't care what they do with the Japs as long as they don't send them back here. A Jap is a Jap." General Delos C. Emmons, who succeeded DeWitt on the West Coast last September, says very little. He is the same General Emmons who decided *not* to order wholesale evacuation of the Japanese from Hawaii.

The longer the Army permits California and the rest of the

Pacific Coast to be closed to everyone of Japanese descent the more time is given the Hearst papers and their allies to convince Californians that they will indeed yield to lawlessness if the unwanted minority is permitted to return. By continuing to keep American citizens in "protective custody," the U.S. is holding to a policy as ominous as it is new. The American custom in the past has been to lock up the citizen who commits violence, not the victim of his threats and blows. The doctrine of "protective custody" could prove altogether too convenient a weapon in many other situations. In California, a state with a long history of race hatred and vigilanteism, antagonism is already building against the Negroes who have come in for war jobs. What is to prevent their removal to jails, to "protect them" from riots? Or Negroes in Detroit, Jews in Boston, Mexicans in Texas? The possibilities of "protective custody" are endless, as the Nazis have amply proved.

*Fortune*, April 1944

# Cassino, Once Thriving, Is Turned Into a Scene of Unrelieved Grimness

by Homer Bigart

WITH THE 8TH ARMY IN CASSINO, Italy, May 19.—Cassino is a bleak, gray, smoking ruin, which, with a little sulphur added, would be more grim than a Calvinist conception of hell.

The city, when we entered it at 12:30 p.m., was silent. For the first time since January no shells crumped down amid the skeleton walls of the few score buildings still erect.

I have seen all the devastated towns on the road to Rome—Capua, Mignano, San Pietro, San Vittore and Cervaro. But not even ghostly San Pietro compares with the utter ruin of this key citadel of the Gustav line.

This once prosperous district center of 15,000, roughly midway between Naples and Rome, is a phantom place of windowless shops and crumbled hotels. Not one Italian crawled from the ruins to cheer the British troops pressing onward for the battle against the Adolf Hitler line. Even in San Pietro part of the population had remained, but here in Cassino none could have endured the four hellish months of siege. The few safe shelters—shallow tunnels and caves along the bleak chalk slopes of Monte Cassino—were exclusively for the young fanatics of the 1st Parachute Division.

Kenneth L. Dixon, of The Associated Press; George Silk, a "Life" photographer, and I were the first reporters to enter the western part of the town, where German paratroopers threw back the American 34th Division in the mid-winter offensive and stalled the New Zealanders in the March assault.

Yesterday two British reporters approaching the abandoned German defenses along Highway No. 6 were killed by mines when they stepped off the road to avoid a sudden spate of

71

enemy mortaring. Today we were lucky—not one shell landed within Cassino during our three hours in the town.

The uncanny stillness, broken only by the rumble of bulldozers wrestling with drifted rubble, intensified rather than lightened the uncompromising grimness of the scene. From the desolate cathedral on the southern outskirts of Cassino we looked across stagnant pools of water to where the ruined shops and houses rose tier on tier against the steep bare slopes of Abbey Hill. The terraced olive orchards rising almost to the monastery were reduced to successive levels of blackened stumps. Not one flower, not one blade of grass, lived in the gardens of the town.

The Germans had diverted the Rapido River, blasting the levee above Cassino so that a considerable stream flowed between the cathedral and the central square, flooding the gutted buildings on the edge of the town and swamping the fields in front of the Hotels Continental and De Rosa, the outposts of their line.

Twisted trees, defoliated by the fragments and concussion of thousands of bombs and shells, reached dead limbs out of pools covered with greenish slime. Across the swamp the scene was solid gray—the gray honeycomb of ruins, then the gray slope of Monte Cassino merging imperceptibly with the steely sky. Only the jagged black outline of the abbey wall, topping the crest 1,300 feet above Cassino, showed where sky and horizon met.

British sappers had thrown a road across the bog. Before crossing we looked inside the cathedral crypt, which served as a command post and first-aid station for the advance spearhead of the three Allied assaults. First, the 100th Battalion of Hawaiians had quartered its wounded there during the opening days of the siege. Then the chapel was intact, but soon enemy guns were reducing it bit by bit. Burial vaults, high up in the walls of the nave, were ripped open. Skeletons disturbed after centuries had rolled down on the startled troops.

After the Hawaiians departed the New Zealanders took over, remaining through the bloody futility of the March assault. When the British forces took over late in March there was nothing left except the underground vaults where fresher corpses lay. The British endured a month of ghastly stench,

hanging sticky paper from the walls to arrest the spring invasion of flies. From this loathesome dungeon no one dared
move during daylight hours, for all approaches were swept by
machine-gun fire from the Hotel Continental across the bog.

Few tourists will remember the Continental, a three-story,
limestone building of perhaps thirty rooms. Baedeker ignores
it. But it was the only hotel in town that had a guest.

The guest squatted black and ugly in the vaulted lobby.
Ever since Feb. 3, when the Americans penetrated the heart of
Cassino, this Mark IV tank had slept there, rousing at intervals to poke its nose into the street and fire at the crypt or the
buildings in the center of the town.

One American patrol got inside the hotel, starting room by
room to mop up the Germans before a counter-attack set
them back. They claimed the destruction of the tank, but it
looked quite formidable today when viewed from a four-foot
pile of rubble at the massive lobby entrance. Its career ended
definitely on March 15, when waves of Allied bombers threw
great drifts of debris against the hotel wall, imprisoning the
tank until the British closed in on the last German strong
points early yesterday.

Sixty yards up Via Casilina in the direction of Rome was the
Hotel de Rosa, another enemy stronghold somewhat less
badly smashed than the Continental. Rooms along the rear
wall were bulwarked with sandbags, and in front of the side
entrance were heaps of discarded clothing and a battered German bazooka.

That was the last building on Highway 6, but across the
fields and abreast of the hotel were a half dozen stone houses
that seemed to have escaped direct hits during the great air
raid, although their walls were punctured by shelling. Elsewhere the Air Force had done a truly remarkable job of flat-
tening Cassino.

There was a stench of death near the smoldering rubble of
the Hotel Continental, but we saw only one German corpse,
which lay near a steel pillbox on the western edge of the
town.

The pillbox was embedded on the left side of the road
where it curved northward along the slope of Hangman's
Hill. It protruded only a foot above the curb and was so well

camouflaged with rocks that it looked like a heap of crushed stones left by a road-repair gang. Its gun had been removed. Through a slit the Germans had an excellent view of the bare flats across which Allied troops must hove to enter Cassino from the east.

Half a mile from the town, toward Rome, were two more German fortresses—on the left of the road, the colossal remains of an ancient amphitheater used by the Germans as a tank park, and opposite the ducal palace a square ruin of considerable dimensions with stone walls three feet thick. Here the Germans had their medical station and a storeroom filled with mortar ammunition.

Except for the Mark IV tanks and a portable pillbox abandoned near the Hotel del Rosa the Germans had left very little equipment of importance. The portable pillbox, mounted on heavy wooden wheels, was designed for a mortar, being opened at the top. Its walls were steel, three inches thick.

All sidestreets leading from the Via Casalina were posted with warnings of mines and booby traps, but a British captain commanding a company of sappers told us that surprisingly few mines were found. However, a considerable part of the town was still unexplored, though by mid-afternoon sappers had cleared a path up the slope through the barbed wire and minefields reaching Castle Hill, a barrier that three great assaults had failed to storm.

Behind Castle Hill is a shallow vale between the ruined castle and Monastery Hill where the Japanese-American battalion had been isolated for nine days while American tank destroyers tried vainly to reduce the thick citadel built in the Hohenstauffen era.

After the Americans withdrew, bombers completed the destruction of the castle, but even then its ruins continued to harbor German machine gunners. Across the vale high up on the slope of Monastery Hill was the celebrated Yellow House, a large stone mansion from which enemy automatic fire took a fearful toll among the attackers trying to advance over the bowlder-strewn pass below.

Neither the castle nor the Yellow House were ever stormed. When the British and Poles closed their trap around the town and monastery two days ago, most of the defenders had vanished.

Fewer than 150 prisoners were taken in Cassino. Many came down the road from the abbey when the Poles approached, preferring to surrender to the British.

Thus ended the bitterest battle of the Italian campaign. In today's quiet, a party of New Zealand tankers returned to Cassino and found the bodies of three comrades killed in the armored thrust following the March 15 air raid. The lead tank halted by drifted rubble was easy prey for German guns.

The New Zealanders dug three graves beside the road, while swallows came back to a town forever dead.

New York *Herald Tribune*, May 20, 1944

# Girl Thrills New Caledonia G.I.'s

by Vincent Tubbs

NEW CALEDONIA—When the first colored USO attraction in the Pacific reached here recently, so many men sought glimpses of "the women" that a special detail of MP's had to be dispatched to the area to clear the roads.

Cpl. Henry White of Cleveland stepped to the microphone, signalled Cpl. Saul Van Kirk of Philadelphia to turn on the juice, and announced the band's opening set of numbers, "Take the A Train," and "Jeep Blues." Then music filled the air.

Soldiers in the front, middle and back rows of the port unit's theatre clapped their hands in rhythm with the music. Soldiers seated on the ground stamped their feet in the dust. One soldier squealed "Ooo-oo-oo-eeee. Send me!" And everybody roared with delight.

The hot midday sun beamed down mercilessly on the backs of the audience. In the middle of the saxophone solo a soldier sitting on the ground rolled over on his stomach and beat the ground. "Lawd, just wait 'til I get home," he told the soil.

Kenneth Spencer, baritone star of stage and screen who played key roles in "Cabin in the Sky," and "Bataan," was introduced to emcee the show, and Julie Gardner crept unobtrusively across the stage with her accordion.

She was the first female of the troupe the boys saw. They did not greet her appearance with applause. A strong hum swept the audience as she crossed the stage, but the men were dubious, for Julie is more than pleasingly plump; she's heavy.

But when she grabbed her squeeze box and began to sing, "that locked it up." She is the star of the show.

*"Hit that jive, Jack,*
*Put it in your pocket*

*'Til I get back.*
*Going downtown to see a man*
*And I ain't got ti-ime to shake your hand."*

To the boys she's a whole constellation. They sat and patted their feet and weaved their heads from side to side as long as they could; then, it was just too much for them. They had to join in, and the whole hillside "jumped."

Julie worked hard on her first number and the sun worked hard on her. She perspired profusely; but for all her effort and discomfort she was richly repaid by the soldiers' howls and applause when she concluded. While they shrieked and nodded to each other their approval, she began again:

*"Are you fer it?*
*Are you fer it?*
*Are you fer it, Sergeant?*
*Well, join this song—and groove with me."*

When she finished this one, the soldiers howled and applauded so loudly she dared not step more than two feet away from the microphone until she had sung "Kow Kow Boogie," and "Don't Cry, Baby," for them.

Reluctantly, then, the audience allowed the show to continue.

With flaming red hair swept up into a wavy pompadour atop her head and wearing a long flowing skirt split up one knee with a bolero that left her midriff exposed, Ann Lewis, throaty-voiced blues singer, sauntered Mae West-ishly onto stage.

She looked at a soldier on the front row and smiled. He slid off his seat and plopped into the dust. He sat there throughout her act. Another soldier stood up and stuck his hand forward. She shook it and as he sat back down he licked his fingers.

She waved to still another soldier in the middle of the audience and he stood up, stared; then pretended to faint.

Although she did, it wouldn't have been necessary for her to do anything more. The mere sight of her was enough.

A soldier who had brought along his native girl friend (and

her family, because that's the way it's done here—take out girl, take out family)—nudged her and yelled in one ear:

"Them's home folk there, baby. That's what I've been trying to tell you about. Them's home folks there. See?"

The completely baffled lass answered: "No compre, no compre."

The soldier looked at her in dismay. His eyes shifted to the accompanying parents and sister who gazed at the stage open-mouthed almost to the drooling point.

He shook his head and said, "Naw, I don't guess you would," then turned back to the stage and yelped "Send me, lady—just stand there and send me."

Ann told the boys that there is nothing left in the States but men who are either "too old, too young or 4F."

Ann sang to them: "It Makes No Difference After Dark." She did the boogie and the Shorty George and her split skirt flew open occasionally. She moaned "Shoo Shoo, Baby" at them, then soothingly gave them "The St. Louis Blues."

> *"Uncle Sam, Uncle Sam,*
> *When does my man get his furlough?*
> *He's been away a long time*
> *And his baby can't stand this much more.*
>
> *Since you went away, baby,*
> *I sure do miss your loving face.*
> *But don't worry, daddy,*
> *No 4F Jodie's gonna take your place."*

Kenneth Spencer, in Robeson-rich baritone, stepped to the mike to sing "Without a Song," followed by "Joshua Fit the Battle of Jericho," and "Old Man River."

He finished with Langston Hughes's "Freedom Road," the words of which kept the boys leaning forward and nodding their approval. The final verse drew applause before the singer could begin the chorus. "Freedom Road" was a definite hit.

Freddie and Flo, the "aristocrats," just completing a tour with a USO Victory unit in the States, had the audience in hand the moment they hit the stage—Flo, shapely and seductive, singing "Basin Street," and Freddie, in black cap and gown, rapping on a box calling for "Order in the court."

The high spot of the show came when Freddie zipped off the gown to reveal an exaggerated zoot suit of loud green and red plaid which he topped off with a scarlet corduroy hat.

The reaction to the suit was terrific. This was Seventh Avenue, Harlem, brought all the way to New Caledonia. The couple did the jitterbug. Flo wiggled wildly. Freddie "stashed." The crowd jumped up and down in glee.

Audiences at the two shows on opening day, 2 p.m. and 7 p.m., totaled several thousand troops, who came from miles around. There were colored and white Army, Navy, Marine and merchant marine personnel. There were Frenchmen, New Zealanders, "Kansakas," Tonkanese and a few Javanese.

Audiences have grown night after night, with many following the performers from one stage to another, until a crowd of 4,000 sitting and standing around a stage built to accommodate 400 is coming to be considered a "normal function."

*Baltimore Afro-American*, May 6, 1944

# Notes from the Kidnap House

by A. J. Liebling

THE SECRET newspapers of France do not give French people much news of the outside world. That is left to the British radio and the Algiers radio, which do not have the paper and distribution problems of the journals in enemy-occupied territory. Since most of the resistance newspapers are no larger than a sheet of typewriter paper and have only four pages, they concentrate on local news and editorial comment. The three largest groups of publications—those in each group are loosely affiliated—are Communist, Socialist, and Mur, this last name being short for Mouvements Unis de Résistance. Mur is an organization of "new men," men who are not connected with the old political parties, and is strongly de Gaullist. The masthead of all Mur papers carries the slogan "One chief, de Gaulle; one struggle, for our liberties." Mur is for "social as well as political democracy," by which it means the nationalization of banks and probably of heavy industry, ruthless punishment of the rich men and Vichy politicians who collaborated openly or tacitly, and the guidance of France by a "new élite" of men who have made their way up through the resistance movements. The editorials in its papers maintain that "the shame of Vichy does not excuse the shortcomings of preceding governments." Some editorials in the Mur papers oppose the presence in Algiers of men like Pierre Cot, Vincent Auriol, and other pre-Vichy government figures, although conceding that in the interest of unity they must be tolerated for a brief while. Mur is nationalistic, occasionally to the point of xenophobia, whereas the Socialist and the Communist newspaper groups place more emphasis on the class struggle and less on the personal leadership of de Gaulle and new élites. Yet these, too, endorse de Gaulle and the Algiers government, and Mur endorses in some degree the class struggle. The difference lies in the importance each faction gives the different aspects of the fight. The Socialists, the largest single party in France before the armistice, defend most of their party record, and the heroic attitude of Léon Blum since his arrest, especially at the Riom trial, has added weight to this defense. Blum, like Edouard Herriot, has become a martyr in his own lifetime. *Populaire*, Blum's old newspaper, has seven regional editions, all clandestine, and reaches at least a million readers. Its preoccupation with the party record sometimes makes it seem to look backward too much. Recently it published a noble but nostalgic appeal to President Roosevelt to vindicate the New Deal by disregarding the demands of American capitalists. The editorialist, in his hideout, apparently had not heard that the term "New Deal" is now in the same limbo as "Popular Front." In almost every issue, *Populaire* runs, under the heading of "Our Martyrs," a list of Socialist resistants shot by the Gestapo or murdered by the Vichy militia, as if to emphasize the fact that the Socialists have at last become a party of action. The Communist press, headed by the several editions of *L'Humanité* and comprising a number of newspapers for various vocational groups of intellectuals and workers, benefits not only from the present prestige of Russia but from the name that Communist resistants have won for courage and austerity.

There are dozens of other resistance papers, of political shades more difficult to classify, ranging from *L'Aurore*, the organ of conservative Republican resistance, to a little sheet called *Le Soviet*, which carries at its masthead the line "Long live Trotsky and Lenin! Down with Stalin, gravedigger of the Third International!" All, however, agree on at least two points. The first of these is the French refusal to be patronized or treated as a decadent nation, especially by the English-speaking nations, whom the French blame for rebuilding Germany between the two great wars, before leaving France to fend for herself in 1939. The resistants look forward to liberation not as a favor but as the first small installment due them on a debt of blood. Smuts' speech last November served to intensify this feeling, which crystallized in the streamer headline of one clandestine paper, *Libération*: "Pétain, Badoglio, Smuts Examples of Intelligence of Marshals." "Great Britain three years ago carried all the hopes of our people;

these are things one does not forget, in spite of the Smutses,"
an editorialist, in hiding from the Gestapo, wrote in *Libération*. "France decadent? Really? Well, if all France were in
ruins, if there survived of all her decimated people only a few
women and old men, the representative of France, whoever
he might be, would have the right to sit with Churchill,
Roosevelt, and Stalin and be treated with the most profound
respect, because, if there hadn't been a certain nation called
France and a certain battle called Verdun, Monsieur Smuts
might now, with a little luck, be a junior native customs official in South Africa. . . . With or without Smuts, the European resistance movement is going to remake the Continent
into a free Europe of free citizens. Taught by our common
experience of slavery, we have more in common with the men
of Free Belgium, of Tito or Ribar, than with most Franco-
phile diplomats. Who knows if the greatest service Smuts
could render us is not to awaken our compatriots to the true
mission of France: to remake Europe and open Africa?" Another clandestine paper, *Franc-Tireur*, says, "The countries
that hoped to save themselves the horrors of war by neutrality
and those who could organize for victory out of the reach of
the enemy while for nine months we held the line — haven't
they also their responsibilities? Didn't they count too much
on France and her Army, on the military qualities of her
people, to conquer a force they had allowed to develop? This
war, in which we were the sacrificed advance guard, has been
waged against a racial dictatorship which intended to hold the
world underfoot. It is unthinkable that it should end in another dictatorship, nationalistic or plutocratic. France, even
defeated, remains great enough and has enough claims to
gratitude not to merit the treatment of a vassal or a servant."
This feeling was also revealed in a statement Daladier made to
the German police who a year ago came to the prison of
Bourrassol to remove him to the Reich. "I congratulate myself," he said, "for having declared war in 1939. A year later
you would have won the war. Today I have the pleasure of
telling you that you are irretrievably lost."

The second point of universal agreement is that France remains intrinsically great. These two basic sentiments make the
resistance press hypersensitive to any hint of infringement on

French sovereignty. A recent report from Washington that General Eisenhower would choose the Frenchmen with whom the Allies would treat meant to many resistants that the Americans would attempt to choose the rulers of France. Since, in the minds of French workingmen, America has always stood for big business and since the de Gaullists feel that the State Department has always worked against them, there is an almost universal fear that the English-speaking powers will try to impose a Kolchak government in striped pants, headed by a shifty *type* like Georges Bonnet. Bonnet was not allowed to participate officially in the Vichy regime because of his association with the Jewish bank of Lazard Frères, and therefore he could now be presented as being free of the Vichy taint. Camille Chautemps, who has been in Washington long enough to be able to disclaim any connection with the "later excesses" of the Vichy regime, is another bogey of the resistance men. The recollection of the high favor Bonnet and his friends enjoyed, back in the Munich days, with men still prominent in the British government, such as Halifax, Hoare, and Simon, does not dispose resistants to look forward to receiving British support against the tendency they think they see in American policy. An extreme statement of the frame of mind that has resulted from the refusal of the Allied governments to commit themselves is the following, in *Combat*: "We think it would be criminal and absurd to have complete confidence in foreign military staffs, in foreign military representatives, or in officers of the French Army of the colonial type to set up a republic and let the citizens of France express themselves. To say everything—if a choice has to be made one day between 'terrorism' and AMG, our choice is made. Of ourselves we are sure, of 'practical men' we are not."

More interesting to me than the editorial opinion of these journalists—who, since they live in constant danger of being captured, tortured to make them give information about their colleagues (usually by having their fingernails torn out), and then shot, lack the calm detachment of, say, Arthur Krock— are the pictures of French life presented, at least by implication, in such publications as *Bulletin des Chemins de Fer*, the clandestine organ of the railroad workers. Railroad men have perhaps the hardest rôle in the resistance movement. A factory saboteur faces the danger of detection and arrest, but when a railroad worker wrecks a train he may not even survive to be arrested. Furthermore, trains and freight yards are constant targets of bombing attacks; a railroader takes the same risks as the German troops among whom he finds himself. There are no air-raid shelters in freight trains as there are in factories. Moreover, railroaders furnish much of the information about troop and ammunition movements that leads to air attacks, and thus they call down the lightning on themselves. These dangers are superimposed upon conditions which are difficult enough in themselves—"overwork, long hours, pathetic remnants of rolling stock left by the Boche, coal dust that hardly burns in place of the good fuel of other days"—and upon the psychological strain of having to work for the Germans. "I know your suffering at feeling yourselves unarmed executioners of your countrymen when you drive trains toward Germany heavy with conscripted French workmen," one writer in *Bulletin* tells his comrades. (Many times, it may be noted, train crews have managed to stop somewhere and give the deportees a chance to escape through the windows of the cars.) "I know how you feel when you drive toward Germany freight trains loaded with all the substance that the Boche has drained from our rich land," the writer continues, "but you must endure, because you alone can on the great day, you eight hundred thousand rail workers, prevent the German from applying his strategy, paralyze his troop movements, isolate his units, immobilize his supplies, break his power, and precipitate his defeat."

The remainder of the same issue of *Bulletin* is more matter-of-fact. There is a prescription for getting rid of a fellow-employee who appears to be spying on resistance activities (accidentally drop a packing case on his toes), a list of the past month's railroad wrecks, and a note on a low *type*, an assistant stationmaster at the Perrache station, in Lyons, who curries favor with the German police. This *type* was present when political prisoners in a train passing through were throwing notes to friends on the platform. He saw a man on the platform cover a note with his foot. "The swine pointed the man out to a cop," *Bulletin* records. "He will not be overlooked." There is also the story of the wrecking of three civilian express passenger trains, with a heavy loss of life. These wrecks were the work not of any resistance group, readers are informed, but of *agents provocateurs* trying to twist public opinion against patriots. Patriot saboteurs do not molest trains of no military importance, especially passenger trains.

Another publication I always like to find in a packet that a friend in the underground movement now and then brings to my flat in London is *La Terre*, which calls itself "the organ of peasant resistance." Farmers, as a group, have always had the temperament and the facilities for resisting official pressure. Readers of *La Terre* are continually enjoined to delay threshing, to hide their harvests until they can be turned over to the *Maquis*, or at least to sell their crops privately to other Frenchmen, since any food delivered to Vichy authorities will be siphoned off to the Germans and sent out of the country. The government has inspectors to check up on agricultural production and delivery. Some of the inspectors, of course, are "reasonable," shutting their eyes to all discrepancies, since they are at heart as anti-Boche as anybody else. Others, not "reasonable," are mobbed or ambushed and beaten up with farm implements. In a Breton village, my latest *La Terre* informs me, three hundred people gathered around an inspector who had complained of the light weight of some pigs delivered by a farmer, and chased him into the mayor's office, from which the gendarmes had to rescue him. In another village, also in Brittany, an officious gendarme tried to make the farm wives stop baking, because the farmers are supposed to deliver all their flour to the government. Enraged women dumped him into a horse trough. In the Yonne department, farmers hide requisitioned horses and cows; in Loir-et-Cher, the farmers deliver no eggs, insisting that the hens stopped laying in 1940. In Seine-et-Oise, the peasants have formed committees to demand high grain prices. Everywhere the peasants unite to hunt informers, just as farmers in Iowa, not long ago, used to chase process servers. *La Terre* holds up the example of the scorched earth set by the Russian peasants. Incidentally, "Le Père Milon," de Maupassant's story of a Norman peasant who spent his nights killing German soldiers

during the 1871 occupation, has been republished, according
to *La Terre*, as a resistance pamphlet.

There are labor papers of all political shades. One, *Les Informations Sociales*, analyzes for French workers, in the tone of
the *New Republic*, the Beveridge Plan and the differences between the C.I.O. and the A.F.L. *Les Informations* describes
itself as "the bulletin of information for militant unionists."
In addition to publishing informative articles, it has reprinted,
without comment, Stalin's decree dissolving the Third International. It reports feelingly the arrest and deportation to
Germany of Léon Jouhaux, president of the Confédération
Général du Travail, for a time a fellow-prisoner of Herriot in
the fortress of Bourrassol, and it denounces several prewar
labor leaders who had accepted posts in fake labor unions set
up by Vichy and are now trying to hedge against the defeat of
Germany. It gives a long list of leaders of miners' unions sentenced for starting a strike against the Germans and it praises
miners for bearing so much of labor's struggle against the
enemy.

  *C.G.T.*, clandestine journal of the now submerged but still
powerful Confédération, argues the necessity of beginning at
once to rebuild a world labor movement and cites an index of
prices which have made life almost impossible for French
workmen in the last few years. In October, 1942, bread was
up, over prewar prices, a hundred and forty per cent, potatoes
two hundred per cent, wine two hundred and thirty per cent,
and shoes three hundred and twenty-five per cent. *Mouve-
ment Ouvrier Français*, another labor publication, says that
the working class is the main object of German attack: the
employers continue to eat well, even though they must pay
high prices, but workers have the choice of producing goods
for the conqueror at starvation wages in France or of being
deported to Germany, where, on rations almost as scanty,
they will be killed by Allied bombers. *Combat*, the most
widely circulated Mur paper, notes, apropos of the deaths of
French workmen in air raids in the Reich, that the French
censor forbids the phrase "Died in Germany" in the death
notices that relatives insert in French papers, although the
German papers, with their usual maudlin bad taste, carry long

accounts of ceremonies held over the graves of French workers killed in the Reich. Germans put pansies on the graves of Frenchmen they have brought to Germany for forced labor, a proof, *Combat* says, of the well-known Boche sensibility.

One of the leading publications in the resistance press is *Cahiers du Témoignage Chrétien*, an excellently printed monthly which sets forth the Catholic arguments in favor of resistance. One issue, discussing whether collaboration is permissible for a Christian, decides that "collaboration with Nazism, perverse in itself, is against the interests and soul of France. Conclusion: *non possumus.*" *Cahiers*, which reaches a large portion of the clergy and Catholic intellectuals, presents religious arguments against racism and anti-Semitism. It is interesting to observe the parallel reactions to Nazism in publications of sections of the clandestine press representing widely divergent groups. *Lettres Françaises*, the underground organ of French writers, charges that "a high proportion of pederasts among the collaborationists is to be expected, for to be against one's own country is against nature." The same sort of thought on the depravity of collaboration occurs in one of the regional clandestine publications, *Combat du Languedoc*. "That the Boche tortures and massacres accords with his business of being a Boche, but that a Frenchman sells other Frenchmen to the enemy, that is the ultimate depth of abjection. On the day of liberation, patriots . . . will sweep away the obscure rabble of informers for the Gestapo. Not even the memory of their crimes must survive in free France."

The regional publications have the strongest and most acrid odor of conflict. One issue of *Combat du Languedoc*, for example, contains a long blacklist of the traitors in surrounding towns and departments. There is in one town an ex-Republican priest who now informs against other clergymen who harbor Jews and *Maquis*; in another there is a Negro doctor, "forgetful of Nazi doctrines," who spies, and "a woman who sent her husband to forced labor and remained with a German soldier." There is a man who took money to betray the place where patriots had hidden the Strasbourg Cathedral's bells, removed to southwest France in 1939. Another man listed was a gunrunner for the Spanish Republicans in the civil war who has now turned coat and informs against refugees escaping across the Pyrenees. There is the president of a chamber of commerce who toasted a German victory, the Germanophile prefect kept by the widow of a former president of the Republic, the French colonel who sent his son to a Schutzstaffel cadet camp. Collaborators are named in print, even down to a man who was seen to tear a Lorraine cross from the neck of a young girl. From another regional publication I cite this excerpt: "Clermont-Ferrand—Our comrade ———— was arrested at sixteen-thirty, October 26th. He was brought to the morgue at two o'clock the next afternoon. His face was swollen almost beyond recognition; his neck bore marks of strangulation. All his fingernails had been torn out. One foot was swollen, enormous. He had two bullet holes in his temple. The executioners are known. They will not be tortured. They will be shot like dogs."

*La Voix du Nord*, the oldest and most powerful regional underground publication in the north of France, which has been occupied by the Germans since 1940, begins the latest issue I have received with a eulogy of Cardinal Lienart, Archbishop of Lille, who in a sermon defended the refusal of labor to work for Germans. This, in strongly Catholic Flanders, is news of the greatest importance. *Le Patriote de l'Oise*, another regional paper, thanks the Bishop of Beauvais for his steadfastness, and *La France Unie*, published in Brittany, praises the leading Catholic preacher of Rennes for his sermons on resistance; he has, the paper says, proved that deportation contradicts the doctrines of Christ. The first two of these publications have a strong Communist tinge, which indicates that the Germans and Laval have brought the French church and the French Communist Party into agreement for the first time in history. *La Voix du Nord* cites as a less appetizing example the local Catholic official of Secours National, a Pétain version of *Winterhilfe*, who takes, for his nephews and nieces, the best shoes and clothes donated to this charity. His sister, *La Voix* declares, then distributes the remainder to the needy, but only to the needy who attend mass regularly. Another local petty grafter it names is a police adjutant who stops people carrying small parcels of food in the streets and confiscates them unless the people can prove that they have been bought legally but who himself levies an illegal tribute of a pound of butter every week from each farm wife. It notifies people living on the coast that Germans billeted in coastal villages have been provided with civilian clothing in which to escape if a surprise landing is made by the Allies. *La Voix* urges its readers to memorize the faces of these Germans, so that they will be able to point them out to Allied troops.

*Le Patriote de l'Oise*, which appears to be Communist, tells of police raids on "our de Gaullist friends" in the district in which it is published. It warns of the presence of Vichy state police in the town of Creil and advises readers to "leave cafés when these *types* enter." *La Voix* tells how gendarmes surrounded a house in which they knew a Communist was hiding, in a village in Flanders; it was his own house, in the town of his birth, and it was a public secret that he had returned there. The man tried to escape by an attic window and the gendarmes shot him off the roof. "We know them," *La Voix* concludes simply. Until some assurance to the contrary is received, many writers in the resistance papers seem to fear that the Allies are coming to rescue the gendarmes.

*The New Yorker*, April 22, 1944

# Working at the Navy Yard

by Susan B. Anthony II

MY FIRST NIGHT on the midnight shift at the Washington Navy Yard, I met Esther, a fellow ordnance worker, who ran the machine next to mine. Dreading the changeover from swing shift to "graveyard," I asked Esther's advice on the best hours for eating and sleeping after 8 a.m.

"When do you go to bed?" I asked.

"Bed!" exclaimed Esther, a swarthy woman of about 35. "I haven't slept in a bed for five months."

Esther, the mother of five children, then told me the seemingly unbelievable schedule she has followed for the five months she has been working on ordnance to pad her husband's daily wage of $4.83, made as a trucker on the railroad.

"I have to run out of here to catch my bus at 8:10 in the morning so I can get home right after he leaves for work," said Esther. "I see that the three older kids are dressed OK for school and have had something to eat. Then I feed the little ones. Tommy is four and Mary is almost three. I feed myself and wash the dishes, straighten up the house, wash if I have to and take the kids out with me to buy groceries. Then I give the little ones lunch and make some sandwiches for the kids that go to school.

"After lunch I try to get some sleep—not in bed though—I just sit in a big chair in the living room and prop my feet up. Have you ever tried getting to sleep and staying asleep while watching two little kids tear the house apart?"

I could only look at Esther's tired face and wonder how many more months she could continue on such a regime. Next month, Tommy will go to half-day kindergarten. There are no nursery schools in the neighborhood for Mary, however, and the only one near the navy yard has a waiting list of 40 children.

Two nights after my talk with Esther, I came in at midnight and found her the center of a buzzing, indignant group of women workers.

"Esther's house almost caught fire this morning," explained Louise excitedly. "The new ruling that we have to take our coats all the way down to the ladies' room at the far end of the shop instead of hanging them in here, made Esther lose her bus. When she got home the kids were fooling with the gas stove and a towel had already caught fire."

The master mechanic, head of the shop, had decreed that we must take a ten-minute round-trip walk to hang up our coats. This meant that women workers had to get to work ten minutes earlier and were delayed ten minutes afterwards.

"Why can't we have lockers right up here near the elevator, like most of the men?" protested one of women.

This led to a petition asking for conveniently located lockers which we planned to get all the women in the shop to sign and then present to the master mechanic. Only four of us had a chance to sign it, however, before a personnel man on his daily check-up rounds, picked it up and turned it over to the master mechanic. We four were called on the carpet.

"Your request for lockers is ridiculous and will never be granted," he said. "Don't ever let me hear another word of this."

Two of the women who had signed were immediately transferred from our room. I was threatened with disciplinary action and was asked to explain my conduct in writing. I did explain. I protested the women's lack of representation on any grievance body. For our locker gripe was the least of our grievances. Working at the navy yard is like working in a completely open shop, since women are not members of the main union at the plant—the International Association of Machinists, AFL. We therefore had no shop steward, no grievance committee, no representation on union bodies and, least of all, no benefits of equal pay, promotion policies or other standards that a union contract would ensure.

Take our wages, for example. Though research for my book* had shown stories of high pay for women workers to

*Out of the Kitchen—Into the War (New York: Stephen Daye, Inc.).

be an utter myth, I had no idea, until I became a war worker myself, how *low* wages actually were. When my skimpy little paycheck of $23 a week came to me, I wondered how on earth I could ever live on that in wartime Washington if I were forced to pay my own room, board, transportation, doctors' bills and other necessities out of it. Then I would look around the shop and wonder how the married women and mothers—the majority there—could support their children and parents as well as themselves on these wages.

Navy-yard women start at $4.65 a day, which, with time and one-half for the sixth day, is $29.64 a week. Deduct the 20-percent withholding tax, and you find that we luxuriate on $23 a week. The highest-paid woman on production in our shop receives $6.95 a day, a peak she has attained after two years at the yard. Men get as high as $22 a day. The same low wages for beginning women workers prevail at most of the other eight navy yards in the country. Welders, however, and others who get preëmployment training are better paid. Welders at one yard receive $1.14 an hour. The wages of mechanics-learners, which is the classification we came under at the Washington yard and in which many women start at other yards, begin at 57 or 58 cents an hour.

Not only do the women start at a low wage—they stay at it. At the Washington yard and at the other navy yards in the East and West, there are no automatic raises. Miriam, who had been in the yard for eighteen months, said to me:

"At this place, it ain't what you know—it's who you know."

Raises were accorded on some indeterminate basis. Promotions to supervisory jobs seem to be unknown not only at Washington but elsewhere in navy yards. I could discover no women foremen, no women job instructors, or "snappers"—the lowest rank in the supervisory hierarchy. Up to last fall, I had heard of only three women "snappers" working at all navy yards. Others may have been promoted since then, but the going is slow.

Equal pay and promotions for women are one of the government standards of employment supported in writing by the Navy Department and seven other federal agencies. The navy yards themselves seem to be unaware of the fact; nor do they observe other standards adhered to on paper by the Department.

A few minutes before my first lunch on the day shift, I saw a woman, crouching almost double, come over to a bucket of dirty water used for cooling tools. She glanced furtively through the glass partitions separating our room from the rest of the shop and then stooped quickly and washed her hands in the filthy water.

"We aren't allowed to go out to the ladies' room and wash our hands before lunch—so this is the only water in the room and at least I can get some of the grease off my hands before I eat. If one of the bosses catches you washing you get docked and suspended," she explained, while keeping an eye out for the bosses.

Following most of the women workers, I quickly adapted myself to eating sandwiches held between grimy hands. I also had to learn to gulp down lunch in 15 minutes. The yard gave us 20 minutes for lunch, but at least five minutes were gone by the time you had raced and waited at the understaffed canteen for cold, watery chocolate milk or cola drinks (no coffee except on the midnight shift). The government standard of 30-minute lunch periods, hot lunches and a decent place to eat them is ignored by the Washington yard, which is nearer being the rule than the exception. Four out of seven yards in the nation give workers lunch periods of less than 30 minutes—15 in one yard, 20 in two and 25 in a fourth. In the other three yards, the lunch period, which is on the workers' own time, is 30, 40 and 45 minutes, respectively. Some of these other yards have hot lunches served from mobile or stationary canteens. We had to choose between cold sandwiches bought from the yard and cold sandwiches which we brought with us.

Another standard neglected by yard officials was the 15-minute rest period, morning and afternoon, advocated for women workers. I don't think many of us at the Washington yard missed these breathing spells, however. The fact was that although the work in our room was physically hard and required standing almost eight hours at a stretch in some cases (such as mine), there was such a slowdown, stemming from the top, that no one hurried. When I first caught on to my particular job, I began working at my normal speed, which is fast. The woman next to me said to me in a blasé tone:

"Don't break your neck working so fast—no one else does and the bosses won't like you any better for it."

Later a boss actually warned me:

"Take it easy; there's no rush. If you finish that there won't be anything else for you to do for a while."

On day shift we were kept fairly busy. The swing shift, from four to midnight, was the slowest. Workers stood around obviously idle for want of work, and would look alert only when a naval officer came by. The workers accepted the slowdown along with the bosses. When I asked one man the cause of it, he replied:

"Oh, it's red tape. The stuff we need in this shop is laying around in another shop and the orders to send it over here are tied up somewhere else."

I do not know whether workers at the other navy yards need rest periods more than those at Washington. Only two out of seven yards reporting have said that their women get formal rest periods, and in one of these, rests were given in the machine shop alone. In the other, women in the sail loft were given a rest period of 10 minutes every two hours. Rest periods for women, just like convenient lunch facilities for all workers, seem to be considered luxuries by yard officials.

At the Washington yard the lack of formal rest periods could not be attributed to the rush of work. Nor could one attribute it to a shortage of workers or overvaluation of the workers' time. I had mistakenly thought before going to work at the yard that minutes were precious in production. Once on the job, personnel officers and posters proclaimed the need for punctuality and perfect attendance. I was naturally surprised to learn after one day's work that the main method of disciplining these "precious" workers was to lay them off for as much as a week at a time.

Bertha, who took two or three days without permission to be with her sailor husband who was shipping out for a long time, was laid off for an entire week as a penalty. If you were one minute late in the morning, you were made to stand idle for one hour and be docked accordingly. If you forgot to tag in upon arrival at work or at lunch time, after three offenses you were laid off for a day.

There were other penalties besides being laid off, I learned when I was on the midnight shift. I saw Miriam, who had held the day shift for months, standing at a machine one night and asked her why she had changed from day work.

"You can bet your life I didn't change because I wanted to. The boss told me today at the end of my shift that I had to come in tonight."

Miriam had just married a soldier. She had accumulated one week's annual leave so she could take her honeymoon when her husband got his furlough. Before her vacation began, however, she took a day's sick leave. When she put in a slip for her vacation, the personnel officer, who had previously promised her the week off, told her:

"You don't get that week's leave now. Taking that day off when you were sick means that you can't take the week."

Miriam decided she would go ahead and take her honeymoon as planned. The result was that her first day back on the job she was forced to work 16 hours, 8 on the day shift and 8 on midnight. She was being punished by assignment to midnight for two weeks.

"Why do you stand for it?" I asked.

"I need the money, that's why," she replied simply.

That was the attitude of most of the women whom I met at the yard. They would stand for practically anything—five months without sleeping in a bed, a solid year on the graveyard shift so as to be home with the kids during the day, the double job, indigestible lunches, long hours and no promise of a future after the war—all for miserably low wages. The longer I worked side by side with them, the more I admired their endurance—but the more I seethed to see them organized in a union that would help solve their problems. And the more I saw the necessity for really planned production, planned community service, labor-utilization inspectors, labor-management committees that function and are recognized, and a program to educate the workers about the issues of the war abroad and at home. I admired the patience of the women who stuck by their jobs, day after day, though it was obvious that their usefulness to the war effort was cut in half by the very working conditions which they endured.

*The New Republic*, May 1, 1944

# 93rd Div. Patrol Kills 20 Japs, Escapes 3 Ambushes

by Vincent Tubbs

BOUGAINVILLE—(By Cable, Censored)—More than twenty Japs died in an attempt to annihilate a patrol of 93rd Division Troops in three ambushes, Tuesday and Wednesday, but our men shot their way out, losing only four men.

The tactical advantages held by the enemy made the encounter one of the worst since the division's arrival here. Superior machine gun and mortar firepower against our two Browning automatic and Thompson submachine guns, plus cunning and secure camouflage, gave the Nips the upper hand.

Our known dead are three noncoms. Missing are another noncom and an officer.

The patrol was assigned to reconnoiter several thousand yards beyond the farthest perimeter outpost near the Saua River and on to the Reini River. On Monday night the men camped beyond the Saua and moved out Tuesday to complete their mission.

When the patrol hit the Jap outpost guard of six men preparing breakfast, five escaped, but Sgt. Nehemian Hodges of Chicago got one. The unit then pushed on 150 yards before running into the first machine gun ambush, from which the entire patrol, and Sgt. Hodges in particular, had a miraculous escape as bullets whizzed through their legs.

The patrol leader drew the troops back, fighting a rear guard action during which Sgt. Rothchild Webb of Indianapolis stunned several Japs with a grenade, and Pfc. Merton Gilliam's automatic rifle fire accounted for three. The leader's report to rear headquarters stated the apparent strength and firepower of the enemy force, which was a remnant of the Jap Sixth Division of Nanking infamy.

Orders converted the reconnaissance patrol into a combat unit and ammunition was dropped by Lt. Darrell Bishop, pilot of an artillery liaison plane, who also directed the artillery fire on Jap positions.

After the barrage, the men moved back down the trail, leaving the artillery group at the command post to keep contact with headquarters. The crafty Japs had deserted the shelled Bivouac area and taken to ridges on both sides of the trail into which the 93rd patrol was allowed to proceed almost to Reini before encountering frontal and cross machine-gun fire from which the unit had its second miraculous escape without casualties.

The patrol leader deployed his men off the trail and skirted through the jungle to a point where they were calculated to meet their rear guard. In the meantime, the rear guard was so far forward that it was now between the patrol body and the Japs.

The patrol then hit an encircling ambush of snipers and machine guns. The lead men fell under the Japs' initial bursts, but Pvt. Deormy Raye of St. Paul, N.C., got three.

Pinned down in the brush beside the trail, Pvt. Gilliam of Cincinnati, firing a Browning automatic rifle, knocked off six, blasting one out of a tree and almost cutting him in half with the rapid fire.

Pfc. James Cofer of Washington, Ga., held the gun in position by its hot barrel with his bare hands, then, firing a Buck Rogers machine gun, crawled forward to cover Pfc. Ed Bradford of Hodge, La., whose machine gun jammed, while Bradford sought cover.

Cofer fired a blinding blast of seventy-five rounds, accounting for two Japs and another probable. Pvt. Ernest Bailery, Bayonne, N.J., silenced a Jap machine gun nest. Pvt. William Tindall of NYC got three snipers. Pvt. Edward Rodes, Richland, N.C., killed three fleeing in crouched positions, while Pvt. Cleotha Simpson of Normangee, Tex., got a ground sniper.

The patrol sneaked off the trail, took to nearby hills, climbing the sheer mountainside to establish a perimeter for a fight.

The rear guard sneaked off-trail through the jungle behind the patrol's ridge and returned to the command post at nightfall, but one man was separated from the guard and was left somewhere on the trail. He was Sgt. James Owens of Cleveland, who wiped out a Jap knee mortar crew setting up to lob shells on the retreating patrol.

The sergeant stayed pinned down by Jap fire until dusk, secreting himself under bushes and leaves, and spent the night listening to enemy troops stomping past, almost over him. Next morning he bravely took to the trail, past the dead Japs, and returned to the command post.

The rear guard section from which he became separated was commanded by T-5 Joshua Roberson of Galveston, Tex., and included Pvt. John Jones, 105 Fiftieth Street, Washington; Pfc. William Blackwell, NYC; Pvt. Cleo Brown, Carthage, Tex.; Pvt. George Turner, Covington, Ky.; Cpl. Doyle Terrence, Camden, Ark.; and Sgt. Owens. The latter three are engineers.

Cpl. Roberson took the men over terrain that the Japs considered impassable and did not defend. They found the command post with aid of a compass. Spotter pilots declare that the journey over the precipitous range was a remarkable feat.

On Wednesday night, while the main patrol was still out of contact, mass preparations were made to send help. At dawn, spotter planes piloted by Lts. Darrell Bishop of Houston and Octave Rainey, New Orleans, searched the jungle at tree top height, oblivious of possible Jap ground fire that could have easily disabled the planes.

Cpl. Thomas Wimbush of Atkins, Ark., mapper with the patrol, led the surviving men to the command post, where they joined Capt. Richard Hearst, white, who dispensed food, cigarettes and a limited water supply before leading the patrol out of the jungle.

A large force of crack infantry men relieved the patrol, fanned out to retrieve our dead, search for the missing, and exact revenge.

That mission is still in progress, with evidences of contact seen in artillery blasts that send whining shells overhead into Jap positions.

Returning members of the reconnaissance patrol were met

by this correspondent at the artillery firing post far in the jungle, beyond which movement is forbidden. They are, besides those mentioned:

T-4 Paul Fisher, Grenada, Mass.; John Medlock, Memphis; William Martin, Florida; Pvt. Melvin Finley, Seattle; Pvt. John James, NYC; Pvt. Marshall Mosely, Springfield, Ill.

At first listed missing, but found by infantrymen, are Saunders Williams, Houston; Pvt. Walter Jeffries, Boston; Clarence Reese, Cotton Plant, Ark.

The tragedy of the home-coming was T-4 Marion Clair of Plataka, Fla., who screamed and yelled with water-filled eyes, from which tears never flowed, when told of the death of a buddy.

*Baltimore Afro-American*, June 3, 1944

# For the Jews—Life or Death?

by I. F. Stone

*Washington, June 1*

THIS LETTER, addressed specifically to fellow-newspapermen and to editors the country over, is an appeal for help. The establishment of temporary internment camps for refugees in the United States, vividly named "free ports" by Samuel Grafton of the New York *Post*, is in danger of bogging down. Every similar proposal here has bogged down until it was too late to save any lives. I have been over a mass of material, some of it confidential, dealing with the plight of the fast-disappearing Jews of Europe and with the fate of suggestions for aiding them, and it is a dreadful story.

Anything newspapermen can write about this in their own papers will help. It will help to save lives, the lives of people like ourselves. I wish I were eloquent, I wish I could put down on paper the picture that comes to me from the restrained and diplomatic language of the documents. As I write, the morning papers carry a dispatch from Lisbon reporting that the "deadline"—the idiom was never more literal—has passed for the Jews of Hungary. It is approaching for the Jews of Bulgaria, where the Nazis yesterday set up a puppet regime.

I need not dwell upon the authenticated horrors of the Nazi internment camps and death chambers for Jews. That is not tragic but a kind of insane horror. It is our part in this which is tragic. The essence of tragedy is not the doing of evil by evil men but the doing of evil by good men, out of weakness, indecision, sloth, inability to act in accordance with what they know to be right. The tragic element in the fate of the Jews of Europe lies in the failure of their friends in the West to shake loose from customary ways and bureaucratic habit, to risk inexpediency and defy prejudice, to be wholehearted, to care as deeply and fight as hard for the big words we use, for justice and for humanity, as the fanatic Nazi does for his master race or the fanatic Jap for his Emperor. A reporter in Washington cannot help seeing this weakness all about him. We are half-hearted about what little we could do to help the Jews of Europe as we are half-hearted about our economic warfare, about blacklisting those who help our enemies, about almost everything in the war except the actual fighting.

There is much we could have done to save the Jews of Europe before the war. There is much we could have done since the war began. There are still things we could do today which would give new lives to a few and hope to many. The hope that all is not black in the world for his children can be strong sustenance for a man starving in a camp or entering a gas chamber. But to feel that your friends and allies are wishy-washy folk who mean what they say but haven't got the gumption to live up to it must brew a poisonous despair. When Mr. Roosevelt established the War Refugee Board in January, he said it was "the policy of this government to take all measures within its power . . . consistent with the successful prosecution of the war . . . to rescue the victims of enemy oppression."

The facts are simple. Thanks to the International Red Cross and those good folk the Quakers, thanks to courageous non-Jewish friends in the occupied countries themselves and to intrepid Jews who run a kind of underground railway under Nazi noses, something can still be done to alleviate the suffering of the Jews in Europe and some Jews can still be got out. Even under the White Paper there are still 22,000 immigration visas available for entry into Palestine. The main problem is to get Jews over the Turkish border without a passport for transit to Palestine. "Free ports" in Turkey are needed, but the Turks, irritated by other pressures from England and the United States, are unwilling to do for Jewish refugees what we ourselves are still unwilling to do, that is, give them a temporary haven. Only an executive order by the President establishing "free ports" in this country can prove to the Turks that we are dealing with them in good faith; under present circumstances they cannot but feel contemptuous of our pleas. And the longer we delay, the fewer Jews there will be left to rescue, the slimmer the chances to get them out. Between 4,000,000 and 5,000,000 European Jews have been killed since August, 1942, when the Nazi extermination campaign began.

There are people here who say the President cannot risk a move of this kind before election. I believe that an insult to the American people. I do not believe any but a few unworthy bigots would object to giving a few thousand refugees a temporary breathing spell in their flight from oppression. It is a question of Mr. Roosevelt's courage and good faith. All he is called upon to do, after all, is what Franco did months ago, yes, *Franco*. Franco established "free ports," internment camps, months ago for refugees who fled across his border, refugees, let us remember, from his own ally and patron, Hitler. Knowing the Führer's maniacal hatred for Jews, that kindness on Franco's part took considerably more courage than Mr. Roosevelt needs to face a few sneering editorials, perhaps, from the Chicago *Tribune*. I say "perhaps" because I do not know that even Colonel McCormick would in fact be hostile.

Official Washington's capacity for finding excuses for inaction is endless, and many people in the State and War departments who play a part in this matter can spend months sucking their legalistic thumbs over any problem. So many things that might have been done were attempted too late. A little more than a year ago Sweden offered to take 20,000 Jewish children from occupied Europe if Britain and the United States guaranteed their feeding and after the war their repatriation. The British were fairly rapid in this case, but it took three or four months to get these assurances from the American government, and by that time the situation had worsened to a point that seems to have blocked the whole project. In another case the Bulgarian government offered visas for 1,000 Jews if arrangements could be made within a certain time for their departure. A ship was obtained at once, but it took seven weeks for British officials to get clearance for the project from London, and by that time the time limit had been passed. The records, when they can be published, will show many similar incidents.

The news that the United States had established "free ports" would bring hope to people who have now no hope. It would encourage neutrals to let in more refugees because we could take out some of those they have already admitted. Most important, it would provide the argument of example and the evidence of sincerity in the negotiations for "free ports" in Turkey, last hope of the Balkan Jews. I ask fellow-newspapermen to show the President by their expressions of opinion in their own papers that if he hesitates for fear of an unpleasant political reaction he badly misconstrues the real feelings of the American people.

*The Nation*, June 10, 1944

# Cross-Channel Trip

by A. J. Liebling

I

THREE DAYS after the first Allied landing in France, I was in the wardroom of an LCIL (Landing Craft, Infantry, Large) that was bobbing in the lee of the French cruiser Montcalm off the Normandy coast. The word "large" in landing-craft designation is purely relative; the wardroom of the one I was on is seven by seven feet and contains two officers' bunks and a table with four places at it. She carries a complement of four officers, but since one of them must always be on watch there is room for a guest at the wardroom table, which is how I fitted in. The Montcalm was loosing salvos, each of which rocked our ship; she was firing at a German pocket of resistance a couple of miles from the shoreline. The suave voice of a B.B.C. announcer came over the wardroom radio: "Next in our series of impressions from the front will be a recording of an artillery barrage." The French ship loosed off again, drowning out the recording. It was this same announcer, I think—I'm not sure, because all B.B.C. announcers sound alike—who said, a little while later, "We are now in a position to say the landings came off with surprising ease. The Air Force and the big guns of the Navy smashed coastal defenses, and the Army occupied them." Lieutenant Henry Rigg, United States Coast Guard Reserve, the skipper of our landing craft, looked at Long, her engineering officer, and they both began to laugh. Kavanaugh, the ship's communications officer, said, "Now what do you think of that?" I called briefly upon God. Aboard the LCIL, D Day hadn't seemed like that to us. There is nothing like a broadcasting studio in London to give a chap perspective.

I went aboard our LCIL on Thursday evening, June 1st. The

little ship was one of a long double file that lay along the dock
in a certain British port. She was fast to the dock, with another LCIL lashed to her on the other side. An LCIL is a
hundred and fifty-five feet long and about three hundred
dead-weight tons. A destroyer is a big ship indeed by comparison; even an LST (Landing Ship, Tanks) looms over an
LCIL like a monster. The LCIL has a flat bottom and draws
only five feet of water, so she can go right up on a beach. Her
hull is a box for carrying men; she can sleep two hundred
soldiers belowdecks or can carry five hundred on a short ferrying trip, when men stand both below and topside. An LCIL
has a stern anchor which she drops just before she goes
aground and two forward ramps which she runs out as she
touches bottom. As troops go down the ramps, the ship naturally lightens, and she rises a few inches in the water; she then
winches herself off by the stern anchor, in much the same way
a monkey pulls himself back on a limb by his tail. Troop space
is about all there is to an LCIL, except for a compact engine
room and a few indispensable sundries like navigation instruments and anti-aircraft guns. LCILs are the smallest ocean-
crossing landing craft, and all those now in the European
theatre arrived under their own power. The crews probably
would have found it more comfortable sailing on the Santa
María. Most LCILs are operated by the Navy, but several
score of them have Coast Guard crews. Ours was one of the
latter. The name "Coast Guard" has always reminded me of
little cutters plying out to ocean liners from the barge office at
the Battery in New York, and the association gave me a definite pleasure. Before boarding the landing craft, I had been
briefed, along with twenty other correspondents, on the flagship of Rear Admiral John L. Hall, Jr., who commanded the
task force of which our craft formed a minute part, so I knew
where we were going and approximately when. Since that
morning I had been sealed off from the civilian world, in the
marshalling area, and when I went aboard our landing craft I
knew that I would not be permitted even to set foot on the
dock except in the company of a commissioned officer.

It was warm and the air felt soporific when I arrived. The
scene somehow reminded me more of the Sheepshead Bay
channel, with its fishing boats, than of the jumping-off place

for an invasion. A young naval officer who had brought me ashore from the flagship took me over the landing craft's gangplank and introduced me to Lieutenant Rigg. Rigg, familiarly known as Bunny, was a big man, thirty-three years old, with clear, light-blue eyes and a fleshy, good-tempered face. He was a yacht broker in civilian life and often wrote articles about boats. Rigg welcomed me aboard as if we were going for a cruise to Block Island, and invited me into the wardroom to have a cup of coffee. There was standing room only, because Rigg's three junior officers and a Navy commander were already drinking coffee at the table. The junior officers—Long, Kavanaugh, and Williams—were all lieutenants (j.g.). Long, a small, jolly man with an upturned nose, was a Coast Guard regular with twenty years' service, mostly as a chief petty officer. He came from Baltimore. Kavanaugh, tall and straight-featured, was from Crary, North Dakota, and Williams, a very polite, blond boy, came from White Deer, Texas. Kavanaugh and Williams were both in their extremely early twenties. The three-striper, a handsome, slender man with prematurely white hair and black eyebrows, was introduced to me by Rigg as the C.O. of a naval beach battalion which would go in to organize boat traffic on a stretch of beach as soon as the first waves of Infantry had taken it over. He was going to travel to the invasion coast aboard our landing craft, and since he disliked life ashore in the marshalling area, he had come aboard ship early. The commander, who had a drawl hard to match north of Georgia, was in fact a Washingtonian. He was an Annapolis man, he soon told me, but had left the Navy for several years to practice law in the District of Columbia and then returned to it for the war. His battalion was divided for the crossing among six LCILs, which would go in in pairs on adjacent beaches, so naturally he had much more detailed dope on the coming operation than normally would come to, say, the skipper of a landing craft, and this was to make conversations in the tiny wardroom more interesting than they otherwise would have been.

Even before I had finished my second cup of coffee, I realized that I had been assigned to a prize LCIL; our ship was to beach at H Hour plus sixty-five, which means one hour and five minutes after the first assault soldier gets ashore. "This ship and No. X will be the first LCILs on the beach," Rigg said complacently. "The first men will go in in small boats, because of mines and underwater obstacles, and Navy demolition men with them will blow us a lane through element C—that's sunken concrete and iron obstacles. They will also sweep the lane of mines, we hope. We just have to stay in the lane."

"These things move pretty fast and they make a fairly small target bow on," Long added cheerfully.

The others had eaten, but I had not, so Williams went out to tell the cook to get me up some chow. While it was being prepared, I went out on deck to look around.

Our landing craft, built in 1942, is one of the first class of LCILs, which have a rectangular superstructure and a narrow strip of open deck on each side of it. Painted on one side of the superstructure I noted a neat Italian flag, with the legend "Italy" underneath so that there would be no mistake, and beside the flag a blue shield with white vertical stripes and the word "Sicily." There was also a swastika and the outline of an airplane, which could only mean that the ship had shot down a German plane in a landing either in Sicily or Italy. Under Britain's double summer time, it was still light, and there were several groups of sailors on deck, most of them rubbing "impregnating grease" into shoes to make them impervious to mustard gas. There had been a great last-minute furore about the possibility that the Germans might use gas against the invasion, and everybody had been fitted with impregnated gear and two kinds of protective ointment. Our ship's rails were topped with rows of drying shoes.

"This is the first time I ever tried to get a pair of shoes pregnant, sir" one of the sailors called out sociably as I was watching him.

"No doubt you tried it on about everything else, I guess," another sailor yelled as he, too, worked on his shoes.

I could see I would not be troubled by any of that formality which has occasionally oppressed me aboard flagships. Most of the sailors had their names stencilled in white on the backs of their jumpers, so there was no need for introductions. One sailor I encountered was in the middle of a complaint about a shore officer who had "eaten him out" because of the way he was dressed on the dock, and he continued after I arrived. "They treat us like children," he said. "You'd think we was the pea-jacket navy instead of the ambiguous farce." The first term is one that landing-craft sailors apply to those on big ships, who keep so dry that they can afford to dress the part. "The ambiguous farce" is their pet name for the amphibious forces. A chief petty officer, who wore a khaki cap with his blue coveralls, said, "You don't want to mind them, sir. This isn't a regular ship and doesn't ever pretend to be. But it's a good working ship. You ought to see our engine room."

A little sailor with a Levantine face asked me where I came from. When I told him New York, he said, "Me too—Hundred twenty-second and First." The name stencilled on his back was Landini. "I made up a song about this deal," he said, breaking into a kind of Off to Buffalo. "I'm going over to France and I'm shaking in my pants."

Through the open door of the galley I could watch the cook, a fattish man with wavy hair and a narrow mustache, getting my supper ready. His name was Fassy, and he was the commissary steward. He appeared to have a prejudice against utensils; he slapped frankfurters and beans down on the hot stove top, rolled them around, and flipped them onto the plate with a spatula. I thought the routine looked familiar and I found out later that in his civilian days Fassy had worked in Shanty restaurants in New York.

While I was standing there, a young seaman stencilled Sitnitsky popped his head into the galley to ask for some soap powder so he could wash his clothes. Fassy poured some out of a vast carton into a pail of hot water the boy held. "'Not recommended for delicate fabrics,'" the steward read from the carton, then roared, "So don't use it on your dainty lingerie!"

Since the frankfurters and beans were ready, I returned to the wardroom. There the board of strategy was again in session. The beach we were headed for was near the American line, only a mile or two from Port-en-Bessin, where the British area began. Eighteen years before I had walked along the tops of the same cliffs the Americans would be fighting under.

In those days I had thought of it as holiday country, not sufficiently spectacular to attract *le grand tourisme* but beautiful in a reasonable, Norman way. This illogically made the whole operation seem less sinister to me. Two pillboxes showed plainly on photographs we had, and, in addition, there were two houses that looked suspiciously like shells built around other pillboxes. Our intelligence people had furnished us with extraordinarily detailed charts of gradients in the beach and correlated tide tables. The charts later proved to be extraordinarily accurate, too.

"What worries me about landing is the bomb holes the Air Forces may leave in the beach before we hit," the commander was saying when I entered. "The chart may show three feet of water, but the men may step into a ten-foot hole anywhere. I'd rather the Air Forces left the beach alone and just let the naval guns knock out the beach defenses. They're accurate."

The general plan, I knew, was for planes and big guns of the fleet to put on an intensive bombardment before the landing. A couple of weeks earlier I had heard a Marine colonel on the planning staff tell how the guns would hammer the pillboxes, leaving only a few stunned defenders for the Infantry to gather up on their way through to positions inland.

"We're lucky," the commander said. "This beach looks like a soft one."

His opinion, in conjunction with frankfurters and beans, made me happy.

We didn't get our passengers aboard until Saturday. On Friday I spent my time in alternate stretches of talk with the men on deck and the officers in the wardroom. Back in Sicily, the ship had been unable to get off after grounding at Licata, a boatswain's mate named Pendleton told me. "She got hit so bad we had to leave her," he said, "and for three days we had to live in foxholes just like Infantrymen. Didn't feel safe a minute. We was sure glad to get back on the ship. Guess she had all her bad luck that trip."

Pendleton, a large, fair-haired fellow who was known to his shipmates as the Little Admiral, came from Neodesha, Kansas. "They never heard of the Coast Guard out there," he said.

"Nobody but me. I knew I would have to go in some kind of service and I was reading in a Kansas City paper one day that the Coast Guard would send a station wagon to your house to get you if it was within a day's drive of their recruiting station. So I wrote 'em. Never did like to walk."

Sitnitsky was washing underclothes at a sink aft of the galley once when I came upon him. When he saw me, he said, "The fois' ting I'm gonna do when I get home is buy my mudder a Washington machine. I never realize what the old lady was up against."

Our neighbor LCIL, tied alongside us, got her soldier passengers late Friday night. The tide was low and the plank leading down to our ship from the dock was at a steep angle as men came aboard grumbling and filed across our deck to the other LCIL. "Didjever see a goddam gangplank in the right place?" one man called over his shoulder as he eased himself down with his load. I could identify a part of a mortar on his back, in addition to a full pack. "All aboard for the second Oran," another soldier yelled, and a third man, passing by the emblems painted on the bridge, as he crossed our ship, yelled, "Sicily! *They* been there, too." So I knew these men were part of the First Division, which landed at Oran in Africa in 1942 and later fought in Sicily. I think I would have known anyway by the beefing. The First Division is always beefing about something, which adds to its effectiveness as a fighting unit.

The next day the soldiers were spread all over the LCIL next door, most of them reading paper-cover, armed-services editions of books. They were just going on one more trip, and they didn't seem excited about it. I overheard a bit of technical conversation when I leaned over the rail to visit with a few of them. "Me, I like a bar [Browning automatic rifle]," a sergeant was saying to a private. "You can punch a lot of tickets with one of them."

The private, a rangy middleweight with a small, close-cropped head and a rectangular profile, said, "I'm going into this one with a pickaxe and a block of TNT. It's an interesting assignment. I'm going to work on each pillbox individually," he added, carefully pronouncing each syllable.

When I spoke to them, the sergeant said, "Huh! A correspondent! Why don't they give the First Division some credit?"

"I guess you don't read much if you say that, Sarge," a tall blond boy with a Southern accent said. "There's a whole book of funnies called 'Terry Allen and the First Division at El Guettar.'"

All three men were part of an Infantry regiment. The soldier who was going to work on pillboxes asked if I was from New York, and said that he was from the Bensonhurst section of Brooklyn. "I am only sorry my brother-in-law is not here," he said. "My brother-in-law is an M.P. He is six inches bigger than me. He gets an assignment in New York. I would like to see him here. He would be apprehensive." He went on to say that the company he was with had been captured near the end of the African campaign, when, after being cut off by the Germans, it had expended all its ammunition. He had been a prisoner in Tunis for a few hours, until the British arrived and set him free. "There are some nice broads in Tunis," he said. "I had a hell of a time." He nodded toward the book he was holding. "These little books are a great thing," he said. "They take you away. I remember when my battalion was cut off on top of a hill at El Guettar, I read a whole book in one day. It was called 'Knight Without Armor.' This one I am reading now is called 'Candide.' It is kind of unusual, but I like it. I think the fellow who wrote it, Voltaire, used the same gag too often, though. The characters are always getting killed and then turning out not to have been killed after all, and they tell their friends what happened to them in the meantime. I like the character in it called Pangloss."

Fassy was lounging near the rail and I called him over to meet a brother Brooklynite. "Brooklyn is a beautiful place to live in," Fassy said. "I have bush Number Three at Prospect Park."

"I used to have bush Number Four," the soldier said.

"You remind me of a fellow named Sidney Wetzelbaum," Fassy said. "Are you by any chance related?"

I left them talking.

Our own passengers came aboard later in the day. There were two groups—a platoon of the commander's beach battalion and a platoon of amphibious engineers. The beach-battalion men were sailors dressed like soldiers, except that they wore black jerseys under their field jackets; among them were a medical unit and a hydrographic unit. The engineers included an M.P. detachment, a chemical-warfare unit, and some demolition men. A beach battalion is a part of the Navy that goes ashore; amphibious engineers are a part of the Army that seldom has its feet dry. Together they form a link between the land and sea forces. These two detachments had rehearsed together in landing exercises, during which they had travelled aboard our LCIL. Unlike the Coastguardsmen or the Infantry on the next boat, they had never been in the real thing before and were not so offhand about it. Among them were a fair number of men in their thirties. I noticed one chief petty officer with the Navy crowd who looked about fifty. It was hard to realize that these older men had important and potentially dangerous assignments which called for a good deal of specialized skill; they seemed to me more out of place than the Infantry kids. Some sailors carried carbines and most of the engineers had rifles packed in oilskin cases. There were about a hundred and forty men in all. The old chief, Joe Smith, who was the first of the lot I got to know, said he had been on battleships in the last war and had been recalled from the fleet reserves at the beginning of this. He took considerable comfort from the fact that several aged battleships would lay down a barrage for us before we went in. You could see that he was glad to be aboard a ship again, even if it was a small one and he would be on it for only a couple of days. He was a stout, red-faced, merry man whose home town was Spring Lake, New Jersey. "I'm a tomato squeezer," he told me. "Just a country boy."

Cases of rations had been stacked against the superstructure for the passengers' use. The galley wasn't big enough to provide complete hot meals for them but it did provide coffee, and their own cook warmed up canned stew and corned beef for them for one meal. The rest of the time they seemed simply to rummage among the cans until they found something they liked and then ate it. They ate pretty steadily, because there wasn't much else for them to do.

Our landing craft had four sleeping compartments belowdecks. The two forward ones, which were given over to passengers, contained about eighty bunks apiece. Most of the crew slept in the third compartment, amidships, and a number of petty officers and noncoms slept in the fourth, the smallest one, aft. I had been sleeping in this last one myself since coming aboard, because there was only one extra bunk for an officer and the commander had that. Four officers who came aboard with the troops joined me in this compartment. There were two sittings at the wardroom table for meals, but we managed to wedge eight men in there at one time for a poker game.

There was no sign of a move Saturday night, and on Sunday morning everybody aboard began asking when we were going to shove off. The morning sun was strong and the crew mingled with the beach-battalion men and the soldiers on deck. It was the same on board every other LCIL in the long double row. The port didn't look like Sheepshead Bay now, for every narrow boat was covered with men in drab-green field jackets, many of them wearing tin hats, because the easiest way not to lose a tin hat in a crowd is to wear it. The small ships and helmets pointed up the analogy to a crusade and made the term seem less threadbare than it usually does. We were waiting for weather, as many times the crusaders, too, had waited, but nobody thought of praying for it, not even the chaplain who came aboard in mid-morning to conduct services. He was a captain attached to the amphibious engineers, a husky man I had noticed throwing a football around on the dock the previous day. He took his text from Romans: "If God be for us, who can be against us?" He didn't seem to want the men to get the idea that we were depending entirely on faith, however. "Give us that dynamic, that drive, which, coupled with our matchless super-modern weapons, will ensure victory," he prayed. After that, he read aloud General Eisenhower's message to the Allied Expeditionary Force.

After the services, printed copies of Eisenhower's message were distributed to all hands on board. Members of our ship's crew went about getting autographs of their shipmates on their "Eisenhowers", which they apparently intended to keep as souvenirs of the invasion. Among the fellows who came to me for my signature was the ship's coxswain, a long-legged, serious-looking young man, from a little town in Mississippi, who had talked to me several times before because he wanted to be a newspaperman after the war. He had had one year at Tulane, in New Orleans, before joining up with the Coast Guard, and he hoped he could finish up later. The coxswain, I knew, would be the first man out of the ship when she grounded, even though he was a member of the crew. It was his task to run a guideline ashore in front of the disembarking soldiers. Then, when he had arrived in water only a foot or two deep, he would pull on the line and bring an anchor floating in after him, the anchor being a light one tied in a life jacket so that it would float. He would then fix the anchor—without the life jacket, of course—and return to the ship. This procedure had been worked out after a number of soldiers had been drowned on landing exercises by stepping into unexpected depressions in the beach after they had left the landing craft. Soldiers, loaded down with gear, had simply disappeared. With a guideline to hold onto, they could have struggled past bad spots. I asked the boy what he was going to wear when he went into the water with the line and he said just swimming trunks and a tin hat. He said he was a fair swimmer.

The rumor got about that we would sail that evening, but late in the afternoon the skipper told me we weren't going to. I learned that the first elements of the invasion fleet, the slowest ones, had gone out but had met rough weather in the Channel and had returned, because they couldn't have arrived at their destination in time. Admiral Hall had told correspondents that there would be three successive days when tide conditions on the Norman beaches would be right and that if we missed them the expedition might have to be put off, so I knew that we now had one strike on us, with only two more chances.

That evening, in the wardroom, we had a long session of a wild, distant derivative of poker called "high low rollem." Some young officers who had come aboard with the troops introduced it. We used what they called "funny money" for chips—five-franc notes printed in America and issued to the troops for use after they got ashore. It was the first time I had seen these notes, which reminded me of old-time cigar-store coupons. There was nothing on them to indicate who authorized them or would pay off on them—just *"Emis en France"* on one side and on the other side the tricolor and *"Liberté, Egalité, Fraternité."* In the game were three beach-battalion officers, a medical lieutenant (j.g.) named Davey, from Philadelphia, and two ensigns—a big, ham-handed college football player from Danbury, Connecticut, named Vaghi, and a blocky, placid youngster from Chicago named Reich. The commander of the engineer detachment, the only Army officer aboard, was a first lieutenant named Miller, a sallow, apparently nervous boy who had started to grow an ambitious black beard.

Next morning the first copy of the *Stars and Stripes* to arrive on board gave us something new to talk about. It carried the story of the premature invasion report by the Associated Press in America. In an atmosphere heavy with unavowed anxiety, the story hit a sour note. "Maybe they let out more than *Stars and Stripes* says," somebody in the wardroom said. "Maybe they not only announced the invasion but told where we had landed. I mean, where we *planned* to land. Maybe the whole deal will be called off now." The commander, who had spent so much time pondering element C, said, "Add obstacles—element A.P." A report got about among the more pessimistic crew members that the Germans had been tipped off and would be ready for us. The Allied high command evidently did not read the *Stars and Stripes*, however, for Rigg, after going ashore for a brief conference, returned with the information that we were shoving off at five o'clock. I said to myself, in the great cliché of the second World War, "This is it," and so, I suppose, did every other man in our fleet of little ships when he heard the news.

II

Peace or war, the boat trip across the English Channel always begins with the passengers in the same mood: everybody hopes he won't get seasick. On the whole, this is a favorable morale factor at the outset of an invasion. A soldier cannot fret about possible attacks by the Luftwaffe or E-boats while he is preoccupied with himself, and the vague fear of secret weapons on the far shore is balanced by the fervent desire to get the far shore under his feet. Few of the hundred and forty passengers on the LCIL (Landing Craft, Infantry, Large) I was on were actively sick the night before D Day, but they were all busy thinking about it. The four officers and twenty-nine men of the United States Coast Guard who made up her complement were not even queasy, but they had work to do, which was just as good. The rough weather, about which the papers have talked so much since D Day and which in fact interfered with the landing, was not the kind that tosses about transatlantic liners or even Channel packets; it was just a bit too rough for the smaller types of landing craft we employed. An LCIL, as its name implies, is not one of the smallest, but it's small enough, and aboard our flat-bottomed, three-hundred-ton job the Channel didn't seem especially bad that night. There was a ground swell for an hour after we left port, but then the going became better than I had anticipated. LCTs (Landing Craft, Tanks), built like open troughs a hundred feet long, to carry armored vehicles, had a much worse time, particularly since, being slow, they had had to start hours before us. Fifty-foot LCMs (Landing Craft, Mechanized) and fifty-foot and thirty-six-foot LCVPs (Landing Craft, Vehicles and Personnel), swarms of which crossed the Channel under their own power, had still more trouble. The setting out of our group of LCILs was unimpressive—just a double file of ships, each a hundred and fifty-five feet long, bound for a rendezvous with a great many other ships at three in the morning ten or fifteen miles off a spot on the coast of lower Normandy. Most of the troops travelled in large transports, from which the smaller craft transferred them to shore. The LCILs carried specially packaged units for early delivery on the Continent doorstep.

Our skipper, Lieutenant Henry Rigg, nicknamed Bunny, turned in early that evening because he wanted to be fresh for a hard day's work by the time we arrived at the rendezvous, which was to take place in what was known as the transport area. So did the commander of a naval beach battalion who was riding with us. The function of this battalion was to organize beach traffic after the Infantry had taken the beach. I stood on deck for a while. As soon as I felt sleepy, I went down into the small compartment in which I had a bunk and went to sleep—with my clothes on, naturally. There didn't

seem to be anything else to do. That was at about eight. I
woke three hours later and saw a fellow next to me being sick
in a paper bag and I went up to the galley and had a cup of
coffee. Then I went back to my bunk and slept until a change
in motion and in the noise of the motors woke me again.

The ship was wallowing slowly now, and I judged that we
had arrived at the transport area and were loafing about. I
looked at my wristwatch and saw that we were on time. It was
about three. So we hadn't been torpedoed by an E-boat. A
good thing. Drowsily, I wondered a little at the fact that the
enemy had made no attempt to intercept the fleet and hoped
there would be good air cover, because I felt sure that the
Luftwaffe couldn't possibly pass up the biggest target of history. My opinion of the Luftwaffe was still strongly influenced
by what I remembered from June, 1940, in France, and even
from January and February, 1943, in Tunisia. I decided to stay
in my bunk until daylight, dozed, woke again, and then decided I couldn't make it. I went up on deck in the gray pre-
dawn light sometime before five. I drew myself a cup of coffee
from an electric urn in the galley and stood by the door drinking it and looking at the big ships around us. They made me
feel proletarian. They would stay out in the Channel and send
in their troops in small craft, while working-class vessels like us
went right up on the beach. I pictured them inhabited by
officers in dress blues and shiny brass buttons, all scented like
the World's Most Distinguished After-Shave Club. The admiral's command ship lay nearby. I imagined it to be gaffed with
ingenious gimmicks that would record the developments of
the operation. I could imagine a terse report coming in of the
annihilation of a flotilla of LCILs, including us, and hear some
Annapolis man saying, "After all, that sort of thing is to be
expected." Then I felt that everything was going to be all right,
because it always had been. A boatswain's mate, second class,
named Barrett, from Rich Square, North Carolina, stopped
next to me to drink his coffee and said, "I bet Findley a pound
that we'd be hit this time. We most always is. Even money."

We wouldn't start to move, I knew, until about six-thirty,
the time when the very first man was scheduled to walk onto
the beach. Then we would leave the transport area so that we
could beach and perform our particular chore—landing one

platoon of the naval beach battalion and a platoon of Army amphibious engineers—at seven-thirty-five. A preliminary bombardment of the beach defenses by the Navy was due to begin at dawn. "Ought to be hearing the guns soon," I said to Barrett, and climbed the ladder to the upper deck. Rigg was on the bridge drinking coffee, and with him was Long, the ship's engineering officer. It grew lighter and the guns began between us and the shore. The sound made us all cheerful and Long said, "I'd hate to be in under that." Before dawn the transports had begun putting men into small craft that headed for the line of departure, a line nearer shore from which the first assault wave would be launched.

Time didn't drag now. We got under way sooner than I had somehow expected. The first troops were on the beaches. The battleship Arkansas and the French cruisers Montcalm and Georges Leygues were pounding away on our starboard as we moved in. They were firing over the heads of troops, at targets farther inland. Clouds of yellow cordite smoke billowed up. There was something leonine in their tint as well as in the roar that followed, after that lapse of time which never fails to disconcert me. We went on past the big ships, like a little boy with the paternal blessing. In this region the Germans evidently had no long-range coastal guns, like the ones near Calais, for the warships' fire was not returned. This made me feel good. The absence of resistance always increases my confidence. The commander of the naval beach battalion had now come on deck, accoutred like a soldier, in greenish coveralls and tin hat. I said to him cheerfully, "Well, it looks as though the biggest difficulty you're going to have is getting your feet in cold water."

He stood there for a minute and said, "What are you thinking of?"

I said, "I don't know why, but I'm thinking of the garden restaurant behind the Museum of Modern Art in New York." He laughed, and I gave him a pair of binoculars I had, because I knew he didn't have any and that he had important use for them.

Our passengers—the beach-battalion platoon and the amphibious engineers—were now forming two single lines on the main deck, each group facing the ramp by which it would leave the ship. Vaghi and Reich, beach-battalion ensigns, were lining up their men on the port side and Miller, an Army lieutenant with a new beard, was arranging his men on the starboard side. I wished the commander good luck and went up on the bridge, which was small and crowded but afforded the best view.

An LCIL has two ramps, one on each side of her bow, which she lowers and thrusts out ahead of her when she beaches. Each ramp is handled by means of a winch worked by two men; the two winches stand side by side deep in an open-well deck just aft of the bow. If the ramps don't work, the whole operation is fouled up, so an LCIL skipper always assigns reliable men to operate them. Two seamen named Findley and Lechich were on the port winch, and two whom I knew as Rocky and Bill were on the other. Williams, the ship's executive officer, was down in the well deck with the four of them.

We had been in sight of shore for a long while, and now I could recognize our strip of beach from our intelligence photographs. There was the house with the tower on top of the cliff on our starboard as we went in. We had been warned that preliminary bombardment might remove it, so we should not count too much upon it as a landmark; however, there it was and it gave me the pleasure of recognition. A path was to have been blasted and swept for us through element C (underwater concrete and iron obstacles) and mines, and the entrance to it was to have been marked with colored buoys. The buoys were there, so evidently the operation was going all right. Our LCIL made a turn and headed for the opening like a halfback going into a hole in the line. I don't know whether Rigg suddenly became solicitous for my safety or whether he simply didn't want me underfoot on the bridge, where two officers and two signalmen had trouble getting around even without me. He said, "Mr. Liebling will take his station on the upper deck during action." This was formal language from the young man I had learned to call Bunny, especially since the action did not seem violent as yet, but I climbed down the short ladder from the bridge to the deck, a move which put the wheelhouse between me and the bow. The upper deck was also the station for a pharmacist's mate named Kallam, who was our reserve first-aid man. A landing craft carries no doctor, the theory being that a pharmacist's mate will make temporary repairs until the patient can be transferred to a larger ship. We had two men with this rating aboard. The other, a fellow named Barry, was up in the bow. Kallam was a sallow, long-faced North Carolinian who once told me he had gone into the peacetime Navy as a youth and had never been good for anything else since. This was his first action, except for a couple of landings in Nicaragua around 1930.

The shore curved out toward us on the port side of the ship and when I looked out in that direction I could see a lot of smoke from what appeared to be shells bursting on the beach. There was also an LCT, grounded and burning. "Looks as if there's opposition," I said to Kallam, without much originality. At about the same time something splashed in the water off our starboard quarter, sending up a high spray. We were moving in fast now. I could visualize, from the plan I had seen so often in the last few days, the straight, narrow lane in which we had to stay. "On a straight line—like a rope ferry," I thought. The view on both sides changed rapidly. The LCT which had been on our port bow was now on our port quarter, and another LCT, also grounded, was now visible. A number of men, who had evidently just left her, were in the water, some up to their necks and others up to their armpits, and they didn't look as if they were trying to get ashore. Tracer bullets were skipping around them and they seemed perplexed. What I hate most about tracers is that every time you see one, you know there are four more bullets that you don't see, because only one tracer to five bullets is loaded in a machine-gun belt. Just about then, it seems in retrospect, I felt the ship ground.

I looked down at the main deck, and the beach-battalion men were already moving ahead, so I knew that the ramps must be down. I could hear Long shouting, "Move along now! Move along!," as if he were unloading an excursion boat at Coney Island. But the men needed no urging; they were moving without a sign of flinching. You didn't have to look far for tracers now, and Kallam and I flattened our backs against the pilot house and pulled in our stomachs, as if to give a possible bullet an extra couple of inches clearance. Something tickled the back of my neck. I slapped at it and discovered that I had most of the ship's rigging draped around my neck and shoulders, like a character in an old slapstick movie about a spaghetti factory, or like Captain Horatio Hornblower. The rigging had been cut away by bullets. As Kallam and I looked toward the stern, we could see a tableau that was like a recruiting poster. There was a twenty-millimetre rapid-firing gun on the upper deck. Since it couldn't bear forward because of the pilot house and since there was nothing to shoot at on either side, it was pointed straight up at the sky in readiness for a possible dive-bombing attack. It had a crew of three men, and they were kneeling about it, one on each side and one behind the gun barrel, all looking up at the sky in an extremely earnest manner, and getting all the protection they could out of the gunshield. As a background to the men's heads, an American flag at the ship's stern streamed across the field of vision. It was a new flag, which Rigg had ordered hoisted for the first time for the invasion, and its colors were brilliant in the sun. To make the poster motif perfect, one of the three men was a Negro, William Jackson, from New Orleans, a wardroom steward, who, like everybody else on the LCIL, had multiple duties.

The last passenger was off the ship now, and I could hear the stern anchor cable rattling on the drum as it came up. An LCIL drops a stern anchor just before it grounds, and pays out fifty to a hundred fathoms of chain cable as it slowly slides the last couple of ship's lengths toward shore. To get under way again, it takes up the cable, pulling itself afloat. I had not known until that minute how eager I was to hear the sound of the cable that follows the order "Take in on stern anchor." Almost as the cable began to come in, something hit the ship with the solid clunk of metal against metal—not as hard as a collision or a bomb blast; just "clink." Long yelled down, "Pharmacist's mate go forward. Somebody's hurt." Kallam scrambled down the ladder to the main deck with his kit. Then Long yelled to a man at the stern anchor winch, "Give it hell!" An LCIL has to pull itself out and get the anchor up before it can use its motors, because otherwise the propeller might foul in the cable. The little engine which supplies power for the winch is built by a farm-machinery company in Waukesha, Wisconsin, and every drop of gasoline that went into the one on our ship was filtered through chamois skin first. That engine is the ship's insurance policy. A sailor now came running up the stairway from the cabin. He grabbed me and shouted, "Two casualties in bow!" I passed this information on to the bridge for whatever good it might do; both pharmacist's mates were forward already and there was really nothing else to be done. Our craft had now swung clear, the anchor was up, and the engines went into play. She turned about and shot forward like a destroyer. The chief machinist's mate said afterward that the engines did seven hundred revolutions a minute instead of the six hundred that was normal top speed. Shells were kicking up waterspouts around us as we went; the water they raised looked black. Rigg said afterward, "Funny thing. When I was going in, I had my whole attention fixed on two mines attached to sunken concrete blocks on either side of the place where we went in. I knew they hadn't been cleared away—just a path between them. They were spider mines, those things with a lot of loose cables. Touch one cable and you detonate the mine. When I was going out, I was so excited that I forgot all about the damn mines and didn't think of them until I was two miles past them."

A sailor came by and Shorty, one of the men in the gun crew, said to him, "Who was it?" The sailor said, "Rocky and Bill. They're all tore up. A shell got the winch and ramps and all." I went forward to the well deck, which was sticky with a mixture of blood and condensed milk. Soldiers had left cases of rations lying all about the ship, and a fragment of the shell that hit the boys had torn into a carton of cans of milk. Rocky and Bill had been moved belowdecks into one of the large forward compartments. Rocky was dead beyond possible doubt, somebody told me, but the pharmacist's mates had given Bill blood plasma and thought he might still be alive. I remembered Bill, a big, baby-faced kid from the District of Columbia, built like a wrestler. He was about twenty, and the other boys used to kid him about a girl he was always writing letters to. A third wounded man, a soldier dressed in khaki, lay on a stretcher on deck breathing hard through his mouth. His long, triangular face looked like a dirty drumhead; his skin was white and drawn tight over his high cheekbones. He wasn't making much noise. There was a shooting-gallery smell over everything, and when we passed close under the Arkansas and she let off a salvo, a couple of our men who had their backs to her quivered and had to be reassured. Long and Kavanaugh, the communications officer, were already going about the ship trying to get things ticking again, but they had little success at first.

Halfway out to the transport area, another LCIL hailed us and asked us to take a wounded man aboard. They had got him from some smaller craft, but they had to complete a mission before they could go back to the big ships. We went alongside and took him over the rail. He was wrapped in khaki blankets and strapped into a wire basket litter. After we had sheered away, a man aboard the other LCIL yelled at us to come back so that he could hand over a half-empty bottle of plasma with a long rubber tube attached. "This goes with him," he said. We went alongside again and he handed the bottle to one of our fellows. It was trouble for nothing, because the man by then had stopped breathing.

We made our way out to a transport called the Dorothea Dix that had a hospital ward fitted out. We went alongside and Rigg yelled that we had four casualties aboard. A young naval doctor climbed down the grapple net hanging on the Dix's side and came aboard. After he had looked at our soldier, he called for a breeches buoy and the soldier was hoisted up sitting in that. He had been hit in one shoulder and one leg, and the doctor said he had a good chance. The three others had to be sent up in wire baskets, vertically, like Indian papooses. A couple of Negroes on the upper deck of the Dix dropped a line which our men made fast to the top of one basket after another. Then the man would be jerked up in the air by the Negroes as if he were going to heaven. Now that we carried no passengers and were lighter, the sea seemed rough. We bobbled under the towering transport and the wounded men swung wildly on the end of the line, a few times almost striking against the ship. A Coastguardsman reached up for the bottom of one basket so that he could steady it on its way up. At least a quart of blood ran down on him, covering his tin hat, his upturned face, and his blue overalls. He stood motionless for an instant, as if he didn't know what had happened, seeing the world through a film of red, because he wore eyeglasses and blood had covered the lenses. The basket, swaying eccentrically, went up the side. After a couple of seconds, the Coastguardsman turned and ran to a sink aft of the galley, where he turned on the water and began washing himself. A couple of minutes after the last litter had been hoisted aboard, an officer on the Dix leaned over her rail and shouted down, "Medical officer in charge says two of these men are dead! He says you should take them back to the beach and bury them." Out there, fifteen miles off shore, they evidently thought that this was just another landing exercise. A sailor on deck said, "The son of a bitch ought to see that beach."

Rigg explained to the officer that it would be impossible to return to the beach and ordered the men to cast off the lines, and we went away from the Dix. Now that the dead and wounded were gone, I saw Kallam sneak to the far rail and be sicker than I have ever seen a man at sea. We passed close by the command ship and signalled that we had completed our mission. We received a signal, "Wait for orders," and for the rest of the day we loafed, while we tried to reconstruct what had happened to us. Almost everybody on the ship had a battle headache.

"What hurts me worst," Lechich said, "is thinking what happened to those poor guys we landed. That beach was hot with Jerries. And they didn't have nothing to fight with— only carbines and rifles. They weren't even supposed to be combat troops."

"I don't think any of them could be alive now," another man said.

As the hours went by and we weren't ordered to do anything, it became evident that our bit of beach wasn't doing well, for we had expected, after delivering our first load on shore, to be employed in ferrying other troops from transports to the beach, which the beach-battalion boys and engineers would in the meantime have been helping to clear.

Other LCILs of our flotilla were also lying idle. We saw one of them being towed, and then we saw her capsize. Three others, we heard, were lying up on one strip of beach, burned. Landing craft are reckoned expendable. Rigg came down from the bridge and, seeing me, said, "The beach is closed to LCILs now. Only small boats going in. Wish they'd thought of that earlier. We lost three good men."

"Which three?" I asked. "I know about Rocky and Bill."

"The coxswain is gone," Bunny said. I remembered the coxswain, an earnest young fellow who wanted to be a newspaperman, and who, dressed in swimming trunks, was going to go overboard ahead of everyone else and run a guideline into shore.

"Couldn't he get back?" I asked.

"He couldn't get anywhere," Rigg answered. "He had just stepped off the ramp when he disintegrated. He must have stepped right into an H. E. shell. Cox was a good lad. We'd recommended him for officers' school." Rigg walked away for the inevitable cup of coffee, shaking his big tawny head. I knew he had a battle headache, too.

A while afterward, I asked Rigg what he had been thinking as we neared the coast and he said he had been angry because the men we were going to put ashore hadn't had any coffee. "The poor guys had stayed in the sack as late as they could instead," he said. "Going ashore without any coffee!"

Long was having a look at the damage the shell had done to our ship, and I joined him in tracing its course. It had entered the starboard bow well above the waterline, about the level of the ship's number, then had hit the forward anchor winch, had been deflected toward the stern of the boat, had torn through the bulkhead and up through the cover of the escape hatch, then had smashed the ramp winch and Rocky and Bill. It had been a seventy-five-millimetre anti-tank shell with a solid-armor-piercing head, which had broken into several pieces after it hit the ramp winch. The boys kept finding chunks of it around, but enough of it stayed in one piece to show what it had been. "They had us crisscrossed with guns in all those pillboxes that were supposed to have been knocked off," Long said. "Something must have gone wrong.

We gave them a perfect landing, though," he added with professional pride. "I promised the commander we would land him dry tail and we did." Long has been in the Coast Guard twenty years and nothing surprises him; he has survived prohibition, Miami and Fire Island hurricanes, and three landings. He is a cheerful soul who has an original theory about fear. "I always tell my boys that fear is a passion like any other passion," he had once told me. "Now, if you see a beautiful dame walking down the street, you feel passion but you control it, don't you? Well, if you begin to get frightened, which is natural, just control yourself also, I tell them." Long said that he had seen the commander start off from the ship at a good clip, run well until he got up near the first line of sand dunes, then stagger. "The commander was at the head of the line about to leave the ship when young Vaghi, that big ensign, came up and must have asked him for the honor of going first," Long said. "They went off that way, Vaghi out ahead, running as if he was running out on a field with a football under his arm. Miller led the soldiers off the other ramp, and he stepped out like a little gentleman, too." The space where the starboard ramp had once been gave the same effect as an empty sleeve or eye socket.

It was Frankel, a signalman who had been on the bridge, who told me sometime that afternoon about how the wounded soldier had come to be on board. Frankel, whose family lives on East Eighteenth Street in Brooklyn, was a slender, restless fellow who used to be a cutter in the garment centre. He played in dance bands before he got his garment-union card, he once told me, and on the ship he occasionally played hot licks on the bugle slung on the bridge. "A shell hit just as we were beginning to pull out," Frankel said, "and we had begun to raise the ramps. It cut all but about one strand of the cable that was holding the starboard ramp and the ramp was wobbling in the air when I saw a guy holding on to the end of it. I guess a lot of us saw him at the same time. He was just clutching the ramp with his left arm, because he had been shot in the other shoulder. I'll never forget his eyes. They seemed to say, 'Don't leave me behind.' He must have been hit just as he stepped off the ramp leaving the ship. It was this soldier. So Ryan and Landini went out and got him.

Ryan worked along the rail inside the ramp and Landini worked along the outside edge of the ramp and they got him and carried him back into the ship. There was plenty of stuff flying around, too, and the ramp came away almost as soon as they got back. That's one guy saved, anyway." Ryan was a seaman cook who helped Fassy, the commissary steward, in the galley, and Landini was the little First Avenue Italian who had made up a special song for himself—"I'm going over to France and I'm shaking in my pants."

Along about noon, an LCVP, a troughlike fifty-footer, hailed us and asked if we could take care of five soldiers. Rigg said we could. The craft came alongside and passed over five drenched and shivering tank soldiers who had been found floating on a rubber raft. They were the crew of a tank that had been going in on a very small craft and they had been swamped by a wave. The tank had gone to the bottom and the soldiers had just managed to make it to the raft. The pharmacist's mates covered them with piles of blankets and put them to bed in one of our large compartments. By evening they were in the galley drinking coffee with the rest of us. They were to stay on the ship for nearly a week, as it turned out, because nobody would tell us what to do with them. They got to be pretty amphibious themselves. The sergeant in command was a fellow from Cleveland named Angelatti. He was especially happy about being saved, apparently because he liked his wife. He would keep repeating, "Gee, to think it's my second anniversary—I guess it's my lucky day!" But when he heard about what we thought had happened to the men we put ashore, he grew gloomy. The tanks had been headed for that beach and should have helped knock out the pillboxes. It hadn't been the tankmen's fault that the waves had swamped them, but the sergeant said disconsolately, "If we hadn't got bitched up, maybe those other guys wouldn't have been killed." He had a soldier's heart.

## III

On the morning of D Day-plus-one, the LCIL (Landing Craft Infantry, Large) on which I lived was like a ship with a hangover. Her deck was littered with cartons of tinned rations left behind by the land fighters she had carried to the Norman shore. There was a gap where the starboard ramp had been and there were various holes in the hull and hatches to mark the path of the anti-tank shell that had hit her while she had been on the beach. Everybody aboard was nursing a headache. The big fellows running the show had found nothing for us to do since our one run to the beach, which we had reached at 7:35 A.M. on D Day. The reason we hadn't been sent in again was that the German resistance was so strong that now the troops were being taken in only on smaller craft, which offered smaller targets. So we hung around in the Channel, waiting for orders and talking over the things that had happened to us. The men in the engine room, which was so clean that it looked like the model dairy exhibit at the World's Fair—all white paint and aluminum trim—had sweated it out at their posts during the excitement on deck and the engine-room log had been punctiliously kept. On the morning of D-plus-one, Cope, the chief machinist's mate, a tall, quiet chap from Philadelphia, told somebody that from the order "Drop stern anchor" to the order "Take in on stern anchor," which included all the time we had spent aground, exactly four minutes had elapsed. Most of us on deck would have put it at half an hour. During those four minutes all the hundred and forty passengers we carried had run off the ramps into three feet of water, three members of our Coast Guard complement of thirty-three had been killed, and two others had rescued a wounded soldier clinging to the end of the starboard ramp, which had been almost shot away and which fell away completely a few seconds later. The experience had left us without appetite. I remember, on the afternoon of D Day, sitting on a ration case on the pitching deck and being tempted by the rosy picture on the label of a roast-beef can. I opened it, but I could only pick at the jellied juice, which reminded me too much of the blood I had seen that morning, and I threw the tin over the rail.

By D-plus-one we were beginning to eat again. That morning I was on the upper deck talking to Barrett, a seaman from North Carolina, when we saw a German mine go off. It threw a column of water high into the air and damaged a ship near it. German planes had been fiddling around above our anchorage during the night, without bombing us; evidently they had been dropping mines. We had seen three of the planes shot down. Barrett looked at the water spout and said, "If we ever hit a mine like that, we'll go up in the air like an arrow." Barrett had bet a pound, even money, that we would be hit during the action. I asked him if he had collected the bet and he said, "Sure. As long as we got hit whether I take the money or not, I might as well take it." In the wardroom, Kavanaugh, the communications officer, talked to me about Bill, one of the Coast Guard boys who had been hit. Kavanaugh, who had censored Bill's letters, said, "Bill began every letter he ever wrote, 'Well, honey, here I am again.'" Long, the engineering officer, told me about a patch he had devised that would expand in water and would close up any underwater holes in the hull, and seemed rather to regret that he had had no chance to try it out. Lieutenant Henry (Bunny) Rigg, commander of the landing craft, kept repeating a tag line he had picked up from Sid Fields, a comedian in a London revue: "What a performance! What a performance!" But the most frequent subject of conversation among both officers and men was the fate of the fellows we had put on the beach—an Army platoon of amphibious engineers and a platoon of a naval beach battalion—usually referred to collectively as "those poor bastards." We had left them splashing through shallow water, with tracer bullets flying around them and only a nearly level, coverless beach immediately in front of them and with a beach pillbox and more of the enemy on a cliff inshore blazing away with everything they had. We had decided that hardly any of our men could have survived.

Late that afternoon our landing craft got an order to help unload soldiers from a big troopship several miles off the French shore. We were to carry the men almost as far as the beach and then transfer them to Higgins boats. One of our ramps was gone and the other one was not usable, and it would have been superfluous cruelty to drop a soldier with a full pack into five feet of water, our minimum draught. We gathered from the order that the Germans were no longer shooting on the beach; this, at least, represented progress.

The soldiers who lined the decks of the transport, all eager to get ashore at once, belonged to the Second Division; they wore a white star and an Indian head on their shoulder flashes. A scramble net hung down the port side of the vessel, and soldiers with full equipment strapped to their backs climbed down it one by one and stepped backward onto our landing craft. As each man made the step, two seamen grabbed him and helped him aboard. It often took as much time to unload the soldiers from a big ship as it did for the ship itself to get from Britain to the Norman coast, and it seemed to me that a small expenditure on gangplanks of various lengths and furnished with grapples, like the ones used in boarding operations in ancient naval battles, would have sped these transfers more than a comparable outlay for any other device could possibly have done. While we were loading the men, a thirty-six-foot craft approached us on the other side. There were two other thirty-six-footers there side by side already. The newest thirty-six-footer got alongside the outer one of the pair of earlier arrivals and the crew boosted up a man who had been standing in the stern of the boat and helped him on to the other craft. The man made his way unsteadily across both of the intervening thirty-six-footers to us, and men on the boats passed his gear, consisting of a typewriter and a gas mask, along after him. He was in a field jacket and long khaki trousers without leggings. The clothes were obviously fresh out of a quartermaster's stores. He wore the war correspondent's green shoulder patch on his field jacket. His face and form indicated that he had led a long and comfortable life, and his eyes betrayed astonishment that he should be there at all, but he was smiling. Some of our Coast-guardsmen helped him over our rail. He said that he was Richard Stokes of the St. Louis *Post-Dispatch*, that he had been a Washington correspondent and a music critic for many years, that he had wanted to go overseas when we got into the war, and that he had finally induced his paper to send him over. He had got airplane passage to Britain, where he had arrived two weeks before, and had been sent to the invasion coast on a Liberty ship that was to land men on D-plus-one. "It seems just wonderful to be here," Stokes said. "I can hardly believe it." He had been very much disappointed when he found out that because of the violence of the German resistance, the Liberty ship was not going to land her passengers for a couple of days. The ship's captain had said to him, "There's another crowd going ashore. Why don't you go with them?" Then the skipper had hailed a boat for him. "And here I am," said Stokes. "It's too good to be true." He was sixty-one years old, and the world seemed marvellous to him. He said he had never been in a battle and he wanted to see what it was like.

We got all our soldiers—about four hundred of them—aboard and started in toward the same stretch of shore we had left in such haste thirty-six hours before. The way in looked familiar and yet devoid of the character it had once had for us, like the scene of an old assignation revisited. The house with the tower on top of the cliff was now gone, I noticed. The naval bombardment, although tardy, had been thorough. Scattered along the shore were the wrecked and burned-out landing craft that had been less lucky than ours. Several of our men told me they had seen the LCT that had been burning off our port quarter on D Day pull out, still aflame, and extinguish the fire as she put to sea, but plenty of others remained. Small craft came out to us from the shore that had so recently been hostile, and soldiers started climbing into them, a less complicated process than the transfer from the troopship because the highest points of the small craft were nearly on a level with our main deck. I could see occasional puffs of smoke well up on the beach. They looked as if they might be the bursts of German shells coming from behind the cliff, and I felt protective toward Stokes. "Mr. Stokes," I said, "it seems to be pretty rough in there." He didn't even have a blanket to sleep on, and he didn't have the slightest idea whom he was going to look for when he got in; he was just going ahead like a good city reporter on an ordinary assignment. He watched two boats load up with soldiers and then, as a third came alongside—I remember that the name painted inside her ramp was "Impatient Virgin"—he said, "Mr. Liebling, I have made up my mind," and went down and scrambled aboard, assisted by everybody who could get a hand on him. He got ashore all right and did some fine stories. A couple of weeks afterward he told me, "I couldn't stand being within sight of the promised land and then coming back."

\* \* \*

There was nothing for us to do during the daylight hours of D-plus-two, but toward eight o'clock in the evening we got an order to go out to another troopship and unload more Second Division soldiers, who were to be taken to a beach next to the one where we had landed on D Day. The ship was an American Export liner. Several other LCILs were also assigned to the job of emptying her. I was on our bridge with Rigg when we came under her towering side, and the smell of fresh bread, which her cooks had evidently been baking, drove all other thoughts from our minds. Rigg hailed a young deck officer who was looking down at us and asked him if he could spare some bread. The officer said sure, and a few minutes later a steward pushed six long loaves across to our bridge from a porthole at approximately our level. They were an inestimable treasure to us. Everything is relative in an amphibious operation; to the four-man crews who operate the thirty-six-foot LCVPs, which are open to the weather and have no cooking facilities, an LCIL seems a floating palace. They would often come alongside us and beg tinned fruit, which they would receive with the same doglike gratitude we felt toward the merchantman for our bread.

The soldiers came aboard us along a single narrow plank, which was put over from the port side of the troopship to our rail, sloping at an angle of forty-five degrees. We pitched continuously in the rough water, and the soldiers, burdened with rifles and about fifty pounds of equipment apiece, slid rather than ran down the plank. Our crew had arranged a pile of ration cases at the rail, right where the gangplank was fastened, and the soldiers stepped from the end of the plank to the top case and then jumped down. We made two trips between the merchantman and the small boats that night, and only one soldier fell, and was lost, between the ships during the whole operation. That, I suppose, was a good percentage, but it still seemed to me an unnecessary loss. On our first trip from ship to shore, while we were unloading soldiers into small boats a couple of hundred yards off the beach, there was an air raid. The soldiers standing on our narrow deck, with their backs to the deckhouse walls, had never been under real fire before, but they remained impassive amid the cascade of

Bofors shells that rose from hundreds of ships. Much of the barrage had a low trajectory and almost scraped the paint off our bridge. On one ship some gunners who knew their business would hit a plane, and then, as it fell, less intelligent gun crews would start after it and follow it down, forgetting that when a plane hits the water it is at the waterline. An anti-aircraft shell travelling upward at an angle of not more than twenty degrees wounded a good friend of mine sleeping in a dugout on the side of a cliff ashore a couple of nights later.

A beach-battalion sailor came out to us on one of the first small boats from the shore. He was a big, smiling fellow whom we had brought from England on our first trip to the invasion coast, one of "those poor bastards" we had all assumed were dead. The cooks hauled him into the galley for sandwiches and coffee, and within a couple of minutes officers as well as men were crowding about him. Nearly everybody we asked him about turned out to be alive—the commander of the beach battalion; Miller, the Army lieutenant; little Dr. Davey; Vaghi and Reich, the poker-playing ensigns; Smith, the beach battalion's veteran chief petty officer; and others whom we had got to know on the ship. They had had a rough time, the sailor said. They had lain for five hours in holes they had scooped in the sand when they went ashore, while one or two American tanks which had landed shot at pillboxes and the pillboxes shot back. Then some infantrymen who had landed in small boats at H Hour worked their way up the beach and took the German positions, releasing our friends from the position in which they were pinned down. They were living on the side of a hill now and getting on with their work of organizing traffic between ship and shore. It was very pleasant news for us aboard the landing craft. We worked all night unloading soldiers, but the Coastguard crew didn't mind; they were in a good mood.

Early the next day, D-plus-three, I thumbed a ride ashore to go visiting. I hailed a passing assault craft, a rocket-firing speedboat, which took me part of the way and then transferred me to an LCVP that was headed inshore. The LCVP ran up onto the beach, dropped her bow ramp, and I walked onto French soil without even wetting my feet. This was the moment I had looked forward to for four years minus nine days, since the day I had crossed the Spanish frontier at Irún after the fall of France. Then the words of de Gaulle—"France has lost a battle but not the war"—were ringing in my ears, for I had just heard his first radio speech from London, but I had not dared hope that the wheel would turn almost full circle so soon. There was the noise of cannonading a couple of miles or so beyond the cliffs, where the First Division was pushing on from the fingerhold it had made good on D Day, but on the beach everything was calm. Troops and sailors of the amphibious forces had cleared away much of the wreckage, so that landing craft coming in would not foul their hulls or anchor chains; metal road strips led up from the water's edge to the road parallel with the shore. Men were going about their work as if there were no enemy within a hundred miles, and this was understandable, because no German planes ever arrived to molest them as they unloaded vehicles and munitions for the troops up ahead. To men who had been in other campaigns, when a solitary jeep couldn't pass down a road without three Messerschmitts' having a pass at it, this lack of interference seemed eerie, but it was true all the same. During the first week after the invasion began, I didn't see one German plane by daylight. Almost in front of me, as I stepped off the boat, were the ruins of the concrete blockhouse that had fired at us as we ran in on D Day. The concrete had been masked by a simulated house, but the disguise had been shot away and the place gaped white and roofless. I had more a sense of coming home to the United States Army than to France, for the first M.P. of whom I inquired the way to the command post of the beach battalion said he didn't know. This is S.O.P., or standard operating procedure, because a soldier figures that if he tells you he knows, he will, at best, have trouble directing you, and if the directions turn out to be wrong you may come back and complain. He has nothing to lose by denying knowledge.

I walked along the beach and met a beach-battalion sailor. He was equally unknowledgeable until I convinced him that I was a friend of the commander. Then he led me two hundred yards up a cliff to the place I had asked about. The commander was not there, but a Lieutenant Commander Watts and a Lieutenant Reardon, both New Yorkers, were. They had gone ashore on another landing craft, but I had met them both while we were in port in Britain awaiting sailing orders. They had landed five hundred yards up the beach from us and had, of course, got the same reception we got. The command post was installed in a row of burrows in the face of the cliff from which the Germans had fired down on the incoming boats and the beach on D Day; now it was we who overlooked the beach. In the side of another cliff, which was almost at a right angle to this one, the Germans had had two sunken concrete pillboxes enfilading the beach, and I realized that the crossfire had centred on our landing craft and the others nearby. Meeting these men reminded me of what a First Division soldier had said to me a few days earlier about "Candide," which he was reading in the Armed Forces edition: "Voltaire used the same gag too often. The characters are always getting killed and then turning out not to have been killed at all, and they tell their friends what happened to them in the meantime." Watts said that after they had left their landing craft, they had run forward like hell and then had thrown themselves down on the beach because there was nothing else to do. The forepart of the beach was covered with large, round pebbles about the size, I imagine, of the one David used on Goliath, and when the German machine-gun bullets skittered among them the stones became a secondary form of ammunition themselves and went flying among the men. "We had infantry up ahead of us, but at first they were pinned down too," Watts said. "A couple of tanks had landed and one of them knocked out a seventy-five up on the side of the hill, but in a short while the Germans either replaced it or got it going again. Then, after a couple of hours, two destroyers came and worked close in to shore, although there were plenty of mines still in there, and really plastered the pillboxes. The infantry went up the hill in the face of machine-gun fire and drove the Germans out of the trench system they had on the crown of the hill. I'll show it to you in a couple of minutes. It's a regular young Maginot Line. By nightfall we felt fairly safe. We found out later from prisoners that the Three Hundred and Fifty-second German

Field Division had been holding anti-invasion exercises here the day before we attacked. They had been scheduled to go back to their barracks D Day morning, but when scouts told them about the big fleet on the way in, they decided to stay and give us a good time. They did." It wasn't until a week later, in London, that I found out that because of this untoward circumstance our beach and those on either side of it had been the toughest spots encountered in the landings, and that the losses there had not been at all typical of the operation.

I was delighted to discover Smith, the old chief petty officer, reclining in a nearby slit trench. He was looking very fit. He was forty-seven, and I had wondered how he would do in the scramble to the beach. He had not only made it but had gathered a large new repertory of anecdotes on the way. "A guy in front of me got it through the throat," Smitty said. "Another guy in front of me got it through the heart. I run on. I heard a shell coming and I threw myself face down. There was an Army colonel on one side of me, a Navy captain on the other. The shell hit. I was all right. I looked up and the captain and the colonel was gone, blown to pieces. I grabbed for my tommy gun, which I had dropped next to me. It had been twisted into a complete circle. I was disarmed, so I just laid there."

While I was listening to Smitty, Reardon, talking over a field telephone, had located the commander somewhere on top of the cliff, along the German trench system, which had been taken over by the amphibious engineers as billets. Watts and I decided to walk up and find him. We made our way along the face of the cliff, on a narrow path that led past clusters of slit trenches in which soldiers were sleeping, and got up to the crest at a point where some Negro soldiers had made their bivouac in a thicket. We followed another path through a tangled, scrubby wood. The Germans had left numbers of wooden skull-and-crossbones signs on the tree trunks. These signs said *"Achtung Minen"* and *"Attention aux Mines."* Whether they indicated that we had taken the enemy by surprise and that he had not had time to remove the signs put up for the protection of his own and civilian personnel, or whether the signs were put there for psychological purposes, like dummy guns, was a question for the engineers to determine. Watts and I took care to stay in the path.

We found the commander, who was in good form. He said he had lost only a couple of the forty-five beach-battalion men who had been on the landing craft with us but that in the battalion as a whole the casualties had been fairly heavy. "Not nearly what I thought they would be when I left that boat, though," he said.

The trench system was a fine monument to the infantrymen of the First Division who had taken it. I couldn't help thinking, as I looked it over, that the German soldiers of 1939–41 would not have been driven from it in one day, even by heroes, and the thought encouraged me. Maybe they were beginning to understand that they were beaten. There were no indications that the position had been under artillery fire and I could see only one trace of the use of a flamethrower. As I reconstructed the action, our fellows must have climbed the hill and outflanked the position, and the Germans, rather than fight it out in their holes, had cleared out to avoid being cut off. They had probably stayed in and continued firing just as long as they still had a chance to kill without taking losses. As the French say, they had not insisted. The trenches were deep, narrow, and so convoluted that an attacking force at any point could be fired on from several directions. Important knots in the system, like the command post and mortar emplacements, were of concrete. The command post was sunk at least twenty-five feet into the ground and was faced with brick on the inside. The garrison had slept in underground bombproofs, with timbered ceilings and wooden floors. In one of them, probably the officers' quarters, there was rustic furniture, a magnificent French radio, and flowers, still fresh, in vases. On the walls were cheap French prints of the innocuous sort one used to see in speakeasies: the little boy and the little girl, and the coyly equivocal captions.

An engineer sergeant who showed us through the place said that the Americans had found hairnets and hairpins in this bombproof. I could imagine an *Oberstleutnant* and his mistress, perhaps the daughter of a French collaborationist, living uneventfully here and waiting for something in which the *Oberstleutnant* had unconsciously ceased to believe, something that he wished so strongly would never happen that he had convinced himself it would happen, if anywhere, on some distant part of the coast. I thought of the Frenchmen I had known in 1939, waiting in a similar mood in the Maginot Line. The sergeant, a straight-featured Jewish fellow in his late thirties, said, "Those infantrymen were like angels. I tell you, I laid there on the beach and prayed for them while they went up that hill with nothing—with bayonets and hand grenades. They did it with nothing. It was a miracle." That made me feel good, because the infantry regiment involved had long been my favorite outfit. The commander was sardonic about one thing. "You remember how I used to worry about how my men would fall into bomb holes and drown on the way in because the Air Forces had laid down such a terrific bombardment?" he asked. "Well, I defy you to find one bomb hole on this whole beach for a mile each way."

The commander and Watts accompanied me back to the shore. On the way, we stopped at a field hospital that had been set up under canvas. There I talked to some Italian prisoners who were digging shelter trenches. They were fine, rugged specimens, as they should have been, because since the Italian surrender they had undoubtedly had plenty of exercise swinging pickaxes for the Todt organization. Their regiment of bridge-building engineers had been disarmed by the Germans in Greece and the men had been given the choice of enrolling in Fascist combat units or in labor service, they told me. They had all chosen labor service. They seemed to expect to be commended for their choice. They had built many of the trenches in the district. "We wouldn't fight for Hitler," they assured me. I thought that the point had been pretty well proved. Now they were digging for us. They said that all Germans were cowards.

We went down to the shore, and the commander, who, being beachmaster, was in charge of all traffic alongshore, hailed a Duck for me. The Duck put me on an LCVP, which took me back to my ship. On the way out, I realized that I had not seen a single French civilian the entire time ashore.

*     *     *

When I came aboard our landing craft, Long, the engineering officer, grinned at me.

"Did you notice a slight list, sometimes on one side, sometimes on the other, the last two days?" he asked.

I said, "You mean the one you said must be on account of
the crew's all turning over in their sleep at the same time?"

"Yes," he said. "Well, today we found an open seam down
in the stern. She started to list that night the big bomb
dropped next to us, but you were sleeping too sound to get
up. So maybe we'll go back to port. She has no ramps, the
forward anchor winch is sheered in half, and she may as well
go into the yard for a couple of days."

The morning of D-plus-four, Rigg signalled the command
ship for permission to put back to Britain. As soon as the
signalman blinked out the message, every man on board knew
there was a chance we would go back, and even fellows who
had expressed a low opinion of the British port at which our
flotilla had been stationed looked extremely happy. While we
were waiting for an answer to our request, an LCIL that acted
as a group leader, a kind of straw boss among the little ships,
passed near us, and the lieutenant on her bridge ordered us
over to help tow a barge of ammunition. We were to be
paired with another LCIL on this job. The barge, a two-
hundred-and-fifty-tonner, was loaded with TNT, and the idea
was for one LCIL to make fast on each side of her and shove
her in to shore. The Diesel motors of an LCIL, although they
can move their craft along at a fair speed, haven't the towing
power of a tug. The two LCILs bounced about in the choppy
sea for quite a while as we tried to get towing lines aboard the
big barge that would hold. Even after we finally got started,
every now and then the lines would snap and we would
bounce against the side of the barge, as we put more lines
aboard her, with a crash that disquieted us, even though we
had been told many times that the explosive was packed so
carefully that no jouncing would possibly set it off. We were
very happy when the barge grounded on the beach according
to plan and we could cast off and leave her. Just before we
had finished, the group leader came along again and an officer
on her bridge shouted over to us through a megaphone, "Re-

port to control-ship shuttle service!" This meant that we were
going back to Britain; control ships organize cross-Channel
convoys. We were not sorry to go.

By Sunday, D-plus-five, when we at last got started, the
water had smoothed out so much that the Channel was like
the Hyde Park Serpentine. The flat-bottomed LCIL will
bounce about in the slightest sea, but today our craft moved
along like a swanboat. The water was full of ration cartons,
life jackets, and shell cases, and on the way over we picked up
one corpse, of a soldier wearing a life jacket, which indicated
that he had never got ashore. Since German planes were
dropping mines every night, the lookout was instructed to
keep a sharp watch for suspicious objects in the water, and
this was almost the only thing it was necessary to think about
as we loafed along. A seaman from Florida named Hurwitz
was lookout on the bow in the early morning. "Suspicious
object off port bow!" he would bawl, and then "Suspicious
object off starboard quarter!" Most of the suspicious objects
turned out to be shell cases. Finally, Hurwitz yelled "Bridge!
The water is just full of suspicious objects!"

The main interest aboard now was whether we would get
to port before the pubs closed, at ten o'clock in the evening.
Long was getting unheard-of speed out of his motors and it
seemed that we would make the pubs easily. Then we happened upon a British LCT that was all alone and was having
engine trouble. She asked us to stand by in case her motors
conked out altogether. We proceeded at four knots. When the
British skipper signalled to us, "Doing my utmost, can make
no more," which meant that our chance of beer had gone
glimmering, Rigg made a gesture that for delicacy and regard
for international relations must have few parallels in naval history. He ordered a signal that may someday be in school-
books along with Nelson's "England expects every man to do
his duty." "Never mind," he signalled the crippled LCT. "We
would have been too late for pub-closing time anyway."

*The New Yorker*, July 1, 8, 15, 1944

# Omaha Beach After D-Day

by Ernie Pyle

### "And Yet We Got On"

NORMANDY BEACHHEAD—(by wireless)—Due to a last-minute alteration in the arrangements, I didn't arrive on the beachhead until the morning after D-day, after our first wave of assault troops had hit the shore.

By the time we got here the beaches had been taken and the fighting had moved a couple of miles inland. All that remained on the beach was some sniping and artillery fire, and the occasional startling blast of a mine geysering brown sand into the air. That plus a gigantic and pitiful litter of wreckage along miles of shoreline.

Submerged tanks and overturned boats and burned trucks and shell-shattered jeeps and sad little personal belongings were strewn all over these bitter sands. That plus the bodies of soldiers lying in rows covered with blankets, the toes of their shoes sticking up in a line as though on drill. And other bodies, uncollected, still sprawling grotesquely in the sand or half hidden by the high grass beyond the beach.

That plus an intense, grim determination of work-weary men to get this chaotic beach organized and get all the vital supplies and the reinforcements moving more rapidly over it from the stacked-up ships standing in droves out to sea.

*        *        *

Now that it is over it seems to me a pure miracle that we ever took the beach at all. For some of our units it was easy, but in this special sector where I am now our troops faced such odds that our getting ashore was like my whipping Joe Louis down to a pulp.

In this column I want to tell you what the opening of the second front in this one sector entailed, so that you can know

and appreciate and forever be humbly grateful to those both
dead and alive who did it for you.

Ashore, facing us, were more enemy troops than we had in
our assault waves. The advantages were all theirs, the dis-
advantages all ours. The Germans were dug into positions that
they had been working on for months, although these were
not yet all complete. A 100-foot bluff a couple of hundred
yards back from the beach had great concrete gun emplacements built right into the hilltop. These opened to the sides
instead of to the front, thus making it very hard for naval fire
from the sea to reach them. They could shoot parallel with
the beach and cover every foot of it for miles with artillery
fire.

Then they had hidden machine-gun nests on the forward
slopes, with crossfire taking in every inch of the beach. These
nests were connected by networks of trenches, so that the
German gunners could move about without exposing themselves.

Throughout the length of the beach, running zigzag a
couple of hundred yards back from the shoreline, was an immense V-shaped ditch 15 feet deep. Nothing could cross it,
not even men on foot, until fills had been made. And in other
places at the far end of the beach, where the ground is flatter,
they had great concrete walls. These were blasted by our naval
gunfire or by explosives set by hand after we got ashore.

Our only exits from the beach were several swales or valleys, each about 100 yards wide. The Germans made the most
of these funnel-like traps, sowing them with buried mines.
They contained, also, barbed-wire entanglements with mines
attached, hidden ditches, and machine guns firing from the
slopes.

This is what was on the shore. But our men had to go
through a maze nearly as deadly as this before they even got
ashore. Underwater obstacles were terrific. The Germans had
whole fields of evil devices under the water to catch our boats.
Even now, several days after the landing, we have cleared only
channels through them and cannot yet approach the whole
length of the beach with our ships. Even now some ship or
boat hits one of these mines every day and is knocked out of
commission.

The Germans had masses of those great six-pronged spiders, made of railroad iron and standing shoulder-high, just beneath the surface of the water for our landing craft to run into. They also had huge logs buried in the sand, pointing upward and outward, their tops just below the water. Attached to these logs were mines.

In addition to these obstacles they had floating mines offshore, land mines buried in the sand of the beach, and more mines in checkerboard rows in the tall grass beyond the sand. And the enemy had four men on shore for every three men we had approaching the shore.

And yet we got on.

*          *          *

Beach landings are planned to a schedule that is set far ahead of time. They all have to be timed, in order for everything to mesh and for the following waves of troops to be standing off the beach and ready to land at the right moment.

As the landings are planned, some elements of the assault force are to break through quickly, push on inland, and attack the most obvious enemy strong points. It is usually the plan for units to be inland, attacking gun positions from behind, within a matter of minutes after the first men hit the beach.

I have always been amazed at the speed called for in these plans. You'll have schedules calling for engineers to land at H-hour plus two minutes, and service troops at H-hour plus 30 minutes, and even for press censors to land at H-hour plus 75 minutes. But in the attack on this special portion of the beach where I am—the worst we had, incidentally—the schedule didn't hold.

Our men simply could not get past the beach. They were pinned down right on the water's edge by an inhuman wall of fire from the bluff. Our first waves were on that beach for hours, instead of a few minutes, before they could begin working inland.

You can still see the foxholes they dug at the very edge of the water, in the sand and the small, jumbled rocks that form parts of the beach.

Medical corpsmen attended the wounded as best they could. Men were killed as they stepped out of landing craft. An officer whom I knew got a bullet through the head just as the door of his landing craft was let down. Some men were drowned.

The first crack in the beach defenses was finally accomplished by terrific and wonderful naval gunfire, which knocked out the big emplacements. They tell epic stories of destroyers that ran right up into shallow water and had it out point-blank with the big guns in those concrete emplacements ashore.

When the heavy fire stopped, our men were organized by their officers and pushed on inland, circling machine-gun nests and taking them from the rear.

As one officer said, the only way to take a beach is to face it and keep going. It is costly at first, but it's the only way. If the men are pinned down on the beach, dug in and out of action, they might as well not be there at all. They hold up the waves behind them, and nothing is being gained.

Our men were pinned down for a while, but finally they stood up and went through, and so we took that beach and accomplished our landing. We did it with every advantage on the enemy's side and every disadvantage on ours. In the light of a couple of days of retrospection, we sit and talk and call it a miracle that our men ever got on at all or were able to stay on.

Before long it will be permitted to name the units that did it. Then you will know to whom this glory should go. They suffered casualties. And yet if you take the entire beachhead assault, including other units that had a much easier time, our total casualties in driving this wedge into the continent of Europe were remarkably low—only a fraction, in fact, of what our commanders had been prepared to accept.

And these units that were so battered and went through such hell are still, right at this moment, pushing on inland without rest, their spirits high, their egotism in victory almost reaching the smart-alecky stage.

Their tails are up. "We've done it again," they say. They figure that the rest of the army isn't needed at all. Which proves that, while their judgment in this regard is bad, they certainly have the spirit that wins battles and eventually wars.

Scripps-Howard wire copy, June 12, 1944

## "The Wreckage Was Vast and Startling"

NORMANDY BEACHHEAD, D Day Plus Two—(by wireless, delayed)—I took a walk along the historic coast of Normandy in the country of France.

It was a lovely day for strolling along the seashore. Men were sleeping on the sand, some of them sleeping forever. Men were floating in the water, but they didn't know they were in the water, for they were dead.

The water was full of squishy little jellyfish about the size of your hand. Millions of them. In the center each of them had a green design exactly like a four-leaf clover. The good-luck emblem. Sure. Hell yes.

I walked for a mile and a half along the water's edge of our many-miled invasion beach. You wanted to walk slowly, for the detail on that beach was infinite.

The wreckage was vast and startling. The awful waste and destruction of war, even aside from the loss of human life, has always been one of its outstanding features to those who are in it. Anything and everything is expendable. And we did expend on our beachhead in Normandy during those first few hours.

\*     \*     \*

For a mile out from the beach there were scores of tanks and trucks and boats that you could no longer see, for they were at the bottom of the water—swamped by overloading, or hit by shells, or sunk by mines. Most of their crews were lost.

You could see trucks tipped half over and swamped. You could see partly sunken barges, and the angled-up corners of jeeps, and small landing craft half submerged. And at low tide you could still see those vicious six-pronged iron snares that helped snag and wreck them.

On the beach itself, high and dry, were all kinds of wrecked vehicles. There were tanks that had only just made the beach before being knocked out. There were jeeps that had burned to a dull gray. There were big derricks on caterpillar treads that didn't quite make it. There were half-tracks carrying office equipment that had been made into a shambles by a single shell hit, their interiors still holding their useless equipage of smashed typewriters, telephones, office files.

There were LCT's turned completely upside down, and lying on their backs, and how they got that way I don't know.

There were boats stacked on top of each other, their sides caved in, their suspension doors knocked off.

In this shoreline museum of carnage there were abandoned rolls of barbed wire and smashed bulldozers and big stacks of thrown-away lifebelts and piles of shells still waiting to be moved.

In the water floated empty life rafts and soldiers' packs and ration boxes, and mysterious oranges.

On the beach lay snarled rolls of telephone wire and big rolls of steel matting and stacks of broken, rusting rifles.

On the beach lay, expended, sufficient men and mechanism for a small war. They were gone forever now. And yet we could afford it.

We could afford it because we were on, we had our toe-hold, and behind us there were such enormous replacements for this wreckage on the beach that you could hardly conceive of their sum total. Men and equipment were flowing from England in such a gigantic stream that it made the waste on the beachhead seem like nothing at all, really nothing at all.

*     *     *

A few hundred yards back on the beach is a high bluff. Up there we had a tent hospital, and a barbed-wire enclosure for prisoners of war. From up there you could see far up and down the beach, in a spectacular crow's-nest view, and far out to sea.

And standing out there on the water beyond all this wreckage was the greatest armada man has ever seen. You simply could not believe the gigantic collection of ships that lay out there waiting to unload.

Looking from the bluff, it lay thick and clear to the far horizon of the sea and on beyond, and it spread out to the sides and was miles wide. Its utter enormity would move the hardest man.

As I stood up there I noticed a group of freshly taken German prisoners standing nearby. They had not yet been put in the prison cage. They were just standing there, a couple of doughboys leisurely guarding them with Tommy guns.

The prisoners too were looking out to sea—the same bit of sea that for months and years had been so safely empty before their gaze. Now they stood staring almost as if in a trance.

They didn't say a word to each other. They didn't need to. The expression on their faces was something forever unforgettable. In it was the final horrified acceptance of their doom.

If only all Germany could have had the rich experience of standing on the bluff and looking out across the water and seeing what their compatriots saw.

Scripps-Howard wire copy, June 16, 1944

### *"This Long Thin Line of Personal Anguish"*

NORMANDY BEACHHEAD—(by wireless)—In the preceding column we told about the D-Day wreckage among our machines of war that were expended in taking one of the Normandy beaches.

But there is another and more human litter. It extends in a thin little line, just like a high-water mark, for miles along the beach. This is the strewn personal gear, gear that will never be needed again, of those who fought and died to give us our entrance into Europe.

Here in a jumbled row for mile on mile are soldiers' packs. Here are socks and shoe polish, sewing kits, diaries, Bibles and hand grenades. Here are the latest letters from home, with the address on each one neatly razored out—one of the security precautions enforced before the boys embarked.

Here are toothbrushes and razors, and snapshots of families back home staring up at you from the sand. Here are pocketbooks, metal mirrors, extra trousers, and bloody, abandoned shoes. Here are broken-handled shovels, and portable radios smashed almost beyond recognition, and mine detectors twisted and ruined.

Here are torn pistol belts and canvas water buckets, first-aid kits and jumbled heaps of lifebelts. I picked up a pocket Bible with a soldier's name in it, and put it in my jacket. I carried it half a mile or so and then put it back down on the beach. I don't know why I picked it up, or why I put it back down.

Soldiers carry strange things ashore with them. In every invasion you'll find at least one soldier hitting the beach at H-Hour with a banjo slung over his shoulder. The most ironic piece of equipment marking our beach—this beach of first despair, then victory—is a tennis racket that some soldier had brought along. It lies lonesomely on the sand, clamped in its rack, not a string broken.

Two of the most dominant items in the beach refuse are cigarets and writing paper. Each soldier was issued a carton of cigarets just before he started. Today these cartons by the thousand, watersoaked and spilled out, mark the line of our first savage blow.

Writing paper and air-mail envelopes come second. The boys had intended to do a lot of writing in France. Letters that would have filled those blank, abandoned pages.

Always there are dogs in every invasion. There is a dog still on the beach today, still pitifully looking for his masters.

He stays at the water's edge, near a boat that lies twisted and half sunk at the waterline. He barks appealingly to every soldier who approaches, trots eagerly along with him for a few feet, and then, sensing himself unwanted in all this haste, runs back to wait in vain for his own people at his own empty boat.

\*          \*          \*

Over and around this long thin line of personal anguish, fresh men today are rushing vast supplies to keep our armies pushing on into France. Other squads of men pick amidst the wreckage to salvage ammunition and equipment that are still usable.

Men worked and slept on the beach for days before the last D-Day victim was taken away for burial.

I stepped over the form of one youngster whom I thought dead. But when I looked down I saw he was only sleeping. He was very young, and very tired. He lay on one elbow, his hand suspended in the air about six inches from the ground. And in the palm of his hand he held a large, smooth rock.

I stood and looked at him a long time. He seemed in his sleep to hold that rock lovingly, as though it were his last link with a vanishing world. I have no idea at all why he went to sleep with the rock in his hand, or what kept him from dropping it once he was asleep. It was just one of those little things without explanation, that a person remembers for a long time.

*    *    *

The strong, swirling tides of the Normandy coastline shift the contours of the sandy beach as they move in and out. They carry soldiers' bodies out to sea, and later they return them. They cover the corpses of heroes with sand, and then in their whims they uncover them.

As I plowed out over the wet sand of the beach on that first day ashore, I walked around what seemed to be a couple of pieces of driftwood sticking out of the sand. But they weren't driftwood.

They were a soldier's two feet. He was completely covered by the shifting sands except for his feet. The toes of his G.I. shoes pointed toward the land he had come so far to see, and which he saw so briefly.

Scripps-Howard wire copy, June 17, 1944

# The First Hospital Ship

by Martha Gellhorn

THERE was nothing to do now but wait. The big ship felt empty and strange. There were 422 beds covered with new blankets; and a bright, clean, well-equipped operating room, never before used; great cans marked "Whole Blood" stood on the decks; plasma bottles and supplies of drugs and bales of bandages were stored in handy places. Everything was ready, and any moment we would be leaving for France.

The ship itself was painfully white. The endless varied ships in this invasion port were gray or camouflaged and they seemed to have the right idea. We, on the other hand, were all fixed up like a sitting pigeon.

Our ship was snowy white with a green line running along the sides below the deck rail, and with many bright new red crosses painted on the hull and painted flat on the boat deck. We were to travel alone. There was not so much as a pistol on board in the way of armament, and neither the English crew and ship's officers nor the American medical personnel had any notion of what happened to large, conspicuous white ships when they appeared at a war, though everyone knew the Geneva agreement concerning such ships, and everyone hoped the Germans would take the said agreement seriously.

There were six nurses aboard, and they were fine girls. They came from Texas and Michigan and California and Wisconsin, and three weeks ago they were in the U.S.A. completing their training for this overseas assignment. They had been prepared to work on a hospital train, which would mean caring for wounded in sensible, steady railway carriages. Instead, they found themselves on a ship, and they were about to move across the dark water of the Channel.

This sudden switch in plans was simply part of the day's work, and each one, in her own excellent way, got through the grim business of waiting for the unknown to start, as elegantly as she could. It was very elegant, indeed, especially if you remembered that no one aboard had ever been on a hospital ship before, and so the helpful voice of experience was lacking.

The nurses had worked day and night for two weeks to get this ship ready to receive wounded. They had scrubbed floors and walls, made beds, prepared supplies, and now their work was finished. They went on working, inventing odd jobs to keep busy during these final empty hours before the real work began. But two tired, brave, tough girls sat on a bench inside the hall of the ship, and painted their fingernails with bright red varnish and talked about wanting their mail and worried about their missing foot lockers, their valuable foot lockers which had in them the vital comfortable shoes and the un-vital, probably never-to-be-worn evening dresses.

One of the British ship's officers, who had been in the Merchant Marine since the beginning of the war, but had never yet set forth in a white ship, came to talk with the girls. He looked tired, too, and he was vastly amused by their nail polish. "It would be nice," he said, "if we could take that nail polish up to London tonight, instead of where we're going."

The tall pretty nurse held her hands out to see whether the job was well done. "No," she said. She was from Texas and spoke in a soft, slow voice. "No. I'm glad to be going just where I'm going. Don't you know how happy those little old boys are going to be when they see us coming?"

Pulling out of the harbor that night we passed a Liberty ship, going the same way. The ship was gray against the gray water and the gray sky, and standing on her decks, packed solidly together, khaki, silent and unmoving, were American troops. No one waved and no one called. The crowded gray ship and the empty white ship sailed slowly out of the harbor toward France.

We crossed by daylight, and the morning seemed longer than other mornings. The captain never left the bridge and, all alone and beautifully white, we made our way through the mine-swept channel. Everyone silently hoped that this would be a lucky number, and we waited very hard.

Then we saw the coast of France and, as we closed in, there was one LCT near us, with washing hung up on a line, and between the loud explosions of mines being detonated on the beach, one could hear dance music coming from its radio. There were barrage balloons, always looking like comic toy elephants, bouncing in the high wind above the massed ships, and you could hear invisible planes flying behind the gray ceiling of cloud. Troops were unloading from big ships to heavy barges or to light craft, and on the shore, moving up brown roads that scarred the hillside, our tanks clanked slowly and steadily forward.

Then we stopped noticing the invasion, the ships, the ominous beach, because the first wounded had arrived. An LCT drew alongside our ship, pitching in the waves. A boy in a steel helmet shouted up to the crew at the aft rail, and a wooden box looking like a lidless coffin was lowered on a pulley, and with the greatest difficulty, bracing themselves against the movement of their boat, the men on the LCT laid a stretcher inside the box. The box was raised to our deck, and out of it was lifted a man who was closer to being a child than a man, dead-white and seemingly dying. The first wounded man to be brought to that ship for safety and care was a German prisoner.

Everything happened at once. We had six water ambulances—light motor launches which swung down from the ship's side and could be raised the same way when full of wounded. They carried six litter cases apiece, or as many walking wounded as could be crowded into them. Now they were being lowered, with shouted orders: "That beach over there where they've got streamers up."

"Take her in slow. . . . Those double round things that look like flat spools are mines. . . . You won't clear any submerged tanks, so look sharp. . . . Ready? . . . Lower her!"

The captain came down from the bridge to watch this. He was feeling very jolly, as well he might, and he now remarked, "I got us in all right, but Heaven only knows how we'll ever get out." He gestured toward the ships that were as thick around us as cars in a parking lot. "Worry about that some other time," he said brightly.

The stretcher-bearers, who were part of the American medical personnel, now started on their long backbreaking job. By the end of that trip, their hands were padded with blisters and they were practically hospital cases themselves. For the wounded had to be got from the shore into our own water ambulances or into other craft, raised over the side, and then transported down the winding stairs of this converted pleasure ship to the wards. The ship's crew became volunteer stretcher-bearers, instantly.

Wounded were pouring in now, hauled up in the lidless coffin, or swung aboard in the motor ambulances, and finally an LST tied alongside and made itself into a sort of landing jetty, higher than the light craft that ran the wounded to us, but not as high as our deck. So the wounded were lifted by men standing on the LST, who raised the stretchers high above their heads and handed them up to men on our deck, who caught hold of the stretcher handles. It was a fast, terrifying bucket-brigade system, but it worked.

Belowstairs, for three decks the inside of the ship was a vast ward with double tiers of bunks. The routine of the ship ran marvelously, though four doctors, six nurses and about fourteen medical orderlies had to be great people to care for four hundred wounded men. From two o'clock one afternoon, until the ship docked in England again the next evening at seven, none of the medical personnel stopped work. And besides plasma and blood transfusions, re-dressing of wounds, examinations, administering of sedatives or opiates or oxygen and all the rest, operations were performed all night long. Only one soldier died on that ship and he had come aboard as a hopeless case.

It will be hard to tell you of the wounded, there were so many of them. There was no time to talk; there was too much else to do. They had to be fed, as most of them had not eaten for two days; their shoes had to be cut off; they needed help to get out of their jackets; they wanted water; the nurses and orderlies, working like demons, had to be found and called quickly to a bunk where a man suddenly and desperately needed attention; plasma bottles must be watched; cigarettes had to be lighted and held for those who could not use their hands; it seemed to take hours to pour hot coffee, from the spout of a teapot, into a mouth that just showed through bandages.

But the wounded talked among themselves, and as time went on you got to know them, by their faces and their wounds, not by their names. They were a magnificent enduring bunch of men. Men smiled who were in such pain that all they really can have wanted to do was turn their heads away and cry, and men made jokes when they needed their strength just to survive.

All of them looked after one another, saying, "Give that boy a drink of water," or "Miss, see that Ranger over there; he's in bad shape. Could you go to him?"

All through the ship, men were asking after other men by name, anxiously, wondering if they were on board and how they were doing.

On A Deck, in a bunk by the wall, lay a very young lieutenant. He had a bad chest wound, his face was white, and he lay too still. Suddenly he raised himself on his elbow and looked straight ahead of him, as if he did not know where he was. He had a gentle oval face and wide blue eyes and his eyes were full of horror and he did not speak. He had been wounded the first day, had lain out in a field for two days and then crawled back to our lines, sniped at by the Germans. He realized now that a German, badly wounded also in the chest, shoulder and legs, lay in the bunk behind him. The gentle-faced boy said very softly, because it was hard to speak, "I'd kill him if I could move." After that he did not speak for a long time; he was given oxygen and later operated on, so that he could breathe.

The man behind him was a nineteen-year-old Austrian. He had fought for a year in Russia and half a year in France; he had been home for six days during this time. I thought he would die when he first came on board but he got better. In the early morning hours he asked whether wounded prisoners were exchanged, would he ever get home again.

I told him that I did not know about these arrangements, but that he had nothing to fear, as he could see. I was not trying to be kind, but only trying to be as decent as the nurses and doctors were. The Austrian said, "Yes, yes." Then he added, "So many men, all wounded, want to get home. Why have we ever fought one another?" Perhaps because he came from a gentler race, his eyes filled up with tears. He was the only wounded prisoner on board who was grateful or polite, who said "Please" or "Thank you," or showed any normal human reaction.

There was an American soldier on that same deck with a head wound so horrible that he was not moved. Nothing could be done for him, and anything, any touch, would have made him worse. The next morning he was drinking coffee. His eyes looked very dark and strange, as if he had been a long way away, so far away that he almost could not get back. His face was set in lines of weariness and pain, but when asked how he felt, he said he was okay. He was never known to say anything more; he asked for nothing and made no complaint, and perhaps he will live, too.

On the next deck, there were many odd and wonderful men, who were less badly wounded and talked more. They talked between bunks with one another, even when they could not see one another's faces. It was all professional talk: where they had landed, at what time, what opposition they had met, how they had got out, when they were wounded.

They spoke of the snipers, and there was endless talk about the women snipers, none of the talk very clear, but everyone believed it. There were no French officers with these boys, who could have interpreted, and the Americans never knew what the villagers were saying.

Two men who thought they were being volubly invited into an old woman's house to eat dinner were actually being warned of snipers in the attic; they somehow caught on to this fact in time. They were all baffled by the French and surprised by how much food there was in Normandy, forgetting that Normandy is one of the great food-producing areas of France. They thought the girls in the villages were amazingly well dressed. Everything was confused and astounding: First, there were the deadly bleak beaches, and then the villages where they were greeted with flowers and cookies—and often by snipers and booby traps.

A French boy of seventeen lay in one of the bunks; he had been wounded in the back by a shell fragment. He lived and worked on his father's land, but he said the Germans had burned their château as they left. Two of the American boys in bunks alongside were very worried about him. They were afraid he'd be scared, a civilian kid all alone and in pain and not knowing any English and going to a strange country. They ignored their respective smashed knee and smashed shoulder and worried about the French kid.

The French boy was very much a man and very tight-lipped. He made no complaints and kept his anxiety inside himself, though it showed in his eyes. His family was still there in the battle zone, and he did not know what had happened to them or how he would ever get back. The American soldiers said, "You tell that kid he's a better soldier than that Boche in the bunk next to him."

We did not like this Boche, who was eighteen and blond and the most demanding of the "master" race aboard. Finally there was a crisp little scene when he told the orderly to move him, as he was uncomfortable, and the orderly said no, he would bleed if moved.

When I explained, the German said angrily, "How long, then, am I to lie here in pain in this miserable position?"

I asked the orderly what to say, and the orderly answered, "Tell him there are a lot of fine boys on this ship lying in worse pain in worse positions."

The American soldiers in the bunks around said, "What a Heinie!" wearily, and then they began wondering how they'd find their old units again and how soon they would get mail.

When night came, the water ambulances were still churning in to the beach looking for wounded. Someone on an LCT had shouted out that there were maybe a hundred scattered along there somewhere. It was essential to try to get them aboard before the nightly air raid and before the dangerous dark cold could get into their hurt bodies.

Going into shore, unable to see, and not knowing this tricky strip of water, was slow work. Two of the launch crew, armed with boat hooks, hung over the side of the boat and stared at the black water, looking for obstacles, sunken ve-hicles or mines, and they kept the hooks ready to push us off the sand as we came closer in. For the tides were a nasty business, too. Part of the time, wounded had to be ferried out to the water ambulances on men's shoulders, and part of the time the water ambulances grounded and stuck on the beach together with other craft, stranded by the fast-moving sea.

We finally got onto a barge near the beach. The motor ambulance could not come inshore near enough to be of any use at this point, so it left us to look for a likelier anchorage farther down. We waded ashore, in water to our waists, having agreed that we would assemble the wounded from this area on board a beach LST and wait until the tide allowed the motor ambulance to come back and call for us. It was almost dark by now, and one had a terrible feeling of working against time.

Everyone was violently busy on that crowded, dangerous shore. The pebbles were the size of apples and feet deep, and we stumbled up a road that a huge road shovel was scooping out. We walked with the utmost care between the narrowly placed white tape lines that marked the mine-cleared path, and headed for a tent marked with a red cross.

Ducks and tanks and trucks were moving down this narrow rocky road, and one stepped just a little out of their way, but not beyond the tapes. The dust that rose in the gray night light seemed like the fog of war itself. Then we got off onto the grass, and it was perhaps the most surprising of all the day's surprises to smell the sweet smell of summer grass, a smell of cattle and peace and the sun that had warmed the earth some other time, when summer was real.

Inside the Red Cross tent, there were two tired, unshaven, dirty, polite young men who said that the trucks were coming in here with the wounded, and where did we want to have them unloaded. We explained the problem of the tides and said the best thing was to run the trucks down to that LST there and carry the wounded aboard, under the canvas roof-covering, and we would get them off as soon as anything floated.

At this point a truck jolted up, and the driver shouted out a question and was told to back and turn. He did not need to be told to do this carefully and not to get off the mine-cleared area. The Red Cross men said they didn't know whether wounded would be coming in all night or not, it was pretty tough to transport them by road in the dark; anyway, they'd send everything down to our agreed meeting place, and everyone said, "Well, good luck, fella," and we left. No one wasted time talking around there. You had a feeling of fierce and driven activity.

We returned to our small, unattractive piece of the beach and directed the unloading of this truck. The tide was coming in, and there was a narrow strip of water between the landing ramp of the LST and the shore. The wounded were carried carefully and laid on the deck inside the great whale's-mouth cavern of the LST. After that, there was a pause, with nothing to do.

Some American soldiers came up and began to talk. This had been an ugly piece of beach from the beginning, and they were still here, living in foxholes and supervising the unloading of supplies. They spoke of snipers in the hills a hundred yards or so behind the beach, and no one lighted a cigarette. They spoke of not having slept at all, but they seemed curiously pleased by the discovery that you could go without sleep and food and still function all right. Everyone agreed that the beach was a stinker, and that it would be a great pleasure to get the hell out of here sometime.

Then there was our favorite American conversation: "Where're you from?" An American always has time to look for someone who knows his home town. We talked about Pittsburgh and Rosemont, Pennsylvania, and Chicago and Cheyenne, not saying much except that they were sure swell places and had this beach licked every way for Sunday. Then one of the soldiers remarked that they had a nice foxhole about fifty yards inland and we were very welcome there, when the air raid started, if we didn't mind eating sand.

My companion, one of the stretcher-bearers from the ship, thanked them for their kind invitation and said that, on the other hand, we had guests aboard the LST and we would have to stay home this evening. I wish I had known his name, because I would like to write it down here. He was one of the best and jolliest boys I've met anyplace, anytime. He joked, no matter what happened, and toward the end of that night, we really began to enjoy ourselves. There is a point where you feel yourself so small and helpless in such an enormous, insane nightmare of a world, that you cease to give a hoot about anything and you renounce care and start laughing. He was

lovely company, that boy was, and he was brave and competent, and I wish I had known his name.

He went off to search for the water ambulances and
returned to say that there wasn't a sign of them, which
meant that they couldn't get inshore yet and we'd just have
to wait and hope they could find this spot when it was black
night. If they never found this place, the LST would float
later, and the British captain said he would run our
wounded out to the hospital ship, though it would not be
for hours.

Suddenly our flak started going up at the far end of the
beach, and it was very beautiful, twinkling as it burst in the
sky, and the tracers were as lovely as they always are; and no
one took pleasure from the beauty of the scene.

"We've had it now," said the stretcher-bearer. "There isn't
any place we can put those wounded."

I asked one of the soldiers, just for interest's sake, what
they did in case of air raids, and he said well, you could
go to a foxhole if you had time, but on the other hand,
there really wasn't much to do. So we stood and watched,
and there was altogether too much flak for comfort. We
could not hear the planes or any bomb explosions, but, as
everyone knows, flak is a bad thing to have fall on your
head.

The soldiers now drifted off on their own business, and we
boarded the LST to keep the wounded company. The
stretcher-bearer and I said to each other gloomily that, as an
air-raid shelter, far better things than the hold of an LST had
been devised, and we went inside, not liking any of it, and
feeling miserably worried about our wounded.

The wounded looked pretty bad and lay very still. In the
light of one bare bulb which hung from a girder, one could
not see them well. Then one of them began to moan, and he
said something. He was evidently conscious enough to notice
this ghastly racket that was going on above us. The Oerlikons
of our LST now opened fire, and the noise inside the steel
hold was as if they were driving rivets into your eardrums.
The wounded man called out again, and I realized that he
was speaking German.

We checked up, then, and found that we had an LST full

of wounded Germans, and the stretcher-bearer said, "Well, that's just dandy! By golly, if that isn't the pay-off!" Then he said, "If anything hits this ship, dammit, they deserve it."

However, there were still the English crew and ourselves aboard and it seemed a rather expensive poetic justice.

The ack-ack lifted a bit, and the stretcher-bearer climbed up to the upper deck, like Sister Anne on the tower, to see where those water ambulances were. I clambered like a very awkward monkey up a ladder to the galley to get some coffee and so missed the spectacle of two German planes, falling like fiery comets from the sky. They hit the beach to the right and left of us and burned in huge bonfires which lighted up the shore.

The beach, in this light, looked empty of human life, cluttered with dark square shapes of tanks and trucks and jeeps and ammunition boxes and all the motley equipment of war. It looked like a vast, uncanny black-and-red-flaring salvage dump, whereas once people actually went swimming here for pleasure.

Our LST crew was delighted because they believed they had brought down one of the German planes, and everyone felt cheerful about the success of the ack-ack. A soldier shouted from shore that we had shot down four planes in all and it was nice work. The wounded were very silent, and those few who had their eyes open had very frightened eyes. They seemed to be listening with their eyes, and fearing what they would hear.

The night, too, went on longer than other nights. Our water ambulances found us, and there was a lot of fine incomprehensible cockney talk among the boatmen while the wounded were loaded from the now floating LST to the small, bucking launch. We set out, happy because we were off the beach and because the wounded would be taken where they belonged.

The trip across that obstacle-studded piece of water was a chatty affair, due to the boat crew. "Crikey, mate, wot yer trying ter do? Ram a destroyer?" And, "By God, man, keep an eye in yer head! That's a tank radio pole."

To which another answered, "Ye expect me to see a bloody piece of grass in this dark?"

So, full of conversation, we zigzagged back to the ship and were at last swung aboard.

The raid had been hard on the wounded because of the terrible helplessness of being unable to move. The ship seemed to lie directly under a cone of ack-ack fire, and perhaps it would have been easier if the wounded had heard the German planes so that, at least through their ears, they would know what was happening.

The American medical personnel, most of whom had never been in an air raid, tranquilly continued their work, asked no questions, showed no sign even of interest in this uproar, and handed out confidence as if it were a solid thing like bread. If I seem to insist too much in my admiration for these people, understand that one cannot insist too much. There is a kind of devotion, coupled with competence, which is almost too admirable to talk about; and they had all of it that can be had.

If anyone had come fresh to that ship in the night, someone unwounded, not attached to the ship, he would probably have been appalled. It began to look very Black Hole of Calcutta, because it was airless and ill-lighted. Piles of bloody clothing had been cut off and dumped out of the way in corners; coffee cups and cigarette stubs littered the decks, plasma bottles hung from cords, and all the fearful surgical apparatus for holding broken bones made shadows on the walls.

There were wounded who groaned in their sleep or called out, and there was the soft steady hum of conversation among the wounded who could not sleep. That is the way it would have looked to anyone seeing it fresh; a ship carrying a load of pain, with everyone waiting for daylight, everyone longing for England.

It was that, but it was something else, too; it was a safe ship, no matter what happened to it. We were together and we counted on one another. We knew that from the British captain to the pink-cheeked little London messboy, every one of the ship's company did his job tirelessly and well. The wounded knew that the doctors and nurses and orderlies belonged to them utterly and would not fail them. And all of us knew that our wounded men were good men, and with their amazing help, their selflessness and self-control, we would get through all right.

There is very little more to write. The wounded looked much better in the morning. The human machine is the most delicate and rare of all, and it is obviously built to survive, if given half a chance. The ship moved steadily across the Channel, and we could feel England coming nearer. Then the coast came into sight, and the green of England looked quite different from how it had looked only two days ago; it looked cooler and clearer and wonderfully safe.

The air of England flowed down through the wards, and the wounded seemed to feel it. The sound of their voices brightened and sharpened, and they began making dates with one another for when they would be on convalescent leave in London. The captain shouted down from the bridge, "Look at it! Just look at it!" He was too proud of the Navy—his Navy and ours—to say more. But he had spoken, in his pride, for all of us.

American ambulance companies were waiting on the pier, the same efficient, swift colored troops I had seen working on the piers and landing ramps before we left. There were conferences on the quay between important shore personages and our captain and chief medical officer; and a few of us, old-timers by now, leaned over the rail and joked about being back in the paper-work department again. Everyone felt very happy and fine, and you could see it in all their faces. The head nurse, smiling though gray with weariness, said, "We'll do it better next time," which seemed to me to be a very elegant thing to say.

As the first wounded were carried from the ship, the chief medical officer, watching them said, "Made it." That was the great thing. Now they would re-stock their supplies, clean the ship, cover the beds with fresh blankets, sleep whatever hours they could, and then they would go back to France. But this trip was done; this much was to the good; they had made it.

*Collier's*, August 5, 1944

# Take Two Parts Sand, One Part Girl, and Stir

by S. J. Perelman

OUTSIDE of the three Rs—the razor, the rope, and the revolver—I know only one sure-fire method of coping with the
simmering heat we may cheerfully expect in this meridian
from now to Labor Day. Whenever the mercury starts inching
up the column, I take to the horizontal plane with a glass
graduate trimmed with ferns, place a pinch of digitalis or any
good heart stimulant at my elbow, and flip open the advertising section of *Vogue*. Fifteen minutes of that paradisiacal
prose, those dizzying non-sequiturs, and my lips are as blue as
Lake Louise. If you want a mackerel iced or a sherbet frozen,
just bring it up and let me read the advertising section of
*Vogue* over it. I can also take care of small picnic parties up
to five. The next time you're hot and breathless, remember
the name, folks: Little Labrador Chilling & Dismaying Corporation.

It would require precision instruments as yet undreamed of
to decide whether *Vogue*'s advertisements contain more
moonbeams per linear inch than those of its competitors, but
the June issue was certainly a serious contender for the ecstasy
sweepstakes. There was, for instance, the vagary which por-
trayed a Revolutionary heroine setting fire to a field of grain
with this caption: "*The Patriotism in Her Heart Burned
Wheat Fields.* It took courage that day in October 1777 for
Catherine Schuyler to apply the torch to her husband's wheat
fields so that food would not fall into the hands of the enemy.
The flames that consumed the wheat fields on the Schuyler
estate near Saratoga burned with no greater brightness than
the patriotism in Catherine Schuyler's heart." Then, with
a triple forward somersault that would have done credit
to Alfredo Codona, the wizard of the trapeze, the copywriter vaulted giddily into an appeal to American women to

augment their loveliness with Avon Cosmetics. Somewhat breathless, I turned the page and beheld a handsome young aviatrix, crouched on a wing of her plane. "Test Pilot—Size 10," read the text. "Nine thousand feet above the flying field, a Hellcat fighter plane screams down in the dark blur of a power dive. Holding the stick of this four-hundred-mile-an-hour ship is a small firm hand." The owner of the small firm hand, I shortly discovered in the verbal power dive that followed, is an enthusiastic patron of DuBarry Beauty Preparations. The transition in logic was so abrupt that it was only by opening my mouth and screaming briefly, a procedure I had observed in the movies, that I was able to keep my eardrums from bursting.

The most singular display of the advertiser's eternal lust for novelty, though, was a bold, full-color photograph of an olive-skinned beauty, buried up to her corsage in sand, in the interests of Marvella Simulated Pearls. A matched string of the foregoing circled her voluptuous throat, and dimly visible in the background were a conch shell and a sponge, identifying the locale as the seaside. The model's face exhibited a resentment verging on ferocity, which was eminently pardonable; anybody mired in a quicksand, with only a string of simulated pearls to show for it, has a justifiable beef. And so have I. The connection between burning wheat field and cosmetic jar, Hellcat fighter and lipstick, is tenuous enough, God knows, but somehow the copywriter managed to link them with his sophistries. Why in Tophet a scowling nude stuck bolt upright in a sand bar should influence the reader to rush to his jeweller for a particular brand of artificial pearl, however, I cannot possibly imagine.

Perhaps if we reconstruct the circumstances under which this baffling campaign was conceived, a clue might be forthcoming. Let us, therefore, don a clean collar and sidle discreetly into the offices of Meeker, Cassavant, Singleton, Doubleday & Tripler, a fairly representative advertising agency.

[Scene: *The Brain Room of the agency, a conference chamber decorated in cerebral gray, Swedish modern furniture, and the inevitable van Gogh reproductions. As the curtain rises, Duckworth, the copy chief, and four members of his staff—Farish,*

*Munkaczi, DeGroot, and Miss Drehdel—are revealed plunged in thought.*]

DUCKWORTH (*impatiently*): Well, what do you say, Farish? Got an angle, DeGroot?

FARISH: I still keep going back to my old idea, V.J.

DUCKWORTH: What's that?

FARISH (*thirstily*): A good red-hot picture of a dame in a transparent shimmy, with plenty of thems and those (*suddenly conscious of Miss Drehdel's presence*)—oh, excuse me.

MISS DREHDEL (*wearily*): That's all right. I read Earl Wilson's column, too.

FARISH: And a balloon coming out of her mouth saying, "I've had my Vita-Ray Cheese Straws today—*have you?*"

DUCKWORTH: No-o-o, it doesn't—it doesn't *sing*, if you know what I mean. I feel there's something gay and youthful and alive about these cheese straws. That's the note I want to hear in our copy.

DEGROOT: How about a gay, newborn baby in a crib? That would include the various elements. I'd like to see a line like "No harsh abrasives to upset tender tummies."

DUCKWORTH: No, it's static. To me it lacks dynamism.

MISS DREHDEL: What's wrong with a closeup of the cheese straws and "20 cents a box" underneath?

DUCKWORTH: Over-simplification. They'd never get it.

MUNKACZI (*violently*): I've got it, V.J., *I've got it!*

DUCKWORTH: What?

MUNKACZI: We'll take one of these Conover models and bury her up to her neck in sand! Maybe some driftwood or a couple of clams for drama!

FARISH: How do we tie in the cheese straws?

MUNKACZI: I haven't worked it out yet, but it smells right to me.

DUCKWORTH (*excitedly*): Wait a minute, now—you threw me into something when you said "sand." What we need is grit—punch—conflict. I see a foxhole at Anzio—shells bursting—a doughboy with shining eyes saying, "This is what I'm fighting for, Ma—freedom of purchase the American Way—the right to buy Vita-Ray Cheese Straws on every drug, grocery, and delicatessen counter from coast to coast!"

FARISH: Man, oh man, that's terrific! I'll buy that!

DeGroot: It's poetic and yet it's timely, too! It's a block-buster, V.J.!

Duckworth (*radiant*): You really mean it? You're sure you're not telling me this just because I'm the boss? (*Indignation in varying degree from all*) O.K. If there's one thing I can't abide, it's a lot of yes men around me. Now let's get on to the Hush-a-Bye Blanket account. Any hunches?

DeGroot: We got a darb. (*Producing two photographs*) This is what the nap of a Hush-a-Bye looks like under the microscope.

Farish: And here's the average blanket. See the difference?

Duckworth: Why, yes. It has twice as many woollen fibers as the Hush-a-Bye.

DeGroot (*happily*): Check. There's our campaign.

Duckworth: Hmm. Isn't that sort of defeatist?

Farish: A little, but it shows we don't make extravagant claims.

DeGroot: We could always switch the photographs.

Farish: Sure, nobody ever looks at their blanket through a microscope.

Duckworth (*dubiously*): We-e-ll, I don't know. I like your approach to the challenge; but I don't think you've extracted its— its thematic milk, shall I say. Now, I for one saw a different line of attack.

Farish (*instantly*): Me too, V.J. What I visualize is a show girl with a real nifty chassis in a peekaboo nightgown. Here, I'll draw you a sketch—

Miss Drehdel: Don't bother. We can read your mind.

Munkaczi: Listen, V.J., do you want a wrinkle that'll revolutionize the business? Answer yes or no.

Duckworth: Does it fit in with the product?

Munkaczi: Fit in? It grows right out of it! You're looking at a beach, see? Voom! Right in front of you is a Powers girl buried up to the bust in sand, with some horseshoe crabs or seaweed as an accent.

Duckworth: Do you see a Hush-a-Bye blanket anywhere in the composition?

Munkaczi: No, that would be hitting it on the nose. Indirection, V.J., that's the whole trend today.

Duckworth: You've realized the problem, Munkaczi, but

your synthesis is faulty. I miss a sense of scope. Who are we rooting for?

MUNKACZI: Well, of course I was only spitballing. I haven't had time to explore every cranny.

DUCKWORTH: Look, kids, if you don't like what I'm about to suggest, will you tell me?

FARISH (*fiercely*): I've never been a stooge for anyone yet.

DEGROOT: You said it. There's not enough money in the world to buy *my* vote.

DUCKWORTH: That's the stuff. I want guts in this organization, not a bunch of namby-pambies scared that I'll kick 'em out into the breadline. Now this is hazy, mind you, but it's all there. A beachhead in the Solomons—a plain, ordinary G.I. Joe in a slit trench, grinning at the consumer through the muck and grime on his face, and asking, "Are you backing me up with Hush-a-Bye Blankets at home? Gee, Mom, don't sabotage my birthright with sleazy, inferior brands!"

DEGROOT: Holy cow, that'll tear their hearts out!

FARISH (*with a sob*): It hits you where you live. It's a portion of common everyday experience.

DUCKWORTH: Remember, men, it isn't sacred. If you think you can improve the phrasing—

DEGROOT: I wouldn't change a word of it.

FARISH: It's got balance and flow and discipline. Say it again, will you, V.J.?

DUCKWORTH: No, it's pretty near lunch and we still need a slant for the Marvella Pearl people.

MUNKACZI (*exalted*): Your troubles are over, boss. I got something that leaps from the printed page into the hearts of a million women! It's four A.M. in the Aleutians. A haggard, unshaven Marine is kneeling in a shell hole, pointing his rifle at you and whispering, "Start thinking, sister! When Johnny comes marching home, are you going to be poised and serene with Marvella Pearls or just another housewife?"

FARISH: Cripes, I had the same notion, V.J. He took the words right out of my mouth!

DEGROOT: I'll go for that! It's as timely as tomorrow's newspaper!

DUCKWORTH: There's only one thing wrong with it. It's *too* timely.

DeGroot (*eagerly*): That's what I meant. It's depressing.

Farish: It reminds people of their troubles. Ugh!

Duckworth: Precisely. Now, I've been mulling a concept which is a trifle on the exotic side but fundamentally sound. Mark you, I'm merely talking out loud. A girl on a bathing beach, almost totally buried in the sand, with a Marvella necklace and a brooding, inscrutable expression like the Sphinx. Haunting but inviting—the eternal riddle of womankind.

DeGroot (*emotionally*): V.J., do you want my candid opinion? I wouldn't tell this to my own mother, but you've just made advertising history!

Farish: It's provocative, muscular, three-dimensional! It's got a *spiral* quality, the more you think of it.

Duckworth: How does it hit you, Munkaczi?

Munkaczi (*warmly*): I couldn't like it more if it was my own idea.

Duckworth: I wonder if Miss Drehdel can give us the woman's reaction, in a word.

Miss Drehdel (*rising*): You bet I can. The word I'm thinking of rhymes with Sphinx. (*Sunnily*) Well, goodbye now. If anybody wants me, I'm over at Tim's, up to here in sawdust and Cuba Libres. (*She goes; a pause.*)

Farish: I always said there was something sneaky about her.

DeGroot: Women and business don't mix.

Munkaczi: You can never tell what they're really thinking.

Farish (*cackling*): Old V.J. smoked her out though, didn't he?

Duckworth (*expansively*): Yes, I may be wrong, but this is one conference she won't forget in a hurry, eh, boys? (*As the boys chuckle loyally and scuffle to light his cigar*).

CURTAIN

*The New Yorker*, July 8, 1944

# Gone to Earth

by Robert Sherrod

WE HAD BEEN inspecting four Jap tanks, which were still burning. One of the tankers' crisp, upraised hands stuck out of his turret as if in supplication to a power beyond his reach. Then three of us sat down in a sacred park near by on the edge of a cement fence built around a pedestaled, steel-shelled Buddha which had suffered considerably from shell fragments—hits in the chest and behind the right ear. We opened a pack of K rations for breakfast.

We had hardly dug into the can of pork and egg yolk when a bullet whizzed close overhead. We hit the dirt behind the cement fence. A marine yelled: "I saw him. He jumped into a cave over there in the rock quarry." Several other marines ran toward the quarry—one of several dozen on Saipan. Caves in the sides of these scooped-out affairs are favorite hiding places for Japs. Then began the familiar game of "flush the sniper."

A marine sergeant took charge of the dozen or more men participating. First he handed a marine a hand grenade. The marine jumped into the quarry and began to edge toward the cave while one of his pals covered him with a Garand. The grenade was tossed into the cave. It burst with a muffled thud. In a movie version of killing Japs, the incident might have ended at this point. But marines have long since learned that one grenade does not always finish off the occupants of a cave or pillbox; almost invariably there are five to 20 Japs in whatever hole you might expect to find one. Besides, the Japs often dig trenches within the caves to avoid the grenade explosions.

One of the marines who fancied himself a linguist—he had been studying the posters labeled "combat language"—took over after the grenade burst. "High de koy!" he shouted into the mouth of the cave. One of the other marines explained to me, "That means 'come out.'" "High de koy!" the linguist

170

repeated, holding his rifle at the ready. But the occupant or occupants of the cave made no move.

"Shippee shenoddy," said the linguist, trying a new tack. I asked him what he was saying now. He said: "That means, 'don't be afraid.'" That seemed a loose choice of words when I looked at the dozen marines surrounding the quarry, with Garands and Browning automatic rifles poised.

"Somebody go get a four-block charge of TNT," said the marine sergeant, who hadn't put much faith in his linguist's coaxing ability in the first place. At this point an armored bulldozer, piloted by a young Seabee, rumbled through the underbrush. The sergeant explained the situation to him. The bulldozer man drove his blade into the earth and started to push dirt from the ground level into the quarry where it fell across the mouth of the cave.

But there was hard coral rock only six inches under the surface and the bulldozer driver finally gave it up. Then the TNT arrived. The sergeant was pretty mad by this time. He snatched it up savagely and said to the spectators: "A lot of muck is going to fly, so all of you people stand back. There's no telling how many bastards may pour out of it."

One of the marines kept on talking about coaxing the Jap or Japs out of the cave. Said he somewhat wistfully: "I wish we had somebody that knew enough Japanese to fetch him out." He said this in a low voice so the sergeant couldn't hear him. Another private first class observed that he didn't believe the Emperor himself knew enough Japanese to coax anybody out of that hole.

The four-block charge of TNT blew black dust high into the air and made a terrific noise. Big waves of black smoke and debris billowed out of the cave. But this was a well-constructed hole which went deep into the earth and heaven knows how far back. About all that came to the surface was the wooden framing of two-inch planks and a cheap suitcase filled with shirts and silk underwear and an empty cloth pocketbook.

The bulldozer driver eyed the result with disappointment and then determination. "Hell, I'll fix him," he said and swung his snorting machine around. He went around to another side of the cave and dipped his blade into the earth.

This time he found soft dirt. He scooped bladeful after bladeful against the mouth of the cave until it was blocked with at least a five-foot thickness of earth. It all ended there. It was not very satisfactory because we never found out what was in the hole. Maybe some day somebody will dig into this piece of earth, and into hundreds of similar pieces of earth on Saipan, and find some answers.

*Time*, July 17, 1944

# The Nature of the Enemy

by Robert Sherrod

WE THOUGHT we had seen everything in the line of Jap military suicides by the time the last charge of the Japs had been beaten off. But we hadn't. Here was something different. During mopping-up operations a detachment of marines on amphibious tractors saw seven Japanese off-shore on a coral reef and drove out to get them. As the amphtracks approached, six of the Japs knelt down on the reef. Then the seventh, apparently an officer, drew a sword and began methodically to hack at the necks of his men. Four heads had rolled into the sea before the marines closed in. Then the officer, sword in hand, charged the amphtracks. He and the remaining two Japs were mowed down.

By this time we had begun to hear a fantastic story that some of the 20,000 civilians on the island (of whom we had interned 10,000) were killing themselves. I headed for the northern tip of Saipan, a place called Marpi Point, where there is a long plateau on which the Japs had built a secondary airfield. At the edge of the plateau there is a sheer 200-ft. drop to jagged coral below; then the billowing sea. The morning I crossed the airfield and got to the edge of the cliff nine marines from a burial detail were working with ropes to pick up the bodies of two of our men, killed the previous day. I asked one of them about the stories I had heard.

"You wouldn't believe it unless you saw it," he said. "Yesterday and the day before there were hundreds of Jap civilians—men, women, and children—up here on this cliff. In the most routine way, they would jump off the cliff, or climb down and wade into the sea. I saw a father throw his three children off, and then jump down himself. Those coral pockets down there under the cliff are full of Jap suicides."

He paused and pointed. "Look," he said, "there's one getting ready to drown himself now." Down below, a young

Japanese, no more than 15, paced back & forth across the rocks. He swung his arms, as if getting ready to dive; then he sat down at the edge and let the water play over his feet. Finally he eased himself slowly into the water.

"There he goes," the marine shouted.

A strong wave had washed up to the shore, and the boy floated out with it. At first, he lay on the water, face down, without moving. Then, apparently, a last, desperate instinct to live gripped him and he flailed his arms, thrashing the foam. It was too late. Just as suddenly, it was all over: the air-filled seat of his knee-length black trousers bobbed on the water for ten minutes. Then he disappeared.

Looking down, I counted the bodies of seven others who had killed themselves. One, a child of about five, clad in a ragged white shirt, floated stiffly in the surf.

I turned to go. "This is nothing," the marine said. "Half a mile down, on the west side, you can see hundreds of them."

Later on I checked up with the officer of a minesweeper which had been operating on the west side. He said: "Down there, the sea is so congested with floating bodies we can't avoid running them down. There was one woman in khaki trousers and a white polka-dot blouse, with her black hair streaming in the water. I'm afraid every time I see that kind of a blouse, I'll think of that woman. There was another one, nude, who had drowned herself while giving birth to a baby. A small boy of four or five had drowned with his arm clenched around the neck of a soldier—the two bodies rocked crazily in the waves. Hundreds & hundreds of Jap bodies have floated up to our minesweeper."

Apparently the Jap soldier not only would go to any extreme to avoid surrender, but would also try to see that no civilian surrendered. At Marpi Point, the marines had tried to dislodge a Jap sniper from a cave in the cliff. For a Jap, he was an exceptional marksman; he had killed two marines (one at 700 yds.) and wounded a third. The marines used rifles, torpedoes and, finally, TNT in a 45-minute effort to force him out. Meantime the Jap had other business.

He had spotted a Japanese group—apparently father, mother and three children—out on the rocks, preparing to drown themselves, but evidently weakening in their decision.

The Jap sniper took aim. He drilled the man from behind, dropping him into the sea. The second bullet hit the woman. She dragged herself about 30 ft. along the rocks. Then she floated out in a stain of blood. The sniper would have shot the children, but a Japanese woman ran across and carried them out of range. The sniper walked defiantly out of his cave, and crumpled under a hundred marine bullets.

Some of the Jap civilians went through considerable ceremony before snuffing out their own lives. The marines said that some fathers had cut their children's throats before tossing them over the cliff. Some strangled their children. In one instance marines watched in astonishment as three women sat on the rocks leisurely, deliberately combing their long black hair.* Finally they joined hands and walked slowly out into the sea.

But the most ceremonious, by all odds, were 100 Japs who were on the rocks below the Marpi Point cliff. All together, they suddenly bowed to marines watching from the cliff. Then they stripped off their clothes and bathed in the sea. Thus refreshed, they put on new clothes and spread a huge Jap flag on a smooth rock. Then the leader distributed hand grenades. One by one, as the pins were pulled, the Japs blew their insides out.

Some seemed to make a little game out of their dying— perhaps out of indecision, perhaps out of ignorance, or even some kind of lightheaded disrespect of the high seriousness of Japanese suicide. One day the marines observed a circle of about 50 Japanese, including several small children, gaily tossing hand grenades to each other—like baseball players warming up before a game. Suddenly six Japanese soldiers dashed from a cave, from which they had been sniping at marines. The soldiers posed arrogantly in front of the civilians, then blew themselves to kingdom come; thus shamed, the civilians did likewise.

What did all this self-destruction mean? Did it mean that the Japanese on Saipan believed their own propaganda which told them that Americans are beasts and would murder them

---

*The marines had obviously never heard that Leonidas and his Spartans did the same before their last stand at Thermopylae.

all? Many a Jap civilian did beg our people to put him to death immediately rather than to suffer the torture which he expected. But many who chose suicide could see other civilians who had surrendered walking unmolested in the internment camps. They could hear some of the surrendered plead with them by loudspeaker not to throw their lives away.

The marines have come to expect almost anything in the way of self-destruction from Japanese soldiers. They have read the story, in Japanese newspapers, of the "dauntless courage of Captain Yamazaki"—in the seventh paragraph it is revealed that Captain Yamazaki's courage consisted in destroying himself. But none were prepared for this epic self-slaughter among civilians. More than one U.S. fighting man was killed trying to rescue a Jap from his wanton suicide.

Saipan is the first invaded Jap territory populated with more than a handful of civilians. Do the suicides of Saipan mean that the whole Japanese race will choose death before surrender? Perhaps that is what the Japanese and their strange propagandists would like us to believe.

*Time*, August 7, 1944

# U.S.A. Tent Hospital

by Lee Miller

As WE FLEW into sight of France I swallowed hard on what were trying to be tears, and remembered a movie actress kissing a handful of earth. My self-conscious analysis was forgotten in greedily studying the soft, grey-skied panorama of nearly a thousand square miles of France . . . of freed France.

The sea and sky joined in a careless watercolour wash . . . below, two convoys speckled the fragile smooth surface of the Channel. Cherbourg was a misty bend far to the right, and ahead, three planes were returning from dropping the bombs which made towering columns of smoke. That was the Front.

Acres of scarred, red-brown soil, pocked with confetti-sized rings, were the result of navy shelling. Three-cornered tears and dots and dashes were the foxholes and slit-trenches where the landing had been fought for and held. A green valley up from a wide, busy beach had been a battleground—at the top, a new cemetery was being dug for six thousand of our dead. No other sign of war except neatly laid-out tents with dazzling Red Cross markers.

It was France. The trees were the same—with little pantaloons like eagles; and the walled farms, the austere Norman architecture. We strapped ourselves in for a bumpy landing on the air strip, but set down more smoothly than we'd travelled. I found that it was no longer France, but a vast military area of planes, soldiers, and gargantuan materiel.

The highways were no longer placid, tree-bordered and grass-edged. New roads had been gouged and bulldozed out, from here to there, in a few days, and the traffic—monstrous dinosaurs and endless convoys moved swiftly—unsnarled, in both directions. A sign warned that civilian cars should not drop below thirty-five miles an hour, but there were none anyway . . . and other boards along the hedges carried a red skull and cross-bones with *"Attention aux mines"* and *"Gefahr Minen"* barring access to herds of poppies and daisies. At every cross-road there were totem poles of arrows, with the code names of units: Missouri Charlie, Missouri Baker, Madonna Charlie, Mahogany Red, Vermont Red, Java Blue—mixed with the names of French villages. The kilométrage had been changed into miles, on the signs and road-stones, and the hedges were draped with dozens of strands of wire, looped into each other like filigree. Crazy cats'-cradles of wire were overhead and on the walls and crossing the arms of a roadside crucifix. Road gangs, civilian and military, were building a road under our passing wheels, and white tape strung by the side advertised that mines had been cleared only to the bank.

We turned through a gap in the dust-stained hedgerow to the Evacuation Hospital. Major Esther McCafferty, Chief Nurse of the First Army, an old acquaintance, met us, and we shared the first real meal which the nurses and medical staff had had in thirty days. It was hot bully beef, tinned peas, tomatoes, and peaches. We ate from white enamel plates, drank from shallow, six-inch basins, caught our breath, and asked questions.

A hospital is sited in an obvious, accessible, well-drained pasture, which, for safety's sake, must be full of cattle. The cows are given a quick chase around and out, to disclose booby traps or mines, and the four hundred-bed tent city is receiving casualties in two-and-one-half hours.

The "Evac" had landed on D Day plus 5, had struggled up the hard-won valley, slept in foxholes, assembled transport, and set up in this dung-spotted field where for a month forty doctors and forty nurses had averaged one hundred operations every twenty-four hours on six operating tables, as well as caring for their four hundred transient patients.

Every few minutes a dusty ambulance rolled in or out . . . full or empty. Medical Soldiers unbuckled the litters, and with gentle, synchronized movements carried them through the receiving tent, fanning out the other end to the pre-ops, shock, or X-ray tents, or directly to the wards.

From the outside, all tents look alike . . . long, dark, greenish-brown, humped at the tent-poles like a dromedary saddle, and bearing on one top side an enormous circle enclosing the red cross. White tape outlines the stakes and entrances, which is a tunnel marquee for blackout and draught-proofing. A few things inside are common to all . . . the sloping, dark, swaying roofs; the swishing grass floor, and the silent wounded.

In one tent the men are somewhat patched, dirty, tired, but reassured . . . they hold their medical tag, confident in the system of priorities which keeps them waiting that others may live.

In the shock ward they are limp and flat under brown blankets, thirty-two at a time, some with plasma-flasks dripping drops of life into an outstretched splinted arm; a doctor and nurse busy on a man with oxygen and plasma—other men sleeping or staring at the dark brown canvas. Patient, waiting, and gathering strength for multiple operations on unorthodox wounds.

The surgical tent had a white floor and white walls, and white mosquito netting to shut off the vestibule from the operating tables. A wing opened out for the preparation of dressings and instruments. The surgeons were changed from their olive "fatigues" into white gown, face-mask, and coif. Discarded helmets were on the floor. Six groups of people were around six operating tables. It was crowded but unconfused; quite enough elbow-room for these unflustered, deft workers, all of whom had been on duty for steady, twelve-hour shifts, often as much as eighteen hours a day since landing. There is no ether smell of hospital, because they use mostly spinal nerve block, sodium pentathol, and nitrous oxide. Voices were unhushed, gestures precise. The wounded were deposited on the tables on the same litters, in the same khaki blankets, that they came in from the Front. A few wore their battle-muddy boots.

Three of the patients were conscious. The far one was nearly completed; that is, his leg had been dealt with and clench-faced men were patting the last of a plaster bandage in place. In the chiaroscuro of khaki and white, I was reminded of Hieronymus Bosch's painting "The Carrying of the Cross." The wounded man had watched me take his photograph and had made an effort, with his good hand, to smooth his hair. I didn't know that he was already asleep with sodium

Maj. Esther McCafferty and patient holding priority card regulating
order of treatment.

pentathol when they started on his other arm. I had turned
away for fear my face would betray to him what I had seen.

The next boy was on his side. They were probing for scattered shell splinters and wood fibres from the vicious, coloured wooden bullets the Huns are using in close fighting.
He'd be all right and in England tomorrow.

Alongside him was a captain, a Medical Corps Surgeon,
from a Battalion Aid Station. His main injury was his knee,
but both legs were covered with abrasions and cuts. The
sulfa-powder sparkled on the edges of the wounds as they
took off the temporary dressings. He was still wearing his field
jacket, and was watching the operation on the fourth table.
Occasionally he winced, and when they started on his knee he
nodded his head. He didn't look or question. He had perfect
confidence in his colleagues. Half-way through he grunted,
"To think I'd be on this end of the knife!" He went to England that evening.

They had been working on the fourth patient for over
two hours. Blood was being slowly transfused into his left
arm. Because of chest wounds, they couldn't turn him over
to work on his back, so he was held up, and the surgeon,
half-kneeling, probed several deep holes by the beam of a
common G.I. flashlight. The anæsthetist, a nurse, spoke
sharply, the surgeon stopped, the patient was lowered . . .
mask and transfusion tube were whisked off. Someone pressed in on his ribs, and a doctor forced a broncho-
scope down his throat. In these few minutes his face had
turned dark blue, his eyes had opened, glazed . . . then he
gasped slowly and started to breathe normally through the
tube. He came alive again, for good. I had thought him
dead.

The other two tables were severe abdominal cases. Belly
wounds have high priority. The magic life-savers in the war—
Sulfa, Penicillin, and Blood—were augmenting the skill of the
surgeons. From the operating room, these two men would go
to the belly ward, known as "Wangensteen Alley," after the
inventor of the suction apparatus. The ward was like a jungle
of banyan trees. A maze of hanging rubber tubes, swaying in
khaki shadow . . . one to the nostril and one to the wound of
each man. They are always hungry on their diet of glucose

and saline. In a short time they will go by air through England to the hospital nearest their home-town in the U.S.A.

The rumour was true, the Evac had closed for reception of new cases. That meant it would fold up gradually as the present cases were well enough to be evacuated, and prepare to leap-frog past two other units to a more forward position. It also meant that the high pressure was let off, that Captain Eva Maclin and her nurses would, in turn, get eight hours' sleep apiece, a leisurely shower, a hair-wash, a chance to write a letter, or read one, or to lie on the grass.

We joined the chow-line and marvelled at the excitement. It wasn't the promised slack in work, as there would still be tough days ahead; it wasn't that it had stopped drizzling— but that the first bakers' bread had been made and delivered. A snowy-white blizzard, it was kissed, caressed, admired, and gobbled. I was even more startled, as I had seen white bread only once in three years—with the British Navy. We hurried through an excellent meal, gossiping, playing "Do you know so-and-so," noting statistics, hearing half-stories with each ear.

With my mouth full of the cherished white bread, I did a zigzag dash through guy ropes to our tent. It was like all the others except that it had no blackout arrangements, and it had a reputation . . . it had just been vacated by a group of captive German army nurses who had been returned to their own lines under a white flag. It appears that they had been deeply impressed with the treatment accorded them, and staggered by our facilities and methods . . . they'll make excellent propaganda agents for us.

I grabbed a pocketful of bulbs and film, and clambered into a command car which was going to take us up to a field hospital about six miles nearer the Front. A field hospital is the nearest completely equipped unit to the fighting lines. The desperately wounded who can't travel the six more miles to the evacuation hospital arrive here. Every case is life or death, and ambulances come in with one or two men instead of waiting for a full load. They are transferred from the pre-ops tent, the X-ray tent, or laboratories to the surgeons' table, with plasma bottles carried above . . . like a silent, dark convoy ship floating a balloon.

In the bluey dusk, the artillery flashes were like summer heat-lightning, and the rumbling was an accompaniment to a sense of strain and urgency. The tempo was quicker than at the Evac—the doctors and nurses were even more tired, and they knew that during the night they were going to run out of blood. The Colonel of the now closing Evac, who had escorted us, offered the surplus from his hospital for the night. One of the eight refrigerated blood-bank trucks would be making its usual delivery round in the morning, distributing the five hundred pints flown daily to Normandy.

I wandered from tent to tent at will. No one found it abnormal that I should be taking photographs, asking questions, helping myself to a mask at an entrance, climbing onto a bale of laundry. I didn't flash a bulb without some warning to the surgeon, but I needn't have bothered, as he never flinched, even for near gunfire. So efficient was the organization, so unflurried and well-planned, that I never once felt in the way, or that it was frivolous to be there at all. Without looking up from his snipping a surgeon asked me to write down for him what exposure he should use if he wanted to take a detailed picture of an operation in that contrast of white towels, concentrated light, and deep shadows. I crossed my fingers and hoped I was right, for my own photos as well as his.

For an hour or so I watched lives and limbs being saved, by skill, devotion, and endurance. Grave faces and tired feet passed up and down the tent aisles. We discussed whether doubling the staff of doctors and nurses would relieve them of overwork—it seemed not, as everyone by his own volition would still do double his duty.

We talked about sulfa and penicillin—there is plenty for all, and they use it generously. Because the wounded are evacuated to England and America so soon, these doctors are unable to check on enough individual cases as to whether it was these drugs which did the saving, or whether it was the fact that immediate definitive surgical or other treatment was given—often less than an hour after the injury. Infection has scarcely the time to develop while the wounded are still in France . . . unlike the last war when a casualty might not even reach first aid for days after his wound. The statistics are not meaningless, dry numbers; they are a vivid tribute to science, organization and personnel: only one and one-tenth per cent. of casualties who reach any medical attention at all, die up to the time they leave France, and the percentage only reaches one and eight-tenths per cent. when it includes all the long-term patients evacuated to the big "general" hospitals in England.

We drove slowly home, caught up in a convoy of carriers returning empty from the front—meeting other convoys of men and equipment thundering by in long, even streams, lit only by the tiniest of "cat's-eye" guide lamps. We stopped for a few moments' chat and a glass of Calvados as we left an officer at the Evacuation hospital, on our way.

It was night, and my day was done. Not so for all these men and women, and the pitiful victims of the pink gunfire on the horizon.

Blackout means blackout—not even a cigarette outdoors—and only a quick look with a hand-covered flashlight inside. After fumbling in the grass for dropped articles, tripping over guy wires on the way to the latrines and lister-bag, I entangled myself with distaste in the blankets of the German nurses. There were occasional sharp bursts of ack-ack during the night, and I put on my helmet sideways, the way I'd been shown. I was aching with cold but felt incompetent to locate more blankets in the darkness, and hopeless about ever finding my way back into the mess I'd made of what I had. I felt infinitely more secure with a millimeter of canvas as a bulwark against the enemy than I felt in London with bricks against the P-Planes. It was probably the knowledge that I was surrounded by hundreds of helpless people who couldn't even put on a helmet if they had one.

In the morning the atmosphere of the 45th had completely changed. It was sunny, a landscape-painter's morning. There was a larger group of nurses around the ablution tanks than yesterday, and they were taking longer to brush their teeth, chatting and teasing. There were even some off duty, digging into the bottom of the other duffle-bag for the first time, scraping mould off the good pair of shoes, and bewailing the condition of their dress uniforms, which they'd probably never have occasion to wear anyway.

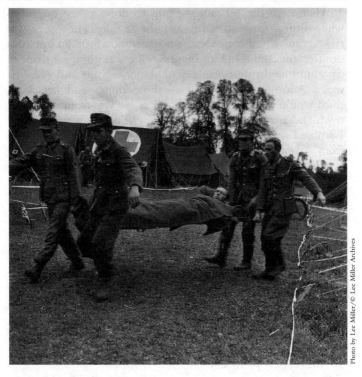

Photo by Lee Miller/© Lee Miller Archives

Under close guard German prisoners are often used as litter bearers in Normandy.

What were the off-duties going to do? I asked questions while sitting, four in a row, in the latrine. The paper was staked on crossed bars, there was grass underfoot, an odour of disinfectant, and a lack of shyness. One was going to sleep all day until night-duty, in a pink satin nightie and woollen socks. Another would wash all those things and herself. A third would go find a boy in Ward 2. He was from her home town and knew someone she knew. The others were on duty. I ambled out, vaguely, and was shown that hot water came from galvanized iron cans into which the bowels of a "bazooka heater" had been stuck, that I should have brought my own basin; that there is a juggling trick to holding the press button of a lister-bag, a toothbrush, and the paste all at once, that there are three positions for squatting, two of which are semi-perched on a helmet; the other—you're using the helmet to wash in, so lean on your left heel.

I poked my head through open tent-flaps at random. Ingenious improvements had been made, sailor-fashion, such as a tall central stake carrying coats, in one. Another had bed-tables from bomb-crates—bits of string and wire hooked up musette-bags, and improvised counterweights held tent-flaps, Rube Goldberg style. Everything was in monochrome of khaki except for pink brassières strung with the brown laundry on every rope in sight.

German prisoners under guard were policing the main grounds. They make fires, carry water, and graduate to being litter-bearers, sometimes without guard. They are not the arrogant, sullen lot who dig a stint of four graves up the hill and get shipped on to prisoner-of-war camps . . . but timid youths who become very much attached to the medical corps, and weep when their twenty days' duty is done. The German wounded are treated exactly like ours, and in one hospital I visited, where there were enough to fill two tents, they were segregated. Otherwise, they mix in the wards as their turn comes around. In the operating tents, a case is scheduled on its surgical urgency, not on the nationality of the patient; and in a hospital where two German surgeons are prisoners, they operate alongside American doctors, taking Reichswehr and U.S. Army casualties as they come. I photographed an American sergeant who lay down laughing to give his blood for a transfusion. He drank a shot of bourbon, carried the bottle to the next tent, and strung it above a German who was howling for nothing on the operating table . . . the only injured man I heard cry aloud in my entire trip.

I stiffened every time I saw a German—and therefore resented my heart softening involuntarily toward German wounded. A group of krauts we interviewed were astonished that we lived and worked in buzz-bombed London, and that the secret weapon was not ending the war for them.

The ground mist was drying off, and a few nurses rolled up the sides of their wall-tents to lie in the sun, wearing their long-handle G.I. underwear. Some appeared in strictly non-G.I. stripes and flowers. A group came single-file between the tent-stakes loosening their surgical whites. They washed away the sweat from all-night duty, and fell on their cots, dead beat. One said, "Nice, isn't it . . . now I can yawn." They were remarkably pretty girls, all of them, now that the strain lines in their faces were slightly erased—lean, fit, and open-hearted.

We went down near the beachhead to be received and have lunch with Major General Albert W. Kenner and Col. John Andrews Rogers, the Chief Surgeon of the 1st Army. They were going to visit medical installations of all types, right up to the combat lines, and we could follow along. It was follow-the-leader, the General wearing a two-star helmet in an open jeep, military, and we in a command car. The roads had been pounded dry during the night and we lurched and bounced through a tunnel of burning yellow dust, as thick as an African sandstorm. The centre of Isigny was being scraped away by machinery I'd thought only existed on the covers of Popular Mechanics. Carentan was the same. The rubble and the skeletons of houses were not much different from Dover, Plymouth, and Coventry. Curiously, the destruction looked less recent, and houses in adjoining streets often had unbroken windows, lace curtains, and geraniums. I can't believe that any French housewife has done a stroke of work since the invasion, as all along the roads they were leaning on rose-garlanded gates and doors, permanently waving to the convoys. Kids, dressed in pinafores and Yank soldier caps, helped the M.P.'s direct traffic. An old woman in black, picking her way across devastation, waved a V-salute.

We passed litter-bearing jeeps, the wounded in racks across the hood, ammunition trucks with cynical names such as "Sudden Death," "Amen," or "You've Had It." There were lots of things, touching, poignant, or queer, I wanted to photograph, but we couldn't stop, partly traffic rules, but mostly because the shoulder of the road was soft, the mines on the edge uncleared, or we'd lose the General. Occasionally we'd pull up for a moment in line, but the swirling dust made zero visibility.

One hospital was pitched alongside the battlefield back of Utah beach . . . a sere, flat area, pitted with trenches, torn with exploding metal, and scraped with hands.

Little roly-poly balloons, with cross-lacing on their stomachs like old-fashioned corsets, sat around all shiny and clean, and the flooded areas were drying up, disclosing vulture-picked limbs of gliders which had crashed. We crossed a trellis-work pontoon bridge which rises and falls with the tide, and fields with whole, transplanted trees sharpened into spikes against our landings . . . another bridge where we spaced out in case of shell fire. There were fewer and fewer inhabited houses as we went on and on, until we reached a deserted but intact row of grey cottages. A hospital flag hung from a telegraph pole and an ambulance was parked back-end to a door . . . a medical soldier was reading that morning's *Stars & Stripes* . . . there were roses, hollyhocks, bumblebees. Until there was a sudden savage noise of firing, I couldn't realize that I was less than one and one-half miles from the fighting.

The first room, piled high with medical supplies, opened into a wall-papered parlour. Bandages, tacked to the ceiling, curled down like flypaper rolls. A group of men knelt around a white-turbanned figure on a litter. No one noticed there were strangers.

This is a Collecting Station. It is the vital heart-point in the branching system of life-saving. Here the front line diagnosis is checked, wounds are re-dressed, splints fitted, and plasma given to strengthen shock cases for further travel.

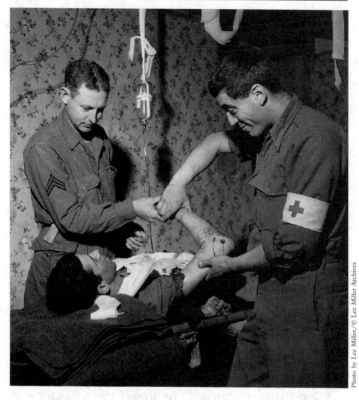

Photo by Lee Miller/© Lee Miller Archives

The collecting station: Plasma has already been attached to the man's left arm.

Those needing the most urgent surgical care are forwarded immediately to the nearest field hospital. Others who can travel a further few miles are sent to an evacuation hospital.

The head-bandaged casualty on the floor was placed back in the nearly-full ambulance, which sped left to an Evac. Another ambulance arrived from the right, and litters were swiftly transferred to the parlour floor. The wounded were not "knights in shining armor," but dirty, dishevelled, stricken figures . . . uncomprehending. They arrived from the front line Battalion Aid Station with lightly laid-on field dressings, tourniquets, blood-soaked slings . . . some exhausted and lifeless.

A badly mangled sergeant was turned over on his chest; his clothes were cut away, he was covered, ticketed, and rushed to a Field Hospital by himself. The doctor with the Raphael-like face turned to a man on a litter which had been placed on up-ended trunks. Plasma had already been attached to the man's outstretched left arm . . . his face was shrunken and pallid under the dirt . . . by the time his pierced left elbow was in its sling, his opaque eyes were clearing, and he was aware enough to grimace as his leg splint was bandaged in place. He was left to rest awhile, covered in blankets, while N.C.O.'s and doctors splinted, sulfa'd and patched the wounded men on the floor, some of whom were well enough to help by holding bandage-ends, or an arm, in midair.

A few "walking wounded" sat around the wall. One man had been brought in with "combat exhaustion"—dazed, slightly amnesiac. He was better already, and thought he'd go back. I don't imagine he was allowed to, but I forgot to ask.

A medic escorted me out back of the cottage, through a well-tended potato and stringbean patch, and up a grassy slope. I walked gingerly in his footsteps as I was frightened of trip-wires and mines, and ducked under branches weighed down with little green apples. Beneath a central tree in the orchard was a pit—in and around it were scattered all kinds of kit and equipment, torn, shabby, abandoned. Plastic canteens, tunics, clips of ammunition, a diary, little coloured bottles, a box with a cake of Gibbs soap, were some of the things I noticed.

We came back through the kitchen of the house. It was as

complete with its *batterie* of copper sauce-pans as when the French had abandoned it to the Germans, later driven out. A corps man was cooking a stew of C-rations on the back, and boiling water for the sterilizer on the front burner. Outside, half tracks whizzed past an odd contraption, mounted on rubber tires. It was a generator, concocted from salvaged German motorcycle-parts, and rigged to head lamps for the dressing-station, where, by now, more wounded had arrived. Four litters were off in twelve minutes, and two men were receiving plasma. I tried three times to take a semi-open flash picture, but each time my hand jerked with near artillery fire . . . our own. The Major General kneeled on the floor to reassure one of the men, and Colonel Rogers said, "There is nothing in this war like the last, except that the wounded are just as dirty. These people won't *look* sick for more than two days. It's not the same."

He described how it would have taken as much as three days to have reached this point from the rear . . . stumbling through muddy trenches, ducking into dugouts, and avoiding crossroads under regular artillery fire. The wounded would often have crawled into shell-holes to be rescued only at night, and arrive here hours or days too late, exhausted and with a very low chance of survival.

The crucial point in the medical services is the prompt diagnosis and redistribution rearwards in stations such as this. The quantity of transport allotted to the Medical Service alone saves scores of lives daily. Then there are the new drugs, new techniques, the super-skill of America's best surgeons and nurses, and finally the quick evacuation by air to England and America.

Next day, before I left, I saw a long queue of planes moving down the airstrip. Ambulances came up in groups from the holding station down the road, and litters were lifted directly into the wide-open double doors of the planes. I recognized a few men I had seen at the Evac hospital. Interlocking looped straps held the stretcher poles in three rigid decks. The nurse and her teammate, a surgical technician sergeant, checked in each patient. The pilot had already started his engines, and the nurse handed out her patients' manifests, as the plane lumbered down the taxi-strip and took off for England.

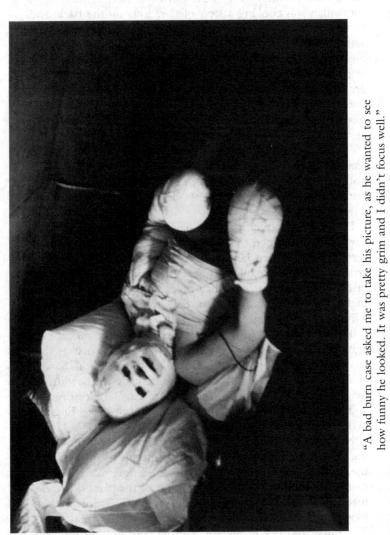

"A bad burn case asked me to take his picture, as he wanted to see how funny he looked. It was pretty grim and I didn't focus well."

It had taken twelve minutes to load twenty-four litters. Over six hundred had been evacuated that day.

Later, I took off from the same airstrip into bad weather. I looked down at the waiting air-ambulances and hoped for them that it wouldn't be a rough ride. The rain closed in behind us, on France.

*Vogue*, September 15, 1944

# Battle and Breakout in Normandy

by Ernie Pyle

### "They Weren't Heroic Figures"

In Normandy — (by wireless) — Lieut. Orion Shockley came over with a map and explained to us just what his company was going to do.

There was a German strong point of pillboxes and machine-gun nests about half a mile down the street ahead of us.

Our troops had made wedges into the city on both sides of us, but nobody had yet been up this street where we were going. The street, they thought, was almost certainly under rifle fire.

"This is how we'll do it," the lieutenant said. "A rifle platoon goes first. Right behind them will go part of a heavy-weapons platoon, with machine guns to cover the first platoon.

"Then comes another rifle platoon. Then a small section with mortars, in case they run into something pretty heavy. Then another rifle platoon. And bringing up the rear, the rest of the heavy-weapons outfit to protect us from behind.

"We don't know what we'll run into, and I don't want to stick you right out in front, so why don't you come along with me? We'll go in the middle of the company."

I said, "Okay." By this time I wasn't scared. You seldom are once you're into something. Anticipation is the worst. Fortunately this little foray came up so suddenly there wasn't time for much anticipation.

*   *   *

The rain kept on coming down, and you could sense that it had set in for the afternoon. None of us had raincoats, and by evening there wasn't a dry thread on any of us. I could go-back to a tent for the night, but the soldiers would have to sleep the way they were.

We were just ready to start when all of a sudden bullets came whipping savagely right above our heads.

"It's those damn 20-millimeters again," the lieutenant said. "Better hold it up a minute."

The soldiers all crouched lower behind the wall. The vicious little shells whanged into a grassy hillside just beyond us. A French suburban farmer was hitching up his horses in a barnyard on the hillside. He ran into the house. Shells struck all around it.

Two dead Germans and a dead American still lay in his driveway. We could see them when we moved up a few feet.

The shells stopped, and finally the order to start was given. As we left the protection of the high wall we had to cross a little culvert right out in the open and then make a turn in the road.

The men went forward one at a time. They crouched and ran, apelike, across this dangerous space. Then, beyond the culvert, they filtered to either side of the road, stopping and squatting down every now and then to wait a few moments.

The lieutenant kept yelling at them as they started:

"Spread it out now. Do you want to draw fire on yourselves? Don't bunch up like that. Keep five yards apart. Spread it out, dammit."

There is an almost irresistible pull to get close to somebody when you are in danger. In spite of themselves, the men would run up close to the fellow ahead for company.

The other lieutenant now called out:

"Now you on the right watch the left side of the street for snipers, and you on the left watch the right side. Cover each other that way."

And a first sergeant said to a passing soldier:

"Get that grenade out of its case. It won't do you no good in the case. Throw the case away. That's right."

\*     \*     \*

Some of the men carried grenades already fixed in the ends of their rifles. All of them had hand grenades. Some had big Browning automatic rifles. One carried a bazooka. Interspersed in the thin line of men every now and then was a medic, with his bags of bandages and a Red Cross arm band on the left arm. The men didn't talk any. They just went.

They weren't heroic figures as they moved forward one at a time, a few seconds apart. You think of attackers as being savage and bold. These men were hesitant and cautious. They were really the hunters, but they looked like the hunted. There was a confused excitement and a grim anxiety in their faces.

They seemed terribly pathetic to me. They weren't warriors. They were American boys who by mere chance of fate had wound up with guns in their hands sneaking up a death-laden street in a strange and shattered city in a faraway country in a driving rain. They were afraid, but it was beyond their power to quit. They had no choice.

They were good boys. I talked with them all afternoon as we sneaked slowly forward along the mysterious and rubbled street, and I know they were good boys.

And even though they aren't warriors born to the kill, they win their battles. That's the point.

Scripps-Howard wire copy, July 13, 1944

## "A Small Assembly Plant"

SOMEWHERE IN NORMANDY—(by wireless)—At the edge of a pasture, sitting cross-legged on the grass or on low boxes as though they were at a picnic, are 13 men in greasy soldiers' coveralls.

Near them on one side is a shop truck with a canvas canopy stretched out from it, making a sort of patio alongside the truck. And under this canopy and all over the ground are rifles—rusty and muddy and broken rifles.

This is the small arms section of our medium ordnance company. To this company comes daily in trucks the picked up, rusting rifles of men killed or wounded, and rifles broken in ordinary service. There are dozens of such companies.

This company turns back around a hundred rifles a day to its division, all shiny and oily and ready to shoot again.

They work on the simple salvage system of taking good parts off one gun and placing them on another. To do this they work like a small assembly plant.

The first few hours of the morning are given to taking broken rifles apart. They don't try to keep the parts of each gun together. All parts are alike and transferable, hence they throw each type into a big steel pan full of similar parts. At the end of the job they have a dozen or so pans, each filled with the same kind of part.

Then the whole gang shifts over and scrubs the parts. They scrub in gasoline, using sandpaper for guns in bad condition after lying out in the rain and mud.

When everything is clean they take the good parts and start putting them back together and making guns out of them again.

When all the pans are empty they have a stack of rifles—good rifles, all ready to be taken back to the front.

Of the parts left over some are thrown away, quite beyond repair. But others are repairable and go into the section's shop truck for working on with lathes and welding torches. Thus the division gets 100 reclaimed rifles a day, in addition to the brand new ones issued to it.

And believe me, during the first few days of our invasion men at the front needed these rifles with desperation. Repairmen tell you how our paratroopers and infantrymen would straggle back, dirty and hazy-eyed with fatigue, and plead like a child for a new rifle immediately so they could get back to the front and "get at them sonsabitches."

One paratrooper brought in a German horse he had captured and offered to trade it for a new rifle, he needed it so badly. During those days the men in our little repair shop worked all hours trying to fill the need.

I sat around on the grass and talked to these rifle repairmen most of one forenoon. They weren't working so frenziedly then for the urgency was not so dire, but they kept steadily at it as we talked.

The head of the section is Sergt. Edward Watts of Welch, Okla., who used to work in the oil fields. Just since the invasion he's invented a gadget that cleans rust out of a rifle barrel in a few seconds whereas it used to take a man about 20 minutes.

Sergeant Watts did it merely by rigging up a swivel shaft on the end of an electric drill and attaching a cylindrical wire brush to the end. So now you just stick the brush in the gun barrel and press the button on the drill. It whirls and in a few seconds all rust is ground out. The idea has been turned over to other ordnance companies.

The soldiers do a lot of kidding as they sit around taking rusted guns apart. Like soldiers everywhere they razz each other constantly about their home states. A couple were from Arkansas, and of course they took a lot of hillbilly razzing about not wearing shoes till they got in the Army and so on.

One of them was Corp. Herschel Grimsley of Springdale, Ark. He jokingly asked if I'd put his name in the paper. So I took a chance and joked back, "Sure," I said, "except I didn't know anybody in Arkansas could read?"

Everybody laughed loudly at this scintillating wit, most of all Corporal Grimsley who can stand anything.

Later Grimsley was telling me how paratroopers used to come in and just beg for another rifle. And he expressed the sincere feeling of the men throughout ordnance, the balance weighing of their own fairly safe job, when he said:

"Them old boys at the front have sure got my sympathy. Least we can do is work our fingers off to give them the stuff."

*     *     *

The original stack of muddy, rusted rifles is a touching pile. As gun after gun comes off the stack you look to see what is the matter with it—

Rifle butt split by fragments; barrel dented by bullet; trigger knocked off; whole barrel splattered with shrapnel marks; gun gray from the slime of weeks in swamp mud; faint dark splotches of blood still showing.

You wonder what became of each owner; you pretty well know.

Infantrymen, like soldiers everywhere, like to put names on their equipment. Just as a driver paints a name on his truck, so does a doughboy carve his name or initials on his rifle butt.

You get crude whittlings of initials in the hard walnut stocks and unbelievably craftsmanlike carvings of soldiers' names, and many and many names of girls.

The boys said the most heart-breaking rifle they'd found was one of a soldier who had carved a hole about silver dollar size and put his wife's or girl's picture in it, and sealed it over with a crystal of flexiglass.

They don't, of course, know who he was or what had happened to him. They only know the rifle was repaired and somebody else is carrying it now, picture and all.

Scripps-Howard wire copy, July 27, 1944

### *"The Heavy Ordnance Company"*

SOMEWHERE IN NORMANDY—(by wireless)—I know of nothing in civilian life at home by which you can even remotely compare the contribution to his country made by the infantry soldier with his life of bestiality, suffering and death.

But I've just been with an outfit whose war work is similar enough to yours that I believe you can see the difference between life overseas and in America.

This is the heavy ordnance company which repairs shot-up tanks, wrecked artillery, and heavy trucks.

These men are not in much danger. They work at shop benches with tools. Compared with the infantry, their life is velvet and they know it and appreciate it. But compared with them your life is velvet. That's what I'd like for you to appreciate.

These men are mostly skilled craftsmen. Many of them are above military age. Back home they made big money. Their jobs here are fundamentally the same as those of you at home who work in war plants. It's only the environment that is different.

These men don't work seven, eight, or nine hours a day. They work from 7 in the morning until darkness comes at night. They work from 12 to 16 hours a day.

You have beds and bathrooms. These men sleep on the ground, and dig a trench for their toilets.

You have meals at the table. These men eat from messkits, sitting on the grass. You have pajamas, and places to go on Sunday. These men sleep in their underwear, and they don't even know when Sunday comes. They have not sat in a chair for weeks. They live always outdoors, rain and shine.

In the War World their life is not bad. By peacetime standards it is outrageous. But they don't complain—because
they are close enough to the front to see and appreciate the
desperate need of the men they are trying to help. They work
with an eagerness and an intensity that is thrilling to see.

*       *       *

This company works under a half-acre grove of trees and
along the hedgerows of a couple of adjoining pastures. Their
shops are in the trucks or out in the open under camouflage
nets.

Most of their work seems unspectacular to describe. It just
consists of welding steel plates in the sides of tanks, of changing the front end of a truck blown up by a mine, or repairing
the barrel of a big gun hit by a bazooka, of re-winding the
coils of a radio, of welding new teeth in a gear.

It's the sincere way they go at it, and their appreciation of
its need that impressed me.

*       *       *

Corp. Richard Kelso is in this company. His home is at 1238
Roscoe st., Chicago.

He is an Irishman from the Old Sod. He apprenticed in
Belfast as a machinist nearly 30 years ago. He went to America
when he was 25 and now he is 45.

He still has folks in Ireland, but he didn't have a chance to
get over there when he was stationed in England. He is thin
and a little stooped, and the others call him Pop. He is quiet
and intent and very courteous. He never did get married.

Kelso operates the milling machine in a shop truck. His
truck is covered deep with extra strips of steel, for these boys
pick up and hoard steel as some people might hoard money.

When I stopped to chat, Kelso had his machine grinding
away on the rough tooth of the gearwheel of a tank.

The part that did the cutting was one he had improvised
himself. In this business of war so much is unforeseen, so
much is missing at the right moment that were it not for
improvisation, wars would be lost.

Take these gearwheels, for instance. Suppose a tank strips
three teeth off some gear. The entire tank is helpless and out
of action. They have no replacement wheels in stock. They
have to repair the broken one.

So they take it to their outdoor foundry, make a form, heat up some steel till it is molten, pour it in the form and mould a rough geartooth which is then welded onto the stub of the broken-off tooth.

Now this rough tooth has to be ground down to the fine dimensions of the other teeth and that is an exact job. At first they didn't have the tools to do it with.

But that didn't stop them. They hacked those teeth down with cold chisels and hand files. They put back into action 20 tanks by this primitive method. Then Kelso and Warrant Officer Henry Moser, of Johnstown, Pa., created a part for their milling machine that would do the job faster and better.

That one little improvisation may have saved 50 Americans' lives, may have cost the Germans a hundred men, may even have turned the tide of a battle.

And it's being done by a man 45 years old wearing corporal stripes who doesn't have to be over here at all, and who could be making big money back home.

He too sleeps on the ground and works 16 hours a day, and is happy to do it—for boys who are dying are not 3000 miles away and abstract; they are 10 miles away and very, very real.

He sees them when they come back, pleading like children for another tank, another gun. He knows how terribly they need the things that are within his power to give.

Scripps-Howard wire copy, August 1, 1944


### "The Great Attack"

IN NORMANDY—(by wireless)—The great attack, when we broke out of the Normandy beachhead, began in the bright light of midday, not at the zero hour of a bleak and mysterious dawn as attacks are supposed to start in books.

The attack had been delayed from day to day because of poor flying weather, and on the final day we hadn't known for sure till after breakfast whether it was on or off again.

When the word came that it was on, the various battalion

staffs of our regiment were called in from their command posts for a final review of the battle plan.

Each one was given a mimeographed sketch of the frontline area, showing exactly where and when each type bomber was to hammer the German lines ahead of them. Another mimeographed page was filled with specific orders for the grand attack to follow.

Officers stood or squatted in a circle in a little apple orchard behind a ramshackle stone farmhouse of a poor French family who had left before us. The stone wall in the front yard had been knocked down by shelling, and through the orchards there were shell craters and tree limbs knocked off and trunks sliced by bullets. Some enlisted men sleeping the night before in the attic of the house got the shock of their lives when the thin floor collapsed and they fell down into the cowshed below.

Chickens and tame rabbits still scampered around the farmyard. Dead cows lay all around in the fields.

\*     \*     \*

The regimental colonel stood in the center of the officers and went over the orders in detail. Battalion commanders took down notes in little books.

The colonel said, "Ernie Pyle is with the regiment for this attack and will be with one of the battalions, so you'll be seeing him." The officers looked at me and smiled and I felt embarrassed.

Then Maj. Gen. Raymond O. Barton, Fourth Division Commander, arrived. The colonel called, "Attention!" and everybody stood rigid until the General gave them, "Carry on."

An enlisted man ran to the mess truck and got a folding canvas stool for the General to sit on. He sat listening intently while the colonel wound up his instructions.

Then the General stepped into the center of the circle. He stood at a slouch on one foot with the other leg far out like a brace. He looked all around him as he talked. He didn't talk long. He said something like this—

"This is one of the finest regiments in the American Army. It was the last regiment out of France in the last war. It was the first regiment into France in this war. It has spearheaded every one of the division's attacks in Normandy. It will spearhead this one. For many years this was my regiment and I feel very close to you, and very proud."

The General's lined face was a study in emotion. Sincerity and deep sentiment were in every contour and they shone from his eyes. General Barton is a man of deep affections. The tragedy of war, both personal and impersonal, hurts him. At the end his voice almost broke, and I for one had a lump in my throat. He ended:

"That's all. God bless you and good luck."

Then we broke up and I went with one of the battalion commanders. Word was passed down by field phone, radio and liaison men to the very smallest unit of troops that the attack was on.

There was still an hour before the bombers, and three hours before the infantry were to move. There was nothing for the infantry to do but dig a little deeper and wait. A cessation of motion seemed to come over the countryside and all its brown-clad inhabitants—a sense of last minute sitting in silence before the holocaust.

The first planes of the mass onslaught came over a little before 10 a.m. They were the fighters and dive bombers. The main road running crosswise in front of us was their bomb line. They were to bomb only on the far side of that road.

Our kickoff infantry had been pulled back a few hundred yards this side of the road. Everyone in the area had been given the strictest orders to be in foxholes, for high-level bombers can, and do quite excusably, make mistakes.

We were still in country so level and with hedgerows so tall there simply was no high spot—either hill or building—from where you could get a grandstand view of the bombing as we used to in Sicily and Italy. So one place was as good as another unless you went right up and sat on the bomb line.

Having been caught too close to these things before, I compromised and picked a farmyard about 800 yards back of the kickoff line.

And before the next two hours had passed I would have given every penny, every desire, every hope I've ever had to have been just another 800 yards further back.

Scripps-Howard wire copy, August 7, 1944

## "A Ghastly Relentlessness"

IN NORMANDY—(by wireless)—Our frontlines were marked by long strips of colored cloth laid on the ground, and with colored smoke to guide our airmen during the mass bombing that preceded our break-out from the German ring that held us to the Normandy beachhead.

Dive bombers hit it just right. We stood in the barnyard of a French farm and watched them barrel nearly straight down out of the sky. They were bombing about half a mile ahead of where we stood.

They came in groups, diving from every direction, perfectly timed, one right after another. Everywhere you looked separate groups of planes were on the way down, or on the way back up, or slanting over for a dive, or circling, circling, circling over our heads, waiting for their turn.

The air was full of sharp and distinct sounds of cracking bombs and the heavy rips of the planes' machine guns and the splitting screams of diving wings. It was all fast and furious, but yet distinct, as in a musical show in which you could distinguish throaty tunes and words.

\*       \*       \*

And then a new sound gradually droned into our ears, a sound deep and all encompassing with no notes in it—just a gigantic faraway surge of doom-like sound. It was the heavies. They came from directly behind us. At first they were the merest dots in the sky. You could see clots of them against the far heavens, too tiny to count individually. They came on with a terrible slowness.

They came in flights of 12, three flights to a group and in groups stretched out across the sky. They came in "families" of about 70 planes each.

Maybe these gigantic waves were two miles apart, maybe they were 10 miles, I don't know. But I do know they came in a constant procession and I thought it would never end. What the Germans must have thought is beyond comprehension.

Their march across the sky was slow and studied. I've never known a storm, or a machine, or any resolve of man that had about it the aura of such a ghastly relentlessness. You had the feeling that even had God appeared beseechingly before them in the sky with palms outward to persuade them back they would not have had within them the power to turn from their irresistible course.

I stood with a little group of men, ranging from colonels to privates, back of the stone farmhouse. Slit trenches were all around the edges of the farmyard and a dugout with a tin roof was nearby. But we were so fascinated by the spectacle overhead that it never occurred to us that we might need the foxholes.

The first huge flight passed directly over our farmyard and others followed. We spread our feet and leaned far back trying to look straight up, until our steel helmets fell off. We'd cup our fingers around our eyes like field glasses for a clearer view.

And then the bombs came. They began ahead of us as the crackle of popcorn and almost instantly swelled into a monstrous fury of noise that seemed surely to destroy all the world ahead of us.

From then on for an hour and a half that had in it the agonies of centuries, the bombs came down. A wall of smoke and dust erected by them grew high in the sky. It filtered along the ground back through our own orchards. It sifted around us and into our noses. The bright day grew slowly dark from it.

By now everything was an indescribable cauldron of sounds. Individual noises did not exist. The thundering of the motors in the sky and the roar of bombs ahead filled all the space for noise on earth. Our own heavy artillery was crashing all around us, yet we could hardly hear it.

\*        \*        \*

The Germans began to shoot heavy, high ack-ack. Great black puffs of it by the score speckled the sky until it was hard to distinguish smoke puffs from planes.

And then someone shouted that one of the planes was smoking. Yes, we could all see it. A long faint line of black smoke stretched straight for a mile behind one of them.

And as we watched there was a gigantic sweep of flame over the plane. From nose to tail it disappeared in flame, and it slanted slowly down and banked around the sky in great wide curves, this way and that way, as rhythmically and gracefully as in a slow motion waltz.

Then suddenly it seemed to change its mind and it swept upward, steeper and steeper and ever slower until finally it seemed poised motionless on its own black pillar of smoke. And then just as slowly it turned over and dived for the earth—a golden spearhead on the straight black shaft of its own creation—and it disappeared behind the treetops.

But before it was done there were more cries of, "There's another one smoking and there's a third one now."

Chutes came out of some of the planes. Out of some came no chutes at all. One of white silk caught on the tail of a plane. Men with binoculars could see him fighting to get loose until flames swept over him, and then a tiny black dot fell through space, all alone.

And all that time the great flat ceiling of the sky was roofed by all the others that didn't go down, plowing their way forward as if there were no turmoil in the world.

Nothing deviated them by the slightest. They stalked on, slowly and with a dreadful pall of sound, as though they were seeing only something at a great distance and nothing existed in between. God, how you admired those men up there and sickened for the ones who fell.

Scripps-Howard wire copy, August 8, 1944

### "The Universe Became Filled with a Gigantic Rattling"

IN NORMANDY—(by wireless)—It is possible to become so enthralled by some of the spectacles of war that you are momentarily captivated away from your own danger.

That's what happened to our little group of soldiers as we stood in a French farmyard, watching the mighty bombing of the German lines just before our break-through.

But that benign state didn't last long. As we watched, there crept into our consciousness a realization that windrows of exploding bombs were easing back toward us, flight by flight, instead of gradually forward, as the plan called for.

Then we were horrified by the suspicion that those machines, high in the sky and completely detached from us, were aiming their bombs at the smokeline on the ground—and a gentle breeze was drifting the smokeline back over us!

An indescribable kind of panic comes over you at such times. We stood tensed in muscle and frozen in intellect, watching each flight approach and pass over us, feeling trapped and completely helpless.

And then all of an instant the universe became filled with a gigantic rattling as of huge, dry seeds in a mammoth dry gourd. I doubt that any of us had ever heard that sound before, but instinct told us what it was. It was bombs by the hundred, hurtling down through the air above us.

Many times I've heard bombs whistle or swish or rustle, but never before had I heard bombs rattle. I still don't know the explanation of it. But it is an awful sound.

We dived. Some got in a dugout. Others made foxholes and ditches and some got behind a garden wall—although which side would be "behind" was anybody's guess.

\*     \*     \*

I was too late for the dugout. The nearest place was a wagon-shed which formed one end of the stone house. The rattle was right down upon us. I remember hitting the ground flat, all spread out like the cartoons of people flattened by steam rollers, and then squirming like an eel to get under one of the heavy wagons in the shed.

An officer whom I didn't know was wriggling beside me. We stopped at the same time, simultaneously feeling it was hopeless to move farther. The bombs were already crashing around us.

We lay with our heads slightly up—like two snakes—staring at each other. I know it was in both our minds and in our eyes, asking each other what to do. Neither of us knew. We said nothing. We just lay sprawled, gaping at each other in a futile appeal, our faces about a foot apart, until it was over.

There is no description of the sound and fury of those bombs except to say it was chaos, and a waiting for darkness. The feeling of the blast was sensational. The air struck you in hundreds of continuing flutters. Your ears drummed and rang. You could feel quick little waves of concussions on your chest and in your eyes.

At last the sound died down and we looked at each other in disbelief. Gradually we left the foxholes and sprawling places, and came out to see what the sky had in store for us. As far as we could see other waves were approaching from behind.

When a wave would pass a little to the side of us we were garrulously grateful, for most of them flew directly overhead. Time and again the rattle came down over us. Bombs struck in the orchard to our left. They struck in orchards ahead of us. They struck as far as half a mile behind us. Everything about us was shaken, but our group came through unhurt.

*        *        *

I can't record what any of us actually felt or thought during those horrible climaxes. I believe a person's feelings at such times are kaleidoscopic and uncatalogable. You just wait, that's all. You do remember an inhuman tenseness of muscle and nerves.

An hour or so later I began to get sore all over, and by mid-afternoon my back and shoulders ached as though I'd been beaten with a club. It was simply the result of muscles tensing themselves too tight for too long against anticipated shock. And I remember worrying about War Correspondent Ken Crawford, a friend from back in the old Washington days, who I knew was several hundred yards ahead of me.

As far as I knew, he and I were the only two correspondents with the Fourth Division. I didn't know who might be with the divisions on either side—which also were being hit, as we could see.

Three days later, back at camp, I learned that AP Photographer Bede Irvin had been killed in the bombing and that Ken was safe.

We came out of our ignominious sprawling and stood up again to watch. We could sense that by now the error had been caught and checked. The bombs again were falling where they were intended, a mile or so ahead.

Even at a mile away a thousand bombs hitting within a few seconds can shake the earth and shatter the air where you are standing. There was still a dread in our hearts, but it gradually eased as the tumult and destruction moved slowly forward.

Scripps-Howard wire copy, August 9, 1944

*"Anybody Makes Mistakes"*

IN NORMANDY—(by wireless)—With our own personal danger past, our historic air bombardment of the German lines holding us in the Normandy beachhead again became a captivating spectacle to watch.

By now it was definite that the great waves of four-motored planes were dropping their deadly loads exactly in the right place.

And by now two Mustang fighters, flying like a pair of doves, patrolled back and forth, back and forth, just in front of each oncoming wave of bombers, as if to shout to them by their mere presence that here was not the place to drop—wait a few seconds, wait a few more seconds.

And then we could see a flare come out of the belly of one plane in each flight, just after they had passed over our heads.

The flare shot forward, leaving smoke behind it in a vivid line, and then began a graceful, downward curve that was one of the most beautiful things I've ever seen.

It was like an invisible crayon drawing a rapid line across the canvas of the sky, saying in a gesture for all to see: "Here! Here is where to drop. Follow me."

And each succeeding flight of oncoming bombers obeyed, and in turn dropped its own hurtling marker across the illimitable heaven to guide those behind.

Long before now the German ack-ack guns had gone out of existence. We had counted three of our big planes down in spectacular flames, and I believe that was all. The German ack-ack gunners either took to their holes or were annihilated.

How many waves of heavy bombers we put over I have no idea. I had counted well beyond 400 planes when my personal distraction obliterated any capacity or desire to count.

I only know that 400 was just the beginning. There were supposed to be 1800 planes that day, and I believe it was announced later that there were more than 3000.

It seemed incredible to me that any German could come out of that bombardment with his sanity. When it was over even I was grateful in a chastened way I had never experienced before, for just being alive.

*          *          *

I thought an attack by our troops was impossible now, for it is an unnerving thing to be bombed by your own planes.

During the bad part a colonel I had known a long time was walking up and down behind the farmhouse, snapping his fingers and saying over and over to himself, "goddamit, goddamit!"

As he passed me once he stopped and stared and said, "goddamit!"

And I said, "There can't be any attack now, can there?" And he said "No," and began walking again, snapping his fingers and tossing his arm as though he was throwing rocks at the ground.

The leading company of our battalion was to spearhead the attack 40 minutes after our heavy bombing ceased. The company had been hit directly by our bombs. Their casualties, including casualties in shock, were heavy. Men went to pieces and had to be sent back. The company was shattered and shaken.

And yet Company B attacked—and on time, to the minute! They attacked, and within an hour they sent word back that they had advanced 800 yards through German territory and were still going. Around our farmyard men with stars on their shoulders almost wept when the word came over the portable radio. The American soldier can be majestic when he needs to be.

*     *     *

There is one more thing I want to say before we follow the ground troops on deeper into France in the great push you've been reading about now for days.

I'm sure that back in England that night other men—bomber crews—almost wept, and maybe they did really, in the awful knowledge that they had killed our own American troops. But I want to say this to them. The chaos and the bitterness there in the orchards and between the hedgerows that afternoon have passed. After the bitterness came the sober remembrance that the Air Corps is the strong right arm in front of us. Not only at the beginning, but ceaselessly and everlastingly, every moment of the faintest daylight, the Air Corps is up there banging away ahead of us.

Anybody makes mistakes. The enemy makes them just the

same as we do. The smoke and confusion of battle bewilder us all on the ground as well as in the air. And in this case the percentage of error was really very small compared with the colossal storm of bombs that fell upon the enemy.

The Air Corps has been wonderful throughout this invasion, and the men on the ground appreciate it.

Scripps-Howard wire copy, August 10, 1944

### *"This Weird Hedgerow Fighting"*

ON THE WESTERN FRONT—(by wireless)—I know that all of us correspondents have tried time and again to describe to you what this weird hedgerow fighting in northwestern France has been like.

But I'm going to go over it once more, for we've been in it two months and some of us feel that this is the two months that broke the German Army in the west.

This type of fighting is always in small groups, so let's take as an example one company of men. Let's say they are working forward on both sides of a country lane, and this company is responsible for clearing the two fields on either side of the road as it advances.

That means you have only about one platoon to a field. And with the company's understrength from casualties, you might have no more than 25 or 30 men in a field.

Over here the fields are usually not more than 50 yards across and a couple of hundred yards long. They may have grain in them, or apple trees, but mostly they are just pastures of green grass, full of beautiful cows.

The fields are surrounded on all sides by immense hedgerows which consist of an ancient earthen bank, waist high, all matted with roots, and out of which grow weeds, bushes, and trees up to 20 feet high.

The Germans have used these barriers well. They put snipers in the trees. They dig deep trenches behind the hedgerows and cover them with timber, so that it is almost impossible for artillery to get at them.

Sometimes they will prop up machine guns with strings attached, so they can fire over the hedge without getting out of their holes. They even cut out a section of the hedge-row and hide a big gun or a tank in it, covering it with brush.

Also they tunnel under the hedgerows from the back and make the opening on the forward side just large enough to stick a machine gun through.

But mostly the hedgerow pattern is this: a heavy machine gun hidden at each end of the field and infantrymen hidden all along the hedgerow with rifles and machine pistols.

\*        \*        \*

Now it's up to us to dig them out of there. It's a slow and cautious business, and there is nothing very dashing about it. Our men don't go across the open fields in dramatic charges such as you see in the movies. They did at first, but they learned better.

They go in tiny groups, a squad or less, moving yards apart and sticking close to the hedgerows on either end of the field. They creep a few yards, squat, wait, then creep again.

If you could be right up there between the Germans and the Americans you wouldn't see very many men at any one time—just a few here and there, always trying to keep hid-den. But you would hear an awful lot of noise.

Our men were taught in training not to fire until they saw something to fire at. But that hasn't worked in this country, because you see so little. So the alternative is to keep shooting constantly at the hedgerows. That pins the Germans in their holes while we sneak up on them.

The attacking squads sneak up the sides of the hedge-rows while the rest of the platoon stay back in their own hedgerow and keep the forward hedge saturated with bul-lets. They shoot rifle grenades too, and a mortar squad a little farther back keeps lobbing mortar shells over onto the Germans.

The little advance groups get up to the far ends of the hedgerows at the corners of the field. They first try to knock out the machine guns at each corner. They do this with hand grenades, rifle grenades and machine guns.

\*        \*        \*

Usually, when the pressure gets on, the German defenders of the hedgerow start pulling back. They'll take their heavier guns and most of the men back a couple of fields and start digging in for a new line.

They leave about two machine guns and a few riflemen scattered through the hedge, to do a lot of shooting and hold up the Americans as long as they can.

Our men now sneak along the front side of the hedgerow, throwing grenades over onto the other side and spraying the hedges with their guns. The fighting is very close—only a few yards apart—but it is seldom actual hand-to-hand stuff.

Sometimes the remaining Germans come out of their holes with their hands up. Sometimes they try to run for it and are mowed down. Sometimes they won't come out at all, and a hand grenade, thrown into their hole, finishes them off.

And so we've taken another hedgerow and are ready to start on the one beyond.

This hedgerow business is a series of little skirmishes like that clear across the front, thousands and thousands of little skirmishes. No single one of them is very big. But add them all up over the days and weeks and you've got a man-sized war, with thousands on both sides being killed.

Scripps-Howard wire copy, August 11, 1944

### "Each One Is a Separate Little War"

ON THE WESTERN FRONT—(by wireless)—What we gave you yesterday in trying to describe hedgerow fighting was the general pattern.

If you were to come over here and pick out some hedge-enclosed field at random, the fighting there probably wouldn't be following the general pattern at all. For each one is a little separate war, fought under different circumstances.

For instance, you'll come to a woods instead of an open field. The Germans will be dug in all over the woods, in little groups, and it's really tough to get them out. Often in cases like that we will just go around the woods and keep going, and let later units take care of those surrounded and doomed fellows.

Or we'll go through the woods and clean it out, and another company, coming through a couple of hours later, will find it full of Germans again. In a war like this one everything is in such confusion I don't see how either side ever gets anywhere.

Sometimes you don't know where the enemy is and don't know where your own troops are. As somebody said the other day, no battalion commander can give you the exact location of his various units five minutes after they've jumped off.

We will by-pass whole pockets of Germans, and they will be there fighting our following waves when our attacking companies are a couple of miles on beyond. Gradually the front gets all mixed up. There will be Germans behind you and at the side. They'll be shooting at you from behind and from your flank.

Sometimes a unit will get so far out ahead of those on either side that it has to swing around and fight to its rear. Sometimes we fire on our own troops, thinking we are in German territory. You can't see anything, and you can't even tell from the sounds, for each side uses some of the other's captured weapons.

\*      \*      \*

The tanks and the infantry had to work in the closest cooperation in breaking through the German ring that tried to pin us down in the beachhead area. Neither could have done it alone.

The troops are of two minds about having tanks around them. If you're a foot soldier you hate to be near a tank, for it always draws fire. On the other hand, if the going gets tough you pray for a tank to come up and start blasting with its guns.

In our breakthrough each infantry unit had tanks attached to it. It was the tanks and the infantry that broke through that ring and punched a hole for the armored divisions to go through.

The armored divisions practically ran amuck, racing long distances and playing hob, once they got behind the German lines, but it was the infantry and their attached tanks that opened the gate for them.

Tanks shuttled back and forth, from one field to another, throughout our breakthrough battle, receiving their orders by radio. Bulldozers punched holes through the hedgerows for them, and then the tanks would come up and blast out the bad spots of the opposition.

It has been necessary for us to wreck almost every farm-house and little village in our path. The Germans used them for strong points, or put artillery observers in them, and they just had to be blasted out.

Most of the French farmers evacuate ahead of the fighting and filter back after it has passed. It is pitiful to see them come back to their demolished homes and towns. Yet it's wonderful to see the grand way they take it.

\*          \*          \*

In a long drive an infantry company may go for a couple of days without letting up. Ammunition is carried up to it by hand, and occasionally by jeep. The soldiers sometimes eat only one K ration a day. They may run clear out of water. Their strength is gradually whittled down by wounds, exhaustion cases and straggling.

Finally they will get an order to sit where they are and dig in. Then another company will pass through, or around them, and go on with the fighting. The relieved company may get to rest as much as a day or two. But in a big push such as the one that broke us out of the beachhead, a few hours is about all they can expect.

The company I was with got its orders to rest about 5 one afternoon. They dug foxholes along the hedgerows, or commandeered German ones already dug. Regardless of how tired you may be, you always dig in the first thing.

Then they sent some men with cans looking for water. They got more K rations up by jeep, and sat on the ground eating them.

They hoped they would stay there all night, but they weren't counting on it too much. Shortly after supper a lieutenant came out of a farmhouse and told the sergeants to pass the word to be ready to move in 10 minutes. They bundled on their packs and started just before dark.

Within half an hour they had run into a new fight that lasted all night. They had had less than four hours' rest in three solid days of fighting. That's the way life is in the infantry.

Scripps-Howard wire copy, August 12, 1944

## "Nothing Left Behind But the Remains"

ON THE WESTERN FRONT—(by wireless)—When you're wandering around our very far-flung front lines—the lines that in our present rapid war are known as "fluid"—you can always tell how recently the battle has swept on ahead of you.

You can sense it from the little things even more than the big things—

From the scattered green leaves and the fresh branches of trees still lying in the middle of the road.

From the wisps and coils of telephone wire, hanging brokenly from high poles and entwining across the roads.

From the gray, burned-powder rims of the shell craters in the gravel roads, their edges not yet smoothed by the pounding of military traffic.

From the little pools of blood on the roadside, blood that has only begun to congeal and turn black, and the punctured steel helmets lying nearby.

From the square blocks of building stone still scattered in the village streets, and from the sharp-edged rocks in the roads, still uncrushed by traffic.

From the burned-out tanks and broken carts still unremoved from the road. From the cows in the fields, lying grotesquely with their feet to the sky, so newly dead they have not begun to bloat or smell.

From the scattered heaps of personal debris around a gun. I don't know why it is, but the Germans always seem to take off their coats before they flee or die.

From all these things you can tell that the battle has been recent—from these and from the men dead so recently that they seem to be merely asleep.

And also from the inhuman quiet. Usually battles are noisy for miles around. But in this recent fast warfare a battle sometimes leaves a complete vacuum behind it.

The Germans will stand and fight it out until they see there is no hope. Then some give up, and the rest pull and run for miles. Shooting stops. Our fighters move on after the enemy, and those who do not fight, but move in the wake of the battles, will not catch up for hours.

There is nothing left behind but the remains—the lifeless debris, the sunshine and the flowers, and utter silence.

An amateur who wanders in this vacuum at the rear of a battle has a terrible sense of loneliness. Everything is dead—the men, the machines, the animals—and you alone are left alive.

*          *          *

One afternoon we drove in our jeep into a country like that. The little rural villages of gray stone were demolished—heartbreaking heaps of still smoking rubble.

We drove into the tiny town of La Detinais, a sweet old stone village at the "T" of two gravel roads, a rural village in rolling country, a village of not more than 50 buildings. There was not a whole building left.

Rubble and broken wires still littered the streets. Blackish gray-stone walls with no roofs still smoldered inside. Dead men still lay in the street, helmets and broken rifles askew around them. There was not a soul nor a sound in town; the village was lifeless.

We stopped and pondered our way, and with trepidation we drove on out of town. We drove for a quarter of a mile or so. The ditches were full of dead men. We drove around one without a head or arms or legs. We stared, and couldn't say anything about it to each other. We asked the driver to go very slowly, for there was an uncertainty in all the silence. There was no live human, no sign of movement anywhere.

Seeing no one, hearing nothing, I became fearful of going on into the unknown. So we stopped. Just a few feet ahead of us was a brick-red American tank, still smoking, and with its turret knocked off. Near it was a German horse-drawn ammunition cart, upside down. In the road beside them was a shell crater.

To our left lay two smashed airplanes in adjoining fields. Neither of them was more than 30 yards from the road. The hedge was low and we could see over. They were both British fighter planes. One lay right side up, the other lay on its back.

We were just ready to turn around and go back, when I spied a lone soldier at the far side of the field. He was standing there looking across the field at us like an Indian in a picture. I waved and he waved back. We walked toward each other.

He turned out to be a second lieutenant—Ed Sasson, of 8137 Mulholland Terrace, Los Angeles. He is a graves registration officer for his armored division, and he was out scouring the fields, locating the bodies of dead Americans.

He was glad to see somebody, for it is a lonely job catering to the dead.

As we stood there talking in the lonely field a soldier in coveralls, with a rifle slung over his shoulder, ran up breathlessly, and almost shouted:

"Hey, there's a man alive in one of those planes across the road! He's been trapped there for days!"

We stopped right in the middle of a sentence and began to run. We hopped the hedgerow, and ducked under the wing of the upside-down plane. And there, in the next hour, came the climax to what certainly was one of the really great demonstrations of courage in this war.

Scripps-Howard wire copy, August 21, 1944

## "Wounded and Trapped"

ON THE WESTERN FRONT—(by wireless)—We ran to the wrecked British plane, lying there upside down, and dropped on our hands and knees and peeked through a tiny hole in the side.

A man lay on his back in the small space of the upside-down cockpit. His feet disappeared somewhere in the jumble of dials and rubber pedals above him. His shirt was open and his chest was bare to the waist. He was smoking a cigaret.

He turned his eyes toward me when I peeked in, and he said in a typical British manner of offhand friendliness, "Oh, hello."

"Are you all right," I asked, stupidly.

He answered, "Yes, quite. Now that you chaps are here."

I asked him how long he had been trapped in the wrecked plane. He said he didn't know for sure as he had got mixed up about the passage of time. But he did know the date of the month he was shot down. He told me the date. And I said out loud, "Good God!"

For, wounded and trapped, he had been lying there for eight days!

His left leg was broken and punctured by an ack-ack burst. His back was terribly burned by raw gasoline that had spilled. The foot of his injured leg was pinned rigidly under the rudder bar.

His space was so small he couldn't squirm around to relieve his own weight from his paining back. He couldn't straighten out his legs, which were bent above him. He couldn't see out of his little prison. He had not had a bite to eat or a drop of water. All this for eight days and nights.

Yet when we found him his physical condition was strong, and his mind was as calm and rational as though he were sitting in a London club. He was in agony, yet in his correct Oxford accent he even apologized for taking up our time to get him out.

The American soldiers of our rescue party cussed as they worked, cussed with open admiration for this British flier's greatness of heart which had kept him alive and sane through his lonely and gradually hope-dimming ordeal.

One of them said, "God, but these Limies have got guts!"

*     *     *

It took us almost an hour to get him out. We don't know whether he will live or not, but he has a chance. During the hour we were ripping the plane open to make a hole, he talked to us. And here, in the best nutshell I can devise from the conversation of a brave man whom you didn't want to badger with trivial questions, is what happened—

He was an RAF flight lieutenant, piloting a night fighter. Over a certain area the Germans began letting him have it from the ground with machine-gun fire.

The first hit knocked out his motor. He was too low to jump, so—foolishly, he said—he turned on his lights to try a crash landing. Then they really poured it on him. The second hit got him in the leg. And a third bullet cut right across the balls of his right-hand forefingers, clipping every one of them to the bone.

He left his wheels up, and the plane's belly hit the ground

going uphill on a slight slope. We could see the groove it had dug for about 50 yards. Then it flopped, tail over nose, onto its back. The pilot was absolutely sealed into the upside-down cockpit.

"That's all I remember for a while," he told us. "When I came to, they were shelling all around me."

\*      \*      \*

Thus began the eight days. He had crashed right between the Germans and Americans in a sort of pastoral no-man's land.

For days afterwards the field in which he lay surged back and forth between German hands and ours.

His pasture was pocked with hundreds of shell craters. Many of them were only yards away. One was right at the end of his wing. The metal sides of the plane were speckled with hundreds of shrapnel holes.

He lay there, trapped in the midst of this inferno of explosions. The fields around him gradually became littered with dead. At last American strength pushed the Germans back, and silence came. But no help. Because, you see, it was in that vacuum behind the battle, and only a few people were left.

The days passed. He thirsted terribly. He slept some; part of the time he was unconscious; part of the time he undoubtedly was delirious. But he never gave up hope.

After we had finally got him out, he said as he lay on the stretcher under a wing, "Is it possible that I've been out of this plane since I crashed?"

Everybody chuckled. The doctor who had arrived said, "Not the remotest possibility. You were sealed in there and it took men with tools half an hour to make an opening. And your leg was broken and your foot was pinned there. No, you haven't been out."

"I didn't think it was possible," the pilot said, "and yet it seems in my mind that I was out once and back in again."

That little memory of delirium was the only word said by that remarkable man in the whole hour of his rescue that wasn't as dispassionate and matter-of-fact as though he had been sitting comfortably at the end of the day in front of his own fireplace.

Scripps-Howard wire copy, August 22, 1944

# *"Rommel — Count Your Men"*

by Bill Davidson

OUTSIDE ST. MALO — The heavy artillery siege of St. Malo on the Brittany coast already had begun when a crack 155-mm howitzer battalion of the 333d Field Artillery, with which I am traveling, received orders to move up. Negro GIs make up this battalion, commanded by white officers.

I took off in a radio command car with the CO, Lt. Col. Harmon Kelsey of Livermore, Calif. At the wheel was T-5 Martin Simmons of Williamstown, N.J., described by the colonel as "the best damned driver I have ever seen and not scared of a damned thing."

We drove slowly up a broad asphalt highway past long rows of doughboys in trucks parked along the road. The battalion's new area was on the fringe of the town less than 10,000 yards from the besieged concrete citadel of St. Malo. The day before, an Infantry battalion had fought a bitter action here and had suffered heavy casualties when the enemy's coastal guns had been turned around to fire inland. We knew those guns were still zeroed in on the area.

The orchards and wheatfields stank with the dead and into many of the caved-in slit trenches had been swept the debris of war — torn GI raincoats, V-mail forms, bloody helmets, riddled rifle stocks and canteens. Three men had died beside the wall of a farmhouse when a tank shell bored a clean, small hole through the stone walls of the house and exploded where they stood talking on the other side.

The artillerymen prodded unconcernedly about the area, which had not yet been cleared of mines. Passing signalmen gingerly stringing their first lines stared at them incredulously. "Fee fie fo fum, I smell the blood of a Boche," said Cpl. David Smith of New York City. Sgt. Gibson Sapp, also of New York City, was looking at the debris-filled slit trenches and composing poetry. "They died under an apple tree," he wrote; "the apples were not yet ripe."

The officers were busy laying out battery areas and gloating about the lack of traffic on the roads this far forward. Some of the men discovered a system of underground fortifications built by the Germans and went foraging for bedroom slippers, shaving mirrors and stationery.

One by one the batteries of the battalion rolled in and began to dig emplacements for SPs and howitzers. By evening they were set up and ready to fire. The big guns pointed short, ugly snouts seaward under camouflage nets. In the battalion fire-direction center men kidded and dug a little deeper while they waited. In the next field a cannoneer sang a song called "Low-down Babe" in a high minor key. At 2035 orders to fire came through and Lt. A. J. Howell of Altus, Okla., left to take off in a Piper Cub. At 2101 Lt. Howell radioed that he could now observe the concrete fortress target. T/Sgt. Henry Washington of New York City and Sgt. Sapp worked furiously over computing charts in the fire-direction center. At 2104 Sgt. Washington picked up the telephone. At 2105 gun No. 2 of Battery B opened fire to register a target for the other 11 guns.

The gun crew went about firing the round quietly and methodically. There was no time for kidding and singing now. No one even muttered the battalion's now-famous battle-cry which goes "Rommel — count your men" before firing and then "Rommel — how many men you got now?" after firing. The projectile slammed into the breech. The crew whirled about rhythmically and the bagged propelling charge flew through the air from man to man. It looked like a well-drilled college backfield handling a tricky lateral-pass play. The breech swung closed. Then No. 1 man, Pfc. Arthur Broadnax of Autaugaville, Ala., pulled the lanyard. There was a blinding flash, a roar and a whistle. Seconds later we heard the 95-pound projectile crash into the crumbling Nazi citadel.

This was the 10,000th round the battalion had fired into the myth of the Aryan superman.

The battalion fired its first round a few hours after debarking on Cherbourg Peninsula June 30. On that occasion the men had barely water-proofed their vehicles and set up for what they thought was a waiting period outside Pont L'Abbe when a strange Piper Cub circling upstairs radioed a code word. The Cub simply said: "The coordinates of the target are such-and-such. Will adjust." That was all.

Col. Kelsey rushed to the map and looked at the target. It was a towering church steeple in the town, which the Germans were using both as a sniper's nest and an OP. "Fire mission," the colonel said into the phone. "Battery adjust shell HE fuse quick, compass 5,000, elevation 300." Four rounds and 90 seconds later three heavy shells crashed into the invisible steeple, completely knocking it out—and the infantry advanced through the town.

That's the kind of shooting the battalion has done ever since. It was the first Negro combat outfit to face the enemy in France. Today it is greatly respected. It is rated by the corps to which it is attached as one of the best artillery units under the corps' control. And I've heard doughboys of five divisions watch men of the battalion rumble past in four-ton prime movers and say: "Thank God those guys are behind us."

The battalion once fired 1,500 rounds in 24 hours, which didn't leave any time for sleeping. I watched the men set a new unofficial record by firing three rounds in a little over 40 seconds. They've developed the reputation of throwing high explosive for anyone who asks for it, regardless of affiliation, and in the Mortain sector they calmly swung their guns over the corps boundary line to help out the 4th Division when it needed some heavy slugging.

The battalion fired steadily for two weeks after it arrived in France and helped pound two vital hills into submission. After that it moved into the fight for La Haye du Puits and on to the bloody Moncastre Forest battle, where C Battery got out in front of the infantry and was so close to the enemy that it was pinned down by machine guns and mortars and couldn't fire. The battalion poured shells across the Periers–St. Lo road the day of the big July 25 attack and swept on through Normandy and Brittany with the big offensive. It was strafed and bombed and it absorbed occasional counterbattery fire from enemy artillery. It got shelled in foxholes and lost valuable men on OP hills. After La Haye du Puits it was issued mine detectors but it has not had time to use them. Its .50-caliber machine guns accounted for one strafing ME-109 and drove away 19 others.

The outfit captured seven prisoners on reconnaissance near Avranches. At Coutances it got out ahead of the infantry and captured a town.

Once when some ME-109s came strafing, the battalion was in a truck column on the road. Cpl. Pink Thomas of Batesville, Miss., stuck at the .50-caliber machine gun atop his truck and traded round for round with a Messerschmitt until it was the Nazi who gave ground and crashed in flames on the next hill. Lt. Joe King's 21-man wire crew was shelled off a hill three times and lost two men to machine-gun fire and shell bursts, but it managed to keep the lines open to OPs. That day the infantry moved ahead to La Haye du Puits under the battalion's protective barrage. Just before the big breakthrough along the Periers–St. Lo road the Germans tried to delay us with concentrations of 88s. Five of the 88s were firing on the battery at one time against our 155s. S/Sgt. Frank Crum of the Bronx, N.Y., crawled forward then up Hill 92 and in five minutes he'd spotted the gun flashes. Two volleys from the battalion silenced the 88s.

One of the things the battalion is most proud of is the time it scored a direct hit on the turret of a Tiger tank from 16,000 yards. When you consider that 16,000 yards is over nine miles, that the 155 howitzer fires a very heavy projectile at a very high arc, that the target was completely out of sight and that even if it were visible a Tiger tank at that distance would have looked about as big as a Maryland chigger—you realize that was some shooting.

The incident took place at Hill 95 north of La Haye du Puits. The position was still obscure on the hill but a three-man reconnaissance patrol took off anyway to look over the site as a forward OP. The patrol consisted of Lt. Edward Claussen of Bridgeport, Conn.; Pfc. Johnny Choice of Milledgeville, Ga., and Cpl. Howard Nesbitt of New York City. As they advanced they strung a telephone line way back to the battalion.

At the foot of the hill they ran into a paratrooper. "Who's up there?" asked Claussen. "Some of us and some of them," said the paratrooper. Whereupon Claussen swapped his pistol for the paratrooper's tommy gun and they proceeded up the hill. On reaching the top they started digging. They stayed there for eight days, observing the fire while an infantry battle surged back and forth around them.

On the ninth day some 88s got zeroed on the top of the hill and shelled it spasmodically day and night. This kept up for three days while Choice and Claussen spotted flashes and the battalion engaged the slippery self-propelled 88s with counter-battery fire. The telephone lines were cut and repaired and cut again.

Suddenly on the thirteenth day Claussen and Choice spotted the turret and apron of a single desert-camouflaged tank just barely showing above a hedgerow on the road alongside a house. Just as they were phoning the information back, the 88s opened up again. One shell burst five feet behind them and cut the telephone wire. Then another burst three feet in front of them and covered them with dirt in their foxholes. "Let's get the hell out of here," said Claussen.

They left with the phone and nothing else. A platoon of paratroopers just in front of them on the slope was falling back at the same time. One paratrooper came bounding over a hedgerow. "This is the first foxhole I've left since I landed 34 days ago," he said, "but, brother, this sure is one I'm saying good-bye to now."

Claussen and Choice moved down the hill 100 yards. Then they plugged into the telephone wire again. They phoned the coordinates of the tank back to the battalion and took chances dashing up to the top of the hill to observe results.

C Battery did the firing. The men used delayed-fuse shells timed to burst after the projectile had penetrated. The first round fell short. The second round dropped right down through the turret. The third smashed through the rear end of the tank. The fourth fell long. The second shell exploded inside the tank. The tank flew in half like a walnut smashed by a hammer.

They told me at gun No. 2 of C Battery that someone had

reverted to the old GI custom and had scribbled some words in chalk on that shell. The words were: "From Harlem to Hitler."

# The Siege of St. Malo

by Lee Miller

I THUMBED a ride on an L.S.T. to the Siege of St. Malo. I had brought my bed, I begged my board, and I was given a grandstand view of fortress warfare reminiscent of Crusader times. I arrived the 13th of August, and there were still armed marauders being dug out of cellars and cleared out of back-yards in the mainland towns . . . snipers who lay in wait for the Brass or the unwitnessed or unwary . . . hoping to rejoin a fighting unit some place else, and not knowing how far behind the real line they were.

So the war wasn't over in this section, and the soldiers who were fighting assault battles, the artillery who were in their turn spotted and shelled by Hun counter-battery, the combat M.P.s who scraped the town for hidden enemies, the Civil Affairs team who aided bewildered civilians and kept them out of the hair of the Army, in fact, all of the Division wondered what they'd tell their grandchildren they'd done in the great war, since it was "all over" where they were still fighting on for weeks . . . bloody, heroic, tricky battles. . . . [ *Censors just released that it was the 83rd Division, 329th Regiment at St. Malo.* ]

The Germans called a truce from the Château in Old St. Malo, and asked that they be allowed to send out all the French people who were sheltering in the burning town. They chose the hour before darkness, typically, and the Civil Affairs sent scouts around quickly to organize hospitalization and food, to find local patriots who would recognize any conspirators or phonies in the lot . . . the *gendarmerie* to control the line. The military sent their counter-intelligence men, and ambulances were provided. From past experience with the Huns, we didn't dare risk sending trucks down to the causeway to meet the refugees, as it might have been a bait to get all our transport concentrated. The shooting suddenly stopped again, and a long stream of people came out into view and passed down the causeway . . . the injured and ill first . . . then old women, with bundles and dazed eyes, little hand-holding groups of girls, stumbling along . . . couples with babies, prams piled with all they had saved of their possessions . . . boys, men shambling from shock . . . prim women, and nuns in immaculate white, and whores. A few were hoisted out of line by the police for their crimes, and a few trustworthy others kept at the bridgehead to help identify any possibly escaping Germans.

There were farewell scenes as the injured were separated and taken off in ambulances . . . and the mass moved on. There were twice the 600 the Germans had announced were on the way. There was no way to control them if they dropped off and went to their own houses, or scattered or got lost, but nearly all wanted the food stocks being given out at the school, and hoped for transport further behind the battle. There was some frigid division among the people, but no haircutting . . . all these people had shared the hardship of battle and were friends again. For the moment.

A couple of counter-intelligence characters came to the Civil Affairs villa, to pick up the prison warden who was there. They wanted to interview a woman they had (on the advice of the *Résistance* people) put in jail the night before. The counter-intelligence deals only with those who are dangerous to the military situation. All other collaborators and such are turned over to the civilian authorities. The jail had a big hole through it, but wasn't blasted at all. The woman and her three children were brought in to the warden's office and her own portfolio of papers put on the desk. Two of the little girls were dressed in blue velvet coats with white bunny collars, and the third was a toddler. The papers contained receipts for salary from the German labour "Todt" organization where she had had a secretarial position. Identity cards and ration books in order . . . and letters signed Heil Hitler, all swastika-ed. There were also some pornographic photographs, which for some strange reason she clung to. When any difficult question came along, she bent over the small child in her lap in madonna-like poses. The CIC man spoke to her in much more halting French than I knew he knew, and with a Bing Crosby voice. It was like snake and bird hypnosis. She claimed that she had never turned in military information to the enemy, and that if her husband or nephew, the authors of the Nazi-minded letters had, she didn't know it, and anyway they had gone away she knew not where.

We parked her back in her cell. She made a pretty pose with her children when I wanted to photograph her. The kids ate some coloured Life-Savers without tasting them, their big, sullen eyes glued to me. They were neither timid nor tough, but gloomy, and I felt like vomiting.

We dodged up to Parame, and found the house where she had lived. It was an ugly cobblestone and brick villa, with a detached shed-garage. We forced the shutters and climbed into a disorderly, slovenly room. Everything in it was sluttish . . . children's clothes and Nazi propaganda were strewn around together . . . unwashed dishes . . . laundry . . . sewing and pornography . . . empty booze bottles and suitcases. In the bathroom, the tub was full of water like all the houses in town, as the water plant had been turned off for a long time. The cupboard was full of men's clothes with the maker's address, "Kiel" inside.

Some young, attractive girls from down the street came in and levelled more accusations at the woman; said that a few nights before, two German officers had come in with suitcases and left in civilian clothes. Also that they had heard that the woman's husband, a Frenchman who organized labour for the Germans, was supposed to be in Rennes and was coming back to fetch her that night. In the garage were the Germans' clothes, also heaps of propaganda material, et cetera. That really clinched the job. It was only a question of picking up the husband. The two girls, by the way, had had a tough time. They were charming and intelligent, if venomous toward their neighbour. Both were students preparing for college, and one has spent 16 months in a concentration camp, accused, rightly, of sheltering and aiding de Gaullists. The other, who was younger, had just done four months for wearing the Cross of Lorraine under her lapel.

*     *     *

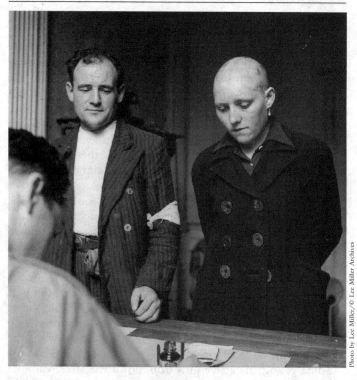

Interrogation of a Frenchwoman who has had her hair shaved for consorting with Germans. Note her earrings.

In the meantime, old St. Malo was busy organizing a surrender. I wasn't allowed to go, as the quai was still under close machine-gun fire, so I called in at the command post of the regiment to see what was cooking there. They seemed to have plenty on their minds, and Major Speedie, the battalion commander, took me on a tour of observation posts which he was setting up for an assault next day on the "Fort de la Cité," the famous Citadel, located on a promontory off St. Servan, and guarding the mouth of the Rance and the Port of St. Malo.

Since 1940 the Germans had been arming the Fort with pillboxes and secret weapons, digging galleries fifty feet into solid granite, building ventilation systems, food stores and 'phone connections to the other fortresses of Cap Frehel, Cézambre, and Grand Bey. When the land fighting of the mainland had driven the Germans to the water's edge, and to surrender, the "Mad Colonel," von Aulock, left his celebrated mistress behind, and decided to make a name for himself by holding out the impregnable "Cité." He had been military governor of the whole area and our people had a wholesome respect for him in a soldier's way. His mistress, a German beauty known for her past with certain Russian royalty, was registered as his secretary interpreter, and was well known by the people of St. Malo and St. Servan, who admire some of the things she did for them on the side, with humanity and discretion . . . for whatever reason she may have had.

The Colonel had now announced that he was going to hold out to the last man. Thus he put the seal of doom on the towns of St. Malo and St. Servan.

Some combat MPs told me of the exploits of various officers of the regiment whom I'd met that day. Captain David Gray, of Topeka, Kansas, had manoeuvred several risky exchanges of prisoner-wounded with Herr Doktor Weller, the interpreter medico of the Fortress. They were always putting up white flags, once to ask for medical supplies in exchange for our wounded prisoners from an unsuccessful night assault on the Fortress. Some of them were recognized truces by both sides, others were risky deals. Walking across the *digue* to meet Weller halfway, with machine-gun fire going on from both sides . . . bargaining for our wounded, shrewdly and fairly . . . taking out Germans and Americans, also two women who had served various purposes in the Fortress.

One of his walks "into the jaws" was to insist on getting a wounded American who had been refused a time before, as too ill to travel. Weller showed the medical chart of his leg amputation, and the Hun marine doctor asked for the return of a captive surgeon we had. It was arranged that a report on the situation should be made under white flag next day at two o'clock, if we recognized their signal. However, Colonel Craibill decided that there should be "no more white flags except for surrender," and enough of this nonsense. Dr. Weller came down, however, on his own, without protection, and was met by Gray and Colonel Craibill who explained that he would not call off the planned aerial bombardment scheduled for one hour from then for just one man, but only for the whole garrison.

There was heavy fire again as the white flag was hauled down on the Fort, Colonel von Aulock having refused the terms. Dr. Gray walked up to the pillbox again to ask for his patient. The Colonel sent word to him that all negotiations were over and "thanks for the fair fighting." There were stories about Captain Boyd, who stamped up to a pillbox with a white flag unrecognized, to see if they'd changed their minds . . . and was waved back by a hand reaching out of the gunhole.

Major Speedie, Gray, and a volunteer named Rifferetti made a reconnaissance with their flag once to see if anyone was left . . . there was. It was confusing enough to catch up with the different exploits without being told that the MP who had been telling me was also guilty of having gone up bare-handed to meet a German white flag, to which we had refused recognition, on the excuse that a combat MP's duties include taking charge of prisoners, and there might have been some. He was an enormous and extraordinary character, and I'm glad he liked me. I take back everything that's been said about MPs . . . they are wonderful.

The next morning I hung around hoping to get into St. Malo proper, and ate breakfast with the MPs who managed everything, including hot water which they boiled in the basement. Fires, like lights and outdoor cigarettes, were strictly forbidden as attracting snipers and enemy OPs, although casual French civilians lit everything, and since the refugees had come back there had been a lot of trouble with shooting at lights, and even some signalling to enemy posts, as well as a few cases of arson. Houses had been fired with German incendiary gadgets within two hours after the refugee truce. Undoubtedly the Huns had sent out saboteurs and soldiers in disguise along with the French, and had confused us also in our inspection by sending more than a thousand people instead of the announced 600.

A company of soldiers was filing out of St. Malo, ready to go into action, grenades hanging on their lapels like Cartier clips, menacing bunches of death. Everybody was leaving as if from the proverbial doomed ship, without even cleaning up the bodies which lay along the streets. War was their business, and they went on in a sloping march across the town of St. Servan, to a small square before the Mairie . . . a nice little square if it had been Bastille Day, but hell now, with its dugout shelters and hand-grenades. I went on to the command post in the boys' school . . . the telephone exchange and the wireless reception were on the courtyard balcony just outside the major's office.

The blackboards were still chalked with German-French lessons and German tourist posters decorated the walls. In the next room it was French or German-English and the silly 1900 pictures of the "Famille Durand" with their cats, canaries, and crowded rooms were on the walls, with a long pointer for reaching to the sideburned gent *"ce monsieur est un soldat."*

In Major Speedie's office, soldiers of all ranks came in and looked at maps and front elevations. There were sketches from prisoners information . . . and drawings of mined areas given by deserters. At the end of the balcony a Captain was briefing his group.

There were flashes from delayed action bombs buried in the earthworks. The next wave was light incendiaries . . . a lot fell in the water to the right. Many hit the sloping earth towards us, and more into the fort. Our artillery started its

Major Speedie (later made Lt. Col.), who received St. Malo's surrender from Col. Von Aulock, in German ex-headquarters.

barrage . . . the soldiers had started moving down the streets with the last air bombs, assembling between the burning buildings at the approach to the fort. The dry, fast cough of our machine guns echoed ghost-like. The enemy's 20mm., 200-a-minute cannons made savage probes . . . our mortars and smokescreen . . . pounded and drifted—our heavy guns battered into the moat . . . on to the fortress and around the pillboxes . . . our soldiers were leaving the houses. I could see them next to the orange-tiled one creeping down to the rocks and moving single-file up the steep approach to the fort, while another platoon crept from the houses to the rocks, crouching, waiting their turn. It was a heavy climb . . . and they were earth-coloured like the burnt soil they were traversing.

I projected myself into their struggle, my arms and legs aching and cramped . . . the first man scrambled over the sharp edge, went along a bit, and turned back to give a hand in hauling up the others . . . on and on the men went up . . . veering off to the right . . . it was awesome and marrow-freezing.

The building we were in and all the others which faced the Fort were being spat at now . . . ping, bang . . . hitting above our window . . . into the next . . . breaking on the balcony below . . . fast, rapid, queer noise . . . impact before the gun noise itself . . . following the same sound pattern . . . hundreds of rounds . . . crossing and recrossing where we were.

Machine-gun fire belched from the end pillbox . . . the men fell flat . . . stumbling and crawling into the shelter of shell-holes . . . some crept on, others sweeping back to the left of the guns' angle, one man reaching the top. He was enormous. A square-shouldered silhouette, black against the sky between the pillbox and the fort. He raised his arm. The gesture of a cavalry officer with sabre waving the others on . . . he was waving to death, and he fell with his hand against the Fort.

The men were flowing away from the path he had followed . . . moving toward the left . . . it was retreat. Singly and together they picked themselves up and threw themselves down into another hole, stooping, hunched . . . scrambling, helping each other. There was silence—poised—desperate. I could hear yells from the slopes . . . orders . . . directions . . . with nightmare faintness. There was a great black explosion where the most forward men had been a minute before. Cézembre was firing on her sister fortress . . . shells which would not penetrate or injure the occupants but which could blast our men, who were oozing down the escarpment . . . and sliding down the path which they had so painfully climbed. Other bursts from Cézembre swept the sides of the Fort. They were directed by telephone, probably from the Cité . . . they followed with hideous knowledge. One burst hiding and shattering the men at the bottom . . . our mortar fire was peppering the pillboxes to keep them silent . . . smoke screens and artillery pummelled the fortress just above our men to keep the krauts from slaughtering them in retreat.

They got back among the houses . . . our machine guns keeping a steady tattoo . . . Cézembre bursts hunting angrily in the rocks, slopes and buildings, hungry for more of the withdrawing soldiers. The Cité guns could not reach them there and turned more attention to us . . . we separated to different rooms . . . everyone was sullen . . . silent . . . and aching, like a terrible hangover. The men came back into the square . . . the ambulance men had the wounded, the dead had been left.

Stricken lonely cats prowled. A swollen horse had not provided adequate shelter for the dead American behind it . . . flower-pots stood in roomless windows. Flies and wasps made tours in and out of underground vaults which stank with death and sour misery. Gunfire brought more stone blocks down into the street . . . I sheltered in a kraut dugout, squatting under the ramparts. My heel ground into a dead detached hand . . . and I cursed the Germans for the sordid ugly destruction they had conjured up in this once beautiful town. I wondered where my friends were . . . that I'd known here before the war . . . how many had been forced into disloyalty and degradation . . . how many had been shot, starved or what. I picked up the hand and hurled it across the street and ran back the way I'd come, bruising my feet and crashing in the unsteady piles of stone and slipping in blood. Christ, it was awful.

Everybody was busy making plans for a new assault on the Citadel in the afternoon. A low level attack—all oil bombs and incendiaries—barrage . . . men . . . that Cézembre should be attacked during the infantry assault to keep its guns silent . . . that St. Malo should be evacuated . . . that the civilians would, for heaven's sake, keep back of the bombline . . . that the fat man in the white helmet refused to leave the bank and had to be taken from St. Malo by the force of civilian police, crying. Streams of refugees haunted the Civil Affairs, tracing families, begging to go into the town of St. Malo.

In the Hotel Victoria the telephone was on the bed, and Major Speedie kept going out too far on the balcony. His sergeant pulled him in by the belt. The attack was scheduled for three. It was nearly that now. There was no fire from the Fort. We weren't bothering either. Somebody thought they saw white flags way down on the left. If they were, they weren't in the agreed position. The wind was the wrong way and it certainly was white and it hadn't been there before. But it looked more like two white sticks, not very straight. Frantic phoning went on. The switchboards tried to break down. Other O.P.'s were contacted. Had they a better view? Could the air attack be called off? Was it a real surrender? A trick? The phones traced air command . . . a General. It couldn't be stopped. They were here . . . on their bomb run.

We could see Capt. Boyd now, running up to the left part of the Fort with his flag-bearer and interpreter. There were other people there. Germans. Somebody else. It was MacFarlane, racing up through the buildings toward them for warning. The planes were nearer. Boyd and his group backed up toward the buildings a few yards. Waving flags, spreading scarlet boundary markers to signal the P-28 pilots that the place was ours. The Major said, "Goddamit, those are my boys!" as a pair of bombs hurled from the first plane over their heads and into the opened belly of the Fort.

There was a burst of flame and billowing smoke, and the second plane veered off without bombing . . . and the third. They circled through the smoke at crazy angles, deprived of their prey, standing by to watch for trickery. We raced down through the streets, up through the causeway buildings. The terrain was soft with shelling, and hard with broken stones, weapons, twisted track rails, scattered ties, unexploded German grenades, and mines to be stepped over. A large metal barrow blocked the narrow street which was still burning.

As we came out into the open we could see Boyd and Mac-Farlane and the others turning over the markers into some other signal pattern. They went down the back of the Fort to the tunnel entrance. Major Speedie made me stay at the markers, and they disappeared at the turn. A messenger went up, the walkie-talkie. A platoon disarmed themselves at the boundary, and carefully spaced out up the hill. It wasn't too late for the Cézembre guns to give us a swipe, and orders were passed back to keep well spread. An armed platoon went up . . . that must mean that the surrender was real and complete.

Captain Boyd had gone to the hole—shouted for a German, and disappeared inside, but I couldn't disobey the Major and had to stay. I caught sight of him escorting a tall figure, certainly not G.I., and preceded by a police dog. It was Colonel von Aulock. He wore a flapping camouflage coat, a battered peaked hat. I took a picture and stepped out in front. Seeing the camera he held a grey-gloved hand up in front of his face. He was pale, monocled. An iron cross and ribbon at his neck. He kept on walking, and obviously, recognized that I was a woman. He said "something Frau" in a loud voice and flushed little red spots in each cheek like rouge. I kept scrambling on in front, turning around to take another shot of him, stumbling, running. He wasted as much energy as I did, and ruined his dignified departure in hiding his face. He seemed awfully thin under his clothes, as he stood in the jeep and said farewell to the men who had carried his bags down. He shook them by the hand, waved the dog away, and was whisked up to headquarters.

I went back to the Citadel, and stood around with Major Speedie and Captain White, while droves of prisoners came down carrying suitcases and bundles. Some straggled, some lingered and had to be ordered to move faster. Some recognized me as a girl and set up conversation, which was forbidden. The German Captain Waller stood nearby. He told our

Col. Von Aulock (the Mad Colonel) waits for jeep after surrender.
On left, Maj. Speedie; on right, Capt. White.

Captain, Dr. Gray, "You understand, that to me this scene is very unhappy." He gave assurances that the tunnels were not mined, that there were no booby traps in return for what they thought was our clean fighting. He picked out six German N. C. O.'s to return with our men into the Fort to act as guides and to keep the ventilation and lights going. Major General Macon raced up the hill like a gazelle and congratulated Major Speedie on having effected the surrender: the last of the hordes of Germans had passed, and the wounded came out.

It was difficult to get the litters out of the crumbled entrance to the tunnel. The bearers had to stoop and crawl, gently, because the first boy was the American prisoner who had been refused evacuation. There were other Americans, too. One, unwounded, who knew the works of the Fort by now, said the aerial bombardment hadn't upset anyone at all. . . . They just went into a deeper tunnel and waited . . . but that many of the gun turrets had been knocked out and could only be used by hand-fire, although that was effective too, and could have made our assault a costly affair. A Polish boy came out very ill. Our Polish-speaking soldiers sat next to him while he got used to the air. The Germans were surprised at the surrender. They had been asked to put all their small arms into a big bonfire of the commander's papers. There had been plenty of food, water, ammunition.

I went into the tunnel. A short, rough-hewn passage turned at an angle into a long higher tunnel. There were rails for a metal barrow, and electric lights at 50 foot intervals. Rooms opened off each side, lofty, rough, curved to the ceiling . . . double-decker bunks in disorder . . . bottles, clothes, photographs, letters, loot from French towns. There were store-rooms, offices, telephones, power plants, dumps of ammunition and cellars of wine, rum and bottled water. Our boys found plenty of souvenirs. The wounded were lying in litters up and down the main passage outside the hospital corridors.

The Hun Marine medical officer refused to be photographed and quoted the Geneva Convention at me through the interpreter. There was only one surgery. It was only "adequate" in equipment. Nothing like what I had seen in our

travelling advance field hospitals. They still had medical supplies of their own in spite of having begged ours in exchange
for wounded.

I went back out into the light. There were crowds of
people now. Reporters had gathered like vultures for the kill,
all the way from Rennes. French people were already trying to
move back into the houses. I didn't walk around the pillbox
to see the man who had waved . . . and I put off going to
the top and walking down where I had seen the little men
crawl up. I never did go. Dr. Gray's American flag was waving
on the top, and that was enough. The war left St. Malo and
me—behind.

*Vogue*, October 1944

# How We Came to Paris

by Ernest Hemingway

NEVER can I describe to you the emotions I felt on the arrival of the armored column of General Leclerc southeast of Paris. Having just returned from a patrol which scared the pants off of me and having been kissed by all the worst element in a town which imagined it had been liberated through our fortuitous entry, I was informed that the general himself was just down the road and anxious to see us. Accompanied by one of the big shots of the resistance movement and Colonel B, who by that time was known throughout Rambouillet as a gallant officer and a *grand seigneur* and who had held the town ever since we could remember, we advanced in some state toward the general. His greeting—unprintable—will live in my ears forever.

"Buzz off, you unspeakables," the gallant general said, in effect, in something above a whisper, and Colonel B, the resistance king and your armored-operations correspondent withdrew.

Later the G-2 of the division invited us to dinner and they operated next day on the information Colonel B had amassed for them. But for your correspondent that was the high point of the attack on Paris.

In war, my experience has been that a rude general is a nervous general. At this time I drew no such deductions but departed on another patrol where I could keep my own nervousness in one jeep and my friends could attempt to clarify the type of resistance we could encounter on the following day between Toussus le Noble and Le Christ de Saclay.

Having found out what this resistance would be, we returned to the Hotel du Grand Veneur in Rambouillet and passed a restless night. I do not remember exactly what produced this restlessness but perhaps it was the fact that the joint was too full of too many people, including, actually, at one time two military police. Or perhaps it was the fact that we had proceeded too far ahead of our supply of Vitamin B., and the ravages of alcohol were affecting the nerves of the hardier guerrillas who had liberated too many towns in too short a time. At any rate I was restless and I think, without exaggeration, I may truly state that those whom Colonel B and I by then referred to as "our people" were restless.

The guerrilla chief, the actual fighting head of "our people," said, "We want to take Paris. What the hell is the delay?"

"There is no delay, Chief," I answered. "All this is part of a giant operation. Have patience. Tomorrow we will take Paris."

"I hope so," the guerrilla chief said. "My wife has been expecting me there for some time. I want to get the hell into Paris to see my wife, and I see no necessity to wait for a lot of soldiers to come up."

"Be patient," I told him.

That fateful night we slept. It might be a fateful night but tomorrow would certainly be an even more fateful day. My anticipations of a really good fight on the morrow were marred by a guerrilla who entered the hotel late at night and woke me to inform me that all the Germans who could do so were pulling out of Paris. We knew there would be fighting the next day by the screen the German army had left. But I did not anticipate any heavy fighting, since we knew the German dispositions and could attack or by-pass them accordingly, and I assured our guerrillas that if they would only be patient, we would have the privilege of entering Paris with soldiers ahead of us instead of behind us.

This privilege did not appeal to them at all. But one of the big shots of the underground insisted that we do this, as he said it was only courteous to allow troops to precede and by the time we had reached Toussus le Noble, where there was a short but sharp fight, orders were given that neither newspapermen nor guerrillas were to be allowed to proceed until the column had passed.

The day we advanced on Paris it rained heavily and everyone was soaked to the skin within an hour of leaving Rambouillet. We proceeded through Chevreuse and St. Remy-lès-Chevreuses where we had formerly run patrols and were well known to the local inhabitants, from whom we had collected information and with whom we had downed considerable quantities of armagnac to still the ever-present discontent of our guerrillas, who were very Paris-conscious at this time. In those days I had found that the production of an excellent bottle of any sort of alcoholic beverage was the only way of ending an argument.

After we had proceeded through St. Remy-lès-Chevreuses, where we were wildly acclaimed by the local *charcutier*, or pork butcher, who had participated in previous operations and been cockeyed ever since, we made a slight error in preceding the column to a village called Courcelle. There we were informed that there were no vehicles ahead of us and, greatly to the disgust of our people who wished to proceed on what they believed to be the shortest route into Paris, we returned to St. Remy-lès-Chevreuses to join the armored column which was proceeding toward Châteaufort. Our return was viewed with considerable alarm by the local *charcutier*. But when we explained the situation to him he acclaimed us wildly again and, downing a couple of quick ones, we advanced resolutely toward Toussus le Noble where I knew the column would have to fight.

At this point I knew there would be German opposition just ahead of us and also on our right at Le Christ de Saclay. The Germans had dug and blasted out a series of defense points between Châteaufort and Toussus le Noble and beyond the crossroads. Past the airdrome toward Buc they had 88s that commanded all that stretch of road. As we came closer to where the tanks were operating around Trappes I became increasingly apprehensive.

The French armor operated beautifully. On the road toward Toussus le Noble, where we knew there were Germans with machine guns in the wheat shocks, the tanks deployed and screened both of our flanks and we saw them rolling ahead through the cropped wheat field as though they were on maneuvers. No one saw the Germans until they came out with their hands up after the tanks had passed. It was a beautiful use of armor, that problem child of war, and it was lovely to see.

When we ran up against the seven tanks and four 88s the Germans had beyond the airfield, the French handled the fight prettily, too. Their artillery was back in another open wheat field, and when the German guns—four of which had been brought up during the night and were firing absolutely in the open—cut loose on the column, the French mechanized artillery slammed into them. You could not hear with the German shells coming in, the 20-mm. firing, and the machine-gun fire cracking overhead, but the French underground leader who had correlated the information on the German dispositions shouted in French into my ear, "The contact is beautiful. Just where we said. Beautiful."

It was much too beautiful for me, who had never been a great lover of contact anyway, and I hit the deck as an 88 shell burst alongside the road. Contact is a very noisy business and, since our column was held up at this point, the more forceful and active of the guerrillas aided in reconstructing the road which had been churned into soup by the armor. This kept their minds from the contact taking place all around us. They filled in the mudholes with bricks and tiles from a smashed house, and passed along chunks of cement and pieces of house from hand to hand. It was raining hard all this time, and by the time the contact was over, the column had two dead and five wounded, one tank burned up, and had knocked out two of the seven enemy tanks and silenced all of the 88s.

"*C'est un bel accrochage,*" the underground leader said to me jubilantly.

This means something like "We have grappled with them prettily" or "We tied into them beautifully," searching in mind for the exact meaning of *accrochage*, which is what happens when two cars lock bumpers.

I shouted, "Prettily! Prettily!"

At which a young French lieutenant, who did not have the air of having been mixed up in too many *accrochages* in his time but who, for all I know, may have participated in hundreds of them, said to me, "Who the hell are you and what are you doing here in our column?"

"I am a war correspondent, monsieur," I replied.

The lieutenant shouted: "Do not let any war correspondents proceed until the column has passed. And especially do not let this one proceed."

"Okay, my lieutenant," the M.P. said. "I will keep an eye on them."

"And none of that guerrilla rabble, either," the lieutenant ordered. "None of that is to pass until all the column has gone through."

"My lieutenant," I said, "the rabble will be removed from sight once this little *accrochage* is finished and the column has proceeded."

"What do you mean—this little *accrochage*?" he demanded, and I feared hostility might be creeping into his voice.

Since we were not to advance farther with the column, I took evasive action at this point and waded down the road to a bar. Numerous guerrillas were seated in it singing happily and passing the time of day with a lovely Spanish girl from Bilbao whom I had last met on the famous two-way, or wide-open patrol point just outside the town of Cognières. This was the town we used to take from the Germans whenever one of their vehicles pulled out of it, and they would return whenever we stepped off the road. This girl had been following wars and preceding troops since she was fifteen and she and the guerrillas were paying no attention to the *accrochage* at all.

A guerrilla chief named C said, "Have a drink of this excellent white wine." I took a long drink from the bottle and it turned out to be a highly alcoholic liqueur tasting of oranges and called Grand Marnier.

A stretcher was coming back with a wounded man on it. "Look," a guerrilla said, "these military are constantly suffering casualties. Why do they not allow us to proceed ahead in a sensible manner?"

"Okay, okay," said another guerrilla in G.I. fatigue clothes, with the brassard of the *francs-tireurs* on his sleeve. "What about the comrades who were killed yesterday on the road?"

Another said, "But today we're going into Paris."

"Let's go back and see if we can make it by Le Christ de Saclay," I said. "The law has arrived and they won't let us go on any farther until the column has passed. The roads are too muddy and torn up here. We could push the light touring cars through, but the truck might bog down and stall things."

"We can push through by a side road," the guerrilla chief named C said. "Since when do we have to follow columns?"

"I think it is best to go back as far as Châteaufort," I said. "Maybe we can go much faster that way."

On the crossroads outside Châteaufort we found Colonel B and Commander A, who had become detached from us before we had run into the *accrochage*, and told them about the beautiful contact up the road. The artillery was still firing in the open wheat field, and the two gallant officers had found some lunch in a farmhouse. French troops from the column were burning the wooden boxes that had held the shells the artillery had been blasting with, and we took off our wet clothes and dried them at the fire. German prisoners were drifting in, and an officer in the column asked us to send the guerrillas up to where a group of Germans had just surrendered in the wheat shocks. They brought them back in good military style, all the prisoners alive and well.

"This is idiotic, you know, my captain," the oldest one of the band said. "Now someone has to feed them."

The prisoners said they were office workers in Paris and had only been brought out and put in the positions at one o'clock this morning.

"Do you believe that sort of stuff?" asked the oldest guerrilla.

"It could be possible. They weren't here yesterday," I said.

"This entire military nonsense disgusts me," the oldest guerrilla said. He was forty-one and had a thin, sharp face with clear blue eyes, and a rare but fine smile. "Eleven of our group were tortured and shot by these Germans. I have been beaten and kicked by them, and they would have shot me if they knew who I was. Now we are asked to guard them carefully and respectfully."

"They are not your prisoners," I explained. "The military took them."

The rain turned to a light drifting mist and then the sky cleared. The prisoners were sent back to Rambouillet in the big German truck that the underground big shot quite rightly was anxious to get out of the column for the moment. Leaving word with the M.P. on the crossroads where the truck could rejoin us, we drove on after the column.

We caught up with the tanks on a side road this side of the main Versailles-Paris highway and moved with them down into a deeply wooded valley and out into green fields where there was an old château. We watched the tanks deploy again, like watching dogs outside a moving band of sheep. They had fought once up ahead of us while we had gone back to see if the road through Le Christ de Saclay was free, and we passed a burned-out tank and three dead Germans. One of these had been run over and flattened out in a way that left no doubt of the power of armor when properly used.

On the main Versailles-Villacoublay highway the column proceeded past the wrecked airdrome of Villacoublay to the crossroads of the Porte Clamart. Here, while the column was stopped, a Frenchman came running up and reported a small German tank on the road that led into the woods. I searched the road with my glasses but could not see anything. In the meantime, the German vehicle, which was not a tank but a lightly armored German jeep mounting a machine gun and a 20-mm. gun, made a turn in the woods and came tearing up the road, firing at the crossroads.

Everyone started shooting at it, but it wheeled and regained the woods. Archie Pelkey, my driver, got in two shots at it but could not be sure that he had hit. Two men were hit and were carried into the lee of the corner building for first aid. The guerrillas were happy now that shooting had started again.

"We have nice work ahead of us. Good work ahead of us," the guerrilla with the sharp face and the light blue eyes said. "I'm happy some of the b——s are still here."

"Do you think we will have much more chance to fight?" the guerrilla named C asked.

"Certainly," I said. "There's bound to be some of them in the town."

My own war aim at this moment was to get into Paris without being shot. Our necks had been out for a long time. Paris was going to be taken. I took cover in all the street fighting —the solidest cover available—and with someone covering the stairs behind me when we were in houses or the entrances to apartment houses.

From now on, the advance of the column was something to see. Ahead of us would be a barricade of felled trees. The tanks would pass around them or butt them around like elephants handling logs. You would see the tanks charge into a barricade of old motorcars and go smashing on ahead with a jalopy bouncing along, its smashed fenders entangled in the tracks. Armor, which can be so vulnerable and so docile in the close hedgerow country where it is a prey to antitank guns, bazookas and anyone who does not fear it, was smashing round like so many drunken elephants in a native village.

Ahead and on our left, a German ammunition dump was burning, and the varicolored antiaircraft projectiles were bursting in the continuous rattle and pop of the exploding 20-mm. stuff. The larger projectiles started to explode as the heat increased, and gave the impression of a bombardment. I couldn't locate Archie Pelkey, but later I found he had advanced on the burning munitions dump, thinking it was a fight.

"There wasn't nobody there, Papa," he said; "it was just a lot of ammunition burning."

"Don't go off by yourself," I said. "How did you know we didn't want to roll?"

"Okay, Papa. Sorry, Papa. I understand, Papa. Only, Mr. Hemingway, I went off with *Frère*—the one who is my brother—because I thought he said there was a fight."

"Oh, hell!" I said. "You've been ruined by guerrillas."

We ran through the road where the munitions dump was exploding, with Archie, who has bright red hair, six years of regular Army, four words of French, a missing front tooth, and a *Frère* in a guerrilla outfit, laughing heartily at the noise the big stuff was making as it blew.

"Sure is popping off, Papa," he shouted. His freckled face was completely happy. "They say this Paris is quite a town, Papa. You ever been into it?"

"Yeah."

We were going downhill now, and I knew that road and what we would see when we made the next turn.

"*Frère*, he was telling me something about it while the

column was held up, but I couldn't make it out," Archie said. "All I could make out was it must be a hell of a place. Something about he was going to *Paname*, too. This place hasn't got anything to do with Panama, has it?"

"No, Arch," I said, "the French call it *Paname* when they love it very much."

"I see," Archie said. "*Compris.* Just like something you might call a girl that wouldn't be her right name. Right?"

"Right."

"I couldn't make out what the hell *Frère* was saying," Archie said. "I guess it's like they call me Jim. Everybody in the outfit calls me Jim, and my name is Archie."

"Maybe they like you," I said.

"They're a good outfit," Archie said. "Best outfit I ever been with. No discipline. Got to admit that. Drinking all the time. Got to admit that. But plenty fighting outfit. Nobody gives a damn if they get killed or not. *Compris?*"

"Yeah," I said. I couldn't say anything more then, because I had a funny choke in my throat and I had to clean my glasses because there now, below us, gray and always beautiful, was spread the city I love best in all the world.

*Collier's*, October 7, 1944

# *Morts pour la Patrie*

by Irwin Shaw

ON THE WALL of the Tuileries, where the Rue de Rivoli joins the Place de la Concorde, there are seven small plaques bearing the names of six men and one woman who died there on August 25th a year ago, the day of the liberation of Paris, fighting the Germans entrenched behind the stone walls of the Ministry of Marine. Today Parisians stop for a moment and look reflectively at the names of Georges Bailly, student of pharmacy, Madeleine Brinet, nurse, Guy Le-Comte, aged twenty-one, and the others, *morts pour la Patrie*, and small wreaths and little pots of flowers decorate the base of the wall where their blood was spilled last summer. "This is the day the war should end," a G.I. of the Twelfth Regiment of the Fourth Division, the first large American unit to enter the city, said on that August 25th. And, looking at the city now, reading the squabbling newspapers, listening to the vague, hurt rhetoric of the politicians along the left bank, seeing the endless, cynical manipulations of the all-embracing black market, hearing the ungenerous mutterings in some quarters against the Americans and the equally unfair mutterings in other quarters against the French, you remember the ripe tide of courage, hope, and gratitude on which we entered the city a year ago and you feel that if history followed any logical or artistic form, the G.I. was completely right as he rolled through the flowers and the wine and the waving girls into the sentimental capital of the world. Recently, as I looked at the plaques on the wall, I felt that the world should return, by an act of will, to its great days. There should not be merely the formal celebration of the anniversary but an attempt by all who were involved to relive the actions, the fears, and the emotions of the ennobling day of triumph.

\*     \*     \*

On August 25, 1944, I was in a Signal Corps camera unit that was attached to the Twelfth Regiment for the day. The unit was made up of two cameramen, a driver, and myself, all of us privates or pfcs. Our jeep was banked with flowers, the gift of the people of the little towns on our route to Paris, and we had a small store of tomatoes and apples and bottles of wine that had been tossed to us as we slowly made our way through the crowds that tore down the barricades that lay in our path. As we came to a halt in the square before Notre Dame, a boy in the truck ahead of us looked up at the spires and said, wonderingly, "And one month ago I was in Bensonhurst."

German prisoners kept going by in droves, in the custody of grinning F.F.I. men, but aside from receiving a few loud, juicy insults from livelier members of the crowds that seemed to flood every street in Paris and having to submit to hearing the "Marseillaise" sung fifteen times an hour, they were not harmed. Among the prisoners, there were many high-ranking officers of the Paris garrison, in pretty uniforms and trying to walk slowly and appear dignified. They were having a hard time of it. It is much easier to appear dignified when surrendering to soldiers in the presence of other soldiers than in the middle of a city full of voluble, newly liberated citizens, mostly women, who have hated you for four years and who spend half their time kissing your conquerors and the other half devising means of breaking through the ranks and taking a quick swipe at the highest officer in your column.

From the direction of the Opéra came the sudden sound of artillery fire. You got to feel that the sound of guns was quite natural and right out in the country, but it always seemed heavy and ominous and strange in a city, especially one bedecked with flags and whose entire population seemed to be on the streets celebrating. We drove up the right bank of the Seine toward the sound of the firing. The streets suddenly were empty, and somewhere, between one block and another, the holiday was ended and the war re-begun.

We stopped our jeep near the Louvre, and, leaving the driver and one cameraman there, the other cameraman — Pfc Philip Drell, of Chicago — and I went on foot toward the Rue de Rivoli. Some tanks of the Second French Armored Division were attacking the Ministry of Marine, at the far end of the Rue de Rivoli, and now and then answering machine-gun fire swept down the long, open, empty boulevard. At each street intersection, hundreds of Parisians stood in little groups behind the protection of the buildings. Occasionally a braver or more curious member of the crowd would dart out for a quick look at the action at the end of the street and come back and report, and one gentleman established himself on the sidewalk behind a very slender lamppost, which he obviously felt afforded him cover, and kept a pair of binoculars trained at the contest, regardless of the bullets that whizzed past him. Several French jeeps sped by and were applauded as they passed each intersection, much the way a favorite pitcher is applauded as he comes in from the bull pen to relieve a faltering teammate in a tight spot at the Polo Grounds.

Hugging the sides of the buildings, Drell and I made our way to a store that had been converted into an F.F.I. first-aid station. There was desultory sniping in the back streets in the neighborhood, and F.F.I. volunteer nurses, carrying bloody litters, kept swooping out onto the bullet-swept Rue de Rivoli to bring back wounded. Dressed in long white smocks, waving large white flags with red crosses on them, running in an awkward, crowded, up-and-down, womanly way, they looked like a group of distracted sea gulls as they rushed back and forth. A wounded German was marched down the street by two cocky F.F.I. boys. The German had been hit in the side, and there was a wide, spreading stain of blood on his uniform and his face was drained and pale, but he somehow made it under his own power to the door of the aid station. A Senegalese, who had been fighting a private war of his own up a back street, came through the crowd with a shattered hand streaming blood, dragging his rifle in his good hand, an abstracted, absent expression on his face as he stared at his wound.

Abruptly one of the tanks that had been firing at the sand-bagged Ministry broke off, turned, and raced at top speed, lurching from side to side, its engine roaring, its treads sparking, down toward us. As it approached each intersection, there was the inevitable hearty round of applause, which suddenly stopped dead as soon as the tank had passed. The top of the tank was open and the tank commander was half out of the hatch, his face gaunt and strained, his eyes wildly staring straight ahead. As he passed us, some of the people around us started to applaud. Then they stopped, too. In the rear plating of the tank, there was a large, neat round hole and from the hole a fierce spurt of fire was whipping back. The tank swept crazily down the street and disappeared. I am not sure what happened to it, but the next day a sergeant in command of another tank in the Second French Armored Division told me that one of the tanks in his company had been hit the day before and all five of the crew had been burned to death, and it may have been the one I saw.

There were three or four huge columns of smoke staining the sky in the distance, and I told Drell that I thought we ought to move closer and get to a high vantage point from which we could take some pictures. A Frenchman standing in the doorway of the first-aid station overheard me and told us, in English, that he'd take us to a good spot. Crouched over, the three of us darted out across the Rue de Rivoli and went down a side street that was completely empty. "Watch the windows," he warned us. "The snipers keep moving from window to window." We watched the windows, with the old, uncomfortable feeling, which you had in any town where there were still snipers, that buildings are made with a ridiculously extravagant number of windows. The Frenchman offered to carry Drell's carbine, so that he would have both hands free for his camera. "Ah," the Frenchman said, admiringly fondling the weapon as we walked close to the sides of the buildings, "it is very handsome. So *légère*. Could you give it to me?" We explained that we could not donate carbines at random to the civilian population of France, and he sighed regretfully.

A door opened and a small bareheaded man with an F.F.I. armband popped out of a building in front of us. He was carrying a pistol in one hand and a German helmet in the other and he was doing a jerky, hopping little dance. The helmet had a bullet hole in it and it was full of brains and blood. "I got him," he said happily, in French, dancing on the pavement. "I got the last pig in the building. Take my picture." We took his picture, as he jigged up and down excitedly, waving the helmet, and he popped back into the building.

We followed our guide into a little square, along one side of which ran a building with an arcade in front of it. On one of the pillars of the arcade a crude red cross had been painted. We ran into the building and I saw that it was a theatre. As we went up the stairs, I saw, too, that the lobby had been transformed into a crude hospital and that there were about thirty wounded lying in litters and on blankets on the floor. Our guide explained that he was an actor and that he had played here. "This is the Comédie-Française," he said. He stopped on the steps to impress us further. "It is the greatest theatre in France."

"Yes," I said, "I know." Outside the sound of the fighting grew stronger and I pointed up toward the roof to show him I was impatient to get there. He resumed climbing.

"You don't understand," he said. "It plays the classics of French dramatic literature. The greatest plays in the world." He stopped again to make this explanation.

"Yes," I said. "I know. Let's get to the roof."

We climbed some more, past the busts of the great actors and actresses of France that adorn each landing of the stairway. "You don't understand," he said. "This is the most famous theatre in the world." He stopped and lectured me from above. There were several bursts of machine-gun fire about four hundred yards away. "The greatest actors of the modern theatre play here—"

"Yes, yes, I understand," I said, gently trying to push him upward. "I know all about the Comédie-Française. I myself write plays," I said, in an attempt to settle the issue and get to the roof.

"A playwright!" he said, and he beamed with pleasure. "An American playwright! Wonderful!" He shook my hand and started down. "You must come downstairs and meet the artists."

I stopped him. There was a fury of firing outside, as though some new crisis had been reached. "Later," I promised him. "After we take our pictures."

Reluctantly he turned around and led us up to the roof. The roofs of Paris, seen from the top of the Comédie-

Française, seemed dangerously bare and quiet. Drell took his pictures with the fussy, lens-adjusting deliberation that is so exasperating in cameramen at moments like that, and we were sniped at once as he finished, the bullet making a nasty, sudden whistle between us. We went down the steps to the floor below, where it was safe. Drell reloaded his camera, and the Frenchman said of the sniper, "It missed by a good deal. Undoubtedly it was a woman." He was the only man I met in the war who could tell the sex of the firer of a gun by the whistle of the bullet as it passed him.

We started down the stairs again and the Frenchman looked in at various offices for artists to whom he wished to introduce me. But all the offices were empty. "Ah, they are all downstairs," he said. "There are a lot of wounded."

We went down to the lobby. There was a smell of antiseptic and a slight smell of ether, and under floodlights in one corner of the large, low room, an operation was taking place. Strong beams of sunlight, with the dust dancing in them, broke into the gloom at several places. Half-naked men were being helped toward the doctors and in a corner lay two bodies wrapped in French flags. Here and there, from one of the men lying on the floor in rows, there came a groan, and the nurses, of whom there were many, trotted busily among them. The nurses, the Frenchman said, were all actresses, most of them from the Comédie-Française company. They were very pretty and dressed in light, soft dresses, and the effect, with the sharp contrasts of the light and shadow, and the white gleam of the wounded bodies, and the piles of bloody bandages and the two dead men in the flags, and the pretty young girls carrying basins and morphine syringes, was that of a painting by Goya for whom the models had been picked by Samuel Goldwyn.

Everybody was very busy and I told our guide that the introductions could wait for another day. A tall, gray-haired man with his sleeves rolled up, who seemed to be in charge, came over and asked, "Are you Americans?"

"Yes," I said.

"Please come with me," he said. He took me by the arm and led me over to the corner where the dead were lying. He bent over and pulled back the flags. The dead were in O.D.s and had been recently killed. One of them was a very young blond boy who had been shot through the temple—a small, exact, round wound from which the blood still seeped out onto the stone floor under his thin, handsome, sunburned, healthy-looking face.

"Are they Americans or French?" the gray-haired man asked me.

I looked. Both the dead were wearing the little enamel badge of the French Army (which had not been seen in Paris until that day) over their right breasts. "French," I said.

The gray-haired man put his hand under the blond boy's armpits and half picked him up and shook him very roughly. "You're all right, *mon copain*," he said, almost smiling. "You're all right." He shook him again and again like a man joking roughly with an old friend in a barracks room. "You're all right." He let the dead boy drop to the floor, smacked him vigorously and almost vulgarly on the shoulder, as though he refused to admit the fact of death, and turned away to his work. I stood looking for a moment at the blond boy and the hole in his temple. He had a streak of rouge on his cheek, like all the soldiers in Paris that day, and there was a dark wine stain down the front of his khaki wool shirt.

Drell and I made our way back toward the Rue de Rivoli. The firing had stopped and we walked down the middle of the street. From all the side streets, thousands of people, seeing us walking unharmed and taking it as a signal of victory, flocked out, applauding, cheering, kissing us, men and women alike, indiscriminately. Of all the hundreds of people who kissed me that day, including, I imagine, some very pretty girls, I remember most clearly a small, fat, middle-aged man—one of the few fat men I saw in Paris—who held me close and kissed me with all the fervor of a husband returned to a loved wife after five years of war.

The smell of perfume from the crowd, now so closely packed in the street down which fifteen minutes before the doomed tank had wavered, was overpoweringly strong, and the variety of rich, sweet odors, as kiss followed kiss, was dazzling and unreal to a soldier who had been living in the field, in mud and dust, for two months. One slender, sharp-eyed

woman came up to me and touched my shoulder affection-
ately but appraisingly, like the man who guesses your weight
at Coney Island. "Ah," she said, smiling pleasantly and without envy, satisfied now by touch as well as by sight that I was
really as large as I looked, "ah, you have eaten well."

The driver and the other cameraman were waiting with the
jeep. They looked very neat and clean, and their hair had been
combed. "What happened to you?" I asked. "An old lady
came out of one of the buildings," the driver said, "and
looked at us and said, 'You're awfully dirty,' and went in and
came back with a basin and pitcher of water and a cake of
soap and a towel and made us wash ourselves. Then she went
away."

We drove slowly through the swarming crowds, over
broken glass, past still-burning German tanks of the recent
battlefield, to the Place de la Concorde, now filling with
people. A thin, fair little woman and her husband came over
to me. The woman said she was American, born in Syracuse.
Her husband was French and she had been in Paris throughout the occupation. Her eyes were shining and she and her
husband kept smiling widely, no matter what the conversation was about. "You're the first American soldier I've seen,"
she said, and started to lean over to kiss my cheek. Then she
checked herself and turned to her husband. "May I kiss him?"
she asked, a little doubtfully. "Certainly," the husband said
gravely. She kissed me on both cheeks.

Suddenly, in the little grove of trees at the end of the Place
de la Concorde near the bridge across the Seine, we saw the
puffs of explosions, small mortar shells bursting at regular intervals. The great square emptied quickly, except for the inevitable F.F.I. Red Cross workers, who ran, swooping, toward
the trees. Some French tanks took up positions along the
river, and one of them, at the approach to the bridge that
leads directly to the steps of the Chambre des Députés, on
the left bank, began to fire sporadically into the huge, pillared
building. Some F.F.I. riflemen appeared and took cover behind the balustrade along the river and added their fire to that
of the tank. A rickety old truck, with an open wooden body
filled with F.F.I. men who had mounted a thirty-calibre machine gun in makeshift fashion, drove furiously to one side of

the square and stopped under a slender little tree, which, I suppose, the driver hopefully imagined concealed them completely. All the F.F.I. men except the machine gunner dropped off and hid behind the monuments with which the Place de la Concorde had been thoughtfully provided. The gunner stood up at his weapon and let loose a fierce, uninterrupted stream of bullets across the river at the august side of the Chambre des Députés. The calmer heads among his comrades recognized the wastefulness of this one-man barrage against thick stone walls and began to group around him, remonstrating. He kept firing with one hand and waving them away with the other, arguing bitterly, until three of them jumped onto the truck, dragged him off, and installed a more conservative machine gunner.

A jeep drove slowly up to the tank, which was still firing, and a young French lieutenant got out and stood, motionless and arrogantly exposed, next to it, directing its fire. It was quite brave, because the mortar fire was dropping unpredictably; he was the sort of lieutenant any soldier crouched behind cover remembers and hates. A nondescript collection of people had taken shelter behind the great stone block at the approach to the bridge, including four or five unarmed members of the F.F.I. and a young girl in a white dress who was holding a bicycle. Off to the right, on our bank of the Seine, a pretty little yacht, which Renoir might have used as a model for his river-outing paintings, burned brightly. A German prisoner was brought up and placed, with a large white flag, on the tank. A French officer took up a position ahead of the tank, and Drell left me to join him. The tank started across the bridge, with the prisoner waving the flag frantically and the officer and Drell walking ahead of it, to demand the surrender of the Germans in the Chambre des Députés. The mortar shells started up again, first hitting in the river, then finding the bridge, finally breaking off a lamppost and wounding several people five yards from the protecting stone block. The officer pulled the German prisoner off the tank and he and the officer and Drell ran across the bridge to the other side, while the tank moved back. The three of them stood there in front of the Chambre des Députés, the prisoner monotonously waving his flag while the mortar fire continued for another ten minutes, roaming along the bridge. Then I saw Drell and the Frenchman run up the steps of the Chambre des Députés and disappear into it. I moved about fifty yards downstream, to where an F.F.I. man was firing his rifle six times a minute at the unresponding official architecture on the other side of the river. A French tank was in position there, its gun trained on the Chambre but not firing. The hatch was open, and a tough, curly-haired French tankman was standing up in it, completely exposed, staring at himself in a small pocket mirror. He noticed me eying him from down below. He shrugged. *"C'est bizarre, n'est-ce pas?"* he said, and turned back to admiring himself in the mirror.

Every once in a while a bullet passed over our heads, but an old sedan loaded with F.F.I. men was able to dash unmolested across the bridge and I followed on foot. When I got to the Chambre des Députés, I found that the three or four hundred Germans there had just surrendered. Drell and the French officer had become separated, and the Germans had tried to surrender to Drell, who was unarmed but American. Drell insisted that he couldn't accept the surrender, and got the Germans to agree to let him take pictures of them surrendering to the French. Negotiations were carried out, on Drell's part in Yiddish, the nearest thing to a common tongue he and the Germans could find.

After the surrender, the Germans drew up in ranks in the courtyard, their arms stacked at one side. (They had left a shambles inside the handsome rooms—a deep litter of sardine tins, used cartridges, biscuit boxes, and empty champagne bottles all over the regal red plush.) A lot of correspondents and photographers had arrived, and the scramble for souvenirs was lively. Suddenly we heard the sound of a shell approaching, the sickening, unmistakable whistle of a shell that is going to land right near you. We all hit the gravel, face down, trying in the awful, traditional way to burrow into the earth even one quarter of an inch before the explosion found us. The noise of the approaching shell grew louder and louder, keeping up for an interminably long time, longer than any artillery sound I had ever heard before. I lay there with the certainty that this was the one that was going to land directly on the exposed back of my neck. Then the noise suddenly stopped. There was no explosion. After a moment, I looked up. All the French and all the Americans were on the ground, fingers and faces deep in the gravel, and all the prisoners were standing absolutely erect, laughing. Every outfit in every army has a mimic who can produce the most deadly, realistic whistle of an approaching shell through his teeth. The captured Germans were no exception, and the comedian had just put on the most successful performance of his career. Drell and I got up sheepishly, dusted ourselves off, collected our loot—Lugers, belts, cameras, and a bicycle—and made our way back to our jeep, where the other camera-man, a very handsome twenty-year-old boy with a deep South Carolina accent, was happily jotting down the addresses of three or four dozen girls who were grouped around the jeep.

We drove off, with a cluster of girls hanging onto the jeep, and found the Hôtel Scribe, where we had been told to re-port with our film. Outside the hotel, inundating the Army vehicles there, were hundreds of Parisians, singing, shaking hands, asking questions, examining jeeps and guns, extending invitations, weeping, kissing the soldiers, kissing the corre-spondents, kissing each other.

As we were unloading our jeep, a Frenchman came up to me and shook my hand. He was dressed with painful neatness in old, threadbare clothes and he seemed more shaken than exhilarated by the events of the day.

"How long does it take a letter to get to the United States?" he asked me in heavily accented English.

"About ten days," I said.

"Where do you live?" he asked.

"New York," I told him.

"I have a sister in Brooklyn," he said. "I have not seen her for nine years. She has not heard from me in four years." He looked around nervously, leaned over, and spoke in a whisper. "I am a Jew. I wonder if it is possible for you to write her for me through your mails."

"Certainly," I said, and I wrote down the address of his sister in Brooklyn. "Now," I said, "what do you want to tell her?"

He looked at me a little dazedly, as though stunned and

frightened by the magnitude of the opportunity being presented to him. He stared around him at the celebrating girls and wrinkled his brow, concentrating intensely. "Tell her," he said, "tell her I'm alive." He shook my hand and went off.

Drell and I went into the hotel and grandly registered for two large rooms, knowing that the day of the pfc in Paris would be short and determined to make the most of it. There was no hot water, but I luxuriated in the bath, nevertheless, listening to the voice of the crowd down below, an endless swelling mixture of cheers, song, and high, feminine laughter. As I lay there, washed of the grit and heat of the long day, listening to the celebrating crowd on the streets below, it was possible to feel that a new age of courage, gallantry, and gratitude was beginning in Europe.

*The New Yorker*, August 25, 1945

# Daily News Writer Sees Man Slain at Her Side in Hail of Lead

by Helen Kirkpatrick

PARIS, Saturday, Aug. 26. — Paris' celebration of its liberation was very nearly converted into a massacre by the Fascist militia's attempt to eliminate French leaders and to start riots during the afternoon's ceremonies.

All Paris streamed into the center of the town — to the Arc de Triomphe, the Place de la Concorde, along the Champs Elysees, at the Hotel de Ville and to Notre Dame Cathedral.

Gens. De Gaulle, Koenig, Leclerc and Juin led the procession from the Etoile to Notre Dame amid scenes of tremendous enthusiasm.

Lt. John Reinhart, U.S.N., and I could not get near enough to the Arc de Triomphe to see the parade, so we turned back to Notre Dame where a Te Deum service was to be held. We stood in the door of the cathedral awaiting the arrival of the French generals at 4 o'clock this afternoon and were about to fight our way through the crowd to leave when they began arriving.

French tanks were drawn up around the square in front of the cathedral. Crowds pushed desperately to get nearer the church, which was already filled with the families of French Forces of the Interior men who had fallen during the Battle of Paris. We stood beside the police who formed a lane into the cathedral.

The generals' car arrived on the dot of 4:15. As they stepped from the car, we stood at salute and at that very moment a revolver shot rang out. It seemed to come from behind one of Notre Dame's gargoyles. Within a split second a machine gun opened from a nearby room — one behind the Hotel de Ville. It sprayed the pavement at my feet. The generals entered the church with 40-odd people pressing from behind to find shelter.

I found myself inside in the main aisle, a few feet behind the generals. People were cowering behind pillars. Someone tried to pull me down.

The generals marched slowly down the main aisle, their hats in their hands. People in the main body were pressed back near the pillars. I was pushed forward down the aisle.

Suddenly an automatic opened up from behind us—it came from behind the pipes of Notre Dame's organ. From the clerestory above other shots rang out and I saw a man ducking behind a pillar above. Beside me F.F.I. men and the police were shooting.

For one flashing instant it seemed that a great massacre was bound to take place as the cathedral reverberated with the sound of guns. Outside, machine guns were rattling. There was a sudden blaze and a machine gun sprayed the center aisle, flecking the tiles and chipping the pillars to my left.

Time seemed to have no meaning. Spontaneously a crowd of widows and bereaved burst forth into the Te Deum as the generals stood bareheaded before the altar.

It seemed hours but it was only a few minutes, perhaps 10, when the procession came back down the aisle. I think the shooting was still going on but, like those around me, I could only stand amazed at the coolness, imperturbability and apparent unconcern of French generals and civilians alike who walked as though nothing had happened. Gen. Koenig, smiling, leaned across and shook my hand.

I fell in behind them and watched them walk deliberately out and into their cars. A machine gun was still blazing from a nearby roof.

Once outside, one could hear shooting all along the Seine. From F.F.I. friends and from Americans I learned later that shooting at the Hotel de Ville, the Tuilleries, the Arc de Triomphe and along the Elysees had started at exactly the same moment.

It was a clearly planned attempt probably designed to kill as many of the French authorities as possible, to create panic and to start riots after which probably the mad brains of the militia, instigated by the Germans, hoped to retake Paris.

It failed for two reasons: First, the militia were such incredibly bad shots that they hit only onlookers in the crowd. Second, the French people did not panic, although all the elements to create a panic were there.

They say today that between 15 and 25 persons were wounded or killed in Notre Dame. I doubt it. I saw one man killed. He stood beside me in the main aisle. A woman behind me fainted, but otherwise the only other person I saw killed was the militiaman who was trapped by the police in the clerestory, and then shot by F.F.I. men from below.

Outside Notre Dame, when only Gen. Leclerc and his staff remained, I saw the police bringing three militiamen, dressed in gray flannels and sleeveless sweaters, from the cathedral.

I was told later that they had caught four there. As we drove past the Crillon, at the Place de la Concorde, they were bringing out a solitary German who apparently had begun shooting at 4:15 with the militia.

Political conflict there may and probably will be in France. But the moment when blood might have been shed on a very large scale was over by 4:30 this afternoon. The prestige of those French generals and the civilians with them is enormous—deservedly so.

Paris was never more beautiful than during the last hours of its fight for freedom Friday afternoon. Friday night it is a madhouse of celebration.

We came through the Porte d'Orleans with French tanks at 2 o'clock in the afternoon, through streets lined with wildly cheering people, heedless of the snipers who were lying low on rooftops and in cellars. We got as far as Boulevard Raspail when we had to turn back because of the fighting ahead.

The police took us in tow to the prefecture of the 6th district, where the honorary mayor of Paris, 70-year-old Henri Boussard, received us with formal dignity and tears.

He presented us to the police commissioner who organized the Paris police for the fight against the Germans. From the windows of the prefecture, St. Sulpice rose majestically in the afternoon sun.

Paris that night was still noisy but behind closed doors. Every few minutes a truck loaded with F.F.I. dashed down the boulevard blowing its horn continuously, and then snipers down at the corner of Raspail opened up. The Palais des Bourbon was burning and the flames made a lurid light.

Germans were still holding out, but Paris was free. Its freedom is heady and intoxicating.

*The Chicago Daily News*, August 26, 1944

# Nazi Mass Killing Laid Bare in Camp

by W. H. Lawrence

LUBLIN, Poland, Aug. 27 (Delayed)—I have just seen the most terrible place on the face of the earth—the German concentration camp at Maidanek, which was a veritable River Rouge for the production of death, in which it is estimated by Soviet and Polish authorities that as many as 1,500,000 persons from nearly every country in Europe were killed in the last three years.

I have been all through the camp, inspecting its hermetically sealed gas chambers, in which the victims were asphyxiated, and five furnaces in which the bodies were cremated, and I have talked with German officers attached to the camp, who admitted quite frankly that it was a highly systemized place for annihilation, although they, of course, denied any personal participation in the murders.

I have seen the skeletons of bodies the Germans did not have time to burn before the Red Army swept into Lublin on July 23, and I have seen such evidence as bone ash still in the furnaces and piled up beside them ready to be taken to near-by fields, on which it was scattered as fertilizer for cabbages.

I have been to Krempitski, ten miles to the east, where I saw three of ten opened mass graves and looked upon 368 partly decomposed bodies of men, women and children who had been executed individually in a variety of cruel and horrible means. In this forest alone, the authorities estimate, there are more than 300,000 bodies.

It is impossible for this correspondent to state with any certainty how many persons the Germans killed here. Many bodies unquestionably were burned and not nearly all the graves in this vicinity had been opened by the time I visited the scene.

But I have been in a wooden warehouse at the camp, approximately 150 feet long, in which I walked across literally tens of thousands of shoes spread across the floor like grain in a half-filled elevator. There I saw shoes of children as young as 1 year old. There were shoes of young and old men or women. Those I saw were all in bad shape—since the Germans used this camp not only to exterminate their victims, but also as a means of obtaining clothing for the German people—but some obviously had been quite expensive. At least one pair had come from America, for it bore a stamp, "Goodyear welt."

I have been through a warehouse in downtown Lublin in which I saw hundreds of suitcases and literally tens of thousands of pieces of clothing and personal effects of people who died here and I have had the opportunity of questioning a German officer, Herman Vogel, 42, of Millheim, who admitted that as head of the clothing barracks he had supervised the shipment of eighteen freightcar loads of clothing to Germany during a two-month period and that he knew it came from the bodies of persons who had been killed at Maidanek.

This is a place that must be seen to be believed. I have been present at numerous atrocity investigations in the Soviet Union, but never have I been confronted with such complete evidence, clearly establishing every allegation made by those investigating German crimes.

After inspection of Maidanek, I am now prepared to believe any story of German atrocities, no matter how savage, cruel and depraved.

As one of a group of nearly thirty foreign correspondents brought to Poland on the invitation of the Polish Committee of National Liberation, I also had an opportunity to sit with the special mixed Soviet-Polish Atrocities Investigation Commission, headed by Vice Chairman Andrey Witos of the Polish Committee, and to question six witnesses, including three German officers—Vogel, Theodore Shoclen and Tanton Earness—who will probably face trial for their part in the administration of the death camp.

For the correspondents, the commission's prosecutor, a Pole, summed up the evidence taken. He said it had been decided that these Germans bore the main responsibility for the crimes committed at Maidanek and in the Krempitski Forest:

> General Globcnik, Gestapo and SS chief of the Lublin district.
>
> Governor Wendler of the Lublin district, described as a distant relative of Heinrich Himmler.
>
> Former Governor Zoerner of the Lublin district.
>
> Lisake, who had charge of all the concentration camps in the Lublin district.
>
> General Weiss, who was in charge of the Maidanek camp.
>
> Company Commander Anton Tumann, who at one time had charge of Maidanek.
>
> Mussfeld, who was in charge of the crematorium.
>
> Klopmann, who was chief of the German political department in the Lublin district.

It is impossible in the space here available to relate details of all the evidence of crimes we saw and heard, but for the benefit of those who have not had the opportunity to see with their own eyes, here is the story as it came from the lips of a German who had been a prisoner in Maidanek and was left behind by the retreating Germans. He is Hans Staub, a 31-year-old, tall, husky man with close-cropped hair, who had been imprisoned for engaging in blackmarket meat operations in Germany.

Despite German orders that prisoners were to keep out of the crematorium area, he managed to slip inside the brick fence one day and secrete himself about the time a truck loaded with about a dozen persons drove up. Among them was a Polish woman he estimated to have been 28 or 29 years old. The prisoners were guarded by tommy-gunners, who ordered them to alight from the truck and undress. The woman refused and this enraged Mussfeld, who beat her. She screamed and Mussfeld lost his temper, shouting, "I'll burn you alive."

According to Staub, Mussfeld then directed two attendants to grab the woman and bind her arms and legs. They then threw her on an iron stretcher, still clothed, and pushed her body into the oven.

"I heard one loud scream, saw her hair flame and then she disappeared into the furnace," Staub said.

According to several witnesses, the peak death production day for Maidanek was Nov. 3, 1943, when for some reason not made clear the Germans executed a total of 18,000 to 20,000 prisoners by a variety of means, including shooting, hanging and gassing.

This is Maidanek as I saw it. It is situated about a mile and a half from the middle of Lublin on the highroad between Chelm and Cracow. As one approaches he gets a view of the concentration camp almost identical with those pictured in American motion pictures. The first sight is a twelve-foot-high double barbed-wire fence, which was charged with electricity.

Inside you see group after group of trim green buildings, not unlike the barracks in an Army camp in the United States. There were more than 200 such buildings. Outside the fence there were fourteen high machine-gun turrets and at one edge were kennels for more than 200 especially trained, savage man-tracking dogs used to pursue escaped prisoners. The whole camp covered an area of 670 acres.

As we entered the camp the first place at which we stopped obviously was the reception center and it was near here that one entered the bath house. Here Jews, Poles, Russians and in fact representatives of a total of twenty-two nationalities entered and removed their clothing, after which they bathed at seventy-two showers and disinfectants were applied.

Sometimes they went directly into the next room, which was hermetically sealed with apertures in the roof, down which the Germans threw opened cans of "Zyklon B," a poison gas consisting of prussic acid crystals, which were a light blue chalky substance. This produced death quickly. Other prisoners were kept for long periods; the average, we were told, was about six weeks.

Near the shower house were two other death chambers fitted for either Zyklon gas or carbon monoxide. One of them was seventeen meters square and there, we were told, the Germans executed 100 to 110 persons at once. Around the floor of the room ran a steel pipe with an opening for carbon monoxide to escape at every twenty-five centimeters.

We were told the victims always received a bath in advance of execution because the hot water opened the pores and generally improved the speed with which the poison gas took effect. There were glass-covered openings in these death chambers so the Germans could watch the effect on their victims and determine when the time had come to remove their bodies. We saw opened and unopened cans of Zyklon gas that bore German labels.

About a mile from the gas chambers was the huge crematorium. Built of brick, it looked and was operated not unlike a small blast furnace for a steel mill, operating with coal as fuel fanned by an electrically operated blower. There were five openings on each side—on one side the bodies were loaded in and on the other ashes were removed and the fire built up. Each furnace held five bodies at a time.

We were told it took fifteen minutes to fill each furnace and about ten to twelve minutes for the bodies to burn. It was estimated that the battery of furnaces had a capacity of 1,900 bodies a day.

Near the furnaces we saw a large number of partial and complete skeletons. Behind a brick enclosure near by were more than a score of bodies of persons who, we were told, had been killed by the Germans on the day the Red Army captured Lublin, which they did not have time to burn before fleeing.

Not far from the furnaces were a large number of earthenware urns, which investigating authorities said witnesses told them were used by the Germans for ashes of some of their victims, which they sold to families for prices ranging up to 2,500 marks.

We saw a concrete table near the furnace and asked its purpose. We were told the Germans laid the bodies of victims there just before cremation and knocked out gold teeth, which were salvaged. We were told that no bodies were accepted for cremation unless the chest bore a stamp certifying that it had been searched for gold teeth.

It is the purpose of the Polish Committee of National Liberation to keep the main parts of Maidanek just as it now exists as an exhibition of German brutality and cruelty for all posterity to see.

M. Witos struck the universal feeling of all who have seen
the camp when he expressed regret that the section of American and British public opinion that favors a soft peace with
the Germans will not have an opportunity in advance of the
peace conference to look at this plain evidence of the brutality
of the Germans practiced toward their victims.

Among the few Polish people whom we had an opportunity
to talk there is a widespread sentiment for stronger means of
vengeance against the Germans, and the belief that some of
those directly responsible for Maidanek should be executed in
the terrible death camp they themselves erected.

*The New York Times*, August 30, 1944

# A Last Word

by Ernie Pyle

THIS final chapter is being written in the latter part of August, 1944; it is being written under an apple tree in a lovely green orchard in the interior of France. It could well be that the European war will be over and done with by the time you read this book. Or it might not. But the end is inevitable, and it cannot be put off for long. The German is beaten and he knows it.

It will seem odd when, at some given hour, the shooting stops and everything suddenly changes again. It will be odd to drive down an unknown road without that little knot of fear in your stomach; odd not to listen with animal-like alertness for the meaning of every distant sound; odd to have your spirit released from the perpetual weight that is compounded of fear and death and dirt and noise and anguish.

The end of the war will be a gigantic relief, but it cannot be a matter of hilarity for most of us. Somehow it would seem sacrilegious to sing and dance when the great day comes— there are so many who can never sing and dance again. The war in France has not been easy by any manner of means. True, it has gone better than most of us had hoped. And our casualties have been fewer than our military leaders had been willing to accept. But do not let anyone lead you to believe that they have been low. Many, many thousands of Americans have come to join the ones who already have slept in France for a quarter of a century.

For some of us the war has already gone on too long. Our feelings have been wrung and drained; they cringe from the effort of coming alive again. Even the approach of the end seems to have brought little inner elation. It has brought only a tired sense of relief.

I do not pretend that my own feeling is the spirit of our

273

armies. If it were, we probably would not have had the power to win. Most men are stronger. Our soldiers still can hate, or glorify, or be glad, with true emotion. For them death has a pang, and victory a sweet scent. But for me war has become a flat, black depression without highlights, a revulsion of the mind and an exhaustion of the spirit.

The war in France has been especially vicious because it was one of the last stands for the enemy. We have won because of many things. We have won partly because the enemy was weakened from our other battles. The war in France is our grand finale, but the victory here is the result of all the other victories that went before. It is the result of Russia, and the western desert, and the bombings, and the blocking of the sea. It is the result of Tunisia and Sicily and Italy; we must never forget or belittle those campaigns.

We have won because we have had magnificent top leadership, at home and in our Allies and with ourselves overseas. Surely America made its two perfect choices in General Eisenhower and General Bradley. They are great men—to me doubly great because they are direct and kind.

We won because we were audacious. One could not help but be moved by the colossus of our invasion. It was a bold and mighty thing, one of the epics of all history. In the emergency of war our nation's powers are unbelievable. The strength we have spread around the world is appalling even to those who make up the individual cells of that strength. I am sure that in the past two years I have heard soldiers say a thousand times, "If only we could have created all this energy for something good." But we rise above our normal powers only in times of destruction.

We have won this war because our men are brave, and because of many other things—because of Russia, and England, and the passage of time, and the gift of nature's materials. We did not win it because destiny created us better than all other peoples. I hope that in victory we are more grateful than we are proud. I hope we can rejoice in victory—but humbly. The dead men would not want us to gloat.

The end of one war is a great fetter broken from around our lives. But there is still another to be broken. The Pacific war may yet be long and bloody. Nobody can foresee, but it would be disastrous to approach it with easy hopes. Our next few months at home will be torn between the new spiritual freedom of half peace and the old grinding blur of half war. It will be a confusing period for us.

Thousands of our men will soon be returning to you. They have been gone a long time and they have seen and done and felt things you cannot know. They will be changed. They will have to learn how to adjust themselves to peace. Last night we had a violent electrical storm around our countryside. The storm was half over before we realized that the flashes and the crashings around us were not artillery but plain old-fashioned thunder and lightning. It will be odd to hear only thunder again. You must remember that such little things as that are in our souls, and will take time.

And all of us together will have to learn how to reassemble our broken world into a pattern so firm and so fair that another great war cannot soon be possible. To tell the simple truth, most of us over in France don't pretend to know the right answer. Submersion in war does not necessarily qualify a man to be the master of the peace. All we can do is fumble and try once more — try out of the memory of our anguish — and be as tolerant with each other as we can.

*Brave Men*, 1944

## "MY BUSINESS IS DRAWING": A CARTOONIST IN COMBAT, 1943–44

# Up Front

by Bill Mauldin

My business is drawing, not writing, and this text is pretty much background for the drawings. It is not a book about my personal life or experiences. I don't think that would be very interesting to anyone but myself.

During the three years I spent in the 45th Division, I was certain that it was not only the best division in the army, but that it *was* the army. Since then I have kicked around in more than fifteen other divisions, and I have found that the men in each of them are convinced that their division is the best and the only division. That's good. Esprit is the thing that holds armies together. But it puts people who write about the army on the spot.

In order to do the right job, you'd have to mention six other outfits if you talked of one, and if you mention one battalion in a regiment, you're going to hear from the other two battalions, and the same with the companies. That is why I have mentioned specific units and persons as little as possible in this book.

Since hanging around many different divisions, I've just about come to the conclusion that when 15,000 men from 48 states are put together in an outfit, their thinking and their actions are going to be pretty much like those of any other 15,000. Their efficiency and their accomplishments are altered to a certain extent by the abilities of their commanders, but the guys themselves are pretty much the same. I certainly have more affection for battered old outfits like the 34th, 3rd, 36th, 1st, 9th, 1st Armored, 2nd Armored, and my old 45th, which have been over here for two or three years and have fought through dozens of campaigns and major battles. I think they and the old divisions in the Pacific have carried the major portion of the burden. And yet when you go through the line companies in those outfits you find, as I did in my old company, only four or five men who have been through the whole war. The rest have died or been crippled. Most of the men in those companies have been over about as long as the fellows in the newer divisions, and they are no different.

I would like to thank the people who encouraged me to draw army cartoons at a time when the gag man's conception of the army was one of mean ole sergeants and jeeps which jump over mountains. They not only encouraged me, but I know that they also backed me up when the drawings did not meet with unanimous approval from high brass. Many of these friends have been brass themselves, and I'm afraid that sometimes the drawings bit the hands that fed them. I wish there were some way to repay these people, and if this book were about my own army life, I might be able to make them feel better.

But it isn't that kind of book, and about all I can say is

thanks to those I know about and many I don't know
about—soldiers, officers, and others—because they encouraged me to draw pictures of an army full of blunders and
efficiency, irritations and comradeship. But, most of all, full of
men who are able to fight a ruthless war against ruthless enemies, and still grin at themselves.

*"You'll get over it, Joe. Oncet I wuz gonna write a book
exposin' the army after th' war myself."*

I'm convinced that the infantry is the group in the army
which gives more and gets less than anybody else. I draw pictures for and about the dogfaces because I know what their
life is like and I understand their gripes. They don't get fancy
pay, they know their food is the worst in the army because
you can't whip up lemon pies or even hot soup at the front,
and they know how much of the burden they bear.

*"Must be a tough objective. Th' old man says we're
gonna have th' honor of liberatin' it."*

But there are some people who object to writers and artists
who consistently publicize one branch of the army. They say
that such exclusive attention lowers the morale of the
branches not publicized, and that it makes for self-pity in the
branch whose troubles are aired. Maybe they are right. But I
understand the infantry well enough to know that very few
combat men are going to pity themselves more because their
gripes are printed in a newspaper.

I felt I was in a pretty good spot to judge any effect the
cartoons might have had on the morale of the rear echelon,
since a lot of my time in the rear was spent pestering ordnance companies to work on my jeep, and bumming cigarettes and condensed milk from ration dumps. The guys back

there never showed any inclination to lynch me—as a matter of fact, they had heard I was in disfavor with a general, and when I came around for a new carburetor jet or more smokes they gave me stories about conditions in the rear, and ideas for cartoons.

*"Tell th' old man I'm sittin' up wit' two sick friends."*

I haven't tried to picture this war in a big, broad-minded way. I'm not old enough to understand what it's all about, and I'm not experienced enough to judge its failures and successes. My reactions are those of a young guy who has been exposed to some of it, and I try to put those reactions in my drawings. Since I'm a cartoonist, maybe I can be funny after the war, but nobody who has seen this war can be cute about it while it's going on. The only way I can try to be a

*"Them wuz his exack words—'I envy th' way you dog-*
*faces git first pick o' wimmen an' likker in towns.'"*

little funny is to make something out of the humorous situations which come up even when you don't think life could be
any more miserable. It's pretty heavy humor, and it doesn't
seem funny at all sometimes when you stop and think it
over.

Since my drawings have been kicking around in some papers in the States, a lot of dogfaces over here have been very
surprised, and so have I. Some of the drawings are meaningless even in Rome, Naples, or Paris. But the guys are glad and
so am I, even if we are still surprised. If it means that people
are interested in seeing how the dogfaces look at themselves,
that's swell. If it means that people at home are beginning to
understand these strange, mud-caked creatures who fight the

*"Ya won't have any trouble pickin' up our trail after th'
first five miles, Joe."*

war, and are beginning to understand their minds and their
own type of humor, that's even more swell, because it means
that the dogfaces themselves are beginning to be appreciated
a little by their countrymen.

They are very different now. Don't let anybody tell you
they aren't. They need a lot of people speaking for them and
telling about them — not speaking for fancy bonuses and extra
privileges. You can't pay in money for what they have done.
They need people telling about them so that they will be
taken back into their civilian lives and given a chance to be
themselves again.

One of the foremost objections to a steady portrayal of the
troubles and lives of combat infantrymen and those who work

*"I'm d'most valooble man in d'third wave. Ever'body give me their cigarettes t' carry in me shirt pocket."*

with them—medical aid men, combat engineers, artillery observers, and others—has been that these guys are going to feel that the nation owes them a living, and that they will become "social problems." This feeling has been so strong in some places that veteran combat men are looked at askance by worried and peaceable citizens. That's a sad thing for a guy who was sent off to war with a blare of patriotic music, and it's really not necessary.

There will be a few problems, undoubtedly, because combat soldiers are made up of ordinary citizens—bricklayers, farmers, and musicians. There will be good ones and some bad ones. But the vast majority of combat men are going to be no problem at all. They are so damned sick and tired of having their noses rubbed in a stinking war that their only ambition will be to forget it.

And there are so few men in the army who have really gone through hell that when they return they will be soaked up and absorbed by their various communities and they couldn't be problems if they wanted to. There are millions who have been inconvenienced. There are millions who have done a great and hard job. But so far there are only a few hundred thousand who have lived through misery, suffering, and death for endless 168-hour weeks and, as I said, they are going to be too tired and sick of it to bother anybody who might be worrying about their becoming problems.

They don't need pity, because you don't pity brave men— men who are brave because they fight while they are scared to death. They simply need bosses who will give them a little time to adjust their minds and their hands, and women who are faithful to them, and friends and families who stay by them until they are the same guys who left years ago. No set of laws or Bill of Rights for returning veterans of combat can do that job. Only their own people can do it. So it is very important that these people know and understand combat men.

Perhaps the American soldier in combat has an even tougher job than the combat soldiers of his allies. Most of his allies have lost their homes or had friends and relatives killed by the enemy. The threat to their countries and lives has been direct, immediate, and inescapable. The American has lost nothing to the Germans, so his war is being fought for more farfetched reasons.

He didn't learn to hate the Germans until he came over here. He didn't realize the immense threat that faced his nation until he saw how powerful and cruel and ruthless the German nation was. He learned that the Nazi is simply a symbol of the German people, as his father learned that the Kaiser was only a symbol. So now he hates Germans and he fights them, but the fact still remains that his brains and not his emotions are driving him.

Many celebrities and self-appointed authorities have returned from quick tours of war zones (some of them getting

*"Able Fox Five to Able Fox. I got a target but ya gotta
be patient."*

within hearing distance of the shooting) and have put out
their personal theories to batteries of photographers and reporters. Some say the American soldier is the same clean-cut
young man who left his home; others say morale is sky-high
at the front because everybody's face is shining for the great
Cause.

They are wrong. The combat man isn't the same clean-cut
lad because you don't fight a kraut by Marquis of Queens-
berry rules. You shoot him in the back, you blow him apart
with mines, you kill or maim him the quickest and most effective way you can with the least danger to yourself. He does
the same to you. He tricks you and cheats you, and if you

*"Run it up th' mountain agin, Joe. It ain't hot enough."*

don't beat him at his own game you don't live to appreciate your own nobleness.

But you don't become a killer. No normal man who has smelled and associated with death ever wants to see any more of it. In fact, the only men who are even going to want to bloody noses in a fist fight after this war will be those who want people to think they were tough combat men, when they weren't. The surest way to become a pacifist is to join the infantry.

I don't make the infantryman look noble, because he couldn't look noble even if he tried. Still there is a certain nobility and dignity in combat soldiers and medical aid men with dirt in their ears. They are rough and their language gets coarse because they live a life stripped of convention and

*"Nonsense. S-2 reported that machine gun silenced hours
ago. Stop wiggling your fingers at me."*

niceties. Their nobility and dignity come from the way they
live unselfishly and risk their lives to help each other. They are
normal people who have been put where they are, and whose
actions and feelings have been molded by their circumstances.
There are gentlemen and boors; intelligent ones and stupid
ones; talented ones and inefficient ones. But when they
are all together and they are fighting, despite their bitching and griping and goldbricking and mortal fear, they are
facing cold steel and screaming lead and hard enemies,
and they are advancing and beating the hell out of the
opposition.

They wish to hell they were someplace else, and they wish
to hell they would get relief. They wish to hell the mud was
dry and they wish to hell their coffee was hot. They want to

go home. But they stay in their wet holes and fight, and then they climb out and crawl through minefields and fight some more.

*"Gimme my canteen back, Willie. I see ya soakin' yer beard full."*

I know that the pictures in this book have offended some people, and I don't blame a lot of them. Some men in the army love their profession, and without those men to build the army we'd be in a sad fix indeed. Some of them I do blame, because the pictures don't offend their pride in their profession—they only puncture their stiff shirt fronts. I love to draw pictures that offend such guys, because it's fun to hear them squawk.

I'm sorry if I disturb the others, but they seldom complain.

*"I'd ruther dig. A movin' foxhole attracks th' eye."*

They know that if their men have a gripe, it is not good for them to sit in their holes and brood about it and work up steam. Men in combat are high-strung and excitable, and unimportant little things can upset them. If they blow that steam off a little bit, whether it is with stories or pictures or cartoons, then they feel better inside.

Not all colonels and generals and lieutenants are good. While the army is pretty efficient about making and breaking good and bad people, no organization of eight million is going to be perfect. Ours are not professional soldiers. They have recently come from a life where they could cuss and criticize their bosses and politicians at will. They realize that an army is held together with discipline, and they know they must have authority. They accept orders and restrictions, but because

*"Awright, awright—it's a general! Ya wanna pass in review?"*

they are fundamentally democratic the insignia on the shoulders of their officers sometimes look a hell of a lot like chips.

I've been asked if I have a postwar plan for Joe and Willie. I do. Because Joe and Willie are very tired of the war they have been fighting for almost two years, I hope to take them home when it is over. While their buddies are readjusting themselves and trying to learn to be civilians again, Joe and Willie are going to do the same. While their buddies are trying to drown out the war in the far corner of a bar, Joe and Willie are going to drink with them. If their buddies find their girls have married somebody else, and if they have a hard time getting jobs back, and if they run into difficulties in the new, strange life of a free citizen, then Joe and Willie are going to do the same. And if they finally get settled and drop slowly into the happy obscurity of a humdrum job and a little wife and a houseful of kids, Joe and Willie will be happy to settle down too.

They might even shave and become respectable.

Soldiers are avid readers: some because they like to read and others because there is nothing else to do. Magazines and newspapers for which they subscribe arrive late and tattered, if they arrive at all. Half the magazines carry serial stories, which are a pain in the neck to the guys who start them and can't finish them as the magazines pass from hand to hand. Newspapers that have enough shreds left to be readable are so old that the only thing guys look for in their own home-town sheets is something about somebody they know. For that reason, the society sections of home papers probably get more attention than the feature pages. Joe's fiancée's picture is printed, showing her engaged to a war-plant worker, and he can pick out Aunt Suzy in the background of the picture taken at the annual tea party for the Quilting Bee Club.

Unfortunately, many papers at home burn soldiers up by printing the news just as it comes to them. If the campaign in Holland is taking up all the space, it burns the guys in Italy to read how "minor patrol action and comparative quiet continue on the Italian front, with no progress reported."

To a soldier in a hole, nothing is bigger or more vital to him than the war which is going on in the immediate vicinity of his hole. If nothing is happening to him, and he is able to relax that day, then it is a good war, no matter what is going on elsewhere. But if things are rough, and he is sweating out a mortar barrage, and his best friend is killed on a patrol, then it is a rough war for him, and he does not consider it "comparatively quiet."

That situation can't be remedied much. Newspapers at home have to print the news as it appears on a world-wide scale, but if they would clamp down a little harder on their enthusiastic rewrite men who love to describe "smashing armored columns," the "ground forces sweeping ahead," "victorious, cheering armies," and "sullen supermen," they wouldn't be doing a bad job. A dogface gets just as tired advancing as he does retreating, and he gets shot at both ways. After a few days of battle, the victorious Yank who has been sweeping ahead doesn't look any prettier than the sullen superman he captures.

*". . . so Archibald kissed her agin an' gently put her
head on th' pillow. She gazed at him wit' half-shut
eyes—tremblin' hard—don't forget to buy next week's
installment at yer newsstand."*

It's tough that a lot of the blame for mistakes of the home-town newspapers is placed upon the war correspondents who cover the army, because they are the only newspapermen the soldiers see. Most war correspondents get the feel of the war

*"Th' hell this ain't th' most important hole in th' world.
I'm in it."*

after they have been around for a while, and some of them
have seen more war than many combat soldiers.

There are bad war correspondents, and there are some who
have been overseas for a long time without poking around to
find out what the score is. A handful of newsmen stuck it out
at Anzio from beginning to end, and they sent back some
wonderful stories. They are the ones who can find real and
honest stuff to write about in a war, regardless of whether or
not that particular phase of the war is making headlines or
getting them by-lines.

Will Lang from *Time* and *Life* became a familiar figure in
several infantry regiments, and the story he wrote while
trapped with a regiment at Salerno made him very popular

*"Fresh, spirited American troops, flushed with victory,
are bringing in thousands of hungry, ragged, battle-
weary prisoners . . ."*
*(News item)*

with the guys. A sawed-off, freckle-faced reporter named Bob
Vermillion voluntarily jumped with the paratroopers over
Southern France, just so his story about them would be accurate. Ken Dixon, another reporter with his heart in the right
place, roasted the pants off the general who commanded
Naples, charging unfairness to combat troops. Ken got into
some trouble over that, but because he lives with and writes
about soldiers he is more interested in writing for them than
for the generals.

Those three guys are among the civilian reporters to whom

the dogfaces are indebted. Their sole idea and purpose is to tell as much as they can about the war.

*"Why ya lookin' so sad? I got out of it okay."*

The mail is by far the most important reading matter that reaches soldiers overseas. This has had so much publicity that if some people aren't writing regularly to their guys in the war, it's because they don't want to. A common excuse at home seems to be that they aren't getting much mail from the guys here. The little lady says, "Okay, if the bum is going to sightsee around Europe and not bother to write, I just won't write him." Some guys do sightsee around Europe without bothering to write. Not the doggie. He doesn't do any sightseeing, and he doesn't have many opportunities to write. If the lady could see him scrawling on a V-mail blank in a dugout, by the light of a candle stuck with its own hot grease on his knee, she would change her way of thinking.

It's very hard to write interesting letters if you are in the infantry. About the only things you can talk about are what you are doing and where you are, and that's cut out by the censor. It's very hard to compose a letter that will pass the censors when you are tired and scared and disgusted with everything that's happening.

A lot of people aren't very smart when they write to a soldier. They complain about the gasoline shortage, or worry him or anger him in a hundred different ways which directly affect his efficiency and morale. Your feelings get touchy and explosive at the front. A man feels very fine fighting a war when his girl has just written that she is thinking that per-haps they made a mistake. He might figure: What the hell, the only thing I was living for was that I knew she would wait for me. He's going to feel pretty low and he might get a little careless because of it, at a place where he can't afford to be careless.

But considerate women have done far more to help their men than they may realize. A soldier's life revolves around his mail. Like many others, I've been able to follow my kid's progress from the day he was born until now he is able to walk and talk a little, and although I have never seen him I know him very well. Jean has sent dozens of snapshots of her-self and the little guy at different intervals, and it makes all the difference in the world.

Soldiers at the front read K-ration labels when the contents are listed on the package, just to be reading something. God knows they are familiar enough with the contents—right down to the last dextrose tablet. That puts *Stars and Stripes*, the only daily newspaper that reaches them with any regular-ity, in a pretty good spot.

*Stars and Stripes* would be an advertiser's dream, if it ac-cepted advertisements. It has no big-scale competition, it reaches hundreds of thousands of readers, and it packs a lot of power because of that.

*"My son. Five days old. Good-lookin' kid, ain't he?"*

The original *Stars and Stripes* of World War I was started by a handful of privates and a sergeant or two, and, although they accumulated several officers along the way, it remained a soldiers' paper throughout the war. The *Stars and Stripes* of this war was started by a colonel. He built a chain of papers stretching from Casablanca to Rome, including Oran, Tunis, Algiers, Palermo, and Naples.

Although Egbert White was a colonel, he had been a private on the first *Stars and Stripes*, and I really think he tried to put out a newspaper for the troops in this war, and not an organ for the high brass. He staffed the papers with as many experienced newspapermen as he could find, and he kept reporters and correspondents in the field covering the troops. Many of his staff members had little journalistic experience

*"Another dang mouth to feed."*

before coming on the paper, and some of them came directly out of combat outfits. But all of them learned the business pretty well, and many of them have become expert newsmen.

When I was transferred to the paper in the early spring of 1944, I thought the old colonel was awfully timid. I had just come from the *45th Division News*, where we thought and wrote what we damned well pleased, just so we got a paper out. Because our paper was exclusively for combat soldiers, we didn't have to worry about hurting the feelings of high brass hats, who had never even heard of us. I couldn't understand the new arrangement, but as I learned a little from day to day I saw that the paper wasn't really timid—it just had to watch its step until it was established. It's established now, and for a long time has been printing a paper which upholds the reputation of the old *Stars and Stripes*.

The great majority of generals and authorities who see the sheet over here leave us strictly alone. There are, as in any big organization, some people who would like to see the editorial staff of the paper drawn and quartered, and there are still a few characters who make life uncomfortable sometimes, but we haven't lost a great deal of sleep over them. As far as I know, the paper has never had any trouble with field generals who actually command troops in combat. While the Italy edition of *Stars and Stripes* runs occasional pictures of General Mark Clark, who commands the Fifth Army in Italy, he gets no preference over anyone else. When Clark got Russia's highest foreign honor, the Order of Suvarov, he was given six lines of type on the last page of an eight-page edition. And he was probably surprised to get that much.

Sometimes the cartoon department of the paper got a little support from the higher brass, including Clark, although I never expected it, because the few cartoons I had done about generals had a definitely insubordinate air about them.

During that first winter in Italy, when *Stars and Stripes* printed letters from outraged combat soldiers in Naples, and when I did a few cartoons on the subject, the disturbance reached the ears of the deputy theater commander. He didn't see eye to eye with the paper and he forbade further distribution of some of the stuff I was doing. It wasn't his first or his last complaint about me, and when brass wearing three stars puts the clamps on you there is nothing much you can do about it. Yet right in the middle of the mess, a corps commander asked for the original of one of the drawings. I took the drawing to him, worrying a little about the fact that my uniform was mixed and my hair wasn't cut, and, besides, I wasn't accustomed to hobnobbing with corps commanders.

The first thing he asked me was, "How's your battle with the rear echelon progressing?" That staggered me. I replied that I had nothing against the rear echelon—only some of its generals—and that I was being accused by them of undermining somebody's morale.

He said, "When you start drawing pictures that don't get a

*"That's okay, Joe—at least we can make bets."*

few complaints, then you'd better quit, because you won't be
doing anybody any good."

I felt a lot better.

I tried to stay completely away from stuff that had an
editorial twist. The only editorializing you can do in the
army is that which is approved by the army. I never could
see any point in doing stuff that didn't show both sides. I
kidded the rear echelon a little, but I also did an occasional
drawing kidding the front about the unnecessary work it
caused the ordnance and maintenance people. But I didn't
do a drawing at all unless I could work in a twist that made it
at least slightly humorous. Once I did get almost editorial
—at the time when it looked as though we weren't going
to get to vote, because the bill was being kicked around in
Congress.

*"Maybe th' sun's comin' up, Joe."*

The only purely editorial cartoon I can remember was when we were all bursting with enthusiasm and optimism about the attempted assassination of Hitler. We felt that this was a sure indication that Germany was cracking, and we would be home by Christmas. I should have remembered we felt the same enthusiasm at Salerno when we first set foot on continental Europe and began pushing inland. The Germans were disorganized after the push started, and they all told us they surrendered because they knew it would be over by Christmas and they didn't want to get killed in the last days of the war.

The only people who see my drawings before they appear in *Stars and Stripes* are the editor and the field press censor. Major Robert Neville, who runs the paper, was an enlisted

*"Let's grab dis one, Willie. He's packed wit' vitamins."*

man of long standing himself, and he lets his staff do its own thinking.

I never have trouble with the censor, because all he is worried about is preventing valuable information from falling into the hands of the Germans, who get the paper regularly through diplomatic channels and irregularly through Americans who are captured while carrying a copy. I do not draw pictures of new equipment until information about such equipment has been officially released, and, anyway, it would be hard in a cartoon to tell the Germans where the second battalion of the umpty-fifth regiment is going to attack. Except for that, I simply try to draw cartoons for the guys.

All that is as it should be. A soldiers' newspaper should

*"I can't git no lower, Willie. Me buttons is in th' way."*

recognize two restrictions—military security and common sense. Outside of that, it should devote itself solely to being a paper that will provide the soldiers with good news coverage and a safety valve to blow off their feelings about things.

We don't have to be indoctrinated or told there is a war on over here. We know there is a war on because we see it. We don't like it a darned bit, but you don't see many soldiers quitting, so fancy propaganda would be a little superfluous.

It's an accepted fact that you must be totalitarian in an army. The guys know that, but sometimes it chafes a little. That's why we do more bitching and groaning than any other army. And that's why it is a tremendous relief to get a little breath of democracy and freedom of speech into this atmosphere of corporals and generals and discipline and officers' latrines. It's a big relief even when it has to come from a little four-page newspaper.

While a guy at home is sweating over his income tax and Victory garden, a dogface somewhere is getting great joy out of wiggling his little finger. He does it just to see it move and to prove to himself that he is still alive and able to move it. Life is stripped down to bare essentials for him when he is living from minute to minute, wondering if each is his last. Because he is fundamentally no different from his countryman at home, he would probably be sweating just as hard over *his* income tax and Victory garden if *he* were home.

But now he has changed. His sense of humor has changed. He can grin at gruesome jokes, like seeing a German get shot in the seat of his pants, and he will stare uncomprehendingly at fragile jokes in print which would have made him rock with laughter before.

Perhaps he will change back again when he returns, but never completely. If he is lucky, his memories of those sharp, bitter days will fade over the years into a hazy recollection of a period which was filled with homesickness and horror and dread and monotony, occasionally lifted and lighted by the gentle, humorous, and sometimes downright funny things that always go along with misery.

I'd like to talk about some of the things he will remember, and then I'd like to forget them myself.

Mud, for one, is a curse which seems to save itself for war. I'm sure Europe never got this muddy during peacetime. I'm equally sure that no mud in the world is so deep or sticky or wet as European mud. It doesn't even have an honest color like ordinary mud.

I made the drawing about the jeep driver and the foot infantry in the mud for a reason. Those guys who have had some infantry, and even those who have had to do a lot of walking in other branches, generally show it by the way they drive. If a man barrels past foot troops, splashing mud or squirting dust all over them because he doesn't bother to slow down — or if he shoots past a hitchhiker in the rain, with half his cozy truck cab empty — then he should spend a week

*"Footprints! God, wotta monster!"*

or two learning how to use his feet, because he doesn't appreciate his job or he's just plain damned stupid.

Unfortunately, there are a lot of them in the army. I saw a big GI truck zoom past an infantry battalion in France, right after the rains began to fall. The driver spattered the troops pretty thoroughly—but they were getting used to being spattered, and they didn't say much. His truck bogged down half a mile up the road, and when the leading company caught up with him he had the unbelievable gall to ask them to push him out. They replied as only long-suffering infantrymen can reply. They shoved his face in the mud.

The worst thing about mud, outside of the fact that it keeps armies from advancing, is that it causes trench foot. There was a lot of it that first winter in Italy. The doggies

"*. . . I'll never splash mud on a dogface again (999).
. . . I'll never splash mud on a dogface again (1000).
. . . Now will ya help us push?*"

found it difficult to keep their feet dry, and they had to stay in wet foxholes for days and weeks at a time. If they couldn't stand the pain they crawled out of their holes and stumbled and crawled (they couldn't walk) down the mountains until they reached the aid station. Their shoes were cut off, and their feet swelled like balloons. Sometimes the feet had to be amputated. But most often the men had to make their agonized way back up the mountain and crawl into their holes again because there were no replacements and the line had to be held.

Sometimes the replacement problem got fierce. Companies were down to thirty or forty men, but they managed to hold

*"So I told Company K they'd just have to work out their
replacement problem for themselves."*

on somehow. It was worse than Valley Forge. I say that because conditions couldn't have been worse, and Washington's
men didn't have to put up with murderous artillery and mortar fire.

I drew "Hit th' dirt, boys!" because I happened to be sliding down one of those mountains in Italy when I got nicked,
and the only thing that saved me from most of the mortar
shell was the fact that sliding down the hill made me as parallel to the earth as if I had been lying horizontally. Many hundreds weren't so lucky on the mountainsides.

This second winter in Italy is just as miserable. A lot of the
guys have the new "shoe packs" which keep their feet reasonably dry, but that comfort is offset by the fact that this year

*"Hit th' dirt, boys!"*

they are getting more enemy artillery. The mountains are just as steep, the Germans just as tough, and the weather just as miserable. And those guys have been getting letters which say, "I'm so glad you're in Italy while the fighting is in France."

All the old divisions are tired—the outfits which fought in Africa and Sicily and Italy and God knows how many places in the Pacific. It doesn't take long to tire an outfit and many of the divisions that saw their first battle in France are undoubtedly feeling very fagged out right now. But only men who have seen actual war at first hand for two years, seeing their buddies killed day after day, trying to tell themselves that they are different—*they* won't get it; but knowing deep inside

*"I feel like a fugitive from th' law of averages."*

them that they *can* get it—only those guys know what real weariness of body, brain, and soul can be.

I've tried to put their weariness and their looks into Willie and Joe, who started with them and are getting tired with them. I tried shaving Willie once, but he just didn't look right, so the next day he had his beard back. I've tried two or three times to bring in replacements, but I've discovered that I have been here too long myself now to understand the feelings or reactions of a replacement fresh from home.

I've seen too much of the army to be funny about first sergeants and corporals, and I've seen too much of the war to be cute and fill it with funny characters.

I wish I could have written this book during my first six months overseas. Then all things in war make a vivid impres-

*"I'm naked!"*

sion on you because they are all new to you. You can describe sorrowful things and funny things with great enthusiasm, and in such a way that people will understand you. But, as the months go on and you see more of war, the little things that are so vivid at first become routine. I haven't tried to describe the activities of the infantry and its weapons because everybody has learned how a BAR man covers a light machine-gunner. I don't describe dead guys being buried in bloody bed sacks because I can't imagine anyone who has not seen it so often that his mind has become adjusted to it. I've simply described some of the feelings which the dogfaces have about different things, and to describe these things I have drawn cartoons about Willie and Joe.

Willie and Joe aren't at all clever. They aren't even good

cartoon characters, because they have similar features which are distinguishable only by their different noses. Willie has a big nose and Joe has a little one. The bags under their eyes and the dirt in their ears are so similar that few people know which is Willie and which is Joe.

True, Joe and Willie don't look much like the cream of young American manhood which was sent overseas in the infantry. Neither of them is boyish, although neither is aged. Joe is in his early twenties and Willie is in his early thirties — pretty average ages for the infantry. While they are no compliment to young American manhood's good looks, their expressions are those of infantry soldiers who have been in the war for a couple of years.

Look at an infantryman's eyes and you can tell how much war he has seen. Look at his actions in a bar and listen to his talk and you can also tell how much he has seen. If he is cocky and troublesome, and talks about how many battles he's fought and how much blood he has spilled, and if he goes around looking for a fight and depending upon his uniform to get him extra-special privileges, then he has not had it. If he is looking very weary and resigned to the fact that he is probably going to die before it is over, and if he has a deep, almost hopeless desire to go home and forget it all; if he looks with dull, uncomprehending eyes at the fresh-faced kid who is talking about the joys of battle and killing Germans, then he comes from the same infantry as Joe and Willie.

I've made it sound as if the only infantry is the kind that spends its time being miserable and scared in foxholes. There are other kinds. There are those who like it and those who have reasons of their own for wanting it. I know two of these notable exceptions: a swamp hunter from Georgia and an exiled baron from Prussia.

The swamp hunter once killed eight krauts with one clip from his M-1 rifle. He loves to go on patrol, all alone, with a rifle, a Luger pistol, a knife, plenty of ammunition, and half a dozen grenades hung to his belt by their safety rings, so he can pluck them and throw them like ripe tomatoes. The fact that hanging grenades by their rings is not a good way to live to a respectable old age doesn't bother him at all. In fact, he tells with great relish how one came loose while he was

*"How ya gonna find out if they're fresh troops if ya don't wake 'em up an' ask 'em?"*

creeping around a German position, and how it exploded under his feet, kicking his legs up in the air, but leaving him miraculously unscratched. He once saved his entire company by sheer guts, and he has been decorated several times. He says war is just like swamp hunting.

The Prussian is a wild character who received a battlefield promotion to lieutenant, after saving a patrol and the officer who commanded it from annihilation. He is famed far and wide for leading his own patrols fantastic distances through enemy lines. He admits he gets scared, but his hatred for the Germans is so intense that he keeps it up. He has been wounded a number of times. His favorite weapon is the tommy gun, although he used a carbine once to shoot a German officer through the throat, and then almost wept because he had shattered the officer's fine binoculars. He has saved many lives and has got a lot of valuable information by the simple process of sneaking into a darkened kraut command post at night, demanding to know the plans and situation in his arrogant Prussian voice, and then sneaking back to our side again.

*"We just landed. Do you know any good war stories?"*

I know of another guy—a former racketeer's bodyguard— who once found two Germans sleeping together to keep warm, remembered an old Ghoum trick, and slit the throat of one, leaving the other alive so he would wake up and see his bunkmate the next morning. Most of the doggies thought it was a good stunt, and it kept the Germans in his sector in a state of uproar and terror for several days.

The army couldn't get along without soldiers like that. They provide wonderful stories, they inspire their comrades to greater feats of arms, and they do a lot to make Jerry fear the American army.

Joe and Willie, however, come from the other infantry—the great numbers of men who stay and sweat in the foxholes that give their more courageous brethren claustrophobia. They go on patrol when patrols are called for, and they don't shirk hazards, because they don't want to let their buddies down. The army couldn't get along without them, either. Although it needs men to do the daring deeds, it also needs men who have the quiet courage to stick in their foxholes and fight and kill even though they hate killing and are scared to death while doing it.

Many people who read and speak of battle and noise and excitement and death forget one of the worst things about a war—its monotony. That is the thing that gets everyone—combat soldier and rear echelon alike.

The "hurry up and wait" system which seems to prevail in every army (double time to the assembly area and wait two hours for the trucks—drive like hell to the docks and wait two days for the ship—fall out at four in the morning to stand an inspection which doesn't come off until late afternoon), that's one of the things that make war tough. The endless marches that carry you on and on and yet never seem to get you anyplace—the automatic drag of one foot as it places itself in front of the other without any prompting from your dulled brain, and the unutterable relief as you sink down for a ten-minute break, spoiled by the knowledge that you'll have to get up and go again—the never-ending monotony of days and weeks and months and years of bad weather and wet clothes and no mail—all this sends as many men into the psychopathic wards as does battle fatigue.

Like fraternity brothers who have had a tough initiation, many of the old-timers over here are ornery enough to kid replacements who begin to feel pretty miserable and homesick after six months. "The first year is the worst," the old-timers say. "The second year isn't so bad, and by the time you begin your third year overseas you are almost used to it."

But it ain't true, brother; it ain't true.

*"I need a couple guys what don't owe me no money fer a little routine patrol."*

My dad used to tell me how in the First World War German and American outfits, living a miserable, monotonous life in the trenches, used to get acquainted with each other. That hasn't happened much in this war, but during the awful winters in Italy things often slowed down to a dead stop, and after a while lonely guys would connect their foxholes and have real old-fashioned trenches. Most of the trenches were pretty well surrounded with barbed wire and minefields, so in many ways it was just like the other war.

The opposing sides often spoke to each other, but seldom in brotherly tones. It was a favorite trick to confuse the enemy

*"She must be very purty. Th' whole column is wheezin'
at her."*

by yapping at him in his own tongue. Both sides did it,
sometimes quite successfully. Once I heard a funny exchange
between a Westerner and a German in the mountains above
Venafro. The American had a machine-gun position on top
of a hill, and the kraut was a sniper, about fifty yards down
the slope. They were well protected, and had been in those
positions for many days. Both had cooties, both had trench
foot, and each had an intense dislike for the other.

   An Italian division was supposed to move into the line near
by. The Nazis, having had experience with the Italians when
they were fighting on the German side, liked this new idea
very much. The Americans, who had seen the Italians as German allies, were not cheered by the prospect.

"How do you like your new ally?" yelled the German to the American in passable English.

"You kin have 'em back," said our guy, having come from a region where diplomacy bows to honesty.

"We don't want them," shouted Jerry, and he lobbed a grenade up the hill. It fell far short.

The American spattered the sniper's rocks with a burst.

"Swine!" jeered the German.

"Horse's ass!" snorted the American, and all was quiet again.

*"I'm depending on you old men to be a steadying influence for the replacements."*

The Germans often accuse us of being low plagiarists when it comes to music, and that we cannot deny. Our musical geniuses at home never did get around to working up a good,

*"Wot kind of voices—Brooklyn or guttural?"*

honest, acceptable war song, and so they forced us to share "Lili Marlene" with the enemy. Even if we did get it from the krauts it's a beautiful song, and the only redeeming thing is the rumor kicking around that "Lili" is an ancient French song, stolen by the Germans. It may not be true, but we like to believe it.

"Lili" got a couple of artillerymen in trouble in France. They were singing it at a bar the day after this particular town had been taken. Some local partisans came over and told them to shut the hell up. The guys understood, apologized, and bought drinks all around.

I read someplace that the American boy is not capable of hate. Maybe we don't share the deep, traditional hatred of

*"Th' krauts ain't followin' ya so good on 'Lili Marlene'
tonight, Joe. Ya think maybe somethin' happened to their
tenor?"*

the French or the Poles or the Yugoslavs toward the krauts,
but you can't have friends killed without hating the men
who did it. It makes the dogfaces sick to read articles by
people who say, "It isn't the Germans, it's the Nazis." Our
army has seen few actual *Nazis*, except when they threw in
special SS divisions. We have seen the Germans—the youth
and the men and the husbands and the fathers of Germany,
and we know them for a ruthless, cold, cruel, and powerful
enemy.

When our guys cringe under an 88 barrage, you don't hear
them say, "Those dirty Nazis." You hear them say, "Those
goddam krauts." Because our men soon learn to be more or
less professional fighters at the front, they have a deep respect

*"Let B Comp'ny go in. They ain't been kissed yet."*

for the German's ability to wage war. You may hear a doggie call a German a skunk, but he'll never say he's not good.

The very professionalism of the krauts which makes the American infantryman respect the German infantryman also makes him hate the German's guts even more. The dogface is quite human about things, and he hates and doesn't understand a man who can, under orders, put every human emotion aside, as the Germans can and do.

Some very unfortunate rumors have drifted over here, from time to time, about the treatment of prisoners of war in America. While the guys here realize it is much more economical to haul krauts back to the States on empty ships, rather than use crowded shipping space to send food over here for them, there is a natural resentment because the enemy gets a privilege that is denied those who fight him. He gets to go back and breathe the air of God's country, even if it is in a prison camp. That's a very human and natural feeling, which can be fully understood only if you have experienced the deep longing for your home country that we have felt here.

*"Hell. When they run we try to ketch 'em. When we ketch 'em we try to make 'em run."*

Since the Germans have many of our own men, and because we are supposed to be a civilized people, we certainly want the krauts to be treated within the rules, but only within the rules.

There is no indication that the rumors were true, but whoever started them was guilty of a criminal thing. One of the rumors was that some Americans gave a dance for Italian

POWs. Another was that a German camp had struck for higher wages for the labor they were forced to do. While most of the soldiers here know that such stuff simply comes from the rumor mills, there are always some who are willing to believe rumors, and there are many who fear that the American people will go soft with the prisoners. Even some American soldiers are lenient with them; but not those who capture them. They have to fight Germans, and they do not like the herrenvolk. Because, as I said, many of them have friends whom the Germans have captured, they don't object to taking krauts alive. But they certainly feel that the prisoners, who should thank God and not their Fuehrer that they have been permitted to remain alive and breathe air which would be much purer without their presence, should remember that they are enemies.

The Germans prefer to surrender to Americans rather than to some Europeans, because they know they will be treated fairly. Being Germans they take advantage of this sometimes. I watched a crippled FFI man working the hell out of a detail of German prisoners at the docks of Marseilles. He was not abusing them; he was simply making certain their hands got calloused. He had been crippled by the Germans and they had wrecked the docks, so his heart was in his work. Then an American sergeant, who had the air of a man freshly arrived in Europe, strolled past and stared at the prisoners. Immediately they began groaning and limping and looking sick, weary, and picked-on. The sergeant stopped the work and gave each man a cigarette. The Frenchman stood and watched him do it and then limped away disgustedly. The American turned his back for a moment, and the entire detail of krauts grinned at each other.

I wouldn't be surprised if a German corporal named Schicklgruber received an American cigarette under similar conditions twenty-six years ago.

Friends in war are different in many ways from friends in peacetime. You depend upon friends in war much more.

The infantrymen can't live without friends. That forces them to be pretty good people and that's the reason men at the front seem so much simpler and more generous than

*"I made it. I owe ya another fifty bucks."*

others. They kid each other unmercifully—sometimes in ways that would seem a little ribald to the uninitiated.

For instance, there's the young guy who got married two weeks before shipping out, has been overseas two years, and is desperately homesick. Some other guys will say to him:

"You wanna go home? Hell, you found a home in the army. You got your first pair of shoes and your first square meal in the army. You're living a clean, healthy, outdoor life, and you want to go back and be henpecked."

He keeps up this apparently heartless tirade until the victim heaves a big rock at him and feels better. But it isn't heartless, because only a man who is terribly homesick himself would dare to say a thing like that. He isn't just pouring it on the other guy—he's trying to kid *himself* into feeling better.

When you lose a friend you have an overpowering desire to go back home and yell in everybody's ear, "This guy was killed fighting for you. Don't forget him—ever. Keep him in your mind when you wake up in the morning and when you go to bed at night. Don't think of him as the statistic which changes 38,788 casualties to 38,789. Think of him as a guy who wanted to live every bit as much as you do. Don't let him be just one of 'Our Brave Boys' from the old home town, to whom a marble monument is erected in the city park, and a civic-minded lady calls the newspaper ten years later and wants to know why that 'unsightly stone' isn't removed."

I've lost friends who were ordinary people and just wanted to live and raise a family and pay their taxes and cuss the politicians. I've also lost friends who had brilliant futures. Gregor Duncan, one of the finest and most promising artists I've ever known, was killed at Anzio while making sketches for *Stars and Stripes*. It's a pretty tough kick in the stomach when you realize what people like Greg could have done if they had lived. It's one of the costs of the war we don't often consider.

Those thoughts are deep in us, and we don't talk about them much.

While men in combat outfits kid each other around, they have a sort of family complex about it. No outsiders may join. Anybody who does a dangerous job in this war has his own particular kind of kidding among his own friends, and sometimes it doesn't even sound like kidding. Bomber crews and paratroopers and infantry squads are about the same in that respect. If a stranger comes up to a group of them when they are bulling, they ignore him. If he takes it upon himself to laugh at something funny they have said, they freeze their expressions, turn slowly around, stare at him until his stature has shrunk to about four inches and he slinks away, and then they go back to their kidding again.

It's like a group of prosperous businessmen telling a risqué joke and then glaring at the waiter who joins the guffaws. Combat people are an exclusive set, and if they want to be that way, it is their privilege. They certainly earn it. New men

*"Why th' hell couldn't you have been born a beautiful woman?"*

in outfits have to work their way in slowly, but they are eventually accepted. Sometimes they have to change some of their ways of living. An introvert or a recluse is not going to last long in combat without friends, so he learns to come out of his shell. Once he has "arrived" he is pretty proud of his clique, and he in turn is chilly toward outsiders.

That's why, during some of the worst periods in Italy, many guys who had a chance to hang around a town for a few days after being discharged from a hospital where they had recovered from wounds, with nobody the wiser, didn't take advantage of it. They weren't eager to get back up and get in the war, by any means, and many of them did hang around a few days. But those who did hang around didn't feel exactly

*"Joe, yestiddy ya saved my life an' I swore I'd pay ya back. Here's my last pair of dry socks."*

right about it, and those who went right back did it for a very simple reason—not because they felt that their presence was going to make a lot of difference in the big scheme of the war, and not to uphold the traditions of the umpteenth regiment. A lot of guys don't know the name of their regimental commander. They went back because they knew their companies were very shorthanded, and they were sure that if somebody else in their own squad or section were in their own shoes, and the situation were reversed, those friends would come back to make the load lighter on *them*.

That kind of friendship and spirit is a lot more genuine and sincere and valuable than all the "war aims" and indoctrination in the world. I think the wise officers who command

*"We'll report we made contack wit' th' enemy an'
walked to our objective."*

these guys realize that. They don't tolerate bootlicking or
petty politicking. Even though, as in the case of the guys ali-
biing for each other because of the smashed jeep, the officer
will be sore as hell, he will have more respect for them than if
one of them had come to him privately and whispered in his
ear, "Joe did it."

There is surprisingly little bickering and jealousy in combat outfits. There might be a little between the company
cooks or the supply sergeant and the company clerk, but the
more action anybody sees the less spiteful he is toward those
around him.

If a man is up for a medal, his friends are so willing to
be witnesses that sometimes they must be cross-examined

*"I brang ya a chaser fer all that plasma, Joe."*

to make sure they are not crediting him with three knocked-out machine guns instead of one. They fight together, argue together, work together, stick together if one is in trouble, and that's a very big reason why infantry guys win wars.

If one man out of a platoon gets a six-hour pass to go back to a town, he will have a good time for himself, of course. It's expected of him. But he will come back with a load of cognac for those who didn't get to go. Guys hitchhike many miles to visit their friends who are in hospitals, and sometimes they will go over to another division to see an old buddy if they have a little time on their hands.

If a man in a rifle squad gets a chance to go home on rotation, his friends congratulate him, tell him they wish to hell they were going themselves, but, as long as they can't, they give him their families' phone numbers, and they wish him a fare-thee-well and join him in the fond hope that he never has to go overseas again. While they envy him like the devil, they aren't low-down about it. The man who goes home carries a huge list of telephone numbers and addresses, and he makes all the calls and writes all the letters, even though it often costs him considerable time and expense during his own precious few days.

Very few of them shoot off their mouths about their own heroism when the inevitable reporter from the home-town paper comes around to see them. They are thinking of their friends who are still having troubles, and how the article will be read by their outfits when the clippings reach them. I've seen few clippings come over here about men who have had a really tough war, and even fewer pictures of them displaying gory souvenirs.

Of course, there are misfits who just can't make friends or who are just plain ornery, but they depart sooner or later. If something doesn't happen to them during battle, they blow their tops or they just leave when there is an opportunity. But you will seldom find a misfit who has been in an outfit more than a few months.

I'm not equipped to talk about Europe because I don't know a darned thing about it. My impressions are simply reactions to what I have seen, and all I can do is offer them as explanations for some of the drawings I made about the experiences soldiers have had with civilians here and there.

While most guys over here swear heartily at the people who always seem to be trying to take advantage of us, we all have to admit that deflating the GI pocketbook is not an activity peculiar to Europe. We still have dim memories of days long ago when shops and restaurants in some American towns kept double price lists for soldiers and civilians, and those of us who had wives can't forget rooming houses whose proprietors hung out "Soldiers' Families Welcome" signs, and then stuck us for all our monthly pay.

Those of us who have spent a long time in Sicily and Italy are

*"Did ya ever see so many furriners, Joe?"*

more amazed every day that such a run-down country could have had the audacity to declare war on anyone, even with the backing of the krauts.

The dogfaces over here have pretty mixed feelings as far as Italy is concerned. A lot of them—but not as many as there used to be—remember that some of their best friends were killed by Italians, and many of our allies can't forget that Italy caused them some grief. I don't belong to that group, even though the first enemies I saw were Italians. You can't work up a good hate against soldiers who are surrendering to you so fast you have to take them by appointment. But the average dogface feels dreadfully sorry for these poor trampled wretches, and wants to beat his brains out doing something for them. I don't belong too strongly to that group, either. The Italians haven't given me a chance to give them anything; they have stolen everything I own except the fillings in my teeth.

Italy reminds a guy of a dog hit by an automobile because it ran out and tried to bite the tires. You can't just leave the critter there to die, but you remember that you wouldn't have run over it if it had stayed on the sidewalk. There is no doubt that the Italians are paying a stiff price for their past sins. The country looks as if a giant rake had gone over it from end to end, and when you have been going along with the rake you wonder that there is anything left at all.

The doggies become accustomed to the abject poverty and hunger of the Italian refugees who stream out of towns which are being fought over, and who hang around bivouac areas, but no dogface ever becomes hardened to it. Also, they get awfully tired of hearing everybody—Fascists, ex-Fascists or non-Fascists—wail about how Mussolini made them do it. Their pity is often strained by the way the Italians seem to wait for somebody else to do something for them, but in spite of the fact that the Italians consider the Americans a gravy train which came to bring them pretty things to eat, the doggies still pity them.

It would take a pretty tough guy not to feel his heart go out to the shivering, little six-year-old squeaker who stands barefoot in the mud, holding a big tin bucket so the dogface can empty his mess kit into it. Many soldiers, veterans of the Italy campaign and thousands of similar buckets, still go back and sweat out the mess line for an extra chop and hunk of bread for those little kids.

But there is a big difference between the ragged, miserable infantryman who waits with his mess kit, and the ragged, miserable civilian who waits with his bucket. The doggie knows where his next meal is coming from. That makes him a very rich man in this land where hunger is so fierce it makes animals out of respectable old ladies who should be wearing cameos and having tea parties instead of fighting one another savagely for a soldier's scraps.

I think that's where the guys direct their sympathies: to-

*"Go ahead, Joe. If ya don't bust it ya'll worry about it all night."*

ward the old people and the little kids, who certainly never had much to say about the sacking of Greece and the invasion of Ethiopia. The men of Italy—the strapping young guys who didn't realize their own country's weakness—evidently sense this, because they don't come around the mess lines. They steal jeep parts instead.

It hits the doggies to see a man staring glassily at the shambles of the home he spent his life building, and they would like to be able to comfort him. Perhaps they feel that way because they realize more and more how lucky our own country is to have escaped all this. It chills a man to see a young girl, with a haunted, hopeless expression in her eyes and a squalling baby which must go on squalling because she is hungry and has no milk for it. Not only does he pity her, but he thinks that this could possibly have happened to his own sister or his wife. He realizes it even more when he considers how near the Germans were to victory when he started fighting them. Thoughts like that sometimes keep guys going.

*The Prince and the Pauper.*

The medical corps has probably done more to endear our army to civilians in stricken areas of Europe than the high-powered agencies which came over with that task in mind.

No one will ever know how many French, Sicilian, and Italian kids will go through life bearing the first names of the doctors who, in their own spare time when they needed rest

*"It's a habit Joe picked up in th' city."*

badly, made the deliveries in chilly stables and leaking aid tents. Nobody ever hesitates to apply to our medics for aid; and the medics, who manage to keep their profession pretty high above the selfish motives which cause wars, usually try to help them.

Nearly everyone who has hung around a battalion aid station in a zone where there are refugees has seen the civilians with banged-up ribs or nicks from stray bullets and shell fragments coming around for treatment. But the most beautiful sight of all is the man you will occasionally see who crumples and uncrumples his battered hat as he paces up and down in front of the aid station with the same worried air, and for the same reason, as a man pacing the tiled floor of a maternity ward at home. The only difference is that here the expectant papa has no cigarettes to smoke.

*"Tell him to look at th' bright side of things, Willie. His trees is pruned, his ground is plowed up, an' his house is air-conditioned."*

Most people in Italy and Sicily gave us a rousing welcome in all their towns and cities, but nowhere was there such excitement as in Rome. We got awful cynical about it, because the enthusiasm seemed to stop, and the complaints seemed to start, twenty-four hours after everybody was kissing everybody else. When were we going to bring shoes and food and clothes and phonograph records? Who was going to pay for Uncle Antonio's bombed vino shop, and why did we have to shell Aunt Amelia's ristorante?

*"It's twins."*

They beefed most about the bombs. Those really did tear hell out of things, and somehow we never did have the heart to ask the Italians when they were going to pay for the damage *they* did in the war.

Some of the housewives were downright furious as they poked through the rubble of what had been their parlors. They seemed to forget that their town was full of German tanks and German supplies; instead, they regarded our fliers as a bunch of irresponsible kids with itchy bombsights.

Europeans have been hardened to centuries of war and invasion and they seem to know what to expect from soldiers. While I have a natural preference for my own countrymen, the contact I have had with other allied troops leads me to

*"Don't look at me, lady. I didn't do it."*

believe that soldiers are pretty much alike, no matter where they come from. They all want to go home more than anything else, and they all feel a certain freedom from the conventions they would observe in their own countries. In fact, about the only factors that decide a soldier's conduct in foreign lands are army regulations, his own conscience, and the way he is treated by civilians.

I've found this to be true all through the army. In the American towns where my division was stationed from time to time during its training, the size of the MP force which policed the town was regulated by how much the local inhabitants tried to gyp us.

If the people were warm and hospitable, as they were in many places, the few drunken soldiers who appeared on the streets were taken in hand by their buddies before anybody saw them. In the towns where soldiers were not only disliked, but actually treated with hostility (and there were plenty of those towns too), we didn't interfere with our more boisterous brethren as they roamed the midnight streets looking for windows to break.

The very guys who caroused so wildly on the streets of Naples behaved themselves pretty well in many towns in France where we were welcomed openly and sincerely.

*"Are you seeking a company of infantry, mon capitaine?"*

We are swindled unmercifully everywhere we go; we've learned to take it for granted. But a lot of the blame is our own. If we find a barbershop where the price equals six cents in American money, we plop down what amounts to fifty cents in tattered European currency. When our change is counted out to us in even more tattered bills—some worth as little as one cent—we tell the barber to keep the change. We'd have paid that price in America, and besides, we hate to have wads of the stuff sticking between our fingers every time we reach into our pockets for a cigarette.

After two or three dogfaces have repeated this performance, the barber decides the stories he has heard about all Americans owning oil wells are true, and the price goes up to fifty cents. Along comes a Canadian, whose government allows him about ten dollars per month and banks the rest for his return, and when the barber tries to soak *him* fifty cents the Canadian tears the shop apart.

All this leads the confused barber to believe that the Canadian is a tightwad and the American is a rich fool.


I've done many drawings of wrecked buildings. Shattered towns and bomb-blasted houses are constant reminders of the war, long after the dead are buried.

There's something very ghostlike about a wall standing in the moonlight in the midst of a pile of broken rubble and staring at you with its single unblinking eye, where a window used to be. There's an awful lot of that in Italy, and it is going to haunt those people for years.

You can usually tell what kind of fighting went on in a town, and how much was necessary to take it, by the wreckage that remains. If the buildings are fairly intact, with only broken windows, doors, and pocked walls, it was a quick, hand-to-hand street fight with small arms and grenades and perhaps a mortar or two.

If most of the walls are still standing, but the roofs have gaping holes, and many rooms are shattered, then the entry was preceded by an artillery barrage. If some of the holes are in the slopes of the roofs facing the retreating enemy, then he gave the town a plastering after he left.

But if there isn't much town left at all, then planes have been around. Bombs sort of lift things up in the air and drop them in a heap. Even the enormous sheet-metal doors with

*"It ain't right to go around leanin' on churches, Joe."*

which shopowners shutter their establishments buckle and balloon out into grotesque swollen shapes.

Only once did a cartoon about civilians give the authorities gray hair and I didn't realize at the time that the drawing had anything to do with civilians. I merely wanted to give pictorial recognition to two of our most formidable allies— Texas and Ireland. The cartoon appeared in the Rome *Stars and Stripes*, a journal which enjoys a more high-brow audience than either the *New Yorker* or *Punch*, because it is the only daily paper available to the various embassies and legations in the city. But because it is published primarily for enlisted soldiers who are fighting a war, some of its

*"You Irishmen woulda lost this war without allies like Texas and Russia."*

contents cause these high brows to wrinkle in puzzled astonishment.

I was informed that the wife of the ambassador from Ireland to the Vatican had called the office and asked what gave in the cartoon department. She was told that no offense was meant and, when the cartoon was explained to her, she asked for copies she might send to Ireland, whose neutrality had not been violated, after all.

No button or shoelace escaped the eyes of the MPs and officers in Naples. I felt sorry for some of them, for I don't doubt that there were many who were nauseated by the job.

Even if you had a pass, and it was typewritten properly (they hooked some combat men on this, because many company clerks tire of lugging typewriters around and fill in passes and reports with a pen), and you had your dogtags around your neck, you were not finished with the investigation.

If your pass showed you were a sergeant, and you didn't have your chevrons, they stuck you—ten dollars per stripe, or thirty for a buck sergeant. Now this was unfair as hell. If they wanted their rear men to wear stripes, that was okay. But an infantry noncom doesn't like to wear his stripes in battle because snipers pick on him. That selfish excuse didn't mean a thing to the inquisitors. He should carry a special set of chevrons, equipped with zipper, for visits to Naples.

So it went. The doggie was snapped up the instant he stepped off the boat coming back from Anzio. One soldier wrote *Stars and Stripes* that he had been arrested and jailed for wearing his combat infantry badge. The MPs didn't know what it was.

It was not enough, the doggies felt, to live in unspeakable misery and danger while these "gumshoe so-and-sos" worked in the comfort and safety of the city. Hell, no. When they came back to try to forget the war for a few days, these "rear echelon goldbrickers" had to pester them to death.

When a man is feeling like this you can't tell him that his tormentors are people like himself, and that they are in the rear because they have been ordered to work there, just as he was ordered to the front.

It wouldn't do any good to show him that these MPs and officers are a part of the tremendous machine that keeps him fed and clothed and supplied. It wouldn't do any good, because the doggie lives a primitive life and hasn't time for reasoning. He says to himself, "This is nothing but a bunch of rear echelon bastards," and goes back and tells his outfit about it. Soldiers who are in danger feel a natural and human resentment toward soldiers who aren't. You'll notice it every time you see men in muddy boots meet men wearing clean ties.

I drew many cartoons about it. I don't know how much

*"Straighten those shoulders! How long you been in the army?"*

trouble they caused the various editors of the paper but I do know that there was enough to go around.

One of the worst plagues for people who draw pictures in the army is the steady stream of requests to do free-lance art work. A cartoonist uses brush and ink; therefore he must also be adept at making signs with Old English letters, copying the Madonna and Child, and doing portraits ("Of course, I'll make it worth your while")—according to the minds of those who need signs, Madonnas, or portraits.

I can't letter worth a damn, I never tried a Madonna, and if I painted George Washington's portrait I'd probably make him look like Willie or Joe before I finished. So I've found a

*"Th' hell with it, sir. Let's go back to the front."*

way to get around those people, and I'll pass it on to others who are in the same predicament.

I pass the request on to the editor, on the grounds that I can't sneeze, much less draw anything, without his orders. Since I keep the editor mystified about how much time I require to do six cartoons a week, he always refuses extracurricular requests because he's afraid I won't meet his deadlines. The more persistent folks who want me to do personal greeting cards and "Off Limits" signs for them have learned that my passing the buck to the editor amounts to a refusal, and soon they go and pick on somebody else whose editor isn't under any illusions about how long it takes to finish a routine drawing.

*"We oughta tell 'em th' whole army don't look like us, Joe."*

But once a request came when I was embroiled in the Battle of Naples, and since it came from a corps commander, I felt I couldn't afford to alienate any possible friends. The corps commander had set up an officers' club in an Italian yacht club. The windows were portholes and had to be blacked out with circular pieces of plywood at night.

The general's aide brought over two wooden disks on which the old man wanted pictures of Willie and Joe. I took a dim view of decorating officers' clubs, because I felt it would ruin my standing as an honorable enlisted man. But I worked out a satisfactory solution. I told the aide the drawings would be finished in a couple of days. It actually took fifteen minutes, but you can't afford to let people know you can work fast.

I painted Willie on one piece of plywood and Joe on the other. They looked like ordinary, life-size portraits until, the evening of the general's party, they were properly mounted in their circular holes.

Next morning, an officer secretly sympathetic with my cause reported that the party was not as lively as it might have been. Every time a beribboned staff officer with a highball in his hand lifted his eyes he found himself staring into the bearded face of a dirty, weary, disapproving dogface peering in the porthole with his fingertips on the sill.

People who make cartoons, according to legend, are supposed never to laugh. Perhaps I'm too young at the game to have the proper attitude, because I got a whale of a laugh out of another incident that occurred in the midst of the Battle of Naples.

I made a drawing of Joe and Willie slouched in a ruined doorway and looking wearily at an admonishing rear echelon corporal.

Says Willie, "He's right, Joe. When we ain't fightin' we should ack like sojers."

The day after the cartoon was printed a pleasant old colonel came into the *Stars and Stripes* office. He was quite evidently a new arrival, for he didn't know I was seditious. He hadn't bothered to study the drawing, which had taken a crack at the rigid regulations with regard to soldierly conduct behind the lines.

All the colonel knew was that when you weren't fighting you *were* supposed to have a military bearing. So he had a brilliant and highly original idea which he thought certain to win him a promotion or the Legion of Merit. He wanted, so help me, to take the original drawing and have thousands of huge poster copies printed. He planned to plaster them on every wall and telephone pole in Italy, as an admonition to GIs to "ack like sojers."

I was in a hell of a spot. He really looked like a nice guy, and I didn't want him slaughtered like a lamb, when he would probably start drawing retirement pay in a couple of years. But surely I couldn't say, "Sir, that's a treacherous cartoon, made to cause riots and rebellion among soldiers, and it would be a mistake to make posters of it and aid and abet my cause."

Instead, I gave him the drawing and, with brigadier's stars in his eyes, he headed for the door.

"The general will love this," he said.

I'm sure the general did.

*"He's right, Joe. When we ain't fightin' we should ack like sojers."*

Of all the world's armies, the American army gets the best equipment. The dogface knows that when he sees other armies. But we missed the boat on one thing. Every other army gets a liquor ration.

Drinking, like sex, is not a question of should or

EDITOR'S NOTE: Sergeant Mauldin has notified the publishers that shortly after he had written this section of the book the War Department granted officers (but not enlisted men) a liquor ration.

shouldn't in the army. It's here to stay, and it seems to us here that the best way to handle it is to understand and recognize it, and to arrange things so those who have appetites can satisfy them with a minimum of trouble for everybody. We have a pretty strong hunch that the army doesn't keep drinkin' likker out of our reach because the War Department is stupid. It's only because the home folks would scream their heads off at any hint of the clean-cut lads overseas besotting themselves. So stuff is bought at very high prices from street vendors over here. The dogfaces love to tell the story of the curious soldier who sent a bottle of cognac to a chemist friend for an analysis. In due time the report came back. It informed the soldier that his horse had kidney trouble. . . .

A liquor ration would seem to be a desirable thing. The British soldier gets a spot of whisky regularly, the size of the spot depending upon his rank. He gets a little beer also. And the Frenchman gets his wine. It's not much, but his palate is soothed with honest liquor which makes him unable to bear the smell, let alone the taste, of the home-distilled stuff the Americans are forced to drink because they can get nothing else.

The Arabs used to gather discarded British whisky bottles, fill them with unmentionable substances, and sell the hooch to the Americans for ten dollars a bottle.

Until some intelligent brass hat repaired a big brewery in Naples and started to send beer to Anzio, the boys at the beachhead were fixing up their own distilleries with barrels of dug-up vino, gasoline cans, and copper tubing from wrecked airplanes. The result was a fiery stuff which the Italians call grappa. The doggies called it "Kickapoo Joy Juice," and took the name from the popular "Li'l Abner" comic strip which *Stars and Stripes* printed daily. It wasn't bad stuff when you cut it with canned grapefruit juice.

Troop commanders, who would seem to be the best judges of discipline and morale in their own outfits, usually looked the other way when they spotted one of these distilleries. Many troop commanders were, in fact, among the distilleries' best customers. I knew one CO who used to tip his boys off

*"It will comfort my ol' woman to know I have gave up
rye whisky an' ten-cent seegars."*

when members of the inspector general's office came around.
He called them "revenooers."

These unauthorized gin mills, in spite of their crude apparatus, produced a drink much less corrosive than the bootleg
stuff the Italian civilians offered. The local rotgut made many
who drank it "crazy" drunk, not "respectable" drunk. That
caused a few cases of ulcers, blindness, and God knows what.

Because drinking is a big thing in a dogface's life, I drew
many pictures of guys wrapped around cognac bottles. I
showed Willie and Joe, stewed to the ears, telling their captain, as an alibi, that they were "jest a coupla red-blooded
American boys."

Too many sharp-eyed people noticed that there were three men in the picture, and *seven* hands; therefore, they were convinced that I was stewed to the ears myself and disqualified as a sober judge of the drinking problem.

*"Hell of a way to waste time. Does it work?"*

Some guys brought the habit overseas with them, but I think the large majority drinks because other recreational facilities are crowded or unavailable, and liquor can dull the sharp memories of war.

That's something the American public just can't seem to realize, and that's why the European armies get good hooch and the Americans don't. The Europeans have seen war and armies at first hand. An army at war is far different from an

*"We're jest a coupla red-blooded American boys."*

army in its own homeland, and all soldiers' instincts are pretty much the same.

The Europeans know that soldiers are going to do some drinking, and, since they don't like to have their windows kicked in by joyful souses, they keep their soldiers' whistles wetted just enough to satisfy the boys, but not enough to souse them.

I'm not trying to say the American army is a drunken army. Most of the men have the same attitude as I have about liquor. I drink very little, and I don't like strong liquor at all. Yet there have been times over here when I have tied one on because I was homesick, or bored, or because I was sitting around with a bunch of guys who had a bottle, and when it came around to me I just naturally took a belt at it. And there were many times that I guzzled wine because the water was questionable.

I don't think I'll carry a confirmed drinking habit back home with me. But until they send me home or send my wife over here, or until they ship over portable soda fountains, I'm going to do a little drinking now and then.

*"Go tell th' boys to line up, Joe. We got fruit juice fer breakfast."*

The Germans seemed to go out of their way to sabotage wineries. They were just like dogs; what they couldn't eat or drink or carry away, they messed up so nobody else could use it.

But they missed one opportunity. Corps headquarters in Anzio was set up in a twisting maze of catacombs far below the earth's surface. The tunnels had been used for wine stor-

*"Them rats! Them dirty, cold-blooded, sore-headed, stinkin' Huns! Them atrocity-committin' skunks . . ."*

age for centuries, and once you got down there it was hard to leave. It wasn't only a good place to stay away from shells. Many of the little niches had big vino barrels.

Only once was the peace of the catacombs and the soft sound of gurgling vino disturbed. That was when a shell hit the officers' latrine on the surface and shattered the wooden stairs which led down into the caves. No officers were in the latrine when the shell struck, but the place was out of commission for some time, and when a high-ranking officer gets off his daily schedule it's a very unhappy day for his subordinates.

The Germans drank a lot of schnapps during that Anzio period. Among the first prisoners captured on the beachhead

were several drunken German officers who had driven a volkswagen into the gaping doors of an LST. They must have had
a terrible hangover when they woke up next morning.

*"Don't startle 'im, Joe. It's almost full."*

I've used Willie and Joe in my cartoons because riflemen like
them are the basic guys and the most important guys in a war.
While there are many other weapons besides rifles even in a
rifle company, and dozens of other branches which are a part
of the general front, I haven't run into many objections because I stick to Willie and Joe and their rifles most of the
time. Those who work nearest the front know that the rifleman has the hardest job. Occasionally, however, I have tried
to branch out a little—with artillery and medics and engineers, mostly.

*"Ordnance? Ah'm havin' trouble with mah shootin' arn."*

(This cartoon was made on the Italian beachhead with inadequate equipment and stamp-pad ink instead of drawing ink.)

Germans respect our artillery, and I don't blame them. Our army seems less reluctant than the German army to expend shells instead of men. If one of our artillery observers in an infantry position sees a few Germans, he's very likely to get excited and throw a concentration of shells at them.

The battered krauts, who come from a land where shells are costly, lives are cheap, and logic governs action, can't understand why we didn't send an infantry patrol instead.

Nevertheless, their artillery is damned good—and in some places they have had us outgunned. Their 88mm. is the terror of every dogface. It can do everything but throw shells

*"I'll let ya know if I find th' one wot invented th' 88."*

around corners, and sometimes we think it has even done that.

The infantryman hates shells more than anything else. He can spend hours camouflaging himself against enemy observation, but the kraut who is twisting the controls on the 88 a couple of mountains away doesn't see what he is shooting at, and so his shell is just as likely to hit the good soldier who is under cover as the dumb one who is standing on top of a knoll.

The doggie becomes a specialist on shells after he has been in the line awhile. Sometimes he hates those that come straight at him more than those that drop, because the high ones give him more warning. On the other hand, if the flat one misses him it keeps on traveling, while the dropped one can kill him even if it misses him by dozens of yards. He has no love for either kind.

Some shells scream, some whiz, some whistle and others whir. Most flat-trajectory shells sound like rapidly ripped canvas. Howitzer shells seem to have a two-toned whisper.

Let's get the hell off this subject.

*"Ever notice th' funny sound these zippers make, Willie?"*

Propaganda leaflets are used by both sides. Because we seem to be winning the war, ours are generally more convincing, but I think theirs sometimes show more ingenuity. They know our fondness for comic strips and often illustrate their leaflets. What these pamphlets lack in truth they make up in reader interest.

I remember one that arrived in Anzio one morning. It was

*"Tell them leaflet people th' krauts ain't got time fer readin' today."*

so well-drawn and attractively colored that a lot of guys risked their necks to scramble out and get copies. It had something to do with a profiteer and an infantryman's wife in America. The continuity was awkward, but the pictures were spicy and the guys were hard up for reading matter.

Once a bunch of sadistic characters in a 105mm. howitzer outfit got a big batch of leaflet shells and didn't know what to do with them. Eventually they made up their minds. They knew that Jerry liked our leaflets. It was an American custom to shoot them over, give them time to scatter and fall to the ground, and then to cease all fire until the krauts could gather them. When they saw our propaganda coming, they would climb out of their cramped holes, light cigarettes, go to the toilet with the leaflets, or take a belt at the schnapps bottle. It was a pleasant five- or ten-minute break.

So the 105 battery crammed its guns full of propaganda and banged away until it was all used up. They waited just long enough for Jerry to get out of his hole and wrap himself around his bottle—then they piled in a concentration of high explosive.

Psychological Warfare probably got as sore about that as the surviving Germans. Our leaflet barrages were distrusted for a long, long time after that.

*"K Comp'ny artillery commander speakin'."*

Mortars are the artillery of an infantry company. Outside of the bazooka, they carry more viciousness and wallop per pound than any weapon the infantry has. The guys who

*"You have completed your fiftieth combat patrol. Con- gratulations. We'll put you on mortars awhile."*

operate them are at a big disadvantage. Because of the mor- tar's limited range, they have to work so close to the front that they are a favorite target for snipers, patrols, shells, and countermortar fire. Knocked-out mortar positions earn Iron Crosses for ambitious young herrenvolk.

The worst thing about mortars is that the Germans make them too. Their nastiest is the "screaming meemie." I never drew pictures about "screaming meemies" because they just aren't funny.

For a long time I loved to throw hooked cartoons at the Air Forces and other branches famed for their comfortable rear echelon accommodations. One of the common gripes among

*"Uncle Willie!"*

the infantry is the way the fliers get to go home after some definite number of missions.

An Air Corps mission amounts to several hours of discomfort and considerable danger, after which the fliers return to their bases. Some of the airfields, particularly the fighter strips, are far from comfortable, but on the whole the flying boys do okay by themselves.

Recently I've changed some of my opinions. After a certain length of time overseas, you stop bitching at the guy who has something. You may wish you had it yourself, but you begin to realize that taking the warm coat off his back isn't going to make your back any warmer. So the more seasoned doggie just sort of wonders why he doesn't get to go home after a certain number of "missions." He laughs about the youthful-

*"Hullo, glamorous."*
*"Howdy, blitzkrieg."*

ness of the Air Corps officers and he wishes somebody looked after him as well as somebody looks after the Air Corps. But he doesn't bitch when he sees a formation of planes going through heavy flak and he feels pretty awful when he sees one go down and thinks of the guys in it.

As the war goes on, a sort of undeclared fraternity develops. It might be called "The Benevolent and Protective Brotherhood of Them What Has Been Shot At." So, while the infantryman may go on griping because *he* doesn't get 50 per cent extra pay for dangerous duty, and because *he* can't go back to a base when his mission is accomplished, when he talks to a man who is flak-happy from too many hours in the substratosphere buzzing with enemy fighters he has a tendency to sympathize with the airman, even when the doggie himself is battle-happy.

It would be pretty hard to define an infantry "mission." It goes on twenty-four hours a day, seven days a week, and the infantryman has everything from planes and tanks to grenades and bullets thrown at him, to say nothing of flame throwers, mines, booby traps, and shells. When he has had a year or two of this he has, in the opinion of many of us, completed enough missions to merit him a hundred "rest cures." He is damned lucky if he gets a three-day pass to a town swarming with other soldiers.

Once I watched a tank battle from as great a distance as I could keep without sacrificing visibility. I wasn't anxious to get any closer because the American tanks were tangling with some very efficient Panzers.

I tried to draw a picture of the battle itself, but no cartoon could have mirrored that scene. The only drawing that came out of the immense spectacle of crawling, turning, spitting, dying monsters was one about the pooped-out crews who crawled out of the tanks for a breath of air before they rumbled back into battle.

Religious services in battle zones offer weird contrast to bursting shells and the twisted wreckage of war. It is strange to see reverence helmeted and armored.

I saw a Catholic chaplain at Salerno gather up his white robes and beat a Focke-Wulf's tracers into a muddy ditch by a split second, then return and carry on the service as if nothing had happened. I have a lot of respect for those chaplains who keep up the spirits of the combat guys. They often give the troops a pretty firm anchor to hang onto.

For some time I experienced a recurring battle between my cartoon deadlines and my sense of respect for the holy. I let the former win in one cartoon, but since then my righteous side has ignored the deadlines.

Once a British friend on the Eighth Army paper asked me why I didn't draw something about them. So I did.

There was a standing joke for a while between the British

*". . . forever, Amen. Hit the dirt."*

division at Anzio and one of the American divisions. The Americans, noted for their wealth of matériel, often littered the area with discarded equipment, and the thrifty British who relieved them just couldn't understand it. If a British colonel draws an unnecessary pair of shoes for his regimental supply, he's likely to get a court-martial out of it, and God help the Tommy who loses his Enfield rifle.

So the British used to accuse the Americans of leaving a messy battlefield, and I drew a picture of a Tommy telling that to two dogfaces. The British up there seemed to like it okay, and the doggies at Anzio caught it. But the British brass in Naples made a complaint. They didn't understand the picture, but they were certain it was anti-British.

I was sorry that happened, because I think the offended

*"You blokes leave an awfully messy battlefield."*

ones belonged to a minority, and the British would have given me quite a lot of opportunities for cartooning.

Their drivers are a little trouble sometimes, because they can't get used to the right-hand side of the highways, and they are often cussed at by our guys. Their brass hats are very stuffy, like a lot of ours, and I think it would have been a pleasure to work on them.

If you can get behind an Englishman's unholy fear of making a friend until he has known the candidate for at least five years, you will find him a pretty good egg. I made a drawing for private circulation among the staff of *Union Jack*, the British army paper, and I had a gratifying feeling that they understood the American sense of humor. The drawing was one of the commanding officer of *Union Jack*.

Chemical Warfare is a big branch which has seldom been noticed because the Germans haven't yet started to gas us. The CWs must have some high-pressure dime-store salesmen working in their midst, judging by the screwy little gadgets with which they love to load the infantry. Still, their 4.2 chemical mortars have done a tremendous and unrecognized job of blasting the pants off the krauts with high explosive and phosphorus.

*"I see Comp'ny E got th' new-style gas masks."*

Once in a while I've been guilty of drawing certain pictures to get a grudge out of my system. One time when I was driving my jeep I got caught in a convoy of quartermaster trucks and I became very unhappy as the miles rolled by. It was the worst convoy I had ever seen. If one driver got tired of

*"You'd hurry home too if you lived in a ration dump!"*

looking at the rear of the preceding truck, he would, without any signal, pull around the offending vehicle and pass it so he could gaze at the rear of the next truck. The whole column was clipping along at sixty miles an hour, hogging the road, and making things very unpleasant indeed for everybody else on the road. I was knocked into the ditch twice.

That made me draw my first Quartermaster cartoon. A little while later the French army started tearing up the roads, and they made our worst quartermaster drivers seem like timid old ladies. All a Frenchman knows about a truck is the general location of the foot throttle. French convoys stop simply by smashing into one another's bumpers.

I made a complete turnabout and did a cartoon favoring

*"Some of you may not come back. A French convoy has
been reported on the road."*

the quartermasters vs. the French. I was merely working off
steam and I doubt very much if I influenced or was even noticed by the quartermasters or the French, who were too busy
denting each other's fenders. There was a slight stink about
the French drawing, because some authorities were afraid our
allies might not take that kind of ribbing. Apparently they
did.

I got downright affectionate toward the quartermasters in
France, where they did a miraculous job of supplying the
combat troops. The gasoline problem was fierce, because the
combat men had moved so far ahead of the supply schedule,
but the QMs delivered the goods.

Army supply is a tremendous machine which works effi-

*"I'll be darned! Here's one wot wuz wrecked in combat."*

ciently and quietly—so quietly that it is hardly noticed by the combat troops, who never wonder where their stuff is coming from and don't hesitate to yell when it fails to arrive.

But I was getting too soft, and so I had to throw one at the quartermasters and the French and everybody else except Ordnance. The ordnance men were too busy patching up the vehicles these gasoline cowboys had wrecked.

I'm sure I didn't hurt any feelings, for nobody paid any attention to me while I was flailing around with my brush and ink bottle. They had more important things to do.

When the mountain fighting in Italy first started to get tough, and it was impossible for trucks or jeeps to bring food, water, and ammo up the mountain trails, mule companies were mustered and calls for experienced mule skinners went out through the divisions. Mules were sought out and bought from farmers. They carried supplies to many soldiers who hadn't seen a jeep for weeks. Many of them were undoubtedly blood relatives of the beloved Maggie of World War I who had been left overseas after she kicked hell out of her regimental commander to the delight of one and all.

It would have gladdened the hearts of those old soldiers at home, who were convinced that this new army was going crazy with newfangled inventions, to see long columns of balky mules being cajoled and threatened up the trails by their bearded, swearing, sweating skinners.

Once I thought I did a very funny cartoon. It was a picture of an old-time cavalryman shooting his jeep, which had a broken axle. It is one of those cartoon ideas you think up rarely; it has simplicity, it tells a story, it doesn't need words. It is, I believe, the very best kind of cartoon.

At the time I was stationed at Fort Devens with my division, the feature editor of *Yank*, the army weekly, asked me to send him some stuff. I did, but he didn't like the material. He had just come from a civilian magazine, where the only army cartoons showed jeeps jumping over mountains. After about a dozen drawings, I stopped sending stuff to him, but he did use the cavalry cartoon. He reduced it to postage-stamp size and ran it on the last column of the last page. One sneeze by the puniest typesetter and I'd have been blown right off the page. Since that time I have found those *Yank* employees whom I have met to be pleasant people, but I have never quite forgiven that feature editor.

I revived the old cavalry sergeant in the *Stars and Stripes*, where I have a regular two-column space which can't be made any smaller. I shall keep reviving that cartoon until somebody appreciates it.

If I were trying to tell somebody about the war, I would certainly say more about the engineers. But I don't know how they bolt braces on Bailey bridges, and I don't know the finer points of neutralizing a Teller mine, so I can't draw many

pictures about them, except as they come into contact with the infantry.

Combat engineers carry rifles and often use them. When they put down their rifles they have to pick up their tools.

I intended the picture of the professional fighting man and the man who is laboring on a road as pure sarcasm. The cartoon was probably understood by few people outside the engineers and infantry. The fighting man won't be able to put his knowledge to good use after the war, and the muddy engineer probably owned a fleet of trucks in civil life.

Mine detectors are always good cartoon material, but unfortunately you can't draw very realistic cartoons about them, because mine detectors are seldom used for anything but detecting mines. That's the trouble with drawing pictures

*"I calls her Florence Nightingale."*

*"Best little mine detector made."*

*"Damn fine road, men!"*

*"Yer lucky. Yer learnin' a trade."*

about specialists and their equipment. All these guys are fighting a war, and some of the time they are doing it in great danger. They develop a rather serious turn of mind, and so an engineer might stare with some wonderment if you tried to show his life with his mine detector in a series of gags. He's usually a little scared when he's poking around in a minefield, and he stopped feeling silly about it a long time ago.

*"Don't hurry for me, son. I like to see young men take*
*an interest in their work."*

The guy who thinks up names for Liberty ships has a relative over here. The relative thinks up names for telephone codes.

Instead of saying, "This is Company A; give me G-3 at Division CP, advance," he says, "Able Jackson company calling

*"This is Fragrant Flower Advance. Gimme yer goddam number."*

Jehoshaphat 3." That's to confuse any wire tappers from the Third Reich who might be listening.

You can take the cartoon and go on from there.

The medics are good subjects for drawings, and anybody who does stuff about the infantry has to throw in the medics once in a while. They are a lot like the other branches. The farther you work toward the front, the simpler and rougher life gets, and a few more human and good things show up.

The aid man is the dogface's family doctor, and he is regarded as an authority on every minor ailment from a blister to a cold in the head. The aid man usually takes this responsibility quite seriously. He lances and patches blisters with all

*"It's okay, Joe. I'm a noncombatant."*

the professional pride of a brain specialist removing a tumor. He watches over his boys and sees that their water is pure or, if there is no water, he looks at the wine barrel.

But the dogface's real hero is the litter bearer and aid man who goes into all combat situations right along with the infantryman, shares his hardships and dangers, and isn't able to fight back. When the infantryman is down, the medic must get up and help him. That's not pleasant sometimes when there's shooting.

The aid men and litter bearers know that their work is often far more important than that of the surgeon at the operating table; because if it were not for the aid man the casualty would not live to reach the surgeon's table.

Let's say the doggie has a shattered leg and is lying in a shell hole out in front of his company, which is pinned down by machine-gun fire. He uses the bandage from his first-aid packet to make a tourniquet, and he takes the sulfa pills, but he knows that if he lies there much longer he will bleed to death.

Nobody is going to blame the aid man if he saves his own neck and doesn't go out after a man who will probably die anyway. But the medic usually goes. If the Germans are feeling pretty good, they might lift their fire when they see his red-cross armband.

Put yourself in the wounded guy's shoes when he sees the medic appear over him, and his pain is dulled by morphine, his bleeding is stopped, and he is lifted out and carried back to safety and good surgery. Sure, he's going to love that medic. And after a few dozen men owe their lives to one man, that little pill roller is going to be very well liked indeed.

Sooner or later, like everybody who works around the infantry, the medic is going to get his. Many aid men have been wounded and many have been killed. It should comfort the families of those who have died to know that there are many friends who grieve with them.

But if I say much more than this the commissioned intern who entered my ward in Naples one winter when I was recovering from pneumonia and ordered me to lie at attention, if I couldn't sit or stand at attention when I saw him coming, will show this around and say:

"See? I told you we medics did a great job!"

It's a hell of a thing that some brass hats have made front-line medics turn in their combat badges. If the brass did it because the medic doesn't fight, and the enemy might take the badge the wrong way if they capture him, that's reasonable. But they should have given him something to replace it—maybe a cross instead of a rifle on the badge.

I say that because it's important. Everybody these days wears combat boots and combat jackets. A lot of people who

EDITOR'S NOTE: The War Department recently restored combat badges to the front-line medics.

*"Hell. Just when I git me practice built up they transfer
me to another regiment."*

never saw more infantry than basic training wear the infantry blue on their caps. The combat badge is about the only thing that sets the front-line man apart, and he has reason to be proud of it.

When they took the badges away, the infantry howled louder than the medics. I'm convinced that the combat badge means much more to the front-line soldier than the small amount of extra pay that goes with it. It is a symbol of what he has been through. Many troops who operate with the infantry should get it and don't and a few who shouldn't get it do.

I was hanging around a regiment in a rest area near Nancy, in France, when a group of doggies brought the subject up. A

*"I'm jest a country doctor. If ya don't mind, I'll consult wit' Pfc. Johnson, th' famous blister specialist."*

medic was in the group. He had plenty of guys speaking for him so he didn't say anything.

"Who's the stupid bastard what did it?"

"What the hell they think they're doing?"

"Our regimental clerks are wearing big combat badges and they take it away from one of our medics two days before a blurp gun cuts him in two!"

"Hell of a goddam note!"

But the direst threat of all came from a little Browning Automatic rifleman with thick glasses:

"Wait'll Ernie Pyle hears about this!"

When a soldier gets out of an army hospital he will most likely

*"Quit beefin' or I'll send ya back to th' infantry."*

be thrown into a "repple depple." This institution, identified in army regulations as a replacement depot, is a sort of clearing-house through which soldiers who have been separated from their outfits or soldiers newly arrived from the States have to pass for reassignment.

I went through a repple depple at Palermo, Sicily, and my experience seems to have been typical. This establishment was operated by a paratrooper lieutenant (I don't know why, either) who spent most of his time convincing us that paratrooping had a great postwar future. Several times I interrupted him to say that my outfit was only fifteen miles away and couldn't I get over to them. Each time he told me that a truck would come within a few hours and pick me up.

*"I think he should at least try to lie at attention."*

I believed this until I discovered two other guys from my outfit who had been waiting for this same truck for three weeks.

I guess the repple depple people didn't trust us, because the place was surrounded by a very high wall and there were guards beyond that.

We waited until night fell, then we plotted our "break." We persuaded one inmate, whose outfit had already gone and who had given up hope of salvation, to distract the guard while we went over the wall. As far as I know they still have my name and I'm still AWOL from a repple depple. I joined my outfit and caught the last boat to Salerno.

Later I learned that soldiers often languish in repple depples for months, only to be snapped up eventually by

*"Ya don't git combat pay 'cause ya don't fight."*

some outfit with which they are not familiar. A soldier's own outfit is the closest thing to home he has over here, and it is too bad when he has to change unnecessarily.

I heard of a soldier who spent his entire time overseas in repple depples, and went home on rotation without ever having been assigned. His home-town paper called him "a veteran of the Italian campaign."

The attitude of the dogface toward America and the home front is a complex thing. Nobody loves his own land more than a soldier overseas, and nobody swears at it more. He loves it because he appreciates it after seeing the horrible mess that has been made of Europe.

He has seen unbelievable degeneracy and filth in Mediter-

*"Who started th' rumor I wuz playin' poker wit' a
beautiful nurse?"*

ranean towns where mothers sell their daughters and daughters sell their mothers and little kids sell their sisters and themselves. He has seen the results of the German occupation of France and the fury of the French people and their savage revenge upon anything German. He has seen stark fear and utter destruction and horrible hunger. But at the same time he has seen families bravely trying to rebuild their shattered homes, and he has seen husbands and wives with rifles fighting ahead of him in France. He knows how they can throw themselves completely and unselfishly into the war when it is necessary.

So he is naturally going to get sore when he thinks of selfishness at home. He got just as sore at the big company which

*"I guess it's okay. The replacement center says he comes
from a long line of infantrymen."*

was caught bribing inspectors and sending him faulty armor for
his tanks as he did at the workers who held up production in
vital factories. He doesn't have time to go into economics and
labor-management problems. All he knows is that he is expected to make great sacrifices for little compensation, and he
must make those sacrifices whether he likes it or not. Don't
expect him to weigh the complicated problem before he gets
sore. He knows he delivered and somebody else didn't.

But, in spite of these irritations, the soldier's pride in his
country is immense. He's proud of the splendid equipment
he gets from home, and sometimes he even gets a little over-
bearing about it.

Often soldiers who are going home say they are going to tell

"*I got a nasty letter from your poor wife, Joe. You better give her an allotment after I pay you back that loan.*"

the people how fortunate we were to stop the enemy before he was able to come and tear up our country. They are also going to tell the people that it is a pretty rough life over here.

I've tried to do that in my drawings and I know that many thousands of guys who have gone back have tried to do it, too. But no matter how much we try we can never give the folks at home any idea of what war really is. I guess you have to go through it to understand its horror. You can't understand it by reading magazines or newspapers or by looking at pictures or by going to newsreels. You have to smell it and feel it all around you until you can't imagine what it used to be like when you walked on a sidewalk or tossed

*"I tried one of them labor-management argyments wit'*
*Lootenant Atkins."*

clubs up into horse chestnut trees or fished for perch or
when you did anything at all without a pack, a rifle, and a
bunch of grenades.

We all used to get sore at some of the ads we saw in magazines from America. The admen should have been required
by law to submit all copy to an overseas veteran before they
sent it to the printers.

I remember one lulu of a refrigerator ad showing a lovely,
dreamy-eyed wife gazing across the blue seas and reflecting
on how much she misses Jack . . . BUT she knows he'll
never be content to come back to his cozy nest (equipped
with a Frosty refrigerator; sorry, we're engaged in vital war

*"Congratulations. You're the 100th soldier who has posed
with that bottle of Icey Cola. You may drink it."*

production now) until the Hun is whipped and the world is
clean for Jack's little son to grow up in.

Chances are that Jack, after eighteen or twenty months of
combat, is rolling his eyes and making gurgling sounds every
time the company commander comes around, so the old man
will think he is battle-happy and send him home on rotation.
Like hell Jack doesn't want to come home now.

And when he does come home you can bet he'll buy some
other brand of refrigerator with his demobilization pay, just
to spite the Frosty adman.

When Bing Crosby returned to America after his visit to the
French front, he told reporters, according to one news dis-

patch, that entertainment is needed most by the dispirited troops of the rear echelon rather than by the front-line soldiers. Up there, it seemed to him, "morale is sky-high, clothes are cleaner and salutes really snap." The dogfaces who read that dispatch in the foxholes didn't know what front Bing was talking about.

Please, God, don't let anybody become a lecturer on frontline conditions until he has spent at least a year talking to the combat men. Many of us over here have been trying to find out about the front for several years and we feel like anything but experts.

One thing that caused a lot of howls among the soldiers was the way celebrities, particularly female ones, were always surrounded by officers.

Some celebrities couldn't help this, some encouraged it, and others just didn't know any better. Most of the blame should go to the officers. It was pretty awful to see a string of them tagging behind some little Hollywood chick. Several memorable ladies of the screen actually managed to break away from the howling pack and escape to the enlisted men, but there were very few such escapes.

I know officers like to see women from home as much as anybody else does, but I think the enlisted men should have been given a chance to see the girls.

Officers around the front were good Joes about it. The success of their jobs depended upon the morale of their men, and very few combat COs tried to horn in on the dogfaces' entertainment.

Decorations are touchy things to talk about. The British kid us because we're overdecorated, and perhaps we are in some ways.

Civilians may think it's a little juvenile to worry about ribbons, but a civilian has a house and a bankroll to show what he's done for the past few years.

I thought the War Department ruined any value the Good Conduct ribbon may have had by passing it out to men who had only one year of service. But it's different with those

medals which are given only for heroism in battle. You can
bet that any man decorated for heroism has earned the award,
because the committee that gave him the decoration first
called in a hell of a lot of witnesses.

I have four ribbons, and I haven't had so many troubles as
a lot of men who finished the last war with a single campaign
ribbon. But sometimes I'm a little proud of those four ribbons, and I often put them on under my sweater and peek at
them when nobody is looking.

*"Don't mention it, lootenant. They mighta replaced ya
wit' one of them salutin' demons."*

To the dogface out on patrol, his platoon command post,
with its machine-gun emplacement, is rear echelon and home
and the safest place in the world.

*"Just gimme a coupla aspirin. I already got a Purple Heart."*

The gunner in the platoon CP is itching to get the hell out of there and back to the safety of company headquarters, where the topkick is equally anxious to find an excuse to visit Battalion.

The radio operators in Battalion like to go after extra tubes at Regimental supply, even though Regimental seldom stocks tubes, and the guys who work at field desks in Regimental hate the guts of those rear echelon bastards in Division. Division feels that way about Corps, Corps about Army, Army about Base Section, and, so help me Hannah, Base Section feels that way about soldiers in the States.

Months after the new combat boots and jackets arrived in

*"Eeeeeek!"*

Italy many front-line soldiers still wore soaked leggings and flimsy field jackets. The new clothing was being short-stopped by some of the rear echelon soldiers who wanted to look like the combat men they saw in the magazines. None of these shortstoppers took the clothing with any direct intention of denying the stuff to guys at the front. I suppose these fellows in the rear just looked at the mountainous heap of warm combat jackets piled in a supply dump and didn't see anything wrong with swiping a couple for themselves. After several hundred thousand men had grabbed at the heap there weren't many new boots and jackets left.

The army had shipped over only enough of the new clothing to supply the men in the foxholes, and because of this rear

*"Wot do ya mean, 'It's nice to git back to th' rear echelon'? Ya been out huntin' souvenirs agin?"*

echelon pilfering, thousands of dogfaces at the front shivered in the mud and the rain while guys at the rear wore the combat clothes in warm offices.

You can see that it was a big gripe, and a justifiable one. If a soldier appeared in combat togs behind the battle zone, he was often stopped by a doggie and asked what he did for a living in the armed service of his country. If his answer was unsuitable, he was shoved into some alley whence he would emerge wearing the thin field jacket and wet leggings of his still outraged but now better dressed challenger.

The cartoon in which Willie tells Joe to grab the kraut's pistol and swap it for combat clothes probably didn't mean much to troops outside the Mediterranean theater. But in

Italy those who understood it best were, strangely, those conscientious souls in the rear who stubbornly insisted that combat suits were for combat men, and not for the guy who pounded a typewriter at Army Headquarters and particularly not for the officer who supervised the pounding.

*"Git his pistol, Joe. I know where we kin swap it fer a combat jacket an' some boots."*

During the winter I acquired a pair of parachutists' jump boots—the most comfortable, well-built footwear issued by the army. They were a present from some guys in the 509th Parachute Battalion and, although I was deeply grateful, I always had a twinge when I wore the boots in town. I felt that a barefoot paratrooper shivered in every alley and followed me wherever I went.

*"We calls 'em garritroopers. They're too far forward to wear ties an' too far back to git shot."*

There is a class of soldiers, midway between the front and rear—"too far forward to wear ties an' too far back to git shot." In this group there were a few men whose conduct, unfortunately, was taken by many combat men as typical of the entire class. I called these few men "garritroopers," to the subsequent protest of some paratroopers who felt that I had intended a crack at them. I really had not.

The garritroopers are able to look like combat men or like the rear soldiers, depending upon the current fashion trend. When the infantry was unpublicized and the Air Forces were receiving much attention, the emphasis was on beauty, and in every Army headquarters and midway supply dump you could shave yourselves with the garritrooper's trouser creases and use his shoes for a mirror. He would not wear ordinary GI trousers and shoes, but went in for sun glasses, civilian oxfords, and officers' forest-green clothing.

This burned up many decidedly unglamorous airplane mechanics who worked for a living and didn't look at all like the Air Force men the garritrooper saw in the magazines. It also burned many honest GIs, who automatically saluted the garritrooper before they noticed that his officer's shirt had no insignia on the collar.

It's true that many of the worst and most confirmed garritroopers were officers, who also affected the dark glasses and crushed caps of the birdmen, but much as he winced, the combat man didn't complain about them.

Some months later the infantry began to get attention. It took the doughfoots a long time to become accustomed to the new combat badges and extra pay. They were like ragged little stepchildren who had found a winning lottery ticket.

It didn't take the garritroopers long to switch clothes. They climbed out of the glamor rags and tossed the twenty-dollar sun glasses into the gutter. "Be dirty, be rough, be scuffed," they shouted. If they rode to town on a truck, they hung their faces over the side to get a coat of dust. They let their whiskers grow. They ripped holes in their pants and pounded their shoes with rocks. You could get five fancy officers' shirts for one tattered combat jacket, and if that jacket had a gen-yu-wine bullet hole you could name your own price.

Bands of the garritroopers would hound a poor khaki-clad clerk, on his way home after a hard day at the office. They would yell, "Haw! Goddam base section. Rear echelon gold-brick." And the base section clerk had to take it, because in his section regulations about clothing were quite strictly enforced.

The average doggie, sick of dirt, will make some effort to clean up when he gets one of those rare opportunities to go back to a city and he certainly doesn't want to start any fighting when he gets there.

So he is rather surprised when he enters a town he remembers having taken last month, and finds it full of rough, bearded wild men, who seem to be in the process of taking it

*"That can't be no combat man. He's lookin' fer a fight."*

again, for they are yelling like hell, smashing windows and tossing empty vino bottles at "those damned rear echelon goldbricks."

Every now and then the garritroopers would mistake a freshly scrubbed infantryman for a rear man. When this happened the doggie was usually too disgusted to protest.

But the saddest thing about the whole business was that a surprisingly large number of those khaki-clad little men far behind the battle, the men resented by doggie and cursed by garritrooper, had seen months of combat before being put on limited service because of wounds or exhaustion.

Dig a hole in your back yard while it is raining. Sit in the hole until the water climbs up around your ankles. Pour cold

*"Let 'im in. I wanna see a critter I kin feel sorry fer."*

mud down your shirt collar. Sit there for forty-eight hours, and, so there is no danger of your dozing off, imagine that a guy is sneaking around waiting for a chance to club you on the head or set your house on fire.

Get out of the hole, fill a suitcase full of rocks, pick it up, put a shotgun in your other hand, and walk on the muddiest road you can find. Fall flat on your face every few minutes as you imagine big meteors streaking down to sock you.

After ten or twelve miles (remember—you are still carrying the shotgun and suitcase) start sneaking through the wet brush. Imagine that somebody has booby-trapped your route with rattlesnakes which will bite you if you step on them. Give some friend a rifle and have him blast in your direction once in a while.

Snoop around until you find a bull. Try to figure out a way to sneak around him without letting him see you. When he does see you, run like hell all the way back to your hole in the back yard, drop the suitcase and shotgun, and get in.

If you repeat this performance every three days for several months you may begin to understand why an infantryman sometimes gets out of breath. But you still won't understand how he feels when things get tough.

*"Maybe Joe needs a rest. He's talkin' in his sleep."*

One thing is pretty certain if you are in the infantry—you aren't going to be very warm and dry while you sleep. If you haven't thrown away your blankets and shelter half during a march, maybe you can find another guy who has kept his shelter half and the two of you can pitch a pup tent. But pup

*"A experienced field sojer will figure out a way to sleep
warm an' dry. Lemme know when ya do."*

tents aren't very common around the front. Neither is sleep,
for that matter. You do most of your sleeping while you
march. It's not a very healthy sleep; you might call it a sort of
coma. You can't hear anybody telling you to move faster but
you can hear a whispering whoosh when the enemy up ahead
stops long enough to throw a shell at you.

You don't feel very good when you wake up, because there
is a thick fuzz in your head and a horrible taste in your mouth
and you wish you had taken your toothbrush out before you
threw your pack away.

It's a little better when you can lie down, even in the mud.
Rocks are better than mud because you can curl yourself
around the big rocks, even if you wake up with sore bruises

*"Ya wouldn't git so tired if ya didn't carry extra stuff.*
*Throw th' joker outta yer decka cards."*

where the little rocks dug into you. When you wake up in the mud your cigarettes are all wet and you have an ache in your joints and a rattle in your chest.

You get back on your feet and bum a cigarette from somebody who has sense enough to keep a pack dry inside the webbing of his helmet liner. The smoke makes the roof of your mouth taste worse but it also makes you forget the big blister on your right heel. Your mind is still foggy as you finger the stubble on your face and wonder why there are no "Burma Shave" signs along the road so you could have fun reading the limericks and maybe even imagine you're walking home after a day's work.

Then you pick up your rifle and your pack and the en-

*"This damn tree leaks."*

trenching tool and the canteen and the bayonet and the first-aid kit and the grenade pouches. You hang the bandoleer around your neck and you take the grenades out of the pouches and hang them on your belt by the handles.

You look everything over and try to find something else you can throw away to make the load on the blister a little lighter. You chuckle as you remember the ad you saw in the tattered magazine showing the infantryman going into battle with a gas mask and full field pack.

Then you discover something and you wonder why the hell you didn't think of it long ago—the M-1 clip pouches on your cartridge belt are just the right size for a package of cigarettes. That will keep the rain off the smokes.

You start walking again but you are getting close now so

*"Me future is settled, Willie. I'm gonna be a expert on types of European soil."*

you keep five yards between yourself and the next guy and you begin to feel your heart pounding a little faster. It isn't so bad when you get there—you don't have time to get scared. But it's bad going there and coming back. Going there you think of what might happen and coming back you remember what did happen and neither is pleasant to think about.

Of course, nothing's really going to get you. You've got too much to live for. But you might get hurt and that would be bad. You don't want to come back all banged up. Why the hell doesn't somebody come up and replace you before you get hurt? You've been lucky so far but it can't last forever.

You feel tighter inside. You're getting closer. Somebody

*"Now that ya mention it, Joe, it does sound like th' patter of rain on a tin roof."*

said that fear is nature's protection for you and that when you get scared your glands make you more alert. The hell with nature. You'd rather be calm the way everybody else seems to be. But you know they're just as jumpy as you are.

Now they're pulling off the road. Maybe you don't have to go up there tonight. You don't. You start to dig a slit trench because the enemy might come to you if you don't go to him. But there's a big root halfway down. Mud and roots seem to follow you wherever you go. You dig around the root and then you try the hole for size. You look at the sky and it looks like rain.

A weapons carrier slithers up the trail and the driver tosses out the packs you all threw away a couple of miles back.

Maybe the army is getting sensible. Hell, you got the wrong pack and somebody else got yours. The blankets are damp but they would have been soaked anyway even if you had carried them.

You throw some brush in the bottom of the trench. You squeeze in. You don't like it. You get out and sleep beside the hole. You wake up two hours later and you're glad you didn't get in the hole because it's raining and the hole is half full of water. Your head still feels fuzzy and your heart is still pounding but it's better because you have been lying down. A pool of water has collected right in the center of the shelter half you threw over yourself and the water is dribbling right through to your skin. You brush the water out and pull the canvas tight around you. The rain continues, the weather is getting colder, and you try to go to sleep quick so you won't feel it.

Sometimes when the doggies are on the march they find a gutted house with part of the roof still hanging out from the top of the wall. This makes very fine shelter indeed and it's a happy time when they go into bivouac near such a house. But when the guys are really lucky they find a barn, and every doggie knows that barns are far better than houses. He knows that vermin are awful things to have and, since he never gets a chance to take a bath, he avoids houses and questionable mattresses if he can find a luxurious barn full of hay. A farmer who has reason to be suspicious of soldiers prefers to have the guys sleep in his barns because even if the doggies swipe some hay they can't carry off his favorite rocking chair and daughter.

When you are in a barn you don't have to bother about being nice to the hostess because she is probably a cow. You can put one blanket under you and one over you and lots of hay on top of that and you will be very, very warm.

The only bad thing about a barn is that you find a lot of rats there. You don't mind it so much when they just scurry over you if they leave your face alone and don't get curious about your anatomy. A barn rat likes nothing better than to bed down with his guest and carry on a conversation in Braille all night.

*"Aim between th' eyes, Joe. Sometimes they charge when they're wounded."*

The best nights I've spent in the field have been in barns. And the best night I ever spent in a barn was when I woke up and found a cow standing over me. She had a calf but I shouldered the little creature aside and milked the mother in my best New Mexico style. The farmer came in when I was almost finished and I pointed to a small lump on the cow's udder. That showed he hadn't stripped her well and I showed him how to do a nice job of stripping with thumb and forefinger. He was well content when I left and so was I because that was the first fresh milk I had drunk since I left the States.

The dogfaces love to find haystacks and an infantry company will tear down a stack in five minutes. They line their

*Breakfast in bed.*

holes with the stuff and, if they've got bedsacks, they'll fill
them too. If they don't have bedsacks they find some stack
that hasn't been torn down and dozens of guys will crawl into
this one stack and disappear. It's wonderfully soft and wonderfully warm but if it's old hay a lot of people who suffer
from hay fever have to pass it up. But even if you don't have
hay fever there's another bad thing about haystacks: the enemy has used them and he figures you are going to use them
too, so he often mines them and, if he is within shooting
range, every now and then throws a shell into them. Bombers
and artillerymen blow up haystacks and barns just on general
principle sometimes.

Caves are nice and you find them sometimes in the mountains. Nice thing about a cave is that you can throw up a little

dirt around the entrance and you're safe from almost anything. Air bursts and butterfly bombs make open holes uncomfortable sometimes.

Barns are still about the best, though.

*"We gotta probe fer Willie."*

Abandoned towns are wonderful places for guys who have time to make homes in them. Many doggies prefer wrecked houses to undamaged houses because as long as there are walls to break the wind and a roof to stop the weather the men can fix the places up without any qualms about scrounging.

There is a difference between scrounging and looting. Looting is the stealing of valuables, but most evacuees take their valuables with them. Scrounging is the borrowing of things which will make life in the field a little more bearable.

*"Who is it?"*

Since the infantryman carries everything on his back, he can scrounge only temporarily, borrowing a chair from this house and bedsprings from that one.

The headquarters units which follow the infantry have a little motor transport and they can carry many things with them. Go into almost any field CP and you'll find a pale-pink upholstered chair which looks pretty silly sitting there in the mud.

In combat, infantry officers usually share the same conditions as the dogfaces. But when the doggies get back to a temporary rest area they have to be careful about fixing up a wrecked house too well because the officers may suddenly remember that they are officers and take over the premises. Noncoms can be just as bad about it, too.

*"Don't tell 'em now, lieutenant. Wait'll they fix th' stove."*

It's strange how memories of peacetime life influence these makeshift homes. If a soldier has fixed himself a dugout or an abandoned house, and has cleaned it up and made it look presentable, his visitors instinctively feel that this is a man's house, and he is its head. They use his C-ration can ash trays and they don't spit on the floor. But no matter how much time or effort a guy is able to spend making his dugout livable, and no matter how many of his friends may come to shoot the breeze with him, there are only a few subjects of conversation: wives and girls and families, just plain women, or home.

Many dugouts in Anzio were fixed up surprisingly well. Some guys sat there for five months without moving, and they had to do something to relieve their boredom. They

*"Take off yer hat when ya mention sex here. It's a reverint subject."*

scrounged a little lumber here, a set of bedsprings there, and some of the boys even found mirrors.

The farther behind the front line the dugouts were made the more elaborate they became. Some blossomed out with reading lamps made from salvaged jeep headlights and batteries, and a few huts had wooden floors and real rugs and charcoal stoves made from German gas cans and the flexible tubing that had been used to waterproof vehicles for the landing. Old brass from shells made good stove parts, and the thick cardboard shell cases were used to line walls and to make "sidewalks" through the mud.

All the dugouts were sunk deep in the sandy, damp ground, and had thick roofs made of layers of logs and planks and dirt. That made them almost invulnerable to shells. Guys

*"Fire two more fer effect, Joe. I'm makin' a stovepipe."*

who were able to find enough planks to line their walls combined insulation and decoration by covering them with cardboard wallpaper from ration boxes. But these more elaborate jobs weren't to be found very often right up at the front, because the guys up there couldn't move around freely enough to do any scrounging.

The Germans must be given credit for rigging up some very fine dwelling places. They had the advantage of time. Their dugouts at Cassino were fantastic. One was so deep that its roof, almost flush with the surface of the ground, consisted of a four-foot layer of dirt and rocks on top, then a section of railroad ties, a thinner layer of stones, a layer of crisscrossed steel rails, and beneath that a ceiling of more thick wooden ties. Its roof indicated that many of our shells and bombs registered direct hits on it, yet I doubt if the explosions even disturbed the sleep of the occupants. The walls were lined with real plywood, nicely fitted, and there were springed bunks which folded into the wall. There was a radio, too, and a number of German magazines. It was easy to see how the krauts were able to snooze blissfully through our worst bombings and shellings, and then come out and fight off our infantry when the big stuff stopped.

The dugout's only weakness was its one entrance—a screen door to protect the delicate krauts from predatory mosquitoes. Cassino was entered by the foot infantry who knocked down the dugout doors with their grenades and bayoneted the occupants.

Then our guys occupied the luxurious dugouts for a while.

Those who look carefully at newspaper pictures have probably observed that many Germans are captured at the front without helmets, while our guys wear them almost all the time. One of the reasons for this is that we were taught very thoroughly that a helmet is a good thing to have around, but the main reason is because the American helmet is a handy instrument even when you're not wearing it. You can dig with it, cook with it, gather fruit with it and bathe with it. The only disadvantage of the helmet is that it is drafty in winter and hot in summer.

The infantryman bathes whenever he has an opportunity, which is about twice during the summer and not quite as often in the winter. He bathes in rivers, seas, and old shell holes which have collected water. The only consistent thing about his bath is that it is always cold.

An infantry company in Italy scrounged a real tin bathtub and they carried it around with them for several weeks until it was riddled by an 88 shell.

In spite of growing resentment against the souvenir hunter, the market for souvenirs is booming. Front-line troops pick them up first-hand, and rear troops buy them or police up what the front-line troops missed. On the local market one hundred bucks is the prevailing price for a Luger pistol. A P-38, the mass-production model of the Luger, will get you

*"No, thanks, Willie. I'll go look fer some mud wot ain't
been used."*

about seventy bucks. German helmets are flooding the market
and aren't worth picking up.

Shortly after Rome fell, all of the city's better hotels were
grabbed by brass hats and the Air Forces. Did the infantry
have a hotel? Hell, no. The sightseeing doggie was out of
luck if he wanted a place to sleep after he had ogled some
of Rome's choicer sights. This was a heck of a note for
the doggie who had sweated out Anzio and Cassino and who
had pushed north to take Rome after nine awful months in
Italy.

It was always a little infuriating for the dogfaces to take a
town away from the Germans by dint of considerable effort,

*"Here's yer money back fer them souvenirs. Ya been scarin'*
*hell outta our replacements."*

to be treated royally by the liberated inhabitants and given the golden key to the city, and, after moving on farther, to come back to that town and find everything changed. All the choice spots are occupied by brass hats and the CIC and AMG and ACC and PWD. All the liquor has been drunk and the pretty babe who kissed the dogface tearfully as he liberated her is already going steady with a war correspondent. It's a bad thing, and even though the doggie realizes all these people have their place in the war, and it is necessary that they follow him, he also gets mad as hell sometimes.

Hence the picture about Joe and Willie being directed to the Catacombs, where Christians used to languish. Whether this sort of cartoon ever did any material good I don't know.

I should like to think that the Catacombs drawing inspired some flinty requisitioning colonel to donate the Grand Hotel to private soldiers in the infantry. But this is a practical world, and if it happened I didn't hear about it.

*"He says we kin git a room in th' Catacombs. They useta keep Christians in 'em."*

Anzio was unique.

It was the only place in Europe which held an entire corps of infantry, a British division, all kinds of artillery and special units, and maintained an immense supply and administration setup without a rear echelon. As a matter of fact, there wasn't any rear; there was no place in the entire beachhead where enemy shells couldn't seek you out.

Sometimes it was worse at the front; sometimes worse at

*"My God! Here they wuz an' there we wuz."*

the harbor. Quartermasters buried their dead and amphibious duck drivers went down with their craft. Infantrymen, dug into the Mussolini Canal, had the canal pushed in on top of them by armor-piercing shells, and Jerry bombers circled as they directed glider bombs into LSTs and Liberty ships. Wounded men got oak leaf clusters on their Purple Hearts when shell fragments riddled them as they lay on hospital beds. Nurses died. Planes crash-landed on the single air strip.

Planes went out to seek the "Anzio Express," that huge gun which made guys in rest areas play softball near slit trenches. The planes would report the Express destroyed and an hour later she would come in on schedule.

The krauts launched a suicidal attack which almost drove

*"Wisht I could stand up an' git some sleep."*

through to the sea. Evacuation was already beginning in the
harbor when a single American battalion broke the point of
the attack, then was engulfed and died. Bodies of fanatical
young Germans piled up in front of the machine guns, and
when the guns ran out of ammunition the Wehrmacht
came through and was stopped only by point-blank artillery.
One American artillery battalion of 155s fired 80,000 rounds
of ammunition at Anzio, and there were dozens of these
battalions.

You couldn't stand up in the swamps without being cut
down, and you couldn't sleep if you sat down. Guys stayed in
those swamps for days and weeks. Every hole had to be covered, because the "popcorn man" came over every night and
shoveled hundreds of little butterfly bombs down on your

head by the light of flares and exploding ack-ack. You'd wake up in the morning and find your sandbags torn open and spilled on the ground.

The krauts used little remote-control tanks filled with high explosives. You wondered how Jerry could see you and throw a shell at you every time you stuck your head up, until you climbed into the mountains after it was all over and were able to count every tree and every house in the area we had held. Tiger tanks grouped together and fired at you. Your artillery thought it was a battery and threw a concentration of shells at the tanks, and by the time your shells struck the Tigers had moved away and were firing at you from another place.

Four American tank destroyers crossed the canal and bounced armor-piercing shells off the turret of a Tiger until it turned its massive gun and disintegrated them with five shells.

German infantry rode their tanks into battle and the dogfaces shot them off like squirrels but they didn't get all of them—some came in and bayoneted our guys in their holes.

This wasn't a beachhead that was secured and enlarged until it eventually became a port for supplies coming in to supplement those being expended as the troops pushed inland. Everything was expended right here. It was a constant hellish nightmare, because when you weren't getting something you were expecting something, and it lasted for five months.

A company of infantry sat on a mountain in Italy in mud, rain, snow, and freezing cold weather. They had inadequate clothing and they didn't get relief. They sat there for weeks, and the only men who came down that mountain were dead ones, badly wounded ones, and those who had trench foot from the icy mud.

During that entire period the dogfaces didn't have a hot meal. Sometimes they had little gasoline stoves and were able to heat packets of "predigested" coffee, but most often they did it with matches—hundreds of matches which barely took the chill off the brew. Soon the guys ran out of matches.

*"By th' way, we spotted some kraut gun positions too."*

Because they were on K rations they had coffee only once a day. The dinner ration had synthetic lemonade—a mixture of carbolic acid and ersatz lemon powder. Try drinking that in a muddy foxhole in freezing weather. The supper ration had a sort of bouillon soup, which was impossible. It takes a lot of water to make it, and a lot more to drown the salty thirst it causes. Usually there wasn't even enough water for the guys to brush their teeth because there weren't enough mules to haul it up.

Our army is pretty well fed behind the lines—as well fed as an army can be. The food advertisers who show a soldier wallowing in goodies aren't far wrong. The abundance of food in

*"Ya know, I ain't worth a dern in th' morning without
a hot cuppa coffee."*

our big ration dumps amazes Europeans. But the advertisers make one mistake. They always show the soldier wallowing in goodies at the front. He doesn't wallow in anything but mud up there.

Usually it's nobody's fault. In Sicily and Southern France things moved so fast it was hard for the supplies to catch up. In Italy the mountains complicated the supply situation.

Since there is not much a cook can do while his company is in combat, his worth depends upon how many ration cases he can carry and not upon how flaky his corn bread turns out. Occasionally a few cooks managed to get hot food up to their boys but this didn't happen very often.

*"Drink it all, boys. Th' guy wot put out that order about
shavin' ain't comin' up here to inspect us."*

Front-line troops got K and C rations because the bulky B
units, which contain fruit juice, flour for pastries, and all the
nice things a guy likes to eat, were too much for the mules
which had to carry everything else, including ammunition and
water. The main trouble with K and C rations was their
monotony. I suppose they had all the necessary calories and
vitamins but they didn't fill your stomach and you got awfully
tired of them.

It's a tragedy that all the advantages of being in the American army never get to those who need them most—the men
at the front. It was the same with the Red Cross and movies
and all the rest of the better things. You just can't have variety
shows and movie screens at the front.

*"I caught KP agin."*

When our planes weren't shooting up kraut supply lines, the German army was pretty well fed. Maybe they didn't know much about vitamins, but their stuff was filling. It was always a great day when our patrols found caches of Jerry food.

Their sausage is good, and they have a marmalade that comes packed in a big wooden box and isn't bad at all. Of course, most of this stuff came from France. Now that they can't get it from the French the German diet will probably get slimmer.

But the Germans have a pretty good chow system, according to prisoners I've talked to. Our guys seldom get a square meal with meat and gravy until they are back in a rest area where the food can be brought up easily. The Germans send all their *best* stuff to the front. One prisoner told me that he had transferred from a cushy job in the rear echelon to the infantry so he could get something to eat.

After having eaten normal German front-line rations, prisoners scream when we throw C rations at them. According to the rules, they are supposed to get the same food as their captors, and they refuse to believe that we also eat C rations.

A captured doggie who escaped and returned to our lines at Anzio reported that he had received three meals a day from the Germans, besides a daily chocolate bar, ten cigarettes, and a bottle of beer. That was a hell of a lot better food than we were getting, and if the krauts fed him like that and then deliberately let him escape, it was a smart trick.

But the kraut wasn't always sleek and well fed. We can thank the fliers and the artillery for the fact that his supplies were shot up a big part of the time. Then he was happy to get black bread and watery soup and didn't object so strongly to C rations if he was taken prisoner.

While the rule books probably frown on it, there are few soldiers who haven't traded army rations for civilian food when it was available. It's funny to watch a civilian, sick of his potato soup, brown bread, and red wine, wolf one of those horrible K rations as eagerly as the soldier tears into the soup and bread and wine.

Every army does some foraging now and then, and I guess European farmers are used to it. In all the Mediterranean areas —especially in Africa and Italy—some of the people more than made up for their losses of fruit, vegetables, and livestock by stealing every piece of army equipment that wasn't nailed down, so they usually got the better end of the deal, as Europeans always seem to do.

The soldiers killed a lot of cows. One rifleman at Anzio insisted that a cow had attacked him and that he had fired in self-defense.

The krauts sometimes used herds of livestock for cover and drove them ahead of the infantry in an attack. Whether the

*"I coulda swore a coupla krauts wuz usin' that cow fer cover, Joe. Go wake up th' cooks."*

attack was successful or not, both sides usually got fresh meat out of it. A dead cow in No Man's Land sometimes was a major objective for patrol activity.

It's astounding how many soldiers before cleaning their rifles squeezed off a couple of rounds to loosen the dirt in the barrels and a cow just happened to be standing there. Anyone who objected to this sort of thing either didn't like fresh meat or hadn't been living on front-line rations.

One American-Canadian division had a neat system for supplementing their GI chow at Anzio. They dug up German anti-tank mines, wired them electrically, dropped them into the sea, exploded them and then harvested bushels of fish. Such highly unorthodox but extremely effective methods of supply persuaded the Germans—fearful, perhaps, that having

*"Drop them cans in th' coffee gentle, Joe. We got a
chicken stewin' in th' bottom."*

exhausted all available sources of provision, the dogfaces
would turn to cannibalism—to keep a respectfully wide No
Man's Land between their lines and our own. The boys took
advantage of this and used to run down rabbits and chickens
far ahead of our forward machine-gun positions.

Back in the rest areas kitchens set up mess lines. The men dig
garbage pits and scrape the rust out of their mess gear. The
infantry seems to get much worse food than any other
branch, but at least the food is hot when the troops get back
to areas where the kitchens are functioning.

Those of us who kick around from outfit to outfit know
where to find the best food. That's one of the first things you

*"We sure got th' goods on this guy, captain. Civilians
wuz supposed to turn in their weapons."*

learn in the field—to scrounge where the scrounging is best.
We know only too well what the infantry gets.

One of my best friends is a cook in an infantry company
when he's not in the klink. I once drove him back to a ration
dump to get a sack of flour. He wanted to make pancakes for
his boys, who hadn't seen pancakes for seven months. I told
the guys at the ration dump that I was scrounging for *Stars
and Stripes*, and that we wanted to do a story, with photographs, about the men who work in ration dumps. They fell
for it, and didn't even stop to wonder why in hell *Stars and
Stripes* wanted a sack of flour. We got the sack but those ration men are still looking for their pictures in the paper.

Halfway back to the company area Mike remembered that we hadn't asked for baking soda. We went back, but they didn't have any soda. Then Mike asked for a few cases of tooth powder, and we got that. After Mike got back to the company, every guy had all the pancakes he could eat. They were made with GI toothpowder, and, in spite of the recipe, they tasted pretty good.

That's how the infantry gets along most of the time.

*"My, sir — what an enthusiastic welcome!"*

As long as you've got to have an army you've got to have officers, so you might as well make the most of it.

The ideal officer in any army knows his business. He is firm and just. He is saluted and given the respect due a man who

*"Beautiful view. Is there one for the enlisted men?"*

knows enough about war to boss soldiers around in it. He is given many privileges, which all officers are happy to accept and he is required, in return, to give certain things which a few officers choose to ignore. I try to make life as miserable as possible for those few.

An officer is not supposed to sleep until his men are bedded down. He is not supposed to eat until he has arranged for his men to eat. He's like a prizefighter's manager. If he keeps his fighter in shape the fighter will make him successful. I respect those combat officers who feel this responsibility so strongly that many of them are killed fulfilling it.

Since I am an enlisted man, and have served under many officers, I have a great deal of respect for the good ones and a great deal of contempt for the bad ones. A man accepts a

*"Dammit, ya promised to bring rations this trip."*

commission with his eyes open and, if he does not intend to take responsibilities as well as privileges, he is far lower than the buck private who realizes his own limitations and keeps that rank.

I never worry about hurting the feelings of the good officers when I draw officer cartoons. I build a shoe, and if somebody wants to put it on and loudly announce that it fits, that's his own affair.

A few of them have done it, to the subsequent enjoyment of the guys who read the letters to the editor in the Mail Call section of *Stars and Stripes*. One poor lieutenant—let's call him Smith to be on the safe side—wrote that instead of picking on officers, I should stop and consider the stupid antics of enlisted men whom he had observed in his three years' service. Several letters came back—not defending me, but putting the blast on the lieutenant for being foolish enough to call soldiers stupid. I remember one of the letters very well. It began:

". . . I pick up the October 23rd issue of *Stars and Stripes* and what do I see but a letter from my old pal, Lt. Smith. The last I heard from 'Stinky' Smith, he was studying for his third attempt to make a score of 110 in his General Classification test in order to qualify for OCS. . . . Now, 'Stinky,' when you worked in my poultry house in 1940, picking turkeys for $14 a week, neither myself nor the other boys regarded you as a mental giant. Quite the contrary . . ."

This undoubtedly provided the boys in Lieutenant Smith's outfit with considerable glee.

A very different and very interesting letter was written by a colonel of artillery. He said:

". . . being Regular Army, my father before me, and his father before him, one of the first things I learned at West Point was to respect the enlisted soldier of the United States Army . . ."

The colonel, for my money, is the perfect officer. He is a professional soldier, he likes the army, he likes his job, he likes the men under him, and he knows his business. He carries his rank easily because he is capable of earning respect without ramming his eagles down somebody's throat. I will throw the gentleman a salute any time I meet him, and I will look him in the eye while I'm doing it. The army is his home, and while I am in it he is the host whose rules I must respect. In civilian life, if he comes into my home, I am the host, and it is obvious that he is going to be enough of a gentleman to abide by my rules.

I've thrown a drawing or two at the regular army, because too many mess sergeants with thirty years in the army have been made temporary majors and lieutenant colonels, and they are making the most of their moments of glory.

Even after four long years in the army I still disagree with some of the officer–enlisted man traditions. But I'm not rabid about it. If the men who wrote the rules prefer their own exclusive bathrooms and latrines, that's okay with me. But if the officer is going to have a tent over his latrine in the field, how about one for me? I might not be as important as he is, but I can get just as wet. And keep him out of *my* latrine when the weather is bad, and his latrine is farther away than mine. If he wishes to eat at his own table, and wants me to wash his dishes because he has weighty problems on his mind and no time for dishwashing, then I understand. But let him keep his hands off my own kitchen's canned orange juice.

*"I wanna long rest after th' war. Mebbe I'll do a hitch in th' regulars."*

Many old line officers are no doubt shocked at a spirit of passive rebellion which occasionally shows itself in this citizen army. That's the whole answer. It is a citizen army, and it has

*"Whistle if you see anybody coming."*

in its enlisted ranks many men who in civil life were not accustomed to being directed to the back door and the servant
quarters. To taking orders, yes; but to taking indignities, no.

It doesn't hurt us. Nearly everybody needs a little hum-
bling from time to time. If the army maintains these customs
to prevent undue fraternization between the ruling class and
the working class, on the theory that familiarity breeds contempt, then perhaps the army is right. But most combat outfits scrap tradition, as they scrap many other things, when
they go into battle. No man who depends upon those below
him—not only for his success, but for his very life—is going
to abuse his men unnecessarily. Not if he has good sense.

An unpleasant noncommissioned officer can often make life a

*"One more crack like that an' ya won't have yer job back after th' war."*

lot more miserable for the men under him than an officer can, simply because there are certain restrictions on the behavior of officers.

An officer can be court-martialed for calling an enlisted man a son of a bitch, but that, coming from some sergeants who have complete mastery of the army language, can be taken as a small compliment. Also, an officer usually lives a little apart from the boys, so if he says there's to be no gambling, it's easy enough to get a flashlight and hold an exclusive little game under a blanket. But a corporal, bucking for a third stripe, can crawl right in there with you and turn you in if he loses.

The infantry in combat doesn't worry much about rank.

One company I know of had two sets of noncoms for a while. One set led squads and patrols when the outfit was committed. After the company was pulled back to a rest area, this first set lined up to be busted, and an entirely different set—those who had more of an eye for regulations and discipline—took over while the others went out and got tight.

*"Looks like we're goin' into th' line, Willie."*

Technicians' ratings have always been good cartoon material. All the boys pick on a technician, but they must call him "sergeant" or "corporal" while they do it.

After I had been a very poor infantry soldier for a year or so, somebody was kind enough to give me an extra cook's rating, which was called a first-third. Although I never saw the kitchen except when I did KP in it, the rating entitled me

*"Sure I got seniority. I got busted a week before you did."*

to one stripe and slightly more than corporal's pay. It was a notable occasion for me, because I got that first-third on my wedding day, and the few extra bucks did a lot to help me get along with my landlady.

A few months before I came overseas the rating was changed to "technician, fourth grade." This gave me three stripes and a T, and sergeant's pay. I wasn't doing my company commander any good, because I was on special duty at division headquarters where I drew pictures for the division paper. My peppery little captain used to trudge over to division every day and try to get those new stripes back.

I've still got them, but I don't wear them. I'd rather look like a respectable buck private than take the ribbing most guys give an ersatz sergeant.

*"He's already gittin' drunk wit' power."*

In many ways you can compare an MP's problems to those of an officer. For the doubtful privilege of maintaining law and order in the armed forces, and being able to put the cuff on just about anything in uniform, the MP has to take a lot of ribbing—some of it funny and some of it nasty. The smart MP realizes this and accepts it, and the not-so-smart MP lets the ribbers get his goat and finishes his hitch a very bitter man.

Military cops come in two sizes—combat and garrison. The combat MP is a handy guy to have around, and he is seldom required to be a fanatic about regulations, so he gets along pretty well with the doggies. He has a dirty job be- cause he has to guard crossroads, and anybody who has been around in this war knows what it is to hang around a cross- roads within artillery range of the enemy. Being in dangerous

*"They must have infiltrated during the night."*

places and associating with dogfaces just naturally gives the combat MP the dogface's point of view. If an MP wearing the insignia of the dogface's own outfit tells him something, the doggie usually listens. That's why commanders try to put their own MPs in towns where their troops are raising hell.

The garrison MP is different. He is often unpopular because he has to enforce those garrison rules which we all hate—proper uniform, saluting, passes, and all that sort of thing. When I'm not cussing them I feel sorry for garrison MPs. I feel particularly sorry for them when they are operating under the orders of an unpleasant area commander, because they are the boys who take the rap for him. If the area commander orders that helmets be worn in blazing hot weather fifty miles behind the lines, the MP is the guy who

*"This must be th' joint."*

has to stand there and see that helmets are worn, and the soldier is naturally going to place the entire blame for his sick headache on the MP who makes him keep that red-hot piece of steel on his knob.

Because he picks up a hundred soldiers a day and hears a hundred dirty cracks, none of them original or amusing, the garrison MP is going to be soured on life in general and soldiers in particular, and he is going to become downright mean. Then a peaceable guy like myself is rudely stopped by the MP who asks:

"Where the hell is yer gawdam helmet?"

I start to say truthfully that I forgot it, but he cuts me off.

"Don't you gimme none of yer gawdam lip, dammit—I heard that one before."

*"Th' yellow one is fer national defense, th' red one wit' white stripes is fer very good conduct, and th' real purty one wit' all th' colors is fer bein' in this theater of operations."*

This goes on until I get sore and blow my top and he takes me to jail or gives me a ticket, and I go off and sulk and draw pictures about him.

I don't think I ever made a lot of the MPs really sore, except once, when I did the one about the MP way down in his hole at the Anzio crossroads, holding up a wooden hand to point directions. That was no gag. Crossroads are good places to stay in holes—especially Anzio crossroads. The MPs at Anzio told me they liked the picture and sent it home in letters, but I got a round robin from an MP battalion doing garrison and traffic duty at Naples.

"We are getting damned sick and tired of you, Mauldin,"

*"Thanks."*

the Naples MPs said. "It's bad enough making fun of us, but your cartoon of March 9 called us yellow and insulted the memory of members of the Military Police who have died performing their duty."

I'm really sorry they took it that way, but when I made the cartoon I wasn't thinking of that particular Naples battalion. I don't doubt that many of them, while performing their duty, were run over by trucks and taxis.

It seems to most dogfaces that five minutes after they have stormed and captured a town the whole place is plastered with "Off Limits" signs. Practically every town in France became off limits immediately after our first troops had cleared it of snipers. Sometimes it seemed like the "Off Limits" signs were there to greet the guys when they shot their way into

*"It's either enemy or off limits."*

the towns. The doggies weren't bothered too much by the signs, anyway, because they seldom had time to go back to the towns they had taken.

One off limits story spread through the army and endeared General Patch, the army commander, to the doggies. According to the story, Patch picked up a hitchhiking paratrooper down in the Riviera district. The general asked the paratrooper where he was going and the paratrooper told him "Cannes." It was off limits and the general told him so. "Hell, that's okay," said the paratrooper. "I can sneak in and nobody will see me until I'm ready to leave." Either the general wasn't wearing his stars on the jeep or the paratrooper didn't give a damn. Anyway, the general was so impressed with such remarkable honesty that he gave the guy a pass. Patch wrote it out in longhand and instructed all the MPs of his command that the paratrooper was not to be picked up.

It doesn't matter whether the story is true or not. If Patch had been a martinet, nobody would have bothered to repeat the yarn. You can learn a lot about a general by listening to the stories told about him by his combat men.

Invasions are magnificent things to watch but awful things to be in. Evidently the army likes to pick certain outfits, train them in landing operations, and then use the same men for every invasion. This is undoubtedly an efficient system, but it gets a little rough on the guys who do the invading.

My old division was one of several whose only rest seemed to come when they were waiting for boats to carry them to other lands where the language was different but the war was the same. These amphibious creatures have seen so much action that when they land back in the States they will, just from force of habit, come off shooting and establish a beachhead around Coney Island. There they will probably dig in and fight until demobilization thins their ranks and allows the local partisans to push the survivors back into the sea.

A lot of these dogfaces have put in more time at sea than half the men in the navy. These salty infantrymen offer fatherly advice to young sailors on how to tie the bowline and they often correct the seafaring language of the officer of the deck when he calls the "head" a "toilet."

The doggies don't envy the navy. They like its excellent food and dry bunks, but they don't like the cramped shipboard life, and bad as the beach may be, they don't want to stay aboard the ship when the Luftwaffe and the shore batteries start operating. A ship is a hellish big target, and there is no place you can hide.

Once he gets ashore the foot soldier is in his element. He breathes easier, even while he scoops up sand by the helmetful to hide himself.

Beaches are awful when they are being subjected to any kind of fire, because they are always crowded with men and equipment coming off the ships, and the enemy can throw a shell almost anywhere in the area and be sure of getting a hit. Strafing planes are the biggest terror, and the Germans always seem to scrape up a sizable number to make beachheads unpleasant. They played hell with our troops at Sicily, Salerno, and Anzio.

*"Try to say sumpin' funny, Joe."*

The best invasion I ever attended was that of Southern France. Part of the easiness I felt was the result of being with my old division, and even though nobody knew whether or not the beachhead was going to be tough, the boys were so accustomed to invasions that they didn't spend their time sweating it out on shipboard. It was almost a rest for the division, because before embarking they had put in some pretty tough training to get their sea legs back again. The training was given, ironically enough, at exactly the same spot where the outfit had gone in below Salerno, and one regi-

*"Hope it ain't a rocky beach. Me feet's tender since they got webbed."*

ment did some climbing exercises on the same mountain they had defended more than a year before. Abandoned, rusted landing craft were still bobbing their sterns as the tide changed, and you would find skeletons washed up on the beaches. It was a very grim place and we all lost friends there.

On shipboard we spent most of our time gambling and chewing the fat and leaning over the rail. The weather was swell.

The invasion came off much better than we had expected, with only one division—the one which had been hurt so terribly at Salerno—meeting really tough resistance. The aerial and naval support was far greater than any of the divisions had ever had before. Everything went off according to schedule.

*"You guys oughta carry a little dirt to dig holes in."*

Every drawing in the set of half a dozen or so I made about that invasion was done before I left Italy. Since it was obvious that we were going to France and that the Germans expected us—but in the wrong place—General Maitland Wilson had a press conference just before the embarkation, and I sneaked in to hear it. After many preliminaries and formalities, General Wilson told his little assembly something they already knew—that they were going to France.

I scrambled back to the *Stars and Stripes* and made up the set of drawings. The editor accepted them with the same air of secrecy as that of a ship's captain receiving his sealed orders. The fact that every Italian on the Mediterranean coast also knew what was coming off did not detract from the solemnity of the ceremony.

*"I'm lookin' fer turtle eggs, Junior."*

I had seen three real beachheads and countless amphibious training maneuvers from Cape Cod to Chesapeake Bay, so I figured the drawings would be quite accurate. But the high brass who arrange such invasions double-crossed me. Any dope knows you can't make invasions unless the dark of very early morning hides your activities. How was I to know that the first wave wasn't scheduled to land until eight A.M.? The first drawing of my series showed the barges going in by the light of flares, and it appeared in Italy about the same time that I was admiring the battered, smoking coast of Southern France from a ship's rail, in the blinding glare of a very high sun.

I got too darn playful with some of my first drawings in

*"Now he's gittin' th' fever, Joe. Let 'im edge in a little."*

Southern France. Even though that campaign was a very fast one for the first few weeks, it was not an easy war. No war is easy for those who fight it.

The guys were tired from constant marching and they were running into stubborn resistance in spots, but it was such a tremendous change from Italy that their morale was a little better. They had expected a tough beachhead, and even tougher mountain fighting. They were very much relieved to find that they could push ahead.

The Maquis and FFI helped a lot, particularly in the mountains. By actually pitching in and helping to chase the krauts out, the French saved many of their towns from destruction. The French were honestly and sincerely glad to see the Americans come, and the farther north we worked the more

*"When ya hit th' water swish yer feet around. They kin
use it."*

hospitable the people became. I had a feeling that we were
regarded truly as liberators, and not as walking bread baskets.
It was a far cry from Italy.

Some towns actually had street lights and sidewalk cafés
open for business and selling real beer, and even though most
of the time the doggies went through too fast to enjoy this
stuff, it was nice to look at.

I didn't really believe atrocity stories until I had been in
France awhile. Now I know why the Germans fight so stubbornly even when they seem to have lost the war. They don't
want to take the rap for what they have done.

*"Seen any signs of partisan activity?"*

The Germans know how much the people hate them. When they surrender, most Germans say, "We are regular army—not SS." Maybe they feel a little less guilty.

No actor on earth could have imitated the thorough contempt and disgust and hatred that was on the face of every French child who watched German prisoners march by. And it was awful to see the grief and horror of the bereaved as they forced the Germans to dig up the bodies of their victims and carry them away for decent burial. You never heard the word "Nazi." The word was "Boche" and it was spat out, not as a name but as an epithet.

You can't be expected to believe such stuff until you have seen it. Once you've seen it, you will understand why the krauts preferred to surrender to the Americans, whose women were safe at home.

In Grenoble, a few miles from the Swiss border, I ran into the five soldiers with whom I had shared the difficulties of publishing the *45th Division News* all over the Mediterranean theater, before I went to *Stars and Stripes.*

Every place the *45th Division News* went, screwy things happened and I felt right at home again. We set up our editorial headquarters at Grenoble directly across the street from a regimental command post, and Fred Sheehan used the CP's portable radio to get the latest BBC news for our "Bulletins" column. One of our biggest scoops, courtesy of BBC, informed the astonished men of the 45th Division that Grenoble had just been captured by troops of the American Army.

Work on the paper was interrupted that first night by reports that a strong force of Germans had appeared on the outskirts of the town. Our French compositors, who were also FFI men, dropped their type sticks and set up machine guns on the street corner. It turned out that an American lieutenant had talked a Jerry major into surrendering a thousand krauts and that the parade was just coming into town. The major was driving a snappy Ford convertible.

All kinds of rumors spring up when troops go a week or so without news. There weren't so many rumors floating around the 45th Division because those boys had a paper. But when I got out to some of the other divisions around Grenoble I heard quite a few rumors. I was told that Hitler had surrendered and that the United States had started to invade the island of Japan. And I heard that General Eisenhower had been killed by a sniper in London. There were many more stories, but those are a few I remember.

The *Stars and Stripes* mobile unit hadn't yet arrived and the troops needed news. So my five irresponsible companions persuaded me to publish a Grenoble edition of *Stars and Stripes.* I batted out a drawing and the engravers did a rush job. Then I waited until the *Division News* was matted and on its way to press. I borrowed their forms, cut out a few items which were of interest only to men of the 45th Division, added several BBC bulletins and finally gave the stuff to the

*"Tell them prisoners to ack sloppier in front of th' lootenant. He might start gittin' ideas."*

pressmen. They showed me that I still had one blank page, so I had the cartoon blown up to full page size. I'm still trying to convince a lot of people that this was the only reason I gave myself a full page.

I told the printer to make 20,000 copies of the paper for me and was told that the bill for that many copies would be fifty dollars. I promised payment as soon as the mobile unit arrived but I kept my fingers crossed for I was beginning to have doubts about the legality of the whole business. It just didn't seem right for a cartoonist without any authority to proclaim himself editor and publisher of one of the largest and most respected army newspapers and it was probably wrong to promise payment in government money for such a

*"Wot's funny about horizontal foxholes?"*

wildcat project. But by that time the presses were running and it was too late to do anything about it.

Next morning I loaded the 20,000 papers into my jeep and started the long and tortuous ride down the winding roads which lead out of the Alps. I was heading back to Corps Headquarters, a hundred miles away. Every mile or so I'd have to stop and pick up papers which had blown out. The men at Corps received me very well and they distributed the papers to the divisions within a few hours. But when I timidly mentioned the matter of fifty bucks which I had to raise some place, they weren't so enthusiastic. Why shouldn't *Stars and Stripes* pay for its own newspaper? Oh, you published it without any authority? Well, that's a little matter between you and *Stars and Stripes*.

*"This is th' town my pappy told me about."*

I started back for Grenoble but less than halfway there I was overtaken by a wild-looking crew on a weapons carrier. God save them if it wasn't the entire *Stars and Stripes* staff— everybody in the organization from editors to linotypers and a few officers. Silently I handed over the bill for fifty bucks. I guess they eventually paid it.

When we got back to Grenoble, *Stars and Stripes* began legitimate publication and, for the first time in its long history, sent the paper *back* to front-line infantry troops, for most of the regimental columns were strung out for a hundred miles along the narrow road leading into Grenoble.

Two of the drawings I did in Southern France were a little

*"I ast her to teach me to yodel. She taught me to yodel."*

bewildering to the guys who were fighting the same war but didn't happen to be in our area.

The first drawing, the one about the girl teaching the dog-faces to yodel, wasn't too obscure, even if most readers wondered how in hell the dogfaces on patrol ever met such a pretty girl. This, they felt, should happen only in novels.

But the second drawing made everybody in Normandy and Italy who saw it wonder what kind of war I was thinking about when I had a CP set up in a beer garden and a return-ing patrol griping because they were shot at. Before I drew the cartoon I really did hear a very surprised soldier in just those circumstances complain to an officer that someone had taken a shot at him. But by the time the cartoon reached the troops in Southern France they had settled back into the same old war themselves, and the only guys who got surprised on patrol were those who didn't get shot at.

I offer those two cartoons as proof that anybody with picture-drawing ambitions shouldn't draw war pictures. He will go nuts trying to keep up with the right war at the right time.

Soldiers are very touchy and explosive persons, especially when they are tired from too much combat. That's why people who sit down and write long books about the war can't please all the soldiers, and one innocent sentence or phrase will cause a hullabaloo from the Atlantic war to the Pacific war.

*"Hell of a patrol. We got shot at."*

I finished the original manuscript for this book shortly after I returned from Italy to France. Most of it was done in Rome, a city two hundred miles south of the war. I stayed in Rome for a couple of weeks because I wanted to finish some drawings I had sketched in France. I also wanted to sleep in a bed and eat at a table. I did all these things and then picked up the manuscript and read it over. It seemed that I had overstated a few things. Sitting there in a warm room with the sun shining outside, I felt a little worried about the book.

So before I sent it off I went north to think some more about it. Two hundred miles is a long way for a jeep, even such a jeep as my pampered and well-manicured "Jeanie" who had covered more than ten thousand miles of Anzio, Italy, and France. The ordnance people called her the most neurotic jeep in Europe. But they cleaned out the carbon, ground the valves, and adjusted the carburetor. In spite of all this tender care, Jeanie developed ignition trouble on the way north and I had to stop every few miles in a pouring rain and get out and get under. After the first one hundred miles I was very glad the mud had obliterated the name "Jeanie" on the jeep's sides because I was swearing at the car in a way that would have crisped her namesake's lovely ears. I was beginning to forget Rome and get back into the right mood.

I traveled up highway 65 until I reached a battalion medical aid station in an old building nestling under a bluff, seven kilometers above Bologna. Dog company was on top of the bluff and they had 50-caliber machine guns and a mortar OP up there. I parked Jeanie under the bluff because the road right around the corner was raked every few minutes by enemy machine guns.

Inside the aid station, I told the medics I was looking for cartoons, and they waved me to a wooden chair beside a small stove. Because the station and the road around it were under observation and fire, the medics couldn't do business until nightfall, so we played hearts with a greasy deck of cards and made horrible pancakes. We were pretty well protected but once a shell hit near by, and I poked my head out to see if Jeanie was still there.

We were high in the mountains, and there was a heavy fog sliced with rain. The mountain earth had been soaked so it

*"I hate to run on a flat. It tears hell outta th' tires."*

couldn't absorb any more, and the rain made the mud a little thinner and colder.

The doctor was a captain from Florida. He had a young, mournful face and a scraggly blond mustache. He didn't know how to play hearts, so while we played he pestered us with a story about "Old Sport." Old Sport was a dog and he belonged to a pack of bird dogs. Every dog in the pack was a bird dog except Old Sport, but he wanted to go hunting too. The doctor drove us crazy, and then Old Sport became a race horse. Every horse in the stable won races but Old Sport, and he won a few races too.

That's silly, but it had us roaring with laughter. After a while a couple of medics started remembering Anzio.

"Were you at Anzio?" one medic asked.

A couple of them hadn't been there.

"Boy, you should have been at Anzio," said a bearded aid man. Then we all started talking about Anzio. Pretty soon the captain said:

"You know where I was during Anzio?"

We told him we didn't know.

"I was in Florida," he said. "Were you in Florida?"

We said no.

"By God, you should have been in Florida," he said. He told us about amphibious maneuvers in Florida, and he kidded the hell out of us. He was a good egg.

After a while we talked about home. Out came the wallets, and although the captain had a pretty wife and one of the men had a lovely fiancée, Jean's picture carried away honors, but the other two guys were prejudiced, of course, and wouldn't admit it.

I showed the captain a picture of my son, and I said he would be two years old soon and I had never seen him. I looked a little gloomy, I guess, because the doc kidded hell out of me and told me how lucky I was I didn't have to change diapers in Florida.

Down the hill an American gun went rat-tatatat-tat-ta-ta, to the rhythm of "shave and a haircut—two bits," and a German with no sense of humor or rhythm came back with a fast blrrrrrrp.

That reminded us of the war in Italy. We agreed that this was just as miserable and cold and muddy as last winter in Italy, only this winter the Germans seemed to have more artillery.

Then we said that everybody in the States seemed to think the Americans and Germans in Italy were dancing beer barrel polkas and all the war was in France. We thought of a couple of dozen German divisions we were keeping off the necks of the guys in France, and we got a little sore when we remembered how last winter's war in Italy was forgotten.

"Were you in Florida on maneuvers last winter?" the captain started, and we grinned and shut up.

It got dark, and pretty soon some sick guys climbed out of

*"Oh, I likes officers. They makes me want to live till the war's over."*

their holes down the hill and came up to the aid station. One had tonsilitis and a fever of 102 degrees. I sat in the corner blowing on the fire and drying the mud on my pants, and watching.

"How would you like to go to the hospital?" the captain asked the dogface. I guess maybe the doggie thought he might be accused of malingering because he said, "I haven't lost anything at the hospital. I wish to hell I hadn't come to the aid station. They need me down at the company."

"There's a cartoon," the captain said to me.

"Hell, nobody would believe it," I said.

"What's the first thing you look for in *Stars and Stripes*?" the doctor asked the soldier and then turned to grin at me.

"The headlines," said the doggie.

*"By th' way, what wuz them changes you wuz gonna
make when you took over last month, sir?"*

"What's the second thing?"

"Hell, nothing else in the rag is worth reading," said the
doggie.

The doctor stopped kidding and examined the doggie.
"You're going to the hospital," the captain said. "You've got
a fever." The medics fixed up a litter in the corner of the
room and put the sick man under blankets.

Pretty soon a guy with a heavy beard and red, sunken eyes
came in with a pain in his chest and a deep cough. He had
been on outpost lying on a muddy embankment for six days
and six nights without being able to stand up or take his
shoes off. It had not stopped raining for six days and six
nights, and it got below freezing at night and he hadn't

*"Sure they's a revolution in Germany. Git down so they won't hit ya wit' a wild shot."*

had any cover. He didn't have a sleeping bag, and he couldn't have used one anyway, because you can't get out of one quickly if Jerry sneaks up on you with a grenade or bayonet.

He had pneumonia, and while he was waiting for the ambulance to come up to the aid station, I talked to him. He had been overseas three months, and he didn't look any different from the men who had been over three years. He talked a little different, though, because he griped about things which three-year men accept with deadened senses. But despite his griping, he had stayed on that muddy embankment with his eyes open for German patrols until his coughing got so bad his buddies were afraid he would die or tip off the Germans to his position, and so they made him come up to the aid station.

Sometimes the doctor kidded the two sick men and some-times he was gruff with them, but they knew what kind of guy he was by the way he acted. When the ambulance came up, both men were evacuated to the hospital.

No men came out of the misery and death and mud below us unless they were awfully sick. They didn't want to stay down there, but they knew they were needed. They were full of bitches and gripes and cynicism about the whole war, but they stayed, and so they had a right to say anything they pleased.

"I wish to hell I could send every man in every hole back to hot food and a hospital bed with sheets," said the captain, and then he realized he had said something serious, so he made a silly crack to neutralize it.

The little field phone rang. One of the guys in the aid sta-tion answered it. It was Charley company with a casualty. The medic took his blankets off the litter he had intended to sleep on, and he carried it out to the medical jeep, which sat in a revetment of sandbags at the side of the building. He asked me if I wanted to go with him. I didn't, but I got up and put on my helmet.

"Now what in hell do you want to go for?" asked one of the Anzio guys I had beaten at hearts. "Haven't you ever seen a foxhole at night before?"

I was grateful to him, because I really didn't want to go. I didn't care if I never saw another foxhole again. But you have to play the game, and so while the two guys were getting ready to go I said:

"Well, you are using barbed wire here, and I guess I ought to see it."

"Haven't you ever seen barbed wire before?" my benefac-tor asked. Still playing the game, I said yes, I had seen barbed wire before, but well, hell, and I fingered my helmet.

"Besides, there's only room for two in the car with the stretcher in back," he said.

"Well, hell," I said again. "If there isn't any room, there isn't any room. Besides, it's an awfully steep hill." I sat down and took off my helmet. The game was over.

They were back in five minutes, because it was only a thou-sand yards, and they used the jeep because the hill was steep

*"We'll be here quite a while, boys. Ya kin take yer shoes off tonight."*

and the machine was faster than men on foot with a litter. The Germans would have killed the medics just as quickly on foot as with the jeep, if they had felt like killing medics that night. I was glad they got back okay.

The boy screamed as the litter bumped the door coming in.

"Goddam it, be careful," said one of the medics to the other.

They laid the litter on two old sawhorses in the middle of the room, and the bantering, good-natured doctor grabbed the kerosene lantern and went to work. He was strangely different now. His warm, sympathetic eyes got cool and quick and his fingers gently unrolled the bandages, now dark red, which the company aid man had wrapped hastily but efficiently around the wounded man's face. The boys who had kidded and bulled about Anzio and Florida maneuvers and Old Sport were very serious now. One took a pair of surgical scissors and slit through layers of muddy, bloody clothing until the boy was stark-naked in the warm room. His face was a pulp, and one arm and a leg were shattered and riddled.

"God, I'm hurt," he said. "God, they hurt me." He couldn't believe it. His unhurt hand reached for his face and one of the medics grabbed his arm and held it—not roughly, but the way a woman would have done.

"Easy, boy," he said.

"God, I'm hurtin'. Give me a shot," the boy screamed.

"We gave you a shot, Jack," said one of the medics who had read his dogtags and was filling out a slip. "Just a minute, and you'll feel better."

While the doctor and the others worked on the bandages and the splint for the shattered arm, the medic with the pencil said:

"What got you, Jack?"

"God, I don't know. It was a tank. Where's the chaplain?"

"You don't need the chaplain, Jack," said the medic. "You're going to be okay. What got you? There weren't any tanks around a while ago."

"It was a grenade," said Jack, his hand still reaching for his face. "Where's the chaplain? God, why do you let me hurt like this?"

"How old are you, Jack?" asked the medic persistently. He had already marked "grenade," because the wounds showed that. It had been a German potato-masher grenade, because the holes in his body looked like bullet wounds, but didn't go clear through him, and they weren't as jagged as shell or mortar fragment wounds. Evidently the German had sneaked up while the boy was down in his hole.

Jack said he was twenty years old, he was a staff sergeant, and he was from Texas.

The questioning seemed heartless at this time, but there is a reason for it. If the patient is able to answer, it distracts him from his pain; and if the information isn't gained here, they have to get it back at the hospital.

*"Do retreatin' blisters hurt as much as advancin' blisters?"*

Jack had guts. Of course he was scared. He knew he was hurt bad, and it's a shock to anybody to get hit. But when they told him he shouldn't reach for his face, he said okay a little sleepily, because the morphine was taking effect.

"Hold a flashlight," the doctor said to me. "The lantern isn't strong enough."

I grabbed a flashlight and held it on the boy while they worked on him. I thought, "Christ, twenty years old!" I felt like an old man at twenty-three. I looked at the holes which had riddled his right arm and practically severed his little finger, and I looked at the swollen bloody gashes on his leg. I looked at his horribly wounded face and head, and I thought of how twenty minutes ago he was sitting quietly in his hole wondering how soon he could get home.

I handed the flashlight to the medic who had finished filling out the slip, and I went over to the litter and sat on it with my head between my knees and tried to keep from being sick on the floor.

The medic took the flashlight without even a glance, and nobody looked at me. They went right on working. Pretty soon Jack's face was fixed and it didn't look so bad with a neat bandage and the blood washed off. His arm was fixed in a splint and it looked very neat indeed. He was wrapped up in blankets, and the ambulance came up and took him away. He was full of morphine and probably dreaming of home.

"I don't know what we'd do without morphine," the doc said.

I guess I looked a little foolish and white, and I started to open my mouth. I don't know what I was going to say, but the medic who had taken the flashlight turned to me and said:

"It's funny. I handle these guys every night, and some of them are really in awful shape. But last night one came in not hurt half as bad as Jack and I did the same thing you did."

Another medic said, "We keep some medicine to take care of those things."

They brought out a miracle—a half-filled bottle of Pennsylvania Rye. Now I know damned well one of those guys got that bottle in a Christmas package, and I know he could have sold it for a hundred dollars cash anyplace between Florence and Bologna. Or he could have kept it to himself, and nobody would have blamed him. But we all had a slug of rye— the doc with his bloody hands and his eyes which were bantering once more, and the medics who were kidding each other again.

Another sick guy came in. The doc asked him if he had been at the front, and the guy said, "No, I was three hundred yards behind it."

Sometimes you can hang around places and guys write cartoon captions for you. I made a note furtively.

I went to sleep on a litter that wasn't being used, and when the odor of coffee woke me up at ten the next morning the aid men told me two more casualties had come in later in the night and that when they picked up my litter and turned it around to make more room I hadn't even budged.

*"Sir, do ya hafta draw fire while yer inspirin' us?"*

I stayed one more day and one night, and when the fog lifted I poked my head up over the sandbags and peered down the valley that led to Bologna. It looked very peaceful and pretty, because you can't see bullets and there was little artillery during those few hours of light before the fog settled down again.

When there is no fog the country is so nice and clear that you don't show more than your helmet even at the battalion aid station.

I hung around and talked with guys who strayed down from Dog company on top of our cliff. Machine-gunners and mortar men, they were feeling very rear echelon and very sorry for the riflemen in the holes below us. Guys in the holes, of course, were feeling sorry for Dog company, because they could see our cliff getting a pounding from time to time.

*"Wisht somebody would tell* me *there's a Santa Claus."*

A moon came out that night, and I decided not to leave until it got murky again, because I had to cover an exposed stretch of road going back. A cloud came over the moon, and I got into Jeanie and turned around slowly so the motor wouldn't make sparks. Then I started crawling back in a very low gear through the cratered and splashy mud. Midway through the open space the motor stopped, and the clouds broke, bathing me in lovely moonlight. I sweated and ground the starter and finally the motor started again.

After I got around the bend I heard a lot of explosions, and I guess maybe they had seen me and threw the stuff too late. Anyway, I kicked hell out of that jeep for the next fifteen or twenty miles.

I felt good when I got back to a building in the rear and, even though I had hardly stuck my nose out from the protection of the aid station sandbags, I felt I had learned something. I sketched sixteen cartoon ideas in three hours.

I came back to Rome, so I could send the book off and finish the sixteen drawings. I read the thing over before I took a bath, and darned if I didn't like it pretty well, even though it may be full of bad grammar. Now I've had the bath and the sixteen drawings are almost finished, and somehow I miss the aid station. It was pretty safe under the cliff, and it was warm and we were able to make coffee. It was full of homesick, tired men who were doing the job they were put there to do, and who had the guts and humanness to kid around and try to make life easier for the other guy.

They are big men and honest men, with the inner warmth that comes from the generosity and simplicity you learn up there. Until the doc can go back to his chrome office and gallstones and the dogface can go back to his farm and I can go back to my wife and son, that is the closest to home we can ever get.

*Up Front*, 1945

# Democracy?

by Rupert Trimmingham and others

Dear YANK:

Here is a question that each Negro soldier is asking. What is the Negro soldier fighting for? On whose team are we playing? Myself and eight other soldiers were on our way from Camp Claiborne, La., to the hospital here at Fort Huachuca. We had to lay over until the next day for our train. On the next day we could not purchase a cup of coffee at any of the lunchrooms around there. As you know, Old Man Jim Crow rules. The only place where we could be served was at the lunchroom at the railroad station but, of course, we had to go into the kitchen. But that's not all; 11:30 A.M. about two dozen German prisoners of war, with two American guards, came to the station. They entered the lunchroom, sat at the tables, had their meals served, talked, smoked, in fact had quite a swell time. I stood on the outside looking on, and I could not help but ask myself these questions: Are these men sworn enemies of this country? Are they not taught to hate and destroy . . . all democratic governments? Are we not American soldiers, sworn to fight for and die if need be for this our country? Then why are they treated better than we are? Why are we pushed around like cattle? If we are fighting for the same thing, if we are to die for our country, then why does the Government allow such things to go on? Some of the boys are saying that you will not print this letter. I'm saying that you will. . . .

*Fort Huachuca, Ariz.*     —Cpl. RUPERT TRIMMINGHAM

*Yank*, April 28, 1944

Dear YANK:

I am writing to you in regard to the incident told in a letter to you by Cpl. Trimmingham (Negro) describing the way he was forced to eat in the kitchen of a station restaurant while a group of German prisoners were fed with the rest of the white civilians in the restaurant. Gentlemen, I am a Southern rebel, but this incident makes me none the more proud of my Southern heritage! Frankly, I think that this incident is a disgrace to a democratic nation such as ours is supposed to be. Are we fighting for such a thing as this? Certainly not. If this incident is democracy, I don't want any part of it! . . . I wonder what the "Aryan supermen" think when they get a first-hand glimpse of our racial discrimination. Are we not waging a war, in part, for this fundamental of democracy? In closing, let me say that a lot of us, especially in the South, should cast the beam out of our own eyes before we try to do so in others, across the seas.

—Cpl. HENRY S. WOOTTON JR.*
*Fairfield-Suisun AAF, Calif.*

* Also signed by S/Sgt. A. S. Tepper and Pfc. Jose Rosenzweig.


Dear YANK:

You are to be complimented on having the courage to print Cpl. Trimmingham's letter in an April issue of YANK. It simply proves that your policy is maturing editorially. He probes an old wound when he exposes the problem of our colored soldiers throughout the South. It seems incredible that German prisoners of war should be afforded the amenities while our own men—in uniform and changing stations—are denied similar attention because of color and the vicious attitude of certain portions of our country. What sort of a deal is this? It is, I think, high time that this festering sore was cut out by intelligent social surgeons once and for all. I can well understand and sympathize with the corporal's implied but unwritten question: why, then, are we in uniform. Has it occurred to anyone that those Boche prisoners of war must be still laughing at us?

*Bermuda*                                    —S/Sgt. ARTHUR J. KAPLAN

Dear YANK:

. . . I'm not a Negro, but I've been around and know what the score is. I want to thank the YANK . . . and congratulate Cpl. Rupert Trimmingham.

*Port of Embarkation*                    —Pvt. GUSTAVE SANTIAGO

*Yank*, June 9, 1944

Dear YANK:

Just read Cpl. Rupert Trimmingham's letter titled "Democracy?" in a May edition of YANK. We are white soldiers in the Burma jungles, and there are many Negro outfits working with us. They are doing more than their part to win this war. We are proud of the colored men here. When we are away from camp working in the jungles, we can go to any colored camp and be treated like one of their own. I think it is a disgrace that, while we are away from home doing our part to help win the war, some people back home are knocking down everything that we are fighting for.

We are among many Allied Nations' soldiers that are fighting here, and they marvel at how the American Army, which is composed of so many nationalities and different races, gets along so well. We are ashamed to read that the German soldier, who is the sworn enemy of our country, is treated better than the soldier of our country, because of race.

Cpl. Trimmingham asked: What is a Negro fighting for? If this sort of thing continues, we the white soldiers will begin to wonder: What are *we* fighting for?

*Burma*                    —Pvt. JOSEPH POSCUCCI (Italian)*

*Also signed by Cpl. Edward A. Kreutler (French), Pfc. Maurice E. Wenson (Swedish) and Pvt. James F. Malloy (Irish).

Dear YANK:

Allow me to thank you for publishing my letter. Although there was some doubt about its being published, yet somehow I felt that YANK was too great a paper not to. . . . Each day brings three, four or five letters to me in answer to my letter. I just returned from my furlough and found 25 letters awaiting me. To date I've received 287 letters, and, strange as it may seem, 183 are from white men and women in the armed service. Another strange feature about these letters is that the most of these people are from the Deep South. They are all proud of the fact that they are of the South but ashamed to learn that there are so many of their own people who by their actions and manner toward the Negro are playing Hitler's game. Nevertheless, it gives me new hope to realize that there are doubtless thousands of whites who are willing to fight this Frankenstein that so many white people are keeping alive. All that the Negro is asking for is to be given half a chance and he will soon demonstrate his worth to his country. Should these white people who realize that the Negro is a man who is loyal—one who would gladly give his life for this our wonderful country—would stand up, join with us and help us to prove to their white friends that we are worthy, I'm sure that we would bury race hate and unfair treatment. Thanks again.

*Fort Huachuca, Ariz.*        —Cpl. RUPERT TRIMMINGHAM

Since YANK printed Cpl. Trimmingham's letter we have received a great number of comments from GIs, almost all of whom were outraged by the treatment given the corporal. His letter has been taken from YANK and widely quoted. The incident has been dramatized on the air and was the basis for a moving short story published recently in the *New Yorker* magazine.

*Yank*, July 28, 1944

# *Young Man Behind Plexiglass*

by Brendan Gill

JOSEPH THEODORE HALLOCK, who has light-blue eyes and an engaging smile and is usually called Ted, is a first lieutenant in the United States Army Air Forces. Two years ago he was an undergraduate at the University of Oregon; today he is a veteran bombardier who has completed thirty missions in a B-17 over Germany and Occupied Europe. Eighteen months ago he fainted when an Army doctor examining him pricked his finger to get a sample of blood; today he wears the Purple Heart for wounds received in a raid on Augsburg, the Air Medal with three oak-leaf clusters, and the Distinguished Flying Cross. Before he got into the Air Forces, he had been rejected by the Navy and Marines because of insufficient chest expansion; he still weighs less than a hundred and thirty pounds, and this gives him an air of tempered, high-strung fragility. When he relaxes, which is not often, he looks younger than his twenty-two years, but he doesn't think of himself as being young. "Sometimes I feel as if I'd never had a chance to live at all," he says flatly, "but most of the time I feel as if I'd lived forever."

Hallock and his wife, Muriel, recently spent a three-week leave in New York, and I met him through friends. I took him aside one morning and talked with him for an hour or two about his part in the war. I was naturally curious to know what it felt like to complete thirty missions in a Flying Fortress, but I also saw, or thought I saw, that he was eager to speak to someone of his experiences. Apparently he considers himself typical of thousands of young men in the armed forces, and he rejects any suggestion that he has done more than was specifically demanded of him. "Whatever I tell you," he said, "boils down to this: I'm a cog in one hell of a big machine. The more I think about it, and I've thought about it a lot lately, the more it looks as if I've been a cog in one thing after another since the day I was born. Whenever I get set to do what I want to do, something a whole lot bigger than me comes along and shoves me back into place. It's not especially pleasant, but there it is.

"As a matter of fact, my father had about the same deal. He'd graduated from Oregon State and was just starting in business when we got mixed up in the first World War. He joined the Navy, and from what he says I guess he disliked the war but liked his job. He'd been trained as a radio engineer, and that was the sort of work they gave him to do, so he got to be a C.P.O. and kept on working for the Navy for quite a while after the war was over. He and Mother moved around from Mare Island to Portland, down to Los Angeles and San Diego, and so on, and they seem to have had a good enough time. Like Muriel and me, they probably didn't try to figure what was going to happen to them next. I was their only child, and I was born on October twenty-fifth, 1921." Hallock shrugged. "In a way, it's funny my being born then. I was arguing about the war with a fellow the other night, and he kept telling me what Wilson should have done and what Wilson shouldn't have done. I got sore finally. Why, hell's bells, I hadn't even been born when Wilson was president! I don't give a hoot about Wilson, I told this guy, Wilson's been dead for years; it's 1944 I'm worrying about.

"Things must have been pretty unsettled when I was a baby, just as they've been ever since I grew up. Whatever that boom was I've heard about, I doubt if it meant anything ritzy for the Hallocks. My father helped found a company that manufactured radios—he was in on the ground floor in radio, from crystal pickup sets to those big old-fashioned jobs with all the knobs and dials—but he figured the fad wouldn't last. That was what he used to say—'Radio won't last.' Those early sets cost too much for the average guy, Dad thought, and it didn't occur to him that the prices were bound to come down someday. So he drifted into one job or another, some good and some bad, up to the time of the crash.

"Naturally, I don't remember anything about Harding and Coolidge. One of my earliest memories is of betting marbles with the kids at school about who was going to win the election, Hoover or Roosevelt. I bet on Roosevelt. I suppose my mother and father had been talking about him at home — about how bad things were and about how the country needed a change. While I don't remember good times, I'd hear Mother and Dad talking about what they'd had once and didn't have any more — nothing like yachts or fur coats, just something like security, whatever that is. It's the same thing Muriel and I talk about sometimes, wondering what the hell it looks and tastes like. Most of the other guys in the Army who grew up when I did feel the same way. We keep trying to figure out what it was our parents had before we grew up, or what our grandparents had. There must have been something back there someplace, or we wouldn't miss it so much.

"Moving around the country during those bad times, I had plenty of trouble with schools, and I guess it's a wonder I managed to learn anything at all. In California, for instance, I'd have to take French but not Latin, and in Maryland I'd have to take Latin but not French. I finally graduated from a Portland, Oregon, high school in 1939. I wasn't very popular at school, partly because I never was in a place long enough to know anybody well, but mostly because I spent my time reading books and listening to good jazz, which can be a lonely thing to do. I was a pretty serious character in those days, and I boned up a lot on the first World War. I listened to my father talk and I read about the munitions kings and I felt sure I'd never be willing to fight in any war about anything. I delivered the commencement address when I graduated from high school, and I called it 'Cannon Fodder?' You can bet I made that question mark a big one.

"Then I began to grow confused. I was disgusted when the League of Nations gave in to Mussolini on the Ethiopian grab, and even before that, when the Spanish War broke out, I saw that that was a war the Loyalists had to fight, and I also saw that it was a war the Loyalists had to win. I was only fifteen or sixteen at the time, but I wanted them to win more than anything else in the world. Besides, there was the Jap attack on China. Naturally, I sided with the Chinese right from the start. What it came down to was that I believed in other people's wars but I didn't believe in any American war.

I guess I was as bad as a lot of people in that respect, like the other kids who were brought up on Senator Nye and the Veterans of Future Wars.

"I wanted to go to Reed College, in Portland, so after I got out of high school I spent a year working as busboy, dishwasher, and things like that to make some money. I also got a job at a radio station, where I had charge of the record library and helped out the announcers on the night shift, and I played drums in a local band. Being on the air when the flash announcing the second World War came through, I remember the time exactly: it was 2:17 A.M., on September third, 1939. As soon as I got home that morning, I asked my father if he thought we'd ever get into the war, and he said, 'No, of course not.' But I suspected we might, and I hated the thought of it. My father had already taken the Civil Service exams for a job with the Federal Communications Commission and passed them, and at about that time he was sent to an F.C.C. job in Texas. I found out that I couldn't afford to go to Reed College unless I was able to live board-free at home, so I had to plan on going to the University of Oregon instead. My family and I got separated back there in 1940, and I've been away from them pretty steadily ever since. There were only the three of us, and we miss each other." Hallock smiled without embarrassment and said, "Damn it, we miss each other a lot."

Hallock and I talked about his family for a while, then got back to the war. "All the time up to Pearl Harbor, I kept trying to pretend that the war wasn't really happening," he said. "I kept telling myself that this was a different kind of war from the Chinese and Spanish wars. When my roommate at college woke me up on Sunday morning, December seventh, 1941, and told me that the Japs had attacked Pearl Harbor, I didn't believe it. It sounded like Warner Brothers stuff to me, so I went back to sleep. Later on I was listening to the André Kostelanetz program when the announcer cut in with some news flashes, and this time I believed it. I guess it's typical of me that as far as I was concerned the war started in the middle of the Coca-Cola program, 'the pause that refreshes on the air.'

"Nearly everybody at college got drunk and burned his books. My roommate and I killed a bottle of kümmel between us and I painted our windows with black enamel as an air-raid precaution. I spent the next two weeks scraping off the enamel with a razor. Undergraduate guards were posted on the library roof, and when the rumor got around that San Francisco had been bombed, 22-calibre rifles started showing up around the campus. Everybody else seemed to be doing something, so I wired my father that I wanted to enlist in the Signal Corps. My father wired back for me to sit tight until the Army told me what to do. In spite of him, I tried enlisting as a cadet in the Navy and Marines, but they said I had insufficient chest expansion and too few college credits. I didn't mind terribly when they turned me down. I had no real convictions about the war in Europe, and I was more or less willing to wait my turn at taking a crack at the Japs. I'd started an orchestra at college called Ted Hallock's Band, which played at sorority and fraternity dances, and during the year I'd had an article on jazz published in *Downbeat*. I'd even made a quick trip to New York and haunted all the night clubs that had good bands. I'd had to hock my Speed Graphic camera to do it, but it was worth it. I felt I was really on my way.

"Besides all that, and a lot more important than all that, I had Muriel, back in Portland. That is, I'd fallen in love with her and I wanted to marry her, but she didn't give me much encouragement. She just wouldn't say anything when I'd ask her to marry me, and I figured that if I got into the Army I might never have a chance to see her again. I wanted time to see her. I wanted time to do a lot of things I hadn't been able to do, and every day outside the Army was worth weeks and months in terms of Muriel and jazz and reading and ordinary living. Finally, in June, 1942, thinking I was bound to be drafted soon, I enlisted as an aviation cadet in the Army Air Forces. I was underweight the first time I took my physical, but I ate fifteen bananas, drank three quarts of milk, passed a second physical, and was sick as a pup for a couple of days afterward.

"The Air Forces told me they'd notify me when to report for training. I didn't feel like going back to college, and I was sore at Muriel because she wouldn't say she'd marry me, so I went down to Galveston to visit my mother and father. I got a job there as a pipe-fitter's apprentice—a fine fate for someone who thought of himself as a rising young authority on jazz and other fine arts. When I couldn't stand not hearing from Muriel, I returned to Portland and got a job in a record shop in a department store. Later, I set up a pitch as a disc jockey at the radio station, playing jazz records and ad-libbing from midnight to eight A.M. I managed to pick up sixty-five or seventy dollars a week, and Muriel and I had some fine times. It seemed as if for once I wasn't just a cog in something bigger than me; I was doing what I wanted to do, but of course that feeling was too good to last. I was ordered to report for duty on February second, 1943, at the A.A.F. base at Santa Ana, California, where I received my pre-flight training.

"That training was really rugged. We had two and a half months of calisthenics led by Fred Perry and Joe DiMaggio, obstacle races, drill, and studies. The saying there was that the discipline was so tough you'd be gigged if they found air under your bed. We took enough mathematics in six weeks to go from two plus two makes four to trig and calculus. I suspected that I might be washed out as pilot material, so to keep from getting a broken heart like a lot of other fellows, I applied to be sent to bombardier school. That was just good strategy on my part, but apparently the officers liked it. We— the bombardier candidates—were sent on to Deming, New Mexico. We arrived there and lined up in one hell of a sandstorm, in terrible heat, feeling a million miles from anywhere. I can still remember the C.O. yelling, as the sand blew down his throat and blinded his eyes, 'Welcome to Deming, men!'

"There were a thousand men at the base and two bars in the town, and things were about as unpleasant as that sounds. We had three months of training with the Norden bomb sight at Deming. The men who had been trained before us had not even been allowed to take notes on what they learned. We could take notes, but we had to burn them as soon as we finished memorizing them. We used to take our notes out to the latrines at night after lights out and study them there. We had to learn how to strip and assemble a bomb sight, a job that became sort of a religious ritual with me. The more I found out about the bomb sight, the more ingenious and inhuman it seemed. It was something bigger, I kept thinking, than any one man was intended to comprehend. I ended up with a conviction, which I still have, that a bombardier can't help feeling inferior to his bomb sight—at least, this bombardier can't. It's not a good feeling to have; it doesn't help you very much when you're over Germany and going into your run to realize that everything depends on your control of something you'll never fully understand, but the feeling is there.

"In July, 1943, I finished the course at Deming and got my wings as a second lieutenant. Muriel had stopped corresponding with me for the umptieth time by then, and I had got so sore that I had written her that I would never see her again. At the last minute, though, I hopped on a train and stood up all the way back to Portland. As soon as I saw Muriel, I told her, 'You know you're going to marry me, don't you?' She said, 'Well, maybe,' which was the greatest encouragement she'd ever given me. I wasted a lot of time—three whole days—making up her mind for her, which left us only three days of my leave in which to get married and have a honeymoon. We spent our honeymoon in a hotel in Portland. Then we took a train to Ephrata, Washington, the training center for B-17s to which I'd been ordered to report.

"Muriel stayed at a hotel in Wenatchee, several miles away. That meant that I was A.W.O.L. a good deal of the time. But I guess I learned something. I didn't like the first pilot to whom I was assigned, so the C.O. assigned me to another pilot, a fellow just my age, with whom I got along fine. It's literally a matter of life and death for everybody in the crew of a Fort to get on well; the ship just won't fly otherwise. There are ten men in a Fort crew—the pilot, co-pilot, navigator, bombardier, and six gunners, and there's more than enough responsibility to go around. The bombardier, for example, is also gunnery officer and in charge of fire control, first aid, and oxygen. Most of those jobs are theoretical in practice flights, but they can all need you at once in a hot raid.

"After a couple of months at Ephrata, where we got the hang of flying a Fort, we were sent on to Rapid City, South

Dakota, for some bomb practice on the target ranges there. Muriel and I felt really married for the first time in Rapid City, because we rented a bungalow and Muriel, who'd never cooked before, practiced her cooking on me. As it turned out, we lived on spaghetti most of the time. Muriel and I had a lot of scraps at Rapid City. I'd come down from a flight looking for trouble, looking for someone to pick on, and Muriel was always the easiest to hurt. That kind of irritability seems to be a characteristic of high flying. I blame it mostly on using oxygen, but, oxygen or no oxygen, there's no doubt the sky does something to you. There it is around you, and it's so damn big, and yet you have a false feeling of having mastered it. And when you come down out of it you feel like elbowing all the civilians you see into the streets that from above looked like little trickles of nothing. The difficulty is, you have to try to live in two different scales of worlds, the one up there and the one down here, and it's not a natural thing to do.

"Muriel must have understood what was going on inside me, because in spite of the way I behaved we had a good time in that cheap little bungalow. As soon as I finished the course at Rapid City, we went to Washington, so I could say good-bye to my parents. My father had been made chief of the Facility Security Division of the F.C.C. when the war broke out, and he and Mother had had to move to Washington. Later, we came up here to New York for a day or two before I went across. We spent most of our time at Nick's, in the Village, getting a last fill of good music. In November, 1943, I shipped out to England, and Muriel went back to Portland and got a job at an advertising agency there."

I asked Hallock a few questions about Muriel, and then he took up his story again. "Right from the start, I liked England. That helped me to stand my separation from Muriel and the fact that I was fighting in a war I'd never particularly believed in fighting. England was so much older physically and spiritually than I had expected that I felt shocked. I understood for the first time that there were people in the world who looked the same as us but thought differently from us, and I began to wonder if the Germans were maybe as much different from the English and us as a lot of writers and politicians claimed. After a day or two in an indoctrination pool, our crew was assigned to an old and well-established operational base south of London and given our Fort, which our pilot christened Ginger. None of us ever found out why he named the ship Ginger, but it's the pilot's privilege to choose any name he likes; probably ginger was the color of his girl's hair or the name of his dog—something like that. We never painted the name on our Fort, because the Forts with names seemed to get shot up more than the ones without.

"My first raid was on December thirty-first, over Ludwigs-haven. Naturally, not knowing what it was going to be like, I didn't feel scared. A little sick, maybe, but not scared. That comes later, when you begin to understand what your chances of survival are. Once we'd crossed into Germany, we spotted some flak, but it was a good long distance below us and looked pretty and not dangerous: different-colored puffs making a soft, cushiony-looking pattern under our plane. A bombardier sits right in the plexiglass nose of a Fort, so he sees everything neatly laid out in front of him, like a living-room rug. It seemed to me at first that I'd simply moved in on a wonderful show. I got over feeling sick, there was so much to watch. We made our run over the target, got our bombs away, and apparently did a good job. Maybe it was the auto-pilot and bomb sight that saw to that, but I'm sure I was cool enough on that first raid to do my job without thinking too much about it. Then, on the way home, some Focke-Wulfs showed up, armed with rockets, and I saw three B-17s in the different groups around us suddenly blow up and drop through the sky. Just simply blow up and drop through the sky. Nowadays, if you come across something awful happening, you always think, 'My God, it's just like a movie,' and that's what I thought. I had a feeling that the planes weren't really falling and burning, the men inside them weren't really dying, and everything would turn out happily in the end. Then, very quietly through the interphone, our tail gunner said, 'I'm sorry, sir, I've been hit.'

"I crawled back to him and found that he'd been wounded in the side of the head—not deeply but enough so he was bleeding pretty bad. Also, he'd got a lot of the plexiglass dust from his shattered turret in his eyes, so he was, at least for the time being, blind. The blood that would have bothered me back in California a few months before didn't bother me at all then. The Army had trained me in a given job and I went ahead and did what I was trained to do, bandaging the gunner well enough to last him back to our base. Though he was blind, he was still able to use his hands, and I ordered him to fire his guns whenever he heard from me. I figured that a few bursts every so often from his fifties would keep the Germans off our tail, and I also figured that it would give the kid something to think about besides the fact that he'd been hit. When I got back to the nose, the pilot told me that our No. 4 engine had been shot out. Gradually we lost our place in the formation and flew nearly alone over France. That's about the most dangerous thing that can happen to a lame Fort, but the German fighters had luckily given up and we skimmed over the top of the flak all the way to the Channel.

"Our second raid was on Lille, and it was an easy one. Our third was on Frankfort. France was the milk run, Germany the bad news. On the day of a raid we'd get up in the morning, eat breakfast, be briefed, check our equipment, crawl into the plane, maybe catch some more sleep. Then the raid, easy or tough, and we'd come back bushed, everybody sore and excited, everybody talking, hashing over the raid. Then we'd take lighted candles and write the date and place of the raid in smoke on our barracks ceiling. Maybe we wouldn't go out again for a week or ten days. Then we'd go out for four or five days in a row, taking chances, waiting for the Germans to come up and give us hell. They have a saying that nobody's afraid on his first five raids, and he's only moderately afraid on his next ten raids, but that he really sweats out all the rest of them, and that's the way it worked with me and the men I knew.

"When we started our missions, we were told that after twenty-five we would probably be sent home for a rest, so that was how we kept figuring things—so many missions accomplished, so many missions still to go. We worked it all out on a mathematical basis, or on what we pretended was a mathematical basis—how many months it would take us to finish our stint, how many missions we'd have to make over Germany proper, what our chances of getting shot down were. Then, at about the halfway mark, the number of mis-sions we would have to make was raised from twenty-five to thirty. That was one hell of a heartbreaker. Supposedly, they changed the rules of the game because flying had got that much safer, but you couldn't make us think in terms of being safer. Those five extra raids might as well have been fifty.

"The pressure kept building up from raid to raid more than ever after that. The nearer we got to the end of the thirty missions, the narrower we made our odds on surviving. Those odds acted on different guys in different ways. One fellow I knew never once mentioned any member of his family, never wore a trinket, never showed us any pictures, and when he got a letter from home he read it through once and tore it up. He said he didn't trust himself to do anything else, but still it took guts. Most of the rest of us would lug a letter around and read it over and over, and show our family pictures to each other until they got cracked and dirty. There was also a difference in the way we faked our feelings. Some of the guys would say, 'Well, if I managed to get through that raid, it stands to reason they'll never get me,' but they didn't mean it. They were knocking on wood. Some of the other guys would say, 'I'm getting it this time. I'll be meeting you in Stalag Luft tonight,' but they were knocking on wood, too. We were all about equally scared all the time.

"My best friend over there was an ardent Catholic. He used to pray and go to confession and Mass whenever he could. I kept telling him, 'What's the use? The whole business is written down in a book someplace. Praying won't make any difference.' But whenever I got caught in a tight spot over Germany, I'd find myself whispering, 'God, you gotta. You gotta get me back. God, listen, you gotta.' Some of the guys prayed harder than that. They promised God a lot of stuff, like swearing off liquor and women, if He'd pull them through. I never tried to promise Him anything, because I figured that if God was really God he'd be bound to under-stand how men feel about liquor and women. I was lucky, anyhow, because I had something to fall back on, and that was music. I went up to London several times between missions and visited some of those Rhythm Clubs that are scattered all over the country. I listened to some good hot records and a few times I even delivered lectures on jazz. The nearest town to our base had its own Rhythm Club, and I spoke there to about a hundred and fifty people on Duke Ellington and Louis Armstrong. Now and then I got a chance to play drums in a band. That helped a lot and made it seem less like a million years ago that I'd been leading Ted Hallock's Band out at Oregon."

Hallock got onto the subject of jazz, then abruptly switched back to his story again. "The missions went on and on," he said, "and the pressure kept on building. Guys I knew and liked would disappear. Somebody I'd be playing ping-pong with one day would be dead the next. It began to look as if I didn't have a chance of getting through, but I tried to take it easy. The worst raid we were ever on was one over Augsburg. That was our twenty-sixth, the one after what we expected to be our last mission. When we were briefed that morning and warned that we might be heading for trouble, I couldn't help thinking, 'By God, I'm getting rooked, I ought to be heading home to Muriel and New York and Nick's this very minute.'

"There was never any predicting which targets the Germans would come up to fight for. I was over Berlin five times, over Frankfort four times, over Saarbrücken, Hamm, Münster, Leipzig, Wilhelmshaven, and I had it both ways, easy and hard. We had a feeling, though, that this Augsburg show was bound to be tough, and it was. We made our runs and got off our bombs in the midst of one hell of a dogfight. Our group leader was shot down and about a hundred and fifty or two hundred German fighters swarmed over us as we headed for home. Then, screaming in from someplace, a twenty-millimetre cannon shell exploded in the nose of our Fort. It shattered the plexiglass, broke my interphone and oxygen connections, and a fragment of it cut through my heated suit and flak suit. I could feel it burning into my right shoulder and arm. My first reaction was to disconnect my heated suit. I had some idea that I might get electrocuted if I didn't.

"I crawled back in the plane, wondering if anyone else needed first aid. I couldn't communicate with them, you see, with my phone dead. I found that two shells had hit in the waist of the plane, exploding the cartridge belts stored there, and that one waist gunner had been hit in the forehead and the other in the jugular vein. I thought, 'I'm wounded, but I'm the only man on the ship who can do this job right.' I placed my finger against the gunner's jugular vein, applied pressure bandages, and injected morphine into him. Then I sprinkled the other man's wound with sulfa powder. We had no plasma aboard, so there wasn't much of anything else I could do. When I told the pilot that my head set had been blown off, the tail gunner thought he'd heard someone say that my head had been blown off, and he yelled that he wanted to jump. The pilot assured him that I was only wounded. Then I crawled back to the nose of the ship to handle my gun, fussing with my wounds when I could and making use of an emergency bottle of oxygen.

"The German fighters chased us for about forty-five minutes. They came so close that I could see the pilots' faces, and I fired so fast that my gun jammed. I went back to the left nose gun and fired that gun till *it* jammed. By that time we'd fallen behind the rest of the group, but the Germans were beginning to slack off. It was turning into a question of whether we could sneak home without having to bail out. The plane was pretty well shot up and the whole oxygen system had been cut to pieces. The pilot told us we had the choice of trying to get back to England, which would be next to impossible, or of flying to Switzerland and being interned, which would be fairly easy. He asked us what we wanted to do. I would have voted for Switzerland, but I was so busy handing out bottles of oxygen that before I had a chance to say anything the other men said, 'What the hell, let's try for England.' After a while, with the emergency oxygen running out, we had to come down to ten thousand feet, which is dangerously low. We saw four fighters dead ahead of us, somewhere over France, and we thought we were licked. After a minute or two, we discovered that they were P-47s, more beautiful than any woman who ever lived. I said, 'I think now's the time for a short prayer, men. Thanks, God, for what you've done for us.'

"When we got back to our base, I found a batch of nineteen letters waiting for me, but I couldn't read a single one of them. I just walked up and down babbling and shaking and listening to the other guys babble. I had my wounds looked at, but they weren't serious. The scars are already beginning to fade a little, and the wounds didn't hurt me much at the time. Still, I never wanted to go up again. I felt sure I couldn't go up again. On the day after the raid I didn't feel any better, and on the second day after the raid I went to my squadron commander and told him that I had better be sent up at once or I'd never be of any use to him again. So he sent me up in another plane on what he must have known would be a fairly easy raid over France, the milk run, and that helped.

"That was my twenty-seventh mission. The twenty-eighth was on Berlin, and I was scared damn near to death. It was getting close to the end and my luck was bound to be running out faster and faster. The raid wasn't too bad, though, and we got back safe. The twenty-ninth mission was to Thionville, in France, and all I thought about on that run was 'One more, one more, one more.' My last mission was to Saarbrücken. One of the waist gunners was new, a young kid like the kid I'd been six months before. He wasn't a bit scared— just cocky and excited. Over Saarbrücken he was wounded in the foot by a shell, and I had to give him first aid. He acted more surprised than hurt. He had a look on his face like a child who's been cheated by grownups.

"That was only the beginning for him, but it was the end for me. I couldn't believe it when I got back to the base. I kept thinking, 'Maybe they'll change the rules again, maybe I won't be going home, maybe I'll be going up with that kid again, maybe I'll have another five missions, another ten, another twenty.' I kept thinking those things, but I wasn't especially bitter about them. I knew then, even when I was most scared, that fliers have to be expendable, that that's what Eaker and Doolittle had us trained for. That's what war is. The hell with pampering us. We're supposed to be used up. If the Army worried one way or another about our feelings, it'd never get any of us out of Santa Ana or Deming."

I asked Hallock how long he had to wait before he was ordered back to the States. "In just a few days," he said, "the word came through that I could go home for a three-week leave. I cabled Muriel and she met me here in New York. I must have looked a lot different to her, and acted different, but she looked and acted the same to me. She brought along whatever money she'd managed to save out of what I'd sent her, so we could shoot it all on a good time. I'd been made a first lieutenant, and I get good pay, but saving any of it is something else again. Muriel and I both figure we'd better spend it while we're here to spend it. After a couple of days in Washington with my mother and father, we settled ourselves here in New York. We've just been eating and sleeping and listening to jazz and wandering around the town in a nice daze. I don't care if things are booming, if the civilians are all pulling down big dough, if no one seems to know there's a war on. For the moment, I don't care about any other damn thing in the world except that I'm here in New York with Muriel.

"We haven't made any plans. Hell's bells, I've *never* been able to make any plans. As soon as my leave's up, I have to report to a rehabilitation centre in Miami, and I suppose I'll be sent on from there to another post. Frankly, I'd like to land a job somewhere on the ground. I don't care where. Even Deming sounds beautiful to me. I don't particularly want to fly again. Pilots and navigators seem to feel different about the flying end of it; they don't seem to get that feeling of never wanting to go up again. Maybe that's because they're really flying the ship. When you're only one of the hired hands, who's being carried along to do the dirty work, to drop the bombs and do the killing, you don't feel so good about it.

"As for after the war, we don't dare to think too much about that. We're not ready to settle down and have kids and all that stuff. We feel as if we'd been cheated out of a good big chunk of our lives, and we want to make it up. I want to go back to college. Damn it, I want to play drums in a band again, in Ted Hallock's Band. I want to feel that maybe I can look two days ahead without getting scared. I want to feel *good* about things. You know what I mean. It seems to me that sooner or later I'm going to be entitled to say to myself, 'O.K., kid, relax. Take it easy. You and Muriel got a lifetime in front of you. Do what you damn please with it.' I want to be able to tell myself, 'Listen, Hallock, all that cannon-fodder stuff never happened. You're safe. You're fine. Things are going to be different for Muriel and you. Things are going to be great. You're not a damn little cog any more. You're on your way.' "

## *The Gothic Line*

by Martha Gellhorn

THE Gothic Line, from where we stood, was a smashed village, an asphalt road and a pinkish brown hill. On this dusty
mined lane leading up to the village, the road and the hill, the
infantry was waiting to attack. They stood single file, spaced
well apart, and did not speak. The noise of our artillery firing
from the hills behind us never stopped. No one listened to it.
Everyone listened to the sudden, woodpecker beats of the
German machine-gun fire ahead and everyone looked to the
sky on the left where the German airbursts made dark, loose,
small clouds.

In front of us a bulldozer was working as bulldozers do,
according to their own laws and in a world of their own. This
machine was trying to fill in a portion of the deep antitank
ditch which the Germans had dug along the entire face of the
Gothic Line. The bulldozer now scraped up two mines in its
wide steel shovel; the mines exploded, the bulldozer shook a
little, and the driver removed his tropical helmet and cursed
the situation. An infantry officer shouted something to him,
and he swerved his big machine, leaving two feet cleared between the side of his shovel and the mined side of the road.
Through this gap the infantry now passed. Each man seemed
very alone, walking slowly and steadily toward the hills he
could not see and to whatever peril those hills would offer.

The great Gothic Line, which the Germans have used as a
threat ever since the Hitler Line was broken, would, under
normal circumstances, be a lovely range of the Apennines. In
this clear and dreaming weather that is the end of summer,
the hills curve up into a water-blue sky: in the hot windless
night you see the very hills only as a soft, rounded darkness
under the moon. Along the Via Emilia, the road that borders
the base of these hills, the Germans dynamited every village

into shapeless brick rubble so that they could have a clear line of fire. In front of the flattened villages they dug their long canal to trap tanks. In front of the tank trap they cut all the trees. Among the felled trees and in the gravel bed and the low water of the Foglia River, they laid down barbed wire and they sowed their never-ending mines, the crude little wooden boxes, the small rusty tin cans, the flat metal pancakes which are the simplest and deadliest weapons in Italy.

On the range of hills that is the actual Gothic Line, the Germans built concrete machine-gun pillboxes which encircle the hills and dominate all approaches. They sank the turrets of tanks, with their long, thin snout-ended 88-mm. guns, in camouflaged pits so that nothing on wheels or tracks could pass their way. They mined some more. They turned the beautiful hills into a mountain trap four miles deep where every foot of our advance could be met with concentrated fire.

And it is awful to die when you know that the war is won anyhow. It is awful, and one would have to be a liar or a fool not to see this and not to feel it like a mystery, so that these days every man dead is a greater sorrow because the end of all this tragic dying is so near. There it was: the Gothic Line carefully planned so that every fold of the earth was used to conceal death, and the young men were walking into it, and because they have seen so much and done so much, they walked into it as if it were part of the day's work. A hellish day but still just part of the work.

It was the Canadians who broke into this line on the Adriatic side by finding a soft place and going through. It makes me ashamed to write that sentence because there is no soft place where there are mines and no soft place where there are Spandaus and no soft place where there are 88-mm. guns, and if you have seen one tank burn on a hillside you will never believe that anything is soft again. But, relatively speaking, this spot was soft, or at any rate the Canadians made it soft and they got across the mined river and past the dynamited villages and over the asphalt road and up into the hills and from then on they poured men and tanks into the gap and they gouged the German positions with artillery fire and they called in the Desert Air Force to bomb it and in two days they had come out on the other side of the Gothic Line at the coast of the Adriatic. But before that, many things had happened.

First of all, the main body of the Eighth Army moved from the center of Italy to the Adriatic coast in three days' time, and the Germans did not know it. That sounds very easy, too, written like that. What it meant was that for three days and three nights the weaving lateral roads across the Apennines and the great highways that make a deep V south from Florence and back up to Ancona were crowded with such traffic as most of us have never seen before.

Trucks and armored cars and tanks and weapon carriers and guns and jeeps and motorcycles and ambulances packed the roads, and it was not at all unusual to spend four hours going twenty miles. The roads were ground to powder by this traffic, and the dust lay in drifts a foot thick and whenever you could get up a little speed the dust boiled like water under the wheels. Everyone's face was greenish-white with dust and it rose in a blinding fog around the moving army and lay high over the land in a brown solid haze.

The road signs were fantastic, too, because more than one hundred thousand men who could not speak Italian were moving through complicated unknown country trying to find places which would never have been too easy to find even with empty roads and complete control of the language. The routes themselves, renamed for this operation, were marked with the symbols of their names, a painted animal or a painted object. There were the code numbers of every outfit, road warnings—bridge blown, crater mines, bad bends—indications of first-aid posts, gasoline dumps, repair stations, prisoner-of-war cages and finally a marvelous Polish sign urging the troops to notice that this was a malarial area: this sign was a large green death's-head with a mosquito sitting on it.

Along the coast the road signs were in Polish and in English, and at one crossroads a mine warning was printed in Polish, English and Hindu. And everywhere you saw the dirty white tapes that limit the safe ground from the treacherous ground, where mines are still buried. On the main highways there were signs saying "Verges Cleared," which means the sides of this road have been de-mined, or "Verges Checked," which means the sides of this road have been rapidly swept and you can suit yourself, if you want to take a chance.

So this enormous army ground its way across Italy and took up positions on a front thirteen miles long. The Eighth Army, which was now ready to attack the last German fortified line outside the Siegfried Line, had fought its way to these mountains from the Egyptian border. In two years since El Alamein, the Eighth Army had advanced across Africa through Sicily and up the peninsula of Italy. And all these men of how many races and nationalities felt that this was the last push and after this they would go home.

We watched the battle for the Gothic Line from a hill opposite, sitting in a batch of thistles and staring through binoculars. Our tanks looked like brown beetles; they scurried up a hill, streamed across the horizon and dipped out of sight. Suddenly a tank flamed four times in great flames, and other tanks rolled down from the sky line seeking cover in the folds of the hill. The Desert Air Force planes, which cavort around the sky like a school of minnows, were signaled to bomb a loaf-shaped hill called Monte Lura. Monte Lura went up in towering waves of brownish smoke and dirt. Our artillery dug into the Gothic Line so that everywhere cotton bolls of smoke flowered on the slopes. Our own air bursts now rained steel fragments over the German positions on Monte Lura.

The young British major who was directing this artillery through a radiophone said happily, "I must say! I do think our air bursts are doing very nicely!" The battle, looking absolutely unreal, tiny, crystal-clear, spread out before us. But there were men in the tanks and men in those trees where the shells landed and men under those bombs.

We had all been awake and roaming the countryside since five o'clock, when our first giant artillery barrage started. We were hot and hungry by now and we went to eat lunch in a tent about fifty yards from our own gun positions. The blast of the guns shook the tent and we could only talk between salvos. All that day and the next the noise of our own guns was physically painful. The Canadian brigadier commanding the brigade which was attacking this sector of the line amused us by outlining a postwar garden party he hoped to give. Dinner would be served on a long wooden table covered with a rather soiled white cloth; the guests would sit on benches which had a tendency to tip over backward. In one corner of the garden a flat voice would start saying: "I am now giving you a short tuning call: Roger over Victory, Victory, Victory," and would go on saying this uninterruptedly for the rest of the evening.

In another corner of the garden some tractors would be organized to act like tanks and they would first race their motors, which is a sound like the end of the world, and then they would roll back and forth on screaming treads. In another corner of the garden some sort of radio apparatus would imitate the sound effect of six-inch guns firing, and it is almost impossible to believe how appalling the sound is. In another corner of the garden a dust machine imported from Hollywood would spray dust imported from the roads of Italy onto the guests. A waiter would then walk in and release one thousand flies at a time.

The dinner would consist of a slab of cold bully beef as appetizer, followed by not very heated-up meat, and beans and hardtack. For dessert there would be hardtack with jam. The tea would have been brewed that morning and would be coal-black and lukewarm. If the guests behaved nicely and did not complain too much, they would be given as a prize a finger of issue rum, a drink guaranteed to burn out anyone's palate. This being a perfect picture of our own meal except that issue rum was lacking, we had a hearty laugh at the expense of the brigadier's mythical guests.

Later—but I don't remember when, because time got very confused—we crossed the Foglia River and drove up the road our tanks had taken and there we saw the remnants of a tank battle. An American Sherman, once manned by an English crew, lay near a farmhouse: across the road a German Tiger tank was burned and its entire rear end had been blown off. The Sherman had received an 88 shell through its turret. Inside the turret were plastered pieces of flesh and much blood. Outside the Tiger, the body of a German lay with straw covering everything except the two black clawlike hands, the swollen blood-caked head and the twisted feet.

Some Canadian soldiers, who were sightseeing, stood around the dead German. It is remarkable how quickly

soldiers start sightseeing where they have fought, perhaps trying now to discover what really happened. "Not much fresh
meat on that guy," one of them said.

You cannot note everything that happens during a battle;
you cannot even see what happens and often you cannot understand it. Suddenly you will see antlike figures of infantry
outlined against the sky; probably they are going in to attack
that cluster of farmhouses. Then they disappear and you do
not know what became of them. Tanks roll serenely across the
crest of a hill, then the formation breaks, you lose most of
them from sight, and then in what was a quiet valley you
unexpectedly see other tanks firing from behind trees. On a
road that is quite empty and therefore dangerous, because
nothing is more suspect at the front than the silent places,
you see a jeep racing in the direction of a town which may or
may not be in our hands. And when you imagine you have
found a nice restful place to camp in for a few minutes, German mortar shells start landing.

A battle is a jigsaw puzzle of fighting men, bewildered, terrified civilians, noise, smells, jokes, pain, fear, unfinished conversations and high explosive. A medical captain in a ruined
first-aid farmhouse speaks with regret of a Canadian padre
who volunteered as a stretcher-bearer to carry wounded men
out of the mine fields in the river bed. The padre lost both his
legs, and though they rushed him out, he died at the first
hospital. Bloody stretchers are stacked all around and now a
jeep arrives with fresh wounded. "Come back and see us any
time," the medical captain says. "Get some more wire splints,
Joe."

A group of English tankists drinking tea outside a smashed
house on Monte Lura invites you into their mansion, which is
mainly fallen beams and the rubble of masonry. The place
smells unbearably, because of two dead oxen at the side of the
road. One of the soldiers who had his tank shot from under
him that morning is waiting for another job. He hopes the
war will be over in time for him to celebrate his twenty-first
birthday in England.

There is a Canadian soldier dead on another roadside with
a coat laid most lovingly over him. If you lie to yourself you
can almost imagine he is asleep. There are two captured

88-mm. guns with a welter of German paper spread around them, for apparently the Germans also are slaves of paper work. Among this paper is a post card with a baby's picture on it addressed presumably to one of the gunners from his wife. And no one feels the slightest pity.

There is a young Italian woman wrapped in a blanket on the doorstep of a poor little hovel that one of our shells had hit during the night; this was in a town the Germans held until a few hours ago. She wakes up and starts to laugh, charming, gay and absolutely mad.

There are twelve parachutist prisoners, the crack troops of the Germans, standing in a courtyard guarded by the Canadian who captured them. They are all young and they wear the campaign medals of the Crimea as well as the medal of Italy. These were the men who held Cassino all winter. You start talking to them without any special feeling and suddenly like a shock, it occurs to you that they really look evil: the sadism which their General Kesselring ordered them to practice in Italy as they retreat shows now in their mouths and their eyes. They are simply a different race of men, and one turns away from them sickened and cold and hoping that such as these will truly perish from the earth.

There was the fat old Italian in Cattolica who had worked for twelve years on the Pennsylvania Railroad and who was now trundling his pitiful possessions home in a handcart. The Germans had occupied Cattolica for three months and had evacuated the citizens one month ago, and during this month they looted with horrid thoroughness like woodworms eating down a house. What they did not wish to steal they destroyed: the pathetic homes of the poor with smashed sewing machines and broken crockery and the coarse linen torn to shreds bear witness to their pointless cruelty. This old man was going home to a gutted house but he was a healthy, happy old man and he was overjoyed to see us and he invited me to visit him and his wife the next day. The next day his wife was dead, as the Germans came over that night and plastered the little town with antipersonnel bombs.

The Canadian troops I had seen two days ago going in to attack the Gothic Line were now swimming in the Adriatic. The beaches were laced with barbed wire, but holes had been cut through it, and engineers appeared with the curious vacuum-cleanerlike mine detectors to sweep the beach, and the infantrymen, sunburned the color of expensive leather, beautifully strong, beautifully alive, were bouncing around in the flat warm sea and racing over the sand as if there was nothing terrible behind them and nothing terrible to come.

Meantime you could sit on the sand with a book and a drink of sweet Italian rum and watch two British destroyers shelling Rimini just up the coast, see German shells landing on the front three kilometers away, follow a pilot in a parachute slowly sinking toward the ground after his plane had been shot down, hear a few German shells whistle overhead to land two hundred yards farther down, and you were getting a fine sunburn, and life seemed an excellent invention.

Historians will think about this campaign far better than we can who have seen it. The historians will note that in the first year of the Italian campaign, in 365 days of steady fighting, the Allied armies advanced 315 miles. They will note this with admiration because it is the first time in history that any armies have invaded Italy from the south and fought up the endless mountain ranges toward the Alps. Historians will be able to explain with authority what it meant to break three fortified lines attacking up mountains, and the historians will also describe how Italy became a giant mine field and that no weapon is uglier, for it waits in silence, and it can kill any day, not only on the day of battle.

But all we know who are here is that the Gothic Line is cracked and that it is the last line. Soon our armored divisions will break into the Lombardy plain and then at last the end of this long Italian campaign will become a fact, not a dream. The weather is lovely and no one wants to think of what men must still die and what men must still be wounded in the fighting before peace comes.

*Collier's*, October 28, 1944

# *Peleliu Landing*

by Tom Lea

*This is not a page from a history book, not an account of a battle. It is the simple narrative of an experience in battle; like combat itself such a narrative is bound to be personal, confused, benumbed and in its deepest sense lonely. D-morning, 15 September, 1944, I landed on Peleliu Island, about fifteen minutes after the first troops hit the beach, with marines under command of Captain Frank Farrell, Headquarters Company, Seventh Regiment. I remained with Farrell and his men under fire for the first thirty-two hours of the assault. As a LIFE War Artist my purpose in going ashore was to record the United States Marines in combat. On the beach I found it impossible to do any sketching or writing; my work there consisted of trying to keep from getting killed and trying to memorize what I saw and felt under fire. On the evening of D-plus-one I returned to a naval vessel offshore where I could record in my sketch book the burden of this memory. Before my hand steadied I put down the words and pictures that compose this book. The narrative is printed here as I first wrote it except for minor chronological rearrangement. The sketches are untouched.*

MY WATCH said *0340* when I woke up on the blacked-out weatherdeck below the bridge. Barefooted and in my skivvies, I got off my cot and stood by the rail rubbing grit from my eyes. Dead ahead, framed between the forward kingposts, there was flickering light on the black horizon. Sick yellow balls of fire flashed low in the clouds like heat lightning, but continuous. It was the Navy shelling Peleliu with the final punch before we landed. The black silhouette of a seaman on watch by the rail turned to me and said, "Them Japs are catching hell for breakfast."

Dawn came dim with low overcast. In the first gray light I saw the sea filled with an awe-inspiring company of strangers to our troop ships. Out to the horizon in every direction were lean men-of-war, fat transports, stubby landing craft, gathered around us like magic in the growing light. It was D-day.

We ate our last meal together, dressed in baggy green dungarees, on the plank benches of the troop officers' mess. We washed the food down our dry throats with big mugs of coffee, and put all the oranges in our pockets. Getting up to go, Captain Farrell repeated his instructions for Martin and me, the two correspondents, "Be at Number Three Net, starboard side, at *0600*."

Growing dawn had brought the ship violently to life. Power winches rumbled, hoisting our landing craft over the side. The marines, after long captivity in their crowded holds, moved at last to their stations by the rail, battle gear buckled, the last oil in the gun, the last whet to the knife. I felt some almost palpable spirit walking the emptying holds and passageways and along the crowded decks, with a word for every man.

In the corner where I kept my gear I checked it carefully and finally. There was the belt with the two filled canteens, first-aid kit and long black-bladed knife; and the pack with the poncho and shovel, the gloves, headnet and K-ration, the waterproofed cigarettes and matches and candy bar—and my sketch book and pencils and camera and films wrapped in the target balloon. All set. I checked my pockets for my watch and identification wrapped in rubbers—and my grizzly coin for luck.

Martin and I buckled our belts, slung our packs and put on our helmets. Inching along through the marines, we found Farrell and his men standing shoulder to shoulder with all their gear on the jampacked maindeck near the rail over Number Three Net. The maindeck looked queer without the landing craft that had loomed overhead on the long convoy days, making shade for marine card games. Now these boats were down in the water ready for the loads.

"Free Boat Two," bellowed the squawkbox on the bridge and Farrell said, "That's us. Let's go."

We gave a hitch to our packs, hoisted our legs over the rail and went down the rope net, down the scaly side of our sea-bitten ship by swinging handgrips and tricky footholds between the swaying knots, down to where the bobbing net met the pitching deck of our little iron tub. When we were loaded the coxswain gunned our engine in a blue stink of smoke and we cast off.

Our ship seemed to fall away from us and grow small as we moved out; there was a kind of finality about leaving it. Yet final or not, there was relief in action, and release from morbid imagination. For a moment we even partook of the gaiety of our bobbing tub on the foam-tracked sea. Emotions of an hour ago seemed suddenly unimportant as we looked back at the transport and remembered the parting words we posted on the bulletin board in the Ship's Officers' Wardroom:

## A MESSAGE OF THANKS

*From:* Marines aboard *U.S.S. Repulsive*
*To:* Officers and Men aboard *U.S.S. Repulsive*

1. It gives us great pleasure at this time to extend our sincere thanks to all members of the crew for their kind and considerate treatment of Marines during this cruise.

2. We non-combatants realize that the brave and stalwart members of the crew are winning the war in the Pacific. You Navy people even go within ten miles of a Japanese island, thereby risking your precious lives. Oh how courageous you are! Oh how our piles bleed for you.

3. Because of your actions during this voyage it is our heartfelt wish that:

    a. The *U.S.S. Repulsive* receives a Jap torpedo immediately after debarkation of all troops.

    b. The crew of the *U.S.S. Repulsive* is stranded on Beach Orange Three where Marine units which sailed aboard the ship may repay in some measure the good fellowship extended by the crew and officers during the trip.

4. In conclusion we Marines wish to say to all you dear, dear boys in the Navy: "Bugger you, you bloody bastards!"

Sixteen thousand yards off the beach the LCVPs circled at the sides of their transports, awaiting H-hour. From the air the big vessels must have seemed like a flock of fat ducks with broods of iron ducklings playing ring-around-the-rosy at their mothers' sides.

We circled until *0714* when our signal came to straighten out and head for the transfer line just outside the reef. The circles of iron ducklings suddenly unwound into parallel files of LCVPs gray with the seriousness of war, heading full speed for the flame.

For an hour we plowed toward the beach, the sun above us coming down through the overcast like a silver burning ball. Peleliu was veiled with the smoke of our shelling. New hits against that veil made brown and gray pillars like graceful ghost-trees by Claude Lorrain. As we drew abreast of our battleships and cruisers 1000 yards outside the reef, the sound of their firing changed from dooming booms to the slamming of huge doors.

At *0747* the carrier planes, hundreds of them, noiseless in the roar of gunfire, started pouring death. I counted 96 over my head at once. I saw one flash and fall in a long slow arc of flame.

Over the gunwale of a craft abreast of us I saw a marine, his face painted for the jungle, his eyes set for the beach, his mouth set for murder, his big hands quiet now in the last moments before the tough tendons drew up to kill.

At *0759* I noticed the amphibious tanks and tractors, the LVTAs and LVTs that would carry us over the reef, being spewed from the maws of LSTs. Sending twin plumes of foam from their tracks aft, they made their way to the transfer line.

At *0800* the rockets from LCI gunboats flashed pink and soared in flaming curves, by salvoes, into the wall of smoke on the beach.

At *0830* we wallowed aft the control boat on the transfer line, the reef a hundred yards ahead, and beyond the edge of the reef 700 yards of green shallow water thick with black niggerheads of coral. The first Jap mortar burst hit just inside the reef as our coxswain worked us up alongside an LVT for transfer. While the two craft bobbed and smashed at each other, we numbly piled ourselves and our gear into the LVT.

Going In—First Wave

The coxswain of the LCVP waved, backed his craft clear, and headed seaward.

The iron bulkheads of the LVT came above our heads—we could see only the sky. Farrell climbed on a pile of gear to see out, preparatory to giving our new coxswain the signal for heading in over the reef. Standing on a field radio case forward, I managed to poke my head up so I could see the first wave of LVTs go in. As I watched, the silence came into my consciousness; our shelling had ceased. Only our tank treads churning the water marred the quietness.

Then on the lip of the beach we saw many pink flashes— the Japs, coming out from under our shelling, were opening up with mortar and artillery fire on the first wave. Dead ahead there was a brighter flash. Looking through his binoculars, Farrell told us, "They hit an LVT."

As our coxswain watched the amphitracks toiling through the black obstructions on the reef, I heard him say to Farrell he doubted if it were possible to get us to our precise point on the far right of Beach Orange Three, and Farrell answered, "Well, take us as close as you can."

Mortar bursts began to plume up all over the reef and walk along the edge of the beach. Farrell, who could have waited another hour to take our Free Boat (not belonging to a specific assault wave) into the beach, abruptly put down his glasses, cupped his hands at the gunner by the coxswain, and bawled, "Let's quit this farting around. Tell him to take us in!"

The clatter of our treads rose to the pitch of a rock crusher and our hell ride began. In that clanking hearse it was impossible to stand without holding on to something, impossible to sit on the deck without the risk of fracturing our tailbones. So we grabbed and lurched and swore. Suddenly there was a cracking rattle of shrapnel on the bulkhead and dousing water on our necks.

"Get down! Squat!" yelled Farrell, and we bent down on our hunkers, grasping at each other's shoulders, at the bulkheads, at anything. That was the first mortar that came close. There were two more, and then the ping and whine of small arms in the air over us.

"Keep down!" yelled Farrell, with his head up over the bulkhead peering at the beach, "Still 300 yards to go."

We ground to a stop, after a thousand years, on the coarse coral. The ramp aft, seaward, cranked down fast and we tightened our holds on our gear. The air cracked and roared, filled our ears and guts with its sound while Farrell bellowed, "OK! Pile out! Scatter! But follow me to the right! The right, goddammit, remember!" And we ran down the ramp and came around the end of the LVT, splashing ankle-deep up the surf to the white beach.

Suddenly I was completely alone. Each man drew into himself when he ran down that ramp, into that flame. Those marines flattened in the sand on that beach were dark and huddled like wet rats in death as I threw my body down among them. There was a rattle and roar under my helmet while I undid the chin strap and smelled the flaming oil and popping ammunition from the burning LVTs around us. Men of the first wave had penetrated about 25 yards inland as I looked up the sandy slope.

Then I ran—to the right—slanting up the beach for cover, half bent over. Off balance, I fell flat on my face just as I heard the *whishhh* of a mortar I knew was too close. A red flash stabbed at my eyeballs. About fifteen yards away, on the upper edge of the beach, it smashed down four men from our boat. One figure seemed to fly to pieces. With terrible clarity I saw the head and one leg sail into the air. Captain Farrell, near the burst, never dodged nor hesitated but kept running, screaming at his men to follow him to their objective down the beach.

I got up to follow him, ran a few steps, and fell into a small shell hole as another mortar burst threw dirt on me. Lying there in terror looking longingly up the slope to better cover, I saw a wounded man near me, staggering in the direction of LVTs. His face was half bloody pulp and the mangled shreds of what was left of an arm hung down like a stick, as he bent over in his stumbling, shock-crazy walk. The half of his face that was still human had the most terrifying look of abject patience I have ever seen. He fell behind me, in a red puddle on the white sand.

I ran farther to the right, angling up the slope. Suddenly I recognized Martin's big back (he was unarmed like myself) under a three-foot ledge on the upper rim of the beach where

The Beach.

My first view as I came around from the ramp of our LVT.

vegetation started. I made a final dash to throw myself under the ledge at Martin's side. The exertion was so great I fell down almost unconscious. When I opened my eyes again my throat burned, yet I was cold with sweat. We were lying with our heads to the ledge, not four feet from the aperture of a Jap "spider trap," a small machine-gun nest built into the face of the ledge with coco logs. Loose sand shovelled away from the aperture in two widening banks at either side made the trough in which we lay and gave additional cover. I wondered how well I could use my knife if a live Jap suddenly should poke an ugly face out at me from the opening formed by the logs.

Mortar shells whished and whapped through the air over our heads. They hit without apparent pattern on the beach and in the reef at our backs. Turning my head seaward I saw a direct center hit on an LVT. Pieces of iron and men seemed to sail slow-motion into the air. As bursts began to creep steadily from the reef in toward the beach, the shells from one mortar rustled through the air directly over our heads at intervals of a few seconds, bursting closer, closer. Then a flat cracking flash nearly buried me with sand. Wriggling out, and trying to wipe the sharp grains from my sweating eyelids, I saw in the clinging gray smoke that a burst had hit about six feet from my left foot, beyond the bank of loose sand at my side. In almost burying me, this sand had also saved me from shrapnel, except for one small spent piece that burned my left shin—which I did not know until later. I yelled to Martin, but he lay with face down, and did not answer. I could see no blood but I thought he was hit. A moment later he raised his head—I shouted, but he could not hear me. The blast had deafened him. Burst followed burst, creeping out to the reef and then back into the beach again. We hugged the earth and hung on.

Abruptly from close by, from over the ledge at our heads came a shuddering explosion, then a wild popping of .50-calibre shells. Later when we got up, we discovered an LVT on fire in the brush above us. It had run over a mine.

A different kind of shellburst began to come at us from a new direction. We judged it was 75-mm. artillery from a Jap battery down the beach on a peninsula to our right. We saw

*The Price*

hits on five or six LVTs as they came jolting in over the reef. As I looked over my shoulder a burst smashed into a file of marines wading toward our beach from a smoking LVT. Jap machine guns lashed the reef with white lines and marines fell with bloody splashes into the green water. The survivors seemed so slow and small and patient coming in, out there.

Our carrier planes were swarming the sky again. Fighters roared in low over our heads almost continuously, strafing beyond our perimeter inland. Dive bombers peeled off by sections, dropping their 1000-pounders, and TBFs made their roaring rocket runs, finishing off with bellies full of 100-pounders for the Japs. We had it all our way in the sky over Peleliu; there was not a Jap plane in the air. Airmen gave marines on Peleliu great support. Martin and I realized their efficiency and close contact with the ground command when we saw dive bombers making runs over the peninsula to our right. The Jap 75's were silenced.

For some reason mortar and sniper fire slackened too, and left us on our lonely beach in comparative quiet. We knew our lines were well toward the airstrip now.

Martin and I lay there weak, grateful and still, in the lull. Suddenly we were conscious of someone crawling up behind us from the beach, and we turned our heads. It was a corpsman. As we moved around to see him, he grinned and rasped, "Christ, I thought you were a couple of corpses!" We agreed.

The delicious lack of bursts in our immediate vicinity was like a life-renewing elixir. Tension broke for a few moments, and we lit cigarettes, the three of us. For myself, I was sampling the sheer joy of being alive.

The sector of the beach we could see from our trough in the sand was empty of living creatures. Two dead bodies and five wrecked LVTs were our closest company. I stared at the sand bank above my head and saw against the smoking sky the tangled, broken wrecks of coco palms and tropical trees with their big leaves hanging burned and dead. Two birds with long bills and short bodies lighted on a smashed palm frond and cried. Then the mortars started again.

Hugging the ground and turning our heads seaward, we watched the next wave of LVTs come in. They had good luck. I saw no hits. The amphitracks crawled in, pushed their snouts against the sand, and the men came up from the surf. Most of them streamed off to our right along the rim of the beach at the edge of the broken trees. Mortar fire shifted far to our left, and there was only the occasional zing of a sniper's bullet. Four men carrying posts and orange beach markers walked by, and another wave of LVTs discharged men along the whole length of the beach. We got up and started walking to our right. I remember the strange quietness, the dead marines in the white sand, the men with heavy loads trudging along in the smoke of the LVTs. Two rows of land mines, sown about six feet apart, lined our beach. The Japs had not tended them well; they were easy to see. We stepped carefully around their rusty bellies and forked horns.

Behind us came a burly man walking fast, as if on eggs. He bawled at the men he passed, "Where's the Seventh's CP?" and always got the reply, "Up that way, Colonel." We recognized him as the CO of our regiment, and fell in behind him, to find Farrell's bunch. When snipers' bullets and occasional mortar shells went over our heads on their way out to the reef, I instinctively pulled in my neck—though I could judge by now when they would be really close. It was interesting to watch the colonel ahead. He never bobbled nor missed a pace, but there was plenty in his stiff stride—almost an expression on the back of his neck—to describe the trouble in his mind.

We followed him inland from the beach, plunging into the burned and twisted jungle trees. We stumbled through debris into an open space where four LVTAs were parked, and thirty paces further into the trees we found our CP being set up in a trench dug by the Japs. It was six feet deep and about twenty yards long. Under our naval shelling the Japs had given it up just before we landed. Farrell had found it, cleared it of Jap machine-gun fire, and had it functioning as a command post when his superiors arrived. It was full of marines now, taking cover from sniper fire and mortars. A burst hit close at our backs just as Martin and I slid down into the trench. There was a yell for corpsmen—somebody was hit.

We sat in the trench, getting our breath. My legs trembled from exertion, but I felt very relieved, very secure. Out some

200 yards ahead, our front line inched forward and our perimeter grew more solid. Firing on our area slackened gradually.

By this time it was *1300*. Some of us climbed out of the trench and walked back in the smashed trees to stretch our cramped legs. Disposal squads were working through the area, digging out dud rockets, bombs and shells. When a projectile could not be disarmed with tools, disposal men would explode it. They would clear the necessary area, pass the word loudly to get down, and let 'er go—*blump!* All through the broken trees we found crude booby traps. Details were busy marking them and the land mines with red tape. Telephone linemen were unrolling their heavy spools of wire. Scout observation planes from warships wheeled high above our heads, directing naval gunfire. Occasionally they would go into a shallow dive and have awkward fun strafing.

Before noon the sun had bitten through the overcast of early morning and burned away all but a few white puffy clouds. Our planes were working against a background of bright, sharp blue. And as the sun, seven degrees above the equator, struck down upon us, it turned Peleliu into a bitter furnace.

Three of us had each carried a can of beer ashore in his pack. Giving each other the high-sign, we gathered behind a broken palm log, punched holes with our knives in the three cans, and drank a toast, *To the Marines on Peleliu*. The beer was hot, foamy and wonderful. When it was gone, we were still dry-mouthed. And not a bit hungry.

About thirty paces back of the Jap trench a sick bay had been established in a big shell crater made by one of our battleship guns. Lying around it were pieces of shrapnel over a foot long. In the center of the crater at the bottom a doctor was working on the worst of the stretcher cases. Corpsmen, four to a stretcher, came in continually with their bloody loads. The doctor had attached plasma bottles to the top of a broken tree stump and was giving transfusions as fast as he could after rough surgery. Corpsmen plied tourniquets, sulpha, morphine, and handled the walking wounded and lighter cases with first aid.

The padre stood by with two canteens and a Bible, helping.

Sick-Bay in a Shellhole:
The Padre read, "I am the Resurrection and the Light."

He was deeply and visibly moved by the patient suffering and death. He looked very lonely, very close to God, as he bent over the shattered men so far from home. Corpsmen put a poncho, a shirt, a rag, anything handy, over the grey faces of the dead and carried them to a line on the beach, under a tarpaulin, to await the digging of graves.

It is hard to remember how the minutes ticked away, while the sun climbed down from the top of the blazing sky. The battle pounded on ahead of us. During flurries of fire I slid down into the trench; during the lulls I tried to find shade from the sun. I was without emotion of any kind. I saw everything around me in sharp focus, yet it no longer crashed into my consciousness. My mind blanked itself for my body's sake.

Our front advanced slowly, if at all; the radio in our trench picked up few reports, and the inactivity began to pall on Martin and me as we grew more and more curious about the battle's progress in other sectors. We had no access to the messages runners brought in to the colonel.

Farrell was sending two men to establish contact with the Division command post which was supposed to be far down the beach to our left. Martin asked if we could go along and get news from the Division command. We buckled our canteen belts and joined the two marines.

It is hard to walk through a jungle that has been subjected to saturation bombing and bombardment for a week. Jagged holes in the scattered stone and dirty sand, splintered trees and tangled vines made a churned, burned wilderness. Strewn through this chaos were not only the remnants and remainders of the marines' advance, but also the new men and new gear that had poured ashore to back up the front line. These men were digging in, making holes for themselves for the long night ahead when the Japs would surely counterattack. We jumped over foxholes, climbed over and around smashed trees, sidestepped tapes denoting mines and booby traps, walked gingerly around those yet unmarked. Telephone wires in crazy criss-cross mazes were stretched along the broken ground. Scattered everywhere were discarded packs, helmets, rifles, boxes, clothes, rubber life belts—the rubbish of battle. Lying on the seared leaves and hot sand were dead bodies yet ungathered by corpsmen, the flesh bluish gray as the pitiless sun began to bring the peculiar and intolerable stench of human dead.

Planes came in strafing over our heads; the whump and chatter of firing to our right made a constant churning of sound. Sweat ran in streams from under our helmets which, without cloth covers, were burning to the touch. Our dungarees, wet with sweat, stuck to our legs and backs. The sand under our clothes scratched like sandpaper.

When we had snaked our way along for about 300 yards, the two marines with us began to ask the men we met where the Division command post was. Nobody knew. We hunted for an hour, and never did find it. Intolerably hot and thirsty, Martin and I left the marines to their search. We turned left and walked down to the edge of the beach, planning to make our way back to our own CP by walking along the beach, the way we had first gotten there. The water's edge was crowded with men bringing equipment ashore.

We had walked fifty paces along the sand, dodging around LVTs, when we heard a mortar shell whirr over us and saw it send up its column of grey water about sixty yards out on the reef. That was the first of several salvoes. They began to get hot.

We were passing by a big hole dug in the sand with a sign above it reading "Shore Party CP" when a burst hit about 25 yards down the beach at the water's edge, where we had been, and set an LVT on fire. We flopped into the very crowded Shore Party CP. The mortar fire lasted for about ten minutes, with most of the hits on that part of the beach we had just traversed. Later that evening we learned from the two marine messengers that in their further search for the Division CP they had been directly under this fire and had four men killed in the same hole with them. They came back shaken and no longer eager.

Meanwhile we lay packed in the hole with the shore party. The supply officer in charge was stretched flat on his belly and holding a telephone in his hand. He wanted to make a call, but he would not get up to crank the box to get the operator. So I cranked it for him, as I was right by it. By the time he got an answer, and I had cranked and cranked, the mortar bursts were hitting further down the beach away from us.

Some guy buried deep in the sand hole stuck his head up and began to gripe, "Goddammit, what are all you bastards in this hole for? Them bursts are a mile off. Scatter, you punks!" Just then a shell came whapping over and hit very close, and the guy buried his head again and said no more. Somebody grunted, "You're a brave son of a bitch walking around out there ain't you?"

In a few minutes Martin and I got up and continued our way down the beach through the welter of men, vehicles and ammunition cases. In some places things were so jammed up that we had to wade out into the surf to get around. The Jap mortars were far from silent, and direct hits on this kind of concentration really played hell. Yet regardless of fire, the marines were pouring everything they could get on the beach before nightfall and the expected counterattack. We watched sweating crews lift light artillery out of the amphitracks and haul them ashore. Martin muttered, "The more of those damn guns they put on here tonight the better I'll feel."

Turning in from the beach toward our CP we found the area thicker than ever with marines digging in for the night. There were foxholes every three or four feet, most of them barricaded with coral stones and logs moved around to help deepen and strengthen the cover. The men worked at their places for the night earnestly, without much conversation except short declarations of fact: "It's the ferking night time I don't like, when them little ferkers come sneakin' into your lap." They dug in the dirt and cleaned their guns.

I saw a big redheaded sergeant I knew, lying in a hole with his eyes closed. It was his first action, and the day's events had bitten too deeply into his mind. At noon, I had seen him sink down on the ground with his hands over his face and cry.

We found our CP. The trench was twice as wide at the bottom as it had been, and cleared of broken tree limbs and big rocks. As we came up a bomb disposal officer was carrying out a dud rocket he had dug from the side of the trench. Improvements were going on. Marines were filling new gunnysacks, making sandbags to pile around the radio set and around the section of the trench where the colonel would spend the night. Men were hacking roots from the sides of the trench and smoothing out bumps, making places to rest their backs. Others were cutting poles from broken trees, laying them crosswise over their part of the trench, and tying their ponchos across the poles. It was getting cosy around the CP.

We asked Farrell if we could spend the night in the trench and he told us he had a place for us down at the extreme left end where he would be.

Very heavy firing suddenly started on our left. The radio operator got busy. When he finished writing out the message he showed it to us before he passed it down the trench to the colonel. It said our center was under heavy counterattack, the enemy using tanks. We knew we had three Shermans ashore, and sat there listening and hoping they would be enough. Gradually the firing died down. The attack stalled after the Shermans had knocked out eleven Jap tanks. A lull settled over us, as both sides prepared for the night.

About sundown we settled into our places at the end of the trench. The low sun cast a sulphurous yellow light through the smoke, then faded. Somewhat to the left and behind us two batteries of 75-mm. were placed. They fired a few rounds over our heads and the crack and blast made me jump. Then there was almost silence in the growing dusk. Our planes left the sky, heading out for their carriers. I got the orange and candy bar out of my pack, ate the candy, split the orange three ways to share with Martin and Farrell. Warm water from my nearly empty canteen was dessert. Word was passed that the "smoking lamp" would be out all night, that if anybody wanted a cigarette this was the last chance before morning. So we sat smoking in the dusk.

Martin and I spread a poncho under us and I hung my knife on a tree root over my head where I could reach it easily. We settled down to sleep, as close into Mother Earth as we could get. Mosquitoes began to swarm and bite. Like everyone else, I finally rummaged in my pack, found my headnet and gloves, and put them on.

We had expected that it might cool off after sundown, but we were wrong. With our headnets over our helmets and tied at the bottom around our necks, and with our gritty gloves on, we sat and steamed in puddles of sweat. Gun flashes occasionally silhouetted the top of the trench against the sky of misty stars. So began the long night in which the waking and the dozing nightmare merged.

A deep and numb kind of weariness both of body and of mind made the trench and the battle, the anxiety and uncertainty unreal, without the power of fact. I did not give a damn. I accepted each moment as it came, as if watching the paying out of a coiled cable, not being able to see when the end would suddenly come, time's end, world's end. Meanwhile the cable unwound. I was neither contented nor disturbed.

Little balls of fire danced under my eyelids when I closed my eyes. Flurries of gunfire rattled and thumped, and I seemed to be drifting off remotely into the sea of sound out there amongst the waves of a death I neither desired nor despised. Somewhere in those great waves was a peace that would lose me everything. Drifting out into the darkness farther, I struggled with those waves like a man on a life raft alone.

The blurred ring of the telephone about five feet from where I lay was like a tug at my sleeve, pulling me back to my fellows, back to my life, back from those huge waves of sound where I struggled alone. The quiet voice of the man on watch was crisp as he relayed information to the officers whose voices answered in the darkness down the trench. I could not help hearing what they said about weakness in our perimeter, about over-extension of Baker Company, about lack of reserves, about failure to contact the Fifth, about our poor position for Jap counterattack. Hunched over in my hole, I had the dreamlike certainty that I was two people—one in a black pit who was too tired to live or die, the other standing by with a disembodied rather benign regret that living and dying were so similar and so confused.

Events were the only measurement of time as the night dragged on. I do not know what time it was when the counterattack came. There was a sudden flurry of rifle fire and blatting machine-guns, a sudden pause, then a crashing answering fire from somewhere out in the blackness ahead of our trench. The phone rang. A battalion CO reported the Japs' infiltration and the beginning of the counterattack. He asked what reserves were available and was told there were none. Small arms fire ahead of us became a continuous rattle. Abruptly three star shells burst in the sky. As soon as they died floating down, others flared to take their place. Then the howitzers just behind us opened up, hurling their charges over our heads, shaking the ground with their blasts. Jap mortars spotted them, and bursts came our way. Some hit very close but I do not know what casualties they caused. The howitzer batteries answered every few seconds. The black air above our trench was gradually filled with the whistle and whine of small arms fire coming our way and crackling in the tattered brush over the banks of our trench. Our machine-guns cracked in short deliberate bursts and were answered by the faster, higher chattering of the Japs' *Nambus.*

Then I heard, in pauses between bursts of fire, the high-pitched, screaming yells of the Japs as they charged, some-where out ahead. The firing would grow to crescendo, drowning out the yells, then the sound would fall dying like the recession of a wave. Four times I heard the screaming Japs; in the firing I could not judge how near they came, though the second wave of yammering seemed closest. From down our trench in the lulls I heard our colonel giving orders to his operations officer who sat by another phone calling out to battalion commanders. Suddenly the colonel stood up and called for one of his junior officers at our end of the trench. I heard him give orders to get forward every available machine-gunner and rifleman from the rear of our position. A runner crawled out to pass the word. Small arms fire over our heads increased. A few moments later three riflemen on their bellies wriggled up behind the coco log that lay broken at the end of our trench about ten feet from where I sat, and started firing over the log. Looking up, I saw the earth, the splintered trees, the men on their bellies all edged against the sky by the light of the star shells like moonlight from a moon dying of jaundice.

I do not know how long it took the marines to beat the Japs back. Perhaps it was an hour, perhaps longer. If my weariness detached me from a sense of bodily peril, it also detached me from a sense of the passage of time. I floated calmly at the bottom of the black eternal well, strangely unconcerned with the fire and the sound that troubled its dark waters. There

Counter attack.
The black well in the shaking earth
the BANZAI, the starshells

was no sudden cessation of battle; it slackened slowly. The words over the telephones were less frequent, the snapping whine of small arms became less steady, the artillery gradually ceased firing. Only the star shells kept going—like bursts of fever in the sky.

The borderline between sleeping and waking melted somewhere within this recession of battle. I dozed, feeling at the same time that I was awake, conscious of the hard stones against my back, the wet gritty sand against my skin, the aches in my bones, the dryness in my mouth. Yet I slept, I'm sure. Martin told me next morning that a fox-like creature with a bushy tail jumped into our hole, ran across my shoulder and up the sliding dirt at my back. I do not remember it. Yet I was awake later when Martin broke his snoring with a violent jerk and curse, and threw a land crab as big as his fist violently down the trench. It had pinched him on the backside and while he rubbed his behind and swore it seemed unbearably funny. I dozed again before daylight, for suddenly I opened my eyes and the sky was gray and the earth was silent. Quickly in the growing light the dark shapes of our trench acquired color, the three riflemen by the coco log grew sharp and clear.

The bottomless black well of night was a lie; the light of heaven had not forgotten us. The world lived again and so did we. Men stood up and grinned and perhaps were ashamed to speak their joy. Then from out of the silence there came a distant hum, growing steadily, becoming a roar. It was our planes: they had not forgotten either. As we climbed out of our trench men popped up out of foxholes everywhere like a magic army conjured from the debris of war.

The staccato rattle of strafing planes, the first rumbling blumps of the dive bombers began the second day of battle after the silence of dawn.

We wiped the slime off our front teeth and lighted cigarettes. Three of us shared our last orange, and I had a stick of chewing gum and the last water in my canteens for breakfast. Ground fire on our perimeter broke out again, and men buckled themselves for battle.

We learned more about what the Japs had done in the night. The nearest dead ones had been found about thirty

yards in front of our position. They had infiltrated behind our
perimeter, even stolen our aircraft markers and planted them
far in our rear. There had been several charges—that explained the *Banzai* screams—but the marines had held them
off in spite of thin spots in our lines. Japs wearing helmets of
dead marines had sneaked into foxholes behind our front and
cut throats. They had been slashed or shot by marines in hand
to hand fighting in the darkness and there were bodies on the
ground now in the morning light.

By *0800* our troops were beginning their day's push, with
heavy air and artillery support. We knew the LVTs were pouring in over the reef again. The 105-mm. guns were at last
being brought ashore and set up. The Jap mortars started
again too, the bastards: corpsmen came in bearing the dead
and the shattered.

Farrell turned to Martin and me. "I'm taking a patrol to see
how things are going at the front. Would you like to go
along?" We said we would, and a few minutes later we strung
out in single file, with Farrell and eight of his marines,
through the shattered jungle. We walked about 400 yards,
skirting the airfield at its southern end.

This airfield was of course the prime reason for the Peleliu
operation. It had big well-graded runways surfaced with finely
crushed gravel. It danced now in the heat waves, wide and
empty under the blistering sun. Although marines held two
sides of the field, the Japs still commanded the 400-foot
height along the left side and could, like the marines, register
fire anywhere on the open space. It was no-man's-land that
morning. Down at our end of the runway there was only one
smashed Zero; up at the other end we could see big piles of
wrecked Jap aircraft (117 by count later in the day).

At the southern end on our side of the field opposite the
hill our artillerymen had dug holes and carried 75-mm. field
howitzers to the sites. As we came down to them these batteries were firing continuously, throwing shells into the Jap
hangars and buildings at the foot of the hill, and at caves in
the hill where Jap mortar and artillery and machine-gun fire
was dealing out misery to marines. The targets were almost
completely obscured by the smoke and dust of the shelling. A
naval scout observation plane spotted fire for our batteries

Field Howitzer at edge of airfield.
Punching at "Bloody Nose"

and carrier aircraft strafed and dive bombed into the murk. Our patrol joined one of the 75-mm. gun crews for awhile, watching them fire. Farrell sent two of his scouts off into the mangrove swamps to locate a battalion commander whose outfit had taken the brunt of the Jap counterattack the night before. Farrell wanted his report for the regimental command. When the scouts returned and reported they had found him, we threaded our way into the tangled mangroves.

We found the battalion commander sitting on a smashed wet log in the mud, marking positions on his map. By him sat his radioman, trying to make contact with company commands on the portable set propped up in the mud. There was an infinitely tired and plaintive patience in the radioman's voice as he called code names, repeating time and again, "This is Sad Sack calling Charlie Blue. This is Sad Sack calling Charlie Blue—"

The whiskery, red-eyed, dirty marines sprawled around us were certainly sad sacks too. They had spent the night fighting in foxholes filled with stinking swamp water; they were slimy, wet and mean now.

The major was trying to establish the exact positions of his companies before moving out of the miserable swamp closer to his day's objective. His people were taking some high ground to our right and had the job of smashing several big blockhouses and pillboxes overlooking the two peninsulas at the southeastern tip of Peleliu. Tanks and flamethrowers were spearheading the advance. We were in the swamp an hour before word came that the high ground had been taken.

As the battalion headquarters group prepared to move forward a supply detail came in carrying cans of water for the outfit. We each filled one of our canteens with the warm brackish stuff that sloshed from the square tins, and had a drink. Just as we were forming up to proceed toward the ridge the Japs laid their mortars and artillery on us. The nearest burst hit about twenty yards from where I ducked down, but the thick trees stopped the shrapnel and none of us was hurt.

There were about sixty of us, including Farrell's patrol. We started eastward in single file, three or four yards between

"This is Sad Sack calling Charlie Blue"

each man, winding tortuously around muddy sink holes and uprooted trees and through the clinging network of vines and broken branches and seared leaves. Gradually we came to higher ground where bare stone sloped up in little ridges and defiles, and vegetation was not so thick. Sniper fire cracked in the trees above our heads, but we were not shelled.

As the sun climbed in the clear sky the heat grew. There was no breeze. Stinging sweat poured from our bodies and kept us wet in our muddy dungarees. That morning marines learned the full force of the sun on Peleliu, where coral rock bakes in the oven of the sky. The heat cut into our very marrow as we trudged up the ridge. The dead Japs we passed were also affected by the heat; they had started to stink before they were stiff.

We could hear the heavy slugging of the tanks and mortars and howitzers, our crackling gunfire and the answering fire of the Japs just ahead as we came into an open pocket near the top of the gentle slope we were climbing. The clearing was a Jap barracks area surrounded by small pillboxes and anti-aircraft positions. It was a smoking heap of rubble as we came into it. Everything in it was smashed, twisted, blasted. There were dead Japs on the ground where they had been hit and in two of the pillboxes I saw some of the bodies were nothing more than red raw meat and blood mixed with the gravelly dust of concrete and splintered logs. I felt no emotion except a kind of gladness that these bodies were dead. An occasional sniper bullet over my head gave some point to my gladness.

Over in some dry grass by a tree I stood a moment looking down at the face of a dead marine. He seemed so quiet and empty and past all the small things a man could love or hate. I suddenly knew I no longer had to defend my beating heart against the stillness of death. There was no defense. The burning hope of remaining restless, unwise and alive, forges frail armor for the beating heart.

The Japs had cleared a trail from their barracks to the top of a ridge where their strong points were. We walked carefully up the side of this trail littered with Jap pushcarts, smashed ammunition boxes, rusty wire, old clothes and tattered gear. Booby traps kept us from handling any of it. Looking up at the head of the trail I could see the big Jap blockhouse that commanded the height. The thing was now a great jagged lump of concrete, smoking. I saw our lead man meet a front line detail posted by the blockhouse while the other troops advanced down the hill with the three tanks and the flame-throwers. Isolated Jap snipers were at work on our slope; small groups of marines fanned out on both sides of the trail to clean them out, while we climbed toward the block-house.

To the left of the trail, about fifty paces from the summit, we came to an open-sided hut with a tattered palm-thatch roof, apparently the mess kitchen for nearby Jap installations. It was filthy and forlorn. Over the open fire pit hung three big blackened cooking pots, with nothing in them but a little charred stuff. On a dusty table were still strewn bright blue enamelware mess bowls with the Jap Navy anchor printed on their sides. A big gunnysack of rice was broken and spilled in the dirt. I looked around for tinned crabmeat or *saki* but

The Blockhouse and the Dead

found nothing worth taking. The Japs had provided fine sanitary arrangements for their kitchen: under the same roof was a chicken roost and pig sty. The poultry was gone, but lying in the sty was a dead hog where a million flies were feasting. A marine came in from the trail and stopped at my side. Looking down at the pig in the puddle of blood, he shook his head and remarked, "Ain't it the goddamdest thing how a dead Jap looks exactly like a stuck hog?"

Just as we walked into the clearing around the blockhouse, a Jap sniper gave us a short machine-gun burst that splattered on the concrete over our heads. We all hit the dirt, most of us bunched up under the blockhouse walls. After a moment somebody got up and yelled, "All right you bastards—break it up and spread out." We did. The Jap did not risk another burst for awhile.

Heavy fighting was in progress just over the brow of the hill beyond the blockhouse clearing. Marine riflemen were still in position along the crest fifty paces ahead of us. Jap mortars from below occasionally overshot our front and burst on the hilltop. The area all around the blockhouse was still subject to sporadic fire and we did not loiter in the open places.

Among the scattered marines on the edge of the clearing I came face to face with a young lieutenant who had been a messmate of mine on the troopship coming to Peleliu. We had seen each other at dawn only the day before, yet we grinned, grimy and proud, as if we had not seen each other for years, shook hands and went our ways. Later I realized we had said a good deal with the handshake.

The battalion headquarters group turned right and went down the slope for better cover, to set up a command post in the trees. Soon Farrell and his men were the only marines left in the immediate area of the blockhouse.

In addition to its primary strongpoint, the hilltop clearing held two concrete pits about thirty feet in diameter constructed as mounts for heavy guns. Their circular walls slanted outward like saucers and around them were neatly painted 360-degree marks. Their decks were about eight feet below ground level and in the circular walls were cut entrances to caves which served as shelters for the gun crews. The pits had been tightly roofed over with brush camouflage now entirely burned off. We found not a trace of the big guns for which the pits had been constructed. Either bombing and bombardment had obliterated them or, more likely, they had never been installed.

Farrell and his patrol had numerous duties in the area, and we sat in one of the gun pits for an hour, taking cover from Jap snipers and mortar fire while members of the patrol completed their work. Three of the six openings in the circular wall around us were blocked up with coral boulders. Peering in the caves behind the other three we found one was empty, another held two dead Japs. The last one, larger than the rest, was full of bloody bodies. They were piled up so tight it was hard to count them, but there were more than twenty. The marines were finding souvenirs, putting bloody Jap flags on the deck to dry in the sun, and examining the firearms and enemy gear scattered around us.

One marine found a beautiful and clean silk "belt of a thousand stitches." It was brilliant yellow with a purple rectangle at the middle top holding the embroidered name of the owner. Below the rectangle were ten lines of one hundred red stitches—little round red dots, embroidered. A thousand ladies had each sewn a stitch of well-wishing for the owner, but this feminine backing had done him damned little good. He was dead now and starting to stink there on the coral rock a long way from home.

The whole gun pit stunk, and the sun cut like a knife. I was glad when Farrell's patrol had covered the blockhouse area, and he decided to go forward, find a place on a ledge overlooking one of the peninsulas to the south, and observe the fighting. The marines were scheduled to take the peninsula that afternoon, but the Japs were putting up a bitter fight as they backed down the slope.

We made our way to the left side of the clearing where we cut into the woods. Then finding a narrow trace in the tangle of trees, we followed it out to the eastern rim of the ridge. At one point a dead Jap lay on his back in the trace. Farrell bent over the body and saw a wire tight around the top of the right shoulder. He tried to peer around under the arm to see if a booby trap grenade was rigged in the armpit, but he couldn't tell. So he said to one of his marines, "We're going on. But go get one of the disposal men, and a line. Secure the line on this arm, get back plenty, and yank—to see if this son of a bitch is rigged. I think he is." I wanted to see that, but I went on with the patrol.

There were mines and booby traps all along the trace, but they were crude and easy to see. Farrell tore narrow strips off his white handkerchief and tied them on the stakes by the trip wires, to mark them for the troops that would come later.

The ledge where we came out, overlooking the beach and the peninsula to the south, had been strongly barricaded by a rough wall of coral boulders. Apparently the Japs had planned some additional work with reinforced concrete, for all along the inland side of the wall we found bundles of steel rods. At first we were careful about lifting our heads above the top of the wall, for now we were the extreme left flank of the marine front that bulged in the center down the hill to our right. After some experimenting, and drawing no fire, we poked our heads up and looked around at will. It was a ringside seat for the battle going on below us, for 400 yards, out to the peninsula's end.

We had been in our position for only a short while when the hot and heavy firing below us eased off into a lull. Farrell explained that the marines were drawing back to positions clear of the area where our aircraft and naval guns were scheduled to soften the Japs on the peninsula for the final ground assault.

While we waited for the fireworks, the sun started down its afternoon journey to the west. It beat upon us unmercifully. The shade from the scraggly brush over our position was thin; the glittering heat simmered us in our own sweat under our iron helmets.

Suddenly 8-inch shells from heavy cruisers started hitting from 250 to 400 yards ahead of us. They burst in tall sprays of flame and grey smoke. The very earth would tremble, and then we would hear the triple booming reports of the salvoes. These giant fountains of flame spouted along the length and breadth of the peninsula again and again—then ceased as suddenly as they had begun.

Immediately from out of the sun dive bombers plummeted with the sound of some huge ripping fabric, as if they were tearing holes in the sky itself. We watched the black eggs leave the plane bellies, and as the divers pulled out and soared, the 1000-pounders would *blump* into the jungle. Over the peninsula there grew again high lazy trees of grey and mustard smoke, where seeds of fire had taken root.

Then torpedo bombers ran down the sky in steep slants, releasing their multiple rockets with a terrifying *whoosh*, and at the end of their runs dropping whole nests full of small black eggs that rattled in the air and roared as they tore into the earth. The torpedo planes did not soar out of their runs, but banked in tight turns and circled over us quite low. We could see their crews distinctly as they banked and peered down at us behind our wall. Two of the pilots waved.

Finally the fighters came, whole squadrons diving in by sections, strafing. We watched the flaming orange paths of their tracers while the air was filled to bursting with the stuttering din of their guns.

The planes were hardly out of sight before the marines below us opened fire to advance. Down the slope the broken trees and the smoke obscured the actual movement of the troops. We could locate the fighting only by the new smoke puffs that rolled up out of the trees. Minute after minute the artillery and small arms slugged and pounded, and the firing positions did not change.

Suddenly Farrell cracked, "All right—you have targets—commence firing!"

We saw a Jap running along an inner ring of the reef, from the stony eastern point of the peninsula below us. Our patrol cut down on him and shot very badly, for he did not fall until he had run a hundred yards along the coral. A moment later, another Jap popped out running—and the marines had sharpened their sights. The Jap ran less than twenty steps when a volley cut him in two, and his disjointed body splattered seaward into the surf.

Our patrol was immensely cheerful when Farrell trained his binoculars and found the caves the Japs had run from. Other Japs were poking their heads out to fire, and for several minutes Farrell and his men peppered the cave mouths with M-1 and carbine bullets. The range was over 350 yards. I strained my eyes until they watered, trying to judge the effect of the firing. The marines claimed at least two more hits, but I did not see them myself.

While we kept our eyes peeled for more Japs Farrell sent one of his men back to the battalion CP to find out how the marine advance was going. About half an hour later he came back with salt sweat rolling over his cracked lips and reported that Jap resistance was very stiff, that our men were catching hell from pillboxes and gaining very little ground in spite of high casualties.

Farrell suggested that we might see more of the fighting under the ridge if we crawled over our wall and made our way down to the beach. Two marines, Farrell, Martin and I decided to go, leaving the rest of the patrol above to cover us.

We crawled over the tearing coral boulders and down the steep slope in the biting sun, heading for a rotten tree about ten feet from the water's edge. Farrell, Martin and I finally squeezed ourselves against the crooked trunk, both for cover and for shade. The two marines squatted by big stones nearby. I suppose we had been there between five and ten minutes, craning our necks at the fighting along the slope to our right—and not getting a very satisfactory view—when suddenly CRACK, a mortar burst hit on the beach to our left, and snipers' bullets splattered on the rocks at our backs. The fire came unexpectedly from the headland up north, toward which Japs from the caves had run. The mortar hadn't ranged us yet, and the riflemen were rotten shots, but we were in a very unhealthy place. We scrambled up the slope and threw ourselves down between big rocks for cover. The heat between the stones out in the fiery sun was intolerable. As I lay there I grew dizzy and began to feel numb. I knew I had to move or I would faint. Without drawing another shot, I slid and crawled and wiggled back up the slope and over the wall. The other four men followed.

I flopped ten feet back of the barricade in a small patch of shade under some limp leaves. Our canteens had been empty since noon; I was very thirsty and infinitely tired. I lay there breathing fiery air over my dry teeth, wishing I had taken some training for this damned beachhead business.

War is Fighting and Fighting is Killing

Every few minutes a mortar would slam into the woods around us; stray rifle and machine-gun bullets sang and ricocheted in the brush over our heads. Down the slope to our right a couple of hundred yards I could hear our tanks trading wallops with Jap pillboxes. Fighter planes came in strafing with a razzle dazzle racket. I took it all for granted, more interested in my aches than in a battle. We waited for the front to advance so we could go down and have a look, but the front stalled, and the afternoon wore on.

About *1600* we heard marines talking as they came up the trace at our backs, then their voices were lost in the grinding and clanking of an LVT mashing a road up the trail we had travelled in the morning. Marines began to slouch by, loaded down with their packs and guns. Some of them went on over the ridge as reinforcements to the front; others filed down the ragged path back of our wall, and trampled through the brush up the slope at our backs. Farrell gave one man hell for stumbling by the strip of handkerchief tied as warning by a land mine about ten feet from where we were sitting. Marines were occupying our position in force to hold it during the night.

When I heard one of the new men say that the LVT had brought up some cans of water, I came to life immediately. I unbuttoned my canteens from my belt and without even putting on my helmet went off at a trot looking for the water cans. I spotted where the LVT had left them in a clearing at the top of the ridge and made for them. About fifteen paces from the water I nearly stepped in a big puddle of fresh blood. Looking up, I saw three marines carrying a man shot in the chest. They were taking him out of the clearing, and there was only one man standing at the water cans. I thought of nothing but getting some of that water and poured it into my canteens without saying a word to the other marine. A moment after I rejoined Farrell and Martin and we were drinking, a marine from our patrol came up puffing with his full canteen and said, "Goddammed snipers got two guys by me while I was pouring this. They got another guy just before that."

I drank several more hot swallows, feeling peculiar.

It appeared that the fighting was mostly finished for the day. Our perimeter for the night was being established; the troops around us were digging in. Farrell decided to go back to his regimental command and report.

Back in the blockhouse clearing we found two LVTs. One of them had brought up the water cans, the other had come up loaded with corpsmen, stretchers and first aid equipment. The coxswain of the one that had brought the water told us he was going to the beach and would take us. So we got in and grabbed hard to the bulkhead as we lurched away. The LVT slammed down the slope batting down trees, rocking over boulders, leaving a swathe of churned hillside and dust. We came out of the brush near the southeastern corner of the airfield, rolled out into the open and headed for the end of the long runway on the southwest edge of the field. As we clanked and roared at our full speed of maybe twelve knots, I stood on an ammunition box to see out over the side and get a look at the scores of Jap aircraft smashed and burned on the ground.

Across the field to the northwest grey skeletons of hangars and barracks and the ruins of a little town lay dead at the foot of the highest hill on Peleliu. Incessant bombardment and bombing had chewed the western end off the ridge, burned from it the living jungle green, shattered its stone into ruinous sawtooth pinnacles and jumbled defiles. Grey against the smoky light of the slanting sun, it stood like the broken wilderness of a dead world. Yet within its crust were living Japs and chattering guns and the blood of dead marines was caked upon the hot and ghostly stone. The gunner of the LVT nudged me and pointed at the hill. "Bloody Nose," he said.

The chartmakers had marked it Umorbrogol Hill; marines had marked it now another way—and found its right name.

Past the howitzer batteries we had visited in the morning we turned into the jungle and found bulldozers scraping roads and carving clearings. The Ducks were thick as ants, carrying supplies to dumps in the trees. Down on the beach where our LVT stopped at the water's edge, we got out to walk to our command post along the way Martin and I had first struggled on D-morning. Now it was totally unfamiliar, covered with vehicles and supplies and teeming with men. I felt lost in the maze of traffic, as if my memory lied about the

Down from BLOODY NOSE
Too Late
He's Finished - Washed Up-Gone

lonely place under the terrible fire so long ago yesterday. Then a mortar burst hit close to the water's edge a hundred yards ahead, and made everything true again.

We got our packs at the CP and thanked Farrell and said good-bye. Marines chewing at K-rations looked up from the trench and did not hide their envy: "Hey, when you get back to that mudscow out there, will you go to the scuttlebutt and drink me about a gallon of that cold water?"

As we passed sick bay, still in the shell hole, it was crowded with wounded, and somehow hushed in the evening light. I noticed a tattered marine standing quietly by a corpsman, staring stiffly at nothing. His mind had crumbled in battle, his jaw hung, and his eyes were like two black empty holes in his head. Down by the beach again, we walked silently as we passed the long line of dead marines under the tarpaulins.

A Duck picked us up and took us out to an LCVP. The sun was going down as we headed seaward. A mortar burst cracked on the reef like a last baleful word from Peleliu.

*Peleliu Landing*, 1945

# My Old Outfit

by Mack Morriss

MAASTRICHT, HOLLAND—We walked at five-yard intervals on either side of the concrete highway and watched without much interest the Typhoons and P-47s that were strafing something off to the left.

The planes went into long dives and pulled out in tight circles to come back and strafe again. The sound of their machine guns reached us long after they had pulled out of the dives. We glanced occasionally at the ready-made German foxholes, dug by impressed civilians and lining the road every 10 yards. They were chest deep and round, with dirt piled neatly beside them; but every one was smooth on the inside so we knew that Jerry had never used them.

We plodded along past wrecked vehicles and modern homes with well-kept yards, and glanced at the terrain off to our left where the war was. Dutch kids by the side of the road, wearing bright orange bows in their hair or on their jackets, reached for our hands.

"Good-bye," they said. They say that either way, whether you're going or coming, as a greeting or as a farewell.

Hutch was walking behind me.

Hutch is Mack Pierce, a mortar sergeant in F Company. He used to be in A Company, where he was a line sergeant, then an artificer and finally mess sergeant. He was a mess sergeant for 18 months, and then he went over the hill and got busted. He transferred to F Company after that, and they finally gave him three stripes again but he didn't care. He never did care much for things like that.

This was our anniversary—Hutch's and mine. We had been in the Army four years. We were members of the Tennessee National Guard, inducted Sept. 16, 1940, among the oldest of the "New Army." Today we were moving up to an assembly

area where our outfit—the 30th (Old Hickory) Division—
would get set for an attack.

It was a bright day, as days go here. The 2d Battalion was
two parallel OD lines moving across the brow of a hill up
ahead and swinging around the shaded curve behind us. They
were leaving Maastricht, a fair-sized town taken two days before. Now—after France and Belgium and Holland—they
were headed for Germany.

I was with Hutch down in F Company because Hutch is
the only line soldier left out of the old bunch from the high-
lands of east Tennessee who came into the Army as Company
A. There were about 150 of us then. Now there are only four
in the regiment. There's Hutch, down in the 2d Battalion.
Then there's Porky Colman, a mess sergeant now; Charlie
Grindstaff, still cooking; and Herman O. Parker, still driving a
truck. They're all that's left of old A Company.

We started out in the Army at Fort Jackson, S.C., when
they were singing the song "I'll Never Smile Again." Lord,
we were sentimental about that song. I remember Hilton
was just married and was leaving his new wife. Crockett
slugged the juke box in the drug store at Columbia; Tommy
Dorsey's arrangement came out soft and smooth, and Hilton
cried. We were all privates then, going into the Army for a
year.

Since then, Hilton's kid brother had become a tail gunner
in a Fort and had gone down over France. Hilton got out of
the Army and his wife had a baby on the same day. Hilton
stayed out of the Army for two years. Now he's in the Navy
somewhere. Crockett went from a basic private up to first sergeant and then to OCS. Now he's a first lieutenant in an
infantry outfit over here.

Hutch Pierce and I walked up the road. Somebody—a replacement—sang briefly and then stopped. The infantry
doesn't sing much, especially moving up. Not after St. Lo and
Mortain, they don't sing much. The replacement chanted:
"Or you might grow up to be a mule. Now, a mule is an
animal with long funny ears."

Hutch and I talked along the way. When we got a break we
lit K-ration cigarettes and tried to reconstruct A Company.

It was a picturesque outfit. Those originals were close-knit, clannish and independent as only hill people can be. It was a company with a heart and a soul. Its code was "Independence." Its motto, in our own language, was "take nothin' offen nobody." That was a philosophy that needed tempering. It works better in combat than in garrison. We had our troubles.

I had seen Col. Crumley in London. He's had a desk job there now since his lungs finally took him out of the field into the hospital. He was a first lieutenant when we went to Jackson, then company commander and then battalion commander. We talked about the old company before it broke up. Crumley was hard, but he loved the company. He was a better soldier than any of us, but he was proud of us—a man who lived by our philosophy and tempered it, too. We learned to take a lot, as the infantry does.

It has been three years since Crumley was with us as a company officer, but Hutch said: "When you're out here you appreciate a man like him."

We tried, Hutch and I, to tell each other what little we knew of the men who came in with us. The outfit had deteriorated slowly in the natural process of transfers and discharges, like an eroded hillside gradually falling away.

Harry Nave, the company clerk, went into the Air Forces as a cadet and got killed in training. Lardo Boring went into the Air Forces, too, and the last we heard, he had pulled his missions and was back home. Lardo used to be in the machine-gun section.

Earl Marshall went into the Paratroops, and so did Bill Longmire. Elmer Simerly was in the Airborne Infantry. Bill Potter went to OCS and the last we knew he was in New Guinea. Red Mason was a lieutenant over there somewhere. Ralph Snavely was one of the first to transfer out. He went down to the Southwest Pacific, too. Lucian Garrison went to Italy and got wounded, and so did Capt. Ritts. Ed Mottern was in Iceland for a long time but he's probably over here now.

Hutch had seen Pony Miller on the beach back in June. Pony is a first now, and an executive officer. Hutch said he'd heard that Howard Fair went in with the 1st Division on

D-Day. Charles Hurt got his jaw broken on maneuvers just before A Company came overseas, so he stayed in the States.

Doc Sharp was transferred; he's down in the Islands with a jungle-training unit, still letting the cards fall the same as always. Jack Ellis came over with another regiment in the division, but he got wounded and we lost track of him. Fred Davis was a captain in the TDS the last we knew.

A Company came to England with only 12 of the old National Guard bunch still left and just a few of our first and second batches of selectees. Now there's only one line soldier left from the first group of selectees we trained—a boy named J. C. Wright. Wright was wounded some time back, but he rejoined the company later as an acting platoon sergeant. Then they got a new lieutenant, and he and J. C. had an argument. J. C. is platoon guide now.

The outfit came to France on D-plus-9. Three weeks went by before they hit it rough. Then, on July 7, the regiment spearheaded the way across the Vire River and fought down through the hedgerows toward St. Lo.

It was a war foreign to the sage fields and pine thickets of South Carolina. It was a war from one piled-up mass of earth and shrubbery to another, with the Artillery blasting savagely and the infantry moving up 50 yards behind it. Those hedges are old, and the decay has built up at their base to form solid walls. Each one of them was a wall of fire, and the open fields between were plains of fire. The flanking hedges on either side belonged to him who could cover them.

Two of the boys from the hills stopped there. One of them was Bill Whitson, black-haired, with a face so dark that his teeth seemed whiter than they really were. He was built like a god—broad and tall. He lived like a happy devil, untamed and untameable. Whit never took anything very seriously. He moved with the corded grace of a panther, lethal and full of power. He could make the sling of his '03 rifle crack like gunfire when the leather hit the hardness of his hand.

Whit raised his head out of a foxhole and a piece of shrapnel caught him flush in the temple. He died somewhere northeast of St. Lo. Bull Bowers got hit there, too, the same day.

Bull is a big boy, almost pudgy, with round cheeks that are a perpetual cherry red. His name is James, but he's always been called Bull because when his voice changed it came out low, deep and throaty, so that whatever Bull said he said it in a rumble with a drawl.

Bull is easygoing. He never pushes anybody unless somebody pushes him. His make-up is not the make-up of a tough platoon sergeant. Bull's a platoon sergeant who swore softly rather often, but never with very much conviction.

So when they pulled Bull out of the foxhole, after the shrapnel had gone into him, he looked at his legs and then said to nobody in particular, without a great deal of violence and in a slow rumble: "Them gawdam sons o' bitches."

Bull was evacuated. Two days later Dale May left the outfit because of sickness. He had stomach trouble—ulcers or something.

Dale got to be a sergeant right after we came into the Army because he was one of the few men in the outfit with service in the Regulars. He had pulled a hitch at Schofield Barracks, and he told us stories about the Old Army—of afternoons off, tailor-made khaki blouses, white gloves and chrome bayonets, and how he was pulling KP when his discharge papers came through and he could go back to the mainland.

Dale was a tech sergeant when he left A Company. The boys in the kitchen hear he's in a Quartermaster outfit now.

The regiment's objective was the high ground to the west overlooking St. Lo. They took it, so they were a protective screen for the outfits that went into St. Lo itself. Then A Company moved south toward Tessy-sur-Vire.

On July 28, the regiment hit trouble. The next day the 1st Battalion went in to attack near a place called Le Mesnil Opac. There were hedgerows again, and a long slope exposed to observation and heavy fire. One of the men wounded in the action was Pfc. James R. Baines.

We always called him Beans. He had been a tech sergeant but had got busted. When he made platoon sergeant he told one of the boys who got another rocker with him: "Well, they

made everybody else, now they made us." That was back in
the States. Nobody cared much for stripes back there any
more than they do over here now. Too many people on your
back, too much worry, too much bother.

Beans got hit by shrapnel and was evacuated. The next
night Clyde Angel was killed.

Clyde was blond and fair. He talked with the nasal twang of
east Tennessee. He was a mess sergeant and before that he
had been a cook in the company, just as his brother Monk
had been a cook for us before him. There were two other
cooks, men who had come to the company later, who were
killed with Clyde.

The kitchens were dispersed and everybody was dug in.
Charlie Grindstaff said Clyde had the best shelter in the
area. He and the other two dug a deep one and covered
it with logs and dirt. Then Jerry came over, dropping big-
stuff bombs that straddled the shelter. The concussion killed
all three of them in the hole. A Company's kitchen was
blown to hell. Now Porky is using the blackout tent of battalion headquarters for his cook tent. It's better than the old
one.

The next night the regiment made its objective beyond
Tessy-sur-Vire and later moved on to relieve elements of the
1st Division near St. Barthelmy. St. Barthelmy is close by
Mortain, not far from the base of the Cherbourg peninsula.
It was between Mortain and Avranches by the sea that our
armor had roared southwest into Brittany after the breakthrough at St. Lo. At St. Barthelmy A Company gave
everything it had. It was there that the regiment was hit—
hard.

The SS had counterattacked with tanks, and the German artillery was trying to cut through to split our forces in Normandy
and Brittany. The Germans hit savagely. They ran over A
Company and C Company. The regiment fought like animals
with everything that would fire and then fought hand-to-
hand with the German infantry that poured in behind the
tanks.

Jerry almost made it. The fight went on for four days while
the division struggled and gave ground but never broke.

Then, on the fifth day, the power was gone and we went back into St. Barthelmy. The *SS* spearhead was blunted and then broken off. But Bud Hale was gone, and Ed Markland.

Bud was the top kick. He was a little guy with delicate hands and a skin that stretched tight across the cheekbones. His eyes were the eyes of all his family. At home the Hales have eyes that are all alike. Frances, Virginia, Luke, Sara, Bud, Mary, Nell and Sonny—they all have eyes that are their medium of expression. Bud played football at home the year we won the state championship and before. He was the kind of boy who drew people to him. Over here one of the new boys in the kitchen put it right: "We had to take the chow up to the line, and when I could see Bud I felt like the whole company was there."

After the *SS* ran over the company, Bud was listed as missing in action. So was Markland.

Ed and I were mortar corporals together for a long time, and our anniversary today would have been a great day for him. The division commander came around this morning presenting medals to a few officers and men in the regiment. The general order for the award of the Silver Star included T/Sgt. George Edward Markland "for gallantry in action in France."

The day after Angel was killed Ed's outfit had been held up by fire from a dug-in position. Ed crawled up ahead, "consistently exposed himself to murderous enemy mortar and artillery fire." We adjusted our own artillery on the strongpoint and the attack went on. Ed wasn't here to get in on the little ceremony by the road this morning, but he may catch the later one. A Company doesn't refer to Bud and Ed as MIA but as captured. Jerry got a lot of prisoners that day. Ernest Oaks was hit there, too.

When the *SS* overran our antitank positions and knocked out four of the guns, Oaks had to be evacuated. He had been in A Company for a long time—part of the triumvirate of Potter, Oaks and Russell. When we came into the Army none of them was 20. They were wild. They laughed and did insane things. Russell—we called him "Reb" although all of us are Southerners—was wide-eyed during our training on the machine gun. The nomenclature delighted him. One day the section sergeant had us naming the parts of the piece and he picked up a tiny pin and asked Reb to identify it.

Reb gazed thoughtfully at the pin.

"That," he said, "is the forward cam lever for the plunger guide on the barrel extension with the swivel pawl."

St. Barthelmy-Mortain was the division's great trial. It was infantry against armor, and the division fought for survival. Col. Frankland, the 1st Battalion's commander, saved his own CP by killing the crew of a German tank with his .45. Parts of five German *Panzer* outfits hit the division, striking along the main highways and the back roads. The division was committed to the last man. The artillery was overrun and fought as infantry. The engineers and cavalry were on the line. Thirty Jerry tanks were destroyed. The engineers got a Mark IV with a bazooka. An AT commander stopped another with a bazooka and killed the crew with a carbine as they tried to get out.

In the fog of the morning of Aug. 7, the regiment and division survived. Our artillery, TDs, rocket-firing planes and armor were thrown in to add strength to a line that was thin. A Company survived.

One battalion of a sister regiment was isolated for three days, cut off on a cliff and blasted mercilessly. When the Germans came forward under a white flag to talk surrender, the battalion said: "Go to hell."

Our 2d Battalion—Hutch's outfit—helped get them out.

Hutch has had the experiences of a line soldier. A machine-gun bullet burned the back of his neck. The blast of Screaming Minnies cart-wheeled him off his feet. A little piece of shrapnel cut across the top of his foot, but he didn't bother to have it treated.

Hutch laughed and said: "The damndest thing I've seen in combat happened that day. We went up after the battalion that was lost. There was a goat up there. He was a sorry-looking goat, sort of a dirty gray.

"Well, we were getting artillery, and every time a shell would come in this goat would dive for a foxhole. Then he would raise his head up and if he didn't hear anything he would come out. There were plenty of foxholes and he knew what they were for. He'd do it every time."

We laughed at the picture of a bewhiskered goat in a fox-hole. One infantryman said: "Yeah. The reason he beat me into one was because he had four legs and me just two."

A Company had two of our originals left in the line after St. Barthelmy. Now both of them are gone—perhaps to come back to the outfit, perhaps not to come back to it at all.

Both went back with fatigue, with nerves that had stood all they could stand for a while.

One of them left just a few days ago, after a river crossing that stirred up a fight. It was a fight like a dozen others the company has had. But it was one too many for him.

The other one who went back is a twin. He and his brother are identical. There were some of us who had soldiered with them every day and still couldn't tell them apart. They're squat and tow-headed and when they laugh their faces crease into a fan of wrinkles from the outside corners of their eyes. They grinned almost always, but when they got mad their lips quivered and they trembled all over, and we were surprised that they did. Not long before the company left the States, one of them was transferred and the other stayed on alone. But part of him was gone.

Yesterday, in a courtyard, Parker and I lay sprawled on the trailer of his jeep and watched as the infantry went past on the outside lane. It was a patrol coming in. "Hit anything?" somebody asked. A voice answered: "Nuh." The patrol went by silently.

"Was that some of us?" I asked Parker.

"Doggone," said Herman, "I don't know. I don't know anybody in the company any more."

*Yank*, December 1, 1944

# Now the Germans Are the Refugees

by William Walton

Aachen, Germany

SOMETIMES war is very personal when you see it all around you. It was that way when we went down from the surrounding hills into Aachen. The shelling and bombing had ceased because our infantrymen were creeping from house to house, rooting out every German with rifles, machine guns and grenades. Gunfire sounded, now loud, now whispering as we entered the streets of Aachen.

Every building was damaged or destroyed. Not a window remained. Dense smoke swirled over rows of houses that looked like the brownstone fronts of New York's East 80s, but in ruins. The air was full of tiny cinders that were grit in your eyes and bitter on your tongue.

We stopped at an intersection to watch spurts of rock thrown up by mortar shells farther down a side street. Then commenced one of the most remarkable sights I have ever seen. Slowly from a huge basement shelter down that street the people of Aachen began streaming out into the smoky sunshine. Heavy with weariness, with fear, and with the bulging bundles of their last possessions, they plodded in double files toward us. One block behind them guns poked from windows and ruined doorways and were blasting at one another, shattering chipped masonry, raising clouds of dust and smoke. The people walked on, casting only occasional frightened looks over their shoulders. For almost 10 days they had lived in that basement; some had been there for months. They blinked in the sunlight.

Three-fourths of them were women, many of them old. The old move very slowly even when the war is breathing hot behind them. They panted under loads of paper, suitcases, packages of clothing, shopping bags stuffed with small possessions. They panted and plodded on. One old crone in wooden-soled shoes pushed a baby carriage full of household goods. She seemed to see and hear nothing. Another passed, muttering gutturally, the wind ruffling her straggling white hair. Middle-aged ones looked more harassed and some were black with anger. In twos and threes they trudged, a long, winding line up the street.

The younger ones herded frightened children. One pushed a baby carriage in which a blank-faced one-year-old sat wedged among sacks of food. Another young woman, her face working with emotion, clutched the hand of her 8-year-old son, who looked wild with terror.

Two girls of 20 came abreast. They gave us a fierce burning look and then turned their faces to the wall as they walked by, not a casual gesture but a slow, studied movement of hate and revulsion.

The only smiles were from an elderly man who walked alone and waved as he passed, and from two blue-eyed women, who looked as though they might be charwomen and seemed to think their struggle with a two-handled basket was uproarious.

The men were old, some shepherding wives. Some pushing carts, some so elderly they barely shuffled, some moved 10 yards, set down mountainous bundles and took a breather before wearily plodding on. Only one old man walked without a single parcel or bag. In his arms was cradled a great gray cat.

Behind a cumbersome steel cart three people struggled up the hill while a fourth guided the cart from the front. One pusher was a fortyish woman in a neat, black, pin-stripe suit with a simple black hat. Twice she faltered on the hill but each time kept grimly on. The muscles in her slim legs bulged with the strain. She gave one more heave and then stumbled to a halt. The cart kept on going. Tears were streaming down her face. She shook convulsively and groped in her pocket for a handkerchief. A poorly dressed woman with a huge bundle strapped to her back walked up beside her and put a comforting arm around the woman in the black suit. She shook her head, then tentatively put one foot forward, then the other, and with infinite weariness continued on up the hill.

One flighty woman stopped to ask if she could wait for her

crippled sister-in-law. In German she said, "We are very glad you have come. Anything to end this terrible war." They were all obedient, turning into another street just as the doughboys directed. When they neared a cross street, some tried to turn off. "These are our homes," they said. "Can't we stay here?"

No. All civilians must leave the city until it is cleaned up entirely. Infantrymen could not risk having Germans, even old ones, at their backs.

Leaning against the wall beside me, Sgt. Eldridge Benefield said in his Texas drawl, "I hope I never live to see anything like this happen in America. These ruins. These people." He shook his head. "But sometimes I wish people over there could at least see it. Sometimes I think they don't quite understand what it's like."

As we watched the people of Aachen straggle down the street we saw them pass two first-aid men carrying a stretcher out of a half-ruined building. On the stretcher was the inert, blood-stained body of an American soldier. Machine guns still echoed behind that building.

More than an hour went by before the last weary refugee plodded out of sight. The sergeant and I had witnessed an historic turning point in World War II. For the first time the people of Germany were joining the long lines of Europe's refugees along the road over which they had forced so many other peoples before them. Now the German people would know how it had been for the Poles, Russians, Greeks, Norwegians and French. Now they would know where their politicians and generals and strutting Nazi youths had led them. Perhaps this was the only way they could learn the fruits of cruelty and oppression which their country had spread over all Europe and far beyond. None of the politicians and generals and strutting youths were in that procession. It was only the very old, the very young and helpless, moving past their ruined homes through the blasted streets of Aachen in poverty and in fear.

*Life*, November 6, 1944

## THE SINKING OF THE PRINCETON:
## OCTOBER 1944

# Death of Carrier Described

by Peggy Hull Deuell

FROM A NAVAL BASE—They may be home now—the several hundred survivors of the light carrier Princeton sunk in the second battle of the Philippine Sea. They may be walking through the quiet streets of their home towns and the people who meet them will not know of that day-long savage fight to save their ship.

None will know because it is difficult and painful for a man to talk about the ship he has lost, more painful than the battle itself. And so they will talk of other things and wait for the call they are eager to hear—orders to report to a new ship.

But this is what happened and if you meet a sailor from the Princeton you will know what his memory holds. Capt. William H. Buracker, the skipper, of Winchester, Mass., shy and slim, soft-spoken and sad, told us about it in the gloomy recesses of the navy's briefing room while a tropical rain beat down to the alleyways and provided a fitting accompaniment to his story.

He wanted to be matter of fact about it. He was a naval officer first and a man, a very human man, second, and the combination of the officer who loved his ship and the man who saw her die brought him close to the breaking point more than once as he talked.

The day of the Princeton's death her combat air patrols shot down 36 of the more than 100 enemy planes which had attempted to attack the task group. It was early morning when this fight took place and the area having been cleared for the time being of the Japanese, the Princeton's planes returned to be serviced and reloaded for another strike at 9 a.m.

Ten had reached the deck safely. The sky was overcast. There were low, thick clouds and it was raining.

Suddenly a gunner picked up a plane starting a gliding run on the ship. Swift orders to maneuver were flashed to the engine room. The antiaircraft batteries let go into the murky ceiling but the Jap pilot came on and over the ship. He dropped a bomb, a 500-pounder, Capt. Buracker thought, and it hit the flight deck squarely between the plane elevators.

"I wasn't too much concerned." The lines from his nose to his mouth grew deeper as he spoke. "I thought it was a small bomb and we could patch up the damage quickly. But, unfortunately, the bomb went through the flight deck into the hangar below where the torpedo bombers were gassed and loaded."

He moved uneasily as if it hurt to remember the shock of the explosions which followed, the fire which broke out immediately, the heavy smoke which filled the ship and interfered with the efficient movement of the crew.

Fire fighting controls were destroyed by the explosions and it was a few moments before the manual controls could be operated. In the meantime, the fire made headway. It was now 9:30 a.m. and Capt. Buracker, watching the fires spread, thought of the bombs stowed aft in an auxiliary stowage compartment.

"I thought," he told us, "that if I could keep the fire away from it we could save the ship. About 10 o'clock the torpedoes on the hangar deck went up and the flight deck buckled. It seemed to me that if that auxiliary compartment was going up, it would have gone then."

In this last explosion the elevators were blown up and the flight deck buckled and conditions made the carrier's nerve center—the island—untenable. Men were trapped aft and the captain turned the ship in the hope that the wind would carry the smoke away from the island.

The Morrison, a destroyer, came alongside and put fire fighting lines aboard but these proved inadequate. Then the Birmingham, a cruiser, brought her more effective equipment to the Princeton's aid. With the destroyer on one side and the cruiser on the other, it looked as if it were going to be possible to save the wounded carrier.

"This is what everyone aboard thought of," said the captain, "to save the ship first. There seemed to be no concern about personal safety."

The fires began to die down and Capt. Buracker's hope mounted. "I didn't think the ship was hurt inside. I was sure we could bring her in. She might not look very pretty, but I knew we could bring her in."

All personnel not engaged in fighting the fire had been ordered to abandon the ship. "Many of those who had the right to go and should have gone refused to leave. They joined the salvage crews as volunteers."

At this point, it was about 1:15 in the afternoon. Japanese planes and submarines were converging on the task force and the Birmingham and Morrison had to cast off. The helpless Princeton was left once more a prey to the fire, which began building up as soon as the ships shoved off.

"We were only 150 miles from Manila," he said, "and the Jap planes could find us easily."

When the all clear came, Capt. Buracker asked for a tow and the Reno, a cruiser, came alongside with the Birmingham.

"It took some time to get the lines aboard, as the Princeton was drifting leeward," said the captain. "I had thought that if the auxiliary bomb stowage was going to go up, it would have gone long before. My air officer, Commander Bruce Harwood of California, was in charge of one of the damage control parties and they went aft to check on the compartment."

He stopped suddenly, moved restlessly, and then, embarrassed by his emotion, continued in a low voice.

"It was as surprising as it was terrifying—that explosion. It was the worst I have ever heard in my life. I can't describe it to you. I was on the flight deck with the captain, who had come aboard a short time before as my relief, Capt. John Hoskins of Bethesda, Md.

"We were all wounded, more or less. I started forward and then looked back to see Capt. Hoskins lying on the deck, his leg hanging by a shred. I called for the doctor, who was wounded himself and who was attending to wounded on the hangar deck. Capt. Hoskins found a piece of line where he had fallen and he applied his own tourniquet. Commander Sala had no kit. He had some morphine, sulfa and a sheath knife, and when he reached Capt. Hoskins, he severed the shred with it."

It was apparent to Capt. Buracker now that he would have to abandon his ship. As Capt. Hoskins was carried overside he said: "Take her home, Bill. You deserve to." But it was Capt. Hoskins who went home, where he is recovering in a Philadelphia naval hospital.

A search was made of the ship for living personnel and at 4:40 the captain went over the side, still hoping it would be possible to tow her home. She was floating on an even keel and he thought he could make it with her. But the task force group commanders decided it would cripple their force; sunset was coming on and the night would be filled with Japanese planes and submarines. She was in more potential danger than her ultimate salvage justified. They decided to sink her with her still unexploded bombs and gasoline, for the storage tanks had not gone up yet.

It was there in the Philippine Sea as the sun went down over the horizon in a red glow that the Princeton shuddered from the death blows of her sister ships and settled beneath the sea.

Capt. Buracker took a muster of the crew at once, and of the 1,548 men aboard, he found that he had lost but 88 enlisted men and 10 officers.

"We never saw Commander Harwood and his party after they had gone to the stowage compartment," he said. "I was afraid we had lost four or five hundred men. It was the only consoling point."

The Princeton had been in a number of strikes previous to the second battle of the Philippine Sea. She had been in the Gilbert show, took part in the Marshall landings, launched strikes at Truk, Palau and Ponape. She had a part in the Marianas landings and had been strafed time and again.

Off Formosa, when the Japs were more than usually effective in their bombing, it seemed that she would surely be hit. But she wasn't.

"It seemed to me that if she had been going to get hurt, it would have been in one of the other shows," said the captain. "I can't reconcile myself to the fact that it was just one bomb that caused it all."

*Cleveland Plain Dealer*, December 7, 1944

# U.S. Board Bares Atrocity Details Told by Witnesses at Polish Camps

by John H. Crider

WASHINGTON, Nov. 25—In the first detailed report by a United States Government Agency offering eyewitness proof of mass murder by the Germans, the War Refugee Board made public today accounts by three persons of organized atrocities at Birkenau and Oswiecim [Auschwitz] in southwestern Poland that transcend the horrors of Lublin. The accounts were vouched for by the WRB.

While at Lublin 1,500,000 persons were said to have been killed in three years, 1,500,000 to 1,765,000 persons were murdered in the torture chambers of Birkenau from April, 1942, to April, 1944, according to these Government-verified reports. Many thousands of other deaths by phenol injection, brutal beatings, starvation, shooting, etc., also are recounted.

"It is a fact beyond denial that the Germans have deliberately and systematically murdered millions of innocent civilians—Jews and Christians alike—all over Europe," the WRB declared.

"This campaign of terror and brutality, which is unprecedented in all history and which even now continues unabated, is part of the German plan to subjugate the free peoples of the world," it added.

"So revolting and diabolical are the German atrocities that the minds of civilized people find it difficult to believe that they have actually taken place," the board stated. "But the Governments of the United States and of other countries have evidence which clearly substantiates the facts."

After describing the nature of the reports now made public, the WRB added:

"The board has every reason to believe that these reports present a true picture of the frightful happenings in these camps. It is making the reports public in the firm conviction that they should be read and understood by all Americans."

Simultaneously with Government publication of the narrative from two young Slovak Jews, who escaped last April 7 — the only Jews to have escaped from Birkenau — and a non-Jewish Polish major — the only survivor of sixty Poles moved to Birkenau from Lublin — Peter H. Bergson, chairman of the Hebrew Committee for National Liberation, announced at a news conference that the United Nations War Crimes Commission had "refused to take into consideration any acts committed against persons other than nationals of the United Nations."

German atrocities against Jews and others of nationalities included in the German sphere of influence have not been recognized by the commission, Mr. Bergson said.

He added that his committee was recommending the following action to the United Nations concerned:

"1. That they issue a joint declaration proclaiming that crimes committed against Hebrews in Europe, irrespective of the territory on which the crime was committed or the citizenship or lack of citizenship of the victim at the time of death, be considered as a war crime and punished as such.

"2. That the Governments of the United Nations concerned instruct their representatives on the War Crimes Commission to see to it that the above-mentioned declaration is put into effect.

"3. That representatives of the Hebrew people be given membership on the War Crimes Commission and that temporarily, until such time as a Hebrew national sovereignty be re-established, the Hebrew Committee of National Liberation be authorized to constitute the Hebrew representation on the War Crimes Commission."

The two Slovak youths cited in the WRB reports estimated the number of Jews gassed and burned at Birkenau in the two-year period at 1,765,000 in the following table, but the Polish officer estimated that about 1,500,000 Jews were killed in Oswiecim in that fashion. Here is the recapitulation by the two escaped Jews:

| | |
|---|---:|
| Poland (transported by truck) | 300,000 |
| Poland (transported by train) | 600,000 |
| Holland | 100,000 |
| Greece | 45,000 |
| France | 150,000 |
| Belgium | 50,000 |
| Germany | 60,000 |
| Yugoslavia, Italy and Norway | 50,000 |
| Lithuania | 50,000 |
| Bohemia, Moravia & Austria | 30,000 |
| Slovakia | 30,000 |
| Camps for foreign Jews in Poland | 300,000 |
| Total | 1,765,000 |

In the report the Jewish youths described the gassing and burning technique as follows:

"At present there are four crematoria in operation at Birkenau, two large ones, I and II, and two smaller ones, III and IV. Those of Type I and II consist of three parts, i.e., (a) the furnace room, (b) the large hall, and (c) the gas chamber. A huge chimney rises from the furnace room, around which are grouped nine furnaces, each having four openings. Each opening can take three normal corpses at once, and after an hour and a half the bodies are completely burned. This corresponds to a daily capacity of about 2,000 bodies.

"Next to this is a large 'reception hall,' which is arranged so as to give the impression of the antechamber of a bathing establishment. It holds 2,000 people, and apparently there is a similar waiting room on the floor below. From there a door and a few steps lead down into the very long and narrow gas chamber. The walls of this chamber are also camouflaged with simulated entries to shower rooms in order to mislead the victims. The roof is fitted with three traps which can be hermetically closed from the outside. A track leads from the gas chamber toward the furnace room.

"The gassing takes place as follows: The unfortunate victims are brought into the hall (b), where they are told to undress. To complete the fiction that they are going to bathe, each person receives a towel and a small piece of soap issued by two men clad in white coats. Then they are crowded into the gas chamber (c) in such numbers that there is, of course, only standing room.

"To compress this crowd into the narrow space, shots are often fired to induce those already at the far end to huddle still closer together. When everybody is inside, the heavy doors are closed. Then there is a short pause, presumably to allow the room temperature to rise to a certain level, after which SS men with gas masks climb the roof, open the traps, and shake down a preparation in powder form out of tin cans labeled 'Cyklon,' for use against vermin, which is manufactured by a Hamburg concern.

"It is presumed that this is a 'cyanide' mixture of some sort which turns into gas at a certain temperature. After three minutes everyone in the chamber is dead. No one is known to have survived this ordeal, although it was not uncommon to discover signs of life after the primitive measures employed in the birch wood.

"The chamber is then opened, aired, and the 'special squad' carts the bodies on flat trucks to the furnace rooms, where the burning takes place. Crematoria III and IV work on nearly the same principle, but their capacity is only half as large. Thus the total capacity of the four cremating and gassing plants at Birkenau amounts to about 6,000 daily."

In his independent report the Polish officer described the mass extermination thus:

"The first large convoys arrived from France and Slovakia. Physically able men and women—those without children or the mothers of grown-up children—were sent to the camp of Birkenau. The remainder, i. e., old or weak men, women with small children and all those unfit for labor, were taken to the Birch Wood (Brzezinki) and killed by means of hydrocyanic gas. For this purpose special gassing barracks had been built there.

"These consisted of large halls, airtight, and provided with ventilators which could be opened or closed according to the need. Inside they were equipped so as to create the impression of bathing establishments. This was done to deceive the victims and make them more manageable. The executions took place as follows: Each death convoy consisted of some eight to ten trucks packed with the 'selectees'; the convoy was unguarded, as the whole frightful drama took place on camp territory."

Then the victims were taken to the gas chambers, according to the report, which continued:

"Everything was hermetically closed, and specially trained SS units threw hydrocyanic bombs through the ventilation openings. After about ten minutes the doors were opened and a special squad composed exclusively of Jews had to clear away the bodies and prepare for a new group of 'selectees.'

"The crematoria had not yet been constructed, although there was a small one at Auschwitz which, however, was not employed for burning these bodies. Mass graves were dug at that time into which the corpses were simply thrown.

"This continued into the autumn of 1942. By this time extermination by gas was being intensified and there was no more time even for such summary burial. Row upon row of bodies of murdered Jews, covered only by a thin layer of earth, were widely dispersed in the surrounding fields, causing the soil to become almost marshy through the putrification of the bodies.

"The smell emanating from these fields became intolerable. In the autumn of 1942 all that remained of the bodies had to be exhumed and the bones collected and burned in the crematoria (by that time four had been completed). An alternative was to gather the remains of the unfortunate victims into heaps, pour gasoline over them, and leave it to the flames to finish the tragedy. The immense quantity of human ashes thus collected was carted away in every direction to be scattered over the fields where these martyrs had found their last rest."

In addition to mass asphyxiations, the Germans resorted to executions, phenol injections and brutality to dispose of victims. Here is one eyewitness account of brutality recorded by the Polish major:

"One day a working comrade discovered a few pieces of turnip, which he carefully hid. He continued his work but, from time to time, took surreptitious bites off his treasure. Another prisoner having 'squealed' on him, the capo arrived a few minutes later.

"It must be remembered that the capo is absolute master of

his commando and that everybody tries to get into his good graces. Unfortunately, this favor often had to be attained to the detriment of the well-being or sometimes even of the lives of other prisoners.

"The capo proceeded to search our comrade and, finding the pieces of turnip, knocked the weakened man to the ground, hitting him brutally about the head and face and in the stomach. He then ordered him to sit up, hands outstretched in front of him on the ground with a weight of bricks on each hand; the pieces of turnip were stuck in his mouth.

"All the men were then assembled and informed that the unfortunate man was to stay in this position for a whole hour. We were warned that this punishment would befall any member of the commando who committed a similar 'offense.' The condemned man underwent this ordeal guarded by one of the foremen, very eager to fulfill his task to the satisfaction of the capo, so that he hit our friend every time he tried to shift his position slightly.

"After fifteen to twenty minutes the man became unconscious, but a bucket of water was poured over him and he was again forced into his original position. After he had slumped over, senseless, for a second time, his body was thrown aside and nobody was allowed to pay further attention to him. After roll call that evening he was taken to the 'infirmary,' where he died two days later."

The use of the hypodermic needle for murder was described by the Polish major as follows:

"The sick were classified into two groups, 'Aryans' and Jews. These groups were again subdivided into further groups, of which the first included the sick, who were to remain in hospital, being considered 'curable.' The second consisted of extremely rundown patients, chronic cases, and the half-starving or mutilated whose recovery could only be effected by a long stay in the hospital.

"This group was practically condemned to death by phenol injections in the heart region. Racial considerations played an important role. An 'Aryan' really had to be seriously ill to be condemned to death by injection, whereas 80 to 90 per cent of the Jews 'hospitalized' there were 'eliminated' in this manner. Many of them knew about this method and applied for admission as so-called 'suicide candidates,' not having the courage to throw themselves on the high tension wires."

The accounts of the Slovaks and the Polish major mentioned a special "hygiene institute" at Oswiecim, which was adjacent to Birkenau, and where mysterious "experiments" were conducted on Jewish prisoners, mostly on females. The Polish major's account, which provided the only clue of what went on in the "institute," said:

"Here sterilizing by X-ray treatment, artificial insemination of women, as well as experiments on blood transfusions, were carried on."

The reports mentioned several well-known individuals, such as Witold Zacharewicz, Polish actor, and a brother of Léon Blum, former French Premier, as having been executed.

"Prominent guests from Berlin were present at the inauguration of the first crematorium in March, 1943," the reports said.

*The New York Times*, November 26, 1944

## "A SOLID MASS OF DARK, IMPENETRABLE GREEN": THE HUERTGEN FOREST, NOVEMBER 1944

# War in the Huertgen Forest

by Mack Morriss

THE FIRS are thick, and there are 50 square miles of them standing dismal and dripping at the approaches to the Cologne plain. The bodies of the firs begin close to the ground, so that each fir interlocks its body with another. At the height of a man standing, there is a solid mass of dark, impenetrable green. But at the height of a man crawling, there is room, and it is like a green cave, low-roofed and forbidding. And through this cave moved the infantry, to emerge cold and exhausted when the forest of Huertgen came to a sudden end before Grosshau.

The infantry, free from the claustrophobia of the forest, went on, but behind them they left their dead, and the forest will stink with deadness long after the last body is removed. The forest will bear the scars of our advance long after our scars have healed, and the infantry has scars that will never heal.

For Huertgen was agony, and there was no glory in it except the glory of courageous men—the MP whose testicles were hit by shrapnel and who said, "Okay, doc, I can take it"; the man who walked forward, firing tommy guns with both hands until an arm was blown off and then kept on firing the other tommy gun until he disappeared in a mortar burst.

Men of the 25th, 43d, and 37th Divisions would know Huertgen—it was like New Georgia. The mud was as deep, but it was yellow instead of black. Trees were as thick, but the branches were stemmed by brittle needles instead of broad jungle leaves. Hills were as steep and numerous, but there were mines—S mines, wooden-shoe mines, teller mines, box mines.

Foxholes were as miserable, but they were covered, because

tree bursts are deadly, and every barrage was a deluge of frag-
mentation from the tops of the neat little firs. Carrying parties
were burdened with supplies on the narrow trails. Rain was as
constant, but in Huertgen it was cold, and on the line there
was constant attack and a stubborn enemy.

For 21 days, the division beat its slow way forward, and
there were two mornings out of those 21 when the order was
to reform and consolidate. Every other morning saw a jump-
off advance, and the moment it stopped, the infantry dug in
and buttoned up, because the artillery and mortars searched
for men without cover and maimed them.

There was counterattack, too, but in time the infantry
welcomed it, because then and only then the German came
out of his hole and was a visible target, and the maddened
infantry killed with grim satisfaction. But the infantry advanced with its battle packs, and it dug in and buttoned up,
and then the artillery raked the line so that there were many
times when the infantry's rolls could not be brought up to
them.

Rolls were brought to a certain point, but the infantry
could not go back for them because to leave the shelter was
insane. So the infantry slept as it fought—if it slept at all—
without blankets, and the nights were long and wet and cold.

But the artillery was going two ways. The division support
fire thundered into the forest, and it was greater than the
enemy fire coming in. A tired battalion commander spoke of
our artillery. "It's the biggest consolation we have," he said.
"No matter how much we're getting, we know the kraut is
getting more." So the infantry was not alone.

Tanks did the best they could, when they could. In the
beginning, they shot up defended bunkers and dueled with
machine guns in the narrow firebreaks, and they waddled
down into the open spaces so that the infantry could walk in
their tracks and feel the comfort of safety from mines. At the
clearing before Grosshau, they lunged forward, and some of
them still dragged the foliage of the forest on their hulls when
they were knocked out.

One crew abandoned its tank, leaving behind all their
equipment in the urgency of the escape. But they took with
them the mascot rooster they had picked up at St. Lo.

The advance through Huertgen was "like wading through the ocean," said S-3 at the regiment. "You walk in it all right, but water is all around you."

There were thickets in the forest where two battalion CPs had been in operation for three days, and physical contact between them had been routine. Thirteen Germans and two antitank guns were discovered between them. The CPs were 800 yards apart. "Four thousand yards from the German lines," said S-3, who had been one of the battalion commanders, "and we had to shoot krauts in our own front yard. Our prisoner-of-war interrogation team got its own captives to question. The engineers bridged the creek, and before they could finish their work they had 12 Germans sitting on a hill 200 yards away, directing artillery fire on them by radio." These things were part of Huertgen, a green monument to the *Wehrmacht*'s defense and the First Army's power.

At that, the monument is a bitter thing, a shattered thing. The Germans had four lines of defense in the forest, and one by one those lines were beaten down and the advance continued. This was for the Fourth Division alone. There were other divisions and other lines. And these MLRs were prepared magnificently.

Huertgen had its roads and firebreaks. The firebreaks were only wide enough to allow two jeeps to pass, and they were mined and interdicted by machine-gun fire. In one break there was a teller mine every eight paces for three miles. In another there were more than 500 mines in the narrow break. One stretch of road held 300 teller mines, each one with a pull device in addition to the regular detonator. There were 400 antitank mines in a three-mile area.

Huertgen had its roads, and they were blocked. The German did well by his abatis, his roadblocks made from trees. Sometimes he felled 200 trees across the road, cutting them down so they interlocked as they fell. Then he mined and booby-trapped them. Finally he registered his artillery on them, and his mortars, and at the sound of men clearing them, he opened fire.

The first two German MLRs were screened by barbed wire in concertina strands. The MLRs themselves were log-and-earth bunkers six feet underground, and they were

nie Pyle in Normandy, France, 1944. *(UPI/Bettmann.)*

Ernie Pyle and U.S. Marines on Okinawa, April 8, 1945. *(AP/Wide World Photos.)*

Vincent Tubbs in the South Pacific. *(Copyright, Afro-American Newspapers Archives and Research Center, Inc., 1991. Reprinted with permission.)*

Homer Bigart during World War II. *(AP/Wide World Photos.)*

A. J. Liebling, 1944. *(Photo: David Scherman. Life Magazine. © Time Warner Inc.)*

nest Hemingway and Martha Gellhorn in New York City, 1940.
*PI/Bettmann Newsphotos.)*

Lee Miller in the bath of Adolf Hitler's abandoned apartment in Munich,
April 30, 1945. *(Photo: David E. Scherman. © Lee Miller Archives.)*

Lee Miller in northern France in 1944 in a helmet of her own design that enabled her to take pictures while wearing it. (© *Lee Miller Archives.*)

Janet Flanner and Ernest Hemingway at *Aux Deux Magots*, Paris. *(Photo: David Scherman. Life Magazine. © Time Inc.)*

Helen Kirkpatrick in England, 1944. *(Army Pictorial Service. Sophia Smith Collection, Smith College.)*

Bill Mauldin in Italy, 1945. *(John Phillips, Life Magazine,* © *Time Inc.)*

Bill Mauldin at press interview in New York City, June 1945. *(UPI/Bettmann.)*

Mack Morriss in Europe, late 1944. *(Photo courtesy of Helen Morriss Wildasin.)*

om Lea on Peleliu, 1944. *(Courtesy Tom Lea.)*

Eric Sevareid with Brig. Gen. John W. O'Daniel in Italy, June 1944.
*(UPI/Bettmann.)*

Anne O'Hare McCormick in 1942. *(UPI/Bettmann.)*

Shelley and Carl Mydans in Goa, India, during their repatriation in 1943.
*(AP/Wide World Photos.)*

helley and Carl Mydans on Guam, May 1945. *(Courtesy Shelley Mydans.)*

John P. Marquand, 1941. *(AP/Wide World Photos.)*

Robert Sherrod in 1944. *(AP/Wide World Photos.)*

Howard Brodie on Guadalcanal, January 1943. *(Courtesy Howard Brodie.)*

James Agee. *(Photo by Walker Evans. The Bettmann Archive.)*

Marguerite Higgins in Japan, 1950. *(AP/Wide World Photos.)*

INSERTION

Marguerite Higgins
with soldiers in Korea.
*(UPI/Bettmann Newsphotos.)*

Edward R. Murrow
broadcasting for CBS.
*(The Bettmann Archive.)*

Virginia Irwin (l.) with other correspondents in Europe.
*(Courtesy St. Louis Post-Dispatch.)*

Edward R. Murrow and William L. Shirer in 1937.
*(AP/Wide World Photos.)*

Philip Hamburger in Charlottesville, Virginia, en route to Europe, spring 1945. *(Courtesy Philip Hamburger.)*

B. White at *The New Yorker* magazine, 1954. *(UPI/Bettmann Newsphotos.)*

John Hersey in 1944. *(AP/Wide World Photos.)*

The sign on the car reads: "PLEASE DONT KILL THE FRENCH CAMERAMEN"

...ench news cameramen during liberation of Paris, 1944. *(UPI/Bettmann.)*

American journalists rushing copy to press radio transmitter, Paris, France, 1944. *(UPI/Bettmann.)*

constructed carefully, and inside them were neat bunks built of forest wood, and the walls of the bunkers were paneled with wood. These sheltered the defenders. Outside the bunkers were the fighting positions.

The infantry went through Huertgen's mud and its splintered forest growth and its mines and its high explosives, mile after mile, slowly and at great cost. But it went through, with an average of perhaps 600 yards gained each day.

The men threw ropes around the logs of the roadblocks and yanked the ropes to explode the mines and booby traps in the roadblock, and then they shoved the trees aside to clear the way. The engineers on their hands and knees probed the earth with number-eight wire to find and uncover nonmetallic shoe mines and box mines that the Germans had planted by the thousands. A wire or bayonet was shoved into the ground at an angle in the hope that it would touch the mines on their sides rather than on the tops, for they detonated at two or three pounds' pressure. Scattered on that ground there were little round mines no larger than an ointment box, but still large enough to blow off a man's foot.

At times, when there was a clearing, the engineers used another method to open a path. They looped primacord onto a rifle grenade and then fired the grenade. As it lobbed forward, it carried with it a length of primacord, which was then touched off and exploded along the ground with enough force to set off or uncover any shoe mines or S mines hidden underground along its path. In other cases, when the area was known to be mined, it was subjected to an artillery concentration that blew up the mines by the force of the concussion. There could be no certainty that every mine was blown. The advance was costly; but the enemy suffered.

One regiment of the Fourth Division claimed the destruction of five German regiments in meeting 19 days of constant attack. The German had been told the value of Huertgen and had been ordered to fight to the last as perhaps never before. He did, and it was hell on him. How the German met our assault was recorded in the brief diary of a medic who later was taken prisoner, and because it is always good for the infantry to know what its enemy is thinking, the diary was published by the Fourth Division. The medic refers to the infantry as "Ami," colloquial for American. These are some excerpts:

It's Sunday. My God, today is Sunday. With dawn the edge of our forest received a barrage. The earth trembles. The concussion takes our breath. Two wounded are brought to my hole, one with both hands shot off. I am considering whether to cut off the rest of the arm. I'll leave it on. How brave these two are. I hope to God that all this is not in vain. To our left, machine guns begin to clatter—and there comes Ami.

In broad waves you can see him across the field. Tanks all around him are firing wildly. Now the American artillery ceases and the tank guns are firing like mad. I can't stick my head out of the hole—finally here are three German assault guns. With a few shots we can see several tanks burning once again. Long smoke columns are rising toward heaven. The infantry takes cover, and the attack slows down—it's stopped. It's unbelievable that with this handful of men we hold out against such attacks.

And now we go forward to counterattack. The captain is leading it himself. We can't go far, though. Our people are dropping like tired flies. We have got to go back and leave the whole number of our dead and wounded. Slowly the artillery begins its monotonous song again—drumming, drumming, drumming without letup. If we only had the munitions and heavy weapons that the American has, he would have gone to the devil a long time ago, but, as it is, there is only a silent holding out to the last man.

Our people are overtired. When Ami really attacks again, he has got to break through. I can't believe this land can be held any longer. Many of our boys just run away and we can't find them and we have to hold out with a small group, but we are going to fight.

Then, two days later, came the final entry:

Last night was pretty bad. We hardly got any sleep, and in the morning the artillery is worse than ever. I can hardly stand it, and the planes are here again. Once more the quiet before the storm. Then, suddenly, tanks and then hordes of Amis are breaking out of the forest. Murderous fire meets him, but he doesn't even take cover anymore. We shoot until the barrels sizzle, and finally he is stopped again.

We are glad to think that the worst is past, when suddenly he breaks through on our left. Hand grenades are bursting, but we cannot hold them any longer. There are only five of us. We have got to go back. Already we can see brown figures through the trees. As they get to within 70 paces, I turn around and walk away very calmly with my hands in my pockets. They are not even shooting at me, perhaps on account of the red cross on my back.

On the road to Grosshau, we take up a new position. We can hear tanks come closer, but Ami won't follow through his gains anyway. He's too cowardly for that.

Perhaps this German who called the infantry cowardly and then surrendered to it will never hear the story of one Fourth Division soldier in Huertgen. He stepped on a mine and it blew off his foot. It was one of those wounds in which the arteries and veins are forced upward so they are in a manner sealed, and bleeding is not so profuse as it otherwise would be.

The man lay there, but he wasn't able to bandage his own wounds. The medics tried to reach him but were fired upon. . One was hit, and the trees around the man were white with scars of the machine-gun bullets that kept the medics away. Finally—after 70 hours—they managed to reach him.

He was still conscious, and for the medics it was a blessing that he was conscious; and for the man himself it was a blessing. For during the darkness the Germans had moved up to the wounded man. They took his field jacket from him, and his cigarettes. They booby-trapped him by setting a charge under his back, so that whoever lifted him would die. So the wounded man, knowing this, lay quietly on the charge and told the men who came to help him what the Germans had done. They cut the wires of the booby trap and carried him away.

The green monument of Huertgen is a bitter thing.

*Yank*, January 5, 1945

# The Price We Pay in Italy

by Eric Sevareid

*London, November 7*

GENERAL SIR HAROLD L. G. ALEXANDER, Allied commander-in-chief in Italy,* has just had his first press conference in some nine months with the war correspondents there.
He defended the Italian campaign as a whole and explained
that the Eighth and Fifth armies cannot reasonably be expected to drive the Germans from the Po valley unless the
enemy makes some mistake which can be exploited. This
most important statement was generally overlooked by the
press.

Here in London one senses that the British public has
never been much taken with the Italian campaign as a vital
contribution to Germany's defeat. Have we, in fact, had a
victory in Italy? A clear-cut victory speaks for itself, and the
very fact that General Alexander felt compelled to state his
claims indicates that public opinion is justified in feeling
doubt about the whole thing and wishing to reserve judgment until all the facts are in. I spent five spring and summer
months in Italy as war correspondent and while men were
dying in their great effort felt constrained from publicly questioning their mission—indeed, the Allied censorship in Italy,
actually run by the British, was always quick to blue-pencil
even implied criticisms. Members of Alexander's staff even
made a habit of telling correspondents not only what they
should not write but what they should. Since the
Commander-in-chief has now spoken about the past, perhaps
a reporter may also take the occasion to look back and issue
some reminders.

*On November 26 General Alexander was made Supreme Commander in
the Mediterranean theater and General Mark Clark became Commander-in-
chief of the Allied forces in Italy.

I for one—and many of my colleagues from that front are of like mind—am impressed by the major miscalculations made in high places. There is not the slightest doubt that the original decision to invade Italy proper was based on a belief that the Germans would not give battle in southern Italy, and that if they did they could not possibly maintain more than three or four divisions there because of their very long supply lines and our own mastery of the sky. The Germans surprised us, and the fight was very hard. It was just the first of many surprises. They held us on the Cassino line, where we lost thousands of men, particularly in the tragic winter attempt by the American Thirty-sixth Division to cross the Rapido River, an attempt which the divisional commander pleaded against with tears. We landed at Anzio in January under the illusion that the Germans, in their alarm, would pull back from the southern front to Rome or beyond. While Churchill was announcing that we would soon have Rome and Alexander was scolding the Anzio reporters for being "alarmists," our cooks and truck drivers were being thrown into the line to stem the German counter-attacks which threatened to drive us into the sea. We recovered our safety, but we lost a strategic, mountainous 10 per cent of the original beachhead and never regained it until the break-out began on May 23. By that date 3,000 Americans lay in the Anzio cemetery; the total of British dead I do not know. We had taken some 4,000 German prisoners, and they had captured "rather more" of our men, as a G-2 colonel put it. After the break-out in May, General Clark's Fifth Army headquarters issued a statement which broadly implied that Anzio was now fully justified—a statement many reporters refused to send to their papers.

We tried to smash the German resistance at Cassino in mid-March with a much-publicized obliteration bombing, followed by an attack by Indians and New Zealanders. It failed completely, and the front went static until the grand offensive opened on May 11 from Cassino to the Tyrrhenian Sea. On that day Alexander issued an order defining his objective as the *destruction of the German armies in Italy*. His troops were told, "You will be supported by overwhelming air forces, and in guns and tanks we are far superior." Nothing was then said about Rome, although of course we expected to take it. Rome was regarded by the generals as purely a political objective, of no military value whatever—actually a liability, since we would have to divert transport and men to feed it. Reporters were told that this offensive was directly connected with the coming invasion of Europe: that we were to oblige the Germans to divert large forces to Italy, that we could accomplish this only by destroying the formations already there, and that if we merely compelled a slow German retreat we would have failed in the primary mission.

Now, in his November 1 statement—I am going by the account in the London *Times*—Alexander says that he aimed to destroy "as much as possible of the enemy forces" and to produce a first-class victory before the second front opened in France, and that "Rome was that victory." He says we inflicted 194,000 casualties on the Germans—though casualty figures for the enemy can never be more than an approximation—at a cost of 116,000 of our own. At the same time he says that only five German divisions were sent into Italy from other fronts after May 11, a reinforcement or replacement of only one-fifth, since twenty-five German divisions were in Italy on that date. Did we, then, give important aid to the second front?

The General, in defending his record, declared further that at no time had he had more than a slight numerical superiority over the Germans. But at various crucial moments of contact we certainly had more than a "slight" superiority. On the southern front, on May 11, we opposed fourteen Allied divisions to the Germans' five. When the battle on the Anzio front opened on May 23, we had seven plus against their five. The Germans, of course, were later reinforced, but it should also be pointed out that the German divisions were nearly always much smaller than ours, running from one-half to two-thirds of our divisional strength. With only a few exceptions, such as the First Parachute and the Hermann Göring divisions, these were hand-me-down enemy divisions, containing troops too old or too young, interspersed with reluctant Russians and other undependable odd lots. The Germans had far fewer guns and tanks, almost no planes at all, and only a fraction of the Allied transport. In May it was estimated we had on the beachhead alone as many vehicles as they had in the whole of Italy.

After Rome, the Allied objective was to capture the Po valley, which we have not done yet. Today General Alexander says he was left with too little strength, because the invasion of southern France took a number of his divisions. It did take several excellent divisions, including all the French and some American. But his statement makes strange reading to any correspondent who was in Rome in early August. When high officers then described their plans for getting the valley, and, indeed, for driving on into South Germany, they had full knowledge—as did the correspondents—of the total diversion for southern France.

We have been fighting in Italy now for fourteen months. We have killed and captured many Germans and wrecked a great deal of their equipment. We knocked the remaining Italian Fascists out of the war. We got bases in the south from which to do important strategic bombing of France, Austria, Hungary, and Rumania and from which we sent considerable aid to Marshal Tito. And, if you find satisfaction in it, we helped to lay waste and impoverish for many years the major part of Italy.

It was the kind of warfare in which wide, sweeping movements are impossible, in which troops have no alternative to orthodox, steam-roller advance, crushing towns and villages in their path, laying waste the countryside. As Churchill said, we have drawn a hot rake up the length of Italy. The consequence is that Italy has become such an economic ruin that the Allies must pour in money and materials for years to come, or be prepared to help millions of Italians to emigrate. I am informed that of the total productive capacity of that part of Italy which has been liberated, approximately one-sixth remains. Destruction of industrial power alone between Rome and Naples is so complete that a year will probably be required to bring it back to 15 per cent of its pre-war level. One can hardly begin to speak of the erasure of ancient Roman towns and monuments, which belonged not to the Italians but to all civilized peoples.

The Italian campaign is not all debit, by any means. But some day people will want to know whether the returns balance the enormous investment of Allied lives, ships, transport, and planes. They will ask if we could not have achieved almost as much by stopping in southern Italy at the Volturno line, securing our ports and our bases and using the bulk of our forces in more fruitful encounters elsewhere. They will ask, "Did not the Italian ground fighting really become a war of attrition and nothing more?"

To this observer at least, it seems very late for commanders to continue to place blame for failure on weather and insufficient forces. Why should we not be frank about Italy and admit that Kesselring, on a very small budget, has done a masterful job in making a primary Allied force pay bitterly for every dubious mile of a secondary battlefield; that no matter what heroism our superb fighters showed, the monstrously difficult terrain of the peninsula, with its few roads winding through precipitous mountains, made encirclement and destruction of a retreating enemy impossible at any stage; that the terrain was not an unknown quantity when the original plans were made?

The Allied peoples—and history—may well ask whether the bloody Italian campaign has been a "victory," whether, indeed, it has accomplished anything of a decisive nature.

*The Nation*, December 9, 1944

# The Italian Ordeal Surprises
# Members of Congress

by Anne O'Hare McCormick

ROME, Dec. 22 — Members of the House Military Affairs Committee who concluded their tour of European battlefields with a visit to the Italian front expressed shocked surprise at the rigors of the campaign in Italy. Nothing they had seen in France, they said, could compare with the terrible terrain of the Apennines, and nothing they had read at home prepared them for the inhuman conditions in which men of the Fifth Army have to fight. The burden of complaint was that they didn't know the Italian battlefield was one of the toughest in the world. They had no idea of the tremendous natural obstacles the GI's have to contend with in addition to the stubbornness of the enemy stand on the best defensive positions he holds in Europe.

The Congressmen charged that the full story of this battlefield has not been told, and declared that the people in the United States should be given more realistic news. Evidently they hadn't a true picture themselves and they wanted to know who was to blame.

The trouble is not with the reporters. It is not at the home copy desk. In this case, at least so far as the terrain is concerned, it isn't even with the censors. Newsmen covering the campaign from Cassino to Bologna have described over and over again the murderous character of this battleground. Who has not heard a hundred times that Italy has been defended throughout history from invasion by her impassable mountains rising, wall after wall, from the toe of the boot to the Po Valley? Who does not know that fighting all the way up this rocky peninsula has never before been attempted?

As to the doughboys grinding their way up steep escarpments under enemy fire from on top, or slithering through muddy valleys in snow and rain, their grim endurance and casual courage have inspired countless newspaper epics. Nobody can do them justice, but the press men who have shared their hardships have tried their best to tell the tale of the heroic fight. "If you write stories we will print them," Representative Shafer of Michigan, a newspaper publisher, told the Rome correspondents.

Stories have been written and have been printed. They have even been overwritten and printed so many times that readers don't see the mud or blood any more. They don't hear the scream of shells or the thunder of fallen rockets. They don't realize what happens when towns are blasted from the earth and human beings are either buried under debris or scattered like ants when somebody steps on an anthill. The boys they know sleep in wet holes, stand in water until their feet freeze, charge up slopes raked by machine guns, but words describing these things are not sensational enough to produce an answering sensation.

The trouble is with the Congressmen. Either they didn't read the accounts of the Italian battle or they couldn't take in the meaning of what they read. They had to see war for themselves before it really registered. And this lack of realization is not their fault. It is because the thing is indescribable. To write about the front is to try in vain to translate one world into another. The United States is in the war as much as Europe, perhaps more, for over here ten miles behind the lines people try to forget it, and over there people try to remember it.

Soldiers from the front don't talk about battle to people in the rear. They can't. An officer just returned from a short leave in the United States says he couldn't discuss at home what he saw and felt in the war theatre, because it didn't seem to fit into the context of normal life. He was desperately homesick after two years of overseas service, but when he got home he felt restless, alien and eager to get back.

This problem of domestication and spiritual readjustment is going to be as difficult as the problem of re-employment and reconversion. There is no getting away from the fact that millions of men in battle zones are leading abnormal lives in an abnormal world that comes in time to seem more normal than the one they have left.

The plaint of the Congressmen on the battlefront, "Why weren't we told about this?" underlines the gap between information and realization. It can be bridged, not wholly but in part, by continual effort at better translation of the abnormal to the normal world by bringing fresh eyes like the Congressmen's to look at the war picture, and more imagination not so much to the reporting end—for no war was ever so fully reported—as to the receiving end.

Perhaps it is more important to bring the normal world closer to the abnormal by keeping soldiers in touch with what is going on at home. A service newspaper like The Stars and Stripes does an excellent job, especially in this theatre, of relaying general home news to men in the battle areas; but several Congressmen came back from the front convinced that overseas editions of home newspapers should be sent to troops. "Boys are dying to know what the people at home are doing and thinking," said one legislator. "They want to know how the war news is reported. They are too much out of contact with American life." This is a more serious gap than the other, for war is a long exile in a strange world, and the future of America depends on the mood and spirit in which the exiles return.

*The New York Times*, December 23, 1944

# The Battle of the Bulge

by Ed Cunningham

IN THE FIRST frantic days of mid-December, the newspapers called it Von Rundstedt's Breakthrough in the Ardennes. Then, as the American line stiffened and held from Elsenborn to Bastogne, it became known as the Battle of the Bulge. In between that time, it was probably the most frightening, unbelievable experience of the war.

At Corregidor and Bataan, it was a lack of men and equipment. At Kasserine Pass, it was inexperienced leadership. At Anzio and Omaha Beach, it was the natural advantage of the defense over the offense. But in the Ardennes, there was no alibi. The odds were all in our favor, yet we were being pushed back.

It was a nightmare of bewilderment for the first few days. Everybody knew we had superiority in men and equipment. There was no questioning the leadership on the grounds of experience. The Germans here were not exploiting fixed defenses.

What was it, then? Why were we falling back? Had the First Army leaders really been caught with their pants down? Were the Germans really turning the tide? Would they reach Liege, cutting off supply lines to the Ninth Army along the Roer?

Everybody asked himself those questions. And nobody knew the answers until the Second Division held at Bullingen, the 30th plugged the gap at Stavelot, and the 101st Airborne stayed put at Bastogne. The answers finally came from the people such answers always come from, the guys in the line.

In most cases, the fighting, the holding, and the winning were done by regular infantrymen and tankmen. But the Breakthrough also made infantrymen out of cooks and clerks and MPs. They gave a few answers to another question, the one about "rear-echelon commandos." More than one

Belgian town in those days owed its continued freedom to Americans who never received a Combat Infantry Badge.

In the middle of December, the people of the town of Hotton, Belgium, heard frightening news. The Boche had driven the Americans from St. Vith and were rolling along relentlessly toward Hotton, just as they had done in the fearful days of 1940. Holiday spirits, bubbling over at the prospect of the first free Noel since 1939, quickly died down. The Boche was coming back for Christmas.

But new hope came to Hotton the week before Christmas, when American tanks and armored vehicles rumbled across the village bridge. Most of them continued north toward the approaching Germans, but some half-tracks and trucks and 100-odd U.S. soldiers stopped in the village. The burgomeister quickly gave permission for the Americans to occupy any buildings they might need.

The people of Hotton went to bed that night confident that the Americans had come back to protect their village from the Boche. They didn't know that the handful of U.S. troops were only rear-echelon men who were not rated as combat soldiers. They were Headquarters Company cooks and clerks, Signal Corps radio operators and linemen, Armored Engineer demolition men and mechanics, and half a dozen MPs from the division Provost Marshal's Office. They had been left behind in this safe spot when Maj. Gen. Maurice Rose took the rest of the Third Armored Division forward to meet the Germans.

Headquarters Company was eating chow in the schoolhouse at 0730 the next morning when eight rounds of mortar fire exploded 40 yards away in the schoolyard. That was Hotton's first warning that elements of a Panzer grenadier division had rolled in from the east to take the main highway at Hotton running north to Liege.

Quick reconnaissance disclosed Jerry infantry and four Mark V tanks in the woods east of the village. Capt. William L. Rodman of Philadelphia, Pennsylvania, Headquarters Company CO, ordered a firing line built up along the hedgerows running from the school to the sawmill at the north end of the main street. Then he told T-4 Paul H. Copeland of

Columbus, Ohio, Special Services noncom, to take three men and a half-track and set up an outpost at the north end of town to protect that flank. Copeland grabbed a .50-caliber and a .30-caliber machine gun and asked for three volunteers to help him man the buildings on the north edge of the village. The first volunteer was his buddy, Cpl. D. A. Henrich of Antigo, Wisconsin, followed by T-5 Peter Brokus of Shamokin, Pennsylvania, half-track driver, and Pvt. Carl Hinz of Chicago, Illinois. Meanwhile, the Armored Engineers under Maj. Jack Fickessen of Waco, Texas, had set up a defense of the southwest section of the village.

Following the heavy burst of mortar fire that ripped off part of the schoolhouse roof and wounded five Yank soldiers, two of the Mark Vs started moving on the village, supported by a small infantry force that stayed a safe distance behind the vehicles. One tank came down the ridge road on the east toward the engineers' CP; the other headed along the railroad tracks that bisected the village just north of the schoolhouse. A partly disabled American M4 tank, which had been left in Hotton for repairs, went out to meet the Jerry tank coming down the ridge road. They met directly in front of the engineers' CP. The U.S. tank threw the first punch and missed. It didn't get another. The heavier enemy tank knocked it out.

The other Mark V bulled through a stone wall and edged out onto the village main street. Waiting for it, game but overmatched, was a U.S. light tank that had stopped in the town the night before. The uneven battle was over in a matter of seconds. Rumbling on, the Mark V stuck its nose up to the window of a house where two Yank bazookamen were firing at it. Firing point-blank, it wrecked the house, but the two bazookamen miraculously escaped injury. One of them, T-5 John Swancik of Melvin, Illinois, was scorched slightly by exploding powder that went off practically under his nose.

As the Mark V backed up, it was jumped from behind by two Headquarters Company bazookamen, T-4 Philip Popp of Lincoln, Nebraska, and Pfc. Carl Nelson of Arcadia, Nebraska. They scored a hit on the turret, and the tank was abandoned by the Jerry crew.

While the tank battles were going on, Maj. Fickessen

notified headquarters by radio that there were German forces trying to move into Hotton. He asked for instructions. He got them. They were: Hold the village at all costs until a relief force arrives.

Hotton, the sleepy little crossroads village, had become an important military objective. Control of it meant control of the road net running west to Belgium's important cities and vital U.S. supply installations. Until combat troops could reach the village, its defense depended on rear-echelon men who'd been left behind while their troops went off to fight.

Loss of the patrol tanks discouraged the Jerries. Instead of following through with an infantry assault, as the outnumbered Americans expected, the Germans started building their own firing line on a ridge that overlooked the village. That gave the Americans time to organize their forces. Maj. Fickessen, senior officer in the village, took over the defense setup and started posting his men—the cooks, clerks, mechanics, and radio operators—in strategic locations. He established strongholds in the schoolhouse, in the sawmill, in the Hotel de la Paix, and in the buildings that commanded the road branching off to the east, where enemy armored attacks might be expected.

Meanwhile, the people of Hotton readied themselves for a siege of their village. With the men unable to work in the sawmill and the children unable to go to school, whole families moved into cellars to sit out the war that had come back.

The Germans continued pouring massed mortars into the village during the afternoon, scoring hits on the theater, where the treatment station was located, and severely damaging several other buildings and homes. The Yanks defending the sawmill area had to take shelter behind piles of lumber to escape the intense mortar fire. The other defenders of the outposts around the village traded small-arms fire with the enemy. But the attack that the Americans expected momentarily failed to develop. It was learned later from PWs that the Germans had sent back a hurried call for reinforcements when their four tanks and company of infantry failed to overrun the 100-odd American rear-echelon men. When they finally made their big bid for Hotton the next night, they had a full battalion of infantry plus 14 tanks and supporting artillery.

Next morning, the village defenders were reinforced by a platoon of 81mm mortars and four medium tanks which came in from the division forward CP. The tanks set up roadblocks on a road east of the village, the most likely route for a German armored attack.

During the night, the Signal Corps had laid a wire net to all the strongholds for constant intradefense communications. A mortar OP was set up in the schoolhouse under the direction of First Lt. Clarence M. McDonald of Long Beach, New York, who happened to be around only because he was in the treatment station suffering from a mild case of pneumonia when the Jerries first struck. He didn't stay in bed long.

The mortar platoon had only 150 rounds, and the men had to make every one count. The OP was located on the top floor of the schoolhouse, the roof of which had been ripped off by mortar fire. It was cold, but McDonald stayed there all day directing the use of the few precious shells.

All day long, Signal Corps maintenance men moved from one stronghold to the next to keep the phone net in operation. Despite mortar fire and MG fire that frequently pinned them to the ground, Pfc. Max D. Troha of Hamtramck, Michigan, and Pfc. Stanley R. Presgrave of Arlington, Virginia, kept the phones working. One mortar burst landed in the Ourthe River only 15 feet from where they were repairing a broken line. They were unhurt by the blast, but several ducks swimming nearby were killed.

Late that afternoon, a Jerry mortar sailed through an open window of the mortar OP in the schoolhouse. Lt. McDonald was knocked 15 feet across the room and suffered minor abrasions of the legs and arms. He was returned to the treatment station he had visited briefly a few hours before. Another officer took over the mortar platoon.

An hour later, the Germans launched a heavy attack—later identified as a full battalion in strength—against the Americans defending the sawmill and lumberyard. First Sgt. Denver Calhoun had 35 men armed with bazookas, a few machine guns, and small arms. The attackers overran part of the position and started infiltrating into the houses on the outskirts of the village. That split the defending force in two, leaving Copeland with 23 men cut off in the north outpost.

Then the Jerries on the ridge brought their newly arrived artillery into action for the first time. They scored three hits on Hotton's main industrial building, leveled the sawmill, and set fire to some of the lumber piles. Two of the Americans were killed and three others wounded in the blast.

Maj. Fickessen ordered Sgt. Calhoun to withdraw his forces to the railroad tracks and told T-4 Copeland to cut back to the west and try to get around the Jerry spearhead set up around the sawmill. An hour later, the special services noncom brought his men, who now numbered 23, including two wounded, and all equipment back to Maj. Fickessen's CP. He had swung 300 yards west, then infiltrated through gaps in the Jerry positions without the loss of a single man or weapon.

Setting up their line along the railroad track, the reconsolidated force of cooks, clerks, and mechanics awaited the next enemy attack. It came about 0200 next morning with an estimated force of two Jerry companies driving against the defenders' line. This time the cooks and clerks held fast.

After their second failure in trying to overrun the Hotton positions, the Germans withdrew to houses on the outskirts of the town. Just before dawn, five U.S. medium tanks with infantry support rolled into Hotton from division headquarters, and more came in later in the day. The cooks, clerks, and company barber had combat support at last. Although they remained at their positions for the next two days, Hotton's original defenders had finished their job. It included the destruction of four Mark IV tanks and five Mark Vs, plus more than 100 German casualties. They pulled out of Hotton on Christmas Day to rejoin the Third Armored Division Headquarters, which had left them behind in this safe place while it went forward to meet the Germans.

Early in the afternoon on the second day of the counteroffensive along the Western Front, a convoy of Battery B, 283d Field Artillery Observation Battalion, was moving along three miles south of Malmedy, Belgium, on a road leading to St. Vith. About 300 yards beyond the crossroad of the cutoff to St. Vith, the convoy was ambushed by riflemen, machine gunners, and mortarmen hidden in the surrounding woods. All the American vehicles halted immediately. The men jumped off and took cover in the ditches lining both sides of the road. Several minutes later, they were flushed out of their hiding place by Tiger tanks from an armored column that lumbered along the ditches spraying machine-gun fire. Other tanks quickly knocked out some 24 American trucks and other vehicles. Armed only with small-caliber weapons, the Americans had no alternative but to surrender. They were ordered by their captors to line up in a snow-covered field south of the crossroads.

While the Americans were lining up, an enemy half-track mounting an 88 gun made an effort to swing around and cover them but was unable to do so. In lieu of that, the Germans parked tanks at either end of the field, where their machine guns had a full sweep over the prisoners. Just then, a German command car drew up. The German officer in the car stood up, took deliberate aim at an American medical officer in the front rank of prisoners, and fired. As the medical officer fell, the German fired again and another front-rank American dropped to the ground. Immediately the two tanks at the end of the field opened up with their machine guns on the defenseless prisoners who were standing with their hands over their heads. No effort had been made to segregate the noncombatant medical corpsmen, all of whom were wearing medic brassards and had red crosses painted on their helmets.

When the massacre started, those who were not wounded dropped to the ground along with those who had been shot. Flat on their stomachs, with their faces pushed into the snow and mud, the Americans were raked by withering machine-gun and small-arms fire from the column of tanks that began to move along the road 25 yards away. Each of the estimated 25 to 50 Tiger tanks and half-tracks took its turn firing on the prostrate group.

Of the approximately 150 American prisoners who were herded up as human targets, only 43 were definitely established as having escaped the German slaughter. More than three-quarters of those who escaped had been wounded. Only 25 men of Battery B's 138 were reported safe.

Pvt. James J. Mattera was the first American to make a dash for freedom and one of the six members of the surviving field artillery men who escaped without injury. Here is his sworn account of what happened when his outfit was ambushed by the Germans:

About three miles outside of Malmedy on the road to St. Vith, our convoy was forced to stop because of machine guns shooting at us and also 88 shells hitting the trucks and blowing them off the road. Everybody dismounted and lay in the ditch along the road for protection. We were forced to surrender because we were not armed heavy enough to stop the tanks.

The outfit was put into one group and a German officer searched us for wristwatches and took our gloves and cigarettes. After the officer was through, we were marched to an open field about 100 feet from the road where the German tanks were moving by. There were about 150 of us, counting officers and medics. We all stood there with our hands up, when a German officer in a command car shot a medical officer and one enlisted man. They fell to the ground. Then the machine guns on the tanks opened up on the group of men and were killing everyone. We all lay on our stomachs, and every tank that came by would open up with machine guns on the group of men lying on the ground. This carried on about 30 minutes and then it stopped all at once.

Then about three or four Germans came over to the group of men lying on the ground. Some officers and noncommissioned officers were shot in the head with pistols. After they left, the machine gunners opened up. I lay there about one hour sweating it out. My buddies around me were getting hit and crying for help. I figured my best bet would be to make a break and run for my life.

I was the first one to raise up and I yelled, "Let's make a break for it!" About 15 fellows raised up, and we were on our way. About 12 of the men ran into a house, and myself and two other soldiers took out over the open field. They fired at us with their machine guns, but by luck we made it into the woods, where we hid until dark. The house into which the 12 men ran was burned down by the Germans. Anyone who tried to escape from the fire was shot by machine guns. After it was dark, my buddy and I made our way back to our troops. We landed with an engineering battalion, told them our story and what had happened. They gave us chow and a safe place to sleep.

Pfc. Homer D. Ford, an American MP of the 518th Military Police Battalion, was directing traffic at the crossroads when the shelling started. Along with several American soldiers who had abandoned their trucks, he took shelter behind a nearby house. Then the Germans knocked an ambulance off the road, and on hearing the blast, Ford and his companions came back to the barn and tried to hide in the hay. They saw the Germans continue on toward the American armored men, who were marching with their hands up at the point of Nazi bayonets. After searching and disarming their prisoners, the Germans ordered them to line up in the field. Then they surrounded the barn where the MP and others were hiding. Realizing they had been spotted, the Americans came out and surrendered. They were herded into the fields with the others after having been disarmed and robbed of their valuables.

Here are excerpts from Ford's sworn testimony as to what happened after the firing started:

They started to spray us with machine-gun fire, pistols, and everything. Everybody hit the ground. Then, as the vehicles came along, they let loose with a burst of machine-gun fire at us. They said: 'You dirty bastards! You will go across the Siegfried Line!' Then they came along with pistols and rifles and shot some that were breathing and hit others in the head with rifle butts. I was hit in the arm, and of the four men who escaped with me, one had been shot in the cheek, one was hit in the stomach, and another in the legs.

The men were all laying around moaning and crying. When the Germans came over, they would say, 'Is he breathing?' And would either shoot or hit them with the butt of the gun. The closest they came to me was about ten feet. After they fired at us, I lay stretched out with my hands out and I could feel that blood was oozing out. I was laying in the snow, and I got wet and started to shiver, and I was afraid they would see me shivering, but they didn't. I had my head down and couldn't see, but they were walking around the whole bunch and then they went over toward the road junction. I heard them shoot their pistols while next to me; I could hear them pull the trigger back and then the click. Then men were moaning and taking on something terrible. I also heard the butt hit their heads and the squishing noise.

As I lay there, I saw about 25 big tanks, and I would hesitate to say how many half-tracks—they went by for two hours. When all the armor and stuff had cleared the road, we got up and ran, and two Germans sprayed us with tracer bullets, but we kept on running. We ran through the field toward Malmedy, and after running for approximately two and a half miles, a jeep picked us up and brought us in.

Testimony of German PWs captured since the massacre has substantiated the account of atrocities as related by the Americans who escaped. Here is an extract of testimony given by a German Prisoner, Pvt. Fritz Steinert, a member of the First *SS* Panzer Division:

On Dec. 17, 1944, at about 3:30 p.m., I saw approximately 50 dead American soldiers lying in a field near an intersection where paved roads radiated in three directions. This point was near Malmedy and between two and three kilometers from Stavelot. The bodies were between 30 and 40 meters from the road and were lying indiscriminately on the ground, and in some instances bodies were lying across each other. There were a burning house at the intersection and a barn and shed.

Questioning the German PWs, together with evidence of *SS* uniforms and insignia supplied by the Americans, convinced First Army officials that members of an *SS* Panzer division were responsible for the atrocity at Malmedy.

During the interrogation of two of the prisoners, both members of the First *SS* Panzer division but not of the outfit near the burning house, one of them—Pvt. George Conrath—was asked about the appearance of the bodies that had caused him to think something improper had happened. "It was such an unusual sight, I thought it was murder," he said.

Asked if anyone told him how these American soldiers met their death, Conrath replied, "No, no one told us. We were all *SS* men on the tanks, and it was strictly forgotten."

The second prisoner, Cpl. Hans Strasdin, who had not personally seen the bodies but who had been told the story by German comrades, was asked if he knew why the German soldiers had killed their American prisoners.

"I have no idea," he replied. "Of course, there are people among us who find great joy in committing such atrocities."

The evacuation of a city is an awesome thing. It gives you the same feeling you get at a wake; you go in, mumble some incoherency to bereaved relatives because you can't think of anything really satisfactory to say, take a brief, self-conscious look at the corpse, and then tiptoe into another room, where you converse with fellow mourners in whispers, even though you know you couldn't possibly be disturbing the person you came to see for the last time.

That's how it is when you are present at what appears to be the last hours of a city before it falls to the enemy. There's no really satisfactory answer when a frightened Belgian woman tearfully asks you if the Americans are going to leave her town to its fate before the advancing vengeful Boche. She doesn't understand when you try to explain in mixed English and French that it is only the rear-echelon troops who are being evacuated, and that the combat men are staying behind to fight, and that this whole thing is really just a consolidation of American lines to stop the German advance before it gains too much momentum. Rear echelons and consolidated lines and the military wisdom of moving back to take advantage of natural defense terrain mean nothing to her. She only remembers the four years the Nazis spent in her town and what their return will mean to her and her people.

It is hard to look at the clusters of old men and women and children standing silently on every street corner, watching the U.S. Army six-by-sixes, command cars, and jeeps assembling in convoy for evacuation. They remind you of a bereaved family at its father's bier.

Then suddenly there is the sound of planes overhead and bombs being dropped on the convoy road that runs west of the town. On a street corner nearby, a little girl with blonde curls buries her head in her mother's coat and cries. The mother pats the blonde curls tenderly and keeps repeating: *"C'est fini. C'est fini."* But there is no belief in her voice.

A little farther down the street is a U.S. Army hospital, formerly a Belgian schoolhouse, which was evacuated this morning. The wounded and sick who slept there last night are now in ambulances and trucks, bouncing over that road which has just been bombed.

The whole population of the town seems to be lining the cobbled streets to watch the Americans leave. The men stand silently, but some of the women and young girls cry softly. Only very small children still smile and wave as their elders did a few short months ago when the Americans first came to town.

Out on the convoy road, the traffic going west is already jammed. Stretched for miles ahead are the six-by-sixes, half-ton trucks, command cars, ambulances, jeeps, weapons carriers, and heavy-ordnance vehicles linked in the moving chain of the bumper-to-bumper escape caravan.

Our jeep stalls beside a bomb crater on the right side of the road. Hanging on a fence post is a pair of torn and muddy OD pants. Half-buried in the mud below are the remains of a GI shirt, matted with blood and torn as if whoever took it off was in a great hurry. In the muddy crater are two American bodies and an abandoned stretcher. They had been pushed off the road so that the passing vehicles would not run them over. An Army blanket covers each corpse. Beside one body is a helmet with a medic's red cross painted on it. There is a hole drilled clean through it.

On the other side of the road, going east, is a long convoy of tanks, TDs, and half-tracks of an armored unit moving up to the front. Our jeep passes slowly through a village, wedged between a weapons carrier and an ordnance truck, and the people of the village line both sides of the street, watching the movement of war. The people on our side are silent and grave, and their eyes have a mixed expression of dread and reproach. They look at our column without warmth, because it is going west. But on the other side there are young girls waving and laughing at the Americans in the tanks and half-tracks who are going east to meet the Germans. Older men and women smile behind their fears and give the V-salute to the men in crash helmets. An old lady stands in the doorway of a house by the road, urging a little boy by her side to wave at the Yanks.

At the edge of the village, still going west, are long lines of refugees, carrying suitcases and blankets and tablecloth packs, plodding slowly and painfully along the shoulders of the road. Some of the more fortunate ride bicycles with their packs balanced on the handlebars. Others push carts loaded with lamps and favorite chairs and loaves of bread and sacks of potatoes. A baby too young to walk sits on a sack of potatoes and smiles at everything.

There is a feeling of security along the road when it gets dark, and there is no longer the fear of planes. The convoy travels blacked out, with only cat's eyes and taillights to mark its progress, and the drivers are very careful to avoid the tanks and half-tracks on the left and the long lines of civilians on the right. Suddenly there is a murmuring from the human line on the right. Everyone turns to the east. There is a low humming sound that grows gradually more ominous, and a long fiery streak flashes through the black sky. It is a German buzz bomb headed toward the Belgian cities to the west. Everyone breathes in half-takes until the flaming arrow has passed over the slow-moving convoy.

Finally the rolling country gives way to scattered black buildings, which can be sensed rather than seen. A city is coming up, far enough away from the lines to be a city of refuge. But it's not that now. Enemy planes are overhead; sirens are moaning, and red and yellow and green antiaircraft tracers are reaching up through the blackness. They make you think of a giant Christmas tree in an enormous room, blacked out except for the red and yellow and green lights on the tree. The lights suddenly shoot up, spend their brilliance, and then sink back into blackness.

Now you start to think about the people who said so confidently that the European war would be over by Christmas, and when you think about them you begin to laugh. You can laugh now—in spite of the ack-ack Christmas tree before you, the little blonde girl who cries at the sound of bombs, the old men pushing rickety carts on a convoy road running west, the Americans in crash helmets and combat overalls who ride east, and the people of the evacuated town that gives you the same feeling you get at a wake.

The battered Belgian village, with its narrow, rubble-heaped streets and worn, cold-looking houses and barns, was a far cry from the spaciousness of the Champs Elysées and the war-forgetting warmth of Paris' swank nightclubs and bars—too damned far for the men of the 82d Airborne Division regiment who had held off on their 48-hour passes so they could spend part of the Christmas holiday in Paris.

Marshal Karl von Rundstedt's counteroffensive screwed up that deal, leaving the paratroopers with nothing more than Paris rainchecks redeemable once the Jerry drive had been rolled back. But the guys in the regiment had one consolation. They, in turn, screwed up a few of Von Rundstedt's holiday plans — and they didn't issue him any rainchecks, either.

According to German prisoners taken since the counter-offensive started, Von Rundstedt had promised they would have Aachen and Antwerp for their Christmas stockings and would spend New Year's Eve in Paris. The Jerries were heading for New Year's Eve in Paris by way of Belgium. That's where they met up with the Yanks, who had similar plans for ushering in 1945.

The meeting took place on a hilly road that leads down into this Belgian village. B Company of the First Battalion started out at 1500 to look over the town, which was reported to be lightly held by the Germans. That was a slight understatement. When the Americans got within half a mile of town, they were promptly tied down by Jerry flakwagons that came out to greet them. Lacking artillery and tank-destroyer support and armed only with M1s, light machine guns, flak, grenades, and bazookas, B Company was in no spot to start trading punches. Regimental headquarters was notified of the situation and urgently requested to send something to get the German flakwagons off B Company's tail. Just about that time, somebody hit on the idea of sending in a previously captured Jerry half-track, mounting a 77, as a pinch-hitter till our own TDs and artillery arrived. A hurry call was sent out for five volunteers to man the German vehicle.

The first guy to stick his neck out was Pfc. Russel Snow of Burbank, California, a regimental code clerk. Snow, who was a clerk in the Los Angeles Board of Education office before the Army got him, volunteered to drive the half-track, although he had never handled one before. Two members of the regiment's 57mm antitank squad — Pfc. Harold Kelly of Chicago, Illinois, and Pfc. Harry Koprowski of Erie, Pennsylvania — offered to work the 77. Pvts. Thomas R. Holliday of Henderson, Kentucky, and Buland Hoover of Hobbs, New Mexico, two BAR men, volunteered to cover the driver and the 77 gunners.

After Kelly and Koprowski had been given a brief orientation on how to operate the 77 — they had never fired one before—Snow drove the half-track onto the frost-hardened rutted road and they went off to relieve the pressure on Company B. For three hours, the Yanks operated their one-vehicle armored patrol up and down the hilly road that led into the German-occupied village. Seven Jerry flakwagons, mounting 20mm guns, and several heavy machine guns were deployed around the edge of the village, well hidden by thick underbrush and heavy ground fog that reduced visibility to 100 or 200 feet. Most of the time, Kelly, who was at the sights of the 77, was firing practically blind, aiming in the direction the 20mm and machine-gun tracers were coming from. Once, however, the men on the half-track saw a column of German infantrymen coming down the road toward positions taken up by B Company. Moving in for the kill, Kelly raked their ranks with his 77, forcing them to abandon the attack. Another time, Hoover, the BAR man, spotted a Jerry machine-gun nest through the fog and silenced it permanently.

Just before dusk, a blast of a 20mm hit the brace of Kelly's gun. He got several pieces of flak in his lower lip and chin. At that point, Snow, the clerk, started doubling in brass. He maneuvered his vehicle into position against the tracers coming from the enemy 20mm or machine gun, then moved back to take Kelly's place on the 77. A moaning German half-track got into Snow's sights on the crossroads just outside of the village and went up in flames, and there were two probables on the machine-gun nests, but Snow couldn't be certain because of bad visibility. Finally, with his ammunition almost gone and Kelly in need of medical attention, Snow turned the captured Nazi vehicle around and headed back to the command post to resume his regular duties there as regimental code clerk.

After determining the real strategy of the German occupying force, Lt. Col. Willard E. Harrison of San Diego, California, battalion commander, ordered an attack on the town that night. The battalion kicked off at 2000 after a 10-minute artillery barrage, with two TDs for support.

It had started to snow, and a thick veil of white covered the huge fir trees that lined the hill road leading into town. B Company, advancing on the right side of the road, yelled over to C Company on its left: "The last ones in town are chicken. Get the lead outta your tails, you guys!"

C Company made contact first, taking on a column of 100 German infantrymen who were supported by 19 flakwagons, several tanks, and a big gun. The first wave was pinned down by murderous fire from Jerry advance machine-gun emplacements. But when the second wave came up, they overran the enemy position and wiped out both guns and crews. S/Sgt. Frank Dietrich of Detroit, Michigan, emptied his tommy gun on a machine-gun crew, and when the last Jerry started to break and run, Dietrich threw the tommy gun at him. The shock of being hit by the gun slowed up the fleeing German just enough for another C Company man to finish him off with a BAR.

Meanwhile, B Company had attacked the flakwagons with bazookas and hand grenades, mixed in with spine-freezing Texas cowboy yells and self-exhortations to "get those bastards!" It was not phony heroics, as one B Company man proved by the way he finished off a Jerry flakwagon gunner who wouldn't surrender. The kraut was injured, but he still leaned over his gun, firing at the advancing Americans. Suddenly, one tough, battle-maddened GI made a direct break for the flakwagon, yelling: "You German sonuvabitch!" He jumped up on the vehicle and stabbed the German with a knife until he fell over dead.

Another Company B man, S/Sgt. William Walsh of Winnetka, Wisconsin, had sneaked up on a flakwagon, ready to throw a grenade inside, when he was hit on the left arm and side by small-arms fire. Unable to pull the pin, Walsh had another GI pull it for him, then turned and hurled the grenade into the flakwagon.

The battalion got into the first building on the outskirts of the town that night, set up a CP there, and dug in. The Germans launched a five-hour counterattack supported by flakwagons and a tank. This failed, but only after the tank had hit the CP three times.

During daylight hours, the Yanks and Jerries fought it out at long range, with nothing particularly startling happening except for the experience of S/Sgt. Edgar Lauritsen, Headquarters Company operations sergeant from Limestone,

Maine, and Pfc. Theodore Watson, a medic. While a German tank was shelling the CP, two jeeploads of soldiers in American uniforms—a captain and eight enlisted men—pulled up in front, got out, and started walking around the other side of the building toward the German lines. Watson hollered to them that they were going too far, but they ignored his warning. That aroused the medic's suspicion. He demanded to know what outfit they were from.

"The 99th," said the captain, and he continued on his way.

Sgt. Lauritsen, who had just come out of the CP, caught the tone of the conversation, got suspicious, and shouted: "What outfit in the 99th?"

"Headquarters," replied the captain in a slightly guttural voice as he kept on walking.

The accented answer convinced Lauritsen. He hollered, "Halt!" and when the eight American-uniformed strangers started running, Lauritsen opened up with his M1. The captain staggered, shot in the back, but his companions grabbed him and hurried him toward a steep embankment that led down into the woods.

The other Americans in the CP, attracted by the firing, thought Lauritsen had gone flak-happy and was shooting Yanks. They were all set to drill Lauritsen himself until they realized what had happened. By that time, the eight fugitives had escaped into the woods, presumably making their way back to German lines.

Regardless of any information the phony Americans may have carried back to the German lines, it didn't do the Nazis who were there much good. That night, the Third Battalion came up the valley and joined with elements of the First Battalion to clear the village, destroying one Mark IV tank and seven flakwagons in the process.

The Joes in the 82d figure that's some solace for the 48-hour passes they didn't get to Paris—but not enough. Mark IV tanks are poor substitutes for G-stringed blondes at the Folies Bergère, and flakwagons and dead Germans will never take the place of champagne and cognac.

The Ardennes campaign was more than a fight against the strongest German attack we had faced since the early days in

Normandy. It was also a fight against almost daily snowstorms in near sub-zero temperatures and face-freezing winds which doubled the difficulty of rolling back the German advance.

We learned a lot about winter warfare in the Ardennes. Some of it was learned the hard way, by frostbitten hands and feet, pneumonia, and even death by freezing. Besides physical difficulties, there was the added trouble of frozen weapons, equipment, and even food. But out of it all came the GIs' usual improvising and homemade remedies.

Line-company men of the 83d Division, who cleared the Bois de Ronce of German opposition in a continuous eight-day push that enabled the armored spearheads to follow through to the vital St. Vith–Houffalize highway, learned a lot of ways to fight winter weather during that operation. Their methods were often makeshift and crude, because there was no time to waste on details. But the men of the 83d are sure those hastily improvised methods of keeping themselves moderately warm and dry and their weapons and equipment workable played an important part in the ultimate success of the operation.

T/Sgt. Wilbur McQuinn of Helechawa, Kentucky, a platoon sergeant in the 331st Regiment, used the usual method for frostbite prevention in his platoon by insisting on frequent toe and finger-clenching exercises to keep the blood circulating. But he and his men learned some other tricks, too.

"Some of the men took off their overshoes and warmed their feet by holding them near burning GI heat rations [fuel tablets] in their foxholes," McQuinn said. "Others used waxed K ration boxes, which burn with very little smoke but a good flame. Both GI heat and K ration boxes are also fine for drying your socks or gloves. I also used straw inside my overshoes to keep my feet warm while we were marching. Some of our other men used newspapers or wrapped their feet with strips of blankets or old cloth."

McQuinn's company commander, Capt. Robert F. Windsor, had another angle on keeping feet warm. "We found our feet stayed warmer if we didn't wear leggings," Capt. Windsor explained. "When they get wet from snow and then freeze, leggings tighten up on your legs and stop the flow of blood to your feet. That's also true of cloth overshoes which are tight-fitting.

"Another must in this weather is to have the men remove their overshoes at night, when that's possible. Otherwise their cloth arctics sweat inside, and that makes the feet cold. Of course, the best deal is to have a drying tent set up so you can pull men out of the line occasionally and let them get thoroughly dried out and warm."

The drying tent to which Capt. Windsor referred is nothing more than a pyramidal tent set up in a covered location several hundred yards behind the front, with a GI stove inside to provide heat. There, an average of seven men at a time can dry their clothes and warm themselves before returning to their foxholes. This procedure takes from 45 minutes to two hours, depending on how wet the men's clothes are. All the front-line outfits in the 83d Division used this method.

Because of their almost continuous advance, it was all but impossible to get sleeping bags and straw up to the front-line troops. In place of straw, the men used branches of trees as matting for their foxholes. Logs and more branches were used as a roof to protect them from tree bursts. GI pioneer tools, which include axes and saws, were issued to each outfit for foxhole-construction work. Raincoats, overcoats, and the usual GI blankets were used for covers. Two or three men slept in each hole, close enough so that they could pool their blankets. Some slept with their helmets on, for an extra measure of warmth.

The chief difficulty men had in carrying their own blankets was that they got wet with snow and then froze, making them hard to roll and heavy to carry. The same was true of GI overcoats, which became water-logged after several days in the snow and slush.

On some of the more frigid nights, the men abandoned any hope of sleep and walked around and exercised all night to keep from freezing.

The front-line troops of the 83d were issued a pair of dry socks each day. However, wading through icy streams and plodding through knee-deep snowdrifts often resulted in men soaking two or three pairs of socks within a few hours. In such cases, the men wrung out their socks thoroughly and placed them inside their shirts or under their shirts or under their belts, where the heat generated by their bodies gradually dried them out. Another sock-drying method was to put them under the blankets and sleep on them at night.

Marshlands in some sections of the Bois de Ronce added to the infantrymen's troubles. When digging in for the night, they hit water two feet down. That meant two or three inches would accumulate in their foxholes before they were ready to go. This also forced them to move around gingerly on branches to avoid sinking into the water. One night, a platoon of the 83d had to dive into muddy foxholes without any preliminaries when a German tank came along a forest path spraying MG bullets. By the time the tank had retreated, every man in the platoon had had the front of his field jacket and pants, plus shoes and socks, thoroughly soaked. Enemy pressure that night was so strong that none of the dripping soldiers could be spared to go back to the drying tent. They spent the entire night in wet clothes with the temperature less than 10 above zero.

The standard GI gloves proved unsatisfactory for winter fighting, 83d men reported. When wet, they froze up and prevented the free movement of the fingers. Nor were they very durable, wearing out in a few days under the tough usage they got in the forest fighting. When their gloves wore out, many of the men used spare pairs of socks as substitutes.

Another improvisation was the use of sleeping bags for combat suits. To be sure of having their bags with them at all times, some of the men cut leg holes in them and drew them up tight, like a pair of combat jumpers. During the day they made a warm uniform; at night they served the original purpose as sleeping bags.

Web equipment was a problem. It froze solidly on cold nights and had to be beaten against a tree in the morning in order to make it pliable enough for use.

Frozen weapons were one of the most dangerous effects of the winter warfare in the Ardennes. Automatic weapons were the chief concern, although some trouble was experienced with M1 rifles and carbines. Small arms had to be cleaned twice daily because of the snow, and none of the larger guns could be left unused for any length of time without freezing up.

"The M1s were okay if we kept them clean and dry," said T/Sgt. Albert Runge, a platoon sergeant from Boston. "You had to be careful not to leave any oil on them, or they would freeze up and get pretty stiff. But you could usually work it out quick by pulling the bolt back and forth a few times. Sometimes the carbines got stiff and wouldn't feed right, but you could always work that out, too."

However, during the fighting at Petit Langlier, Pvt. Joseph Hampton found himself in a spot where he had no time to fool around with the above method. Just as his outfit started into action, Hampton found that ice had formed in the chamber of his M1. With no time to waste, Hampton thought and acted fast. He urinated into the chamber, providing sufficient heat to thaw it out. Not five minutes later, he killed a German with his now-well-functioning rifle. Hampton's company commander vouches for that story.

"The BARs gave us the most trouble," Runge said. "They froze up easily when not in use. Ice formed in the chamber and stopped the bullet from going all the way in, besides retarding the movement of the bolt. We thawed them out by cupping our hands over the chamber or holding a heat ration near it until it let loose."

Some other outfits reported that the lubricants in their light machine guns and antitank guns froze. Heat tablets were ignited to thaw out the machine guns that couldn't be cocked. But blowtorches were needed before the antitank guns were put back into firing condition.

Communications men of the 83d had headaches in the Ardennes fighting. Breath vapors wet the inside of their radio mouthpieces and then froze, cutting off transmission of their speech. Most of the time, the mikes were thawed out with cupped hands or by placing them inside sweaters.

Pfc. Frank Gaus of Pittsburgh, Pennsylvania, solved the problem by inserting a piece of cellophane inside the mouthpiece to prevent the moisture from accumulating there.

Other communications difficulties were experienced when radio batteries froze up and went dead. Signal Corps wire-maintenance crews were kept on 24-hour duty by numerous torn-out lines that resulted when tanks and other vehicles slid off the icy roads and ripped out wires.

The 83d medics also were hampered greatly by winter wartime conditions. Not only did snowdrifts make their litter-bearing jobs doubly difficult, but the severe cold caused their morphine syrettes and blood plasma to freeze. The medics remedied the morphine situation by keeping the syrettes under their armpits, thawing them out with body heat. When stoves were not available to melt the frozen plasma, they stuck it under the hood of a jeep whose motor was running. Slippery roads and snowdrifted fields often stymied jeeps, half-tracks, and tanks, which were pressed into service to haul supplies and evacuate the wounded. Some units improvised crude toboggans made of strips of tin taken from shell-shattered roofs with two-by-four planks as runners.

The 83d men found only one compensating factor amid all the misery of the Ardennes. That was when they occasionally plodded across snow-covered German mine fields without incident because the mines failed to explode. Melted snow seeped down around the firing pins of some of the mines and then froze them up when the temperature fell at night, thus preventing them from detonating. Chemicals in other mines turned to mush and failed to go off.

That was the only good thing the 83d men could find about winter war in the Ardennes.

*Yank*, March 2, 1945

# Retreat in Belgium

by Jack Belden

THERE WERE no regular combat units in the town at that moment, only some army engineers, medics and ack-ack officers and men who had come to try and find out what had happened to their cut-off units. In the upper-story windows of houses a few G.I.s rested rifles on sills while women civilians looked on, some with fright, some with scorn, some with amusement and some with the air of "we're all in this together."

As we stood there some colored soldiers drove up and began wrestling a pile of logs into position as a road block. It seemed amazing, but that was all there was between us and the Germans.

Toward dusk we left the town. Some medics who had lost their units were walking. We gave them a lift. None knew what had happened. The road was crowded with trucks. One of them was driven by a Red Cross girl who waved spiritedly to us.

Already many vehicles were going toward the rear. Gasoline supply trucks, portable bridges that we might have used to cross rivers, all things that we could use again went back so that the decks could be cleared for action. The inhabitants of the town watched these precautions with frightened faces. Many were refugees from bombed cities and now they had jumped from the frying pan into the fire and didn't know where to go.

I noticed in myself a feeling that I had not had for some years. It was the feeling of guilt that seems to come over you whenever you retreat. You don't like to look anyone in the eyes. It seems as if you have done something wrong. I perceived this feeling in others too.

More people now stood in the roads, alarm plainly stamped on their faces. Our planes were swooping and diving and circling close overhead and sometimes you could hear the sputter of machine-gun fire and the sharp crump of a bomb falling in the valley behind the hills encircling the town. Once there was a tremendous crash close by, the windows rattled and a column of smoke leaped out of a small wooded hill a few hundred yards away. The people rushed for the buildings. Our blood began to race a little faster.

A middle-aged woman grabbed me by the arm and began pouring out words of broken English in a pleading, tortured voice. She wanted us to take her children, a boy aged ten and a girl aged twelve, with us. "Just a little way on the road," she said, "then you can drop them off. My husband, he's been in the resistance movement. He'll have to get out. The collaborators will report him. It doesn't matter about me. But only take my children with you." Her eyes were red and I realized she would have been crying if her need for saving her children had not been stronger than her grief. A French photographer finally agreed to take her in his civilian car.

The road was jammed with every conceivable kind of vehicle. A plane came down out of a formation and bombed and strafed the column, knocking three trucks off the road, shattering trees and causing everyone to flee to ditches.

We went down roads along which we had advanced to the tune of cheers and applause three months before, but now there were not many people about and they no longer looked ecstatically happy, but only glum. Many, however, gave us the V sign and waved bravely. At dusk we came to a city. The buzz of the robombs was loud and clear over the hubbub of the traffic, and we saw a trail of red fire coming across the grey sky on the darkened city. It fell with a loud clatter and flames shot up and people ran hurriedly through the streets.

It was like that all night. There must have been a buzz bomb or a piloted plane raid somewhere every five minutes. The next day in a jeep we saw the tail flame on one robomb overhead suddenly go out and then the big frame of the bomb dove down on us in perfect silence, an inhuman Moloch coming to devour us. We threw ourselves to the ground and it burst near-by, breaking all the windows but not hurting anyone. I went to a café where I had been the first American three months previously and was kissed and embraced by the barmaid and given free drinks of cognac. The people told me: "We can stand the buzz bombs. That is nothing. But the Germans. We couldn't stand the Germans here again."

*Time*, January 1, 1945

# The Battle of the Bulge

by Martha Gellhorn

THEY all said it was wonderful Kraut-killing country. What it looked like was scenery for a Christmas card: smooth white snow hills and bands of dark forest and villages that actually nestled. The snow made everything serene, from a distance. At sunrise and sunset the snow was pink and the forests grew smoky and soft. During the day the sky was covered with ski tracks, the vapor trails of planes, and the roads were dangerous iced strips, crowded with all the usual vehicles of war, and the artillery made a great deal of noise, as did the bombs from the Thunderbolts. The nestling villages, upon closer view, were mainly rubble and there were indeed plenty of dead Krauts. This was during the German counteroffensive which drove through Luxembourg and Belgium and is now driven back. At this time the Germans were being "contained," as the communiqué said. The situation was "fluid"—again the communiqué. For the sake of the record, here is a little of what containing a fluid situation in Kraut-killing country looks like.

The road to Bastogne had been worked over by the Ninth Air Force Thunderbolts before the Third Army tanks finally cleared the way. A narrow alley was free now, and two or three secondary roads leading from Bastogne back to our lines. "Lines" is a most inaccurate word and one should really say "leading back through where the Germans weren't to where the Americans were scattered about the snowscape." The Germans remained on both sides of this alley and from time to time attempted to push inward and again cut off Bastogne.

A colleague and I drove up to Bastogne on a secondary road through breath-taking scenery. The Thunderbolts had

created this scenery. You can say the words "death and destruction" and they don't mean anything. But they are awful
words when you are looking at what they mean. There were
some German staff cars along the side of the road: they had
not merely been hit by machine-gun bullets, they had been
mashed into the ground. There were half-tracks and tanks
literally wrenched apart, and a gun position directly hit by
bombs. All around these lacerated or flattened objects of steel
there was the usual riffraff: papers, tin cans, cartridge belts,
helmets, an odd shoe, clothing. There were also, ignored and
completely inhuman, the hard-frozen corpses of Germans.
Then there was a clump of houses, burned and gutted, with
only a few walls standing, and around them the enormous
bloated bodies of cattle.

The road passed through a curtain of pine forest and came
out on a flat, rolling snow field. In this field the sprawled or
bunched bodies of Germans lay thick, like some dark shapeless vegetable.

We had watched the Thunderbolts working for several
days. They flew in small packs and streaked in to the attack in
single file. They passed quickly through the sky and when
they dived you held your breath and waited; it seemed impossible that the plane would be able to pull itself up to safety.
They were diving to within sixty feet of the ground. The
snub-nosed Thunderbolt is more feared by the German
troops than any other plane.

You have seen Bastogne and a thousand other Bastognes
in the newsreels. These dead towns are villages spread over
Europe and one forgets the human misery and fear and
despair that the cracked and caved-in buildings represent.
Bastogne was a German job of death and destruction and it
was beautifully thorough. The 101st Airborne Division, which
held Bastogne, was still there, though the day before the
wounded had been taken out as soon as the first road was
open. The survivors of the 101st Airborne Division, after being entirely surrounded, uninterruptedly shelled and bombed,
after having fought off four times their strength in Germans,
look—for some unknown reason—cheerful and lively. A
young lieutenant remarked, "The tactical situation was always
good." He was very surprised when we shouted with

laughter. The front, north of Bastogne, was just up the road and the peril was far from past.

At Warnach, on the other side of the main Bastogne road, some soldiers who had taken, lost and retaken this miserable village were now sightseeing the battlefield. They were also inspecting the blown-out equipment of two German tanks and a German self-propelled gun which had been destroyed here. Warnach smelled of the dead; in subzero weather the smell of death has an acrid burning odor. The soldiers poked through the German equipment to see if there was anything useful or desirable. They unearthed a pair of good bedroom slippers alongside the tank, but as no one in the infantry has any chance to wear bedroom slippers these were left. There was a German Bible but no one could read German. Someone had found a German machine pistol in working order and rapidly salted it away; they hoped to find other equally valuable loot.

The American dead had been moved inside the smashed houses and covered over; the dead horses and cows lay where they were, as did a few dead Germans. An old civilian was hopelessly shoveling grain from some burned and burst sacks into a wheelbarrow; and farther down the ruined street a woman was talking French in a high angry voice to the chaplain, who was trying to pacify her. We moved down this way to watch the goings-on. Her house was in fairly good shape; that is to say, it had no windows or door and there was a shell hole through the second-floor wall, but it was standing and the roof looked rainproof. Outside her parlor window were some German mines, marked with a white tape. She stood in her front hall and said bitterly that it was a terrible thing, she had left her house for a few moments that morning, and upon returning she found her sheets had been stolen.

"What's she saying?" asked an enormous soldier with red-rimmed blue eyes and a stubble of red beard. Everyone seems about the same age, as if weariness and strain and the unceasing cold leveled all life. I translated the woman's complaint.

Another soldier said, "What does a sheet look like?"

The huge red-bearded man drawled out, "My goodness," a delicious expression coming from that face in that street. "If she'd of been here when the fighting was going on, she'd act different."

Farther down the street a command car dragged a trailer; the bodies of Germans were piled on the trailer like so much ghastly firewood.

We had come up this main road two days before. First there had been a quick tempestuous scene in a battalion headquarters when two planes strafed us, roaring in to attack three times and putting machine-gun bullets neatly through the second-story windows of the house. The official attitude has always been that no Germans were flying reclaimed Thunderbolts, so that is that. No one was wounded or killed during this brief muck-up. One of the battalion machine-gunners, who had been firing at the Thunderbolts, said, "For God's sake, which side are those guys fighting on?" We jumped into our jeep and drove up nearer the front, feeling that the front was probably safer.

A solitary tank was parked close to a bombed house near the main road. The crew sat on top of the tank, watching a village just over the hill which was being shelled, as well as bombed by the Thunderbolts. The village was burning and the smoke made a close package of fog around it, but the flames shot up and reddened the snow in the foreground. The armed forces on this piece of front consisted, at the moment, of this tank, and out ahead a few more tanks, and somewhere invisibly to the left a squadron of tanks. We did not know where our infantry was. (This is what a fluid situation means.) The attacked village would soon be entered by the tanks, including the solitary watchdog now guarding this road.

We inquired of the tank crew how everything went. "The war's over," said one of the soldiers, sitting on the turret. "Don't you know that? I heard it on the radio, a week ago. The Germans haven't any gasoline. They haven't any planes. Their tanks are no good. They haven't any shells for their guns. Hell, it's all over. I ask myself what I'm doing here," the tankist went on. "I say to myself, boy, you're crazy, sitting out here in the snow. Those ain't Germans, I say to myself, didn't they tell you on the radio the Germans are finished?"

As for the situation, someone else on the tank said that they would gratefully appreciate it if we could tell them what was going on.

"That wood's full of dead Krauts," said another, pointing across the road. "We came up here and sprayed it just in case there was any around and seems the place was full of them, so it's a good thing we sprayed it all right. But where they are right now, I wouldn't know."

"How's your hen?" asked the Captain, who had come from Battalion HQ to show us the way. "He's got a hen," the Captain explained. "He's been sweating that hen out for three days, running around after it with his helmet."

"My hen's worthless," said a soldier. "Finished, no good, got no fight in her."

"Just like the Germans," said the one who listened to the radio.

Now two days later the road was open much farther and there was even a rumor that it was open all the way to Bastogne. That would mean avoiding the secondary roads, a quicker journey, but it seemed a good idea to inquire at a blasted German gun position. At this spot there were ten Americans, two sergeants and eight enlisted men; also two smashed German bodies, two dead cows and a gutted house.

"I wouldn't go up that road if I was you," one of the sergeants said. "It's cut with small-arms fire about a quarter of a mile farther on. We took about seventeen Heinies out of there just a while back, but some others must of got in."

That seemed to settle the road.

"Anyhow," the sergeant went on. "They're making a counterattack. They got about thirty tanks, we heard, coming this way."

The situation was getting very fluid again.

"What are you going to do?" I said.

"Stay here," said one of the soldiers.

"We got a gun," said another.

War is lonely and individual work; it is hard to realize how small it can get. Finally it can boil down to ten unshaven gaunt-looking young men, from anywhere in America, stationed on a vital road with German tanks coming in.

"You better take that side road if you're going to Bastogne," the second sergeant said.

It seemed shameful to leave them. "Good luck," I said, not knowing what to say.

"Sure, sure," they said soothingly. And later on they got a tank and the road was never cut and now if they are still alive they are somewhere in Germany doing the same work, as undramatically and casually—just any ten young men from anywhere in America.

About a mile from this place, and therefore about a mile and a half from the oncoming German tanks, the General in command of this tank outfit had his headquarters in a farmhouse. You could not easily enter his office through the front door, because a dead horse with spattered entrails blocked the way. A shell had landed in the farmyard a few minutes before and killed one cow and wounded a second, which was making sad sounds in a passageway between the house and the barn.

The air-ground-support officer was here with his van, checking up on the Thunderbolts who were attacking the oncoming German tanks. "Argue Leader," he said, calling on the radiophone to the flight leader. "Beagle here. Did you do any good on that one?"

"Can't say yet," answered the voice from the air.

Then over the loud-speaker a new voice came from the air, talking clearly and loudly and calmly. "Three Tigers down there with people around them."

Also from the air the voice of Argue Leader replied rather peevishly, "Go in and get them. Don't stand there talking about it." They were both moving at an approximate speed of three hundred miles an hour.

From the radio in another van came the voice of the Colonel commanding the forward tank unit, which was stopping this counterattack on the ground. "We got ten and two more coming," said the Colonel's voice. "Just wanted to keep you posted on the German tanks burning up here. It's a beautiful sight, a beautiful sight, over."

"What a lovely headquarters," said a soldier who was making himself a toasted cheese sandwich over a small fire that served everyone for warmth and cookstove. He had opened the cheese can in his K ration and was doing an excellent job, using a German bayonet as a kitchen utensil.

"Furthermore," said a lieutenant, "they're attacking on the other side. They got about thirty tanks coming in from the west too."

"See if I care," remarked the soldier, turning his bread carefully so as to toast it both ways. A shell landed, but it was farther up the road. There had been a vaguely sketched general ducking, a quick reflex action, but no one of course remarked it.

Then Argue Leader's voice came exultantly from the air. "Got those three. Going home now. Over."

"Good boys," said the ground officer. "Best there is. My squadron."

"Listen to him," said an artillery officer who had come over to report. "You'd think the Thunderbolts did everything. Well, I got to get back to work."

The cow went on moaning softly in the passageway. Our driver, who had made no previous comment during the day, said bitterly, "What I hate to see is a bunch of livestock all beat up this way. Goddammit, what they got to do with it? It's not their fault."

Christmas had passed almost unnoticed. All those who could, and that would mean no farther forward than Battalion Headquarters, had shaved and eaten turkey. The others did not shave and ate cold K rations. That was Christmas. There was little celebration on New Year's Eve, because everyone was occupied, and there was nothing to drink. Now on New Year's Day we were going up to visit the front, east of Luxembourg City. The front was quiet in the early afternoon, except for artillery, and a beautiful fat-flaked snowstorm had started. We decided, like millions of other people, that we were most heartily sick of war; what we really wanted to do was borrow a sled and go coasting. We borrowed a homemade wooden sled from an obliging little boy and found a steep slick hill near an abandoned stone quarry. It was evidently a well-known hill, because a dozen Luxembourg children were already there, with unsteerable sleds like ours. The sky had cleared and the ever present Thunderbolts returned and were working over the front less than four kilometers away. They made a lot of noise, and the artillery was pounding away too. The children paid no attention to this; they did not watch the Thunderbolts, or listen to the artillery. Screaming with joy, fear, and good spirits, they continued to slide down the hill.

Our soldier driver stood with me at the top of the hill and watched the children. "Children aren't so dumb," he said. I said nothing. "Children are pretty smart," he said. I said nothing again. "What I mean is, children got the right idea. What people ought to do is go coasting."

When he dropped us that night he said, "I sure got to thank you folks. I haven't had so much fun since I left home."

On the night of New Year's Day, I thought of a wonderful New Year's resolution for the men who run the world: get to know the people who only live in it.

There were many dead and many wounded, but the survivors contained the fluid situation and slowly turned it into a retreat, and finally, as the communiqué said, the bulge was ironed out. This was not done fast or easily; and it was not done by those anonymous things, armies, divisions, regiments. It was done by men, one by one—your men.

*The Face of War*, 1959

# *"My God! It's Carl Mydans"*

by Carl Mydans

WE WERE 700 strong, headed by tanks and followed by jeeps, weapon carriers, command cars, trucks and engineering and service outfits, with more tanks bringing up the rear. Our task was to slash through 60 miles of Jap-held territory to liberate and secure 3,700 American men, women and children who had been interned by the Japanese at camp Santo Tomás in Manila for more than three years. We started on Feb. 1 from a sugar-cane field 60 miles from Manila.

Our outfit, the 2nd Squadron of the 8th Cavalry Regiment of the 1st Cavalry Division, was commanded by Lieut. Colonel Haskett Conner, who gave his final orders to the men in a Luzon sugar-cane field, speaking in a quiet voice to the undertones of tank engines spitting and growling.

The trucks and jeeps were loaded with men and bulged with heavy and light machine guns and 20- and 40-mm. cannon. This was the modern version of a mounted cavalry unit, designed to use mobility and firepower to blast through the Japs, killing those ahead of us, pushing off flank attacks and letting the enemy then flow in behind us after we had passed. It was a proud outfit and it did itself proud.

Late on Feb. 2 we reached Bigaa, 18 miles from Manila. Sometimes we rode on highways, more frequently on carabao paths. In places we cut our way through areas where roads had not been before. We had to ford most of the rivers because the Japs had blown out the bridges. Constantly we ran into pockets of the enemy. But we moved so fast that we met only those surprised along the route. We shot them up with racketing fire of everything from everyone in our train, firing both sides of the road, and kept moving.

We were to break into Manila and enter camp Santo Tomás on Feb. 3. We started from Bigaa in full moonlight precisely at midnight and by dawn we were at the tiny village of Santa Maria where the bridge was out and Japs were contesting our river crossing. But we had been through this kind of thing before. Reconnaissance was sent out to find a ford. Our mortars ripped across the river and Jap fire ceased. Then church bells in the village began to toll and that was the old signal the Japs had fled and the village was liberated. A tired lieutenant sprawled at the base of a tree said, "There goes the bell. Another town's been liberated—for a day or two."

At 10 o'clock we were assembling to push on when a radioman rushed up to Colonel Conner and reported, "Our recon has been ambushed. They're calling for help and mortar fire." In a moment we were all on the move forward, priority being given to those units which were needed at the fight first. Again tanks and mortars did their job and we rolled through burning Jap trucks, houses and Jap bodies. There was no time to examine the battlefield. There were Japs around, so we pushed through and kept going. Every man and every vehicle in the squadron had a fixed position, but there was frequent debate as to whether it was safest at the head or tail of the column.

We would pass through barrio after barrio, where every man, woman and child would be out waving, shouting victory, handing us flowers, eggs, asking for cigarets, and there could be no doubt of where their warm and deep convictions lay. I was more moved by these people welcoming us than by the victory marches I have been on as we liberated southern France.

Then we would pass into country with barrio after barrio emptied of all its people, pigs and chickens. Here we sat with our guns at the ready, for this was an inevitable sign that Japs were near. "It's almost impossible to prevent ambush when we move troops through the countryside in this manner," Colonel Conner said, looking sharply into the trees on both sides of the road as we passed. "It's about the same thing as following a trail in the jungle. The first men get knocked off."

We rode on into the afternoon and the colonel showed his first impatience. "We ought to have been in Manila by now," he said, and sent a messenger forward with an order to speed up and not stop and fight unless Jap fire was heavy.

The Jap fire became heavier and heavier as we cut down the miles to Manila. Now it was raining and we were wet and the lead tanks were squashing the dirt road into a slippery mess. At Vicente, Jap fire stopped us for an hour. It's an exciting sight to watch well-trained troops run suddenly into the enemy, halt in a split second, dismount and take cover, move on into the fight. No football team moved with more coordination and cooperation than the 2nd Squadron did that day. In the midst of the fight and with pinging bullets all around, I found myself watching, fascinated at the squadron's fighting skill.

When the last enemy shot was fired, the signal was passed. Every man leaped into his vehicle as he would onto a horse and we were off again, guns blasting from both sides of the road to cover us.

My position was four jeeps back of the two leading tanks and the rattle of their 50s and of intermittent 75s, filled my ears every time we passed a wood or house or knoll that could harbor a Jap. I have not yet got this sound out of my ears and I hear it even now as the typewriters rattle beside me.

Colonel Conner was pressing his squadron and, as the lead tankman in his turret looked back, we were sure to see the colonel's fisted hand jerking up and down, the signal to speed up. We were now moving into the area where the Japs had not yet blown bridges, and as we roared into Novaliches, eight miles from Manila, it was after 5 o'clock. Tanks were just making the turn onto the bridge over the river which headed them due south for Manila when all hell opened up from both sides of the road. Brakes ground to an instant stop and tank hatches closed. We all hit the sides of the road and, behind jeeps and trucks, each column faced outward, covering its side of the road. For a few moments there was heavy firing from the Japs but overpowering concentration from our column cut the enemy's fire down moment by moment. The tanks were now concentrating on a two-story house and, after raking it with machine guns, they burst a 75 into it. Foot soldiers were now combing both sides of the road, shooting small groups of Japs here and there. Major James C. Gerhart, executive officer of the squadron, rushed up and asked Lieut. James P. Sutton of the Navy's Mobile Explosion Investigating

Unit, who was attached to us, to "come over here quick, the bridge is mined and the fuse is burning." Sutton, who had been firing steadily beside me from cover of the road, jumped up and, ignoring all cover, followed Gerhart to the bridge. The fuse had about 14 minutes to go. It would have set off over 400 pounds of TNT and 3,000 pounds of picric acid if Sutton had not come up to stop it.

Again the colonel's clenched fist jerked up and down and we were on our last leg to Manila. The train was already under way when Gerhart, running to toss himself into his jeep, spotted a Jap running 75 yards away. Without slowing his pace and shooting with his carbine stock at his belly, he drilled the Jap sentry through the back and swung himself on his jeep.

Later, when I commended him on his shooting, he said, "Hell, I've been teaching my boys to shoot from the waist for three years. I sure had to show them I could do it myself." Gerhart comes from Santa Fé, N.M. and is the organizer of the "Revenge Bataan Unit" for New Mexico boys from Carlsbad who were antiaircraft gunners at Clark Field on Dec. 8 when the war started, and who did such a brilliant job on Bataan. Sgt. Joe Smith, whose story appeared in LIFE (Dec. 22, 1941), is one of their idols.

The sun was setting now in a huge red globe and tenseness in the column increased as we approached the city's outskirts. We had just run through a small group of waving, cheering Filipinos and had a moment to relieve the pain in our backs, shoulders and necks which comes from constant and unconscious stooping to keep low when expecting enemy fire at any second. But now we were again in a deserted area and we were passing a column of loaded Japanese military trucks which had been abandoned by the road. They were intact and loaded with Japanese supplies and we knew they had just been abandoned and Japs were close by in the houses and fields we were passing through.

The men about me looked tired now and word was constantly passed, "Be alert," and there was not a rifle or machine gun in the column which was not pointing outward, trigger fingered.

Suddenly a Chinese boy came up out of a ditch, flagged

down our jeep and shouted, "Japanese in cemetery," and pointed to a small hilly cemetery right alongside of us. The men in the jeeps on either side of us had already dismounted and, kneeling or in prone position, were covering when two Japanese jumped up and rushed for the knoll of the cemetery. The cavalry boys, quick on the trigger, fired. The Japs made it over the knoll, right into the 50s of jeeps on the other side of the hill and were cut down. The Chinese boy shouted, "Good, good," and then something waved from behind a gravestone and Gerhart was on it in a flash but the Chinese boy shouted, "No, no. Filipino." We waited until he came out for fear the following cars, with men trained to shoot first and investigate later, would cut him down.

When we got to Grace Park airfield at the edge of Manila the hangars were burning briskly and had obviously just been set. It was getting dark and speed was everything. We passed a street with Japs a hundred yards away, hurriedly getting into trucks, but we let them be. As we entered the north end of Manila itself hysterical Filipinos greeted us.

Suddenly we swung into the area down Rizal Avenue where Filipinos had deserted their shops and homes. I saw someone down the street and waved frantically for him to come up. He would not move. A soldier threatened him with a carbine and he came, slowly, reluctantly. He was Chinese and very nervous. He told us that there were many Japs on the other side of the barricade and that the barricade was mined. Then he backed off and fled, shouting, "I am afraid. The Japanese will come back. They will kill me."

We pushed on down a side street, returning on Rizal. A quarter mile from the great China University we were brought under fire. It was dark now and we hit the pavement again. Tanks swept the area with guns and then we broke up into two columns. One went straight down Rizal to run into heavy Jap ambush in the university. When it got under windows, Japs opened from every one with light and heavy machine guns and tossed TNT bundles into the three leading trucks. Casualties were heavy before the column was able to gather its wounded and back off.

But my route turned left with Colonel Conner rather than into the ambush and in a few moments the black, swale covered fence of my old prison camp of Santo Tomás was flanking us. For just a moment I felt a flush of illness. This was the moment I'd been living for for three years. But then I was caught in the scramble of dismounted infantry now crouching at the ready as they moved in black silhouetted columns on either side of the vehicles. Fires were burning over much of the city and the red-lighted sky and stealth of the scene and pitch of emotion had me shaking so that my camera bag pounded against me. Behind me was Frank Hewlett of United Press, no less gripped with emotion than I was. We had come all the way together and he had come for his wife Virginia, who got caught in Manila and put in Santo Tomás while Frank went through Bataan and Corregidor and got out to Australia.

Half the front gate was open, the inside was black. We shouted and got no answer. Two tanks rumbled up facing the gate and turned on powerful lights. I cut a hole through the fence and looked in but could see nothing. Then we threw up flares. A swale fence had been constructed across the front since my days there, cutting off the view of the building. There was some delay and Frank lay beside me alongside the fence. Then impatience got me and I turned to Frank and said, "The gate's half open and I'm sure the Japs have gone. Let's slip in." Frank followed. As we reached the guardhouse at the gate entrance and approached the grass-covered bunker a Jap jumped from the other side four feet away, shrieked and fired point-blank at us. The blue flame blinded us for a moment as we hit the ground. The bullet had gone neatly between our heads. We lay there for a moment, then dragged ourselves on our stomachs along the side of the fence, breathing hard. Frank said simply, "There are Japs in there."

Then, like many such scenes in war, I never did know the sequence for as I moved over toward Colonel Conner, who was directing the operation on foot by the edge of the road, someone shouted "grenade!" and I hit the ground with my face in the gutter. Several men were wounded near by.

Then Colonel Conner shouted to the leading tank: "Run that tank in through the fence," and behind him to several men huddled together, "Keep the flares going up as she goes in."

The "Battling Basic" medium tank got straightened away and walked through the concrete fence as if it were corrugated paper. The area was bright now for flares were hanging overhead. There was shooting behind us and on the other side of the camp. Jeeps with headlights on followed in and then the infantry, which spread out at once. Frank and I walked up to the second fence and I could see the building as I had once seen it before. There was the "big house" I had lived in so long. I walked farther in and shouted, "Any Americans in there?" There was no answer. Later we learned they had answered me with a chorus of "Yes, yes" but we did not hear them. Then tank lights caught three Japs with rifles in the beam and we took cover.

A moment later a long-coated American appeared from nowhere. He was an internee. He said simply, "You Americans?" A few voices answered tiredly, "Yes."

"Good," he said, "I'll lead you in."

Two tanks were just ahead and foot soldiers moved forward over the driveway outside of the main building where my wife Shelley and I had paced back and forth for so long. Frank and I were right behind the tank. Then our guide said suddenly, "There's a Jap machine-gun nest on the left side of the building," and as the tanks and soldiers turned left, I shouted to Frank, "I'm going in across the lawn," and I made my last dash with Frank behind me. I tripped once, recovered myself and pushed into an hysterical mob of internees waving, shouting, screaming, some weeping. The feeble, shadowy light from several candles only partly lighted the large lobby. I could not say anything, the din was so terrific. Hands just felt me, pressed me, and voices cried, "Thank God you are here." "It's been so long."

Crowds pressed in on me so closely that I could not move and then suddenly the crowd picked me up, 40-pound camera kit and all, and passed me from hand to hand overhead.

I was helpless, nor was I able to talk above the din. Then I was put down and a stern voice rang above all the others. "You are an American soldier? Put the light on yourself so we can see." I turned the flashlight on myself and said, "I'm Carl Mydans."

For a moment no one said anything. Then a woman's voice

came, "Carl Mydans. My God! It's Carl Mydans," and Betty Wilborne broke through the crowd and threw her arms around my neck and cried.

I was pushed through the crowds to the stairs in the main lobby with shouts of "speech" and for a moment I was unable to talk. I mumbled something about I never knew how good it could feel to be back here in Santo Tomás. Then I made my way out of the building, everyone feeling me, holding on to me as I struggled through the crowd. I brushed past a woman holding a weeping child. "No, darling, no," she was saying, "he's an American. He's an American soldier. They have come for us, darling. Don't be afraid."

Outside I found a sight I had dreamed about many times. In the brilliant light beside the Battling Basic stood three Japanese in officers' uniforms, ringed by soldiers pointing rifles at them. The Japanese were part of the administrative staff of this and other prison camps on Luzon. But they were strangers to me. The staff I knew had left some time ago.

Now I was aware of the crowds in the windows above, cheering and cheering. They had been there during my dash across the lawn but I was unaware of them. "God bless America." "Oh what a sight for sore eyes you are." "Oh how long we've waited," were some of the things they shouted at us.

Suddenly there was firing in the Education Building to the right of the main building. There were 65 Jap officers and men in there with 221 American internees. The Japs were on the second floor, Americans on the third. The Education Building was the newest in the compound and was of steel reinforced concrete. All night we attempted to break into the building but the Japs had an overwhelming advantage. They went up to the third floor with the Americans so that our shooting into the second was useless.

Intermittently during Feb. 4 there were short exchanges of fire between our men surrounding the building under cover and the Japs inside, and we suffered some light casualties as the day wore on. Many women in the main building had husbands in the structure under siege and the strain was growing throughout the camp. So that night Lieut. Colonel Charles E. Brady walked into the Japanese lair and discussed a compromise with the Japanese commanding officer, Colonel Hayashi. Japanese demands were clear and short: safe conduct into the area of Manila where they would have a fair chance of fighting their way out, each man carrying side arms, rifles, ammunition and rations. His alternative was clear, too: the lives of the 221 Americans who were his hostages within the building. Hayashi strutted back and forth, suddenly reached both hands over his hips where hung two pistols and, glaring at Colonel Brady, flipped the pistols back and forth into their holsters.

Brady is a dapper officer with a waxed mustache who hails from West Orange, N.J. Later in reporting this meeting to General Chase he said, "My right hand twitched so I had to twirl my mustache."

That night the decision was made. The first job was to save the lives of the American internees. Jap demands were agreed to.

In the predawn darkness of the next morning one of the strangest dramas of the war took place. Colonel Brady addressed the troops lined up before the Education Building in the area which, for a few hours, was no man's land. "Men, there are 65 Japs in that building and we're going to give them safe conduct out. They will have side arms and rifles but no machine guns or grenades. We shall march in a column of two with columns of Japanese between us. I want each man to carry his rifle with a cartridge in the chamber and with the rifle off his shoulder. Each man is to cover a Jap. At a certain point agreed between the Japs and me, we will halt and they will continue. Under no condition is any man to be trigger happy. We hope to get away with it without anyone being hurt. But if they shoot first, get them."

Headed by their officers, the Japanese came out. As they appeared our men tensed up and fingers played with triggers. These Americans had seen many Japs before but they had always shot at them or were shot at. There was nervousness all around.

Brady gave the command, headed the column and started off. There was firing in the city as we marched down side streets. Colonel Brady warned the Filipinos who were rushing out at this strange sight to be silent and stay back.

There were many stops and conferences between Brady and Hayashi as to where they would go and how far, the Japanese urging us to conduct them farther and farther. But at Legarda and Aviles Streets Brady called a halt and told Hayashi, "This is as far as we go. This is the front line. You are on your own." Hayashi now showed nervousness for the first time. He talked with two of his officers, then sent them forward a block. They came back and Hayashi again asked for further safe conduct, but Brady shook his head. "This is where we leave you."

Then Hayashi called a command, turned to Brady and saluted smartly. Brady returned it as the Japanese fell in step and began to move forward. As they passed out of our column, each officer and each man either saluted or bowed to Brady.

Ahead of the Japs down Legarda was massed a large troop of Filipinos and, as the Jap column approached them, several Filipinos near us broke out of line. Brady shouted, "Stand back and keep quiet." At this advice one of the Filipinos yelled loudly in Tagalog to the mass across the street. They broke and ran, madly stumbling into each other. The Japs with their backs to us now could see only the Filipinos. They broke ranks, falling and tripping over each other, taking cover in doorways. Only their officers forward held ranks.

Then Hayashi rushed back and pushed and shoved his men back into formation and they disappeared up the street. The last little act of disorder and utter fear on the part of the Japs had ruined their whole carefully planned show.

The situation in Santo Tomás had changed much since I left there Sept. 12, 1942. All access to outside supplementary food-stuffs had been discontinued by the Japanese. There is not one of the 3,700 people in Santo Tomás who isn't suffering from malnutrition, and most of them are so thin that I did not recognize them.

I walked the same walks Shelley and I had been over so many times, stood in the same food line where we had stood so long, washed at the same troughs and saw the same lines of people standing patiently to get to the shabby toilets. There were the same old hats and the same old clothes the people wore when I was there. But they were mended and re-mended. And there was the same docility on the part of the internees toward us that the Japs had so indoctrinated into us. Even with husky welcoming Americans on the main gate the internees would not venture past the swale fence which marked the out-of-bounds area. Three years of Jap militarism left its mark on our people and many of them, like withered plants, will not begin to perk their heads up again until nour-ishment restores the vitality which humans must have to live.

This does not mean that our people are a broken people. They are anything but that. There is not one of them who has not kept faith these long three years. There is not one of them but knew we were coming back. Their only comment has been, "It's been a long time."

Sunday morning we raised the American flag over Santo Tomás. The internees stood by breathlessly as the colors were carried to the front of the building. They shouted and cheered when they were raised. Then someone started singing *God Bless America* and the entire camp picked it up. I have never heard it sung as it was sung that day. I have never heard people singing *God Bless America* and weeping openly. And they have never seen soldiers—hard-bitten youngsters such as make up the 1st Cavalry—stand unashamed and weep with them.

Apart from liberation and the food that came with it, noth-ing had meant more to the internees. And to the internees today the GIs are the epitome of everything that is great and good. They talk about them endlessly. They are amazed at the quiet way they speak to each other. "Perhaps it's because they've lived in the jungle so long," one internee explained. They are struck by the politeness they have toward one an-other, and by their cooperation and generosity. They are amused at their "duckhunting caps and duckhunting pock-ets." Many were moved to tears when, several days later, they learned that the soldiers who spearheaded in there with streamlined rations gave everything they had to the internees the first few hours in camp and went several days without any themselves until additional supplies arrived. But mostly they are thrilled by the kind of army we've now got. When they last saw us, we were different. They stand in little groups admiring the tanks, sitting in jeeps, taking helmet liners from helmets. They beg for little bits of Army clothing—hats, insignia, canteen covers, anything that they can have or wear that makes them feel a part of us again. My hat went in the first few hours and no appeal could bring it back.

The youngsters are playing soldiers now, too. They say things the youngsters back home have never thought to say: "I am a soldier. I am an American soldier." The children here are worldly-wise. Perhaps nobody understands the Japanese better than they. Sgt. Homer Brown of Tucson was confused when, marching away with the group of Japanese civilian administrators of the camp, he was met with a chorus of tiny voices shouting, "Make them bow. Make them bow."

*Life*, February 19, 1945

# Iwo Jima Before H-Hour

by John P. Marquand

LIFE on a battleship is largely conducted against a background of disregarded words. For example, upon leaving Saipan, the radio loudspeaker on the open bridge produced a continuous program somewhat along the following lines:

"This is Peter Rabbit calling Audacity One — Peter Rabbit calling Audacity One — over . . . Audacity One calling Peter Rabbit . . . Come in, Peter Rabbit — over . . . Peter Rabbit to Audacity One — Shackle. Charley. Abel. Oboe. Noel Coward. Unshackle — over . . . Audacity One to Peter Rabbit — Continue as directed. Over . . . Peter Rabbit to Audacity One — Roger. Over . . ."

Sometimes these guarded code conversations, all conducted with flawless diction in clear unemotional tones, would reach a degree of subtlety that bordered on the obvious.

"Tiger Two is now in a position to give the stepchildren a drink. Will Audacity One please notify the stepchildren? . . . Bulldog calling Turtle. A pilot is in the water, southeast of Hot Rock. Pick him up. I repeat: In the water, southeast of Hot Rock. Pick him up. . . ."

There was never any way of telling whether or not the stepchildren received the drinks which Tiger was kind enough to offer, or whether or not the pilot was rescued from the slightly chilly waters off that unpleasant island of Iwo. Moreover, no one seemed particularly to care. The Admiral and the Captain sat upon the bridge in comfortable high-chairs, not unlike those used by patrons in a billiard parlor. Their staff officers stood near them, and behind the staff officers stood the men with earphones and mouthpieces tethered by long insulated cords, and next came the Marine orderlies with their .45 automatics. Occasionally a Filipino mess boy would appear from the small kitchenette below — doubtless called a galley—with sandwiches and coffee for the Admiral and the Captain. He would carry these on a tray, sparkling with bright silver, china, and napery, up two dark companion ladders to the open bridge. Once when the main battery of 14-inch guns was firing, some freak of concussion lifted him a good six inches off the deck. But guns or not, no one appeared to listen to the voices on that radio.

However, as hours merged into days during those vigils on the bridge, that constant flow of words could not help but appeal to the imagination of anyone whose experience on battleships and with naval affairs had been previously limited almost exclusively to an acquaintance with Pinafore and Madame Butterfly. Charley and Abel and Peter Rabbit, who kept shackling and unshackling themselves, gradually became old friends. You began to wonder what was happening now to Audacity and Oboe. It would not have been tactful to ask, since each was a special ship, a unit of the task force, but once one of those characters revealed its identity. This was when Little Abner had words with Audacity off the beach of Iwo Jima on D-day minus two.

"Little Abner calling Audacity," Little Abner said. "We've got three holes and so we're going back to the line."

"What line do you mean?" Audacity asked.

"What the hell line do you think?" Little Abner answered. "The firing line."

Little Abner was an LCI—Landing Craft Infantry, in case you do not understand naval initials. She was one of the LCI's equipped with rockets, assigned to strafe the beach, and the Jap batteries had taken her under fire at eight hundred yards.

In addition to the radio on the bridge, there was also entertainment down below. When the great ship withdrew from the area, and when General Quarters had changed to Condition Two, some unknown hands would place recordings of radio programs from home upon a loud-speaker that reached the crew's mess, the warrant officers' mess, and the wardroom. Thus, above the shufflings on the deck, the clatter of mess tins and dishes, would come blasts of music, roars of laughter and blatant comedy. There was no way of escaping it if you wanted to eat. Though you were seven hundred-odd miles from Tokyo, you were back home again.

"And now Dr. Fisher's tablets for intestinal sluggishness present Willie Jones, and all the little Jones boys, and the Jones boys' orchestra." (Whistles, laughter, and applause from an unknown audience.) "But first a brief, friendly word from our sponsor. Folks, do you feel headachy and pepless in the morning? Just take one with a glass of warm water. But here he is, Willie Jones himself." (Whistles, applause, and cheers from that unknown audience.) "How are you tonight, Willie?"—"Well, frankly, Frank, I'm feeling kind of dumb." —"You mean you're just your old self, then?" (Shrieks, whistles, and applause from the unknown audience.)

There was no way of turning the thing off, but no one seemed to mind. Perhaps after having been at sea almost continuously for thirty months, as had many members of that crew, these sounds gave a sort of reassurance that a past to which everyone was clinging still waited back at home. At the ship's service, days before the ship was cleared for action, you could buy all sorts of reminders of that past. The shaving creams and toothpastes were like old acquaintances. There was even Williams' Aqua Velva, though this line was finally discontinued when it was found that certain members of the crew were taking it internally. There was a selection of homely literature, such as *The Corpse in the Coppice* and *Murder Walks at Midnight* and *The Book of Riddles*, and there were fragile volumes of comics and nationally known brands of gum and candy. When men went to battle stations nearly all of them took a few of these things along. When the ship was closed into hermetically sealed compartments and the ventilating system was cut off you could see them reading by the ammunition hoist. You could see the damage control groups, with their gas masks, their tools and telephones, reclining on the decks slowly devouring those pages and chewing gum. They may not have enjoyed this literature for itself but it must have given them about the only illusion of privacy that there was in a life at sea where privacy does not exist.

"If you write this thing just the way you see it," an officer said, "maybe it might mean something to people back home.

They might see what we're going through. They might understand—they never understand back home."

That was what nearly everyone aboard said. They all had a
pathetic desire for people at home to know. Of course, if they
had thought about it, they would have realized that this was
impossible. There was too great a gap between civilian and
naval life. There were too few common values. The life
aboard a ship in enemy waters was even more complex and
difficult of explanation than the life of troops ashore. There
was a combination of small personal comforts and of impending danger verging on calamity that was ugly and incongru-
ous. The living quarters of the crew were overcrowded, but
they had hot water and soap, hot showers, and all sorts of
things you would never get ashore. There were clean clothes,
and all the coffee you wanted day and night, and red meat
and other hot food, and butter and ice cream. Yet, at the
same time, the sense of danger was more intense. You could
not run away from it as you could on land. It might come at
any minute of the day and night from torpedoes, from the air,
from a surface engagement. Almost any sort of blow meant
casualties and damage. Even a light shell on the superstructure might cause complications incomparable to the results of
a similar blow on land.

## II

There had been some hope that the task force of battleships,
cruisers, and destroyers that was scheduled to bombard Iwo
Jima for three days before the transports and the amphibious
craft appeared, might arrive there undetected, but the force
was spotted by an enemy plane on the evening of February
15th. No one aboard saw that speck in the dark sky.

In the junior officers' wardroom there was a complete collection of all the intelligence which had been gathered regard-
ing the island of Iwo. Nothing was a secret any longer. It was
possible to scan the latest airplane photographs, which had
been taken early in the month. There were maps showing the
target areas assigned every unit, with batteries, pillboxes, and
anti-aircraft installations marked in red. There were reports on
the soil of the island. The beach would be coal-black lava

sand, and the land rose up from it quite sharply in terraces. Each terrace had been a former beach, since in the past few years the island had been rising from the sea. As one moved in from the water's edge the soil was a soft sand of volcanic ash, almost barren of vegetation and exceedingly difficult for any sort of vehicle to negotiate. Higher on the island were the cliffs of brown volcanic stone, suitable for construction of underground galleries. There were patches of coarse grass full of the mites that cause scrub typhus. There were hot springs, and there was the sulphur mine from which Iwo draws its name (Sulphur Island), and a small sugar plantation to the north near a single town called Motoyama. There were believed to be fifteen hundred troops on the island. The defensive installations were all underground or carefully camouflaged. There was only one practical beach on which to land and there was no chance for tactical subtlety.

The most interesting unit of this informational material was a large relief map made out of soft, pliable rubber, that gave a bird's-eye view of the island we were approaching. Every contour of it was there in scale—the cliffs to the northward, the vegetation, the roads, the air strips (two finished and one nearing completion), and Mount Suribachi, the low, brown volcanic cone on the southern tip.

There have already been a good many ingenious descriptions of the shape of Iwo Jima, including comparisons to a mutton chop and a gourd. The whole thing was about five miles long. Mount Suribachi, to the south, was a walled-in crater. Its northern slope was known to be studded with pillboxes and with artillery. Bushes and boulders on this slope ran down to the lowest and narrowest stretch on the island, which had beaches on the east and west. (The west beach, however, would not permit landing operations on account of the prevailing winds.) From here the land gradually rose upward, and the island broadened until it finally reached a width of two and one-half miles. The air strips were on its central spine. The northern shores came down to the sea in cliffs. There were only eight square miles of this bleak, unpromising, and porous dry land.

Anyone could tell that the plans for the seizure of Iwo Jima must have been the main occupation of a large group of specialists for a long, long time. Heaps of secret orders showed the disposition at any given moment of every one of the hundreds of craft that would take part in the invasion. The thousands of pages made a scenario for an operation which might take place in an hour or a minute. Veterans of other invasions were not impressed by the infinite detail. They spoke of the plans for Normandy and the south of France, or they discussed the arrangements for Guam and Saipan.

"If you've seen one of them," they said, "you've seen them all."

No one spoke much on the bridge. It was chilly and rain was falling before daylight. We were a silent, blacked-out ship, moving slowly, and as far as one could tell, alone—except for voices on the bridge radio.

"Battleaxe One," the radio was saying, "Area Zebra. Shackle. Charley. Oswald. Henry. Abel. Unshackle."

"We'll start firing at about ten thousand yards," someone said.

Then the first daylight began to stir across the water and we were among the shadows of other heavy ships, moving very slowly.

"Look," someone said, "there's the mountain."

There was a faint, pinkish glow on the rain clouds above the horizon and the first faint rays of an abortive sunrise struggling against the rain fell on a rocky mass some five miles dead ahead. It was the cone of Suribachi emerging from a misty haze of cloud, and cloud vapor covered the dark mass of the rest of Iwo Jima. After one glance at its first vague outlines, it would have been hard to have mistaken it for anything but a Japanese island, for it had the faint delicate colors of a painting on a scroll of silk.

Our spotting plane was warming up on the catapult aft and you could hear the roar of the motor clearly over the silent ship. Then there was a flat explosion as the plane shot over the water. When it circled for altitude and headed for the island, there was already light enough to see the faces on the bridge.

The Captain dropped his binoculars and lighted a cigarette. The clouds were gradually lifting above the island. It was unexpectedly tedious waiting and wondering when we would begin to fire. The island lay there mute and watchful. A bell was ringing. "Stand by," someone said, and seconds later one of our 14-inch projectiles was on its way to Iwo Jima. The noise was not as bad as the concussion, for your chest seemed to be pushed by invisible hands when the big guns went off. There was a cloud of yellow smoke, not unlike the color of Mount Suribachi. Then everyone crowded forward to gaze at the island. It seemed a very long while before a cloud of smoke and gray sand rose up almost like water from land. Then another ship fired. The bombardment of Iwo Jima had begun and the island lay there in the dingy, choppy sea, taking its punishment stoically without a sound.

Even at a distance of five miles, which somehow does not seem as far at sea as it does on land, one had the inescapable impression that Iwo Jima was ready for it and accustomed to taking a beating. This was not strange, as we had bombed it from the air for successive dozens of days, and fleet units had already shelled it twice. Nevertheless, this lack of reaction was something that you did not expect, even though common sense told you that there would not possibly be any land fire until we closed the range.

Another aspect of that three-day bombardment before D-day was even more unexpected, especially when one retained memories of the heavy and continuous fire by land batteries upon prepared positions in the last World War. The bombardment turned out to be a slow, careful probing for almost invisible targets, with long dull intervals between the firing. Occasionally one could see a cloud of drab smoke arise from another ship, and a long while afterward the sound of the explosion would come almost languidly across the water, and then there would be another plume of dust and rubble on another target area of Iwo Jima. Sometimes, when the breeze was light, the smoke from the big guns of another ship would rise in the air in a huge perfect ring. Of course common sense again gave the reason for this deliberate firing. The fleet had come too long a distance to waste its limited ammunition, and consequently the effect of every shot had to undergo careful professional analysis.

In the lulls between the firing there was always an atmosphere of unremitting watchfulness. While the crews of the anti-aircraft batteries below us sat by their guns, smoking and talking, hundreds of eyes were examining the sky and land. There was air cover far above us. In the distance were under-water listeners on the destroyers and DE's that were screening us. Our own air watch, besides, was covering every sector of the sky—and you also knew that the enemy looked back at us from his hidden observation posts. That consciousness of eye-strain and listening never entirely vanished in those days at Iwo Jima, and, because of it, not a moment on the bridge was restful.

The slow approach on Iwo Jima was somewhat like the weaving and feinting of a fighter watching for an opening early in the first round. To put it another way, our task force was like a group of big-game hunters surrounding a slightly wounded but dangerous animal. They were approaching him slowly and respectfully, endeavoring to gauge his strength and at the same time trying to tempt him into action. We moved all through the day, nearer and nearer to Iwo Jima. Planes from the carrier force came from beyond the horizon, peeling off through the clouds and diving toward the air strip; but except for an occasional burst of automatic fire and a few black dots of flak, the enemy was very listless. Our mine-sweeps, small, chunky vessels, began operating very close to the island. There were a few splashes near them, but that was all. The Japanese commander was too good a soldier to show his hand.

As the day wore on, we crowded close and objects loomed very large ashore. You could see the coal-black strip of beach where our assault waves would land, and the sea broke on the rusting hulls of a few old wrecks. Above the beach were the gray terraces we had read about, mounting in gradual, uneven steps to the air strip. Beside the air strip there was a tangle of planes, smashed by our bombings and pushed carelessly aside, like rubbish on a city dump. To the north were the quarries which had been mentioned by the Intelligence. You could see caves to the south on Mount Suribachi. We were very close for a battleship and we knew the enemy had 8-inch coast de-fense guns.

We continued firing at pillboxes and at anti-aircraft emplacements, but there was no return fire and no trace of life upon the island. We stayed there until the light grew dim, and then we turned to leave the area until next morning. Twelve hours of standing on the bridge and the concussion of the guns left everyone very tired. We must have done some damage but not enough to hurt.

### III

It was different the next morning—D-day minus two. When we returned to the dull work the island was waiting with the dawn. Today the sky was clearer and the sea was smoother, and the ships closed more confidently with the shore. The schedule showed that there was to be a diversion toward the middle of the morning, and the force was obviously moving into position.

"We're going to reconnoiter the beach with small craft," an officer explained. "And the LCI's will strafe the terraces with rockets."

It was hard to guess where the LCI's had come from, for they had not been with us yesterday—but there they were just behind us, on time and on order, like everything else in amphibious war. The sun had broken through the cloud ceiling and for once the sea was almost blue. The heavy ships had formed a line, firing methodically. Two destroyers edged their way past us and took positions nearer shore.

"Here come the LCI's," someone said. "You can see the small craft with them," and he gave the initials by which the small boats were identified. They were small open launches, manned by crews with kapok life jackets. They were twisting and turning nervously as they came to join the LCI's.

"Where are they going in those things?" I asked.

"They are going to see what there is along the beach," my friend answered. "Someone has to see." He spoke reprovingly, as though I should have known the routine that had been followed again and again in the Pacific.

Eight or ten LCI's—it was difficult to count them—were passing among the battleships, with their crews at their battle stations. They were small vessels that had never been designed for heavy combat. They had been built only to carry infantry ashore, but in the Pacific they were being put to all sorts of other uses—as messenger ships to do odd jobs for the fleet, as gunboats, and as rocket ships. Each had a round tower amidships where the commanding officer stood. Each had open platforms with light automatic guns, and now they were also fitted with brackets for the rockets. They were high and narrow, about a hundred feet overall, dabbed with orange and green paint in jungle camouflage. They were a long way from jungle shores, however, as they moved toward the beach of Iwo Jima.

Suddenly the scene took concrete shape. They would approach within a quarter of a mile of shore under the cover of our guns. Without any further protection their crews stood motionless at their stations.

Afterward a gunner from one of the LCI's spoke about it.

"If we looked so still," he said, "it was because we were scared to death. But then everyone had told us there was nothing to be scared of. They told us the Japs never bothered to fire at LCI's."

They were wrong this time, probably because the small craft that followed gave the maneuver the appearance of a landing. For minutes the LCI's moved in and nothing happened. They had turned broadside to the beach, with small boats circling around them like water beetles, before the enemy tipped his hand and opened up his batteries. Then it became clear that nothing we had done so far had contributed materially to softening Iwo Jima. The LCI's were surrounded with spurts of water, and spray and smoke. They twisted and backed to avoid the fire, but they could not get away. It all seemed only a few yards off, directly beneath our guns. Then splashes appeared off our own bows. The big ships themselves were under fire.

"The so-and-so has taken a hit," someone said. "There are casualties on the such-and-such." He was referring to the big ships, but at the moment it did not seem important. All you thought of were the LCI's just off the beach. We were inching into line with the destroyers.

It appeared later that when we had been ordered to withdraw we had disregarded the order, and thus all at once we were in a war of our own, slugging it out with the shore.

There had been a great deal of talk about our gunnery and the training of our crews. There was no doubt that they knew their business when they began firing with everything that could bear. The 14-inch guns and the 5-inch batteries were firing as fast as they could load. The breeze from the shore blew the smoke up to the bridge in bilious clouds. The shore line of Iwo Jima became cloaked in white smoke as we threw in phosphorus. Even our 40-millimeters began to fire. It was hard to judge the lapse of time, but the LCI's must have let off their rockets according to the schedule while the Japanese were blinded by the smoke and counterfire. When the LCI's began to withdraw, we also moved off slowly. It was the first mistake the enemy had made, if it was a mistake—revealing those batteries, for the next day was mainly occupied in knocking them out.

The LCI's were limping back. One of them was listing and small boats were taking off her crew. Another was asking permission to come alongside. When she reached us the sun was beating on the shambles of her decks. There was blood on the main deck, making widening pools as she rolled on the sluggish sea. A dead man on a gun platform was covered by a blanket. The decks were littered with wounded. They were being strapped on wire stretchers and passed up to us over the side, since nothing as small as an LCI had facilities for wounded. The men who were unhurt were lighting cigarettes and talking quietly, but no one was smiling. The commanding officer was tall, bare-headed, and blond, and he looked very young. Occasionally he gave an order and then he, also, lighted a cigarette. When they began to hose off the blood on the deck, the crew must have asked for fresh water, because our men, gathered by the rail, began tossing down canteens. Then there was a call from our bridge.

"Can you proceed under your own power?"

The blond CO looked up. He evidently had not heard, because the question was repeated.

"Can you proceed under your own power?"

"We can't proceed anywhere for three days," the CO said.

They had passed up the wounded—seventeen of them—and then they passed up five stretchers with the dead—twenty-two out of a crew of about sixty.

"That officer ought to get a medal," I said to someone on the bridge.

"They don't give medals for things like that in the Navy," I was told.

It may be so, but I still hope he gets the medal.

That evening the Japanese reported that they had beaten off two landings on Iwo Jima and that they had sunk numerous craft, including a battleship and a destroyer. There was a certain basis of fact in this, since what had happened must have looked like a landing. One LCI was sinking, waiting for a demolition charge, as disregarded as a floating can.

After the reconnaissance of the beach had been accomplished, the pounding of Iwo Jima continued through the afternoon and through the whole next day. Planes dove in with bomb loads, while the ring of ships kept up their steady fire. At night the "cans," as the destroyers were called, continued a harassing fire. Incendiary bombs were dumped on the slopes of Suribachi. Rockets were thrown at it from the air. Fourteen-inch shells pounded into its batteries. The ship to starboard of us attacked the battery to the north on the lip of the quarry. The earth was blown away, exposing the naked concrete gun emplacements, but now that the novelty had worn off it was all a repetition of previous hours. The scene grew dull and very fatiguing, but the voices on the radio loudspeaker continued tirelessly.

"Dauntless reports a contact. . . . Bulldog is ready to give a drink to any of our pigeons that may need it. Audacity One to Tiger—I repeat: Did you get our message? Over. . . ."

The island lay still, taking it. No visible life appeared until the last day, when an installation was blown up and a few men staggered out from it. Some of us on the bridge saw them and some did not. One Japanese ran a few steps and seemed to stop and stoop to pick up something. Then he was gone. We had probably seen him dying.

The Japanese commander was playing his cards close to his chest, revealing no more targets by opening fire. It was clear that he also had his plan, less complicated than ours, but rational. He might damage our heavy ships, but he could not sink them, or conceivably prevent the inevitable landing. He had clearly concluded to wait and take his punishment, to keep his men and weapons under cover, until our assault waves were on the beach. Then he would do his best to drive them off, and everyone at Iwo knows it was not such a bad plan, either. He did not come so far from doing it when he opened up his crossfire on the beach. Some pessimists even admit that he might have succeeded if it had not been for that coarse, light sand which embedded the mortar shells as they struck, so that they only killed what was very near them.

IV

At the end of D-day minus one our task force was still there, without many new additions, but it was different the next morning. At dawn on D-day the waters of Iwo looked like New York harbor on a busy morning. The transports were there with three divisions of Marines—a semicircle of gray shipping seven miles out. Inside that gray arc the sea, turned choppy by the unsettled weather, was dotted by an alphabet soup of ships.

There were fleets of LST's filled with amphibious tanks and alligators; there were LSM's; there were the smaller LCT's, and packs of LCI's gathering about the kill. The ring of warships was drawing tighter. Small boats were moving out bearing flags to mark the rallying points from which the landing waves would leave. It looked like a Hollywood production, except that it was a three-billion-, not a three-million-dollar extravaganza. There must have been as many as eight hundred ships clustered off Iwo Jima, not counting the small boats being lowered. The officers and crew faced it without surprise. Instead they pointed out small incidents and made critical remarks.

"See the LCVP's," someone said. He was pointing out the tiny dots around the transports where the landing craft were loading. "They'll be moving into position. Here come the planes." It was all working without a hitch, with H-hour not so far away. At nine o'clock exactly the first assault wave was due to hit the beach, but before that Iwo Jima was due to receive its final polishing. Its eight square miles were waiting to take everything we could pour into them, and they must have already received a heavier weight of fire than any navy in the world had previously concentrated upon so small an area.

Anyone who has been there can shut his eyes and see the place again. It never looked more aesthetically ugly than on D-day morning, or more completely Japanese. Its silhouette was like a sea monster with the little dead volcano for the head, and the beach area for the neck, and all the rest of it with its scrubby, brown cliffs for the body. It also had the minute, fussy compactness of those miniature Japanese gardens. Its stones and rocks were like those contorted, wind-scoured, water-worn boulders which the Japanese love to collect as landscape decorations. "I hope to God," a wounded Marine said later, "that we don't get to go on any more of those screwy islands."

An hour before H-hour it shook and winced as it took what was being dished out to it. In fact, the whole surface of the island was in motion as its soil was churned by our shells and by the bombs from the carrier planes that were swooping down across its back. Every ship was firing with a rising tempo, salvo after salvo, with no more waiting for the shell-burst to subside. Finally Iwo Jima was concealing itself in its own debris and dust. The haze of battle had become palpable, and the island was temporarily lost in a gray fog.

"The LST's are letting down their ramps," someone said.

There could not have been a better place to observe the whole spectacle than from the air lookout station above the bridge, but there was too much to see. Only an observer familiar with the art and theory of amphibious warfare could possibly have unraveled all the threads, and an ordinary witness could only give as inaccurate an account as the innocent bystander gives to circumstances surrounding a killing on the street. There was no time any longer to ask questions or to digest kindly professional explanations. All the facts that one had learned from the secret documents were confused by the reality.

The LST's had let down their ramps and the amphibious vehicles which they had carried were splashing through the water, like machines from a production line. Watching them,

I found myself speaking to a chief petty officer who was standing next to me.

"It's like all the cats in the world having kittens," I said, and the idea appeared to interest him.

The amphibious vehicles, churning up the sea into foaming circles, organized themselves in lines, each line following its leader. Then the leaders moved out to the floating flags, around which they gathered in circling groups, waiting for their signal to move ashore. The gray landing craft with the Marines had left the transports some time before for their own fixed areas and they also were circling, like runners testing their muscles before the race. The barrage which had been working over the beach area had lifted, and the beach, with the smoldering terraces above it, was visible again. It was time for the first wave to be starting.

It was hard to pick the first wave out in that sea of milling craft, but suddenly a group of the barges broke loose from its circle, following its leader in a dash toward shore. Close to land the leader turned parallel to the beach, and kept on until the whole line was parallel. Then the boats turned individually and made a dash for it. The Navy had landed the first wave on Iwo Jima—at nine o'clock on the dot—or, at least, not more than a few seconds after nine.

*Harper's Magazine*, May 1945

# The First Three Days

by Robert Sherrod

BY WIRELESS FROM IWO JIMA
THE JAPS had expected for a long time that we would land on
Iwo Jima and they prepared accordingly. Into their defense
they poured all the ingenuity they could command, all the
lessons they learned from Tarawa, Kwajalein, Saipan, Guam
and Peleliu. For our attack on Iwo Jima, the island they could
not afford to lose, they had saved their newest and best
weapons.

Besides their meticulously built pillboxes and their concentrated hillside caves, the Japs had dozens of big guns, a new
rocket projectile, hundreds of smaller guns and machine guns
and the most fantastic array of mortars man ever assembled in
defense of one island. Their soldiers—perhaps 20,000 of
them—lived underground because our planes could destroy
topside barracks. It is no wonder that Vice Admiral Richmond Kelly Turner, veteran of the toughest Pacific amphibious operations, said, "Iwo Jima is as well defended as any
fixed position that exists in the world today."

Yet it is possible to say after three days that the Japs will
lose Iwo Jima and we will have airfields within 675 miles of
Tokyo. One reason is sheer power, including naval and air
supremacy which made available some 800 ships and a total of
perhaps 1,200 planes. But the ultimate factor in the fall of Iwo
Jima will be the character and courage of the U.S. Marines.

Iwo Jima is shaped roughly like South America. The northern half of Iwo Jima's five-mile length is a high plateau rising
over 300 feet and having steep cliffs around the perimeter as
well as in between the various levels of the plateau. The
southern tip of Iwo Jima is Mt. Suribachi, a volcano shaped
like a scoop of ice cream which rises 554 feet. The only
beaches on the island are between the plateau and the volcano

at the southern tip. Our landings were made on the east beaches.

The island had been bombed for 74 straight days before D-Day. In January it had been thoroughly shelled by cruisers and battleships. For three days prior to D-Day many cruisers, battleships and destroyers poured more than 8,000 tons of high explosives on the eight square miles of Iwo Jima. To a British observer aboard our transport it seemed "that nothing could possibly be alive." The naval gunfire stripped away many tons of earth from the east side of Mt. Suribachi and from the cliffs at the underside of the bulge on the right flank. Thus the concrete-framed caves of the molelike Japs were revealed—rectangular frames leading to holes which extended far into the cliffs. Some of these concrete frames were wrecked. But from many others, though they had been laid bare, the Japs kept firing.

Several hundred carrier planes dropped their last bombs and completed their final strafing runs as the first wave of assault boats reached the shore of Iwo Jima's east beaches. It was 9 o'clock when regimental combat teams from the 4th Marine Division of Major General Clifton Cates and the new 5th Marine Division under Major General Keller Rockney landed abreast on the black sand.

The first objective was Motoyama Airfield No. 4 which lies midway between the east and west beaches of Iwo Jima. The airfield itself is on a plateau that looks deceptively low. But from the beach the airfield looks as high as a mountain. Furthermore the sand on Iwo Jima beaches is a coarse, loose, black sand which can be negotiated only by tracked vehicles—and not always by them. Many of our indispensable tanks stalled in the sand soon after they hit the beaches. There they became easy marks for heavy gunfire.

The first two hours were not easy. Mortars from Mt. Suribachi and the northern plateau rained on the beaches. The 4th Division was sprinkled by machine-gun fire from the cliffs. By 11 o'clock one division had advanced 300 yards to the steep embankment below the airfield, had almost crossed the island at its narrow neck just above Suribachi. But the first two hours were a picnic compared to what followed.

We had a toehold and it looked like a good one. Then,

before noon, all hell broke loose. From the north and from the south the hidden Japs poured artillery and six-inch mortars into the marines on the beachhead. Nearly all our tanks were clustered near the beaches like black beetles struggling to move on tar paper. A few others waddled up the steep, sandy incline toward the airfield, spouting flames now and then into the pillboxes.

Viewing the scene later, I could only marvel that any men got past those pillboxes. Their openings were mostly to the north and south. Naval gunfire might have destroyed them had their vents been exposed to the sea. But somehow these incredible marines had swept past the pillboxes, tossing grenades into them or shooting flame into them as they inched uphill toward the airfield.

It was sickening to watch the Jap mortars crash into the men as they climbed. These huge explosive charges—"floating ash cans" we called them—would crash among the thin lines of marines or among the boats bringing reinforcements to the beach, throwing sand, water and even pieces of human flesh a hundred feet into the air. Supporting naval gunfire and planes with bombs managed to knock out some of the mortars but the Japs continued throwing their deadly missiles all afternoon. By noon the assault battalions reported 20% to 25% fatalities.

Some units crossed the island in midafternoon and overran the southern extremity of the airfield but others were knocked back every time they struggled over the eastern embankments. Five tanks actually got on the airfield but three of them were quickly knocked out and the other two had to return. Our trouble was that the Japs had us covered from both ends of the island, from any point on the island. The marines could only advance and die, paving with their bodies a way for the men who came behind them.

By late afternoon we held perhaps 10% of the island, the most dangerous 10%. It was about 5 o'clock when orders came for Colonel Walter Irvine Jordan to take his 24th Regiment of the 4th Division to the beach. I had been assigned a spot in the boat of Jordan's executive officer, Lieut. Colonel Austin R. Brenelli.

The Higgins boat crunched on the shore. We ran up the

steep beach and started digging in for the night. Fashioning a foxhole out of that loose sand was, in the words of a marine from the Deep South, "like trying to dig a hole in a barrel of wheat." But we all finally managed to spade holes deep enough to protect our bodies against the shelling that was to come.

All night the Japs rained heavy mortars and rockets and artillery on the entire area between the beach and the airfield. Twice they hit casualty stations on the beach. Many men who had been only wounded were killed. The command post of one of the assault battalions received a direct hit which killed several officers. An artillery battalion based near the beach had 12 men killed and one of its guns knocked out. A six-inch mortar killed the captain of one assault company with two of his officers and five of his men. When the night had ended one group of medical corpsmen had been reduced from 28 to 11. The corpsmen were taking it as usual.

Many times during the night we blessed our naval gunfire and the few pieces of land-based artillery. They plastered the Jap nine tenths of the island so thoroughly that the enemy could never gather for a counterattack against our thinly held lines. Once a hundred Nips managed to rush against the 5th Division lines. Those who were not killed fled.

During the entire second day I saw only 12 dead Japs, though many others had undoubtedly been burned in their pillboxes by flamethrowers. The Jap plan of defense was plain. Only a few men would defend the beaches. The mortars and machine guns from the hillside caves, long ago registered on the beaches, would stop the landing. The Jap plan of defense failed because we had so much power we could stun them if we could not kill them, because the Navy's guns and planes could keep them down during our attacks. And it failed because the marines kept advancing despite their losses.

About the dead, whether Jap or American, there was one thing in common. They died with the greatest possible violence. Nowhere in the Pacific war have I seen such badly mangled bodies. Many were cut squarely in half. Legs and arms lay 50 feet away from any body. In one spot on the sand, far from the nearest cluster of dead men, I saw a string of guts 15 feet long. There are 250 wounded aboard the transport where this story is being written. One of the doctors tells me that 90% of them require major surgery. Off Normandy last summer, he says, only 5% who were brought aboard this transport needed such surgery. On the beach this morning I saw at least 50 men still fighting despite their wounds. Only the incapacitated request evacuation.

On the second day the 4th and 5th Divisions completed occupation of the airfield and pushed northward toward Motoyama Airfield No. 2, about 400 yards north of No. 1. The second night ashore was bitter cold but Jap firepower had decreased. After three days we hold about one quarter of Iwo Jima and we have finally gained some high ground. It seems certain that we will take Iwo Jima at a smaller cost in casualties than Saipan's 16,000. Probably no large percentage of the Jap defenders have yet been killed, but henceforth the Japs will kill fewer marines and the marines will kill more Japs.

*Life*, March 5, 1945

# Jump-Off

by Howard Brodie

WITH THE NINTH ARMY—I joined K Company, 406th Regiment, 102d Division, the night before the shove-off, as an artist, not an infantryman.

We were part of a reserve regiment several miles behind the line and would not be committed until after the Roer had been crossed by forward elements.

I felt everyone of us sweated it out as we went to sleep that night. At 0245 our barrage awoke us, but we stayed in our sacks until 0400. After hot chow we saddled our packs and headed for an assembly area in a wrecked town about five miles away. It was a silent company of men spaced on either side of the road—the traditional soldier picture of silhouettes against the crimson flashes of shells bursting on the enemy lines in the distance.

In the assembly town, we waited in the shattered rooms of a crumbling building. It was not pleasant waiting, because a dead cow stank in an adjoining room. We shoved off at daylight and came to gutted Rurdorf. I remember passing crucifixes and a porcelain pee pot on the rubble-laden road and pussy willows as we came to the river. A pool of blood splotched the side of the road. We crossed the Roer on a pontoon bridge and moved on. The forward elements were still ahead of us a few miles.

We passed a still doughboy on the side of the road with no hands; his misshapen, ooze-filled mittens lay a few feet from him. Knots of prisoners walked by us with their hands behind their heads. One group contained medics. In their knee-length white sacks, emblazoned with red crosses, they resembled crusaders. In another group were a couple of German females, one of them in uniform. Mines like cabbages lay on either side of the road.

We entered the town of Tetz and set up the CP in a cellar. Two platoons went forward a few hundred yards to high ground overlooking the town and dug in. We were holding the right flank of the offensive finger. Several enemy shells burst in the town. Some tracers shot across the road between the CP and the dug-in platoons. The tracers seemed to be below knee level. Night fell.

The CP picked up reports like a magnet: "The Jerries are counterattacking up the road with 40 Tiger tanks . . . The Jerries are attacking with four medium tanks." Stragglers reported in from forward companies. One stark-faced squad leader had lost most of his squad. The wounded were outside, the dead to the left of our platoon holes. It was raining. I went to sleep.

The next day I went to our forward platoons. I saw a dough bailing his hole out with his canteen cup . . . saw our planes dive-bomb Jerry in the distance . . . saw our time-fire burst on Jerry, and white phosphorus and magenta smoke bombs. I saw platoon leader Lt. Joe Lane playing football with a cabbage. I saw a dead GI in his hole slumped in his last living position—the hole was too deep and too narrow to allow his body to settle. A partially smoked cigarette lay inches from his mouth, and a dollar-sized circle of blood on the earth offered the only evidence of violent death.

Night fell and I stayed in the platoon CP hole. We didn't stay long because word came through that we would move up to the town of Hottorf, the forward position of the offensive finger, preparatory to jumping off at 0910.

K Company lined up in the starlit night—the CO, the first platoon, MGs, third platoon, heavy weapons, headquarters and the second platoon in the rear—about 10 paces between each man and 50 between the platoons. The sky overhead was pierced by thousands of tracers and AA bursts as Jerry planes flew over. Again it was a silent company.

At Hottorf we separated into various crumbling buildings to await H-hour. We had five objectives, the farthest about 2¼ miles away. All were single houses but two, which were towns of two or three houses. We were the assault company of the Third Battalion.

H-hour was approaching. A shell burst outside the win-

*"I saw a GI in his hole, slumped in his last living position."*

dow, stinging a couple of men and ringing our ears. We huddled on the floor.

It was time to move now. The first platoon went out on the street followed by the MGs and the third platoon and the rest of us. We passed through doughs in houses on either side of the street. They wisecracked and cheered us on. We came to the edge of town and onto a broad rolling field. The third and first platoons fanned out in front of us. Headquarters group stayed in the center.

I followed in the footsteps of Pfc. Joe Esz, the platoon runner. He had an aluminum light case upon which I could easily focus the corner of my eye to keep my position and still be free to observe. Also, I felt if I followed in his footsteps I would not have to look down at the ground for mines. He turned to me and commented on how beautifully the company was moving, properly fanned and well-spaced.

Several hundred yards away I noticed Jerries running out of a gun position waving a white flag. A black puff of smoke a few hundred yards to my right caught my attention, then another closer. I saw some men fall on the right flank. The black puffs crept in. There were whistles and cracks in the air and a barrage of 88s burst around us, spaced like the black squares of a checkerboard surrounding the reds. I heard the zing of shrapnel as I hugged the earth. We slithered into the enemy 88 position from which I had seen the prisoners run. Somebody threw a grenade into the dugout.

We moved on. Some prisoners and a couple of old women ran out onto the field from a house, Objective One. There was the zoom and crack of 88s again. A rabbit raced wildly away to the left. We went down. I saw a burst land on the running Jerries. One old woman went down on her knees in death, in an attitude as though she were picking flowers.

A dud landed three feet in front of T/Sgt. Jim McCauley, the platoon sergeant, spraying him with dirt. Another dud ricocheted over Pfc. Wes Maulden, the 300 radio operator. I looked to the right flank and saw a man floating in the air amidst the black smoke of an exploding mine. He just disappeared in front of the squad leader, S/Sgt. Elwin Miller. A piece of flesh sloshed by Sgt. Fred Wilson's face. Some men didn't get up. We went on. A couple of men vomited. A piece of shrapnel cut a dough's throat as neatly as Jack the Ripper might have done it.

The right flank was getting some small-arms fire. I was so tired from running and going down that it seemed as though my sartorius muscles would not function. The 300 radio wouldn't work and we couldn't get fire on those 88s. Pfc. George Linton went back through that barrage to get another one from Hottorf. Medic Oliver Poythress was working on wounded in that barrage.

*"A dud landed . . ."*

Objective Two loomed ahead—a large building enclosing a courtyard. Cow shed, stables, tool shed, hay loft, living quarters opened on the inner court. I saw an 88 explode over the arched entrance.

We filtered into the courtyard and into the surrounding rooms. The executive officer started to reorganize the company. The platoons came in. 1st Sgt. Dick Wardlow tried to make a casualty list. Many didn't make it. A plan of defense was decided on for the building. A large work horse broke out from his stable and lumbered crazily around the courtyard. T-4 Melvin Fredell, the FO radio operator, lay in the courtyard relaying artillery orders. An 88 crashed into the roof. The cows in their shed pulled on their ropes. One kicked a sheep walking around in a state of confusion.

A dying GI lay in the tool room; his face was a leathery yellow. A wounded GI lay with him. Another wounded dough lay on his belly in the cow shed, in the stench of dung and decaying beets. Another GI quietly said he could take no more. A couple of doughs started frying eggs in the kitchen. I went into the tool shed to the dying dough. "He's cold, he's dead," said Sgt. Charles Turpen, the MG squad leader. I took off my glove and felt his head, but my hand was so cold he felt warm. A medic came and said he was dead.

Lt. Bob Clark organized his company and set up defense. FO Phillip Dick climbed the rafters of the hay loft to report our artillery bursts. The wounded dough in the cow shed sobbed for more morphine. Four of us helped carry him to a bed in another room. He was belly down and pleaded for someone to hold him by the groin as we carried him: "I can't stand it. Press them up, it'll give me support." A pool of blood lay under him.

*"One dough was hit as he ran."*

I went to the cowshed to take a nervous leak. A shell hit, shaking the roof. I ducked down and found I was seeking shelter with two calves. I crossed the courtyard to the grain shed where about 60 doughs were huddled.

Tank fire came in now. I looked up and saw MG tracers rip through the brick walls. A tank shell hit the wall and the roof. A brick landed on the head of the boy next to me. We couldn't see for the cloud of choking dust. Two doughs had their arms around each other; one was sobbing. More MG tracers ripped through the wall, and another shell. I squeezed between several bags of grain. Doughs completely disappeared in a hay pile.

We got out of there and our tanks joined us. I followed a tank, stepping in its treads. The next two objectives were taken by platoons on my right, and I don't remember whether any 88s came in for this next quarter mile or not. One dough was too exhausted to make it.

We were moving up to our final objective now—a very large building, also enclosing a courtyard, in a small town. Jerry planes were overhead but for some reason did not strafe. Our tanks spewed the town with fire and led the way. Black bursts from Jerry time-fire exploded over our heads this time. We passed Jerry trenches and a barbed-wire barrier. Lt. Lane raced to a trench. A Jerry pulled a cord, setting off a circle of mines around him, but he was only sprayed with mud. S/Sgt. Eugene Flanagan shot at the Jerry, who jumped up and surrendered with two others.

Jerries streamed out of the large house. Women came out too. An 88 and mortars came in. I watched Pfc. Bob de Valk and Pfc. Ted Sanchez bring out prisoners from the basement, with Pfc. Ernie Gonzalez helping. An 88 crashed into the roof and a platoon leader's face dripped blood but it was a surface wound. Jerries pulled out their wounded on an old bed spring and chair.

We made a CP in the cellar. The wounded were brought down. Stray Jerries were rounded up and brought to the rear. Jittery doughs relaxed for a moment on the beds in the basement. Pfc. Frank Pasek forgot he had a round in his BAR and frayed our nerves by letting one go into the ceiling. A pretty Jerry girl with no shoes on came through the

*"Two doughs had their arms around each other; one was sobbing."*

basement. Doughs were settling down now. The CO started to prepare a defense for a counterattack. Platoons went out to dig in. L and M Companies came up to sustain part of our gains.

Most of us were too tired to do much. The battalion CO sent word he was relieving us. All of us sweated out going back over the field, although this time we would go back a sheltered way. We were relieved and uneventfully returned to a small town. The doughs went out into the rain on the outskirts and dug in. A few 88s came into the town and some time-fire near the holes. Early the next morning, K Company returned to its former position in the big house with the courtyard as the final objective. Just when I left, Jerry started counterattacking with four tanks and a company of men.

*Yank*, March 11, 1945 (Continental Edition)

# Big Jump into Germany

by Richard C. Hottelet

WE GOT HIT the first time as we swung over the drop zone. Out of the left waist window we were watching parachutes bubble out of a C-47. And then we heard the hammering straight down below us. You could tell by the sound that it was 20- or 37-mm., and at 700 feet, our B-17 was a fat, lazy bird. We should have known when the first shell knocked against our ship that we ought to get out of the area and stay out. But we didn't, and that's how it happened.

We should not have been there in the first place. But the great airborne offensive across the northern Rhine on March 24th was probably one of the last big stories of the European war, and from a news as well as from a technical reporting angle, the Army wanted complete coverage. So the U.S. Troop Carrier Forces put aside a beautiful silver Flying Fortress, loaded it with their combat cameramen and observers, let me get on board with my sound-recording equipment and sent us out to cover the operation.

The plan was to take a small, but very important bite out of the German east bank of the Rhine. To the south, other armies were poised and ready to jump the river but, up in the north near the Dutch border, the British Second was held up by heavy opposition coming from around Wesel.

D-Day was set for March 24th, and two divisions, the British Sixth Airborne and the U.S. Seventeenth Airborne, were to be flown low across the Rhine inland five miles to the high ground northwest of Wesel and dropped there. Simultaneously, the engineers were to blanket 30 miles of the area with smoke, and General Miles C. Dempsey's British Second was to effect a Rhine crossing six hours before the air drops, push inland and join the paratroopers.

In effect, this was a better planned Arnhem job. You may

remember that unsuccessful paratrooper landing in Holland last year. The job was carried out well, except that the paratroopers were so far ahead of the ground troops that the Germans in between held the ground troops back while cutting the airborne invaders to ribbons.

This time, the chunk of land was to be much smaller and much more vital. Days before the operation, the four areas selected for landing of paratroopers and gliders were given a careful going over by tactical aircraft, which stitched up and down the roads around the areas and smashed the antiaircraft gun positions and spotted German reinforcement columns miles east of Wesel and left them wrecked and blazing.

Meanwhile, the U.S. Seventeenth Airborne, which had not had combat jump experience, practiced drops in northern France. It had only reached Europe in December. The British Sixth Airborne, a combat-wise group, was in England practicing drops.

On the 22d, all paratroopers were brought to airports and placed in special stockades for security reasons. The next morning, pilots, navigators and radiomen were briefed before big maps marked "Top Secret." After dark, the jumpmasters were taken from the stockades and briefed. They were to jump low—700 feet. Forward speed was to be 105 miles per hour over the drop zones. The planes were to be emptied of 15 paratroopers in no more than eleven seconds.

At 8:30 A.M. on the 24th, a great parade of English planes and another great column of American planes met over Brussels, Belgium. There were five thousand ships in all, counting fighter escort, and they swung northeastward to the Rhine. As they crossed the river, the quiet paratroopers were hooking up to the guide lines and could see great globs of black smoke arising from the drop zones. The heavy bombers were just finishing the softening up.

The weather was on our side. For eleven superb days the sun had crossed the sky, brilliant from the moment it rose to its last setting red. It helped the men patrolling the sky, and the bomber fleets that went out day after day and night after night. It helped the men on the ground by drying out the soil over which they would have to move. Along the sacred German River Rhine it was the enemy who prayed for clouds and rain and overcast to help him against our supremacy in the air and the massive weight of our superiority on the ground. But on this day of decision the good weather held.

To me the only worrying thing about the enterprise was the fact that I was not in the least worried. It's not superstition. It is just that after seven years of crisis and war, I have come to feel that things are most likely to go wrong when it seems inevitable that they will go completely well.

But this slight twinge disappeared after half an hour in the air. Because the sight of airfield after airfield in northern France loaded with planes and gliders taking off and ready to take off was too real a sign of strength to brook any doubt.

The sky above was pale blue. Below us, golden soil and bright green meadows were cut by long morning shadows. Flying at a few hundred feet, banking steeply to let the cameramen get their shots, we saw the solid phalanxes of olive-green troop carriers and tow planes and gliders nose to tail on the perimeter tracks of the ground bases. From one field to another we went until it got monotonous, until we sat down on our flak suits and parachutes in the waist and just watched the sky. I no longer even felt worried that I was not worried.

On my right was Colonel Joel O'Neal, the Deputy Chief of Staff of the U.S. Carrier Forces, come to see the execution of what he had helped to plan. He chewed gum and looked at his map. Tech Sergeant Clarence Pearce and Staff Sergeant Fred Quandt sat silent, with their knees drawn up, and smoked. We all watched dark-bearded Sergeant George Rothlisberg, who sat and slept on the upended little khaki suitcase that carried his equipment. He just sat upright, with no support, and slept.

It was warm, despite the fact that we had taken the windows out of the waist, and the wind was rushing through. Outside, the sun was climbing, and you had just about absorbed the roaring of the four great engines and the screaming of the slipstream into the open fuselage as a thoroughly acceptable part of a perfect day, when someone nudged you and pointed out of the side.

You got up and looked, and there they were—hundreds of C-47s flying along in tight formation. This was the realization of months of training and planning. It was an airborne dream come true. It was a mighty olive-green river that surged steadily and inevitably over Germany, and over the Germans crouched behind their last great defense line below. It was a mightier river than the German Rhine, and this day would prove it. From now on in, it was business, strict and cold. The troop carriers looked sleek and well fed, bobbing up and down in the air currents and propwash like fat men in a gentle surf. But inside them there were thousands of desperate young men, trained to a fine edge and armed to the teeth. Slung under the green bellies of the planes were the bundles of explosives and ammunition and supplies for dropping to the paratroops. They nosed ahead inexorably, and behind them came other serials (large formations), and behind them still others, until the procession disappeared in the thin March mist.

Colonel O'Neal put his flak suit on over his parachute harness and strapped the steel flaps of his flak helmet down over his ears. We all did the same. The three photographers, their cameras clicking away, jostled one another at the waist windows as we swooped around the drop ships.

P-Hour, the drop hour for the paratroops, was 10 A.M. Just after 9:45 we passed our last check point. It was called the IP, or Initial Point, the same as a bombing run. Its code name was Yalta. All of a sudden the ground below us, which had been golden in the morning sunlight, turned gray. For a moment I thought that we had run into clouds. It seemed impossible. Then we caught a whiff. It was chemical smoke. Below us and around us was a bank of misty smoke that ran for miles up and down the west bank of the Rhine, across the river and over the east bank.

Here there was no sunlight; here in the center of green and fertile land was a clearly marked area of death. The smoke seemed a shroud. Outlines below us were indistinct. What had seemed warm now appeared ominously cold, and almost clammy. On our left was the first serial of paratroop pathfinders. We were flying at 700 feet.

Below us there was no sign of life. We looked for troops going across, for the familiar invasion LCVPs and LCMs of our Rhine navy. We saw none. The river below us was a slate-gray ribbon winding through a dull gray land; on our left the troop carriers, pregnant dolphins in an eerie sea; and down to our right, straight into the sun, the dark mass of the city of Duisburg. From its broad, regular inland harbor the sun reflected panels of light into the battle area.

Over the roar of the engines and the screaming of air in the waist windows we heard a faint thumping. Colonel O'Neal grabbed me by the shoulder and pointed. The intercom crackled and a dry voice said, "Flak at twelve o'clock and nine o'clock. But they're off the beam." Outside, coming up from Duisburg, were the shells from Nazi 88s. Black puffs of smoke feathered pretty far off to our right. All of a sudden I felt how tense I had become. There was no more flak for a moment and I began to relax.

And just at that moment we were over the first drop zone. It was 9:50, ten minutes early. On our left, paratroopers were tumbling out of the C-47s, their green camouflage chutes blending with the dark gray ground. The troop-carrier serial seemed like a snail, leaving a green trail as it moved along. And it was crawling indeed—about 115 miles an hour. Our big Fort seemed to me to be close to stalling speed.

We were watching the bright blue and red and yellow supply parachutes mix with the falling troopers, admiring the concentration of that first jump, when we first got it. I was surprised and pained. The ground, as far as we could see it through the smoke, was torn up as if a gigantic seed drill had passed over it. It was an insult that anyone should be left down there to shoot at us.

It sounded like a riveting machine, a heavy one. For a split-second I didn't catch on. Then I smelled the explosive—a stench that always nauseates me. You get it in outward-bound bombers when the gunners clear their guns. But we had no gunners. Our turret guns were taped up and our waist guns had been unmounted. We were here to photograph and record, not to fight. There was a sharp rap on the ship somewhere. We had been hit.

The drop run was finished, so we swung up in a banking climb to our left while the first serial turned sharply right and headed out. I listened to the engines. They roared healthily on. The sound of the slipstream was the same, and the crackling of the aluminum skin.

I looked around the waist with new eyes. I noted the sheet of armor below each waist window and decided to stick close there. The men were busy with their cameras, their knees bent, and hunched slightly over to keep balance. I hung on to one of the innumerable pipes that run down the top of the fuselage, like a strap-hanger in a New York subway, swaying slightly as we banked and heeled. I looked at Quandt. He looked back, and nodded his head with the corners of his mouth turned down. I knew exactly what he meant, so I did likewise. Colonel O'Neal's Irish face remained impassive.

We turned and circled for a minute or two, and then joined another serial going into its drop zone. On the ground we could see occasional gun flashes, but no sign of life apart from them. No flak was coming near, so again a gradual relaxation made me see how tense I had become in every muscle. We watched the serial, with its fifteen tight little three-ship V formations, drop its load.

A hundred yards away from us, one of its ships, spawning parachutes from the rear, suddenly blossomed with yellow light up forward. It was not the reflection of the sun on the windshield. It was flame. And the ship turned off to the left in a steep glide. I remembered that two ships in the first serial had also slipped away, but with no apparent damage. Probably the pilots were hit by flak.

This bunch finished its work and turned for home. We turned off and joined a third formation, flying level with them at their speed and altitude. One of the photographers, crowded away from the window, was probably thinking along identical lines with me. There were a couple of extra flak suits back with us, and he stretched the double aprons flat out on the wooden floor.

It suddenly seemed extremely silly to me that we should be there, because we were a huge bright silver B-17 flying along at almost stalling speed. We were probably the most conspicuous thing in the sky.

The Germans must have arrived at the same conclusion. We had been over the drop zone twenty or twenty-five minutes. We were turning again to pick up the first incoming serial of C-46s. These ships, the Curtiss Commandos, carried more paratroopers and jumped them out of two doors at once. They were used in this operation for the first time.

We were banking to head back to the Rhine and pick them up. Hanging from my pipe, I could look almost straight down through the waist window through the tattered smoke at the ground. By now, there were several blobs of drop zones where the colored parachutes reminded you of a Mardi Gras sidewalk strewn with confetti.

And then we really hit trouble. It may have been the same gun. I did not see it. Radio Operator Roy Snow watched the tracers come up from the ground and lifted his feet to let the shells pass under him. In the waist we heard the riveter again. A short burst, then a longer one. The heavy steel-scaled flak suit and the heavy flak helmet, which had been weighing me down, now felt light and comforting. Then we got hit in a ripple. The ship shuddered, I grabbed my pipe. And then, as if it had been rehearsed, all five of us in the waist stepped onto the flak suits, spread on the flooring.

Over the intercom, Snow was telling our pilot, Lieutenant Colonel Benton Baldwin, that the left wing had been hit, and that fire was breaking out between the engines. The flak stopped. Baldwin was gaining altitude in a climbing turn. Smoke began to pour down through the plane, and in the left waist window. A tongue of flame licked back as far as the window, and the silver inner skin of the ship reflected its orange glow. The crew chief told Lieutenant Albert Richey that gasoline was sloshing around in the bomb bay.

Sitting in a plane that is being peppered by flak and being able to do nothing at all about it is a miserable feeling. But even that is nothing to the sensation of sitting in a burning plane. Baldwin used both extinguisher charges in a vain attempt to put out the fire. There was nothing to do but bail out.

This Fortress carried two thousand gallons of aviation fuel, which can almost ignite in a hot wind. One engine was burning; the one next to it was catching fire. The ship was still under control. But there was no telling for how long.

As we staggered out, we watched the C-46s come in and apparently walk into a wall of flak. I could not see the flak, but one plane after another went down. All our attention was concentrated on our own ship. It could blow up in mid-air any moment. We moved close to the windows. From the pilot's compartment came streams of stinging smoke. The intercom went out.

Up in the cockpit, Colonel Baldwin was keeping the ship under control, watching the fire eat a larger and larger hole in the left wing like a smoldering cigarette in a tablecloth. Looking down on the wing from above, he could not see a large fire. The flame was mainly below the wing.

Suddenly we went into a sharp dip. Back aft we did not know what was happening. All we had was the smoke and the deafening noise, and the tiny fragments of molten metal which the wing was throwing back and which twinkled in the sun as they raced past the waist window.

We pulled off our flak suits and helmets. I reached down and buckled on my chest chute. It was obvious we would have to jump. But down below was still the cold, gray smoky country east of the Rhine. Impossible to tell what was happening down there. If it was not in enemy hands, it was a battlefield.

As we went into the dip, I thought the pilots had been hit, and I put my hands on the edge of the window to vault out. But the colonel brought her back under control, and we hung on. There was no movement among the men in the waist. We stood and waited—for flak, or more flames or explosion or for the Rhine to slide by below. There was nothing else to do. After what seemed hours, the Rhine was below us at last. The left wing was blazing, but three motors were still running.

We were hardly across the river when Roy Snow came back and told us that the pilot wanted us to jump. That and the Rhine River were all we had been waiting for.

Colonel O'Neal went back and began to struggle with the handle that jettisons the rear door. I jogged my chest pack up and down, made sure it was secure. The other men did the same. Colonel O'Neal was still wrestling with the door. I went back to help.

There was no panic. But if this telling sounds cool and collected, the actuality was not so. Uppermost in everyone's mind was just physically getting out of that ship. We were still flying at less than a thousand feet, which left not much time. I abandoned, with hardly a thought, my recording equipment and typewriter and notes and jacket in the radio compartment. Of the cameramen, only Quandt thought to take the film out of his camera. There was no point in trying to jump with anything in your hand because the opening of the chute will make you drop anything that is not tied to you.

The colonel got the door open and crouched in it for a moment. I shouted, "Okay, Colonel, get going." He didn't hear, but tumbled out. I got into the doorway.

All my life, one of the sensations I have disliked most has been the feeling of falling. As a boy I avoided the big slides in the amusement parks at Coney Island. Even now, working at the front, when I go up in a Cub or observation L-5, I always hope fervently that the pilot will not do those steep banking dives they like so much. The sinking feeling in my stomach when I fall is sickening.

Standing in the doorway of the burning Fortress, I somehow hardly thought of that. Down below, the ground was green and golden and friendly again. We had left the smoke zone, the sun was bright and the air was warm. Everything seemed friendly. It was the most natural thing in the world to want to leave the doomed plane and, anyway, behind me were three men waiting to jump, too. So I simply let myself tumble forward on my face. As I left the ship, the slipstream caught me, and it was like a big friendly hand that I could dig my shoulder into. The black rubber de-icer on the stabilizer was above me. And then all was confusion.

We were jumping at about six hundred feet, so I pulled the rip cord almost immediately. I pulled it so hard I almost jerked my shoulder out. There was more confusion. I felt as if I had come to a dead stop. The harness straps were digging into my flesh. My main thought was to save the ring, and I put it in my pocket. My next thought was gentle surprise that I should have been successful in parachuting the first time I tried.

For a moment there was relaxation, and enjoyment of the wonderful quiet that the departing Fort had left me in. Up above my head, the chute was glistening white, billowing like a sail full of wind. I began to sway, so I turned my attention to the ground.

I tried to remember everything I had read about parachuting—like pulling the shrouds to stop swaying. But I was afraid to try anything that might spill the chute. So I concentrated on worrying about where I was going to fall. Below me were a farmhouse, some open fields, a clump of trees and a pond. Men were running in my direction from one side of the house. Away in the next field Colonel O'Neal, who had also been swaying, had just come down.

I landed in a pasture. Trying to gauge my height to brace myself for the fall, I kept opening and closing my eyes, but was barely able to keep pace. I remembered to flex my knees. The next second I hit with a grunt. I snapped off the parachute and got to my feet. To my surprise I stayed there, getting my wind back.

It was the British Second Army area, and—true to the old Battle of Britain tradition—the parachuting visitor was promptly filled with tea and whisky.

I reached in my pocket for the ring. It is parachuting tradition to keep the ring to prove you have been in command of the situation at all times. The ring was not there. I had obviously been out of control.

Word came that the colonel was all right, but that Pearce, who jumped right after me, had been killed when his chute streamed like an exclamation mark instead of opening. Our pilot pulled his rip cord in the cockpit by accident while putting his chute on after we had all got out. So he rode the Fort into a crash landing and came out safe.

All around us, as we stood on this approach route for the airborne forces, burning and disabled C-47s crashed into the fields. In every case the pilot stayed with his ship until his crew and passengers were out before bailing out himself. In some cases he stayed too long. It was a thrilling demonstration of the highest kind of courage to see a burning troop carrier come gliding in, to see two or three or four chutes blossom out under it, a pause as the ship turned away, and then another lone chute as the pilot got out. We stood looking up and cheered.

After a while, I noticed that my eye was hurting, and found that the chest chute had given me the start of a beautiful shiner as it was ripped up past my face. On hitching my way back to Paris next day, I found a telegram from my boss in London saying: "Better a purple eye than a Purple Heart."

By that time, there was good news from the front. Some 6,400 Nazis had been taken prisoner in the drop zones; the whole operation was a great success, and the British Second Army was slashing across the top of Germany—east of the Rhine.

*Collier's*, May 5, 1945

# *"These Terrible Records of War"*

by James Agee

THE PARAMOUNT newsreel issue about Iwo Jima subjects the tremendous material recorded by Navy and Marine Corps and Coast Guard camera men to an unusually intelligent job of editing, writing, and soundtracking. I noticed with particular respect a couple of good uses of flat silence; the use of a bit of dialogue on "intercoms," recorded on the spot, in a tank; and the use, at the end, of a still photograph down whose wall the camera moved slowly. Still photographs of motionless objects have a very different quality from motion-picture photographs of motionless objects; as Jean Cocteau observed, time still moves in the latter. The still used here was of dead men, for whom time no longer moved. The device is not a new one; Griffith (or William Bitzer) used it for the same purpose at the end of a battle in "The Birth of a Nation," and René Clair used stop-shots for a somewhat related purpose in "The Crazy Ray." But it is a device too basic to poetic resource on the screen to discard as plagiarized, and I am glad to see it put back into use so unpretentiously and well.

The Fox version of the same battle—the only other version I could find—drew on the same stock, and is interesting to compare with the Paramount. In one way it is to its credit that it is much less noisy and much less calculated to excite; it is in other words less rhetorical, and the temptations to rhetoric must be strong in handling such material, and usually result in falseness. But in this Paramount issue it seems to me that rhetoric was used well, to construct as well as might be in ten hours' work and in ten minutes on the screen an image of one of the most terrible battles in history. And that is not to mention plain sense: the coherent shape of violence in the Paramount version, which moves from air to sea to land; its intact, climactic use of the footage exposed through a tank-slit, which in the Fox version is chopped along through the picture; and its use of the recorded dialogue, which Fox didn't even touch. The Fox version does on the other hand have two shots—a magically sinister slashing of quicksilvery water along the sand, and a heartrending picture of a wounded Marine, crawling toward help with the scuttling motions of a damaged insect—which I am amazed to see omitted from a piece of work so astute as Paramount's.

Very uneasily, I am beginning to believe that, for all that may be said in favor of our seeing these terrible records of war, we have no business seeing this sort of experience except through our presence and participation. I have neither space nor mind, yet, to try to explain why I believe this is so; but since I am reviewing and in ways recommending that others see one of the best and most terrible of war films, I cannot avoid mentioning my perplexity. Perhaps I can briefly suggest what I mean by this rough parallel: whatever other effects it may or may not have, pornography is invariably degrading to anyone who looks at or reads it. If at an incurable distance from participation, hopelessly incapable of reactions adequate to the event, we watch men killing each other, we may be quite as profoundly degrading ourselves and, in the process, betraying and separating ourselves the farther from those we are trying to identify ourselves with; none the less because we tell ourselves sincerely that we sit in comfort and watch carnage in order to nurture our patriotism, our conscience, our understanding, and our sympathies.

*The Nation*, March 24, 1945

# Letter from Cologne

by Janet Flanner (Genêt)

MARCH 19 (BY WIRELESS)
COLOGNE-ON-THE-RHINE is now a model of destruction. The nearby city of Aachen died in a different way: its handsome, melancholy skeleton is left upright; behind its elegant, carved façades, it was burned out. Cologne and its heavy, medieval pomp were blown up. By its river bank, Cologne lies recumbent, without beauty, shapeless in the rubble and loneliness of complete physical defeat. Through its clogged side streets trickles what is left of its life, a dwindled population in black and with bundles—the silent German people appropriate to the silent city.

Most of the people in Cologne have little to say. Dazed by a week of defeat, three years of bombings, and twelve years of propaganda, the old men and the women and children who now inhabit the city sound as if they had lost all ability to think rationally or to tell the truth. Nor did the last orders from their departing Nazi government encourage accurate conversation. One brand-new, fragile-looking item that is seen again and again along the sodden Cologne streets, battered by weather and war, is a propaganda poster pasted on the remaining walls. In Gothic letters, and with exclamation point, the poster advises *"Schweigen siegen!"*—"To keep silent is to win." This poster was put up just before the American First Army's triumphant entrance into the city. Having lost the war of arms, defeated Germany is apparently counting again on the psychological victory she won in the last peace—the victory of silence, lies, whining, energy, devotion, and guile. Even the children seem to have been given their orders to tell the same old patriotic little Nazi fibs. Some small boys I saw who were patently wearing their Hitlerjugend caps, from which the insignia had been removed, told me, with no

662

timidity whatever, that these were ordinary winter caps. Then, overcome by the farcical ease of their first trick on the decadent democratic foreigner, they fled, giggling, to hide behind a ruined doorway. Theirs was the only laughter I have heard in Cologne. The other day, from the nearby city of Bonn, which our troops were then entering, news came to Cologne of an extraordinary proposition. Being a university town, Bonn felt competent to offer, for our American Army's help, the city's own selected corps of interpreters, all speaking perfect Oxford English and high German, who could thus replace, in our relations with the Bonn civilians, our own Army interpreters, many of whom are German Jews.

The only Cologne German I have talked to who has made sense began with the customary subservient lies but ended, at least, with his version of Teutonic truth. He lives near the gate of the Klingelpütz Gestapo prison and for forty years was a paper bundler for the *Kölnische Zeitung*, which was the town's leading conservative Catholic newspaper. He opened our conversation by mumbling mendaciously that no Germans had ever believed Germany could win the war, then admitted that the shocking idea of losing it had come to him and everyone else only when their Army failed to capture Stalingrad. I asked him if the Germans had not been discouraged when Japan pulled the powerful, productive United States into the conflict. He said that they had, on the contrary, rejoiced and had at once intelligently declared war on us themselves. By doing that, he explained, they forced upon us that war on two fronts which had long been the German high command's formula for military defeat. He actually seemed able to accept philosophically the idea of Germany's fast-approaching defeat—on two fronts—since it proved that the German high command had been, for Germany anyhow, absolutely right. He furthermore felt that somehow England had failed to keep a date with history by not falling by 1941.

He and his patient, nervous wife, whom I also talked with, had been bombed out three times, but she had been buried alive with him only twice, since in the terrible daylight bombing of September 17, 1944, she had been away from home in a food queue and had popped into one of the available *Bunker*, as the Germans call their air-raid shelters. It had never oc-

curred to them to leave Cologne, where food was fairly easy
to get. Anyway, every other place was being bombed, too,
and refugees were resented. The couple showed me their cellar room, where they had been sleeping, cooking, and hoping
for the past fourteen months. It looked and smelled orthodox
in the circumstances—damp, dark, crowded with a mixture
of bedding and skillets, family photographs, and mudstained
clothes. The mud of Cologne is part wallpaper from the city's
bombed homes, part window panes, part books, part slate
roofs fallen from fine old buildings, and surely part blood
from the two hundred thousand dead, the fourth of
Cologne's population now in peace. The paper bundler and
his wife were planning to sleep upstairs now that the Americans had come. *"Gott sei Dank,"* the woman said bleakly.
"Anyhow, they bring an end to the war."

The power of survival of the poor apartment house in
which this couple live was shared by few of the city's grand
mansions. The bombs had left the paper bundler's ground-
floor bedroom intact. From its single window was visible, in
the rubble-strewn areaway outside, a discarded Nazi flag. It
could have been tossed only from that room. Like all the Nazi
flags that had been dumped, like scarlet garbage, into the corners of alleys, its arrival there was dated. It had surely lain
there from precisely four-thirty of the Tuesday afternoon on
which the American Army officially took over the city and
began its appreciative collection of such German souvenirs as
Nazi flags. Cologne was so thoroughly destroyed by bombings that the German Army did not bother to boobytrap its
ruins, presumably figuring, incorrectly, that they contained
nothing attractive to the American soldier.

The hundred thousand inhabitants of Cologne who lived like
troglodytes in their caves during all our blitzes are now coming up from underground to present themselves, with pale
servility, to the U.S. Army's Military Government, which has
already got a census under way. Three hours after our Army
had fought its last bleeding step in, this military government
started to operate. Much of the impression we make on captive Germany and it makes on us will be formalized in our
first civilian relations with Cologne, our first big conquered

city. The dangerous, comfortable moment in Germany may come when the American administrators, quite naturally, find the obedient, obsequious, efficient enemy Germans easier to deal with than the scatter-brained, individualistic French have been, or the captious Belgians, or the obstinate Dutch.

Fraternization carries a heavy penalty in Cologne. What was called in Aachen, where we began our first relations with the Germans en masse, the sixty-five-dollar question—the amount of the fine, as ordered by General Eisenhower, a soldier had to pay for talking to a German *Mädchen*—has been raised in Cologne to a ten-year prison sentence. I saw a soldier take longer than necessary to discuss with a Cologne *Fräulein* the problem of getting his laundry done, in itself a permitted brief platonic dialogue. An M.P. picked him up, theoretically for ten years. Another soldier nipped by an M.P. proved to be a Pennsylvania Dutch reconnaissance man who was lost and asking his way, in bad German, along the ruined streets. Our Army captured some splendid colored *Stadtpläne*, or city maps, of Cologne, but unfortunately the streets they indicate are often no longer there. Even the city parks are plowed under. To the Germans, with their worshipful sense of iconography, it must be shocking to sit for a moment's rest in a park beneath a blasted tree and a headless statue of the beautiful old Kaiserin Louise.

Cologne contains two important chambers of horrors. It was good that a half dozen of us American journalists viewed them together, so that our eyewitness reports would be unanimous and would be believed. Sometimes it appears that Americans in general and the good-and-bad-Germans school in particular do not wish to hear about Nazi atrocities. One of the great differences between some officers and their men here is that the officers are inclined to believe, even at this late date, that German sadism is a lot of hysterical bunk, whereas their men usually know that it is an unpleasant truth. Certainly the wrecked human beings whom I saw tumbling to liberty through the grilled doorway of the Klingelpütz Gestapo prison on the cold Saturday after our Army had entered Cologne were scarred, starved, in-the-flesh proofs of the existence of very bad Germans indeed. During their first half hour's delirium of freedom and fresh air, these men and women who had been imprisoned for the adultness of their political faith acted like lunatics—sobbing, falling down on the cobblestones of the courtyard, wagging their heads, and holding their temples, where they had most often been beaten. From the nose of one French boy the blood spurted in a pale-pink, excited, pulsing jet. A tall, once strong Dutch workingman kept shouting, in German, "We must never forget! Swear it!" A thin young Belgian, in what had once been good tweeds, stood praying over a mound of earth in the prison courtyard. His father and four other prisoners had been buried there the night before our soldiers came in. The son had made a cross by binding two bits of wood together with a frayed strap he had been using as a belt for his trousers. Then he had prayed. He apologized to me in English for not being shaved. At first he refused a cigarette—"for fear of depriving you." He and his dead father had been resistance men. The most startling member of the group was the still exquisitely pretty Brussels girl in a saintly blue rain cape who had spent nineteen months of her nineteen years in Gestapo prisons for having helped R.A.F. fliers to escape. Another surprise was a seventy-year-old Dutch grandmother, complete with dignity, four languages, gold-rimmed glasses, and a decent black fur coat. She had listened to the London B.B.C. broadcasts. There were also several blond, tubercular Russian girls, some terrified-looking, speechless Poles, and three completely crazed Germans. One liberated Frenchman was a Montmartre café waiter who had refused to go to Germany to work and had therefore been sent there and put in a concentration camp, the first of a series of nine camps. He had escaped nine times and been caught nine times. His eyes, teeth, hands, head, and feet had all been injured by the beatings the Germans had given him. In one camp, on the Vistula River, he had labored one summer, along with some starving Poles, dredging sand to make a bathing beach for the *Herrenvolk* officers.

The second horror chamber was the Gestapo office in the Apellhof Platz, across from the court of appeals it had ignored. Near the curiously undamaged office, on a mattress in the middle of a wrecked street, lay three young non-German corpses. These were the bodies of men who were being dragged by two Gestapo men to the questioning room when an American shell fell and, perhaps fortunately, killed all five men. High above them lay a sixth victim of the same shell: a well-to-do, stay-at-home old German, still wearing a nice blue suit and his wedding ring, his prosperous person caught, but still intact, underneath the staircase on the second-floor landing of his big house, half of which had been sheared away just an inch from where he lay. Below the Gestapo office was a small sub-basement cell where, the Klingelpütz prisoners said, the Gestapo had hung other prisoners six at a time by crowding them into a row, standing them on stools, dropping nooses around their necks from an overhead bar, and then kicking the stools out from beneath their feet. One Italian became a legend by kicking his stool loose himself and shouting, as his final strangled words, *"Viva l'Italia! Viva la libertà!"*

The Gestapo sub-basement smelled of a rotting haunch of horsemeat from which a hoof still dangled. Supplies, apparently, had run low as the Americans approached the city. In the office were files containing some copies of an S.S. French-language leaflet destined for French slave-labor gangs in Germany. The leaflet said, "French comrades, conscious of the future of thy country, thou canst not remain neutral in this conflict, thou shouldst take up arms to fight at thy European brothers' sides. Thy country sinks beneath Jewish-Anglo-American bombs. Thy parents lie amid the ruins. Come avenge them. Come with us to chase these assassins from France, give thyself the honor of not leaving this task to Germans alone. Come combat with us the true enemies of thy land, those who turn it into a vast cemetery, the Jews. France will relive, thanks to thee, and thou wilt participate with us in its arising again in the new National Socialist regime which we will set up after our victory. Offer thy services to the French Armed Elite Guard or to the French National Socialist movement, 7 Freytagstrasse, in Düsseldorf."

The buildings of architectural interest in Cologne have been seventy-five-per-cent destroyed, the Fine Arts and Monuments section of our Army reports. The Wallraf-Richartz Museum, which contained good paintings of the South German and Cologne schools of 1300–1550, including various Altdorfers, Cranachs, and Dürers, and Stephan Lochner's famous "Madonna in an Arbor of Roses," was demolished, a loss in itself because of its fine cloisters, but the paintings had been evacuated. Our art experts figure only a ten-percent damage to Cologne Cathedral, which typical Hohenzollern egotism put over as one of the sublimest in the world, although its pleasant Gothic nave was finished in exactly 1880 (a priest was still on hand with a throwaway historical booklet to give our tourist soldiers) and is only slightly better than Fifth Avenue's St. Patrick's. The really great loss to Cologne and the world are its eleventh-century Romanesque churches, such as the decagonal St. Gereon, which has been cut in two, and, above all, the Apostles' Church, with its twelfth-century side aisles, superb mosaics, and magnificent domed crossing. I stumbled and crawled up a nobly proportioned aisle into which the mosaic dome had crumbled in colored ruin. Overhead, four of the dome's ribs and its lantern, miraculously intact, were outlined as naked, resistant, architectural principles—nearly a thousand years old in wisdom and balance—against the dull modern sky. Across that sky flew a gaggle of nine planes. The mortar shells of the Nazis still fighting on the other side of the Rhine began dropping, a long way off, into what had once been their fine city. The air shook and from the church's injured choir great drops of red mosaics bled down onto the altar.

It is reasonable to think that Cologne's panorama of ruin will be typical of what our rapidly advancing Army will see in city after city. Because Germany is populous, more cities have been destroyed there than in any other country in Europe. Defeat in the last war did not cost Germany a stone. This time the destroyer of others is herself destroyed. This physical destruction of Germany is the one positive reason for thinking that this time the Allies may win the peace. However they decide to divide Germany, her cities, if they are like Cologne, are already divided into morsels of stone no bigger than your hand.

*The New Yorker*, March 31, 1945

# Freed Captives Fill Roads
# That Lead to France

by Marguerite Higgins

FRANKFURT AM MAIN, April 2.—At least 10,000 Polish, Russian, French and other former European slave laborers are roaming through Frankfurt and thousands more are streaming down the roads toward France.

The sudden sweep of the Allied armies liberated large groups of these laborers with such swiftness that it has been impossible to gather the majority into "displaced persons" centers. In fact, in some places there has not even been time to set up centers.

Spontaneously formed battalions, made up primarily of French men and women, many of whom have not seen their homeland for five years, are hurrying down the roads south from Frankfurt and Worms. Smiling and gayly shouting to the jeeps that pass them, the French affect a semi-military formation, marching proudly four abreast and in columns of about twenty deep. Most seemed to be headed for Saarbruecken and Metz.

The foreign workers in this town, which was one of Germany's great industrial centers, are still in a state of bewilderment. A sizable number took to the woods, following the instructions dropped from Allied planes, and only now are filtering back. The military government, with a staff of some twenty people to deal with this whole city, which has a remaining population of some 150,000, has managed to set up a "displaced persons" center. But it has been impossible under the circumstances to inform all the foreign laborers about its existence.

It is a difficult situation. The Russians, French, Poles and others who have been maltreated are looting the food and wine cellars of the Germans now that they are liberated. The military government has not the man power at its disposal at present to station sufficient guards at these places, yet from the military government's point of view these food depots should rightfully be kept intact, so the Germans can depend on themselves for supplies and will not need help from the Allied armies.

But, as one military government officer emphasized, the foreign-workers-vs.-Germans situation is extremely delicate. "I asked a 3d Army lieutenant the other day to help me out by assigning a member of the military police to guard a food store that had been broken into," the officer said. "The lieutenant asked me why, and I said the Russians were looting the store. He replied that as far as he was concerned he would a hell of a lot rather see the Russians eating the food than the Germans."

A graphic example of the attitude of the newly released foreign workers was the case of the group of some 3,000 at a propeller plant at Hedernheim, in the northern suburbs of Frankfurt. Many of the workers had previously escaped into the fields, but after Frankfurt fell they returned to the factory where they had once been slaves, simply because they had no idea what else to do. The long years of docility and subservience to the Germans had left their mark, and they were still taking orders from the guards and directors of the factory.

None of the laborers knew that arrangements had been made to repatriate them. They clamored for information from the reporters. One Frenchman, who has been here since 1940, asked with disbelief, "Do they really still remember us at home?"

New York *Herald Tribune*, April 3, 1945

# Das Deutsches Volk

by Martha Gellhorn

No one is a Nazi. No one ever was. There may have been some Nazis in the next village, and, as a matter of fact, in that town about twenty kilometers away it was a veritable hotbed of Nazidom. To tell you the truth confidentially, there were a lot of Communists here. Oh, the Jews? Well, there weren't really many Jews in this neighborhood. I hid a Jew for six weeks. I hid a Jew for eight weeks. All God's chillun hid Jews.

We have been waiting for the Americans. You came to befriend us. The Nazis are *Schweinhunde*. The Wehrmacht wants to give up but they do not know how. No, I have no relatives in the army. I worked on the land. I worked in a factory. That boy wasn't in the army, either; he was sick. Ach! How we have suffered! The bombs. We lived in the cellars for weeks. We have done nothing wrong. We were never Nazis! . . .

It would sound better if it were set to music. Then the Germans could sing this refrain. They all talk like this. One asks oneself how the Nazi government to which no one paid allegiance managed to carry on this war for five and a half years. Obviously not a man, woman or child in Germany ever approved of the war.

On the other hand, we are not having any of this story and we stand around looking blank and contemptuous, and we listen without friendliness and certainly without respect. To see a whole nation passing the buck is not an enlightening spectacle. At night the Germans take pot shots at Americans or string wires across roads, apt to be fatal to men driving jeeps. They burn the houses of Germans who accept posts in our Military Government or they booby-trap ammunition dumps or motorcycles or anything that is likely to be touched. But that is at night. In the daytime we are the answer to the German prayer.

At the moment we are sitting on the west bank of the Rhine facing the Ruhr pocket. The Germans here are peeved and wish us to push the pocket back ten miles so they will no longer be troubled by their own artillery, which fires into their villages whenever it can spare some shells. The 504th Regiment of the 82d Airborne Division sent a company across the Rhine in landing craft one night and took and held a town for thirty-six hours. On the other side was the Wehrmacht, which was not giving up by any manner of means.

The company of paratroopers drew onto themselves a great deal of armed attention—two German divisions, it was estimated. This relieved pressure at another part of the front but the company lost heavily. When they got back, two officers and four sergeants were decorated with the Silver Star. This ceremony took place in a nondescript street amidst brick rubble and fallen telephone wires outside the regimental command post. The six who received medals were not dressed for the occasion. They had come directly from their work. Their faces were like gray stone from weariness, and their eyes were not like eyes you will see every day around you, and no one was talking about what he'd seen across the river.

The German civilians looked with wonder at this row of dirty, silent men standing in the street. It makes little or no difference to anyone around here whether the Germans are Nazis or not; they can talk their heads off; sing The Star-Spangled Banner. They are still Germans and they are not liked. No one has forgotten yet that our dead stretch back all the way to Africa.

The villages along the Rhine here are in pretty good shape. In the middle, of course, is Cologne, one of the great morgues of the world, but, by and large, these adjacent villages have nothing to complain of. There is food and clothing, coal, bedding, all household equipment and livestock. The Germans are nice and fat, too; clean, orderly and industrious. They carry on their normal lives within seven hundred yards of their army which is now their enemy.

The burgomasters whom we appoint rule the people by decrees which we publish and slap up on the walls. The Germans seem to love decrees and they stand in line busily to read anything new that appears. We went to call on one burgo-

master of a front-line village; he was, he said, a Communist
and a half-Jew and he may be, for all I know, but it is amazing
how many Communists and half-Jews there are in Germany.
He was a workingman before and he says there are plenty of
people in the village who are furious about him being burgomaster; he has got above himself, they think, just because of
the Americans.

If the Americans fired him he would be killed, he said. He
stated this in a perfectly matter-of-fact way.

We said, "Then that means the people here are Nazis."

"No, no," he said. "It is that they think I have too good a
position."

He spoke with some despair about the future of Germany
and finished by saying that America must help Germany to
recover. We listened to this remark with surprise and asked
him why. He admitted that perhaps we had a reason to hate
Germany, but the Germans were relying on our well-known
humanitarianism.

"Nuts," said a sergeant who spoke German.

"Translate nuts," said a lieutenant.

The burgomaster went on to say that if the Americans did
not occupy Germany for fifty years, there would be war again.

"Some man," he said, "with a bigger mouth than Hitler
will come along and promise them everything, and they will
follow, and there will be war again."

"I believe him," said the lieutenant.

"I'd just as soon leave him a little present when we go," the
sergeant said. "I'd just as soon slip him in his pocket a hand
grenade with the pin pulled—him and all the others."

After the tidy villages, Cologne is hard to believe. We are
not shocked by it, which only goes to prove that if you see
enough of anything, you stop noticing it. In Germany when
you see absolute devastation you do not grieve. We have
grieved for many places in many countries, but this is not one
of the countries. Our soldiers say, "They asked for it."

Between two mountains of broken brick and backed by a
single jagged wall, a German had set up a pushcart and was
selling tulips, narcissuses and daffodils. The flowers looked a
little mad in this *décor*, and considering there are no houses to
put flowers in, the whole setup seemed odd. Two young men

on bicycles rode up, and one of them bought a bunch of tulips. We asked him what he wanted tulips for, and he said he was Dutch. So of course he needed the tulips. He had been in forced labor in this city for three years. He and his friend came from Rotterdam. Anything that happened to Cologne was all right with them.

The flower vendor then came over to talk. He made very little money, but before we came, he sold his flowers to the hospitals as well as to some old customers. He was alone in the world now. His family, forty-two of them including his grandparents and parents, his wife and children, his sisters and their children and husbands, had all been buried in one cellar during one air raid. He brought pictures out of his wallet.

The two soldiers and I sat in the jeep and wondered why he talked to us; if forty-two members of our families had been killed by German bombs we would not talk pleasantly to Germans.

A crowd gathered around us; since no one speaks to Germans except on official business, you can collect a crowd anywhere simply by saying *"Guten Tag."* This desire to be chummy baffles us as much as anything. The crowd was varied and everyone talked at once. I asked them when things had started to go bad in Germany. I had a private bet with myself on the answer and I won. Things have been bad in Germany since 1933, they all said loudly.

I said, "No, I am talking about since the war. Since 1941 it has been bad. Why?"

"Because of the bombs."

*"Danke schön,"* said I. Then I asked what form of government they hoped for after the war.

"Democracy," they cried.

But one day in another village it came out much better than that and much more truly; the women said that if they had enough to eat and could live quietly they did not care *who* ruled them. The men said they had not talked politics for eleven years and no longer knew anything about government. However, democracy is a fine word and in frequent use in Germany.

Then I asked them whether they had traveled during the war. Had anyone made a side trip to Paris? No one had traveled anywhere at all: they were assigned their work and they stayed to do it, twelve hours a day. After that, the talk degenerated into the usual condemnation of the Nazis.

We went down to the river front to call on some airborne pals. The company command post was in a candy factory and we were taken to see the vast stocks of sugar, chocolate, cocoa, butter, almonds and finished candies that remained. Then we were led to a huge wine cellar, only one of three they had located. Next we visited a flour warehouse which had more flour in it than any of us had seen at one time. After this (and by now we were all in a temper thinking how well off the Germans had been) we went through a jumble of factory buildings used as a general food depot and we looked with anger on rooms full of Dutch and French cheese, Portuguese sardines, Norwegian canned fish, all kinds of jams and canned vegetables, barrels of sirup and so on.

The Germans had not given up butter for guns but had done very nicely producing or stealing both.

There was a line of German women sitting outside the white tape which marked off the military zone. They were watching their houses. No roof or window remains, and often there is not a wall left, either, and almost everything in those houses has been blown about. But there they sat and kept mournful guard on their possessions. When asked why they did this, they started to weep. We have all seen such beastly and fantastic suffering accepted in silence that we do not react very well to weeping. And we certainly do not react well to people weeping over furniture.

I remembered Oradour, in France, where the Germans locked every man, woman and child of the village into the church and set the church afire, and after the people were burned, the village was burned. This is an extremely drastic way to destroy property. The Germans have taught all the people of Europe not to waste time weeping over anything easy like furniture. Farther down the river, the Military Government was registering German civilians in the villages.

During all the war this village had lost ten civilians dead; during the last week German shells had killed seven more. We talked with some German women about the horrors of war.

"The bombs," they said. "O God, the bombs! Two thousand eight hundred bombs fell on this village alone," they said.

"Don't be crazy," we told them. "There would be no sign of a village if that were true."

"Ah, the bombs!" they said, firmly convinced that their village was flat and they were all dead.

Just across the river the German ack-ack continues to operate. Yesterday it operated effectively and a B-26 was shot down and a column of black smoke rose straight and mountain-high. It looked like a funeral pyre to all of us. The tanks of the Thirteenth Armored Division were moving up across the river behind the burning plane, but the crew were there in a belt of Krauts and no one could reach them. From a 505th observation post, some paratroopers had seen four men get out of the plane. That was at about one o'clock on a soft clear day.

At six o'clock, across the river on the green bank, someone started waving a white flag. This was ignored because it does not necessarily mean anything. Then a procession came down to a landing pier. They carried a Red Cross flag; through binoculars we could see a priest, a medic, and two German soldiers carrying a stretcher. A landing craft put out from our bank, well covered by our machine guns in case this was all a sinister joke. Presently on both banks of the Rhine there was an audience. Normally you would never have moved in this area in daylight. Now we stood cheerfully in the sun and gaped.

Slowly three more stretchers were carried down to our boat. We could see civilians over there, children, German soldiers; everyone was out staring at everyone else. We could not quite believe it and were still prepared to dive for cover. Then the little boat was launched into the current. It landed, and our medic who had gone over to get these four wounded men—the survivors of the B-26 crew—shouted to clear the banks, because the Krauts said they'd give the ambulance time to load and then they would open up.

The war had stopped for approximately an hour on a hundred-yard front.

"I never saw the Krauts act so nice," one soldier said.

"They know our tanks are coming up," another soldier said. "Krauts don't act nice for nothing."

The DPs (Displaced Persons, if you have forgotten) tell us that Krauts never act nice. There are tens of thousands of Russians and Poles and Czechs and French and Yugoslav and Belgian slave laborers around here, and they pour in every day in truckloads to the camps which the 82d Airborne now runs.

There is apparently an inexhaustible supply of human beings who have been torn from their families and have lived in misery with no medical care and on starvation rations while working twelve hours a day for their German masters. They do not feel very kindly toward the Germans, as you can imagine. The only time I have seen a Russian cry was when a Russian nurse, a girl of twenty-five, wept with rage telling of the way her people were treated. They had all seen their dead thrown into huge lime-filled pits which were the communal graves.

"Everywhere the graves became as high as a mountain," she said. The anger of these people is so great that you feel it must work like fire in the earth.

British prisoners of war are starting to come through now, still joking, still talking in understatement but with bitterness behind the jokes and the quiet words. The ones we saw had walked for fifty-two days from the Polish frontier to Hannover, where their tank columns freed them, and on that fearful march those who fell out from hunger and exhaustion died. Their Red Cross parcels kept them alive during five years, but since last November no parcels had arrived. In one small group, nine men had died of starvation after the long march, and their bodies lay for six days in their crowded barracks because for some unknown reason the Germans did not feel like burying them or allowing them to be buried.

"They're not human is all," a New Zealander said.

"I wish they'd let us take charge of the German prisoners," a boy from Wales said.

A man who was lying on the grass near him now spoke up thoughtfully. "You can't really learn to like those people," he said, "unless they're dead."

Meantime, the Germans, untroubled by regret (because after all they did nothing wrong; they only did what they were

told to do), keep on saying with energy, "We are not Nazis."
It is their idea of the password to forgiveness, probably to be
followed by a sizable loan. "We were never Nazis! We are
friends."

There are hundreds of thousands of people in khaki around
here—and equal numbers of foreigners in rags—who simply
cannot see it that way.

*Collier's*, May 26, 1945

# *"A Soldier Died Today"*

by James Agee

IN Chungking the spring dawn was milky when an MP on the graveyard shift picked up the ringing phone in U.S. Army Headquarters. At first he heard no voice on the other end; then a San Francisco broadcast coming over the phone line made clear to him why his informant could find no words. A colonel came in. The MP just stared at him. The colonel stared back. After a moment the MP blurted two words. The colonel's jaw dropped; he hesitated; then without a word he walked away.

It was fresh daylight on Okinawa. Officers and men of the amphibious fleet were at breakfast when the broadcast told them. By noon the news was known to the men at the front, at the far sharp edge of the world's struggle. With no time for grief, they went on with their work; but there, while they worked, many a soldier wept.

At home, the news came to people in the hot soft light of the afternoon, in taxicabs, along the streets, in offices and bars and factories. In a Cleveland barbershop, 60-year-old Sam Katz was giving a customer a shave when the radio stabbed out the news. Sam Katz walked over to the water cooler, took a long, slow drink, sat down and stared into space for nearly ten minutes. Finally he got up and painted a sign on his window: "Roosevelt Is Dead." Then he finished the shave. In an Omaha poolhall, men racked up their cues without finishing their games, walked out. In a Manhattan taxicab, a fare told the driver, who pulled over to the curb, sat with his head bowed, and after two minutes resumed his driving.

Everywhere, to almost everyone, the news came with the force of a personal shock. The realization was expressed in the messages of the eminent; it was expressed in the stammering and wordlessness of the humble. A woman in Detroit said: "It doesn't seem possible. It seems to me that he will be back on the radio tomorrow, reassuring us all that it was just a mistake."

It was the same through that evening, and the next day, and the next: the darkened restaurants, the shuttered night-clubs, the hand-lettered signs in the windows of stores: "Closed out of Reverence for F.D.R."; the unbroken, 85-hour dirge of the nation's radio; the typical tributes of typical Americans in the death-notice columns of their newspapers (said one, signed by Samuel and Al Gordon: "A Soldier Died Today").

It was the same on the cotton fields and in the stunned cities between Warm Springs and Washington, while the train, at funeral pace, bore the coffin up April's glowing South in re-enactment of Whitman's great threnody.

It was the same in Washington, in the thousands on thousands of grief-wrung faces which walled the caisson's grim progression with prayers and with tears. It was the same on Sunday morning in the gentle landscape at Hyde Park, when the burial service of the Episcopal Church spoke its old, strong, quiet words of farewell; and it was the same at that later moment when all save the gravemen were withdrawn and reporters, in awe-felt hiding, saw how a brave woman, a widow, returned, and watched over the grave alone, until the grave was filled.

*Time*, April 23, 1945

# *"For Most of It I Have No Words"*

---

by Edward R. Murrow

---

APRIL 15, 1945

During the last week, I have driven more than a few hundred miles through Germany, most of it in the Third Army sector—Wiesbaden, Frankfurt, Weimar, Jena and beyond. It is impossible to keep up with this war. The traffic flows down the superhighways, trucks with German helmets tied to the radiators and belts of machine-gun ammunition draped from fender to fender. The tanks on the concrete roads sound like a huge sausage machine, grinding up sheets of corrugated iron. And when there is a gap between convoys, when the noise dies away, there is another small noise, that of wooden-soled shoes and of small iron tires grating on the concrete. The power moves forward, while the people, the slaves, walk back, pulling their small belongings on anything that has wheels.

There are cities in Germany that make Coventry and Plymouth appear to be merely damage done by a petulant child, but bombed houses have a way of looking alike, wherever you see them.

But this is no time to talk of the surface of Germany. Permit me to tell you what you would have seen, and heard, had you been with me on Thursday. It will not be pleasant listening. If you are at lunch, or if you have no appetite to hear what Germans have done, now is a good time to switch off the radio, for I propose to tell you of Buchenwald. It is on a small hill about four miles outside Weimar, and it was one of the largest concentration camps in Germany, and it was built to last. As we approached it, we saw about a hundred men in civilian clothes with rifles advancing in open order across the fields. There were a few shops; we stopped to inquire. We were told that some of the prisoners had a couple of SS men cornered in there. We drove on, reached the main gate. The prisoners crowded up behind the wire. We entered.

And now, let me tell this in the first person, for I was the least important person there, as you shall hear. There surged around me an evil-smelling horde. Men and boys reached out to touch me; they were in rags and the remnants of uniform. Death had already marked many of them, but they were smiling with their eyes. I looked out over that mass of men to the green fields beyond where well-fed Germans were ploughing.

A German, Fritz Kersheimer, came up and said, "May I show you round the camp? I've been here ten years." An Englishman stood to attention, saying, "May I introduce myself, delighted to see you, and can you tell me when some of our blokes will be along?" I told him soon and asked to see one of the barracks. It happened to be occupied by Czechoslovakians. When I entered, men crowded around, tried to lift me to their shoulders. They were too weak. Many of them could not get out of bed. I was told that this building had once stabled eighty horses. There were twelve hundred men in it, five to a bunk. The stink was beyond all description.

When I reached the center of the barracks, a man came up and said, "You remember me. I'm Peter Zenkl, one-time mayor of Prague." I remembered him, but did not recognize him. He asked about Benes and Jan Masaryk. I asked how many men had died in that building during the last month. They called the doctor; we inspected his records. There were only names in the little black book, nothing more—nothing of who these men were, what they had done, or hoped. Behind the names of those who had died there was a cross. I counted them. They totalled 242. Two hundred and forty-two out of twelve hundred in one month.

As I walked down to the end of the barracks, there was applause from the men too weak to get out of bed. It sounded like the hand clapping of babies; they were so weak. The doctor's name was Paul Heller. He had been there since 1938.

As we walked out into the courtyard, a man fell dead. Two others—they must have been over sixty—were crawling toward the latrine. I saw it but will not describe it.

In another part of the camp they showed me the children,

hundreds of them. Some were only six. One rolled up his sleeve, showed me his number. It was tattooed on his arm. D-6030, it was. The others showed me their numbers; they will carry them till they die.

An elderly man standing beside me said, "The children, enemies of the state." I could see their ribs through their thin shirts. The old man said, "I am Professor Charles Richer of the Sorbonne." The children clung to my hands and stared. We crossed to the courtyard. Men kept coming up to speak to me and to touch me, professors from Poland, doctors from Vienna, men from all Europe. Men from the countries that made America.

We went to the hospital; it was full. The doctor told me that two hundred had died the day before. I asked the cause of death; he shrugged and said, "Tuberculosis, starvation, fatigue, and there are many who have no desire to live. It is very difficult." Dr. Heller pulled back the blankets from a man's feet to show me how swollen they were. The man was dead. Most of the patients could not move.

As we left the hospital I drew out a leather billfold, hoping that I had some money which would help those who lived to get home. Professor Richer from the Sorbonne said, "I should be careful of my wallet if I were you. You know there are criminals in this camp, too." A small man tottered up, saying, "May I feel the leather, please? You see, I used to make good things of leather in Vienna." Another man said, "My name is Walter Roeder. For many years I lived in Joliet. Came back to Germany for a visit and Hitler grabbed me."

I asked to see the kitchen; it was clean. The German in charge had been a Communist, had been at Buchenwald for nine years, had a picture of his daughter in Hamburg. He hadn't seen her for almost twelve years, and if I got to Hamburg, would I look her up? He showed me the daily ration—one piece of brown bread about as thick as your thumb, on top of it a piece of margarine as big as three sticks of chewing gum. That, and a little stew, was what they received every twenty-four hours. He had a chart on the wall; very complicated it was. There were little red tabs scattered through it. He said that was to indicate each ten men who died. He had to account for the rations, and he added, "We're very efficient here."

We went again into the courtyard, and as we walked we talked. The two doctors, the Frenchman and the Czech, agreed that about six thousand had died during March. Kersheimer, the German, added that back in the winter of 1939, when the Poles began to arrive without winter clothing, they died at the rate of approximately nine hundred a day. Five different men asserted that Buchenwald was the best concentration camp in Germany; they had had some experience of the others.

Dr. Heller, the Czech, asked if I would care to see the crematorium. He said it wouldn't be very interesting because the Germans had run out of coke some days ago and had taken to dumping the bodies into a great hole nearby. Professor Richer said perhaps I would care to see the small courtyard. I said yes. He turned and told the children to stay behind. As we walked across the square I noticed that the professor had a hole in his left shoe and a toe sticking out of the right one. He followed my eyes and said, "I regret that I am so little presentable, but what can one do?" At that point another Frenchman came up to announce that three of his fellow countrymen outside had killed three S.S. men and taken one prisoner. We proceeded to the small courtyard. The wall was about eight feet high; it adjoined what had been a stable or garage. We entered. It was floored with concrete. There were two rows of bodies stacked up like cordwood. They were thin and very white. Some of the bodies were terribly bruised, though there seemed to be little flesh to bruise. Some had been shot through the head, but they bled but little. All except two were naked. I tried to count them as best I could and arrived at the conclusion that all that was mortal of more than five hundred men and boys lay there in two neat piles.

There was a German trailer which must have contained another fifty, but it wasn't possible to count them. The clothing was piled in a heap against the wall. It appeared that most of the men and boys had died of starvation; they had not been executed. But the manner of death seemed unimportant. Murder had been done at Buchenwald. God alone knows how many men and boys have died there during the last twelve years. Thursday I was told that there were more than twenty thousand in the camp. There had been as many as sixty thousand. Where are they now?

As I left that camp, a Frenchman who used to work for Havas in Paris came up to me and said, "You will write some- thing about this, perhaps?" And he added, "To write about this you must have been here at least two years, and after that—you don't want to write any more."

I pray you to believe what I have said about Buchenwald. I have reported what I saw and heard, but only part of it. For most of it I have no words. Dead men are plentiful in war, but the living dead, more than twenty thousand of them in one camp. And the country round about was pleasing to the eye, and the Germans were well fed and well dressed. Ameri- can trucks were rolling toward the rear filled with prisoners. Soon they would be eating American rations, as much for a meal as the men at Buchenwald received in four days.

If I've offended you by this rather mild account of Buchen- wald, I'm not in the least sorry. I was there on Thursday, and many men in many tongues blessed the name of Roosevelt. For long years his name had meant the full measure of their hope. These men who had kept close company with death for many years did not know that Mr. Roosevelt would, within hours, join their comrades who had laid their lives on the scales of freedom.

Back in 1941, Mr. Churchill said to me with tears in his eyes, "One day the world and history will recognize and ac- knowledge what it owes to your President." I saw and heard the first installment of that at Buchenwald on Thursday. It came from men from all over Europe. Their faces, with more flesh on them, might have been found anywhere at home. To them the name "Roosevelt" was a symbol, the code word for a lot of guys named "Joe" who are somewhere out in the blue with the armor heading east. At Buchenwald they spoke of the President just before he died. If there be a better epitaph, history does not record it.

CBS Radio Broadcast, April 15, 1945

# Ernie Pyle

by Evan Wylie

OKINAWA—Ernie Pyle covered Okinawa on D-Day with the Marines. Many of them did not recognize him at first and stared curiously at the small oldish-looking man with the stubby white whiskers and frayed woolen cap. When they did recognize him they said: "Hi, Ernie. What do you think of the war here in the Pacific?" And Pyle smiled and said a little wearily: "Oh, it's the same old stuff all over again. I am awful tired of it." The men watched him climb from the boat, his thin body bent under the weight of his field pack and draped in fatigue clothes that seemed too big for him and they said: "That guy is getting too old for this kind of stuff. He ought to go home."

Ie Shima, where Pyle died, is a small, obscure island off the western coast of Okinawa. The operation was on such a small scale that many correspondents didn't bother to go along. Pyle had been in the ship's sick bay for a week with one of his famous colds. The weather was perfect, with balmy air and bright sunshine. Pyle was ashore on D-plus-one. He stretched out on the sunny slope with Milton Chase, WLW radio correspondent, soaking up the sun and gazing at the picturesque landscape and gently rolling fields dotted with sagebrushlike bushes and clumps of low pine trees. The country, he said, was the way Italy must be in summertime. That was only a guess, he added, because he was in Italy in the middle of winter. Most of all, it reminded him of Albuquerque. "Lots of people don't like the country around Albuquerque," he said, "but it suits me fine. As soon as I finish this damned assignment I'm going back there and settle down for a long time."

A young officer came up to report that the Japs were blowing themselves up with grenades. "That's a sight worth seeing," he said. Chase asked Pyle what his reaction to the Jap dead was. Pyle said dead men were all alike to him, and it made him feel sick to look at one. A wounded soldier with a bloody bandage on his arm came up the slope and asked Pyle for his autograph. "Don't usually collect these things," he told Pyle sheepishly, "but I wanted yours. Thanks a lot."

The operation was going so well that most of the correspondents left that night. There had been hardly any casualties and only a very few of these were killed. Pyle was in the midst of preparing a story on a tank-destroyer team, so he stayed on. He was wearing green fatigues and a cap with a Marine emblem. He was with a few troops when he died, standing near Lt. Col. Joseph B. Coolidge of Helena, Mont. The Jap machine gun that got him took the group by surprise.

Pyle had proceeded to the front in a jeep with Col. Coolidge. As they reached a crossroads, still some distance from the front lines, the Jap machine gun, hidden in a patch of woods, suddenly opened up on them. The gun was a sleeper. Our troops had been moving up and down the road all morning and most of the day before. This was the first time it had revealed itself.

Pyle and the others jumped from the jeep and took cover in a ditch beside the road. The machine gun fired another long burst, and Pyle was dead. The rest withdrew. Several groups attempted to recover the body, once with the support of tanks, but each time they were driven back.

At 1500, Chaplain N. B. Saucier of Coffeeville, Miss., received permission to attempt to recover the body with litter-bearers. T-5 Paul Shapiro of Passaic, N.J., Sgt. Minter Moore of Elkins, W. Va., Cpl. Robert Toaz of Huntington, N.Y., and Sgt. Arthur Austin of Tekamah, Neb., volunteered to go with him. The crossroads lay in open country that offered no cover. The men crawled up the ditch, dragging the litter behind them. Army Signal Corps photographer Cpl. Alexander Roberts of New York City preceded them and was the first man to reach the body.

Pyle lay on his back in a normal resting position. His unmarked face had the look of a man sleeping peacefully. He had died instantly from a bullet that penetrated the left side of his helmet and entered the left temple. His hands folded across his chest still clutched his battered cap, said to be the same one he carried through his previous campaigns. The litter-bearers placed the body on the stretcher and worked their way slowly back along the ditch under sniper fire. The battle for Ie Shima still remained to be won.

The island probably will be remembered only as the place where America's most famous war correspondent met the death he had been expecting for so long.

*Yank*, May 18, 1945

# Letters from Paris

by Janet Flanner (Genêt)

### *"Let Us Weep For This Man": The French Mourn Roosevelt*

APRIL 19 (BY WIRELESS)

THE DEATH of President Roosevelt caused a more personal grief among the French than the deaths of their own recent great men. On the demise of both Papa Clemenceau and Marshal Foch, their grief was a nationalistic, patriotic emotion, since these men, the one with his sabre-sharp tongue, the other with his sword, had saved France. The sorrow the French felt at losing Roosevelt seemed like someone's private unhappiness multiplied by millions. Friday morning, when the news was first known here, French men and women approached the groups of Americans in uniform standing on street corners and in public places and, with a mixture of formality and obvious emotion, expressed their sorrow, sometimes in French, sometimes in broken English. On the Rue Scribe, a sergeant in a jeep held up traffic while he received the condolences of two elderly French spinsters. In the Jardin des Tuileries, an American woman was stopped beneath the white-flowering chestnut trees by a French schoolboy who, with trembling voice, spoke for his father, a dead Army officer, to express his father's love for the dead President. At the outdoor flower stalls of the Place de la Madeleine, a patriarchal flower vendor gave a passing and startled paratrooper a free pink tulip, with the statement "Today they will be sending beautiful flowers for your great man. How sad." A café waitress naïvely touched the sublime when she said of his death, *"C'est ennuyeux pour toute l'humanité."*

On Friday morning, the Germans' Stuttgart radio, the first enemy station to show signs of life that day, interrupted a hysterical patriotic harangue to announce Roosevelt's death, without comment. By Saturday it had worked out its new anti-American propaganda line. It no longer mentioned the man it had consistently heckled as President Rosenfeldt, but declared that President Truman was already viewed with skepticism by the United States and that if he fulfilled his promise to follow those White House policies which had started this second World War, he would have the distinction of starting the third.

Since the American system for filling the Presidential chair when it is left vacant by death was unknown to most French citizens, the journals here carried an official explanatory paragraph headed *"Monsieur Truman Sera Président Jusqu'en 1948"* and quoted our Constitution. The Paris press wrote of F.D.R. with sober magnificence and sincere superlatives. Under the spirited Gallic headline *"Vive Roosevelt!,"* the *Libération-Soir* spoke of "the unjust destiny and yet the ancient grandeur of the event." *Le Monde*, in an editorial entitled *"Après Roosevelt,"* began by saying, "The great voice which directed American political destinies has been hushed, but its echo continues in French souls." In conclusion, it praised "his charm, his beautiful and great words," and said, "Let us weep for this man and hope that his wise and generous conception of the human communities remains like a light to brighten the path for all men of good will." De Gaulle's Minister of Foreign Affairs said, "It is not only appropriate but necessary to express the depth of the sadness of the government and of the French people. Roosevelt was one of the most loved and venerated men in France. He takes with him the tenderness of the French nation." Which is true.

The increasing malaise, now that Roosevelt must be absent from the peace, and the unexpected return last Saturday of thousands of French prisoners liberated from Germany, juxtaposed fear and happiness in a way Parisians will probably always remember in recalling that historic weekend. On Saturday, eight thousand French male prisoners were flown back from Germany in American transport planes, which afterward tumultuously circled the city while the men were being unpacked from trucks outside the newly decorated reception center in the Gare d'Orsay. On its walls these weary men saw an astonishing series of modernistic bas-reliefs depicting their welcome return to the freedom of what explanatory signs called *"la liberté d'aimer"* and the liberty to play, to sleep, to work, to eat, to drink, and to breathe freely. Few of the prisoners, in their hasty flight from the German Army and their later flight with the Americans in the skies, had heard our sad news. When they did hear it, one thin, bitter blond Frenchman said, "*Voyez-vous.* We've come home too late."

The next day, the first contingent of women prisoners arrived by train, bringing with them as very nearly their only baggage the proofs, on their faces and their bodies and in their weakly spoken reports, of the atrocities that had been their lot and the lot of hundreds of thousands of others in the numerous concentration camps our armies are liberating, almost too late. These three hundred women, who came in exchange for German women held in France, were from the prison camp of Ravensbrück, in the marshes midway between Berlin and Stettin. They arrived at the Gare de Lyon at eleven in the morning and were met by a nearly speechless crowd ready with welcoming bouquets of lilacs and other spring flowers, and by General de Gaulle, who wept. As he shook hands with some wretched woman leaning from a window of the train, she suddenly screamed, *"C'est lui!,"* and pointed to her husband, standing nearby, who had not recognized her. There was a general, anguished babble of search, of finding or not finding. There was almost no joy; the emotion went beyond that, to something nearer pain. So much suffering lay behind this homecoming, and it showed in the women's faces and bodies.

Of the three hundred women whom the Ravensbrück *Kommandant* had selected as being able to put up the best appearance, eleven had died en route. One woman, taken from the train unconscious and placed on a litter, by chance opened her eyes just as de Gaulle's color guard marched past her with the French tricolor. She lifted an emaciated arm, pointed to the flag, and swooned again. Another woman, who still had a strong voice and an air of authority, said she had been a camp nurse. Unable to find her daughter and son-in-law in the crowd, she began shouting "Monique! Dominique!" and crying out that her son and husband had been killed fighting in the resistance and now where were those two who were all she had left? Then she sobbed weakly. One woman, six years ago renowned in Paris for her elegance, had become a bent, dazed, shabby old woman. When her smartly attired brother, who met her, said, like an automaton, "Where is your luggage?," she silently handed him what looked like a dirty black sweater fastened with safety pins around whatever small belongings were rolled inside. In a way, all the women looked alike: their faces were gray-green, with reddish-brown circles around their eyes, which seemed to see, but not to take in. They were dressed like scarecrows, in what had been given them at camp, clothes taken from the dead of all nationalities. As the lilacs fell from inert hands, the flowers made a purple carpet on the platform and the perfume of the trampled flowers mixed with the stench of illness and dirt.

The Ravensbrück prisoners were only an unexpected addition to a day of memorable gloom in Paris. An hour before their arrival, a brief and dramatic memorial service for our President had been held in Notre Dame. Great crowds of silent Parisians thronged the *Parvis* before the cathedral. Inside, behind the high altar, taps was sounded by a trumpet. "The Star-Spangled Banner" was played slowly as a dead march, and a prayer of intercession to the Virgin Queen of Heaven for the soul of a Democratic, Episcopalian President and the "Kyrie Eleison" were splendidly chanted, in fine diction, into a microphone by an Army chaplain. At the conclusion, the Garde Républicaine, in white breeches and gold helmets, made a semicircle inside the cathedral and an honor line outside its door, through which marched the cameo-faced Parisian Cardinal Suhard, with his ebony cane; a purple-robed Bishop; Madame L'Ambassadrice Américaine, with His Excellency; and General de Gaulle, followed by his Cabinet, including its assembly speaker, Le Père Blanc Carrière, white-haired, white-socked, and in his religious order's hooded white-wool robe.

The death of a global figure like Roosevelt produces a political vacuum. It is already being filled here by an inrush of worldly suppositions. These are diverse. According to them, de Gaulle will benefit from Roosevelt's death, bourgeois France will lose, Republican France will gain by coming closer, through her alliance with Russia and against England, to her goal of a nonmonarchial Latin bloc—a non-Fascist, kingless Italy, Spain, Portugal, and France, which will establish an anti-Queen Victorian Mediterranean. Churchill, London, and all royalty, including the Greek, will lose insofar as their old-fashioned balance-of-power notion of a controlled Europe will suffer. Germany will lose, because Roosevelt was her worthy enemy; Germany will gain, because the international and local rich he fought will revive Germany's cartelized industrial power. Europe as a whole, these speculations continue, will gain, insofar as it will settle its own fate, free of the too carefully guiding White House hand and the power of the Downing Street cigar. These notions, too, are tributes to that rare American figure who has, on the Continent, left his own great mark—a void.

*The New Yorker*, April 28, 1945

### "A Sad Homecoming": Prisoners from Ravensbrück

APRIL 25 (BY WIRELESS)
RAVENSBRÜCK is not in the prewar "Baedeker" of northern Germany. It will figure, however, as a very important name in any post-war handbook that stars places for their exceptional interest as historical Nazi torture centers. Ravensbrück has already become famous as the *Straflage*, or punishment camp, for women of all the occupied nations, is at this writing still in German-held Germany, and has more than thirty thousand inmates. In exchange for four hundred stout German women, three hundred of the healthiest French women that could be found were recently selected by the Ravensbrück *Kommandantur* and returned to Paris. Only eleven of them died on the homeward journey, which took nearly two weeks.

I talked to one of the younger survivors, the friend of a friend of mine. She had been part of the French bourgeois resistance movement. In May, 1943, she had been arrested by the Gestapo in her parents' comfortable flat in the St. Sulpice quarter of Paris. Her job in the resistance was the passing on of orders transmitted to her, as they were to hundreds of others, by the de Gaulle Free French of London, via the radio, in a surrealistic code that produced announcements like "Message for Colette. The China pears are dancing in my grandmother's garden." Somebody in France, perhaps under torture, gave both the code key and the code names to the Germans. The young woman was identified, thrown into the suburban prison of Fresnes, and, in March, 1944, shipped in a freight car, as a political deportee, to Ravensbrück. Colette— that is not her name—was twenty-five and, according to her friend, was a big-boned, attractive, still adolescent-looking brunette, individualistic, healthy, strong-willed. I saw her three days after her arrival in Paris on April 14, 1945. Her sorrowing blue eyes looked like the eyes of someone who has almost died. She said she had always been thin; her torso now seemed to consist only of her broad shoulder bones. Her black, curly hair looked lifeless, but, by whatever laws of chance account for the survival of anything in a Nazi camp, it had never been shaved. Her mind seemed quiet and clear. Her only trouble was loss of memory, which embarrassed her; she had suffered intermittent amnesia because she had been starved. She had lived through constant and humiliating horrors, some of which *"on ne peut pas nommer."* What she remembered most explicitly and chose to talk about were the thirty thousand women she had lived among in Ravensbrück.

Thousands of women dwelt and died at Ravensbrück, in terror, confusion, pain, and despair, without even knowing where they were. They were on a flat, featureless marshland lying between Stettin and Berlin. The camp is made up of twenty-five buildings, each of which was intended to house five hundred but in the past year has been crammed with twelve hundred. While Colette was there, the women slept four to a single bunk. They had to lie on their sides, the feet of two of them in the faces of the other two. Even the thirty to fifty who died every day afforded only a temporary relief, when their bedfellows carried them off to the pile of corpses which accumulated each night on the cold tile floor of the washroom and which crowded the living the next morning as they cleaned up for the first, pre-dawn roll call, in which there were always newcomers to take the places of the dead. The first call came at 2 or 2:30 A.M. Dressed in their blue-and-white striped prison dresses, with their numbers on their sleeves and a red triangle for political deportees, green for common criminals, and black for slave laborers who had refused to work, the horde lined up out of doors, in the cold and dark, to be counted. They were speechless and motionless, even when the woman next in line fainted or fell dead. It took about two hours for the counting call, which conveniently overlapped with the work call, which ended at 6 A.M. with orders telling what battalions were to do what labor for the day. The calls were supervised by uniformed women guards—superior Germans called *Offizierinnen*, who were the bosses, and inferior Poles called *Blokowas*, each of whom supervised a *Blok*, or house, and *Stubewas*, each of whom was merely in charge of a *Stube*, or room. Since Hitler had declared the Poles to be subhuman, the rank they had been accorded was apparently calculated to humiliate the other Europeans, who actually minded only their cruelty. The Poles, terrified at the prospect of losing their jobs, all too humanly terrorized the prisoners as a means of holding onto those jobs, and they outdid the *Offizierinnen* in lashing the wavering women with the straps all the guards carried. Some of the straps had a heavy rubber weight at the tip.

On Colette's first day at camp, she was ordered, with several other women, to appear naked for a medical examination before an S.S. doctor, who made personal comments. Then he perfunctorily examined each woman's throat and carefully examined her mouth for gold teeth, which were noted down, since in death the woman who had them would still be valuable. The last six months Colette was in Ravensbrück, breakfast, which had consisted of a cup of ersatz coffee and a sliver of black bread, was omitted, because of Germany's increasing food shortage. After what should have been the breakfast hour, some women were marched off to the neighboring sandy marshes to dig drainage ditches, part of a *Geopolitik* arable-land scheme. Others were put to work sorting dead or captured Russians' uniforms, always without the buttons, which had already been salvaged by Nazi war-metal scavengers. The uniforms were always dirty, often bloody, and frequently lousy. The women thought it was from these lice that the many cases of typhus came, as well as what they supposed was cholera. Cholera or not, many of their comrades turned black when they died. Once, before Colette's arrival at the camp, some of the prisoners worked in the camp tailoring shop on the white Nazi uniforms destined for the final, disastrous winter campaign in Russia. Colette at first was marched two miles four times a day to and from work in an isolated, marshbound factory belonging to Siemens, the great German electrical firm, in peacetime admired by doctors for the world-famous and helpful therapeutic machines it produced. Her first march was to the factory after breakfast, or the lack of breakfast; her second and third marches were back and forth for the noon dinner—thin soup and black bread—which during her last six months there was the only meal of the day, for there never had been a supper. Toward the end, as the women trained for the factory work died faster and the Wehrmacht's needs increased, a Siemens factory unit was set up nearer the camp, to save strength and time.

Whatever the women worked at, they worked an eleven-hour day without a breathing spell, except for the noon meal. If they paused even for a deep sigh, they were lashed or kicked by the women guards. The women around the age of forty stood it all best. The young became desperate. The old, usually bewildered mothers, arrested as hostages because they had sons or husbands in the resistance, perished fast. Colette came back after work at six-thirty, to a camp that stank of dysentery and death. In wintertime, the plumbing froze. The toilets were clogged to their brim. It was always at least eight o'clock before she could find a place to wash in the wash-room, less crowded than it was mornings, when the dead were also there. Washing every night was an act of morale which kept the more intelligent women going. Colette said that it was at first her will and then her hate that kept her alive. She had never hated anybody before. She learned to hate the Germans because what they had carefully organized and what she lived in, as part of a planned political program, made them different from all other modern peoples and iso-lated them from civilization. The theory that sadism was the thing that made the cruelties of the camp bearable to those who inflicted them seemed to her disproved by the fact that the guards who lashed at her were women, who in abnormal-ity are more inclined to masochism. In the end, she felt that the cruelties were merely natural to a fanatical race, that it was the German spirit which inflicted them.

With difficulty, I put to Colette the final, frightful question:

Was there a gas chamber and a crematorium at Ravensbrück? This proved to be one of the things which, perhaps for a double reason, Colette said *"on ne peut pas nommer."* Before leaving the camp, the released French prisoners had been blackmailed by the Nazi camp *Kommandant* into promising not to reveal "the worst" of the camp; if such news reached the press in France, "the worst," whatever it was, would be meted out at random among those thousands of women remaining behind. So Colette spoke instead of the worst at Auschwitz, the Silesian camp for Poles and Jews, some of whose overflow of Jewish women seeped into Ravensbrück. Wherever gas chambers and crematoriums existed, she said, they had lately been used only once a month, because of Germany's cob shortage.

The severest Ravensbrück punishment, which often led to death, was twenty-five blows on the bare buttocks with a heavy stick. This was administered by an S.S. officer. An S.S. doctor was always present to test the victim's heart reaction. If the prisoner's heart could stand only ten blows, the doctor called a halt; the remaining fifteen were administered the next day. Septicemia developing in unhealed flesh wounds caused by such beatings was a commonplace. Prisoners were beaten for the possession of jewelry or of a prayer book of any faith, those two disparate treasures here on earth.

All the prisoners' watches, wedding rings, money, clothes, blankets, and other possessions were taken from them when they entered; a receipt, a typical legal Nazi flourish, was given them. In Auschwitz there were daughters of the three or four most famous, rich, and powerful Jewish families in all Christendom—girls who, after the Nuremberg law, had proudly worn around their throats a gold star of David on a beautiful gold chain. These emblems had been snatched from them. In Ravensbrück no one ever got anything back which had once been handed over.

Every day Colette's mother mailed her a parcel from Paris; in a year she received only ten. The Swiss Red Cross whose young Dr. Mayer was responsible for the delicate negotiations that finally released the three hundred French women, apparently left thousands of packages at the Ravensbrück outer office; few were ever seen inside the barracks. According to

Colette, the German *Offizierinnen* and the Polish *Blokowas* and *Stubewas* took charge of the packages—as they did of the slightly thicker soup and toasted black bread which were the S.S. doctors' concession to women palpably sick to death with starvation and dysentery—and then occasionally tossed sweaters and scarves (sent from occupied, bombed-out homes) to a few lucky prisoners to prevent their freezing and stopping work.

In prison, where there was no money, everything yet had its price. The women were entitled to a mark or so a day for their labor, provided they signed a paper declaring that they were voluntary laborers for Germany. Being a political deportee and anti-Fascist, Colette refused to sign. A few German women in the camp wore the black badge which indicated that they had refused to work for the *Partei* in labor gangs. Yet even these Germans showed no spirit of fellowship with the other women.

Up to the day Colette left, new wretches from everywhere were constantly being brought into camp, and this gave it an air of dreadful busyness, dramatized by the new arrivals' shrieks of fear throughout their first night and by their first beatings the next morning. Ravensbrück was not only the *Straflage* but the liberation camp for the women of all the occupied countries, so general despair was mixed with the exultation of those few who came there only to go on to liberty. Like all German prison camps, it was run exclusively by S.S. men. Aside from the constant comings and occasional goings of prisoners, which provided a little weak talk, and aside from a dazed curiosity to know who had just died, there was almost no conversation in the monotony of horrors at Ravensbrück. At night, when each set of four women had fitted themselves, with disgust, head to feet and stomach against buttocks so as not to fall from their narrow bunk, they lay, without whispering, in agonizing exhaustion instead of sleep. They could hear the baying of the guardian dogs, fine German police and Belgian breeds, trained so that even when on leash in the daytime they would leap at and bite passing prisoners. At night, on the loose, the dogs snuffled and growled outside the barracks.

As the Allied armies swung over the Rhine, Ravensbrück began to change and seemed to be getting ready for the inevitable. Some Dutch women who had appeared at the camp early this spring, when the English began making inroads into Holland, were set, under the lash, to planting hastily prepared flower gardens, which would brighten up the grounds if the Allies didn't arrive too soon, and the barracks were given a fresh coat of paint on the outside. Inside, the deaths continued.

When Colette was told that she had been chosen as one of the three hundred French women to be exchanged, she didn't believe that any of them would actually leave. Three days before the great day, the three hundred were ordered into the camp showers, which terrified them, since they knew that in camps in which gas is used, the victims were often sent into the showers beforehand so that their pores would be well opened for the gas. After bathing, Colette and the two hundred and ninety-nine others were given cotton dresses and drawers and their shoes and stockings and prison blankets were taken away from them. For three days, in bed and out, they shivered with confusion, expectancy, incredulity, hope, and cold, in the damp, German spring. On the last day, they were given some dead civilians' clothes — coats, shoes, and stockings, and scarves for their heads. In a final parade of authority, the *Offizierinnen*, *Blokowas*, and *Stubewas* accompanied them to the camp gate, lashing at them with the leather straps in farewell.

Outside the camp, the prisoners climbed into trucks driven by Canadian prisoners of war. The Canadians were like the first figures in a good dream. Then came three days of nightmares when the trucks ran out of gasoline and were held up in a small Bavarian town. Only when the prisoners crossed the border into Switzerland did they feel safe. In relief, a few of the older women died. The two hundred and eighty-nine living French women arrived in Paris at the Gare de Lyon on the Saturday morning after President Roosevelt died. As Colette said, it would have been a sad homecoming in any case. Neither she nor any of the other women could forget what they had learned by heart and in body. On their minds, and in their memories, were the thirty thousand other women still in Ravensbrück.

*The New Yorker*, May 5, 1945

# The Russians

by Martha Gellhorn

THERE was one Russian guard standing on the ponton bridge on our side of the Elbe. He was small and shaggy and bright-eyed. He waved to us to stop and came over to the jeep and spoke Russian very fast, smiling all the time. Then he shook hands and said, *"Amerikanski?"* Then he shook hands again, and we saluted each other.

A silence followed, during which we all smiled. I tried German, French, Spanish and English in that order: We wanted to cross the Elbe to the Russian side and pay a visit to our allies. None of these languages worked. The Russians speak Russian. The G.I. driver now made a few remarks in Russian which filled me with wonder and admiration.

"How did you ever learn?" I asked.

"You got to talk a little bit of everything to get around these days," he said modestly.

The Russian guard had listened and digested our request and he now answered. The operative word in his answer was *niet*. It is the only word in Russian I know but you hear it a lot, and afterward there is no use arguing.

So we drove back to the command post of a Russian officer who perhaps controlled that bridge. Here we had another brilliant and enjoyable conversation filled with handshakes, laughter and good will. The operative word again was *niet*. It was suggested that I go to a building in Torgau, a little way farther back from the river, where I would find more of my compatriots who were waiting for one thing or another. This was a gray, square German house outside of which were parked jeeps and staff cars belonging to various American and English officers waiting to cross the Elbe on business.

The situation seemed to be permanently snafu. The atmosphere was one of baffled but cordial resignation. Officers stood in the street and speculated on Russian time, which was either one or two hours earlier or later than ours. They asked themselves whether the Russian general who was due today (they thought) but who had actually arrived and departed yesterday would possibly come tomorrow and, if so, at whose hour—ours or theirs?

They said that it was pointless to try to telephone across the river because the telephone which was located in the first office I had visited was in a purely experimental stage, and anyhow you never got an answer to anything by telephone—if in the first place the telephone worked and you happened to reach anyone at the other end. They said, "This is the way it is, chum, and you may as well get used to waiting because wait is what you do." You could only cross the Elbe to the Russian side if accompanied by a Russian officer who had come to take you to a specific place for a specific purpose. There was no nonsense about walking across a few hundred yards of ponton bridge and fraternizing with your allies.

It was quite agreeable in the sun and the street was interesting. Two Russian girl soldiers passed, and a Russian nurse wearing a pistol very competently on her hip. A Russian soldier, in a blue coverall, with lovely blue eyes to match, wandered up and said, *"Amerikanski?"* and shook everyone's hand and was treated to a flood of G.I. jokes, to which he responded with smiles and the word *"Russki."* Then he said *"Na"* with a little sigh, and shook hands all around again and went about his business.

The morning wore on, and obviously nothing was going to happen, so we drove through the Russian part of Torgau and across a bridge guarded by M.P.s and went to battalion headquarters for lunch. There we found a very large, jolly, soiled Russian colonel and his interpreter doing their best to cope with the plateful of K rations. They were no more enthusiastic about K rations than we are, which proves them to be men of taste, but they did like the coffee.

No one was looking very spic and span in battalion headquarters, due to the fact that combat troops have a tendency to be too hurried and occupied to look spic and span. Also there is usually no water in newly liberated towns. However, the Russians all looked as if they hadn't had time for a bath since Stalingrad, so we felt perfectly cozy.

The colonel was delightful and had a handshake like the final death squeeze of a grizzly bear. Through his interpreter he said he would take me across the Elbe tonight, as he was going back to his division headquarters, and he would call for me at 5:30.

After a certain amount of discussion we agreed on whose 5:30 that would be, his or ours, and everyone was happy. At 5:30, he had not come, and runners went out to search for him. At 6:30, I went back to the Russian part of Torgau and tracked him down.

He insisted that I come and eat with them as they were having a little snack. The little snack was a dream—hard-boiled eggs, three kinds of sausage, pickles, butter, honey and various wines. I decided then and there that the Russians had a more sensible approach to rationing than we have; it may be old-fashioned but it is effective and it saves a lot of trouble. You live off the land, and any land can beat K rations.

Then we began to talk about crossing the Elbe. It appeared that the colonel had not understood my request; no, it would be impossible to go unless the general gave his permission. Then could he telephone the general? What? Now? Yes, now.

"Time is money," said the interpreter sagely.

"Oh, hell!" said I, not so sagely.

"You are in such a hurry," said the colonel. "We will talk this all over later."

"You do not understand," I said. "I am a wage slave. I work for a bunch of capitalist ogres in New York who drive me night and day and give me no rest. I will be severely punished if I hang around here eating with your citizens when it is my duty to my country to cross the Elbe and salute our gallant allies."

They thought this was fine, but still nothing happened.

"Go and call the general," I said, trying the wheedle angle. "What difference will it make to the general if one insignificant female correspondent pays him a visit?"

"Hokay," said the colonel, that being an English word he knew. He went out to telephone the general and more time passed.

There was another colonel and between mouthfuls of hard-boiled eggs we had a splendid talk. We discussed the Germans and were in perfect agreement all along the line. We discussed the American Army and were in perfect agreement all along the line. I was told of the wonders of Russia, which I have never seen, and was urged to visit the Crimea in the summer since it is of surpassing beauty. I said I would. I was asked what I thought about the Russian army. I said I would give anything to see it, but in the meantime I thought it was won-derful—the whole world thought it was wonderful.

We had a few toasts. We toasted *"Trumann"* for quite a while before I realized we were toasting the President; the way they said it, I imagined it was some crisp Russian term meaning "Bottoms up!" Then the colonel came back. The operative word again was *niet*. I do not really think he had telephoned the general but it was *niet* anyhow.

The conversation had been purely gay, and then all of a sudden it got serious. We were talking about their medals. They do not wear ribbons, they wear the entire medal—offi-cers and men alike—and they are worn on both sides of the chest and look terrific. There are handsome enamel decora-tions for killing Germans. I believe each decoration equals fifty dead Germans but I am not sure of this, and there are medals for individual heroism and for battles.

"Let us go out and walk," said the colonel. "We must not be sad. We hate war and we would like to go home, for it is many years since we have been home. But we kill Germans as long as they ask for it, and meantime it is a nice night so we will go walking."

Torgau in the evening was a very picturesque place; from one building there came the lovely, sad sound of Russian singing, low and slow and mourning; from another a young man leaned out of a window and played a very fast bright tune on a harmonica. Rare-looking types wandered around the street; there is the greatest possible variety in the faces and uniforms of the Russian soldiery. There were blonds and Mongols and fierce-looking characters with 19th century mus-taches, and children of about sixteen; it felt like a vast en-campment of nomad people when everyone is eating around campfires, singing, playing cards and getting ready to roll in blankets and sleep.

There were a few stray shots and a few stray drunks, and no

one paid the slightest attention naturally. We then passed a couple of burning houses which looked very pretty indeed, and a yard where a wealth of Torgau bicycles had been collected and stashed. Tomorrow, no doubt, more of the Russian army would be mobile.

I said it was all charming. But how about getting across the Elbe?

"In two weeks," the colonel said, "I am sure it will be arranged."

If there was anything I was sure of, it was that I wouldn't be waiting around Torgau for two weeks. "It is a political question," said the interpreter. "You are capitalists and we are Communists."

I told them very heatedly that I did not consider it any of my business whether they were Mormons, cannibals or ballet-omanes, the point being that we were allies and very naturally we were interested in each other and each other's armies. No one, said I crossly, minded where *they* went; their correspondents moved freely with our armies, and everyone was delighted to see them. If, on the other hand, they acted in this suspicious and unfriendly manner it would make everyone very peeved and it would be their own fault. We were eager to understand them and none of us in these parts was interested in politics; it would be nice if they acted more open-hearted for a change.

They agreed to this but said that in their army nothing was done without permission. The permission had not been granted as yet.

"All right," I said, "but unless we can all circulate freely amongst each other, there will be no trust and no confidence, and that will be very terrible."

"It will be arranged in time; you will see," said the colonel.

In the morning the ponton bridge was the center of interest. The day before, to the vast amazement of the G.I.s, some Russian soldiers had appeared and washed the boats which supported the wooden treadway. Today more Russians appeared with pots of green paint and painted the boats. Small fir trees were stuck up along the treadway and it was the prettiest bridge you could hope to see.

Now in the early sunlight a procession of displaced persons

appeared. These were the Russians who had been taken into slavery by the Germans and they were crossing the Elbe to go home. They looked weary and thin and quiet, and it was somehow a sad sight. The Elbe is not very wide and the banks are soft green grass, but as soon as anyone crossed that bridge and disappeared up the opposite bank he might as well have gone to Tibet, because it was forbidden, unimaginable territory.

For a little while, there was relative calm and we sat on a stone wall and watched the river and smoked and talked about nothing. Then gradually the Russian army began to cross the bridge. The army came in like a sort of tide; it had no special shape; there were no orders given. It came and flowed over the stone quay and up onto the roads behind us like water rising, like ants, like locusts. It was not so much an army as a whole world on the move. Knowing nothing of the formation of the Russian army (and never being told by the Russians), one does not know whether this was a regiment or a division or six regiments or six divisions. But it came on and on and on, inchoate, formless and amazing. It was very noisy and slightly mad and it knew exactly what it was doing.

First came men. Men are the mainstay—hordes of them wearing tunics, greatcoats, baggy khaki-ish clothing and carrying a light sort of tommy gun, pistols, grenades and generally assorted munitions. They did not seem to march and they did not seem to be numerically divided into any known groups; they were simply a mass. They looked tired and indifferent and definitely experienced.

Then some trucks bumped over the bridge—God knows what sort of trucks or where manufactured. Quantities of men rode on these; also women. These women were uniformed like the men and equally armed and they looked young, absolutely square in build and tough as prize fighters. We were told that the women were wonderful snipers and that they serve as MPs. At this point a woman arrived at the near end of the bridge carrying two flags, like semaphore flags, and took up her position. She was an MP, and with her flags and a look of authority she proceeded to handle this endless traffic.

A pack train now rumbled across the bridge. It was a honey. It consisted of very beat-up carts and wagons and strong but shabby horses. The drivers handled the horses with a competence that was inspiring and rather like the chariot races in Ben-Hur. The pack trains had everything on them: bedding and clothing and pots and pans and ammunition and also women, because Russian women go to war with their men and it seems a very reasonable idea. These were no glamor girls; they were peasants and they looked as if no hardship would be too much for them.

After the pack train, something like the first locomotive appeared; it was short and had a huge smokestack and it towed two huge wooden cars. The G.I.s on the wall above the river broke into applause, saying, "Here comes the motorized stuff." Men on bicycles pedaled across the bridge, and more men on foot, and then some trucks carrying pontons. The noise was lovely; a sort of splendid Slavic roar and the clang of iron wheels on cobbles and occasional shouts which may have been orders or curses.

There was no visible plan to this exodus. It was entirely unlike anything we had ever seen before and it would be impossible to describe the feeling of power that came from this chaos of men and beat-up material. We thought how bitterly the Germans must have regretted attacking the Russians. We thought anyone would be extremely silly to bother these people, for in these great shapeless numbers they were as overwhelming and terrible as a flow of lava.

And by a miracle this welter of humanity vanished from Torgau and proceeded to infiltrate inland to take up the Russian line along the Mulde River some fifty miles west. I have no idea how this was done: It happened. Many of these men wore the medal of the Battle of Stalingrad, and the whole lot had certainly fought their way west for some 3,000 miles, probably pretty largely on their own feet.

Now it was lunchtime and the exodus stopped temporarily. "The show's over," said a G.I. sitting next to me. Then summing up the whole matter, he said with awe, "My God!" We walked back to the bridge which leads to the American side of Torgau. Two G.I.s were guarding the bridge, and a Russian soldier, about eighteen, stood across the street apparently guarding it also. Three Russian soldiers were leaning over the stone railing in the middle of the bridge. Suddenly there was a loud explosion and a fountain of water coming up from the stream below.

"That's nothing," one of the American guards said, "they're just throwing hand grenades in the water. They're crazy about that. I don't know what it does to them, but if you see one anywhere near a bridge, he's pretty sure to throw a hand grenade in the water."

The Russian guard now crossed the street and said in a voice of wonder, *"Amerikanski?"* To which the G.I.s replied in a tone of equal wonder, *"Russki?"*

Then we all shook hands.

"You can't turn around for Russians shaking hands," the short G.I. said. "Now this Joe, for instance, he's been on this bridge all morning and this is the fourth time he comes over and says *'Amerikanski'* and gives us the handshaking treatment."

"It's to show we're allies," the tall G.I. explained.

"Sure," said the short one. "That's okay by me. I only ask myself how many more times this Joe is going through this routine."

"Look at that ambulance, will you," said the tall one.

We turned and saw something that looked like a furniture van painted green, with small red crosses on its side. It had stopped farther down the street, and now a rank of wounded crawled, limped or hopped out. They had been packed in on a welter of quilts and mattresses, and they disappeared into a house which may have been an aid station.

"That's the first ambulance I've seen," the tall one said. "Seems like if you can walk, you go right along in their army. You see more guys with bandages on their heads. Don't seem to bother them none."

"I used to think we were rugged," the other G.I. said, "until I saw these *Russkis.* Boy, they're really rugged, I mean."

"They're crazy," the tall one said flatly.

"What's the matter?" I asked. "Don't you like them?"

"Sure I like them. They seem like pretty good guys. They're crazy is all."

"I guess they'll push us back to the Rhine pretty soon," the short one said. "They shoved a lot of men over this morning."

"Suits me," his colleague answered. "I hope they push us back quick. I hope they take all of Germany. They know how to handle it, brother. They really know. Suits me. What I want is to go home."

# *"A Giant Whirlpool of Destruction"*

---

by Virginia Irwin

---

BERLIN, Germany, April 27.—I am one of the first three Americans to enter Berlin. After a fantastic journey northward, after we crossed the Elbe River where the Russians and Americans made contact this afternoon, I arrived at Berlin at dark tonight with Andrew Tully, reporter for the Boston Traveler, and jeep driver Sgt. John Wilson of Roxbury, Mass.

The air is heavy with smoke. Everywhere around us is the clatter of small arms fire. Russian artillery is pouring an almost constant barrage into the heart of the city.

But in this Russian command post, where we are guests of Guards Major Nikolai Kovaleski, there is a terrific celebration going on. The arrival of three Americans in Berlin was the signal for the Russians to break out their best vodka and toss a terrific banquet in our honor.

I have just finished eating all sorts of strange Russian concoctions and being toasted by every officer in this command post. I have danced with at least a dozen Russians of various rank and degrees of terpsichorean ability. I have even been initiated into that great knee-bend brand of acrobatics which the Guards-Major says is "Russian Kosachec."

We arrived in Berlin a few minutes before 8 o'clock after the strangest journey I have ever undertaken. It was a nerve-shattering experience. We "ran off" the map and had to navigate by guess.

None of us understood Russian. German road signs had been removed and replaced with their Russian equivalent. We got to Berlin on the strength of a crude hand-made American flag flying from our jeep, several hundred handshakes and repeated assurances to fierce Russians who repeatedly stopped us that we were "Amerikanski."

And everywhere, as soon as we had convinced the Russians of our identity, we were mobbed. Russian infantry piled out of their horse-drawn wagons and crowded round. Refugees of all nationalities closed in around us and time after time the road had to be cleared almost by force before we could proceed.

Shortly after noon today at Torgau, east of the Elbe, we dined with Maj. Gen. Emil Reinhardt, commander of the Sixty-ninth American Division; Maj. Gen. Clarence R. Huebner, commander of the American Fifth Corps; Maj. Gen. Gleb Zlabimirovitzch Baklanoff, commander of the Thirty-fourth Russian Corps, and Gen. Vladimir Rusakov, commander of the Fifty-eighth Guards Infantry Division. The dinner was the official celebration of the meeting of the American and Russian troops at the Elbe River.

From Torgau we started north, behind the Russian lines, traveling sometimes over deserted roads, through dark forests. At other times, we hit highways clogged with the great body of the Russian Army, beating along in its motley array of horse-drawn vehicles of all sorts.

There were Russian troops riding in American 2½-ton trucks. There were Russian troops riding in two-wheeled carts, phaetons, in old-fashioned pony carts, in gypsy wagons, and surreys with fringed tops. They rode in everything that could be pulled.

The wagons were filled with hay and the soldiers lay on top of the hay like an army taking a holiday and going on a great mass hayride. It was the most fantastic sight I have ever seen. The fierce fighting men of the Red Army in their tunics and great boots, shabby and ragged after their long war, riding toward Berlin in their strange assortment of vehicles, singing their fighting songs, drinking vodka, were like so many holiday-makers going on a great picnic.

Before 8, we were well into Berlin with the forward elements of the Russian troops in the German capital.

German dead lay on the sidewalks, in the front yards of the bomb-shattered homes of the Berlin suburbs.

All streets were clogged with Russian tanks, guns, infantry in their shaggy fur hats, and everywhere the horses of the Russian Army ran loose about the streets.

But the Russians were happy—with almost indescribable wild joy. They were in Berlin. In this German capital lies their true revenge for Leningrad and Stalingrad, for Sevastopol and Moscow.

And the Russians are having their revenge. All along the road into Berlin, the fields along the roadways are littered with the carts and belongings of the Germans who tried to escape from the German capital. For the Russians are not so polite as the Americans are to Germans who clog the roads in the paths of American traffic. Americans wait for the Germans to pull off the road to let traffic pass, but the Russians drive over the German carts, push them off the road and upset them.

In the territory over which I traveled to reach Berlin, I saw very few Germans. They fear the Russians as no nation has ever feared a conquering army. The Russian Red Army is a mad, wonderful lot of fierce fighting men. They are also wonderful hosts.

American prisoners of war liberated from the great prison camps I passed on the way to Berlin told me that the Russians insisted on sharing their last morsel of food and their last drop of drink with every American they encounter. And tonight, here in Berlin, I am sampling Russian hospitality at its best.

This command post is in what is left of a German home in the battered city of Berlin, almost leveled by American bombers. There are no electric lights, no running water, but the Guards-Major is a kind of host who can rise above such difficulties. The minute I arrived he had his Cossack orderly, a fierce Mongolian with a great scar on his left cheek, ready with a dishpan of water. After I had washed my face the Guards-Major produced some German face powder, a quarter-full bottle of German perfume, and a cracked mirror.

I made myself as presentable as possible and sat down to a candlelit, flower-bedecked dinner table. The candelabra was upturned milk bottles and the flower vase was an old pickle jar, but the dinner was served with all the formality of a State function in Washington. At each toast the Russian officers stood up, clicked their heels, bowed deeply and drained tumblers of vodka. Besides vodka, there was cognac and a drink of dynamite strength the Major described simply as "spirits."

The food was served by a German woman and a Russian

laundress attached to artillery headquarters. The "appetizer" was huge platefuls of something that tasted like spiced salmon. Then came in huge platefuls of a strange dish that tasted like mutton cooked over charcoal, huge masses of mashed potatoes with meat oil poured all over them, a huge Russian cheese, and for dessert, platefuls of Russian-made pastries.

After each course there were toasts to "The late and great President Roosevelt," to Stalin, to President Truman, to Churchill, to "Capt. Andre Tooley," to "Capt. Veergeenee Erween," to the "Red Army," to "the American Army," to "Sarjaunt Wilson," and "to the American jeep."

As we drank our toasts the battle of Berlin raged only a few blocks away. As the artillery roared, the house shook and the candles fluttered. The candles are still fluttering as I write this story, this story of the most exciting thing that could ever happen to a newspaper reporter. It is all unreal.

Russian officers in their worn but military tunics bedecked with the medals of Leningrad, Stalingrad, and all the other great Russian battles, are unreal. The whole battle is somehow unreal.

And the thought keeps coming into my mind that here is the greatest city-dump in the world, with the remains of bombed buildings all dumped in the same place with the dead.

I asked the Guards-Major if Berlin was his greatest battle.

He smiled and said sadly, "No. To us there were greater battles. In those we lost our wives and children."

And then the Guards-Major told the story of the strange staff he has gathered around him. Every officer on that staff had lost his entire family to the Germans.

In that Major's story, I thought, lay the answer to the success of the fierce battle the Russians are waging for a Berlin that is almost all now in Russian hands.

————

BERLIN, April 28.—I almost had a jeep ride down the Unter den Linden today. After repeated attempts to reach the center of the city, I finally stopped at a Russian infantry command post about 200 yards north of the intersection of the Tempel-hofstrasse and Eberstrasse.

To have gone farther than this command post on the north-ern boundary of the Schoeneberg section of the city would have been suicide. Russian artillery was laying down a merci-less barrage on the heart of Berlin. Snipers were everywhere on rooftops, in sewers, and behind road blocks that had been thrown up at all main intersections.

The last 16 blocks that stand between me and the Unter den Linden are too hot to navigate.

With me here in Berlin are Andy Tully, reporter for the Boston Traveler, and jeep driver Johnny Wilson. We are the only three Americans here, and even the Russians think we are slightly mad to have dared the trip from Torgau on the Elbe through the Russian lines.

It is now about 3 o'clock in the afternoon. We have spent the day probing the main highways that lead into the heart of the city. On our first three tries we were turned back after running into pitched battles.

On the fourth try, we penetrated to within 10 blocks of the Wilhelmstrasse. To get there we drove north, up the Berliner-strasse, turned left on a Ringbahn near the Templehof and then took a sharp right turn down the Sachsendamm to the Innsbrueckerplatz. There we took another right turn and edged our way about 200 yards down the Eberstrasse to the Russian command post.

The Russians are fighting madly and doggedly beyond this point.

As each block is cleared of organized resistance, there still remains the job of fine-combing the buildings for snipers. The crack of small-arms fire is everywhere. German dead still lie in the streets.

This section of Berlin is not so badly damaged as I had expected it to be. There are still plenty of houses and build-ings that remain intact to provide good hiding places and snipers. The few German civilians that have remained are in a state of abject and shivering terror. They know that for them the least suspicion of sniping means death.

The sight of our crude Russian-made American flag from our jeep brings all German civilians running.

"When will the Americans be here?" is their one question.

Several Germans who spoke English have begged for the answer and it has given me considerable pleasure to reply: "The Americans will not be here. Berlin belongs to the Russians."

At this command post today we were told that somewhere in this section were two American flyers who had escaped from a prison camp and were fighting with the Russians. We spent about an hour trying to find them, but it was no use — hunting anybody in Berlin is like trying to find a dime on the bottom of the Atlantic.

At one point we thought we were within reach of them. We found a German woman who spoke English, but she was too frightened to be coherent and when we tried to follow her directions we were hopelessly lost.

This German woman tried to tell us how the Russians were treating the civilians in Berlin, but we paused only long enough to get the information about the American flyers. For us to be seen talking to a German behind the Russian lines might easily have meant death for us.

One look at this German woman told more than she could have said in words. There were circles under her eyes so deep and dark that they might have been etched there with lamp black. She shivered like some one with the ague.

The Russians have shown no mercy. They have played the perfect game of tit-for-tat. They have done to Berlin what the German Army did to Leningrad and Stalingrad.

Last night in the artillery command post where we three Yanks were guests of the Russian Guards-Maj. Nikolai Kovaleski, I heard from Russian officers the staggering numbers of Russian civilians killed in the battles of Smolensk, Sevastopol, Leningrad and Stalingrad; and as they talked the Russian artillery boomed the revenge of these cities.

Last night was a fantastic night. The artillery barrage went almost all night long. Between rounds there were unearthly sounds—the cracking of machine-gun fire tearing the night, the rumbling sounds of great buildings collapsing under the battering of the artillery barrage.

But in the guard-major's command post there was a great celebration. By the time the great feast was over, we had established beyond doubt in the guard-major's mind that we were not spies, but only three foolhardy Yanks who had taken our lives in our hands to get to Berlin. Once all suspicion was gone from the minds of the officers in the party, there was an air of camaraderie that is hard to describe.

They practically gave us the keys to Berlin. The guard-major insisted that "our brave and courageous Sergeant" Johnny Wilson have a seat of honor near the head of the table. Johnny was without appetite in the excitement, but the guard-major slapped his gun, pointed to Johnny's plate and roared good-naturedly "Mange, mange." Johnny understands a little French and knew that the Major was commanding him to eat. So, wide-eyed and almost choking with emotion over being the first American GI to enter Berlin, Johnny ate.

After the dinner, there was dancing to a beaten-up victrola. One young Captain was the Russian equivalent of the American jitterbug and danced, not only with me, but with Johnny. I am still puffing from the exertion.

At about 1 o'clock in the morning we three exhausted Yanks begged off from more dancing and vodka drinking and the Major showed us to our rooms. Still the perfect host, he gave up his bed to our Sergeant. While Johnny slept in style, the Major disposed himself on a divan in the living room.

Everywhere today the sight of three Yanks in Berlin was the sign for great mobs of Russian soldiers to gather around us. I have shaken hands until my right wrist is paralyzed. I have smiled and laughed until my ears ache.

———

BERLIN, April 28.—The Red Army in action is terrific. On the move it looks like a mixture of a scene from a De Mille movie of the Crusades and newsreel shots of American motorized supply columns.

American Studebaker trucks rub axles with antiquated farm carts loaded down with Russian infantry. Great herds of sheep and cows are mixed in with armored cars and half-tracks with household belongings lashed to their sides. Super tanks tangle with a fantastic mess of horse-drawn buggies, phaetons, surreys, pony carts and farm wagons, all loaded down with ammunition, food, women, wounded and animals.

To an American observer used to the ordered precision of the American Army on the move, the scene is unbelievable, but behind this seeming confusion there is an order, or purpose, that has already carried the Russians into the heart of Berlin.

As I write, the Russian artillery is pounding the heart of the city with a barrage I have never heard equaled in an American battle. The earth shakes. The air stinks of cordite and the dead. All Berlin seems confusion.

The fierce Russian infantry are pushing into the heart of the city. Wild horses turned loose after pulling supply carts roam the streets. German dead lie everywhere. Here and there, a horse, caught by some sniper's bullet, lies sprawled amidst the wreckage of the buildings.

We three Yanks, Andy Tully of the Boston Traveler, a jeep driver, Johnny Wilson of the Twenty-sixth U.S. Division, and I are the first Americans to see the Russian fighting army in action. They have practically given us the keys to the city and we have spent the day trying to keep the Russian infantry from sweeping us before them on their way down the Unter den Linden.

The ruthlessness and the determination of the Russian fighting men is hard to describe. Nobody seems to have any set duty. They all just pitch in and fight like hell wherever there is fighting to be done.

Today we managed to make ourselves understood to a Russian infantryman who acted as a sort of guide around the city. This fierce-looking youngster in a great fur shako took off without bothering to ask a superior officer's permission. He perched on the hood of our jeep and motioned directions with his riot gun. Finally, when we had had all we could take, we made him understand that we were going back toward the rear, where things were a little quieter, but, instead of going back with us to his command post where we had picked him up about a mile back, he shook hands with us and set off on foot to join some Russian infantrymen who were going into the heavy fighting right in the heart of Berlin.

The Russian Army does a fantastic job of mixing work and play. They fight like mad and play with a sort of barbaric abandon.

This morning after eating a heavy breakfast of charred veal and potatoes swimming in fat—all washed down with alternate drinks of hot milk and vodka—we three Yanks set off alone to try to see something of Berlin.

We made a wrong turn some place off the Berlinerstrasse and at a road block that had not been cleared got scared out of our field boots by a terrific burst of machine-gun fire off to our right.

Retracing our way, we went back to the command post of our friend, the Guards Maj. Nikolai Kovalesky.

When we returned, there was a mid-morning dance in full swing. Russian officers, their medals clanking on their chests, were dancing with a young Russian WAC Lieutenant; and there, practically in the middle of Berlin and in the middle of one of the bloodiest battles in history, I danced for an hour before we could pry ourselves away from the festivities.

I waltzed to the tune of "Kannst Du Mir Gut Sein," which I think was a German record of "Sonny Boy." I danced to "Magnolia" and "Love and Kisses" by Paul Whiteman and his orchestra. In fact, they swung me around until the scratchy old Victrola hopped on the table and I was a dripping mess of mud composed of three parts perspiration and one part German bomb rubble dust.

In between times, Russian noncoms would come in, click their heels smartly, salute and receive their orders for the fighting at hand.

At about 10:30 our Russian host insisted we eat another breakfast, well basted again with cognac and vodka. My Russian orderly, a fierce-looking Mongolian named Rachmann, turned up with a fresh bouquet of flowers and escorted me out into the hall for a shoeshine. He put enough black polish on my brown Army shoes to last a lifetime. He also blacked my stockings halfway to the knee.

The whole day was like being transported to another and strange world. I felt as though I had been caught in a giant whirlpool of destruction. There was such an air of unreality about the whole of the battle for Berlin that I thought at times I had lost my reason and was only imagining these strange and unearthly sights.

It was too much for my reason to accept the Russian women—in the uniforms of secretaries, laundresses and traffic cops—riding in the hay-filled ricks with the infantry.

It was too much to get out of our jeep to shake hands with a furiously milling mob of Russian soldiers—one of whom was serenading me on an accordion—and find that I was standing practically in the middle of a yard full of German dead.

All of these two days I have spent with the Russian Army is like a dream. I have only to close my eyes to see again the fantastic scene of the Russian Army on the move. The horse-drawn carts are, many of them, driven by infantrymen with their heads swathed in bandages. In the Russian Army, evidently, you have to be pretty seriously wounded to be relieved of duty and taken to a hospital.

I have only to close my eyes to see again the horses and cattle, American trucks and almost medieval carts, and anti-tank guns and tanks and the phaetons and buggies and gaily painted gypsy wagons are rolling down a road into Berlin.

The U.S. Army allows the German civilian to keep his cattle and chickens and sheep, so the Army won't have to feed him. The Russian Army sweeps the countryside and drives before it all the livestock in its path.

This was the most nerve-racking day of my life. We were continually caught in traffic jams. When I wasn't worried about being killed by a bursting shell or a German sniper, I was panic-stricken lest a horse chew my arm off.

Whenever a column would halt, there would be an unearthly din of truck horns mixed with the neighing of horses, the bleating of sheep and the cackling of chickens loaded in coops, with the infantry riding in farm carts. Over all could usually be heard the strains of some Russian tune being "rendered" on an accordion or a violin. Always there was the shouting in, to me, unintelligible Russian.

And over all this there has been the almost hysterical shouting of our American Sergeant, Jeep Driver Johnny Wilson of Roxbury, Mass., yelling "Amerikanski" and acting like the Grover Whalen of World War II. Johnny is the greatest ambassador of good will a nation ever had. He looks like a sad sack, but he is the personality kid with the Russians. He shows me off like Evelyn MacLean sporting the Hope diamond. If the Russians don't notice me at every hand, Johnny yells, "American woman," and brings to their attention that an American female is in Berlin, and he is right now telling a bunch of Russian officers that Andy Tully should be a battalion commander in the Red Army.

It has been a mad day, but a wonderful one.

If the pay was in something besides rubles, I'd join the Russian Army and try to help take Berlin.

St. Louis *Post-Dispatch*, May 9–11, 1945

# *33,000 Dachau Captives Freed by 7th Army*

by Marguerite Higgins

DACHAU, Germany, April 29 (Delayed).—Troops of the United States 7th Army liberated 33,000 prisoners this afternoon at this first and largest of the Nazi concentration camps. Some of the prisoners had endured for eleven years the horrors of notorious Dachau.

The liberation was a frenzied scene. Inmates of the camp hugged and embraced the American troops, kissed the ground before them and carried them shoulder high around the place.

[At Moosburg, north of Munich, the United States 14th Armored Division liberated 110,000 Allied prisoners of war, including 11,000 Americans, from Stalag 7A.

[From United States 12th Army Group headquarters came the story of a captured Nazi doctor, Gustav Wilhelm Schuebbe, who said that the Nazi annihilation institute at Kiev, Russia, killed from 110,000 to 140,000 persons "unworthy to live" during the nine months he worked there. He himself, he said, murdered about 21,000 persons.]

The Dachau camp, in which at least a thousand prisoners were killed last night before the S.S. (Elite Guard) men in charge fled, is a grimmer and larger edition of the similarly notorious Buchenwald camp near Weimar.

This correspondent and Peter Furst, of the army newspaper "Stars and Stripes," were the first two Americans to enter the inclosure at Dachau, where persons possessing some of the best brains in Europe were held during what might have been the most fruitful years of their lives.

While a United States 45th Infantry Division patrol was still fighting a way down through S.S. barracks to the north, our jeep and two others from the 42d I..fantry drove into the camp inclosure through the southern entrance. As men of the patrol with us busied themselves accepting an S.S. man's surrender, we impressed a soldier into service and drove with him to the prisoners' barracks. There he opened the gate after pushing the body of a prisoner shot last night while attempting to get out to meet the Americans.

There was not a soul in the yard when the gate was opened. As we learned later, the prisoners themselves had taken over control of their inclosure the night before, refusing to obey any further orders from the German guards, who had retreated to the outside. The prisoners maintained strict discipline among themselves, remaining close to their barracks so as not to give the S.S. men an excuse for mass murder.

But the minute the two of us entered a jangled barrage of "Are you Americans?" in about sixteen languages came from the barracks 200 yards from the gate. An affirmative nod caused pandemonium.

Tattered, emaciated men, weeping, yelling and shouting "Long live America!" swept toward the gate in a mob. Those who could not walk limped or crawled. In the confusion, they were so hysterically happy that they took the S.S. man for an American. During a wild five minutes he was patted on the back, paraded on shoulders and embraced enthusiastically by prisoners. The arrival of the American soldier soon straightened out the situation.

I happened to be the first through the gate, and the first person to rush up to me turned out to be a Polish Catholic priest, a deputy of August Cardinal Hlond, Primate of Poland, who was not a little startled to discover that the helmeted, uniformed, begoggled individual he had so heartily embraced was not a man.

In the excitement, which was not the least dampened by the German artillery and the sounds of battle in the northern part of the camp, some of the prisoners died trying to pass through electrically charged barbed wire. Some who got out after the wires were decharged joined in the battle, when some ill-advised S.S. men holding out in a tower fired upon them.

The prisoners charged the tower and threw all six S.S. men out the window.

After an hour and a half of cheering, the crowd, which

would virtually mob each soldier that dared to venture into the excited, milling group, was calmed down enough to make possible a tour of the camp. The only American prisoner, a flyer, with the rank of major, took some of the soldiers through.

According to the prisoners, the most famous individuals who had been at the camp had been removed by S.S. men to Innsbrueck. Among them were Leon Blum, former French Premier, and his wife; the Rev. Martin Niemoeller, German church leader; Kurt Schuschnigg, Chancellor of Austria at the time of the anschluss (he was said to have been alive a few days ago); Gabriel Piquet, Bishop of St. Etienne; Prince Leopold of Prussia; Baron Fritz Cirini, aide to Prince Leopold; Richard Schmitz, former Mayor of Vienna, and Marshal Stalin's son, Jacob.

The barracks at Dachau, like those at Buchenwald, had the stench of death and sickness. But at Dachau there were six barracks like the infamous No. 61 at Buchenwald, where the starving and dying lay virtually on top of each other in quarters where 1,200 men occupied a space intended for 200. The dead—300 died of sickness yesterday—lay on concrete walks outside the quarters and others were being carried out as the reporters went through.

The mark of starvation was on all the emaciated corpses. Many of the living were so frail it seemed impossible they could still be holding on to life.

The crematorium and torture chambers lay outside the prisoner inclosures. Situated in a wood close by, a new building had been built by prisoners under Nazi guards. Inside, in the two rooms used as torture chambers, an estimated 1,200 bodies were piled.

In the crematorium itself were hooks on which the S.S. men hung their victims when they wished to flog them or to use any of the other torture instruments. Symbolic of the S.S. was a mural the S.S. men themselves had painted on the wall. It showed a headless man in uniform with the S.S. insigne on the collar. The man was astride a huge inflated pig, into which he was digging his spurs.

The prisoners also showed reporters the grounds where men knelt and were shot in the back of the neck. On this very spot a week ago a French general, a resistance leader under General Charles de Gaulle, had been killed.

Just beyond the crematorium was a ditch containing some 2,000 more bodies, which had been hastily tossed there in the last few days by the S.S. men, who were so busy preparing their escape they did not have time to burn the bodies.

Below the camp were cattle cars in which prisoners from Buchenwald had been transported to Dachau. Hundreds of dead were still in the cars due to the fact that prisoners in the camp had rejected S.S. orders to remove them. It was mainly the men from these cattle cars that the S.S. leaders had shot before making their escape. Among those who had been left for dead in the cattle cars was one man still alive who managed to lift himself from the heap of corpses on which he lay.

New York *Herald Tribune*, May 1, 1945

# *Dachau*

by Martha Gellhorn

WE CAME out of Germany in a C-47 carrying American prisoners of war. The planes were lined up on the grass field at
Regensburg, and the passengers waited sitting in the shade
under the wings. They would not leave the planes: this was a
trip no one was going to miss. When the crew chief said "All
aboard," we got in as if we were escaping from a fire.

No one looked out the windows as we flew over Germany. No one ever wanted to see Germany again. They
turned away from it with hatred and sickness; everything
about it was evil. At first they did not talk but when it became real that Germany was behind forever they began talking of their prisons. We did not comment on the Germans:
they are past words.

"No one will believe us," a soldier said.

They agreed on that: No one would believe them.

"Where were you captured, miss?" a soldier asked.

"I am only bumming a ride; I've been down to see
Dachau."

One of the men said suddenly, "We got to talk about it,
see? We got to talk about it if anyone believes us or not.". . .

Behind the barbed wire and the electric fence, the skeletons
sat in the sun and searched themselves for lice. They have no
age and no faces; they all look alike and like nothing you will
ever see if you are lucky. We crossed the wide, crowded, dusty
compound between the prison barracks and went to the hospital. In the hall sat more of the skeletons and from them
came the smell of disease and death. They watched us but did
not move: No expression shows on a face that is only yellow-
ish stubbly skin stretched across bone.

What had been a man dragged himself into the doctor's
office; he was a Pole and he was about six feet tall and he

724

weighed less than a hundred pounds and he wore a striped prison shirt, a pair of unlaced boots and a blanket which he tried to hold around his legs. His eyes were large and strange and stood out from his face, and his jawbone seemed to be cutting through his skin. He had come to Dachau from Buchenwald on the last death transport.

There were fifty boxcars of his dead traveling companions still on the siding outside the camp, and for the last three days the American Army had forced Dachau civilians to bury these dead.

When this transport arrived, the German guards locked the men, women and children in the cars and there they slowly died of hunger and thirst. They screamed and they tried to fight their way out; from time to time the guards fired into the cars to stop the noise.

This man had survived; he was found under a pile of dead. Now he stood on the bones that were his legs and talked, and then suddenly he wept. "Everyone is dead," he said, and the face that was not a face twisted with pain or sorrow or horror. "No one is left. Everyone is dead. I cannot help myself," he said. "Here I am and I am finished and cannot help myself. Everyone is dead."

The Polish doctor who had been a prisoner here for five years said, "In four weeks, you will be a young man again. You will be fine."

Perhaps his body will live and take strength, but one cannot believe that his eyes will ever be like other people's eyes.

The doctor spoke with great detachment about the things he had watched in this hospital. He had watched them, and there was nothing he could do to stop them. All the prisoners talked in the same way—quietly, with a strange little smile as if they apologized for talking of such loathsome things to someone who lived in a real world and could hardly be expected to understand Dachau.

"The Germans made here some unusual experiments," he said. "They wished to see how long an aviator could go without oxygen; how high in the sky he could go. So they had a closed car from which they pumped the oxygen. It is a quick death," he said. "It does not take more than fifteen minutes. But it is a hard death. They killed not so many people, only eight hundred, in that experiment. It was found that no one can live above 36,000 feet altitude without oxygen."

"Whom did they choose for this experiment?" I asked.

"Any prisoner," he said, "so long as he was healthy. They picked the strongest. The mortality was one hundred per cent, of course."

"It is very interesting, is it not?" said another doctor. We did not look at one another. I do not know how to explain it, but aside from the terrible anger you feel, you are ashamed. You are ashamed for mankind.

"There was also the experiment of the water," said the first doctor. "This was to see how long pilots could survive when they were shot down over water like the Channel, let us say. For that, the German doctors put the prisoners in great vats of sea water, and they stood in water up to their necks. It was found that the human body can resist for two hours and a half in water eight degrees below zero. They killed six hundred people on this experiment. Though sometimes a man had to suffer three times, for he fainted early in the experiment and then he was revived, and a few days later the experiment was again undertaken."

"Didn't they scream? Didn't they cry out?" I said.

He smiled at that question. "There was no use in this place for a man to scream or cry out. It was no use for any man ever."

A colleague of the doctor's came in. He was the one who knew about the malaria experiment. The German doctor who was chief of the army tropical medicine research used Dachau as an experimental station. He was attempting to find a way to immunize German soldiers against malaria. To that end, he inoculated 11,000 Dachau prisoners with tertiary malaria. The death rate from the malaria was not too heavy; it simply meant that these prisoners weakened by fever died more quickly afterward from hunger. However, in one day three men died of overdoses of pyramidon with which, for some unknown reason, the Germans were then experimenting. No immunization for malaria was ever found.

Down the hall in the surgery, the Polish surgeon got out the record book to look up some data on operations performed by the SS doctors. These were castration and sterilization operations. The prisoner was forced to sign a paper beforehand saying that he willingly undertook this self-destruction. Jews and gypsies were castrated; any foreigner who had had relations with a German woman was sterilized. The woman was sent to a concentration camp.

The surgeon mentioned another experiment, really a very bad one, he said, and obviously quite useless. The guinea pigs were Polish priests. (Over two thousand Catholic priests passed through Dachau, but only one thousand are alive.) The German doctors injected streptococcus germs in the upper leg of the prisoners between the muscle and the bone. An extensive abscess formed, accompanied by fever and extreme pain.

The Polish doctor knew of more than a hundred cases who had been treated this way; there may have been more. He had a record of thirty-one deaths, but it took usually from two to three months of ceaseless pain before the patient died, and all of them died after several operations performed during the last few days of their lives. The operations were a further experiment to see if a dying man could be saved, but the answer was that he could not. Some prisoners recovered entirely because they were treated with the already known and proved antidote, but there were others who were now moving around the camp as best they could, crippled for life.

And then because very simply I could listen to no more, my guide who had been in Dachau for ten and a half years took me across the compound to the jail. In Dachau if you want to rest from one horror you go and see another.

The jail was a long clean building with small white cells in it. Here lived the people whom the prisoners called the N.N. men. N.N. stands for *nacht und nebel*, which means "night and mist." Translated into less romantic terms, this means that the prisoners in these cells never saw a human being; were never allowed to speak to anyone; were never taken out into the sun and the air. They lived in solitary confinement on the watery soup and a slice of bread which was the camp diet.

There was, of course, the danger of going mad. But no one ever knew what happened to them in the years of their silence. And on Friday before the Sunday when the Americans entered Dachau, eight thousand men were removed by the SS on a final death transport. Amongst these were all the prisoners from the solitary cells. None of these men have been heard of since.

In Dachau if a man was found with a cigarette butt in his pocket he received twenty-five to fifty lashes with a bull whip. If he failed to stand at attention with his hat off six feet away from any SS trooper who happened to pass, he had his hands tied behind his back and he was hung by his bound hands from a hook on the wall for an hour. If he did any other little thing which displeased the jailers he was put in the box. "The box" is a room the size of a telephone booth. It is so constructed that being in it alone, a man cannot sit down nor kneel down nor, of course, lie down. It was usual to put four men in it together. Here they stood for three days and nights without food or water or any form of sanitation. Afterward they went back to the sixteen-hour day of labor and the diet of watery soup and a slice of bread like soft gray cement.

It is not known how many people died in this camp in the twelve years of its existence but at least 45,000 are known to have died in the last three years. And last February and March, 2,000 were killed in the gas chamber because, though they were too weak to work, they did not have the grace to die, so it was arranged for them.

The gas chamber is part of the crematorium. The crematorium is a brick building outside the camp compound standing in a grove of pine trees. A Polish priest had attached himself to us and, as we walked there, he said, "I started to die twice of starvation but I was very lucky. I got a job as a mason when we were building this crematorium, so I received a little more food and that way I did not die."

I said nothing and I would like to know what there is to say.

Then he said, "Have you seen our chapel, Madam?"

I said I had not, and my guide said I could not; it was within the zone where the 2,000 typhus cases were more or less isolated.

"It is a pity," the priest said. "We finally got a chapel and we had Holy Mass there almost every Sunday. There are very beautiful murals. The man who painted them died of hunger two months ago."

Now we were at the crematorium, and there suddenly but never to be believed were the bodies of the dead. They were everywhere. There were piles of them inside the oven room, outside the door and alongside the building. They were all naked and behind the crematorium the ragged clothing of the dead was neatly stacked—shirts, jackets, trousers and shoes awaiting sterilization and further use. The clothing was handled with order but the bodies were dumped like garbage rotting in the sun.

We have all seen the dead like bundles lying on all the roads of half the earth, but nowhere was there anything like this. Nothing about war was ever as insanely wicked as these starved and outraged naked, nameless dead. Behind one pile of dead lay the clothed healthy bodies of the German guards who had been found in this camp. They were killed at once by the prisoners when the American Army entered. And for the first time anywhere, one could look at a dead man with gladness.

Just behind the crematorium stood the hothouses and they were fine big modern hothouses. Here the prisoners grew the flowers that the SS officers loved. Next to the hothouses were the vegetable gardens and very rich ones, too, where the starving prisoners cultivated the vitamin foods that kept the SS strong. But if a man dying of hunger furtively pulled up and gorged himself on a head of lettuce he would be beaten until he was unconscious. And in front of the crematorium separated from it by a stretch of garden stood a long row of well-built commodious homes. The families of the SS officers lived here: their wives and children lived here quite happily while the chimneys of the crematorium spewed out the unending human ashes.

The American soldier in the plane said, "We got to talk about it."

You cannot talk about it very well, because there is a kind of shock that sets in and makes it almost unbearable to go back and remember what you have seen.

I have not talked about the women who were moved to Dachau three weeks ago from their own concentration camps. Their crime was that they were Jews. There was the lovely girl from Budapest who somehow was still lovely, and the woman with mad eyes who had watched her sister walk into the gas chamber at Auschwitz and been held back, and the Austrian woman who pointed out quite calmly that they all had the dresses they wore on their backs, that they had never had anything more, and that they worked sixteen hours a day, too, in the long winters and that they, too, were "corrected," as the Germans say, for any offense, real or imaginary.

I have not talked about how it was the day the American Army arrived, though the prisoners told me. In their joy to be free and longing to see the friends who had come at last, the prisoners rushed to the fence and died—electrocuted. There were those who died cheering, because that effort of happiness was more than their bodies could endure. There were those who died because at last they had food and they ate before they could be stopped and it killed them. I do not know words fine enough to talk of the men who have lived in this horror for years—three years, five years, ten years—and whose minds are as clear and unafraid as the day they entered.

I was in Dachau when the German armies surrendered unconditionally to the Allies. It was a suitable place to be. For surely this war was made to abolish Dachau and all the other places like Dachau and everything that Dachau stands for. To abolish it forever. That these cemetery prisons existed is the crime and shame of the German people.

We are not entirely guiltless, we the Allies, because it took us twelve years to open the gates of Dachau. We were blind and unbelieving and slow, and that we can never be again. We must know now that there can never be peace if there is cruelty like this in the world.

And if ever again we tolerate such cruelty we have no right to peace.

*Collier's*, June 23, 1945

# The War in Europe Is Ended!
# Surrender Is Unconditional;
# V-E Will Be Proclaimed Today

by Edward Kennedy

REIMS, France, May 7—Germany surrendered unconditionally to the Western Allies and the Soviet Union at 2:41 A.M. French time today. [This was at 8:41 P.M. Eastern Wartime Sunday.]

The surrender took place at a little red schoolhouse that is the headquarters of Gen. Dwight D. Eisenhower.

The surrender, which brought the war in Europe to a formal end after five years, eight months and six days of bloodshed and destruction, was signed for Germany by Col. Gen. Gustav Jodl. General Jodl is the new Chief of Staff of the German Army.

The surrender was signed for the Supreme Allied Command by Lieut. Gen. Walter Bedell Smith, Chief of Staff for General Eisenhower.

It was also signed by Gen. Ivan Susloparoff for the Soviet Union and by Gen. Francois Sevez for France.

[The official Allied announcement will be made at 9 o'clock Tuesday morning when President Truman will broadcast a statement and Prime Minister Churchill will issue a V-E Day proclamation. Gen. Charles de Gaulle also will address the French at the same time.]

General Eisenhower was not present at the signing, but immediately afterward General Jodl and his fellow delegate, Gen. Admiral Hans Georg Friedeburg, were received by the Supreme Commander.

They were asked sternly if they understood the surrender terms imposed upon Germany and if they would be carried out by Germany.

They answered Yes.

Germany, which began the war with a ruthless attack upon Poland, followed by successive aggressions and brutality in internment camps, surrendered with an appeal to the victors for mercy toward the German people and armed forces.

After having signed the full surrender, General Jodl said he wanted to speak and received leave to do so.

"With this signature," he said in soft-spoken German, "the German people and armed forces are for better or worse delivered into the victors' hands.

"In this war, which has lasted more than five years, both have achieved and suffered more than perhaps any other people in the world."

*The New York Times*, May 8, 1945

# The A.P. Surrender

by A. J. Liebling

THE GREAT ROW over Edward Kennedy's Associated Press story of the signing of the German surrender at Reims served to point up the truth that if you are smart enough you can kick yourself in the seat of the pants, grab yourself by the back of the collar, and throw yourself out on the sidewalk. This is an axiom that I hope will be taught to future students of journalism as Liebling's Law. The important aspect of the row, I am sure, is not that Kennedy got his dispatch out of Europe before the SHAEF Public Relations bosses wanted him to but that only three representatives of the American press were admitted to one of the memorable scenes in the history of man, and they only on condition that they promise not to tell about it until the brigadier general in charge of public relations gave them permission. *No* correspondent of a newspaper published in the United States was invited to the signing; besides Kennedy, Boyd Lewis of the United Press, and James Kilgallen of Hearst's International News Service, the official list included four radio men, an enlisted correspondent for *Stars & Stripes*, and a collection of French, Russian, Australian, and Canadian correspondents. Whether a promise extorted as this one was, in an airplane several thousand feet up, has any moral force is a question for theologians. The only parallel I can think of offhand is the case of Harold the Saxon, who was shipwrecked in the territories of William of Normandy at a time when Edward the Confessor was getting on in years. William, taking Harold into protective custody, made him swear not to claim the English throne after Edward died, but when Harold got home he cocked a snoot at William. Anglo-Saxon historians have since expressed a good deal of sympathy for Harold's point of view, but the Church held with William. I suppose that Kennedy should have refused to promise anything and thus made sure of missing an event that no newspaperman in the world would want to miss, but I can't imagine any correspondent's doing it.

I do not think Kennedy imperilled the lives of any Allied soldiers by sending the story, as some of his critics have charged. He probably saved a few, because by withholding the announcement of an armistice you prolong the shooting, and, conversely, by announcing it promptly you make the shooting stop. Moreover, the Germans had broadcast the news of the armistice several hours before Kennedy's story appeared on the streets of New York, and Absie, the O.W.I.'s American Broadcasting Station in Europe, broadcast it in twenty-four languages, including English, within an hour after. The thing that has caused the most hard feeling is that Kennedy broke a "combination," which means that he sent out a story after all the correspondents on the assignment had agreed not to. But the old-fashioned "combination" was an agreement freely reached among reporters and not a pledge imposed upon the whole group by somebody outside it. Incidentally, the *Times* used to make its reporters at Police Headquarters stay out of combinations. The willingness of the large American news organizations in the European Theatre of Operations to be herded into the new-style combination, in return for favors that independent journalists didn't get, had led directly to the kind of official contempt for the press that the Reims arrangements indicated, with the accompanying view that opportunity to report history was what SHAEF calls a "SHAEF privilege," like a Shubert pass. The Associated Press was a leader in establishing this form of organized subservience, and the jam it now finds itself in is therefore a good illustration of the workings of Liebling's Law.

For many years before this war, the editorial end of the American newspaper business had been turning from news gathering to shopping for a packaged, mass-produced wordage sold by the press associations and syndicates. A few newspapers, such as the *Times* and *Herald Tribune* here and the *Tribune* and *Daily News* in Chicago, went into wholesaling in a modest way themselves by setting up their own syndicates, principally to peddle European news. The war, coupled with the excess-profits tax (which made many businessmen decide that they might as well pay their extra money to employees as to the tax collector), put an end, in a number of cases, to the newspapers' depending entirely on this sort of ready-made, or store, news, and scores of writers for magazines and newspapers began to arrive in the European Theatre of Operations. The large news organizations then faced the problem of proving that boughten coverage was not only cheaper but better than "original" reporting—say, Ernest Hemingway's. To accomplish this, they either suggested or accepted enthusiastically—it is not quite clear which—the Army's present principle of "limited facilities" for the coverage of news events. This meant that they concurred in the rear-area military maxim that there were never enough accommodations for the number of correspondents who wanted to see anything. The military, in return, conceded that the correspondents of the organizations which had large London bureaus should have first call on whatever accommodations there were. These bureaus established their importance with a SHAEF Public Relations personnel that seldom got out of London. The clearing house for the allotment of "facilities," which from then on assumed the character not of rights but of favors, was the Association of American Correspondents, whose headquarters were in London and which was dominated by the representatives of the large press organizations, and any facilities that were left over were distributed among the independent correspondents whom the members found most "reasonable." The key members of the Association further impressed the Public Relations soldiers with statistics about the number of readers each of their organizations served. The Associated Press claims to "fill the news needs of eight hundred million people," I.N.S. two hundred and twenty-five million, United Press (unaccountably modest) fifty-five million "in the United States alone," the Chicago *Tribune* syndicate a hundred and ten million, the *Herald Tribune* syndicate ten million, the *Times* syndicate six million, and Time-Life, Inc., which managed to wedge its way into the Association at an early date, twenty-two million. Together with the major radio chains, which reach a good billion people each, these press associations and syndicates served about twice the population of the world. This total does not even include the readers of the Chicago *Daily News* syndicate, figures for which are not on hand at this writing. Having once accepted the principle of limitation (i.e., to members of the Correspondents' Association) and having made a habit, for thirty months, of shouting publicly, "Headquarters is always right!," the dozen or so ruling members were hardly in a position to object when the Army decided on a further limitation of newspaper facilities—this time to zero.

The story that amused me most during armistice week was the one that appeared in the *Times* of Wednesday, May 9th, under the headline "Fiasco by SHAEF at Reims Is Bared: Reporters Barred from Seeing Historic Signing of the German Surrender." It was signed by Raymond Daniell, a sententious little man who, as chief of the *Times'* London bureau, had been the chief promoter of the limitations scheme, back in 1942. "The correspondents never liked the Army's plan, but they accepted it with reservations," Daniell wrote. "What made them especially angry, however, was the fact that when the time came for the surrender, it was the Army's plan for coverage in Berlin that was adopted, instead of an order of precedence drawn up at Dieppe by the newspaper representatives and followed ever since until last Sunday night by the Army where space was limited." Daniell, as president of the Correspondents' Association, had practically imposed the "order of precedence" on the Army press-relations chief in London after the Dieppe what-was-it. His reason was that it turned out after the raid that Quentin Reynolds of *Collier's* had been along without the sanction of the Association. It was never hinted that Reynolds' presence had anything to do with the sanguinary unsuccess at Dieppe, but Daniell and his opposite numbers in the other large news organizations nevertheless felt that magazine men should be discouraged. The bureau chiefs of the syndicates, conspicuously including Robert Bunnelle of the A.P., who is now involved in the Kennedy trouble, simply transferred to Europe the tendency of American district reporters to play ball with the police lieutenant on the desk. It is that which makes the rather spluttery rage of Brigadier General Frank Allen, the Supreme Headquarters Press Relations chief, so comprehensible. The Brigadier feels like a keeper at the Zoo who has been butted in the behind by his favorite gazelle. What made Daniell especially angry, apparently, was that the military found room at the surrender ceremony for twenty women friends of officers but left him standing outside. He seemed to feel that this was rubbing it in.

The Kennedy explosion has, I imagine, done no harm, except possibly to Kennedy—one of my favorite reporters, I might add. The Russians have not declined to end the war because of it. Maybe, in the absence of opposition, the Russians would have had to stop anyway, although this does not seem to have occurred to Supreme Headquarters spokesmen. The Russians had their own surrender show in Berlin, and probably had a better publicity break on it than they would have had if the two surrenders had been announced simultaneously. (They could do with a public-relations counsel, anyway.) One unconditional surrender of the Reich a day is about as much as the public can absorb. Moreover, the row can do a lot of good if it brings into the clear the whole disturbing question of military censorship imposed for political, personal, or merely capricious reasons and reveals the history of the prodigious amount of pure poodle-faking that has gone on under the name of Army Public Relations. I remember the period in North Africa when, for reasons of "military security," no correspondent was allowed to say anything against Admiral Darlan even after he was dead, and when a dispatch of my own was censored because I said that anti-Fascist Frenchmen thought our indulgence of the Fascists silly (information which obviously would have been of great interest to the German General Staff). In France, last summer, another of my stories was held up a week because I wrote about the torture and execution of an American parachutist by Vichy militiamen. It was evidently important to military security that the American public shouldn't think hard of our enemies. "Horror stuff," by which the censors meant any mention of ugly wounds or indecorous deaths, was for a long time forbidden, but recently it has been found compatible with security. Somebody must have told whoever makes the rules that the Germans know about it. But the worst form of censorship was the preventive kind exercised by Public Relations, which, in any echelon higher than an army in the field, acted on the principle that an inactive correspondent was potentially a source of less bother than a correspondent who was going somewhere. While the correspondent was in the United States, the object was to keep him from crossing to England, and once he got to England the game was to stop him from reaching Africa, Italy, France, or any other place he might find subject matter. If he arrived in any of those countries, there was one more line of defense—P.R.O. would try to hold him in Algiers, Naples, or Paris, as the case might be. Actually, he was safe only when he got to a front. He had nothing to worry him there but shells, for the higher echelons of Public Relations left him alone. To give Army Public Relations the only credit due it, some of the younger officers in the field were helpful, hard-working, and at times even intelligent.

The Public Relations situation reached a high point in *opera-buffa* absurdity in London in the spring of a year ago, before the invasion of France. There were at one time nine separate echelons of Public Relations in London at once: P.R.O. SHAEF; P.R.O. Twenty-first Army Group (Montgomery's command); P.R.O. FUSAG (First Army Group, which later became Twelfth Army Group); P.R.O. First Army; P.R.O. ETOUSA (European Theatre of Operations, U.S. Army), which handled the correspondents' mail, gave out ration cards, did publicity for Services of Supply, and tried to horn in on everything else; P.R.O. Eighth Air Force; P.R.O. Ninth Air Force; the P.R.O. for General Spaatz's highest echelon of the Air Forces command; and the Navy P.R.O. The Air Forces publicity people were unpretentious but aggressive; the Navy was helpful; the five other echelons spent most of their time getting in each other's way.

The P.R.O.s, mostly colonels and lieutenant colonels (a major, in this branch of service, was considered a shameful object, to be exiled to an outer office), had for the most part been Hollywood press agents or Chicago rewrite men in civilian life. They looked as authentic in their uniforms as dress extras in a B picture, but they had learned to say "Army" with an unction that Stonewall Jackson could never have achieved. One rewrite lieutenant colonel used to predict casualties as high as eighty per cent in the first assault wave on D Day. He had never heard a shot fired in anger. Others would seriously tell correspondents, that they, the correspondents, couldn't go along on D Day because there wouldn't be space enough on the landing craft to hold another man. The P.R.O.s were perhaps under the impression that you load ships for an invasion the way you would ferry boats, without regard to the organization of combat units. There was room for ninety more men on the Coast Guard LCI on which I finally crossed. The one point on which all the London officers were united was their detestation of the field army. One division commander who requested that a certain correspondent be allowed to accompany his outfit into action stirred such resentment in the London army that he was reprimanded by the Chief of Staff of SHAEF. The London P.R.O.s felt that the division commander, being a mere major general rich in battle experience, was guilty of insubordination when he disagreed with non-combatant lieutenant colonels. Daniell, Bunnelle, and the rest of the news-agency men adapted themselves to this squalid milieu and flourished in it. They agreed with everything the dress extras said, especially with the thesis that on fifty miles of Norman coast there would be room for only about twenty correspondents, who would of course represent the larger news organizations. The habit of saying yes to people you don't respect is hard to break, which is one reason I think well of Edward Kennedy for breaking it. Also, I think that if any severe punishment is inflicted on the first journalist to disobey an unreasonable order, an era of conformity will set in that will end even the pretense of freedom of the press in any area where there is a brigadier general to agree with.

Having finished with what I consider the deeper implications of the Kennedy case, I would like to say that it has produced some delightful examples of journalism right here in this country. On the afternoon of Tuesday, May 8th, after most of the papers had played up Kennedy's story real big and the Army had then denounced it as "unauthorized," Roy W. Howard, president of the Scripps-Howard newspapers and overlord of the United Press, the A.P.'s chief rival, broke into print with a plea for the Associated Press. Howard said that he himself had been pilloried like Kennedy in November, 1918, when he had reported the armistice four days before it had happened. The two cases were an exact parallel except that Kennedy's report was right and Howard's was wrong.

The *Times*, on that same Tuesday morning, carried Kennedy's story in two columns on the right-hand side of the front page, in twelve-point type, under two cross-lines and two banks dropping from its four-line streamer headline. On Thursday it published an editorial saying Kennedy had done a "grave disservice to the newspaper profession." A *Times* man I met in a saloon that afternoon said they had run the story because it looked authentic but they had run the editorial because they didn't like the way the story had been sent out. On Tuesday they also carried a boxed dispatch from Drew Middleton, one of their own men in Paris, saying that all the correspondents except Kennedy had been caught in "the most colossal 'snafu' in the history of the war."

Wednesday morning brought Daniell's remarkable *Times* story, cited above (which read exactly the way a *Nebelwerfer* sounds) and a perfectly deadpan account of the Reims function by Drew Middleton, who presumably had not been there, since he wasn't on the list of correspondents invited by SHAEF. Middleton's story appeared twenty-four hours after the *Times* had carried the Kennedy story and was practically a duplicate of it. The *Herald Tribune* had an equally deadpan account by John O'Reilly, who presumably wasn't there either, and an editorial, better-tempered than the *Times'*, chiding Kennedy. It also had on its front page an excellent eyewitness story about Berlin in the final days of the Russian attack upon it, written by its own correspondent Seymour Freidin, who was still under suspension by SHAEF for having gone to Berlin without Brigadier General Allen's permission. The story had been held up six days. The *Times* had a similar story by the equally excommunicated John Groth, but it wasn't so good. *PM*, that same P.M., had a long, involved "Letter from the Editor," by the Editor, toward the end of which it came out that the Editor was in favor of the decision Kennedy had made.

After that, the excitement seemed to be dying away, but Friday morning, Robert McLean, publisher of the Philadelphia

*Bulletin* and president of the Associated Press, issued a statement censuring Kennedy. Friday afternoon brought an editorial in *Editor & Publisher*, the trade journal of the newspaper
business, a publication that usually reflects high-echelon
newspaper sentiment. *Editor & Publisher* made a magnificent
grab for the best of both worlds simultaneously, just as if it
were a newspaper. It said, "We agree with Kennedy that no
military security was involved and that it was political censorship. . . . The Paris correspondents also declare they have no
degree of confidence in the Public Relations Division of
SHAEF, and we don't blame them. [Actually, when a motion
of no confidence was proposed at a correspondents' meeting
in Paris after the surrender incident, the correspondents
tabled it, preferring to gang up on their colleague Kennedy.]
We hope this will serve as a lesson to the military and political
leaders of the Allied nations that a story of that magnitude
cannot be kept secret." But the editorial also said, "Kennedy
apparently violated one of the cardinal principles of good
journalism—that of respecting a confidence. No amount of
explanation . . . is justification." Of course, the Allied leaders
would not have learned the lesson if Kennedy had not repu-
diated the confidence. Neither McLean nor *Editor & Publisher* challenged SHAEF's right to impose such a condition.
The top side of the newspaper business obviously believes
that freedom of the press goes no farther than the right to
complain about corporation taxes.

To wind up, and illustrate, my morality tale, the *Times*, on
Saturday morning, carried a story that SHAEF was going to
retain control over correspondents in Europe even though
fighting has ceased and that censors have been empowered to
suppress anything they consider "unauthorized, inaccurate, or
false reports, misleading statements and rumors, or reports
likely to injure the morale of the Allied forces (or nations)."
This means that correspondents may send no news, even
though it is verified and vital to American understanding of
what is happening, unless it is "authorized" by some Army
political adviser like Robert Murphy, who in 1942 gave a
sample of his stuff by stopping all stories unfavorable to the
State Department filed in North Africa. It also means that
the censors—or rather, in the last analysis, the censors' Army

superiors—will decide what is true and accurate or false and misleading, and what is calculated to injure the morale of Allied forces. For example, a correspondent might say there was a strong republican movement in Italy, but the censor might decide that such knowledge would diminish the Royal Italian Army's enthusiasm for the Royal House the Allies insist on propping up. So he would stop the correspondent from sending the story to America. And so it might go—and will, if the press continues to truckle to the dress extras.

*The New Yorker*, May 19, 1945

# Letter from Rome

by Philip Hamburger

MAY 8 (BY WIRELESS)

HAVING LIVED for a year in a troubled semblance of peace, Rome has accepted the news of peace itself with the helpless and tired shrug of the defeated. My guess is that few cities are sadder today. V-E Day has pointed up an unpleasant fact many people here had tried to forget: that Italy lost the war and can advance no claims for the rewards of peace. To the Italians I've talked with, peace in Europe means at the moment little more than a dreary continuation of their present misery—fantastic prices, black markets, unemployment, the struggle to regain national pride, and the even more difficult struggle to get people to think for themselves after two decades of stupefaction. The German surrender seems to have increased the Roman's capacity for introspection; his comprehension of the situation his country is in is almost morbid, and his personal problems have suddenly loomed larger and become more pressing: how can a young man get to Turin to discover whether his parents survived the German occupation; does the American know someone who will deliver a letter to a lady's husband, a Partisan, in Milan; please, will the United States permit Italians to leave home and settle in America; at the far end of town a wealthy friend has food enough for his friends tonight, but can the American arrange to get them there and back by jeep?

Today, Tuesday, is V-E Day, but the bars and restaurants are deserted, the streets practically empty. No more bells than usual have been rung. To be sure, some flags are out and the sirens have sounded, but something is lacking. Occasional noisy groups of young Italians parade the streets, trying with almost pathetic desperation to crash the gate of victory, but the victory is not theirs and the enthusiasm is hollow. One such procession—fifteen to twenty poorly dressed young men, a boy beating a drum, and another boy carrying a large red flag—straggled down the Via Sistina this afternoon and stopped before a British mess. Through the door they could see men laughing and drinking. *"Finita, finita, la guerra è finita!"* cried the paraders, and a British sergeant, glass in hand, stepped outside, bowed gracefully, and thanked the parade for stopping by. "Good of you to come," he said, and went inside. The procession slowly moved down the street a few doors to a hotel where some Americans live. *"Finita, finita, la guerra è finita!"* the Italians cried. Several Americans stuck their heads out of windows, and yelled "Hooray!," and one man with a camera leaned out and said, "Hold it till I get this!" Then everybody stuck his head back in again. The parade disappeared around a corner, the drummer half-heartedly sounding a roll. Of all the troops in town, only the British seem to be in a rejoicing mood. Arm in arm and six or eight abreast, groups of them have been marching through the city, singing. Victory in Europe appears to have accented only the homesickness of the American troops, and, knowing very well that for most of them the end of one war means simply the beginning of another, still farther from home, they have shown little enthusiasm. Tonight I saw hundreds of them sitting alone on curbstones staring into space or ambling along the streets, hands in pockets, looking into shop windows.

Italy last week was Milan, and, unlike Rome, Milan had its victory, a victory all the more pleasant, perhaps, because it came from within rather than from without. Our troops were greeted there almost with hysteria, but this exhilaration had already been touched off, first by the Partisan uprising in the city and then by the execution of Mussolini and his most infamous henchmen. When the Germans in Italy finally surrendered, the news went almost unnoticed in Milan. The newspapers welcomed the capitulation in modest headlines but continued to devote their biggest ones to Partisan activities. On the whole, the efficiency and triumph of the Partisan tactics seemed to stun even the Partisans, and for the first three or four days after the liberation large groups of them—almost all of whom were dashing around town in captured

German cars, rounding up or finishing off lingering Fascists—could be seen embracing one another in the streets.

Because Milan is in the plains and would have been difficult to defend against any reinforcements the Germans might send in to aid the garrison troops, the Committee of National Liberation had to move slowly. Nevertheless, from the beginning of the German occupation, in September, 1943, at least fifteen thousand copies of clandestine newspapers were circulated every week. The newsprint for them was bought on the black market. In March, 1944, the Committee put on a successful eight-day general strike in Milan. In September of that year the Partisans began to attack the Fascists and Germans in the mountains of northern Italy, but they knew that it would be futile to attempt a fight in Milan yet. "Justice and Liberty" squads—one squad to almost every block in the city—were formed and told to provide themselves with arms. The main source of weapons was the garrison of twenty thousand Fascist troops, many of whom were willing to sell their arms if paid high enough prices. Many others were killed at night and robbed of their arms. The acquiring of arms was accelerated last December, when the Allies gave the Committee of National Liberation the task of leading the resistance movement in northern Italy. The Allies not only began to supply arms but also gave a lot of money to a trusted Partisan in Rome, a banker. By intricate financial maneuvering, he was able to transfer the money to the north.

Meanwhile, in Milan, the Partisans shifted their headquarters about once a week, settling now in the office of an obscure razor-blade distributor, now across town in a dismal restaurant. Mussolini, who had a villa on Lake Garda, north of Verona, appeared less and less frequently in Milan. When he did appear, he and his heavily armed cavalcade usually raced through the city, bound for somewhere beyond. By last January, work in the factories making supplies for the Germans had almost entirely stopped because Allied bombing of the Brenner Pass had cut the railway over which coal was sent into the country. In April, the Committee of National Liberation ordered railroad and tramway workers in Milan to strike, snubbed the Fascists when they suggested that everybody let bygones be bygones and that one big brotherly "sacred union" of all Italians might be created, formed a Committee of Revolt, mobilized the Justice and Liberty squads, and finally, on the twenty-fifth, told its ten thousand armed and ten thousand unarmed Partisans to start taking over the city. By noon the following day, a hundred Fascists had been killed and the Committee was in control of Milan. The Germans fought in the suburbs until the twenty-eighth, the day of Mussolini's execution, but those inside the town barricaded themselves in several hotels and refused to come out and fight, preferring to await the arrival of the Allies and to surrender to them.

Although many Romans—and quite a few American correspondents—deplore what went on in the Piazza Loreto on the morning of Sunday, the twenty-ninth, to the Milanese these events will probably always be symbols of the north's liberation. To an outsider like myself, who happened to be on hand to see Mussolini, Clara Petacci, Pavolini, Starace, and some of the other Fascists dangling by their heels from a rusty beam in front of a gas station, the breathless, bloody scene had an air of inevitability. You had the feeling, as you have at the final curtain of a good play, that events could not have been otherwise. In many people's minds, I think, the embellishments of this upheaval—thousands of Partisans firing their machine guns into the air, Fascist bodies lying in a heap alongside the gas station, the enormous, pressing crowd—have been overemphasized and its essential dignity and purpose have been overlooked. This is best illustrated by the execution of Starace—the fanatical killer who was once secretary of the Fascist Party—who was brought into the square in an open truck at about ten-thirty in the morning. The bodies of Mussolini and the others had been hanging for several hours. I had reached the square just before the truck arrived. As it moved slowly ahead, the crowd fell back and became silent. Surrounded by armed guards, Starace stood in the middle of the truck, hands in the air, a lithe, square-jawed, surly figure in a black shirt. The truck stopped for an instant close to the grotesque corpse of his old boss. Starace took one look and started to fall forward, perhaps in a faint, but was pushed back to a standing position by his guards. The truck drove ahead a few feet and stopped. Starace was taken out and placed near a white wall at the rear of the gas station. Beside him were baskets of spring flowers—pink, yellow, purple, and blue—placed there in honor of fifteen anti-Fascists who had been murdered in the same square six months before. A firing squad of Partisans shot Starace in the back, and another Partisan, perched on a beam some twenty feet above the ground, turned toward the crowd in the square and made a broad gesture of finality, much like a highly dramatic umpire calling a man out at the home plate. There were no roars or bloodcurdling yells; there was only silence, and then, suddenly, a sigh—a deep, moaning sound, seemingly expressive of release from something dark and fetid. The people in the square seemed to understand that this was a moment of both ending and beginning. Two minutes later, Starace had been strung up alongside Mussolini and the others. "Look at them now," an old man beside me kept saying. "Just look at them now."

No city could long remain in the emotional fever of the first days of liberation in Milan, and by the middle of that week there were signs of weariness. Fewer Partisans roamed the streets, and they were less rambunctious. Only isolated shootings took place, and these at night. The slow process of rounding up the twenty-four hundred Fascists in the city continued; they were placed in San Vittoria Jail, in cells recently occupied by their captors. A good many Partisans dropped their clandestine names and resumed their own, which created some confusion among the Partisans themselves, who had never known one another's real names. It suddenly became apparent that the days ahead, like any morning after, meant a slow and complicated readjustment.

As for the city itself, its population has, in a few years, jumped from a million to a million seven hundred thousand. A sixth of Milan's buildings were bombed, a considerable number of them in the center of town. The Duomo, however, has survived; only two of the hundreds of delicate statues along its sides were chipped by bomb fragments, although five of its seven organs were wrecked by the concussions of nearby explosions. On the first day of liberation, a crude sign over the door of La Scala (whose roof had been bombed out) said, "We Want Toscanini," but someone took it down after the entrance of the Allied troops and substituted the American, British, and Russian flags. Most of the church of Santa Maria delle Grazie and all of its cloisters are now rubble, but there are hopes that da Vinci's "Last Supper," in the refectory, is intact. Before the first bombings of the war, the fresco was lovingly buttressed with heavy wooden scaffolding and bags filled with stones. The framework withstood the bombings and looks sturdy enough from the outside, amid the wreckage, but so far, understandably, no one has had time to begin the painstaking work of removing the wood and the bags of stones to find out whether da Vinci's masterpiece has survived the second World War.

*The New Yorker*, May 19, 1945

# *Beautiful Upon a Hill*

by E. B. White

SAN FRANCISCO, MAY 4

IF YOU hold a press card in San Francisco, you can go far. You get free bus rides, free Coca-Cola, free sandwiches, and a free seat at all sorts of big and small parleys. You find yourself falling into the vicious habit of attending meetings merely to establish your right to be there. This leads nowhere. There is an air of fantasy about the place, as penetrating as the high fogs which swirl in from sea in the early morning and twist around the tops of buildings. One day last week, soon after arriving in town, I saw a large gray bus labelled "Conference." I entered, showed my press card to the girl at the wheel, and sat down. Except for me, there were no passengers. Immediately the door closed, a motorcycle escort drew alongside and signalled to us to go ahead, and we roared away—all three of us—toward the halls of peace. Later I asked the girl about the escort. "Oh, he doesn't do any good," she said, "but I get a big bang out of having him."

During the past few days I have been at press conferences conducted by Molotov, by Stettinius, and by Stassen. Molotov has been holding his in the St. Francis Hotel. When he and his staff of interpreters, secretaries, and guards enter the room, they come swiftly, heavily, and with a curious emanation of vitality. They walk erect and determined, and there is no casualness about them. The Russian plainclothesmen caused talk at first. Americans don't like the idea of strong-arm stuff, but after a few days the guards seemed more comical than sinister, and their clothes were not exactly plain— there was always some quick giveaway, like a pair of Sears Roebuck shoes, or a hat with no dents. Whatever Foreign Commissar Vyacheslav M. Molotov may think, or not think, about the institution of a free press, he gives a good imitation of enjoying it and he is well equipped to meet its peculiar challenge. His manner is direct, and despite the lag caused by interpretation he is able to create a conversational mood. Pavlov, his interpreter, is a youngish fellow, scholarly in appearance and with a high, sustained voice that sounds as though he were drawing a bow across his vocal strings. He seems earnest and overworked, but indestructible. Molotov himself also seems to possess unlimited endurance, both physical and mental. He is never ruffled, never doubtful, and (as in the case of the Argentine affair) he often has the Press with him.

Stettinius tries hard to develop an easy manner with the boys and girls of the Press, but it doesn't always come off. His weekend with Argentina and Poland was, of course, rough going, since it presented him with the job of explaining matters which, for one reason or another, couldn't be explained. I have noticed that at his press conferences he makes a point of calling reporters by their first names, but when he pronounces the word Bill it sounds strangely like William. He is at his best in parliamentary procedure. Whenever life takes a parliamentary turn, you see Stettinius's chest expand; he draws himself up contentedly and a look of assurance comes over him, and he suddenly appears very double-breasted and Chairman-of-the-Board. When he is being needled, and the subject slips out of the parliamentary area into the realm of diplomatic sleight-of-hand, he leans forward over the table, thrusts an ear out to catch the question, licks his lips as he prepares to reply, and clearly shows embarrassment if he is withholding information for diplomatic reasons.

Stassen is direct and unruffled when the Press is in the room. He analyzes questions quickly and comes up with answers. Whenever it is possible to answer in one word, he answers in one word. A word like yes, or a word like no— two fine little words that seldom turn up these days in San Francisco.

I have watched the United Nations Conference on International Organization for more than a week now, and it has all the endearing and frightening potentials of an Airedale puppy. One minute you look at it and you are sure it will grow rabid and destroy the family. The next minute you look again and you feel certain it will someday pull a drowning child from a stream and win the gratitude of the whole community. The first day or two, the Conference lived in awe of itself. The speeches were subdued, lofty, and long. The atmosphere was that of a cathedral. Over the first weekend, the Conference developed labor pains, and, much to everyone's embarrassment, gave birth to a set of triplets, including a puppy named Argentina, which didn't look at all like its mother and which immediately ruined the rug. Yesterday morning, its strange travail over, the Conference developed growing pains and began trying to digest the objectives proposed by the U.S. delegation.

The meeting yesterday morning at which these proposals were given out to the Press seemed to me by far the best thing that has happened to date. It was the first time the Conference clearly put on record that it had in mind the people of the world as well as the nations of the world. And although justice, law, and human rights still had no effective international status, at least they were being written into the proceedings, with the implication that something would certainly have to be done later to blow life into them. I went up about eleven o'clock to attend this meeting and found the Press assembling in the Red Room of the Fairmont Hotel, described in my souvenir booklet as "beautifully situated on Nob Hill, overlooking the harbor and the financial section." It was in many respects a memorable occasion. The reporters, although beautiful upon a hill, were well aware that most of the people of the earth, for whom these principles of justice and human rights were being written, were not beautifully situated at all. There was a feeling in the room (or at any rate it appeared so to me) that an old order was dead and a new one was about to begin. The occasion seemed far more like a turning point in time than did the twenty-fifth of April, in the Opera House, when the Conference got under way. It seemed more like a turning point than any day I had ever known. Benito Mussolini and Clara Petacci had just been placed in a cheap coffin lined with sawdust and lowered into a potter's-field grave. Hitler and Goebbels were reported dead. The Red flag flew over Berlin. In Italy, the war was over. In a grave in Hyde Park lay the man to whom hundreds of millions had looked for guidance and comfort. And here, beautifully situated upon a hill, were a handful of architectural apprentices whose drawing board contained a neat and precise blueprint labelled the Future.

After a few minutes, Stassen came into the room and walked to the speakers' table. Sol Bloom sat beside him as he addressed the reporters. Nobody was there who didn't hold what is called, in these parts, an "A" card. Speaking for the U.S. delegation, Stassen began reading the list of the nine "objectives"—the principle of justice, the development of law, the recognition of human rights, the concept of peaceful change, the idea of trusteeship, the inclusion of China's clause about cultural objectives, and so on. The reporters took notes busily. Twice they asked him to go back and repeat. It was an on-the-record conference, but not for quotation. There were the usual questions which are fired at anyone who stands up at a desk in San Francisco these days: how about remodelling the Polish government before lunchtime, what about India's independence? For the most part, however, the Press was in an inquiring rather than a challenging mood. When one reporter asked what the word "cultural" meant, Stassen smiled and said that he had been studying his Webster hard in an attempt to find out himself.

One thing that has struck me, hanging around these press conferences, is how greatly the function of the American press has been enlarged. The quality of the reporting here is high, and the questioning is done by men who know what they are talking about. Two days earlier, for instance, there had been another conference in this same Red Room. Argentina was on the fire and Stettinius was being backed against the wall and made to explain how a peace-loving nation could also be a Fascist-loving nation, or vice versa. A good many newspaper people, that day, were sore right up to their armpits, and although they were present in the capacity of recorders—to ask questions and take down answers—actually they were extending that function and were managing, in the course of asking questions, to make short, hot speeches from the floor. Thus the Press, in the process of being told, was right in there telling. It was a fascinating moment in the pungent laboratory of democracy, with test tubes and flashbulbs exploding with a cosmic crackle, exposing the world's almost impenetrable gloom.

The persistence, the knowingness, and the courage of a free press is the one best hope in this meeting ground, and when, the other day, I came upon a nest of burned-out flashbulbs in an out-of-the-way corner of the Veterans' Building, I had a strong impulse to sit on them and brood them back to life. Instead, I just went on down the hall to the big press room, where forty or fifty men and women, of several shades of color and of many shades of opinion, were belaboring the keys. The room had the wonderful sound that orchestras make just before they swing into action. I sat down and began tuning an Underwood and studying the notes of the New World Symphony. Next to me sat a girl reporter from, I think, one of the local papers. She was relaxed in front of a still typewriter and was deep in a magazine. I glanced cautiously at the title. It was called *Fantastic Adventures*.

*The New Yorker*, May 12, 1945

# Attack on Carrier Bunker Hill

by Phelps Adams

ABOARD A FAST CARRIER IN THE FORWARD PACIFIC AREA, May 11 (Delayed). — Two Japanese suicide planes carrying 1,100 pounds of bombs plunged into the flight deck of Admiral Marc A. Mitscher's own flagship early today, killing several hundred officers and men, and transforming one of our biggest and finest flattops into a floating torch, with flames soaring nearly a thousand feet into the sky.

For eight seemingly interminable hours that followed, the ship and her crew fought as tense and terrifying a battle for survival as has ever been witnessed in the Pacific, but when dusk closed in the U.S.S. Bunker Hill — horribly crippled and still filmed by thin wisps of smoke and steam from her smoldering embers, was valiantly plowing along under her own power on the distant horizon — safe! Tomorrow she will spend nearly eight equally interminable hours burying at sea the men who died to save her.

Only once before during the entire war against Japan has any American carrier suffered such wounds, fought such fires, and lived — and that was when the battered, gutted hulk of the Franklin managed miraculously to steam away from these waters under her own power.

Like the Franklin, the Bunker Hill took everything the Japs could give her, under the most unfavorable circumstances, and survived it. And tonight, as she licks at her wounds and nurses her wounded, she stands as a living monument to the fact that no major unit of the American fleet has ever been sunk by a suicide plane or by any combination of them. She constitutes one more link in the chain of evidence which must, by now, have convinced the Japs that all the maniacal, suicidal fury that they can unleash against us cannot save them.

From the deck of the neighboring carrier a few hundred yards distant I watched the Bunker Hill burn, and I do not yet see how she lived through it. It is hard to believe that men could survive those flames, or that metal could withstand such heat.

I still find it incredible, too, that death could strike so swiftly and so wholly unexpectedly into the very heart of our great Pacific fleet. At one minute our task force was cruising in lazy circles about sixty miles off Okinawa without a care in the world and apparently without a suggestion of the presence of an enemy plane in any direction. In the next minute the Bunker Hill was a pillar of flame. It was as quick as that—like summer lightning without any warning rumble of thunder.

The Oriental equivalent of Lady Luck was certainly riding with Japan's suicide corps today. Everything broke for them with unbelievable good fortune.

A series of fleecy-white, low-hanging clouds that studded a bright sky concealed the intruders from the vigilant eyes of all the lookouts manning all the stations on all of the ships that go to make up this great armada called Task Force 58. Not until they began their final screaming plunge from the cover of these clouds did the Jap kamikazes become visible.

And it was sheer luck, of course, that they happened to strike on the particular day and at the exact hour when their target was most vulnerable. Because there was no sign of the enemy and because the Bunker Hill and the men aboard her were weary after fifty-eight consecutive days in the battle zones off Iwo Jima, Tokyo, the Inland Sea and Okinawa her crew was not at General Quarters when she was hit. For the first time in a week our own ship had secured from General Quarters an hour or two before. Some of the watertight doors that imprisoned men in small, stifling compartments were thrown open. The ventilators were unsealed and turned on, and those men not standing the regular watch were permitted to relax from the deadly sixteen-hour vigil that they had put in at their battle stations every day since we had entered the danger zone.

So it was on the Bunker Hill. Exhausted men not on watch were catching a catnap. Aft on the flight deck thirty-four planes were waiting to take off. Their tanks were filled to the last drop of capacity with highly volatile aviation gasoline.

Their guns were loaded to the last possible round of ammunition. Earnest young pilots, mentally reviewing the briefing they had just received, were in the cockpits warming up the motors. On the hangar deck below more planes—also crammed with gasoline and ammunition—were all set to be spotted on the flight deck, and in the pilots' ready rooms other young aviators were kidding around while waiting their turn aloft.

Just appearing over the horizon were the planes returning from the early mission. They jockeyed into the landing circle and waited until the Bunker Hill should launch her readied craft and clear the deck for landing.

And it was at this precise moment that a keen-eyed man aboard our ship caught the first glimpse of three enemy planes and cried a warning. But before General Quarters could be sounded on this ship, and before half a dozen shots could be fired by the Bunker Hill, the first kamikaze had dropped his 550-pound bomb and plunged squarely into the midst of the thirty-four waiting planes in a shower of burning gasoline.

The bomb, fitted with a delayed action fuse, pierced the flight deck at a sharp angle, passed out through the side of the hull and exploded in mid-air before striking the water. The plane—a single-engined Jap fighter—knocked the parked aircraft about like ten-pins, sent a huge column of flame and smoke belching upwards and then skidded crazily over the side.

Some of the pilots were blown overboard, and many managed to scramble to safety; but before a move could be made to fight the flames another kamikaze came whining out of the clouds, straight into the deadly anti-aircraft guns of the ship. This plane was a Jap dive bomber—a judy. A five-inch shell that should have blown him out of the sky, set him afire and riddled his plane with metal, but still he came. Passing over the stern of the ship, he dropped his bomb with excellent aim right in the middle of the blazing planes. Then he flipped over and torched through the flight deck at the base of the island. The superstructure, which contains many of the delicate nerve centers from which the vessel is controlled, was instantly enveloped in flames and smoke which were caught in turn by the maws of the ventilating system and sucked down into the inner compartments of the ship, where the watertight doors and hatches had just been swung shut and battened down. Scores of men were suffocated in these below deck chambers.

Minutes later a third Jap suicider zoomed down to finish the job. Ignoring the flames and the smoke that swept around them, the men in the Bunker Hill's gun galleries stuck courageously to their posts, pumping ammunition into their weapons and filling the sky with a curtain of protective lead. It was a neighboring destroyer, however, which finally scored a direct hit on the Jap and sent him splashing harmlessly into the sea.

That was the end of the attack and beginning of an heroic and brilliant fight for survival. The entire rear end of the ship was burning with uncontrollable fury. It looked very much like the newsreel shots of a blazing oil well, only worse — for this fire was feeding on highly refined gasoline and live ammunition. Greasy black smoke rose in a huge column from the ship's stern, shot through with angry tongues of cherry-red flame. Blinding white flashes appeared continuously as ready ammunition in the burning planes or in the gun galleries was touched off. Every few minutes the whole column of smoke would be swallowed in a great burst of flame as another belly tank exploded or as the blaze reached another pool of gasoline flowing from the broken aviation fuel lines on the hangar deck below.

For more than an hour there was no visible abatement in the fury of the flames. They would seem to be dying down slightly as hundreds of thousands of gallons of water and chemicals were poured on them, only to burst forth more hungrily than ever as some new explosion occurred within the stricken ship.

The carrier itself had begun to develop a pronounced list, and as each new stream of water was poured into her the angle increased more dangerously. Crippled as she was, however, she ploughed ahead at top speed and the wind that swept her decks blew the flame and smoke astern over the fantail and prevented the blaze from spreading forward on the flight deck and through the island structure. Trapped on the fantail, men faced the flames and fought grimly on, with only the ocean behind them, and with no way of knowing how much of the ship remained on the other side of that fiery wall.

Then, somehow, other men managed to break out the huge openings in the side of the hangar deck, and I got my first glimpse of the interior of the ship. That, I think, was the most horrible sight of all. The entire hangar deck was a raging blast furnace, white-hot throughout its length. Even from where I stood the glow of molten metal was unmistakable.

By this time the explosions had ceased and a cruiser and three destroyers were able to venture alongside with hoses fixed in their rigging. Like fireboats in New York Harbor, they pumped great streams of water into the ship and the smoke at last began to take on that greyish tinge which showed that somewhere a flame was dying.

Up on the bridge, Capt. George A. Seitz, the skipper, was growing increasingly concerned about the dangerous list his ship had developed, and resolved to take a gambling chance. Throwing the Bunker Hill into a 70-degree turn, he heeled her cautiously over onto the opposite beam so that tons of water which had accumulated on one side were suddenly swept across the decks and overboard on the other. By great good fortune this wall of water carried the heart of the hangar deck fire with it.

That was the turning point in this modern battle of the Bunker Hill. After nearly three hours of almost hopeless fighting, she had brought her fires under control, and, though it was many more hours before they were completely extinguished, the battle was won and the ship was saved.

A thick book could not record all the acts of heroism that were performed aboard that valiant ship today. There was the executive officer, Commander H. J. Dyson, who was standing within fifty feet of the second bomb when it exploded and who was badly injured; yet he refused medical aid and continued to fight the blaze until it was safely under control.

Then there was a squad of Marines who braved the white heat of the hangar deck and threw every bomb and rocket out of a nearby storage room.

But the most fruitful work of all, perhaps, was performed

by the pilots of the almost fuelless planes that had been circling overhead for a landing when the ship was struck. In the hours that followed, nearly three hundred men went overboard, and the fact that 269 of these were picked up by other ships in the fleet later was due, in no small measure, to the work of these sharp-eyed airmen.

Although our own flight deck had been cleared for their use and they had been instructed to land on it, these pilots kept combing every inch of the surface of the sea, tearing packets of dye marker from their own life jackets and dropping them to guide destroyers and other rescue vessels to the little clusters of men they saw clinging to bits of wreckage below them. Calculating their fuel supply to a hairbreadth nicety, some of them came aboard us with such a close margin that a single wave-off would have sent them and their planes into the sea before they could make another swing of the landing circle and return.

In all, I am told, 170 men will be recommended for awards as a result of this day's work.

Late today Admiral Mitscher and 60 or more members of his staff came aboard us to make this carrier his new flagship. He was unhurt—not even singed by the flames that swept the Bunker Hill, but he had lost three officers and six men of his own staff and a number of close friends in the ship's company. It was the first time in his long years of service that he had personally undergone such an experience.

As he was hauled aboard in a breeches buoy across the churning water that separated us from the speedy destroyer that had brought him alongside, he looked tired and old and just plain mad. His deeply lined face was more than weather beaten—it looked like an example of erosion in the dust-bowl country—but his eyes flashed fire and vengeance. He was a man who had a score to settle with the Japs and who would waste no time going about it. He had plans that the Japs will not like.

But as a matter of fact, the enemy is already on the losing end of the Bunker Hill box score. Since she arrived in the Pacific in the fall of 1943 the Bunker Hill has participated in every major strike that has occurred. She was initiated at Rabaul, she took part in the invasions of the Gilberts and the

Marshalls, pounding at Kwajalein and Eniwetok. With Task Force 58, she has struck twice at Tokyo and also at Truk, the China Coast, the Ryukyus, Formosa, the Bonins, Iwo Jima and Okinawa.

During this period the pilots of her air groups have sunk, probably sunk and damaged, nearly a million tons of Jap shipping. They have shot 475 enemy planes out of the air, 169 of them during the past two months. In two days here off Okinawa they splashed sixty-seven Nipponese aircraft, and the ship herself has brought down fourteen more by anti-aircraft fire.

On a raid last March at Kure Harbor when the Japanese fleet was hiding out in the Inland Sea, Bunker Hill planes scored direct bomb hits on three carriers and one heavy cruiser, and then sent nine torpedoes flashing into the side of the enemy's beautiful new battleship, the Yamato, sinking her.

That is our side of the box score.

In the Jap column stands the fact that at the cost of three pilots and three planes today the enemy killed a probable total of 392 of our men, wounded 264 others, destroyed about 70 planes and wrecked a fine and famous ship. The flight deck of that ship tonight looks like the crater of a volcano. One of the great fifty-ton elevators has been melted almost in half. Gun galleries have been destroyed and the pilots' ready rooms demolished. Virtually the entire island structure with its catwalks and platforms is a twisted mass of steel, and below decks tonight hospital corpsmen are preparing 352 bodies for burial at sea, starting at noon tomorrow.

But the ship has not been sunk. Had it been it would have taken years to build another. As it is the Bunker Hill will steam back to Bremerton Navy Yard under her own power and there will be repaired. While she remains there one American carrier with a hundred or so planes and a crew of 3,000 men will be out of action, but within a few weeks she will be back again, sinking more ships, downing more planes, and bombing out more Japanese airfields.

Perhaps her next task will be to cover the Invasion of Tokyo itself. Who knows?

*The New York Sun*, June 28, 1945

# Guam Holdouts Give Up

by Shelley Mydans

AFTER a year of hiding in the jungle, the Japanese officer had become a Guam legend. Now he stood in the clearing, ready to surrender to the Americans. With him was his lieutenant, his orderly—who from time to time wiped the sweat from the officer's forehead—and 33 ragged soldiers. When Colonel Howard Stent, USMC, arrived in his jeep, the Japanese officer snapped his men to attention. "You are now prisoners of war," he said. "This is no disgrace. It is a mistake to think of it as such." The 35 men turned toward their emperor in Tokyo and bowed, eyes closed. Then they went off to the prisoners' stockade.

This was the biggest single haul of Jap prisoners since Guam was secured last August. Their surrender was a significant success for Colonel Stent and his psychological-warfare men. With sound truck and leaflets they had been on the trail of the officer since September, trying to get him to surrender. Not until April did they get any hint of results. Then a Jap soldier, who gave himself up, revealed that he had first asked the officer's permission to surrender. "Go ahead," the officer answered. "I'm thinking of it myself."

On June 2 the officer himself approached the sound truck in the hills, wanting to speak to Colonel Stent. He told the colonel that he had been reading the leaflets and stolen copies of *Time*, then made a strange request: "Let me live in the jungle until the end of the war. I will not molest you and you will not hunt for me." This, Colonel Stent replied, was impossible. The Jap officer said he was considering hara-kiri. The Colonel argued that Japan would need responsible officers like him after the war.

The Jap asked for a week to think it over. In a week he asked for two more days. On June 11, one year after the first

U.S. shell landed on Guam—as had probably been carefully planned—he finally gave up.

The victory over the stubborn officer came after a war of nerves which is proving more successful in routing out Japs on Guam than the most adroit patrolling. At first the American sound trucks used Japanese-speaking Americans and Nisei, whose strange voices and accent brought meager results. After one Japanese prisoner volunteered to speak to his comrades in the jungle, surrenders came more frequently. Other stockade Japs were used. Willing to help, they suggested useful changes in the surrender appeals. Today the favorite themes addressed to the Japs are: 1) *Jungle life is so difficult. What is the use of dying out there when you can surrender and save your life for Japan?* 2) *Your family and friends are worrying about you. Give up now and live to rebuild Japan for them.*

Leaflets and a weekly newspaper dropped into areas where Japs lurk show pictures of cleanliness, food and tobacco enjoyed in the prison stockades. The Japanese written character is a revealing and personal thing, even more than handwriting. When they were in the bush, the prisoners had mistrusted the strange hand of the Nisei and Americans. Now they offer to write the leaflets themselves. Some prisoners even volunteer to go out and talk face to face with their fellow soldiers. Not one has broken his word that he would come back. Almost always they come back with new prisoners.

The Japs, however, are hard to persuade. One little fellow decided to see for himself whether all this was talk or truth. He sneaked up to the stockade and hid under the officers' shower cabin, drinking the shower water—which he figured must be good if officers used it—and watching his friends in the stockade. After two days he decided the propaganda was really true, gave himself up.

Life, July 9, 1945

# Atomic Bombing of Nagasaki
# Told by Flight Member

by William L. Laurence

WITH THE ATOMIC BOMB MISSION TO JAPAN, Aug. 9 (De-layed)—We are on our way to bomb the mainland of Japan. Our flying contingent consists of three specially designed B-29 "Superforts," and two of these carry no bombs. But our lead plane is on its way with another atomic bomb, the second in three days, concentrating in its active substance an explosive energy equivalent to 20,000 and, under favorable conditions, 40,000 tons of TNT.

We have several chosen targets. One of these is the great industrial and shipping center of Nagasaki, on the western shore of Kyushu, one of the main islands of the Japanese homeland.

I watched the assembly of this man-made meteor during the past two days, and was among the small group of scientists and Army and Navy representatives privileged to be present at the ritual of its loading in the "Superfort" last night, against a background of threatening black skies torn open at intervals by great lightning flashes.

It is a thing of beauty to behold, this "gadget." In its design went millions of man-hours of what is without doubt the most concentrated intellectual effort in history. Never before had so much brain-power been focused on a single problem.

This atomic bomb is different from the bomb used three days ago with such devastating results on Hiroshima.

I saw the atomic substance before it was placed inside the bomb. By itself it is not at all dangerous to handle. It is only under certain conditions, produced in the bomb assembly, that it can be made to yield up its energy, and even then it gives only a small fraction of its total contents—a fraction, however, large enough to produce the greatest explosion on earth.

The briefing at midnight revealed the extreme care and the tremendous amount of preparation that had been made to take care of every detail of the mission, to make certain that the atomic bomb fully served the purpose for which it was intended. Each target in turn was shown in detailed maps and in aerial photographs. Every detail of the course was rehearsed—navigation, altitude, weather, where to land in emergencies. It came out that the Navy had submarines and rescue craft, known as Dumbos and Superdumbos, stationed at various strategic points in the vicinity of the targets, ready to rescue the fliers in case they were forced to bail out.

The briefing period ended with a moving prayer by the chaplain. We then proceeded to the mess hall for the traditional early morning breakfast before departure on a bombing mission.

A convoy of trucks took us to the supply building for the special equipment carried on combat missions. This included the "Mae West," a parachute, a lifeboat, an oxygen mask, a flak suit and a survival vest. We still had a few hours before take-off time, but we all went to the flying field and stood around in little groups or sat in jeeps talking rather casually about our mission to the Empire, as the Japanese home islands are known hereabouts.

In command of our mission is Maj. Charles W. Sweeney, 25, of 124 Hamilton Avenue, North Quincy, Mass. His flagship, carrying the atomic bomb, is named The Great Artiste, but the name does not appear on the body of the great silver ship, with its unusually long, four-bladed, orange-tipped propellers. Instead it carried the number 77, and someone remarks that it was "Red" Grange's winning number on the gridiron.

Major Sweeney's co-pilot is First Lieut. Charles D. Albury, 24, of 252 Northwest Fourth Street, Miami, Fla. The bombardier, upon whose shoulders rests the responsibility of depositing the atomic bomb square on its target, is Capt. Kermit K. Beahan of 1004 Telephone Road, Houston, Tex., who is celebrating his twenty-seventh birthday today.

Captain Beahan has the awards of the Distinguished Flying Cross, the Air Medal and one Silver Oak Leaf Cluster, the

Purple Heart, the Western Hemisphere Ribbon, the European Theatre Ribbon and two battle stars. He participated in the first Eighth Air Force heavy bombardment mission against the Germans from England on Aug. 17, 1942, and was on the plane that transported Gen. Dwight D. Eisenhower from Gibraltar to Oran at the beginning of the North African invasion. He has had a number of hair-raising escapes in combat.

The navigator on The Great Artiste is Capt. James F. Van Pelt Jr., 27, of Oak Hill, W. Va. The flight engineer is M/Sgt. John D. Kuharek, 32, of 1054 Twenty-second Avenue, Columbus, Neb.; S/Sgt. Albert T. De Hart of Plainview, Tex., who celebrated his thirtieth birthday yesterday, is the tail gunner; the radar operator is S/Sgt. Edward K. Buckley, 32, of 529 East Washington Street, Lisbon, Ohio. The radio operator is Sgt. Abe M. Spitzer, 33, of 655 Pelham Parkway, North Bronx, N.Y.; Sgt. Raymond Gallagher, 23, of 572 South Mozart Street, Chicago, is assistant flight engineer.

The lead ship is also carrying a group of scientific personnel, headed by Comdr. Frederick L. Ashworth, USN, one of the leaders in the development of the bomb. The group includes Lieut. Jacob Beser, 24, of Baltimore, Md., an expert on airborne radar.

The other two Superfortresses in our formation are instrument planes, carrying special apparatus to measure the power of the bomb at the time of explosion, high speed cameras and other photographic equipment.

Our "Superfort" is the second in line. Its commander is Capt. Frederick C. Bock, 27, of 300 West Washington Street, Greenville, Mich. Its other officers are Second Lieut. Hugh C. Ferguson, 21, of 247 Windermere Avenue, Highland Park, Mich., pilot; Second Lieut. Leonard A. Godfrey, 24, of 72 Lincoln Street, Greenfield, Mass., navigator; and First Lieut. Charles Levy, 26, of 1954 Spencer Street, Philadelphia, bombardier.

The enlisted personnel of this "Superfort" are: T/Sgt. Roderick F. Arnold, 28, of 130 South Street, Rochester, Mich., flight engineer; Sgt. Ralph D. Curry, 20, of 1101 South Second Avenue, Hoopeston, Ill., radio operator; Sgt. William C. Barney, 22, of Columbia City, Ind., radar operator; Corp. Robert J. Stock, 21, of 415 Downing Street, Fort Wayne, Ind., assistant flight engineer, and Corp. Ralph D. Belanger, 19, of Thendara, N.Y., tail gunner.

The scientific personnel of our "Superfort" includes S/Sgt. Walter Goodman, 22, of 1956 Seventy-fourth Street, Brooklyn, N.Y., and Lawrence Johnson, graduate student at the University of California, whose home is at Hollywood, Calif.

The third "Superfort" is commanded by Maj. James Hopkins, 1311 North Queen Street, Palestine, Tex. His officers are Second Lieut. John E. Cantlon, 516 North Takima Street, Tacoma, Wash., pilot; Second Lieut. Stanley C. Steinke, 604 West Chestnut Street, West Chester, Pa., navigator; and Second Lieut. Myron Faryna, 16 Elgin Street, Rochester, N.Y., bombardier.

The crew are Tech. Sgt. George L. Brabenec, 9717 South Lawndale Avenue, Evergreen, Ill.; Sgt. Francis X. Dolan, 30-60 Warren Street, Elmhurst, Queens, N.Y.; Corp. Richard F. Cannon, 160 Carmel Road, Buffalo, N.Y.; Corp. Martin G. Murray, 7356 Dexter Street, Detroit, Mich., and Corp. Sidney J. Bellamy, 529 Johnston Avenue, Trenton, N.J.

On this "Superfort" are also two distinguished observers from Britain, whose scientists played an important role in the development of the atomic bomb. One of these is Group Capt. G. Leonard Cheshire, famous Royal Air Force pilot, who is now a member of the British military mission to the United States. The other is Dr. William G. Penney, Professor of Applied Mathematics, London University, one of the group of eminent British scientists that has been working at the "Y-Site" near Santa Fe, N.M., on the enormous problems involved in taming the atom.

Group Captain Cheshire, whose rank is the equivalent to that of colonel in the United States Army Air Forces, was designated as an observer of the atomic bomb in action by Winston Churchill when he was still Prime Minister. He is now the official representative of Prime Minister Clement R. Attlee.

We took off at 3:50 this morning and headed northwest on a straight line for the Empire. The night was cloudy and threatening, with only a few stars here and there breaking through the overcast. The weather report had predicted storms ahead part of the way but clear sailing for the final and climactic stages of our odyssey.

We were about an hour away from our base when the storm broke. Our great ship took some heavy dips through the abysmal darkness around us but it took these dips much more gracefully than a large commercial airliner, producing a sensation more in the nature of a glide than a "bump," like a great ocean liner riding the waves, except that in this case the air waves were much higher and the rhythmic tempo of the glide much faster.

I noticed a strange eerie light coming through the window high above the navigator's cabin and as I peered through the dark all around us I saw a startling phenomenon. The whirling giant propellers had somehow became great luminous disks of blue flame. The same luminous blue flame appeared on the plexiglass windows in the nose of the ship, and on the tips of the giant wings it looked as though we were riding the whirlwind through space on a chariot of blue fire.

It was, I surmised, a surcharge of static electricity that had accumulated on the tips of the propellers and on the dielectric material in the plastic windows. One's thoughts dwelt anxiously on the precious cargo in the invisible ship ahead of us. Was there any likelihood of danger that this heavy electric tension in the atmosphere all about us might set it off?

I expressed my fears to Captain Bock, who seems nonchalant and imperturbed at the controls. He quickly reassures me:

"It is a familiar phenomenon seen often on ships. I have seen it many times on bombing missions. It is known as St. Elmo's Fire."

On we went through the night. We soon rode out the storm and our ship was once again sailing on a smooth course straight ahead, on a direct line to the Empire.

Our altimeter showed that we were traveling through space at a height of 17,000 feet. The thermometer registered an outside temperature of 33 degrees below zero centigrade, about 30 below Fahrenheit. Inside our pressurized cabin the temperature was that of a comfortable air-conditioned room, and a pressure corresponding to an altitude of 8,000 feet. Captain Bock cautioned me, however, to keep my oxygen mask handy in case of emergency. This, he explained, might mean either something going wrong with the pressure equipment inside the ship or a hole through the cabin by flak.

The first signs of dawn came shortly after 5 o'clock. Sergeant Curry, who had been listening steadily on his earphones for radio reports, while maintaining a strict radio silence himself, greeted it by rising to his feet and gazing out the window.

"It's good to see the day," he told me. "I get a feeling of claustrophobia hemmed in in this cabin at night."

He is a typical American youth, looking even younger than his 20 years. It takes no mind-reader to read his thoughts.

"It's a long way from Hoopeston, Ill.," I find myself remarking.

"Yep," he replies, as he busies himself decoding a message from outer space.

"Think this atomic bomb will end the war?" he asks hopefully.

"There is a very good chance that this one may do the trick," I assure him, "but if not, then the next one or two surely will. Its power is such that no nation can stand up against it very long."

This was not my own view. I had heard it expressed all around a few hours earlier, before we took off. To anyone who had seen this man-made fireball in action, as I had less than a month ago in the desert of New Mexico, this view did not sound overoptimistic.

By 5:50 it was real light outside. We had lost our lead ship, but Lieutenant Godfrey, our navigator, informs me that we had arranged for that contingency. We have an assembly point in the sky above the little island of Yakoshima, southeast of Kyushu, at 9:10. We are to circle there and wait for the rest of our formation.

Our genial bombardier, Lieutenant Levy, comes over to invite me to take his front-row seat in the transparent nose of the ship and I accept eagerly. From that vantage point in space, 17,000 feet above the Pacific, one gets a view of hundreds of miles on all sides, horizontally and vertically. At that height the vast ocean below and the sky above seem to merge into one great sphere.

I was on the inside of that firmament, riding above the giant mountains of white cumulous clouds, letting myself be suspended in infinite space. One hears the whirl of the motors behind one, but it soon becomes insignificant against the immensity all around and is before long swallowed by it. There comes a point where space also swallows time and one lives through eternal moments filled with an oppressive loneliness, as though all life had suddenly vanished from the earth and you are the only one left, a lone survivor traveling endlessly through interplanetary space.

My mind soon returns to the mission I am on. Somewhere beyond these vast mountains of white clouds ahead of me there lies Japan, the land of our enemy. In about four hours from now one of its cities, making weapons of war for use against us, will be wiped off the map by the greatest weapon ever made by man. In one-tenth of a millionth of a second, a fraction of time immeasurable by any clock, a whirlwind from the skies will pulverize thousands of its buildings and tens of thousands of its inhabitants.

Our weather planes ahead of us are on their way to find out where the wind blows. Half an hour before target time we will know what the winds have decided.

Does one feel any pity or compassion for the poor devils about to die? Not when one thinks of Pearl Harbor and of the Death March on Bataan.

Captain Bock informs me that we are about to start our climb to bombing altitude.

He manipulates a few knobs on his control panel to the right of him and I alternately watch the white clouds and ocean below me and the altimeter on the bombardier's panel. We reached our altitude at 9 o'clock. We were then over Japanese waters, close to their mainland. Lieutenant Godfrey motioned to me to look through his radar scope. Before me was the outline of our assembly point. We shall soon meet our lead ship and proceed to the final stage of our journey.

We reached Yakoshima at 9:12 and there, about 4,000 feet ahead of us, was The Great Artiste with its precious load. I saw Lieutenant Godfrey and Sergeant Curry strap on their parachutes and I decided to do likewise.

We started circling. We saw little towns on the coastline,

heedless of our presence. We kept on circling, waiting for the third ship in our formation.

It was 9:56 when we began heading for the coastline. Our weather scouts had sent us code messages, deciphered by Sergeant Curry, informing us that both the primary target as well as the secondary were clearly visible.

The winds of destiny seemed to favor certain Japanese cities that must remain nameless. We circled about them again and again and found no opening in the thick umbrella of clouds that covered them. Destiny chose Nagasaki as the ultimate target.

We had been circling for some time when we noticed black puffs of smoke coming through the white clouds directly at us. There were fifteen bursts of flak in rapid succession, all too low. Captain Bock changed his course. There soon followed eight more bursts of flak, right up to our altitude, but by this time were too far to the left.

We flew southward down the channel and at 11:33 crossed the coastline and headed straight for Nagasaki about 100 miles to the west. Here again we circled until we found an opening in the clouds. It was 12:01 and the goal of our mission had arrived.

We heard the prearranged signal on our radio, put on our arc-welder's glasses and watched tensely the maneuverings of the strike ship about half a mile in front of us.

"There she goes!" someone said.

Out of the belly of The Great Artiste what looked like a black object went downward.

Captain Bock swung around to get out of range; but even though we were turning away in the opposite direction, and despite the fact that it was broad daylight in our cabin, all of us became aware of a giant flash that broke through the dark barrier of our arc-welder's lenses and flooded our cabin with intense light.

We removed our glasses after the first flash, but the light still lingered on, a bluish-green light that illuminated the entire sky all around. A tremendous blast wave struck our ship and made it tremble from nose to tail. This was followed by four more blasts in rapid succession, each resounding like the boom of cannon fire hitting our plane from all directions.

Observers in the tail of our ship saw a giant ball of fire rise as though from the bowels of the earth, belching forth enormous white smoke rings. Next they saw a giant pillar of purple fire, 10,000 feet high, shooting skyward with enormous speed.

By the time our ship had made another turn in the direction of the atomic explosion the pillar of purple fire had reached the level of our altitude. Only about forty-five seconds had passed. Awe-struck, we watched it shoot upward like a meteor coming from the earth instead of from outer space, becoming ever more alive as it climbed skyward through the white clouds. It was no longer smoke, or dust, or even a cloud of fire. It was a living thing, a new species of being, born right before our incredulous eyes.

At one stage of its evolution, covering millions of years in terms of seconds, the entity assumed the form of a giant square totem pole, with its base about three miles long, tapering off to about a mile at the top. Its bottom was brown, its center was amber, its top white. But it was a living totem pole, carved with many grotesque masks grimacing at the earth.

Then, just when it appeared as though the thing has settled down into a state of permanence, there came shooting out of the top a giant mushroom that increased the height of the pillar to a total of 45,000 feet. The mushroom top was even more alive than the pillar, seething and boiling in a white fury of creamy foam, sizzling upward and then descending earthward, a thousand Old Faithful geysers rolled into one.

It kept struggling in an elemental fury, like a creature in the act of breaking the bonds that held it down. In a few seconds it had freed itself from its gigantic stem and floated upward with tremendous speed, its momentum carrying into the stratosphere to a height of about 60,000 feet.

But no sooner did this happen when another mushroom, smaller in size than the first one, began emerging out of the pillar. It was as though the decapitated monster was growing a new head.

As the first mushroom floated off into the blue it changed its shape into a flowerlike form, its giant petal curving downward, creamy white outside, rose-colored inside. It still retained that shape when we last gazed at it from a distance of about 200 miles.

*The New York Times*, September 9, 1945

# *Japan Signs, Second World War Is Ended*

by Homer Bigart

ABOARD U. S. S. MISSOURI, Tokyo Bay, Sept. 2 (Sunday). — Japan, paying for her desperate throw of the dice at Pearl Harbor, passed from the ranks of the major powers at 9:05 a.m. today when Foreign Minister Mamoru Shigemitsu signed the document of unconditional surrender.

If the memories of the bestialities of the Japanese prison camps were not so fresh in mind, one might have felt sorry for Shigemitsu as he hobbled on his wooden leg toward the green baize covered table where the papers lay waiting. He leaned heavily on his cane and had difficulty seating himself. The cane, which he rested against the table, dropped to the deck of this battleship as he signed.

No word passed between him and General Douglas MacArthur, who motioned curtly to the table when he had finished his opening remarks.

Lieutenant General Jonathan M. Wainwright, who surrendered Corregidor, haggard from his long imprisonment, and Lieutenant General A. E. Percival, who surrendered Singapore on another black day of the war, stood at MacArthur's side as the Allied Supreme Commander signed for all the powers warring against Japan.

Their presence was a sobering reminder of how desperately close to defeat our nation had fallen during the early months of 1942.

The Japanese delegation of eleven looked appropriately trim and sad. Shigemitsu was wearing morning clothes — frock coat, striped pants, silk hat and yellow gloves. None of the party exchanged a single word or salute while on board, except the foreign minister's aide, who had to be shown where to place the Japanese texts of the surrender documents.

Shigemitsu, however, doffed his silk hat as he reached the top of the starboard gangway and stepped aboard the broad deck of the Missouri.

New York *Herald Tribune*, September 2, 1945

# A Month After the Atom Bomb: Hiroshima Still Can't Believe It

by Homer Bigart

HIROSHIMA, Japan, Sept. 3 (Delayed).—We walked today through Hiroshima, where survivors of the first atomic-bomb explosion four weeks ago are still dying at the rate of about one hundred daily from burns and infections which the Japanese doctors seem unable to cure.

The toll from the most terrible weapon ever devised now stands at 53,000 counted dead, 30,000 missing and presumed dead, 13,960 severely wounded and likely to die, and 43,000 wounded. The figures come from Hirokuni Dadai, who as "chief of thought control" of Hiroshima Prefecture is supposed to police subversive thinking.

On the morning of Aug. 6 the 340,000 inhabitants of Hiroshima were awakened by the familiar howl of air-raid sirens. The city had never been bombed—it had little industrial importance. The Kure naval base lay only twelve miles to the southeast and American bombers had often gone there to blast the remnants of the imperial navy, or had flown mine-laying or strafing missions over Shimonoseki Strait to the west. Almost daily enemy planes had flown over Hiroshima, but so far the city had been spared.

At 8 a.m. the "all clear" sounded. Crowds emerged from the shallow raid shelters in Military Park and hurried to their jobs in the score of tall, modern, earthquake-proof buildings along Hattchobori, the main business street of the city. Breakfast fires still smoldered in thousands of tiny ovens—presently they were to help to kindle a conflagration.

Very few persons saw the Superfortress when it first appeared more than five miles above the city. Some thought they saw a black object swinging down on a parachute from the plane, but for the most part Hiroshima never knew what hit it.

A Japanese naval officer, Vice-Admiral Masao Kanazawa, at the Kure base said the concussion from the blast twelve miles away was "like the great wind that made the trees sway." His aide, a senior lieutenant who was to accompany us into the city, volunteered that the flash was so bright even in Kure that he was awakened from his sleep. So loud was the explosion that many thought the bomb had landed within Kure.

When Lieutenant Taira Ake, a naval surgeon, reached the city at 2:30 p.m., he found hundreds of wounded still dying unattended in the wrecks and fields on the northern edge of the city. "They didn't look like human beings," he said. "The flesh was burned from their faces and hands, and many were blinded and deaf."

Dadai was standing in the doorway of his house nearly two miles from the center of impact. He had just returned from Tokyo.

"The first thing I saw was a brilliant flash," he said. "Then after a second or two came a shock like an earthquake. I knew immediately it was a new type of bomb. The house capsized on top of us and I was hit with falling timbers.

"I found my wife lying unconscious in the debris, and I dragged her to safety. My two children suffered cuts, and for the next hour or so I was too busy to think of what was happening in the city."

Doctors rushed from the Kure naval base—including Lieutenant Ake—were prevented from entering the city until six hours after the blast because of the searing heat of the explosion. City officials said that many indoors who were buried under collapsing walls and roofs subsequently were burned to death in the fires that broke out within a few minutes after the blast.

The first impression in the minds of the survivors was that a great fleet of Superfortresses flying at great height had somehow sneaked past the defenses and dropped thousands of fire bombs. Even today there are many who refuse to believe that a single bomb wiped out the city.

A party of newspaper men led by Colonel John McCrary was the first group of Americans to reach Hiroshima. We flew in today in a B-17, our pilot, Captain Mark Magnan, finding a hole in the clouds over Kure and setting the plane down on the tiny runway of the naval air base there with about seventy feet to spare.

The admiral in charge of the base, after telling us what he had seen and knew of the bombing, gave us two sedans and a truck, and we drove down a mountain, through ruined Kure and past the navy yard. A tall fence set up along the road to block the view of the yard had been removed, and we could see ten destroyers, two submarines and some gunboats anchored in the harbor.

Across the bay, beached on an island and listing to port so that the waves broke over her deck, was the battleship Haruna. Farther on we passed close to another beached warship, an old three-stacker that flaunted the silhouettes of ten American planes on her mid-stack. A four-engine bomber was among the planes the destroyer claimed to have shot down.

Several tunnels and deep cuts along the highway to Hiroshima were stacked with airplane motors and other vital equipment, leaving only a narrow lane for passage. Our driver, speeding at fifty miles an hour along the concrete highway, slammed into one crated engine and swerved across the road and struck another, shearing the rear fender.

Three miles outside Hiroshima we saw the first signs of blast damage—loose tiles torn from roofs and an occasional broken window. At the edge of town there were houses with roofs blown off, while the walls facing the center of the city had caved inward.

Finally we came to the river and saw the Island of Hiro, which holds, or rather held, the main districts of Hiroshima, which means "Hiro Island."

In the part of town east of the river the destruction had looked no different from a typical bomb-torn city in Europe. Many buildings were only partly demolished, and the streets were still choked with debris.

But across the river there was only flat, appalling desolation, the starkness accentuated by bare, blackened tree trunks and the occasional shell of a reinforced concrete building.

We drove to Military Park and made a walking tour of the ruins.

By all accounts the bomb seemed to have exploded directly

over Military Park. We saw no crater there. Apparently the full force of the explosion was expended laterally.

Aerial photographs had shown no evidence of rubble, leading to the belief that everything in the immediate area of impact had been literally pulverized into dust. But on the ground we saw this was not true. There was rubble everywhere, but much smaller in size than normal.

Approaching the Hattchobori, we passed what had been a block of small shops. We could tell that only because of office safes that lay at regular intervals on sites that retained little else except small bits of iron and tin. Sometimes the safes were blown in.

The steel door of a huge vault in the four-story Geibi Bank was flung open, and the management had installed a temporary padlocked door. All three banking houses—Geibi, Mitsubishi and the Bank of Japan—were conducting business in the sturdy concrete building of the Bank of Japan, which was less damaged than the rest.

Since the bank and the police station were the only buildings open for business, we asked our naval lieutenant guide if we could enter. He disappeared and was gone for several minutes.

We stood uneasily at the corner of the bank building, feeling very much like a youth walking down Main Street in his first long pants. There weren't many people abroad—a thin trickle of shabbily dressed men and women—but all of them stared at us.

There was hatred in some glances, but generally more curiosity than hatred. We were representatives of an enemy power that had employed a weapon far more terrible and deadly than poison gas, yet in the four hours we spent in Hiroshima none so much as spat at us, nor threw a stone.

We later asked the naval lieutenant, who once lived in Sacramento, to halt some pedestrians and obtain eyewitness accounts of the blast. He was very reluctant to do so.

"They may not want to talk to you," he said. But finally he stopped an old man, who bared his gold teeth in an apparent gesture of friendship.

"I am a Christian," said the old man, making the sign of the cross. He pointed to his ears, indicating deafness, and the lieutenant, after futile attempts to make him hear, told us that the old man, like many others, apparently had suffered permanent loss of his hearing when the crashing blast of the atomic bomb shattered his ear drums.

The lieutenant stopped a few more middle-aged civilians, but they backed off, bowing and grinning. They said they were not in Hiroshima on Aug. 6.

Two boys walking barefoot through the rubble displayed no fear of infection, although no doctor could say positively that the danger had ended. The boys said they had been brought in from the countryside to help clean up the city.

The cloying stench of death was still very noticeable in the street, and we were glad when the lieutenant finally motioned us inside the bank.

Except for broken windows and chipped cornices, the Bank of Japan presented an intact facade outside. Inside, however, we saw that the concussion had smashed the frail stalls and reduced the furnishings to matchwood. Under the lofty vaulted roof spaces had been roped off, and skeleton staffs of the three banking institutions sat behind crude wooden tables handing the government's new yen currency to waiting lines.

Several persons showed bad burns about their necks and faces, and nearly half the population seemed to be wearing gauze bandages over noses and mouths to protect them from germs.

Those who entered Hiroshima and stayed only a few hours appeared to suffer no ill effects, doctors said, but many who attempted to live in the ruins developed infections that reacted on the blood cells as destructively as leukemia, except that the white blood corpuscles and not the red were consumed. Victims became completely bald; they lost all appetite; they vomited blood.

A few of the main streets of Hiroshima have been cleared. Trolleys ran through the blighted areas down to the waterfront. But the public is forbidden to drink from wells, and water has to be brought in from the countryside.

Down one street was the ruined wall of a Christian church, and near it the site of the Japanese 2d Army headquarters. Hiroshima was an embarkation point for the invasion which threatened Kyushu, and the city had been filled with soldiers when the bomb fell. How many of them perished no one yet knows, for all records were destroyed by fire. Among the army staff members killed was the chief of military police.

The city and the prefectural (provincial) government had moved to a motorcycle plant in the outskirts of town, and there we met Dadai. He was introduced at first as "a high government official," but later admitted he was Chief of Thought Control.

Dadai's appearance fitted his role. He looked like a man who could not only suppress a thought, but could torture it. He wore a white bandage across his brow, tied in back of his head, and the face beneath it was sallow and repressive. His tight, grim mouth hardly opened as he answered questions put to him through the naval interpreter.

He told us that the wounded were doomed by the disintegrating effects of the uranium on the white blood corpuscles. This statement, however, was not substantiated by doctors, who said they knew so little about the strange disorders that it was useless to speculate on how high the death toll would run. They cited the case of the woman who suffered only a slight cut in the explosion, yet died eighteen days later.

Neither Dadai nor local correspondents who asked for an interview seemed to believe that the atomic bomb would end war. One of the first questions asked by Japanese newspaper men was: "What effect will the bomb have on future wars?" They also asked whether Hiroshima "would be dangerous for seventy years." We told them we didn't know.

New York *Herald Tribune*, September 5, 1945

# *Hiroshima*

by John Hersey

## I. A NOISELESS FLASH

AT EXACTLY fifteen minutes past eight in the morning, on
August 6, 1945, Japanese time, at the moment when the
atomic bomb flashed above Hiroshima, Miss Toshiko Sasaki, a
clerk in the personnel department of the East Asia Tin Works,
had just sat down at her place in the plant office and was
turning her head to speak to the girl at the next desk. At that
same moment, Dr. Masakazu Fujii was settling down cross-
legged to read the Osaka *Asahi* on the porch of his private
hospital, overhanging one of the seven deltaic rivers which
divide Hiroshima; Mrs. Hatsuyo Nakamura, a tailor's widow,
stood by the window of her kitchen, watching a neighbor
tearing down his house because it lay in the path of an air-
raid-defense fire lane; Father Wilhelm Kleinsorge, a German
priest of the Society of Jesus, reclined in his underwear on a
cot on the top floor of his order's three-story mission house,
reading a Jesuit magazine, *Stimmen der Zeit*; Dr. Terufumi
Sasaki, a young member of the surgical staff of the city's large,
modern Red Cross Hospital, walked along one of the hospital
corridors with a blood specimen for a Wassermann test in his
hand; and the Reverend Mr. Kiyoshi Tanimoto, pastor of the
Hiroshima Methodist Church, paused at the door of a rich
man's house in Koi, the city's western suburb, and prepared
to unload a handcart full of things he had evacuated from
town in fear of the massive B-29 raid which everyone expected Hiroshima to suffer. A hundred thousand people were
killed by the atomic bomb, and these six were among the
survivors. They still wonder why they lived when so many
others died. Each of them counts many small items of chance
or volition—a step taken in time, a decision to go indoors,

catching one streetcar instead of the next—that spared him.
And now each knows that in the act of survival he lived a
dozen lives and saw more death than he ever thought he
would see. At the time, none of them knew anything.

The Reverend Mr. Tanimoto got up at five o'clock that morning. He was alone in the parsonage, because for some time his
wife had been commuting with their year-old baby to spend
nights with a friend in Ushida, a suburb to the north. Of all
the important cities of Japan, only two, Kyoto and Hiroshima, had not been visited in strength by *B-san*, or Mr. B, as
the Japanese, with a mixture of respect and unhappy familiarity, called the B-29; and Mr. Tanimoto, like all his neighbors and friends, was almost sick with anxiety. He had heard
uncomfortably detailed accounts of mass raids on Kure,
Iwakuni, Tokuyama, and other nearby towns; he was sure
Hiroshima's turn would come soon. He had slept badly the
night before, because there had been several air-raid warnings. Hiroshima had been getting such warnings almost every
night for weeks, for at that time the B-29s were using Lake
Biwa, northeast of Hiroshima, as a rendezvous point, and no
matter what city the Americans planned to hit, the Superfortresses streamed in over the coast near Hiroshima. The
frequency of the warnings and the continued abstinence of
Mr. B with respect to Hiroshima had made its citizens jittery;
a rumor was going around that the Americans were saving
something special for the city.

Mr. Tanimoto is a small man, quick to talk, laugh, and cry.
He wears his black hair parted in the middle and rather long;
the prominence of the frontal bones just above his eyebrows
and the smallness of his mustache, mouth, and chin give him
a strange, old-young look, boyish and yet wise, weak and yet
fiery. He moves nervously and fast, but with a restraint which
suggests that he is a cautious, thoughtful man. He showed,
indeed, just those qualities in the uneasy days before the
bomb fell. Besides having his wife spend the nights in Ushida,
Mr. Tanimoto had been carrying all the portable things from
his church, in the close-packed residential district called Naga-
ragawa, to a house that belonged to a rayon manufacturer
in Koi, two miles from the center of town. The rayon man, a

Mr. Matsui, had opened his then unoccupied estate to a large number of his friends and acquaintances, so that they might evacuate whatever they wished to a safe distance from the probable target area. Mr. Tanimoto had had no difficulty in moving chairs, hymnals, Bibles, altar gear, and church records by pushcart himself, but the organ console and an upright piano required some aid. A friend of his named Matsuo had, the day before, helped him get the piano out to Koi; in return, he had promised this day to assist Mr. Matsuo in hauling out a daughter's belongings. That is why he had risen so early.

Mr. Tanimoto cooked his own breakfast. He felt awfully tired. The effort of moving the piano the day before, a sleepless night, weeks of worry and unbalanced diet, the cares of his parish—all combined to make him feel hardly adequate to the new day's work. There was another thing, too: Mr. Tanimoto had studied theology at Emory College, in Atlanta, Georgia; he had graduated in 1940; he spoke excellent English; he dressed in American clothes; he had corresponded with many American friends right up to the time the war began; and among a people obsessed with a fear of being spied upon—perhaps almost obsessed himself—he found himself growing increasingly uneasy. The police had questioned him several times, and just a few days before, he had heard that an influential acquaintance, a Mr. Tanaka, a retired officer of the Toyo Kisen Kaisha steamship line, an anti-Christian, a man famous in Hiroshima for his showy philanthropies and notorious for his personal tyrannies, had been telling people that Tanimoto should not be trusted. In compensation, to show himself publicly a good Japanese, Mr. Tanimoto had taken on the chairmanship of his local *tonarigumi*, or Neighborhood Association, and to his other duties and concerns this position had added the business of organizing air-raid defense for about twenty families.

Before six o'clock that morning, Mr. Tanimoto started for Mr. Matsuo's house. There he found that their burden was to be a *tansu*, a large Japanese cabinet, full of clothing and household goods. The two men set out. The morning was perfectly clear and so warm that the day promised to be uncomfortable. A few minutes after they started, the air-raid

siren went off—a minute-long blast that warned of approaching planes but indicated to the people of Hiroshima
only a slight degree of danger, since it sounded every morning at this time, when an American weather plane came over.
The two men pulled and pushed the handcart through the
city streets. Hiroshima was a fan-shaped city, lying mostly on
the six islands formed by the seven estuarial rivers that branch
out from the Ota River; its main commercial and residential
districts, covering about four square miles in the center of the
city, contained three-quarters of its population, which had
been reduced by several evacuation programs from a wartime
peak of 380,000 to about 245,000. Factories and other residential districts, or suburbs, lay compactly around the edges
of the city. To the south were the docks, an airport, and the
island-studded Inland Sea. A rim of mountains runs around
the other three sides of the delta. Mr. Tanimoto and Mr. Matsuo took their way through the shopping center, already full
of people, and across two of the rivers to the sloping streets of
Koi, and up them to the outskirts and foothills. As they
started up a valley away from the tight-ranked houses, the
all-clear sounded. (The Japanese radar operators, detecting
only three planes, supposed that they comprised a reconnaissance.) Pushing the handcart up to the rayon man's house
was tiring, and the men, after they had maneuvered their load
into the driveway and to the front steps, paused to rest
awhile. They stood with a wing of the house between them
and the city. Like most homes in this part of Japan, the house
consisted of a wooden frame and wooden walls supporting a
heavy tile roof. Its front hall, packed with rolls of bedding and
clothing, looked like a cool cave full of fat cushions. Opposite
the house, to the right of the front door, there was a large,
finicky rock garden. There was no sound of planes. The
morning was still; the place was cool and pleasant.

Then a tremendous flash of light cut across the sky. Mr.
Tanimoto has a distinct recollection that it travelled from east
to west, from the city toward the hills. It seemed a sheet of
sun. Both he and Mr. Matsuo reacted in terror—and both
had time to react (for they were 3,500 yards, or two miles,
from the center of the explosion). Mr. Matsuo dashed up the
front steps into the house and dived among the bedrolls and

buried himself there. Mr. Tanimoto took four or five steps and threw himself between two big rocks in the garden. He bellied up very hard against one of them. As his face was against the stone, he did not see what happened. He felt a sudden pressure, and then splinters and pieces of board and fragments of tile fell on him. He heard no roar. (Almost no one in Hiroshima recalls hearing any noise of the bomb. But a fisherman in his sampan on the Inland Sea near Tsuzu, the man with whom Mr. Tanimoto's mother-in-law and sister-in-law were living, saw the flash and heard a tremendous explosion; he was nearly twenty miles from Hiroshima, but the thunder was greater than when the B-29s hit Iwakuni, only five miles away.)

When he dared, Mr. Tanimoto raised his head and saw that the rayon man's house had collapsed. He thought a bomb had fallen directly on it. Such clouds of dust had risen that there was a sort of twilight around. In panic, not thinking for the moment of Mr. Matsuo under the ruins, he dashed out into the street. He noticed as he ran that the concrete wall of the estate had fallen over—toward the house rather than away from it. In the street, the first thing he saw was a squad of soldiers who had been burrowing into the hillside opposite, making one of the thousands of dugouts in which the Japanese apparently intended to resist invasion, hill by hill, life for life; the soldiers were coming out of the hole, where they should have been safe, and blood was running from their heads, chests, and backs. They were silent and dazed.

Under what seemed to be a local dust cloud, the day grew darker and darker.

At nearly midnight, the night before the bomb was dropped, an announcer on the city's radio station said that about two hundred B-29s were approaching southern Honshu and advised the population of Hiroshima to evacuate to their designated "safe areas." Mrs. Hatsuyo Nakamura, the tailor's widow, who lived in the section called Nobori-cho and who had long had a habit of doing as she was told, got her three children—a ten-year-old boy, Toshio, an eight-year-old girl, Yaeko, and a five-year-old girl, Myeko—out of bed and dressed them and walked with them to the military area known as the East Parade Ground, on the northeast edge of the city. There she unrolled some mats and the children lay down on them. They slept until about two, when they were awakened by the roar of the planes going over Hiroshima.

As soon as the planes had passed, Mrs. Nakamura started back with her children. They reached home a little after two-thirty and she immediately turned on the radio, which, to her distress, was just then broadcasting a fresh warning. When she looked at the children and saw how tired they were, and when she thought of the number of trips they had made in past weeks, all to no purpose, to the East Parade Ground, she decided that in spite of the instructions on the radio, she simply could not face starting out all over again. She put the children in their bedrolls on the floor, lay down herself at three o'clock, and fell asleep at once, so soundly that when planes passed over later, she did not waken to their sound.

The siren jarred her awake at about seven. She arose, dressed quickly, and hurried to the house of Mr. Nakamoto, the head of her Neighborhood Association, and asked him what she should do. He said that she should remain at home unless an urgent warning—a series of intermittent blasts of the siren—was sounded. She returned home, lit the stove in the kitchen, set some rice to cook, and sat down to read that morning's Hiroshima *Chugoku*. To her relief, the all-clear sounded at eight o'clock. She heard the children stirring, so she went and gave each of them a handful of peanuts and told them to stay on their bedrolls, because they were tired from the night's walk. She had hoped that they would go back to sleep, but the man in the house directly to the south began to make a terrible hullabaloo of hammering, wedging, ripping, and splitting. The prefectural government, convinced, as everyone in Hiroshima was, that the city would be attacked soon, had begun to press with threats and warnings for the completion of wide fire lanes, which, it was hoped, might act in conjunction with the rivers to localize any fires started by an incendiary raid; and the neighbor was reluctantly sacrificing his home to the city's safety. Just the day before, the prefecture had ordered all able-bodied girls from the secondary schools to spend a few days helping to clear these lanes, and they started work soon after the all-clear sounded.

Mrs. Nakamura went back to the kitchen, looked at the rice, and began watching the man next door. At first, she was annoyed with him for making so much noise, but then she was moved almost to tears by pity. Her emotion was specifically directed toward her neighbor, tearing down his home, board by board, at a time when there was so much unavoidable destruction, but undoubtedly she also felt a generalized, community pity, to say nothing of self-pity. She had not had an easy time. Her husband, Isawa, had gone into the Army just after Myeko was born, and she had heard nothing from or of him for a long time, until, on March 5, 1942, she received a seven-word telegram: "Isawa died an honorable death at Singapore." She learned later that he had died on February 15th, the day Singapore fell, and that he had been a corporal. Isawa had been a not particularly prosperous tailor, and his only capital was a Sankoku sewing machine. After his death, when his allotments stopped coming, Mrs. Nakamura got out the machine and began to take in piecework herself, and since then had supported the children, but poorly, by sewing.

As Mrs. Nakamura stood watching her neighbor, everything flashed whiter than any white she had ever seen. She did not notice what happened to the man next door; the reflex of a mother set her in motion toward her children. She had taken a single step (the house was 1,350 yards, or three-quarters of a mile, from the center of the explosion) when something picked her up and she seemed to fly into the next room over the raised sleeping platform, pursued by parts of her house.

Timbers fell around her as she landed, and a shower of tiles pommelled her; everything became dark, for she was buried. The debris did not cover her deeply. She rose up and freed herself. She heard a child cry, "Mother, help me!," and saw her youngest—Myeko, the five-year-old—buried up to her breast and unable to move. As Mrs. Nakamura started frantically to claw her way toward the baby, she could see or hear nothing of her other children.

In the days right before the bombing, Dr. Masakazu Fujii, being prosperous, hedonistic, and, at the time, not too busy,

had been allowing himself the luxury of sleeping until nine or
nine-thirty, but fortunately he had to get up early the morning the bomb was dropped to see a house guest off on a train.
He rose at six, and half an hour later walked with his friend to
the station, not far away, across two of the rivers. He was
back home by seven, just as the siren sounded its sustained
warning. He ate breakfast and then, because the morning was
already hot, undressed down to his underwear and went out
on the porch to read the paper. This porch—in fact, the
whole building—was curiously constructed. Dr. Fujii was the
proprietor of a peculiarly Japanese institution, a private,
single-doctor hospital. This building, perched beside and over
the water of the Kyo River, and next to the bridge of the
same name, contained thirty rooms for thirty patients and
their kinfolk—for, according to Japanese custom, when a
person falls sick and goes to a hospital, one or more members
of his family go and live there with him, to cook for him,
bathe, massage, and read to him, and to offer incessant famil-
ial sympathy, without which a Japanese patient would be miserable indeed. Dr. Fujii had no beds—only straw mats—for
his patients. He did, however, have all sorts of modern equipment: an X-ray machine, diathermy apparatus, and a fine tiled
laboratory. The structure rested two-thirds on the land, one-
third on piles over the tidal waters of the Kyo. This overhang,
the part of the building where Dr. Fujii lived, was queer-
looking, but it was cool in summer and from the porch,
which faced away from the center of the city, the prospect of
the river, with pleasure boats drifting up and down it, was
always refreshing. Dr. Fujii had occasionally had anxious moments when the Ota and its mouth branches rose to flood,
but the piling was apparently firm enough and the house had
always held.

Dr. Fujii had been relatively idle for about a month because
in July, as the number of untouched cities in Japan dwindled
and as Hiroshima seemed more and more inevitably a target,
he began turning patients away, on the ground that in case of
a fire raid he would not be able to evacuate them. Now he
had only two patients left—a woman from Yano, injured in
the shoulder, and a young man of twenty-five recovering
from burns he had suffered when the steel factory near Hiro-

shima in which he worked had been hit. Dr. Fujii had six nurses to tend his patients. His wife and children were safe; his wife and one son were living outside Osaka, and another son and two daughters were in the country on Kyushu. A niece was living with him, and a maid and a manservant. He had little to do and did not mind, for he had saved some money. At fifty, he was healthy, convivial, and calm, and he was pleased to pass the evenings drinking whiskey with friends, always sensibly and for the sake of conversation. Before the war, he had affected brands imported from Scotland and America; now he was perfectly satisfied with the best Japanese brand, Suntory.

Dr. Fujii sat down cross-legged in his underwear on the spotless matting of the porch, put on his glasses, and started reading the Osaka *Asahi*. He liked to read the Osaka news because his wife was there. He saw the flash. To him—faced away from the center and looking at his paper—it seemed a brilliant yellow. Startled, he began to rise to his feet. In that moment (he was 1,550 yards from the center), the hospital leaned behind his rising and, with a terrible ripping noise, toppled into the river. The Doctor, still in the act of getting to his feet, was thrown forward and around and over; he was buffeted and gripped; he lost track of everything, because things were so speeded up; he felt the water.

Dr. Fujii hardly had time to think that he was dying before he realized that he was alive, squeezed tightly by two long timbers in a V across his chest, like a morsel suspended between two huge chopsticks—held upright, so that he could not move, with his head miraculously above water and his torso and legs in it. The remains of his hospital were all around him in a mad assortment of splintered lumber and materials for the relief of pain. His left shoulder hurt terribly. His glasses were gone.

Father Wilhelm Kleinsorge, of the Society of Jesus, was, on the morning of the explosion, in rather frail condition. The Japanese wartime diet had not sustained him, and he felt the strain of being a foreigner in an increasingly xenophobic Japan; even a German, since the defeat of the Fatherland, was unpopular. Father Kleinsorge had, at thirty-eight, the look of a boy growing too fast—thin in the face, with a prominent Adam's apple, a hollow chest, dangling hands, big feet. He walked clumsily, leaning forward a little. He was tired all the time. To make matters worse, he had suffered for two days, along with Father Cieslik, a fellow-priest, from a rather painful and urgent diarrhea, which they blamed on the beans and black ration bread they were obliged to eat. Two other priests then living in the mission compound, which was in the Nobori-cho section—Father Superior LaSalle and Father Schiffer—had happily escaped this affliction.

Father Kleinsorge woke up about six the morning the bomb was dropped, and half an hour later—he was a bit tardy because of his sickness—he began to read Mass in the mission chapel, a small Japanese-style wooden building which was without pews, since its worshippers knelt on the usual Japanese matted floor, facing an altar graced with splendid silks, brass, silver, and heavy embroideries. This morning, a Monday, the only worshippers were Mr. Takemoto, a theological student living in the mission house; Mr. Fukai, the secretary of the diocese; Mrs. Murata, the mission's devoutly Christian housekeeper; and his fellow-priests. After Mass, while Father Kleinsorge was reading the Prayers of Thanksgiving, the siren sounded. He stopped the service and the missionaries retired across the compound to the bigger building. There, in his room on the ground floor, to the right of the front door, Father Kleinsorge changed into a military uniform which he had acquired when he was teaching at the Rokko Middle School in Kobe and which he wore during air-raid alerts.

After an alarm, Father Kleinsorge always went out and scanned the sky, and this time, when he stepped outside, he was glad to see only the single weather plane that flew over Hiroshima each day about this time. Satisfied that nothing would happen, he went in and breakfasted with the other Fathers on substitute coffee and ration bread, which, under the circumstances, was especially repugnant to him. The Fathers sat and talked a while, until, at eight, they heard the all-clear. They went then to various parts of the building. Father Schiffer retired to his room to do some writing. Father Cieslik sat in his room in a straight chair with a pillow over his stomach to ease his pain, and read. Father Superior LaSalle stood at the window of his room, thinking. Father Kleinsorge went up to a room on the third floor, took off all his clothes except his underwear, and stretched out on his right side on a cot and began reading his *Stimmen der Zeit.*

After the terrible flash—which, Father Kleinsorge later realized, reminded him of something he had read as a boy about a large meteor colliding with the earth—he had time (since he was 1,400 yards from the center) for one thought: A bomb has fallen directly on us. Then, for a few seconds or minutes, he went out of his mind.

Father Kleinsorge never knew how he got out of the house. The next things he was conscious of were that he was wandering around in the mission's vegetable garden in his underwear, bleeding slightly from small cuts along his left flank; that all the buildings round about had fallen down except the Jesuits' mission house, which had long before been braced and double-braced by a priest named Gropper, who was terrified of earthquakes; that the day had turned dark; and that Murata-*san*, the housekeeper, was nearby, crying over and over, "*Shu Jesusu, awaremi tamai!* Our Lord Jesus, have pity on us!"

On the train on the way into Hiroshima from the country, where he lived with his mother, Dr. Terufumi Sasaki, the Red Cross Hospital surgeon, thought over an unpleasant nightmare he had had the night before. His mother's home was in Mukaihara, thirty miles from the city, and it took him two hours by train and tram to reach the hospital. He had slept uneasily all night and had wakened an hour earlier than usual, and, feeling sluggish and slightly feverish, had debated whether to go to the hospital at all; his sense of duty finally forced him to go, and he had started out on an earlier train than he took most mornings. The dream had particularly frightened him because it was so closely associated, on the surface at least, with a disturbing actuality. He was only twenty-five years old and had just completed his training at the Eastern Medical University, in Tsingtao, China. He was something of an idealist and was much distressed by the inadequacy of medical facilities in the country town where his mother lived. Quite on his own, and without a permit, he had begun visiting a few sick people out there in the evenings, after his eight hours at the hospital and four hours' commuting. He had recently learned that the penalty for practicing without a permit was severe; a fellow-doctor whom he had asked about it had given him a serious scolding. Nevertheless, he had continued to practice. In his dream, he had been at the bedside of a country patient when the police and the doctor he had consulted burst into the room, seized him, dragged him outside, and beat him up cruelly. On the train, he just about decided to give up the work in Mukaihara, since he felt it would be impossible to get a permit, because the authorities would hold that it would conflict with his duties at the Red Cross Hospital.

At the terminus, he caught a streetcar at once. (He later calculated that if he had taken his customary train that morning, and if he had had to wait a few minutes for the streetcar, as often happened, he would have been close to the center at the time of the explosion and would surely have perished.) He arrived at the hospital at seven-forty and reported to the chief surgeon. A few minutes later, he went to a room on the first floor and drew blood from the arm of a man in order to perform a Wassermann test. The laboratory containing the incubators for the test was on the third floor. With the blood specimen in his left hand, walking in a kind of distraction he had felt all morning, probably because of the dream and his restless night, he started along the main corridor on his way toward the stairs. He was one step beyond an open window when the light of the bomb was reflected, like a gigantic photographic flash, in the corridor. He ducked down on one knee and said to himself, as only a Japanese would, "Sasaki, *gambare!* Be brave!" Just then (the building was 1,650 yards from the center), the blast ripped through the hospital. The glasses he was wearing flew off his face; the bottle of blood crashed against one wall; his Japanese slippers zipped out from under his feet—but otherwise, thanks to where he stood, he was untouched.

Dr. Sasaki shouted the name of the chief surgeon and rushed around to the man's office and found him terribly cut by glass. The hospital was in horrible confusion: heavy partitions and ceilings had fallen on patients, beds had overturned, windows had blown in and cut people, blood was spattered on the walls and floors, instruments were everywhere, many of the patients were running about screaming, many more lay dead. (A colleague working in the laboratory to which Dr. Sasaki had been walking was dead; Dr. Sasaki's patient, whom he had just left and who a few moments before had been dreadfully afraid of syphilis, was also dead.) Dr. Sasaki found himself the only doctor in the hospital who was unhurt.

Dr. Sasaki, who believed that the enemy had hit only the building he was in, got bandages and began to bind the wounds of those inside the hospital; while outside, all over Hiroshima, maimed and dying citizens turned their unsteady steps toward the Red Cross Hospital to begin an invasion that was to make Dr. Sasaki forget his private nightmare for a long, long time.

Miss Toshiko Sasaki, the East Asia Tin Works clerk, who is not related to Dr. Sasaki, got up at three o'clock in the morning on the day the bomb fell. There was extra housework to do. Her eleven-month-old brother, Akio, had come down the day before with a serious stomach upset; her mother had taken him to the Tamura Pediatric Hospital and was staying there with him. Miss Sasaki, who was about twenty, had to cook breakfast for her father, a brother, a sister, and herself, and— since the hospital, because of the war, was unable to provide food—to prepare a whole day's meals for her mother and the baby, in time for her father, who worked in a factory making rubber earplugs for artillery crews, to take the food by on his way to the plant. When she had finished and had cleaned and put away the cooking things, it was nearly seven. The family lived in Koi, and she had a forty-five-minute trip to the tin works, in the section of town called Kannon-machi. She was in charge of the personnel records in the factory. She left Koi at seven, and as soon as she reached the plant, she went with some of the other girls from the personnel department to the factory auditorium. A prominent local Navy man, a former employee, had committed suicide the day before by throwing himself under a train—a death considered honorable enough to warrant a memorial service, which was to be held at the tin works at ten o'clock that morning. In the large hall, Miss Sasaki and the others made suitable preparations for the meeting. This work took about twenty minutes.

Miss Sasaki went back to her office and sat down at her desk. She was quite far from the windows, which were off to her left, and behind her were a couple of tall bookcases containing all the books of the factory library, which the personnel department had organized. She settled herself at her desk, put some things in a drawer, and shifted papers. She thought that before she began to make entries in her lists of new employees, discharges, and departures for the Army, she would chat for a moment with the girl at her right. Just as she turned her head away from the windows, the room was filled with a blinding light. She was paralyzed by fear, fixed still in her chair for a long moment (the plant was 1,600 yards from the center).

Everything fell, and Miss Sasaki lost consciousness. The ceiling dropped suddenly and the wooden floor above collapsed in splinters and the people up there came down and the roof above them gave way; but principally and first of all, the bookcases right behind her swooped forward and the contents threw her down, with her left leg horribly twisted and breaking underneath her. There, in the tin factory, in the first moment of the atomic age, a human being was crushed by books.

## II. THE FIRE

Immediately after the explosion, the Reverend Mr. Kiyoshi Tanimoto, having run wildly out of the Matsui estate and having looked in wonderment at the bloody soldiers at the mouth of the dugout they had been digging, attached himself sympathetically to an old lady who was walking along in a daze, holding her head with her left hand, supporting a small boy of three or four on her back with her right, and crying, "I'm hurt! I'm hurt! I'm hurt!" Mr. Tanimoto transferred the child to his own back and led the woman by the hand down the street, which was darkened by what seemed to be a local column of dust. He took the woman to a grammar school not far away that had previously been designated for use as a temporary hospital in case of emergency. By this solicitous behavior, Mr. Tanimoto at once got rid of his terror. At the school, he was much surprised to see glass all over the floor and fifty or sixty injured people already waiting to be treated. He reflected that, although the all-clear had sounded and he had heard no planes, several bombs must have been dropped. He thought of a hillock in the rayon man's garden from which he could get a view of the whole of Koi—of the whole of Hiroshima, for that matter—and he ran back up to the estate.

From the mound, Mr. Tanimoto saw an astonishing panorama. Not just a patch of Koi, as he had expected, but as much of Hiroshima as he could see through the clouded air was giving off a thick, dreadful miasma. Clumps of smoke, near and far, had begun to push up through the general dust. He wondered how such extensive damage could have been dealt out of a silent sky; even a few planes, far up, would have been audible. Houses nearby were burning, and when huge drops of water the size of marbles began to fall, he half thought that they must be coming from the hoses of firemen fighting the blazes. (They were actually drops of condensed moisture falling from the turbulent tower of dust, heat, and fission fragments that had already risen miles into the sky above Hiroshima.)

Mr. Tanimoto turned away from the sight when he heard Mr. Matsuo call out to ask whether he was all right. Mr. Matsuo had been safely cushioned within the falling house by the bedding stored in the front hall and had worked his way out. Mr. Tanimoto scarcely answered. He had thought of his wife and baby, his church, his home, his parishioners, all of them down in that awful murk. Once more he began to run in fear—toward the city.

Mrs. Hatsuyo Nakamura, the tailor's widow, having struggled up from under the ruins of her house after the explosion, and seeing Myeko, the youngest of her three children, buried breast-deep and unable to move, crawled across the debris, hauled at timbers, and flung tiles aside, in a hurried effort to free the child. Then, from what seemed to be caverns far below, she heard two small voices crying, "*Tasukete! Tasukete!* Help! Help!"

She called the names of her ten-year-old son and eight-year-old daughter: "Toshio! Yaeko!"

The voices from below answered.

Mrs. Nakamura abandoned Myeko, who at least could breathe, and in a frenzy made the wreckage fly above the crying voices. The children had been sleeping nearly ten feet apart, but now their voices seemed to come from the same place. Toshio, the boy, apparently had some freedom to move, because she could feel him undermining the pile of wood and tiles as she worked from above. At last she saw his head, and she hastily pulled him out by it. A mosquito net was wound intricately, as if it had been carefully wrapped, around his feet. He said he had been blown right across the room and had been on top of his sister Yaeko under the wreckage. She now said, from underneath, that she could not move, because there was something on her legs. With a bit more digging, Mrs Nakamura cleared a hole above the child and began to pull her arm. "*Itai!* It hurts!" Yaeko cried. Mrs. Nakamura shouted, "There's no time now to say whether it hurts or not," and yanked her whimpering daughter up. Then she freed Myeko. The children were filthy and bruised, but none of them had a single cut or scratch.

Mrs. Nakamura took the children out into the street. They had nothing on but underpants, and although the day was very hot, she worried rather confusedly about their being cold, so she went back into the wreckage and burrowed underneath and found a bundle of clothes she had packed for an emergency, and she dressed them in pants, blouses, shoes, padded-cotton air-raid helmets called *bokuzuki*, and even, irrationally, overcoats. The children were silent, except for the five-year-old, Myeko, who kept asking questions: "Why is it night already? Why did our house fall down? What happened?" Mrs. Nakamura, who did not know what had happened (had not the all-clear sounded?), looked around and saw through the darkness that all the houses in her neighborhood had collapsed. The house next door, which its owner had been tearing down to make way for a fire lane, was now very thoroughly, if crudely, torn down; its owner, who had been sacrificing his home for the community's safety, lay dead. Mrs. Nakamoto, wife of the head of the local air-raid-defense Neighborhood Association, came across the street with her head all bloody, and said that her baby was badly cut; did Mrs. Nakamura have any bandage? Mrs. Nakamura did not, but she crawled into the remains of her house again and pulled out some white cloth that she had been using in her work as a seamstress, ripped it into strips, and gave it to Mrs. Nakamoto. While fetching the cloth, she noticed her sewing machine; she went back in for it and dragged it out. Obviously, she could not carry it with her, so she unthinkingly plunged her symbol of livelihood into the receptacle which for weeks had been her symbol of safety—the cement tank of water in front of her house, of the type every household had been ordered to construct against a possible fire raid.

A nervous neighbor, Mrs. Hataya, called to Mrs. Nakamura to run away with her to the woods in Asano Park—an estate, by the Kyo River not far off, belonging to the wealthy Asano family, who once owned the Toyo Kisen Kaisha steamship line. The park had been designated as an evacuation area for their neighborhood. Seeing fire breaking out in a nearby ruin (except at the very center, where the bomb itself ignited some fires, most of Hiroshima's citywide conflagration was caused by inflammable wreckage falling on cook-stoves and live wires), Mrs. Nakamura suggested going over to fight it. Mrs. Hataya said, "Don't be foolish. What if planes come and drop more bombs?" So Mrs. Nakamura started out for Asano Park with her children and Mrs. Hataya, and she carried her rucksack of emergency clothing, a blanket, an umbrella, and a suitcase of things she had cached in her air-raid shelter. Under many ruins, as they hurried along, they heard muffled screams for help. The only building they saw standing on their way to Asano Park was the Jesuit mission house, alongside the Catholic kindergarten to which Mrs. Nakamura had sent Myeko for a time. As they passed it, she saw Father Kleinsorge, in bloody underwear, running out of the house with a small suitcase in his hand.

Right after the explosion, while Father Wilhelm Kleinsorge, S. J., was wandering around in his underwear in the vegetable garden, Father Superior LaSalle came around the corner of the building in the darkness. His body, especially his back, was bloody; the flash had made him twist away from his window, and tiny pieces of glass had flown at him. Father Kleinsorge, still bewildered, managed to ask, "Where are the rest?" Just then, the two other priests living in the mission house appeared—Father Cieslik, unhurt, supporting Father Schiffer, who was covered with blood that spurted from a cut above his left ear and who was very pale. Father Cieslik was rather pleased with himself, for after the flash he had dived into a doorway, which he had previously reckoned to be the safest place inside the building, and when the blast came, he was not injured. Father LaSalle told Father Cieslik to take Father Schiffer to a doctor before he bled to death, and suggested either Dr. Kanda, who lived on the next corner, or Dr. Fujii, about six blocks away. The two men went out of the compound and up the street.

The daughter of Mr. Hoshijima, the mission catechist, ran up to Father Kleinsorge and said that her mother and sister were buried under the ruins of their house, which was at the back of the Jesuit compound, and at the same time the priests noticed that the house of the Catholic-kindergarten teacher at the front of the compound had collapsed on her. While Father LaSalle and Mrs. Murata, the mission housekeeper, dug the teacher out, Father Kleinsorge went to the catechist's fallen house and began lifting things off the top of the pile. There was not a sound underneath; he was sure the Hoshijima women had been killed. At last, under what had been a corner of the kitchen, he saw Mrs. Hoshijima's head. Believing her dead, he began to haul her out by the hair, but suddenly she screamed, "*Itai! Itai!* It hurts! It hurts!" He dug some more and lifted her out. He managed, too, to find her daughter in the rubble and free her. Neither was badly hurt.

A public bath next door to the mission house had caught fire, but since there the wind was southerly, the priests thought their house would be spared. Nevertheless, as a precaution, Father Kleinsorge went inside to fetch some things he wanted to save. He found his room in a state of weird and illogical confusion. A first-aid kit was hanging undisturbed on a hook on the wall, but his clothes, which had been on other hooks nearby, were nowhere to be seen. His desk was in splinters all over the room, but a mere papier-mâché suitcase, which he had hidden under the desk, stood handle-side up, without a scratch on it, in the doorway of the room, where he could not miss it. Father Kleinsorge later came to regard this as a bit of Providential interference, inasmuch as the suitcase contained his breviary, the account books for the whole diocese, and a considerable amount of paper money belonging to the mission, for which he was responsible. He ran out of the house and deposited the suitcase in the mission air-raid shelter.

At about this time, Father Cieslik and Father Schiffer, who was still spurting blood, came back and said that Dr. Kanda's house was ruined and that fire blocked them from getting out of what they supposed to be the local circle of destruction to Dr. Fujii's private hospital, on the bank of the Kyo River.

Dr. Masakazu Fujii's hospital was no longer on the bank of the Kyo River; it was in the river. After the overturn, Dr. Fujii was so stupefied and so tightly squeezed by the beams gripping his chest that he was unable to move at first, and he hung there about twenty minutes in the darkened morning. Then a thought which came to him—that soon the tide would be running in through the estuaries and his head would be submerged—inspired him to fearful activity; he wriggled and turned and exerted what strength he could (though his left arm, because of the pain in his shoulder, was useless), and before long he had freed himself from the vise. After a few moments' rest, he climbed onto the pile of timbers and, finding a long one that slanted up to the river-bank, he painfully shinnied up it.

Dr. Fujii, who was in his underwear, was now soaking and dirty. His undershirt was torn, and blood ran down it from bad cuts on his chin and back. In this disarray, he walked out onto Kyo Bridge, beside which his hospital had stood. The bridge had not collapsed. He could see only fuzzily without his glasses, but he could see enough to be amazed at the number of houses that were down all around. On the bridge, he encountered a friend, a doctor named Machii, and asked in bewilderment, "What do you think it was?"

Dr. Machii said, "It must have been a *Molotoffano hana-*

*kago*"—a Molotov flower basket, the delicate Japanese name
for the "bread basket," or self-scattering cluster of bombs.

At first, Dr. Fujii could see only two fires, one across the
river from his hospital site and one quite far to the south. But
at the same time, he and his friend observed something that
puzzled them, and which, as doctors, they discussed: although there were as yet very few fires, wounded people were
hurrying across the bridge in an endless parade of misery,
and many of them exhibited terrible burns on their faces
and arms. "Why do you suppose it is?" Dr. Fujii asked.
Even a theory was comforting that day, and Dr. Machii stuck
to his. "Perhaps because it was a Molotov flower basket," he
said.

There had been no breeze earlier in the morning when Dr.
Fujii had walked to the railway station to see his friend off,
but now brisk winds were blowing every which way; here on
the bridge the wind was easterly. New fires were leaping up,
and they spread quickly, and in a very short time terrible
blasts of hot air and showers of cinders made it impossible to
stand on the bridge any more. Dr. Machii ran to the far side
of the river and along a still unkindled street. Dr. Fujii went
down into the water under the bridge, where a score of
people had already taken refuge, among them his servants,
who had extricated themselves from the wreckage. From
there, Dr. Fujii saw a nurse hanging in the timbers of his
hospital by her legs, and then another painfully pinned across
the breast. He enlisted the help of some of the others under
the bridge and freed both of them. He thought he heard the
voice of his niece for a moment, but he could not find her; he
never saw her again. Four of his nurses and the two patients
in the hospital died, too. Dr. Fujii went back into the water of
the river and waited for the fire to subside.

The lot of Drs. Fujii, Kanda, and Machii right after the explosion—and, as these three were typical, that of the majority of
the physicians and surgeons of Hiroshima—with their offices
and hospitals destroyed, their equipment scattered, their own
bodies incapacitated in varying degrees, explained why so
many citizens who were hurt went untended and why so
many who might have lived died. Of a hundred and fifty doc-

tors in the city, sixty-five were already dead and most of the rest were wounded. Of 1,780 nurses, 1,654 were dead or too badly hurt to work. In the biggest hospital, that of the Red Cross, only six doctors out of thirty were able to function, and only ten nurses out of more than two hundred. The sole uninjured doctor on the Red Cross Hospital staff was Dr. Sasaki. After the explosion, he hurried to a storeroom to fetch bandages. This room, like everything he had seen as he ran through the hospital, was chaotic—bottles of medicines thrown off shelves and broken, salves spattered on the walls, instruments strewn everywhere. He grabbed up some bandages and an unbroken bottle of mercurochrome, hurried back to the chief surgeon, and bandaged his cuts. Then he went out into the corridor and began patching up the wounded patients and the doctors and nurses there. He blundered so without his glasses that he took a pair off the face of a wounded nurse, and although they only approximately compensated for the errors of his vision, they were better than nothing. (He was to depend on them for more than a month.)

Dr. Sasaki worked without method, taking those who were nearest him first, and he noticed soon that the corridor seemed to be getting more and more crowded. Mixed in with the abrasions and lacerations which most people in the hospital had suffered, he began to find dreadful burns. He realized then that casualties were pouring in from outdoors. There were so many that he began to pass up the lightly wounded; he decided that all he could hope to do was to stop people from bleeding to death. Before long, patients lay and crouched on the floors of the wards and the laboratories and all the other rooms, and in the corridors, and on the stairs, and in the front hall, and under the porte-cochère, and on the stone front steps, and in the driveway and courtyard, and for blocks each way in the streets outside. Wounded people supported maimed people; disfigured families leaned together. Many people were vomiting. A tremendous number of schoolgirls—some of those who had been taken from their classrooms to work outdoors, clearing fire lanes—crept into the hospital. In a city of two hundred and forty-five thousand, nearly a hundred thousand people had been killed or doomed at one blow; a hundred thousand more were hurt. At least ten thousand of the wounded made their way to the best hospital in town, which was altogether unequal to such a trampling, since it had only six hundred beds, and they had all been occupied. The people in the suffocating crowd inside the hospital wept and cried, for Dr. Sasaki to hear, "*Sensei!* Doctor!," and the less seriously wounded came and pulled at his sleeve and begged him to come to the aid of the worse wounded. Tugged here and there in his stockinged feet, bewildered by the numbers, staggered by so much raw flesh, Dr. Sasaki lost all sense of profession and stopped working as a skillful surgeon and a sympathetic man; he became an automaton, mechanically wiping, daubing, winding, wiping, daubing, winding.

Some of the wounded in Hiroshima were unable to enjoy the questionable luxury of hospitalization. In what had been the personnel office of the East Asia Tin Works, Miss Sasaki lay doubled over, unconscious, under the tremendous pile of books and plaster and wood and corrugated iron. She was wholly unconscious (she later estimated) for about three hours. Her first sensation was of dreadful pain in her left leg. It was so black under the books and debris that the borderline between awareness and unconsciousness was fine; she apparently crossed it several times, for the pain seemed to come and go. At the moments when it was sharpest, she felt that her leg had been cut off somewhere below the knee. Later, she heard someone walking on top of the wreckage above her, and anguished voices spoke up, evidently from within the mess around her: "Please help! Get us out!"

Father Kleinsorge stemmed Father Schiffer's spurting cut as well as he could with some bandage that Dr. Fujii had given the priests a few days before. When he finished, he ran into the mission house again and found the jacket of his military uniform and an old pair of gray trousers. He put them on and went outside. A woman from next door ran up to him and shouted that her husband was buried under her house and the house was on fire; Father Kleinsorge must come and save him.

Father Kleinsorge, already growing apathetic and dazed in the presence of the cumulative distress, said, "We haven't much time." Houses all around were burning, and the wind was now blowing hard. "Do you know exactly which part of the house he is under?" he asked.

"Yes, yes," she said. "Come quickly."

They went around to the house, the remains of which blazed violently, but when they got there, it turned out that the woman had no idea where her husband was. Father Kleinsorge shouted several times, "Is anyone there?" There was no answer. Father Kleinsorge said to the woman, "We must get away or we will all die." He went back to the Catholic compound and told the Father Superior that the fire was coming closer on the wind, which had swung around and was now from the north; it was time for everybody to go.

Just then, the kindergarten teacher pointed out to the priests Mr. Fukai, the secretary of the diocese, who was standing in his window on the second floor of the mission house, facing in the direction of the explosion, weeping. Father Cieslik, because he thought the stairs unusable, ran around to the back of the mission house to look for a ladder. There he heard people crying for help under a nearby fallen roof. He called to passers-by running away in the street to help him lift it, but nobody paid any attention, and he had to leave the buried ones to die. Father Kleinsorge ran inside the mission house and scrambled up the stairs, which were awry and piled with plaster and lathing, and called to Mr. Fukai from the doorway of his room.

Mr. Fukai, a very short man of about fifty, turned around slowly, with a queer look, and said, "Leave me here."

Father Kleinsorge went into the room and took Mr. Fukai by the collar of his coat and said, "Come with me or you'll die."

Mr. Fukai said, "Leave me here to die."

Father Kleinsorge began to shove and haul Mr. Fukai out of the room. Then the theological student came up and grabbed Mr. Fukai's feet, and Father Kleinsorge took his shoulders, and together they carried him downstairs and outdoors. "I can't walk!" Mr. Fukai cried. "Leave me here!" Father Kleinsorge got his paper suitcase with the money in it

and took Mr. Fukai up pickaback, and the party started for
the East Parade Ground, their district's "safe area." As they
went out of the gate, Mr. Fukai, quite childlike now, beat on
Father Kleinsorge's shoulders and said, "I won't leave. I
won't leave." Irrelevantly, Father Kleinsorge turned to Father
LaSalle and said, "We have lost all our possessions but not our
sense of humor."

The street was cluttered with parts of houses that had slid
into it, and with fallen telephone poles and wires. From every
second or third house came the voices of people buried and
abandoned, who invariably screamed, with formal politeness,
"*Tasukete kure!* Help, if you please!" The priests recognized
several ruins from which these cries came as the homes of
friends, but because of the fire it was too late to help. All the
way, Mr. Fukai whimpered, "Let me stay." The party turned
right when they came to a block of fallen houses that was one
flame. At Sakai Bridge, which would take them across to the
East Parade Ground, they saw that the whole community on
the opposite side of the river was a sheet of fire; they dared
not cross and decided to take refuge in Asano Park, off to
their left. Father Kleinsorge, who had been weakened for a
couple of days by his bad case of diarrhea, began to stagger
under his protesting burden, and as he tried to climb up over
the wreckage of several houses that blocked their way to the
park, he stumbled, dropped Mr. Fukai, and plunged down,
head over heels, to the edge of the river. When he picked
himself up, he saw Mr. Fukai running away. Father Kleinsorge
shouted to a dozen soldiers, who were standing by the
bridge, to stop him. As Father Kleinsorge started back to get
Mr. Fukai, Father LaSalle called out, "Hurry! Don't waste
time!" So Father Kleinsorge just requested the soldiers to take
care of Mr. Fukai. They said they would, but the little, broken
man got away from them, and the last the priests could see of
him, he was running back toward the fire.

Mr. Tanimoto, fearful for his family and church, at first ran
toward them by the shortest route, along Koi Highway. He
was the only person making his way into the city; he met
hundreds and hundreds who were fleeing, and every one of
them seemed to be hurt in some way. The eyebrows of some

were burned off and skin hung from their faces and hands. Others, because of pain, held their arms up as if carrying something in both hands. Some were vomiting as they walked. Many were naked or in shreds of clothing. On some undressed bodies, the burns had made patterns—of undershirt straps and suspenders and, on the skin of some women (since white repelled the heat from the bomb and dark clothes absorbed it and conducted it to the skin), the shapes of flowers they had had on their kimonos. Many, although injured themselves, supported relatives who were worse off. Almost all had their heads bowed, looked straight ahead, were silent, and showed no expression whatever.

After crossing Koi Bridge and Kannon Bridge, having run the whole way, Mr. Tanimoto saw, as he approached the center, that all the houses had been crushed and many were afire. Here the trees were bare and their trunks were charred. He tried at several points to penetrate the ruins, but the flames always stopped him. Under many houses, people screamed for help, but no one helped; in general, survivors that day assisted only their relatives or immediate neighbors, for they could not comprehend or tolerate a wider circle of misery. The wounded limped past the screams, and Mr. Tanimoto ran past them. As a Christian he was filled with compassion for those who were trapped, and as a Japanese he was overwhelmed by the shame of being unhurt, and he prayed as he ran, "God help them and take them out of the fire."

He thought he would skirt the fire, to the left. He ran back to Kannon Bridge and followed for a distance one of the rivers. He tried several cross streets, but all were blocked, so he turned far left and ran out to Yokogawa, a station on a railroad line that detoured the city in a wide semicircle, and he followed the rails until he came to a burning train. So impressed was he by this time by the extent of the damage that he ran north two miles to Gion, a suburb in the foothills. All the way, he overtook dreadfully burned and lacerated people, and in his guilt he turned to right and left as he hurried and said to some of them, "Excuse me for having no burden like yours." Near Gion, he began to meet country people going toward the city to help, and when they saw him, several exclaimed, "Look! There is one who is not wounded." At Gion, he bore toward the right bank of the main river, the Ota, and ran down it until he reached fire again. There was no fire on the other side of the river, so he threw off his shirt and shoes and plunged into it. In midstream, where the current was fairly strong, exhaustion and fear finally caught up with him—he had run nearly seven miles—and he became limp and drifted in the water. He prayed, "Please, God, help me to cross. It would be nonsense for me to be drowned when I am the only uninjured one." He managed a few more strokes and fetched up on a spit downstream.

Mr. Tanimoto climbed up the bank and ran along it until, near a large Shinto shrine, he came to more fire, and as he turned left to get around it, he met, by incredible luck, his wife. She was carrying their infant son. Mr. Tanimoto was now so emotionally worn out that nothing could surprise him. He did not embrace his wife; he simply said, "Oh, you are safe." She told him that she had got home from her night in Ushida just in time for the explosion; she had been buried under the parsonage with the baby in her arms. She told how the wreckage had pressed down on her, how the baby had cried. She saw a chink of light, and by reaching up with a hand, she worked the hole bigger, bit by bit. After about half an hour, she heard the crackling noise of wood burning. At last the opening was big enough for her to push the baby out, and afterward she crawled out herself. She said she was now going out to Ushida again. Mr. Tanimoto said he wanted to see his church and take care of the people of his Neighborhood Association. They parted as casually—as bewildered—as they had met.

Mr. Tanimoto's way around the fire took him across the East Parade Ground, which, being an evacuation area, was now the scene of a gruesome review: rank on rank of the burned and bleeding. Those who were burned moaned, "*Mizu, mizu!* Water, water!" Mr. Tanimoto found a basin in a nearby street and located a water tap that still worked in the crushed shell of a house, and he began carrying water to the suffering strangers. When he had given drink to about thirty of them, he realized he was taking too much time. "Excuse me," he said loudly to those nearby who were reaching out their hands to him and crying their thirst. "I have many people to take care of." Then he ran away. He went to the river again, the basin in his hand, and jumped down onto a sandspit. There he saw hundreds of people so badly wounded that they could not get up to go farther from the burning city. When they saw a man erect and unhurt, the chant began again: *"Mizu, mizu, mizu."* Mr. Tanimoto could not resist them; he carried them water from the river—a mistake, since it was tidal and brackish. Two or three small boats were ferrying hurt people across the river from Asano Park, and when one touched the spit, Mr. Tanimoto again made his loud, apologetic speech and jumped into the boat. It took him across to the park. There, in the underbrush, he found some of his charges of the Neighborhood Association, who had come there by his previous instructions, and saw many acquaintances, among them Father Kleinsorge and the other Catholics. But he missed Fukai, who had been a close friend. "Where is Fukai-*san?*" he asked.

"He didn't want to come with us," Father Kleinsorge said. "He ran back."

When Miss Sasaki heard the voices of the people caught along with her in the dilapidation at the tin factory, she began speaking to them. Her nearest neighbor, she discovered, was a high-school girl who had been drafted for factory work, and who said her back was broken. Miss Sasaki replied, "I am lying here and I can't move. My left leg is cut off."

Some time later, she again heard somebody walk overhead and then move off to one side, and whoever it was began burrowing. The digger released several people, and when he had uncovered the high-school girl, she found that her back was not broken, after all, and she crawled out. Miss Sasaki spoke to the rescuer, and he worked toward her. He pulled away a great number of books, until he had made a tunnel to her. She could see his perspiring face as he said, "Come out, Miss." She tried. "I can't move," she said. The man excavated some more and told her to try with all her strength to get out. But books were heavy on her hips, and the man finally saw that a bookcase was leaning on the books and that a heavy beam pressed down on the bookcase. "Wait," he said. "I'll get a crowbar."

The man was gone a long time, and when he came back, he was ill-tempered, as if her plight were all her fault. "We have no men to help you!" he shouted in through the tunnel. "You'll have to get out by yourself."

"That's impossible," she said. "My left leg . . ." The man went away.

Much later, several men came and dragged Miss Sasaki out. Her left leg was not severed, but it was badly broken and cut and it hung askew below the knee. They took her out into a courtyard. It was raining. She sat on the ground in the rain. When the downpour increased, someone directed all the wounded people to take cover in the factory's air-raid shelters. "Come along," a torn-up woman said to her. "You can hop." But Miss Sasaki could not move, and she just waited in the rain. Then a man propped up a large sheet of corrugated iron as a kind of lean-to, and took her in his arms and carried her to it. She was grateful until he brought two horribly wounded people—a woman with a whole breast sheared off and a man whose face was all raw from a burn—to share the simple shed with her. No one came back. The rain cleared and the cloudy afternoon was hot; before nightfall the three grotesques under the slanting piece of twisted iron began to smell quite bad.

The former head of the Nobori-cho Neighborhood Association, to which the Catholic priests belonged, was an energetic man named Yoshida. He had boasted, when he was in charge of the district air-raid defenses, that fire might eat away all of Hiroshima but it would never come to Nobori-cho. The bomb blew down his house, and a joist pinned him by the legs, in full view of the Jesuit mission house across the way and of the people hurrying along the street. In their confusion as they hurried past, Mrs. Nakamura, with her children, and Father Kleinsorge, with Mr. Fukai on his back, hardly saw him; he was just part of the general blur of misery through which they moved. His cries for help brought no response from them; there were so many people shouting for help that they could not hear him separately. They and all the others went along. Nobori-cho became absolutely deserted, and the fire swept through it. Mr. Yoshida saw the wooden mission

house—the only erect building in the area—go up in a lick
of flame, and the heat was terrific on his face. Then flames
came along his side of the street and entered his house. In a
paroxysm of terrified strength, he freed himself and ran down
the alleys of Nobori-cho, hemmed in by the fire he had said
would never come. He began at once to behave like an old
man; two months later his hair was white.

As Dr. Fujii stood in the river up to his neck to avoid the heat
of the fire, the wind blew stronger and stronger, and soon,
even though the expanse of water was small, the waves grew
so high that the people under the bridge could no longer
keep their footing. Dr. Fujii went close to the shore,
crouched down, and embraced a large stone with his usable
arm. Later it became possible to wade along the very edge of
the river, and Dr. Fujii and his two surviving nurses moved
about two hundred yards upstream, to a sandspit near Asano
Park. Many wounded were lying on the sand. Dr. Machii was
there with his family; his daughter, who had been outdoors
when the bomb burst, was badly burned on her hands and
legs but fortunately not on her face. Although Dr. Fujii's
shoulder was by now terribly painful, he examined the girl's
burns curiously. Then he lay down. In spite of the misery all
around, he was ashamed of his appearance, and he remarked
to Dr. Machii that he looked like a beggar, dressed as he was
in nothing but torn and bloody underwear. Later in the afternoon, when the fire began to subside, he decided to go to his
parental house, in the suburb of Nagatsuka. He asked Dr.
Machii to join him, but the Doctor answered that he and his
family were going to spend the night on the spit, because of
his daughter's injuries. Dr. Fujii, together with his nurses,
walked first to Ushida, where, in the partially damaged house
of some relatives, he found first-aid materials he had stored
there. The two nurses bandaged him and he them. They went
on. Now not many people walked in the streets, but a great
number sat and lay on the pavement, vomited, waited for
death, and died. The number of corpses on the way to Nagatsuka was more and more puzzling. The Doctor wondered:
Could a Molotov flower basket have done all this?

Dr. Fujii reached his family's house in the evening. It was

five miles from the center of town, but its roof had fallen in and the windows were all broken.

All day, people poured into Asano Park. This private estate was far enough away from the explosion so that its bamboos, pines, laurel, and maples were still alive, and the green place invited refugees—partly because they believed that if the Americans came back, they would bomb only buildings; partly because the foliage seemed a center of coolness and life, and the estate's exquisitely precise rock gardens, with their quiet pools and arching bridges, were very Japanese, normal, secure; and also partly (according to some who were there) because of an irresistible, atavistic urge to hide under leaves. Mrs. Nakamura and her children were among the first to arrive, and they settled in the bamboo grove near the river. They all felt terribly thirsty, and they drank from the river. At once they were nauseated and began vomiting, and they retched the whole day. Others were also nauseated; they all thought (probably because of the strong odor of ionization, an "electric smell" given off by the bomb's fission) that they were sick from a gas the Americans had dropped. When Father Kleinsorge and the other priests came into the park, nodding to their friends as they passed, the Nakamuras were all sick and prostrate. A woman named Iwasaki, who lived in the neighborhood of the mission and who was sitting near the Nakamuras, got up and asked the priests if she should stay where she was or go with them. Father Kleinsorge said, "I hardly know where the safest place is." She stayed there, and later in the day, though she had no visible wounds or burns, she died. The priests went farther along the river and settled down in some underbrush. Father LaSalle lay down and went right to sleep. The theological student, who was wearing slippers, had carried with him a bundle of clothes, in which he had packed two pairs of leather shoes. When he sat down with the others, he found that the bundle had broken open and a couple of shoes had fallen out and now he had only two lefts. He retraced his steps and found one right. When he rejoined the priests, he said, "It's funny, but things don't matter any more. Yesterday, my shoes were my most important possessions. Today, I don't care. One pair is enough."

Father Cieslik said, "I know. I started to bring my books along, and then I thought, 'This is no time for books.'"

When Mr. Tanimoto, with his basin still in his hand, reached the park, it was very crowded, and to distinguish the living from the dead was not easy, for most of the people lay still, with their eyes open. To Father Kleinsorge, an Occidental, the silence in the grove by the river, where hundreds of gruesomely wounded suffered together, was one of the most dreadful and awesome phenomena of his whole experience. The hurt ones were quiet; no one wept, much less screamed in pain; no one complained; none of the many who died did so noisily; not even the children cried; very few people even spoke. And when Father Kleinsorge gave water to some whose faces had been almost blotted out by flash burns, they took their share and then raised themselves a little and bowed to him, in thanks.

Mr. Tanimoto greeted the priests and then looked around for other friends. He saw Mrs. Matsumoto, wife of the director of the Methodist School, and asked her if she was thirsty. She was, so he went to one of the pools in the Asanos' rock gardens and got water for her in his basin. Then he decided to try to get back to his church. He went into Nobori-cho by the way the priests had taken as they escaped, but he did not get far; the fire along the streets was so fierce that he had to turn back. He walked to the riverbank and began to look for a boat in which he might carry some of the most severely injured across the river from Asano Park and away from the spreading fire. Soon he found a good-sized pleasure punt drawn up on the bank, but in and around it was an awful tableau—five dead men, nearly naked, badly burned, who must have expired more or less all at once, for they were in attitudes which suggested that they had been working together to push the boat down into the river. Mr. Tanimoto lifted them away from the boat, and as he did so, he experienced such horror at disturbing the dead—preventing them, he momentarily felt, from launching their craft and going on their ghostly way—that he said out loud, "Please forgive me for taking this boat. I must use it for others, who are alive." The punt was heavy, but he managed to slide it into the water. There were no oars, and all he could find for propulsion was a thick bamboo pole. He worked the boat upstream to the most crowded part of the park and began to ferry the wounded. He could pack ten or twelve into the boat for each crossing, but as the river was too deep in the center to pole his way across, he had to paddle with the bamboo, and consequently each trip took a very long time. He worked several hours that way.

Early in the afternoon, the fire swept into the woods of Asano Park. The first Mr. Tanimoto knew of it was when, returning in his boat, he saw that a great number of people had moved toward the riverside. On touching the bank, he went up to investigate, and when he saw the fire, he shouted, "All the young men who are not badly hurt come with me!" Father Kleinsorge moved Father Schiffer and Father LaSalle close to the edge of the river and asked people there to get them across if the fire came too near, and then joined Tanimoto's volunteers. Mr. Tanimoto sent some to look for buckets and basins and told others to beat the burning underbrush with their clothes; when utensils were at hand, he formed a bucket chain from one of the pools in the rock gardens. The team fought the fire for more than two hours, and gradually defeated the flames. As Mr. Tanimoto's men worked, the frightened people in the park pressed closer and closer to the river, and finally the mob began to force some of the unfortunates who were on the very bank into the water. Among those driven into the river and drowned were Mrs. Matsumoto, of the Methodist School, and her daughter.

When Father Kleinsorge got back after fighting the fire, he found Father Schiffer still bleeding and terribly pale. Some Japanese stood around and stared at him, and Father Schiffer whispered, with a weak smile, "It is as if I were already dead." "Not yet," Father Kleinsorge said. He had brought Dr. Fujii's first-aid kit with him, and he had noticed Dr. Kanda in the crowd, so he sought him out and asked him if he would dress Father Schiffer's bad cuts. Dr. Kanda had seen his wife and daughter dead in the ruins of his hospital; he sat now with his head in his hands. "I can't do anything," he said. Father Kleinsorge bound more bandage around Father Schiffer's head, moved him to a steep place, and settled him so that his head was high, and soon the bleeding diminished.

The roar of approaching planes was heard about this time. Someone in the crowd near the Nakamura family shouted, "It's some Grummans coming to strafe us!" A baker named Nakashima stood up and commanded, "Everyone who is wearing anything white, take it off." Mrs. Nakamura took the blouses off her children, and opened her umbrella and made them get under it. A great number of people, even badly burned ones, crawled into bushes and stayed there until the hum, evidently of a reconnaissance or weather run, died away.

It began to rain. Mrs. Nakamura kept her children under the umbrella. The drops grew abnormally large, and someone shouted, "The Americans are dropping gasoline. They're going to set fire to us!" (This alarm stemmed from one of the theories being passed through the park as to why so much of Hiroshima had burned: it was that a single plane had sprayed gasoline on the city and then somehow set fire to it in one flashing moment.) But the drops were palpably water, and as they fell, the wind grew stronger and stronger, and sud-denly—probably because of the tremendous convection set up by the blazing city—a whirlwind ripped through the park. Huge trees crashed down; small ones were uprooted and flew into the air. Higher, a wild array of flat things revolved in the twisting funnel—pieces of iron roofing, papers, doors, strips of matting. Father Kleinsorge put a piece of cloth over Father Schiffer's eyes, so that the feeble man would not think he was going crazy. The gale blew Mrs. Murata, the mission house-keeper, who was sitting close by the river, down the embank-ment at a shallow, rocky place, and she came out with her bare feet bloody. The vortex moved out onto the river, where it sucked up a waterspout and eventually spent itself.

After the storm, Mr. Tanimoto began ferrying people again, and Father Kleinsorge asked the theological student to go across and make his way out to the Jesuit Novitiate at Naga-tsuka, about three miles from the center of town, and to re-quest the priests there to come with help for Fathers Schiffer and LaSalle. The student got into Mr. Tanimoto's boat and went off with him. Father Kleinsorge asked Mrs. Nakamura if she would like to go out to Nagatsuka with the priests when they came. She said she had some luggage and her children were sick—they were still vomiting from time to time, and so, for that matter, was she—and therefore she feared she could not. He said he thought the fathers from the Novitiate could come back the next day with a pushcart to get her.

Late in the afternoon, when he went ashore for a while, Mr. Tanimoto, upon whose energy and initiative many had come to depend, heard people begging for food. He consulted Father Kleinsorge, and they decided to go back into town to get some rice from Mr. Tanimoto's Neighborhood Association shelter and from the mission shelter. Father Cieslik and two or three others went with them. At first, when they got among the rows of prostrate houses, they did not know where they were; the change was too sudden, from a busy city of two hundred and forty-five thousand that morning to a mere pattern of residue in the afternoon. The asphalt of the streets was still so soft and hot from the fires that walking was uncomfortable. They encountered only one person, a woman, who said to them as they passed, "My husband is in those ashes." At the mission, where Mr. Tanimoto left the party, Father Kleinsorge was dismayed to see the building razed. In the garden, on the way to the shelter, he noticed a pumpkin roasted on the vine. He and Father Cieslik tasted it and it was good. They were surprised at their hunger, and they ate quite a bit. They got out several bags of rice and gathered up several other cooked pumpkins and dug up some potatoes that were nicely baked under the ground, and started back. Mr. Tanimoto rejoined them on the way. One of the people with him had some cooking utensils. In the park, Mr. Tanimoto organized the lightly wounded women of his neighborhood to cook. Father Kleinsorge offered the Nakamura family some pumpkin, and they tried it, but they could not keep it on their stomachs. Altogether, the rice was enough to feed nearly a hundred people.

Just before dark, Mr. Tanimoto came across a twenty-year-old girl, Mrs. Kamai, the Tanimotos' next-door neighbor. She was crouching on the ground with the body of her infant daughter in her arms. The baby had evidently been dead all day. Mrs. Kamai jumped up when she saw Mr. Tanimoto and said, "Would you please try to locate my husband?"

Mr. Tanimoto knew that her husband had been inducted into the Army just the day before; he and Mrs. Tanimoto had entertained Mrs. Kamai in the afternoon, to make her forget. Kamai had reported to the Chugoku Regional Army Head-quarters—near the ancient castle in the middle of town—where some four thousand troops were stationed. Judging by the many maimed soldiers Mr. Tanimoto had seen during the day, he surmised that the barracks had been badly damaged by whatever it was that had hit Hiroshima. He knew he hadn't a chance of finding Mrs. Kamai's husband, even if he searched, but he wanted to humor her. "I'll try," he said.

"You've got to find him," she said. "He loved our baby so much. I want him to see her once more."

### III. DETAILS ARE BEING INVESTIGATED

Early in the evening of the day the bomb exploded, a Japa-nese naval launch moved slowly up and down the seven rivers of Hiroshima. It stopped here and there to make an an-nouncement—alongside the crowded sandspits, on which hundreds of wounded lay; at the bridges, on which others were crowded; and eventually, as twilight fell, opposite Asano Park. A young officer stood up in the launch and shouted through a megaphone, "Be patient! A naval hospital ship is coming to take care of you!" The sight of the shipshape launch against the background of the havoc across the river; the unruffled young man in his neat uniform; above all, the promise of medical help—the first word of possible succor anyone had heard in nearly twelve awful hours—cheered the people in the park tremendously. Mrs. Nakamura settled her family for the night with the assurance that a doctor would come and stop their retching. Mr. Tanimoto resumed ferrying the wounded across the river. Father Kleinsorge lay down and said the Lord's Prayer and a Hail Mary to himself, and fell right asleep; but no sooner had he dropped off than Mrs. Murata, the conscientious mission housekeeper, shook him and said, "Father Kleinsorge! Did you remember to repeat your evening prayers?" He answered rather grumpily, "Of course," and he tried to go back to sleep but could not. This, apparently, was just what Mrs. Murata wanted. She began to chat with the exhausted priest. One of the questions she raised was when he thought the priests from the Novitiate, for whom he had sent a messenger in midafternoon, would arrive to evacuate Father Superior LaSalle and Father Schiffer.

The messenger Father Kleinsorge had sent—the theological student who had been living at the mission house—had arrived at the Novitiate, in the hills about three miles out, at half past four. The sixteen priests there had been doing rescue work in the outskirts; they had worried about their colleagues in the city but had not known how or where to look for them. Now they hastily made two litters out of poles and boards, and the student led half a dozen of them back into the devastated area. They worked their way along the Ota above the city; twice the heat of the fire forced them into the river. At Misasa Bridge, they encountered a long line of soldiers making a bizarre forced march away from the Chugoku Regional Army Headquarters in the center of the town. All were grotesquely burned, and they supported themselves with staves or leaned on one another. Sick, burned horses, hanging their heads, stood on the bridge. When the rescue party reached the park, it was after dark, and progress was made extremely difficult by the tangle of fallen trees of all sizes that had been knocked down by the whirlwind that afternoon. At last—not long after Mrs. Murata asked her question—they reached their friends, and gave them wine and strong tea.

The priests discussed how to get Father Schiffer and Father LaSalle out to the Novitiate. They were afraid that blundering through the park with them would jar them too much on the wooden litters, and that the wounded men would lose too much blood. Father Kleinsorge thought of Mr. Tanimoto and his boat, and called out to him on the river. When Mr. Tanimoto reached the bank, he said he would be glad to take the injured priests and their bearers upstream to where they could find a clear roadway. The rescuers put Father Schiffer onto one of the stretchers and lowered it into the boat, and two of them went aboard with it. Mr. Tanimoto, who still had no oars, poled the punt upstream.

About half an hour later, Mr. Tanimoto came back and excitedly asked the remaining priests to help him rescue two children he had seen standing up to their shoulders in the river. A group went out and picked them up—two young girls who had lost their family and were both badly burned. The priests stretched them on the ground next to Father Kleinsorge and then embarked Father LaSalle. Father Cieslik thought he could make it out to the Novitiate on foot, so he went aboard with the others. Father Kleinsorge was too feeble; he decided to wait in the park until the next day. He asked the men to come back with a handcart, so that they could take Mrs. Nakamura and her sick children to the Novitiate.

Mr. Tanimoto shoved off again. As the boatload of priests moved slowly upstream, they heard weak cries for help. A woman's voice stood out especially: "There are people here about to be drowned! Help us! The water is rising!" The sounds came from one of the sandspits, and those in the punt could see, in the reflected light of the still-burning fires, a number of wounded people lying at the edge of the river, already partly covered by the flooding tide. Mr. Tanimoto wanted to help them, but the priests were afraid that Father Schiffer would die if they didn't hurry, and they urged their ferryman along. He dropped them where he had put Father Schiffer down and then started back alone toward the sandspit.

The night was hot, and it seemed even hotter because of the fires against the sky, but the younger of the two girls Mr. Tanimoto and the priests had rescued complained to Father Kleinsorge that she was cold. He covered her with his jacket. She and her older sister had been in the salt water of the river for a couple of hours before being rescued. The younger one had huge, raw flash burns on her body; the salt water must have been excruciatingly painful to her. She began to shiver heavily, and again said it was cold. Father Kleinsorge borrowed a blanket from someone nearby and wrapped her up, but she shook more and more, and said again, "I am so cold," and then she suddenly stopped shivering and was dead.

Mr. Tanimoto found about twenty men and women on the sandspit. He drove the boat onto the bank and urged them to get aboard. They did not move and he realized that they were too weak to lift themselves. He reached down and took a woman by the hands, but her skin slipped off in huge, glove-like pieces. He was so sickened by this that he had to sit down for a moment. Then he got out into the water and, though a small man, lifted several of the men and women, who were naked, into his boat. Their backs and breasts were clammy, and he remembered uneasily what the great burns he had seen during the day had been like: yellow at first, then red and swollen, with the skin sloughed off, and finally, in the evening, suppurated and smelly. With the tide risen, his bamboo pole was now too short and he had to paddle most of the way across with it. On the other side, at a higher spit, he lifted the slimy living bodies out and carried them up the slope away from the tide. He had to keep consciously re-peating to himself, "These are human beings." It took him three trips to get them all across the river. When he had fin-ished, he decided he had to have a rest, and he went back to the park.

As Mr. Tanimoto stepped up the dark bank, he tripped over someone, and someone else said angrily, "Look out! That's my hand." Mr. Tanimoto, ashamed of hurting wounded people, embarrassed at being able to walk upright, suddenly thought of the naval hospital ship, which had not come (it never did), and he had for a moment a feeling of blind, mur-derous rage at the crew of the ship, and then at all doctors. Why didn't they come to help these people?

Dr. Fujii lay in dreadful pain throughout the night on the floor of his family's roofless house on the edge of the city. By the light of a lantern, he had examined himself and found: left clavicle fractured; multiple abrasions and lacerations of face and body, including deep cuts on the chin, back, and legs; extensive contusions on chest and trunk; a couple of ribs pos-sibly fractured. Had he not been so badly hurt, he might have been at Asano Park, assisting the wounded.

By nightfall, ten thousand victims of the explosion had in-vaded the Red Cross Hospital, and Dr. Sasaki, worn out, was moving aimlessly and dully up and down the stinking corri-dors with wads of bandage and bottles of mercurochrome, still wearing the glasses he had taken from the wounded nurse, binding up the worst cuts as he came to them. Other doctors were putting compresses of saline solution on the worst burns. That was all they could do. After dark, they worked by the light of the city's fires and by candles the ten remaining nurses held for them. Dr. Sasaki had not looked outside the hospital all day; the scene inside was so terrible and so compelling that it had not occurred to him to ask any questions about what had happened beyond the windows and doors. Ceilings and partitions had fallen; plaster, dust, blood, and vomit were everywhere. Patients were dying by the hundreds, but there was nobody to carry away the corpses. Some of the hospital staff distributed biscuits and rice balls, but the charnel-house smell was so strong that few were hungry. By three o'clock the next morning, after nineteen straight hours of his gruesome work, Dr. Sasaki was incapable of dressing another wound. He and some other survivors of the hospital staff got straw mats and went outdoors—thousands of patients and hundreds of dead were in the yard and on the driveway—and hurried around behind the hospital and lay down in hiding to snatch some sleep. But within an hour wounded people had found them; a complaining circle formed around them: "Doctors! Help us! How can you sleep?" Dr. Sasaki got up again and went back to work. Early in the day, he thought for the first time of his mother, at their country home in Mukaihara, thirty miles from town. He usually went home every night. He was afraid she would think he was dead.

Near the spot upriver to which Mr. Tanimoto had transported the priests, there sat a large case of rice cakes which a rescue party had evidently brought for the wounded lying thereabouts but hadn't distributed. Before evacuating the wounded priests, the others passed the cakes around and helped themselves. A few minutes later, a band of soldiers came up, and an officer, hearing the priests speaking a foreign language, drew his sword and hysterically asked who they were. One of the priests calmed him down and explained that they were Germans—allies. The officer apologized and said that there were reports going around that American parachutists had landed.

The priests decided that they should take Father Schiffer first. As they prepared to leave, Father Superior LaSalle said he felt awfully cold. One of the Jesuits gave up his coat, another his shirt; they were glad to wear less in the muggy night. The stretcher bearers started out. The theological student led the way and tried to warn the others of obstacles, but one of the priests got a foot tangled in some telephone wire and tripped and dropped his corner of the litter. Father Schiffer rolled off, lost consciousness, came to, and then vomited. The bearers picked him up and went on with him to the edge of the city, where they had arranged to meet a relay of other priests, left him with them, and turned back and got the Father Superior.

The wooden litter must have been terribly painful for Father LaSalle, in whose back scores of tiny particles of window glass were embedded. Near the edge of town, the group had to walk around an automobile burned and squatting on the narrow road, and the bearers on one side, unable to see their way in the darkness, fell into a deep ditch. Father LaSalle was thrown onto the ground and the litter broke in two. One priest went ahead to get a handcart from the Novitiate, but he soon found one beside an empty house and wheeled it back. The priests lifted Father LaSalle into the cart and pushed him over the bumpy road the rest of the way. The rector of the Novitiate, who had been a doctor before he entered the religious order, cleaned the wounds of the two priests and put them to bed between clean sheets, and they thanked God for the care they had received.

Thousands of people had nobody to help them. Miss Sasaki was one of them. Abandoned and helpless, under the crude lean-to in the courtyard of the tin factory, beside the woman who had lost a breast and the man whose burned face was scarcely a face any more, she suffered awfully that night from the pain in her broken leg. She did not sleep at all; neither did she converse with her sleepless companions.

In the park, Mrs. Murata kept Father Kleinsorge awake all night by talking to him. None of the Nakamura family were able to sleep, either; the children, in spite of being very sick,

were interested in everything that happened. They were delighted when one of the city's gas-storage tanks went up in a
tremendous burst of flame. Toshio, the boy, shouted to the
others to look at the reflection in the river. Mr. Tanimoto,
after his long run and his many hours of rescue work, dozed
uneasily. When he awoke, in the first light of dawn, he looked
across the river and saw that he had not carried the festered,
limp bodies high enough on the sandspit the night before.
The tide had risen above where he had put them; they had
not had the strength to move; they must have drowned. He
saw a number of bodies floating in the river.

Early that day, August 7th, the Japanese radio broadcast for
the first time a succinct announcement that very few, if any,
of the people most concerned with its content, the survivors
in Hiroshima, happened to hear: "Hiroshima suffered considerable damage as the result of an attack by a few B-29s. It is
believed that a new type of bomb was used. The details are
being investigated." Nor is it probable that any of the survivors happened to be tuned in on a short-wave rebroadcast of
an extraordinary announcement by the President of the
United States, which identified the new bomb as atomic:
"That bomb had more power than twenty thousand tons of
TNT. It had more than two thousand times the blast power
of the British Grand Slam, which is the largest bomb ever yet
used in the history of warfare." Those victims who were able
to worry at all about what had happened thought of it and
discussed it in more primitive, childish terms — gasoline
sprinkled from an airplane, maybe, or some combustible gas,
or a big cluster of incendiaries, or the work of parachutists;
but, even if they had known the truth, most of them were too
busy or too weary or too badly hurt to care that they were the
objects of the first great experiment in the use of atomic
power, which (as the voices on the short wave shouted) no
country except the United States, with its industrial know-
how, its willingness to throw two billion gold dollars into an
important wartime gamble, could possibly have developed.

Mr. Tanimoto was still angry at doctors. He decided that he
would personally bring one to Asano Park—by the scruff of

the neck, if necessary. He crossed the river, went past the Shinto shrine where he had met his wife for a brief moment the day before, and walked to the East Parade Ground. Since this had long before been designated as an evacuation area, he thought he would find an aid station there. He did find one, operated by an Army medical unit, but he also saw that its doctors were hopelessly overburdened, with thousands of patients sprawled among corpses across the field in front of it. Nevertheless, he went up to one of the Army doctors and said, as reproachfully as he could, "Why have you not come to Asano Park? You are badly needed there."

Without even looking up from his work, the doctor said in a tired voice, "This is my station."

"But there are many dying on the riverbank over there."

"The first duty," the doctor said, "is to take care of the slightly wounded."

"Why—when there are many who are heavily wounded on the riverbank?"

The doctor moved to another patient. "In an emergency like this," he said, as if he were reciting from a manual, "the first task is to help as many as possible—to save as many lives as possible. There is no hope for the heavily wounded. They will die. We can't bother with them."

"That may be right from a medical standpoint—" Mr. Tanimoto began, but then he looked out across the field, where the many dead lay close and intimate with those who were still living, and he turned away without finishing his sentence, angry now with himself. He didn't know what to do; he had promised some of the dying people in the park that he would bring them medical aid. They might die feeling cheated. He saw a ration stand at one side of the field, and he went to it and begged some rice cakes and biscuits, and he took them back, in lieu of doctors, to the people in the park.

The morning, again, was hot. Father Kleinsorge went to fetch water for the wounded in a bottle and a teapot he had borrowed. He had heard that it was possible to get fresh tap water outside Asano Park. Going through the rock gardens, he had to climb over and crawl under the trunks of fallen pine trees; he found he was weak. There were many dead in the gardens. At a beautiful moon bridge, he passed a naked, living woman who seemed to have been burned from head to toe and was red all over. Near the entrance to the park, an Army doctor was working, but the only medicine he had was iodine, which he painted over cuts, bruises, slimy burns, everything—and by now everything that he painted had pus on it. Outside the gate of the park, Father Kleinsorge found a faucet that still worked—part of the plumbing of a vanished house—and he filled his vessels and returned. When he had given the wounded the water, he made a second trip. This time, the woman by the bridge was dead. On his way back with the water, he got lost on a detour around a fallen tree, and as he looked for his way through the woods, he heard a voice ask from the underbrush, "Have you anything to drink?" He saw a uniform. Thinking there was just one soldier, he approached with the water. When he had penetrated the bushes, he saw there were about twenty men, and they were all in exactly the same nightmarish state: their faces were wholly burned, their eyesockets were hollow, the fluid from their melted eyes had run down their cheeks. (They must have had their faces upturned when the bomb went off; perhaps they were anti-aircraft personnel.) Their mouths were mere swollen, pus-covered wounds, which they could not bear to stretch enough to admit the spout of the teapot. So Father Kleinsorge got a large piece of grass and drew out the stem so as to make a straw, and gave them all water to drink that way. One of them said, "I can't see anything." Father Kleinsorge answered, as cheerfully as he could, "There's a doctor at the entrance to the park. He's busy now, but he'll come soon and fix your eyes, I hope."

Since that day, Father Kleinsorge has thought back to how queasy he had once been at the sight of pain, how someone else's cut finger used to make him turn faint. Yet there in the park he was so benumbed that immediately after leaving this horrible sight he stopped on a path by one of the pools and discussed with a lightly wounded man whether it would be safe to eat the fat, two-foot carp that floated dead on the surface of the water. They decided, after some consideration, that it would be unwise.

Father Kleinsorge filled the containers a third time and

went back to the riverbank. There, amid the dead and dying, he saw a young woman with a needle and thread mending her kimono, which had been slightly torn. Father Kleinsorge joshed her. "My, but you're a dandy!" he said. She laughed.

He felt tired and lay down. He began to talk with two engaging children whose acquaintance he had made the afternoon before. He learned that their name was Kataoka; the girl was thirteen, the boy five. The girl had been just about to set out for a barbershop when the bomb fell. As the family started for Asano Park, their mother decided to turn back for some food and extra clothing; they became separated from her in the crowd of fleeing people, and they had not seen her since. Occasionally they stopped suddenly in their perfectly cheerful playing and began to cry for their mother.

It was difficult for all the children in the park to sustain the sense of tragedy. Toshio Nakamura got quite excited when he saw his friend Seichi Sato riding up the river in a boat with his family, and he ran to the bank and waved and shouted, "Sato! Sato!"

The boy turned his head and shouted, "Who's that?"

"Nakamura."

"Hello, Toshio!"

"Are you all safe?"

"Yes. What about you?"

"Yes, we're all right. My sisters are vomiting, but I'm fine."

Father Kleinsorge began to be thirsty in the dreadful heat, and he did not feel strong enough to go for water again. A little before noon, he saw a Japanese woman handing something out. Soon she came to him and said in a kindly voice, "These are tea leaves. Chew them, young man, and you won't feel thirsty." The woman's gentleness made Father Kleinsorge suddenly want to cry. For weeks, he had been feeling oppressed by the hatred of foreigners that the Japanese seemed increasingly to show, and he had been uneasy even with his Japanese friends. This stranger's gesture made him a little hysterical.

Around noon, the priests arrived from the Novitiate with the handcart. They had been to the site of the mission house in the city and had retrieved some suitcases that had been stored in the air-raid shelter and had also picked up the remains of melted holy vessels in the ashes of the chapel. They now packed Father Kleinsorge's papier-mâché suitcase and the things belonging to Mrs. Murata and the Nakamuras into the cart, put the two Nakamura girls aboard, and prepared to start out. Then one of the Jesuits who had a practical turn of mind remembered that they had been notified some time before that if they suffered property damage at the hands of the enemy, they could enter a claim for compensation with the prefectural police. The holy men discussed this matter there in the park, with the wounded as silent as the dead around them, and decided that Father Kleinsorge, as a former resident of the destroyed mission, was the one to enter the claim. So, as the others went off with the handcart, Father Kleinsorge said goodbye to the Kataoka children and trudged to a police station. Fresh, clean-uniformed policemen from another town were in charge, and a crowd of dirty and disarrayed citizens crowded around them, mostly asking after lost relatives. Father Kleinsorge filled out a claim form and started walking through the center of the town on his way to Nagatsuka. It was then that he first realized the extent of the damage; he passed block after block of ruins, and even after all he had seen in the park, his breath was taken away. By the time he reached the Novitiate, he was sick with exhaustion. The last thing he did as he fell into bed was request that someone go back for the motherless Kataoka children.

Altogether, Miss Sasaki was left two days and two nights under the piece of propped-up roofing with her crushed leg and her two unpleasant comrades. Her only diversion was when men came to the factory air-raid shelters, which she could see from under one corner of her shelter, and hauled corpses up out of them with ropes. Her leg became discolored, swollen, and putrid. All that time, she went without food and water. On the third day, August 8th, some friends who supposed she was dead came to look for her body and found her. They told her that her mother, father, and baby brother, who at the time of the explosion were in the Tamura Pediatric Hospital, where the baby was a patient, had all been given up as certainly dead, since the hospital was totally destroyed. Her friends then left her to think that piece of news over. Later, some men picked her up by the arms and legs and carried her quite a distance to a truck. For about an hour, the truck moved over a bumpy road, and Miss Sasaki, who had become convinced that she was dulled to pain, discovered that she was not. The men lifted her out at a relief station in the section of Inokuchi, where two Army doctors looked at her. The moment one of them touched her wound, she fainted. She came to in time to hear them discuss whether or not to cut off her leg; one said there was gas gangrene in the lips of the wound and predicted she would die unless they amputated, and the other said that was too bad, because they had no equipment with which to do the job. She fainted again. When she recovered consciousness, she was being carried somewhere on a stretcher. She was put aboard a launch, which went to the nearby island of Ninoshima, and she was taken to a military hospital there. Another doctor examined her and said that she did not have gas gangrene, though she did have a fairly ugly compound fracture. He said quite coldly that he was sorry, but this was a hospital for operative surgical cases only, and because she had no gangrene, she would have to return to Hiroshima that night. But then the doctor took her temperature, and what he saw on the thermometer made him decide to let her stay.

That day, August 8th, Father Cieslik went into the city to look for Mr. Fukai, the Japanese secretary of the diocese, who had ridden unwillingly out of the flaming city on Father Kleinsorge's back and then had run back crazily into it. Father Cieslik started hunting in the neighborhood of Sakai Bridge, where the Jesuits had last seen Mr. Fukai; he went to the East Parade Ground, the evacuation area to which the secretary might have gone, and looked for him among the wounded and dead there; he went to the prefectural police and made inquiries. He could not find any trace of the man. Back at the Novitiate that evening, the theological student, who had been rooming with Mr. Fukai at the mission house, told the priests that the secretary had remarked to him, during an air-raid alarm one day not long before the bombing, "Japan is dying. If there is a real air raid here in Hiroshima, I want to die with our country." The priests concluded that

Mr. Fukai had run back to immolate himself in the flames. They never saw him again.

At the Red Cross Hospital, Dr. Sasaki worked for three straight days with only one hour's sleep. On the second day, he began to sew up the worst cuts, and right through the following night and all the next day he stitched. Many of the wounds were festered. Fortunately, someone had found intact a supply of *narucopon*, a Japanese sedative, and he gave it to many who were in pain. Word went around among the staff that there must have been something peculiar about the great bomb, because on the second day the vice-chief of the hospital went down in the basement to the vault where the X-ray plates were stored and found the whole stock exposed as they lay. That day, a fresh doctor and ten nurses came in from the city of Yamaguchi with extra bandages and antiseptics, and the third day another physician and a dozen more nurses arrived from Matsue—yet there were still only eight doctors for ten thousand patients. In the afternoon of the third day, exhausted from his foul tailoring, Dr. Sasaki became obsessed with the idea that his mother thought he was dead. He got permission to go to Mukaihara. He walked out to the first suburbs, beyond which the electric train service was still functioning, and reached home late in the evening. His mother said she had known he was all right all along; a wounded nurse had stopped by to tell her. He went to bed and slept for seventeen hours.

Before dawn on August 8th, someone entered the room at the Novitiate where Father Kleinsorge was in bed, reached up to the hanging light bulb, and switched it on. The sudden flood of light, pouring in on Father Kleinsorge's half sleep, brought him leaping out of bed, braced for a new concussion. When he realized what had happened, he laughed confusedly and went back to bed. He stayed there all day.

On August 9th, Father Kleinsorge was still tired. The rector looked at his cuts and said they were not even worth dressing, and if Father Kleinsorge kept them clean, they would heal in three or four days. Father Kleinsorge felt uneasy; he could not yet comprehend what he had been through; as if he were

guilty of something awful, he felt he had to go back to the
scene of the violence he had experienced. He got up out of
bed and walked into the city. He scratched for a while in the
ruins of the mission house, but he found nothing. He went to
the sites of a couple of schools and asked after people he
knew. He looked for some of the city's Japanese Catholics,
but he found only fallen houses. He walked back to the Novitiate, stupefied and without any new understanding.

At two minutes after eleven o'clock on the morning of August 9th, the second atomic bomb was dropped, on Nagasaki.
It was several days before the survivors of Hiroshima knew
they had company, because the Japanese radio and newspapers were being extremely cautious on the subject of the
strange weapon.

On August 9th, Mr. Tanimoto was still working in the park.
He went to the suburb of Ushida, where his wife was staying
with friends, and got a tent which he had stored there before
the bombing. He now took it to the park and set it up as a
shelter for some of the wounded who could not move or be
moved. Whatever he did in the park, he felt he was being
watched by the twenty-year-old girl, Mrs. Kamai, his former
neighbor, whom he had seen on the day the bomb exploded,
with her dead baby daughter in her arms. She kept the small
corpse in her arms for four days, even though it began smelling bad on the second day. Once, Mr. Tanimoto sat with her
for a while, and she told him that the bomb had buried her
under their house with the baby strapped to her back, and
that when she had dug herself free, she had discovered that
the baby was choking, its mouth full of dirt. With her little
finger, she had carefully cleaned out the infant's mouth, and
for a time the child had breathed normally and seemed all
right; then suddenly it had died. Mrs. Kamai also talked about
what a fine man her husband was, and again urged Mr. Tanimoto to search for him. Since Mr. Tanimoto had been all
through the city the first day and had seen terribly burned
soldiers from Kamai's post, the Chugoku Regional Army
Headquarters, everywhere, he knew it would be impossible to
find Kamai, even if he were living, but of course he didn't tell

her that. Every time she saw Mr. Tanimoto, she asked whether he had found her husband. Once, he tried to suggest that perhaps it was time to cremate the baby, but Mrs. Kamai only held it tighter. He began to keep away from her, but whenever he looked at her, she was staring at him and her eyes asked the same question. He tried to escape her glance by keeping his back turned to her as much as possible.

The Jesuits took about fifty refugees into the exquisite chapel of the Novitiate. The rector gave them what medical care he could—mostly just the cleaning away of pus. Each of the Nakamuras was provided with a blanket and a mosquito net. Mrs. Nakamura and her younger daughter had no appetite and ate nothing; her son and other daughter ate, and lost, each meal they were offered. On August 10th, a friend, Mrs. Osaki, came to see them and told them that her son Hideo had been burned alive in the factory where he worked. This Hideo had been a kind of hero to Toshio, who had often gone to the plant to watch him run his machine. That night, Toshio woke up screaming. He had dreamed that he had seen Mrs. Osaki coming out of an opening in the ground with her family, and then he saw Hideo at his machine, a big one with a revolving belt, and he himself was standing beside Hideo, and for some reason this was terrifying.

On August 10th, Father Kleinsorge, having heard from someone that Dr. Fujii had been injured and that he had eventually gone to the summer house of a friend of his named Okuma, in the village of Fukawa, asked Father Cieslik if he would go and see how Dr. Fujii was. Father Cieslik went to Misasa station, outside Hiroshima, rode for twenty minutes on an electric train, and then walked for an hour and a half in a terribly hot sun to Mr. Okuma's house, which was beside the Ota River at the foot of a mountain. He found Dr. Fujii sitting in a chair in a kimono, applying compresses to his broken collarbone. The Doctor told Father Cieslik about having lost his glasses and said that his eyes bothered him. He showed the priest huge blue and green stripes where beams had bruised him. He offered the Jesuit first a cigarette and then whiskey, though it was only eleven in the morning. Father Cieslik thought it would please Dr. Fujii if he took a little, so he said yes. A servant brought some Suntory whiskey, and the Jesuit, the Doctor, and the host had a very pleasant chat. Mr. Okuma had lived in Hawaii, and he told some things about Americans. Dr. Fujii talked a bit about the disaster. He said that Mr. Okuma and a nurse had gone into the ruins of his hospital and brought back a small safe which he had moved into his air-raid shelter. This contained some surgical instruments, and Dr. Fujii gave Father Cieslik a few pairs of scissors and tweezers for the rector at the Novitiate. Father Cieslik was bursting with some inside dope he had, but he waited until the conversation turned naturally to the mystery of the bomb. Then he said he knew what kind of bomb it was; he had the secret on the best authority—that of a Japanese newspaperman who had dropped in at the Novitiate. The bomb was not a bomb at all; it was a kind of fine magnesium powder sprayed over the whole city by a single plane, and it exploded when it came into contact with the live wires of the city power system. "That means," said Dr. Fujii, perfectly satisfied, since after all the information came from a newspaperman, "that it can only be dropped on big cities and only in the daytime, when the tram lines and so forth are in operation."

After five days of ministering to the wounded in the park, Mr. Tanimoto returned, on August 11th, to his parsonage and dug around in the ruins. He retrieved some diaries and church records that had been kept in books and were only charred around the edges, as well as some cooking utensils and pottery. While he was at work, a Miss Tanaka came and said that her father had been asking for him. Mr. Tanimoto had reason to hate her father, the retired shipping-company official who, though he made a great show of his charity, was notoriously selfish and cruel, and who, just a few days before the bombing, had said openly to several people that Mr. Tanimoto was a spy for the Americans. Several times he had derided Christianity and called it un-Japanese. At the moment of the bombing, Mr. Tanaka had been walking in the street in front of the city's radio station. He received serious flash burns, but he was able to walk home. He took refuge in his Neighbor-

hood Association shelter and from there tried hard to get
medical aid. He expected all the doctors of Hiroshima to
come to him, because he was so rich and so famous for giving
his money away. When none of them came, he angrily set out
to look for them; leaning on his daughter's arm, he walked
from private hospital to private hospital, but all were in ruins,
and he went back and lay down in the shelter again. Now he
was very weak and knew he was going to die. He was willing
to be comforted by any religion.

Mr. Tanimoto went to help him. He descended into the
tomblike shelter and, when his eyes were adjusted to the
darkness, saw Mr. Tanaka, his face and arms puffed up and
covered with pus and blood, and his eyes swollen shut. The
old man smelled very bad, and he moaned constantly. He
seemed to recognize Mr. Tanimoto's voice. Standing at the
shelter stairway to get light, Mr. Tanimoto read loudly from a
Japanese-language pocket Bible: "For a thousand years in Thy
sight are but as yesterday when it is past, and as a watch in the
night. Thou carriest the children of men away as with a flood;
they are as a sleep; in the morning they are like grass which
groweth up. In the morning it flourisheth and groweth up; in
the evening it is cut down, and withereth. For we are consumed by Thine anger and by Thy wrath are we troubled.
Thou hast set our iniquities before Thee, our secret sins in the
light of Thy countenance. For all our days are passed away in
Thy wrath: we spend our years as a tale that is told. . . ."

Mr. Tanaka died as Mr. Tanimoto read the psalm.

On August 11th, word came to the Ninoshima Military Hospital that a large number of military casualties from the Chugoku Regional Army Headquarters were to arrive on the island that day, and it was deemed necessary to evacuate all
civilian patients. Miss Sasaki, still running an alarmingly high
fever, was put on a large ship. She lay out on deck, with a
pillow under her leg. There were awnings over the deck, but
the vessel's course put her in the sunlight. She felt as if she
were under a magnifying glass in the sun. Pus oozed out of
her wound, and soon the whole pillow was covered with it.
She was taken ashore at Hatsukaichi, a town several miles to
the southwest of Hiroshima, and put in the Goddess of Mercy

Primary School, which had been turned into a hospital. She lay there for several days before a specialist on fractures came from Kobe. By then her leg was red and swollen up to her hip. The doctor decided he could not set the breaks. He made an incision and put in a rubber pipe to drain off the putrescence.

At the Novitiate, the motherless Kataoka children were inconsolable. Father Cieslik worked hard to keep them distracted. He put riddles to them. He asked, "What is the cleverest animal in the world?," and after the thirteen-year-old girl had guessed the ape, the elephant, the horse, he said, "No, it must be the hippopotamus," because in Japanese that animal is *kaba*, the reverse of *baka*, stupid. He told Bible stories, beginning, in the order of things, with the Creation. He showed them a scrapbook of snapshots taken in Europe. Nevertheless, they cried most of the time for their mother.

Several days later, Father Cieslik started hunting for the children's family. First, he learned through the police that an uncle had been to the authorities in Kure, a city not far away, to inquire for the children. After that, he heard that an older brother had been trying to trace them through the post office in Ujina, a suburb of Hiroshima. Still later, he heard that the mother was alive and was on Goto Island, off Nagasaki. And at last, by keeping a check on the Ujina post office, he got in touch with the brother and returned the children to their mother.

About a week after the bomb dropped, a vague, incomprehensible rumor reached Hiroshima—that the city had been destroyed by the energy released when atoms were somehow split in two. The weapon was referred to in this word-of-mouth report as *genshi bakudan*—the root characters of which can be translated as "original child bomb." No one understood the idea or put any more credence in it than in the powdered magnesium and such things. Newspapers were being brought in from other cities, but they were still confining themselves to extremely general statements, such as Domei's assertion on August 12th: "There is nothing to do but admit the tremendous power of this inhuman bomb."

Already, Japanese physicists had entered the city with Lauritsen electroscopes and Neher electrometers; they understood the idea all too well.

On August 12th, the Nakamuras, all of them still rather sick, went to the nearby town of Kabe and moved in with Mrs. Nakamura's sister-in-law. The next day, Mrs. Nakamura, although she was too ill to walk much, returned to Hiroshima alone, by electric car to the outskirts, by foot from there. All week, at the Novitiate, she had worried about her mother, brother, and older sister, who had lived in the part of town called Fukuro, and besides, she felt drawn by some fascination, just as Father Kleinsorge had been. She discovered that her family were all dead. She went back to Kabe so amazed and depressed by what she had seen and learned in the city that she could not speak that evening.

A comparative orderliness, at least, began to be established at the Red Cross Hospital. Dr. Sasaki, back from his rest, undertook to classify his patients (who were still scattered everywhere, even on the stairways). The staff gradually swept up the debris. Best of all, the nurses and attendants started to remove the corpses. Disposal of the dead, by decent cremation and enshrinement, is a greater moral responsibility to the Japanese than adequate care of the living. Relatives identified most of the first day's dead in and around the hospital. Beginning on the second day, whenever a patient appeared to be moribund, a piece of paper with his name on it was fastened to his clothing. The corpse detail carried the bodies to a clearing outside, placed them on pyres of wood from ruined houses, burned them, put some of the ashes in envelopes intended for exposed X-ray plates, marked the envelopes with the names of the deceased, and piled them, neatly and respectfully, in stacks in the main office. In a few days, the envelopes filled one whole side of the impromptu shrine.

In Kabe, on the morning of August 15th, ten-year-old Toshio Nakamura heard an airplane overhead. He ran outdoors and identified it with a professional eye as a B-29. "There goes Mr. B!" he shouted.

One of his relatives called out to him, "Haven't you had enough of Mr. B?"

The question had a kind of symbolism. At almost that very moment, the dull, dispirited voice of Hirohito, the Emperor Tenno, was speaking for the first time in history over the radio: "After pondering deeply the general trends of the world and the actual conditions obtaining in Our Empire today, We have decided to effect a settlement of the present situation by resorting to an extraordinary measure. . . ."

Mrs. Nakamura had gone to the city again, to dig up some rice she had buried in her Neighborhood Association air-raid shelter. She got it and started back for Kabe. On the electric car, quite by chance, she ran into her younger sister, who had not been in Hiroshima the day of the bombing. "Have you heard the news?" her sister asked.

"What news?"

"The war is over."

"Don't say such a foolish thing, sister."

"But I heard it over the radio myself." And then, in a whisper, "It was the Emperor's voice."

"Oh," Mrs. Nakamura said (she needed nothing more to make her give up thinking, in spite of the atomic bomb, that Japan still had a chance to win the war), "in that case . . ."

Some time later, in a letter to an American, Mr. Tanimoto described the events of that morning. "At the time of the Post-War, the marvelous thing in our history happened. Our Emperor broadcasted his own voice through radio directly to us, common people of Japan. Aug. 15th we were told that some news of great importance could be heard & all of us should hear it. So I went to Hiroshima railway station. There set a loud-speaker in the ruins of the station. Many civilians, all of them were in boundage, some being helped by shoulder of their daughters, some sustaining their injured feet by sticks, they listened to the broadcast and when they came to realize the fact that it was the Emperor, they cried with full tears in their eyes, 'What a wonderful blessing it is that Tenno himself call on us and we can hear his own voice in person. We are thoroughly satisfied in such a great sacrifice.' When they came to know the war was ended—that is, Japan was defeated, they, of course, were deeply disappointed, but followed after their Emperor's commandment in calm spirit, making whole-hearted sacrifice for the everlasting peace of the world—and Japan started her new way."

## IV. PANIC GRASS AND FEVERFEW

On August 18th, twelve days after the bomb burst, Father Kleinsorge set out on foot for Hiroshima from the Novitiate with his papier-mâché suitcase in his hand. He had begun to think that this bag, in which he kept his valuables, had a tal-ismanic quality, because of the way he had found it after the explosion, standing handle-side up in the doorway of his room, while the desk under which he had previously hidden it was in splinters all over the floor. Now he was using it to carry the yen belonging to the Society of Jesus to the Hiroshima branch of the Yokohama Specie Bank, already reopened in its half-ruined building. On the whole, he felt quite well that morning. It is true that the minor cuts he had received had not healed in three or four days, as the rector of the Novi-tiate, who had examined them, had positively promised they would, but Father Kleinsorge had rested well for a week and considered that he was again ready for hard work. By now he was accustomed to the terrible scene through which he walked on his way into the city: the large rice field near the Novitiate, streaked with brown; the houses on the outskirts of the city, standing but decrepit, with broken windows and di-shevelled tiles; and then, quite suddenly, the beginning of the four square miles of reddish-brown scar, where nearly every-thing had been buffeted down and burned; range on range of collapsed city blocks, with here and there a crude sign erected on a pile of ashes and tiles ("Sister, where are you?" or "All safe and we live at Toyosaka"); naked trees and canted tele-phone poles; the few standing, gutted buildings only accentu-ating the horizontality of everything else (the Museum of Science and Industry, with its dome stripped to its steel frame, as if for an autopsy; the modern Chamber of Com-merce Building, its tower as cold, rigid, and unassailable after the blow as before; the huge, low-lying, camouflaged city hall; the row of dowdy banks, caricaturing a shaken economic system); and in the streets a macabre traffic—hundreds of crumpled bicycles, shells of streetcars and automobiles, all halted in mid-motion. The whole way, Father Kleinsorge was oppressed by the thought that all the damage he saw had been done in one instant by one bomb. By the time he reached the center of town, the day had become very hot. He walked to the Yokohama Bank, which was doing business in a temporary wooden stall on the ground floor of its building, deposited the money, went by the mission compound just to have another look at the wreckage, and then started back to the Novitiate. About halfway there, he began to have peculiar sensations. The more or less magical suitcase, now empty, suddenly seemed terribly heavy. His knees grew weak. He felt excruciatingly tired. With a considerable expenditure of spirit, he managed to reach the Novitiate. He did not think his weakness was worth mentioning to the other Jesuits. But a couple of days later, while attempting to say Mass, he had an onset of faintness and even after three attempts was unable to go through with the service, and the next morning the rector, who had examined Father Kleinsorge's apparently negligible but unhealed cuts daily, asked in surprise, "What have you done to your wounds?" They had suddenly opened wider and were swollen and inflamed.

As she dressed on the morning of August 20th, in the home of her sister-in-law in Kabe, not far from Nagatsuka, Mrs. Nakamura, who had suffered no cuts or burns at all, though she had been rather nauseated all through the week she and her children had spent as guests of Father Kleinsorge and the other Catholics at the Novitiate, began fixing her hair and noticed, after one stroke, that her comb carried with it a whole handful of hair; the second time, the same thing happened, so she stopped combing at once. But in the next three or four days, her hair kept falling out of its own accord, until she was quite bald. She began living indoors, practically in hiding. On August 26th, both she and her younger daughter, Myeko, woke up feeling extremely weak and tired, and they stayed on their bedrolls. Her son and other daughter, who had shared every experience with her during and after the bombing, felt fine.

At about the same time—he lost track of the days, so hard

was he working to set up a temporary place of worship in a private house he had rented in the outskirts—Mr. Tanimoto fell suddenly ill with a general malaise, weariness, and feverishness, and he, too, took to his bedroll on the floor of the half-wrecked house of a friend in the suburb of Ushida.

These four did not realize it, but they were coming down with the strange, capricious disease which came later to be known as radiation sickness.

Miss Sasaki lay in steady pain in the Goddess of Mercy Primary School, at Hatsukaichi, the fourth station to the southwest of Hiroshima on the electric train. An internal infection still prevented the proper setting of the compound fracture of her lower left leg. A young man who was in the same hospital and who seemed to have grown fond of her in spite of her unremitting preoccupation with her suffering, or else just pitied her because of it, lent her a Japanese translation of de Maupassant, and she tried to read the stories, but she could concentrate for only four or five minutes at a time.

The hospitals and aid stations around Hiroshima were so crowded in the first weeks after the bombing, and their staffs were so variable, depending on their health and on the unpredictable arrival of outside help, that patients had to be constantly shifted from place to place. Miss Sasaki, who had already been moved three times, twice by ship, was taken at the end of August to an engineering school, also at Hatsukaichi. Because her leg did not improve but swelled more and more, the doctors at the school bound it with crude splints and took her by car, on September 9th, to the Red Cross Hospital in Hiroshima. This was the first chance she had had to look at the ruins of Hiroshima; the last time she had been carried through the city's streets, she had been hovering on the edge of unconsciousness. Even though the wreckage had been described to her, and though she was still in pain, the sight horrified and amazed her, and there was something she noticed about it that particularly gave her the creeps. Over everything—up through the wreckage of the city, in gutters, along the riverbanks, tangled among tiles and tin roofing, climbing on charred tree trunks—was a blanket of fresh, vivid, lush, optimistic green; the verdancy rose even from the foundations of ruined houses. Weeds already hid the ashes, and wild flowers were in bloom among the city's bones. The bomb had not only left the underground organs of plants intact; it had stimulated them. Everywhere were bluets and Spanish bayonets, goosefoot, morning glories and day lilies, the hairy-fruited bean, purslane and clotbur and sesame and panic grass and feverfew. Especially in a circle at the center, sickle senna grew in extraordinary regeneration, not only standing among the charred remnants of the same plant but pushing up in new places, among bricks and through cracks in the asphalt. It actually seemed as if a load of sickle-senna seed had been dropped along with the bomb.

At the Red Cross Hospital, Miss Sasaki was put under the care of Dr. Sasaki. Now, a month after the explosion, something like order had been reëstablished in the hospital; which is to say that the patients who still lay in the corridors at least had mats to sleep on and that the supply of medicines, which had given out in the first few days, had been replaced, though inadequately, by contributions from other cities. Dr. Sasaki, who had had one seventeen-hour sleep at his home on the third night, had ever since then rested only about six hours a night, on a mat at the hospital; he had lost twenty pounds from his very small body; he still wore the ill-fitting glasses he had borrowed from an injured nurse.

Since Miss Sasaki was a woman and was so sick (and perhaps, he afterward admitted, just a little bit because she was named Sasaki), Dr. Sasaki put her on a mat in a semi-private room, which at that time had only eight people in it. He questioned her and put down on her record card, in the correct, scrunched-up German in which he wrote all his records: *"Mittelgrosse Patientin in gutem Ernährungszustand. Fraktur am linken Unterschenkelknochen mit Wunde; Anschwellung in der linken Unterschenkelgegend. Haut und sichtbare Schleimhäute mässig durchblutet und kein Oedema,"* noting that she was a medium-sized female patient in good general health; that she had a compound fracture of the left tibia, with swelling of the left lower leg; that her skin and visible mucous membranes were heavily spotted with *petechiae*, which are hemorrhages about the size of grains of rice, or even as big as soybeans; and, in addition, that her head, eyes, throat, lungs, and heart were apparently normal; and that she had a fever. He wanted to set her fracture and put her leg in a cast, but he had run out of plaster of Paris long since, so he just stretched her out on a mat and prescribed aspirin for her fever, and glucose intravenously and diastase orally for her undernourishment (which he had not entered on her record because everyone suffered from it). She exhibited only one of the queer symptoms so many of his patients were just then beginning to show—the spot hemorrhages.

Dr. Fujii was still pursued by bad luck, which still was connected with rivers. Now he was living in the summer house of Mr. Okuma, in Fukawa. This house clung to the steep banks of the Ota River. Here his injuries seemed to make good progress, and he even began to treat refugees who came to him from the neighborhood, using medical supplies he had retrieved from a cache in the suburbs. He noticed in some of his patients a curious syndrome of symptoms that cropped out in the third and fourth weeks, but he was not able to do much more than swathe cuts and burns. Early in September, it began to rain, steadily and heavily. The river rose. On September 17th, there came a cloudburst and then a typhoon, and the water crept higher and higher up the bank. Mr. Okuma and Dr. Fujii became alarmed and scrambled up the mountain to a peasant's house. (Down in Hiroshima, the flood took up where the bomb had left off—swept away bridges that had survived the blast, washed out streets, undermined foundations of buildings that still stood—and ten miles to the west, the Ono Army Hospital, where a team of experts from Kyoto Imperial University was studying the delayed affliction of the patients, suddenly slid down a beautiful, pine-dark mountainside into the Inland Sea and drowned most of the investigators and their mysteriously diseased patients alike.) After the storm, Dr. Fujii and Mr. Okuma went down to the river and found that the Okuma house had been washed altogether away.

Because so many people were suddenly feeling sick nearly a month after the atomic bomb was dropped, an unpleasant rumor began to move around, and eventually it made its way to the house in Kabe where Mrs. Nakamura lay bald and ill. It was that the atomic bomb had deposited some sort of poison on Hiroshima which would give off deadly emanations for seven years; nobody could go there all that time. This especially upset Mrs. Nakamura, who remembered that in a moment of confusion on the morning of the explosion she had literally sunk her entire means of livelihood, her Sankoku sewing machine, in the small cement water tank in front of what was left of her house; now no one would be able to go and fish it out. Up to this time, Mrs. Nakamura and her relatives had been quite resigned and passive about the moral issue of the atomic bomb, but this rumor suddenly aroused them to more hatred and resentment of America than they had felt all through the war.

Japanese physicists, who knew a great deal about atomic fission (one of them owned a cyclotron), worried about lingering radiation at Hiroshima, and in mid-August, not many days after President Truman's disclosure of the type of bomb that had been dropped, they entered the city to make investigations. The first thing they did was roughly to determine a center by observing the side on which telephone poles all around the heart of the town were scorched; they settled on the torii gateway of the Gokoku Shrine, right next to the parade ground of the Chugoku Regional Army Headquarters. From there, they worked north and south with Lauritsen electroscopes, which are sensitive to both beta rays and gamma rays. These indicated that the highest intensity of radioactivity, near the torii, was 4.2 times the average natural "leak" of ultra-short waves for the earth of that area. The scientists noticed that the flash of the bomb had discolored concrete to a light reddish tint, had scaled off the surface of granite, and had scorched certain other types of building material, and that consequently the bomb had, in some places, left prints of the shadows that had been cast by its light. The experts found, for instance, a permanent shadow thrown on the roof of the Chamber of Commerce Building (220 yards from the rough center) by the structure's rectangular tower; several others in the lookout post on top of the Hypothec Bank (2,050 yards); another in the tower of the Chugoku Electric Supply Building (800 yards); another projected by the handle of a gas pump (2,630 yards); and several on granite tombstones in the Gokoku Shrine (385 yards). By triangulating these and other such shadows with the objects that formed them, the scientists determined that the exact center was a spot a hundred and fifty yards south of the torii and a few yards southeast of the pile of ruins that had once been the Shima Hospital. (A few vague human silhouettes were found, and these gave rise to stories that eventually included fancy and precise details. One story told how a painter on a ladder was monumentalized in a kind of bas-relief on the stone façade of a bank building on which he was at work, in the act of dipping his brush into his paint can; another, how a man and his cart on the bridge near the Museum of Science and Industry, almost under the center of the explosion, were cast down in an embossed shadow which made it clear that the man was about to whip his horse.) Starting east and west from the actual center, the scientists, in early September, made new measurements, and the highest radiation they found this time was 3.9 times the natural "leak." Since radiation of at least a thousand times the natural "leak" would be required to cause serious effects on the human body, the scientists announced that people could enter Hiroshima without any peril at all.

As soon as this reassurance reached the household in which Mrs. Nakamura was concealing herself—or, at any rate, within a short time after her hair had started growing back again—her whole family relaxed their extreme hatred of America, and Mrs. Nakamura sent her brother-in-law to look for the sewing machine. It was still submerged in the water tank, and when he brought it home, she saw, to her dismay, that it was all rusted and useless.

By the end of the first week in September, Father Kleinsorge was in bed at the Novitiate with a fever of 102.2, and since he seemed to be getting worse, his colleagues decided to send him to the Catholic International Hospital in Tokyo. Father Cieslik and the rector took him as far as Kobe and a Jesuit from that city took him the rest of the way, with a message from a Kobe doctor to the Mother Superior of the International Hospital: "Think twice before you give this man blood transfusions, because with atomic-bomb patients we aren't at all sure that if you stick needles in them, they'll stop bleeding."

When Father Kleinsorge arrived at the hospital, he was terribly pale and very shaky. He complained that the bomb had upset his digestion and given him abdominal pains. His white blood count was three thousand (five to seven thousand is normal), he was seriously anemic, and his temperature was 104. A doctor who did not know much about these strange manifestations—Father Kleinsorge was one of a handful of atomic patients who had reached Tokyo—came to see him, and to the patient's face he was most encouraging. "You'll be out of here in two weeks," he said. But when the doctor got out in the corridor, he said to the Mother Superior, "He'll die. All these bomb people die—you'll see. They go along for a couple of weeks and then they die."

The doctor prescribed suralimentation for Father Kleinsorge. Every three hours, they forced some eggs or beef juice into him, and they fed him all the sugar he could stand. They gave him vitamins, and iron pills and arsenic (in Fowler's solution) for his anemia. He confounded both the doctor's predictions; he neither died nor got up in a fortnight. Despite the fact that the message from the Kobe doctor deprived him of transfusions, which would have been the most useful therapy of all, his fever and his digestive troubles cleared up fairly quickly. His white count went up for a while, but early in October it dropped again, to 3,600; then, in ten days, it suddenly climbed above normal, to 8,800; and it finally settled at 5,800. His ridiculous scratches puzzled everyone. For a few days, they would mend, and then, when he moved around, they would open up again. As soon as he began to feel well, he enjoyed himself tremendously. In Hiroshima he had been one of thousands of sufferers; in Tokyo he was a curiosity. American Army doctors came by the dozen to observe him. Japanese experts questioned him. A newspaper interviewed him. And once, the confused doctor came and shook his head and said, "Baffling cases, these atomic-bomb people."

Mrs. Nakamura lay indoors with Myeko. They both continued sick, and though Mrs. Nakamura vaguely sensed that their trouble was caused by the bomb, she was too poor to see a doctor and so never knew exactly what the matter was. Without any treatment at all, but merely resting, they began gradually to feel better. Some of Myeko's hair fell out, and she had a tiny burn on her arm which took months to heal. The boy, Toshio, and the older girl, Yaeko, seemed well enough, though they, too, lost some hair and occasionally had bad headaches. Toshio was still having nightmares, always about the nineteen-year-old mechanic, Hideo Osaki, his hero, who had been killed by the bomb.

On his back with a fever of 104, Mr. Tanimoto worried about all the funerals he ought to be conducting for the deceased of his church. He thought he was just overtired from the hard work he had done since the bombing, but after the fever had persisted for a few days, he sent for a doctor. The doctor was too busy to visit him in Ushida, but he dispatched a nurse, who recognized his symptoms as those of mild radiation disease and came back from time to time to give him injections of Vitamin $B_1$. A Buddhist priest with whom Mr. Tanimoto was acquainted called on him and suggested that moxibustion might give him relief; the priest showed the pastor how to give himself the ancient Japanese treatment, by setting fire to a twist of the stimulant herb moxa placed on the wrist pulse. Mr. Tanimoto found that each moxa treatment temporarily reduced his fever one degree. The nurse had told him to eat as much as possible, and every few days his mother-in-law brought him vegetables and fish from Tsuzu, twenty miles away, where she lived. He spent a month in bed, and then went ten hours by train to his father's home in Shikoku. There he rested another month.

Dr. Sasaki and his colleagues at the Red Cross Hospital watched the unprecedented disease unfold and at last evolved a theory about its nature. It had, they decided, three stages. The first stage had been all over before the doctors even knew they were dealing with a new sickness; it was the direct reaction to the bombardment of the body, at the moment when the bomb went off, by neutrons, beta particles, and gamma rays. The apparently uninjured people who had died so mysteriously in the first few hours or days had succumbed in this first stage. It killed ninety-five per cent of the people within a half mile of the center, and many thousands who were farther away. The doctors realized in retrospect that even though most of these dead had also suffered from burns and blast effects, they had absorbed enough radiation to kill them. The rays simply destroyed body cells—caused their nuclei to degenerate and broke their walls. Many people who did not die right away came down with nausea, headache, diarrhea, malaise, and fever, which lasted several days. Doctors could not be certain whether some of these symptoms were the result of radiation or nervous shock. The second stage set in ten or fifteen days after the bombing. The main symptom was falling hair. Diarrhea and fever, which in some cases went as high as 106, came next. Twenty-five to thirty days after the explosion, blood disorders appeared: gums bled, the white-blood-cell count dropped sharply, and *petechiae* appeared on the skin and mucous membranes. The drop in the number of white blood corpuscles reduced the patient's capacity to resist infection, so open wounds were unusually slow in healing and many of the sick developed sore throats and mouths. The two key symptoms, on which the doctors came to base their prognosis, were fever and the lowered white-corpuscle count. If fever remained steady and high, the patient's chances for survival were poor. The white count almost always dropped below four thousand; a patient whose count fell below one thousand had little hope of living. Toward the end of the second stage, if the patient survived, anemia, or a drop in the red blood count, also set in. The third stage was the reaction that came when the body struggled to compensate for its ills— when, for instance, the white count not only returned to normal but increased to much higher than normal levels. In this stage, many patients died of complications, such as infections in the chest cavity. Most burns healed with deep layers of pink, rubbery scar tissue, known as keloid tumors. The duration of the disease varied, depending on the patient's constitution and the amount of radiation he had received. Some victims recovered in a week; with others the disease dragged on for months.

As the symptoms revealed themselves, it became clear that

many of them resembled the effects of overdoses of X-ray, and the doctors based their therapy on that likeness. They gave victims liver extract, blood transfusions, and vitamins, especially $B_1$. The shortage of supplies and instruments hampered them. Allied doctors who came in after the surrender found plasma and penicillin very effective. Since the blood disorders were, in the long run, the predominant factor in the disease, some of the Japanese doctors evolved a theory as to the seat of the delayed sickness. They thought that perhaps gamma rays, entering the body at the time of the explosion, made the phosphorus in the victims' bones radioactive, and that they in turn emitted beta particles, which, though they could not penetrate far through flesh, could enter the bone marrow, where blood is manufactured, and gradually tear it down. Whatever its source, the disease had some baffling quirks. Not all the patients exhibited all the main symptoms. People who suffered flash burns were protected, to a considerable extent, from radiation sickness. Those who had lain quietly for days or even hours after the bombing were much less liable to get sick than those who had been active. Gray hair seldom fell out. And, as if nature were protecting man against his own ingenuity, the reproductive processes were affected for a time; men became sterile, women had miscarriages, menstruation stopped.

For ten days after the flood, Dr. Fujii lived in the peasant's house on the mountain above the Ota. Then he heard about a vacant private clinic in Kaitaichi, a suburb to the east of Hiroshima. He bought it at once, moved there, and hung out a sign inscribed in English, in honor of the conquerors:

M. FUJII, M.D.
MEDICAL & VENEREAL

Quite recovered from his wounds, he soon built up a strong practice, and he was delighted, in the evenings, to receive members of the occupying forces, on whom he lavished whiskey and practiced English.

Giving Miss Sasaki a local anaesthetic of procaine, Dr. Sasaki made an incision in her leg on October 23rd, to drain the infection, which still lingered on eleven weeks after the injury. In the following days, so much pus formed that he had to dress the opening each morning and evening. A week later, she complained of great pain, so he made another incision; he cut still a third, on November 9th, and enlarged it on the twenty-sixth. All this time, Miss Sasaki grew weaker and weaker, and her spirits fell low. One day, the young man who had lent her his translation of de Maupassant at Hatsukaichi came to visit her; he told her that he was going to Kyushu but that when he came back, he would like to see her again. She didn't care. Her leg had been so swollen and painful all along that the doctor had not even tried to set the fractures, and though an X-ray taken in November showed that the bones were mending, she could see under the sheet that her left leg was nearly three inches shorter than her right and that her left foot was turning inward. She thought often of the man to whom she had been engaged. Someone told her he was back from overseas. She wondered what he had heard about her injuries that made him stay away.

Father Kleinsorge was discharged from the hospital in Tokyo on December 19th and took a train home. On the way, two days later, at Yokogawa, a stop just before Hiroshima, Dr. Fujii boarded the train. It was the first time the two men had met since before the bombing. They sat together. Dr. Fujii said he was going to the annual gathering of his family, on the anniversary of his father's death. When they started talking about their experiences, the Doctor was quite entertaining as he told how his places of residence kept falling into rivers. Then he asked Father Kleinsorge how he was, and the Jesuit talked about his stay in the hospital. "The doctors told me to be cautious," he said. "They ordered me to have a two-hour nap every afternoon."

Dr. Fujii said, "It's hard to be cautious in Hiroshima these days. Everyone seems to be so busy."

A new municipal government, set up under Allied Military Government direction, had gone to work at last in the city hall. Citizens who had recovered from various degrees of radiation sickness were coming back by the thousand—by

November 1st, the population, mostly crowded into the outskirts, was already 137,000, more than a third of the wartime
peak—and the government set in motion all kinds of projects
to put them to work rebuilding the city. It hired men to clear
the streets, and others to gather scrap iron, which they sorted
and piled in mountains opposite the city hall. Some returning
residents were putting up their own shanties and huts, and
planting small squares of winter wheat beside them, but the
city also authorized and built four hundred one-family "barracks." Utilities were repaired—electric lights shone again,
trams started running, and employees of the waterworks fixed
seventy thousand leaks in mains and plumbing. A Planning
Conference, with an enthusiastic young Military Government
officer, Lieutenant John D. Montgomery, of Kalamazoo, as
its adviser, began to consider what sort of city the new Hiroshima should be. The ruined city had flourished—and had
been an inviting target—mainly because it had been one of
the most important military-command and communications
centers in Japan, and would have become the Imperial headquarters had the islands been invaded and Tokyo been captured. Now there would be no huge military establishments
to help revive the city. The Planning Conference, at a loss as
to just what importance Hiroshima could have, fell back on
rather vague cultural and paving projects. It drew maps with
avenues a hundred yards wide and thought seriously of pre-
serving the half-ruined Museum of Science and Industry more
or less as it was, as a monument to the disaster, and naming it
the Institute of International Amity. Statistical workers gathered what figures they could on the effects of the bomb. They
reported that 78,150 people had been killed, 13,983 were missing, and 37,425 had been injured. No one in the city government pretended that these figures were accurate—though the
Americans accepted them as official—and as the months went
by and more and more hundreds of corpses were dug up from
the ruins, and as the number of unclaimed urns of ashes at the
Zempoji Temple in Koi rose into the thousands, the statisticians began to say that at least a hundred thousand people
had lost their lives in the bombing. Since many people died of
a combination of causes, it was impossible to figure exactly
how many were killed by each cause, but the statisticians cal-

culated that about twenty-five per cent had died of direct burns from the bomb, about fifty per cent from other injuries, and about twenty per cent as a result of radiation effects. The statisticians' figures on property damage were more reliable: sixty-two thousand out of ninety thousand buildings destroyed, and six thousand more damaged beyond repair. In the heart of the city, they found only five modern buildings that could be used again without major repairs. This small number was by no means the fault of flimsy Japanese construction. In fact, since the 1923 earthquake, Japanese building regulations had required that the roof of each large building be able to bear a minimum load of seventy pounds per square foot, whereas American regulations do not normally specify more than forty pounds per square foot.

Scientists swarmed into the city. Some of them measured the force that had been necessary to shift marble gravestones in the cemeteries, to knock over twenty-two of the forty-seven railroad cars in the yards at Hiroshima station, to lift and move the concrete roadway on one of the bridges, and to perform other noteworthy acts of strength, and concluded that the pressure exerted by the explosion varied from 5.3 to 8.0 tons per square yard. Others found that mica, of which the melting point is 900° C., had fused on granite gravestones three hundred and eighty yards from the center; that telephone poles of *Cryptomeria japonica*, whose carbonization temperature is 240° C., had been charred at forty-four hundred yards from the center; and that the surface of gray clay tiles of the type used in Hiroshima, whose melting point is 1,300° C., had dissolved at six hundred yards; and, after examining other significant ashes and melted bits, they concluded that the bomb's heat on the ground at the center must have been 6,000° C. And from further measurements of radiation, which involved, among other things, the scraping up of fission fragments from roof troughs and drainpipes as far away as the suburb of Takasu, thirty-three hundred yards from the center, they learned some far more important facts about the nature of the bomb. General MacArthur's headquarters systematically censored all mention of the bomb in Japanese scientific publications, but soon the fruit of the scientists' calculations became common knowledge among Japanese physicists, doctors, chemists, journalists, professors, and, no doubt, those statesmen and military men who were still in circulation. Long before the American public had been told, most of the scientists and lots of non-scientists in Japan knew—from the calculations of Japanese nuclear physicists— that a uranium bomb had exploded at Hiroshima and a more powerful one, of plutonium, at Nagasaki. They also knew that theoretically one ten times as powerful—or twenty—could be developed. The Japanese scientists thought they knew the exact height at which the bomb at Hiroshima was exploded and the approximate weight of the uranium used. They estimated that, even with the primitive bomb used at Hiroshima, it would require a shelter of concrete fifty inches thick to protect a human being entirely from radiation sickness. The scientists had these and other details which remained subject to security in the United States printed and mimeographed and bound into little books. The Americans knew of the existence of these, but tracing them and seeing that they did not fall into the wrong hands would have obliged the occupying authorities to set up, for this one purpose alone, an enormous police system in Japan. Altogether, the Japanese scientists were somewhat amused at the efforts of their conquerors to keep security on atomic fission.

Late in February, 1946, a friend of Miss Sasaki's called on Father Kleinsorge and asked him to visit her in the hospital. She had been growing more and more depressed and morbid; she seemed little interested in living. Father Kleinsorge went to see her several times. On his first visit, he kept the conversation general, formal, and yet vaguely sympathetic, and did not mention religion. Miss Sasaki herself brought it up the second time he dropped in on her. Evidently she had had some talks with a Catholic. She asked bluntly, "If your God is so good and kind, how can he let people suffer like this?" She made a gesture which took in her shrunken leg, the other patients in her room, and Hiroshima as a whole.

"My child," Father Kleinsorge said, "man is not now in the condition God intended. He has fallen from grace through sin." And he went on to explain all the reasons for everything.

*      *      *

It came to Mrs. Nakamura's attention that a carpenter
from Kabe was building a number of wooden shanties in Hiroshima which he rented for fifty yen a month—$3.33, at the
fixed rate of exchange. Mrs. Nakamura had lost the certifi-
cates for her bonds and other wartime savings, but fortunately
she had copied off all the numbers just a few days before the
bombing and had taken the list to Kabe, and so, when her
hair had grown in enough for her to be presentable, she went
to her bank in Hiroshima, and a clerk there told her that after
checking her numbers against the records the bank would
give her her money. As soon as she got it, she rented one of
the carpenter's shacks. It was in Nobori-cho, near the site of
her former house, and though its floor was dirt and it was
dark inside, it was at least a home in Hiroshima, and she was
no longer dependent on the charity of her in-laws. During the
spring, she cleared away some nearby wreckage and planted a
vegetable garden. She cooked with utensils and ate off plates
she scavenged from the debris. She sent Myeko to the kindergarten which the Jesuits reopened, and the two older children
attended Nobori-cho Primary School, which, for want of
buildings, held classes out of doors. Toshio wanted to study
to be a mechanic, like his hero, Hideo Osaki. Prices were
high; by midsummer Mrs. Nakamura's savings were gone.
She sold some of her clothes to get food. She had once had
several expensive kimonos, but during the war one had been
stolen, she had given one to a sister who had been bombed
out in Tokuyama, she had lost a couple in the Hiroshima
bombing, and now she sold her last one. It brought only a
hundred yen, which did not last long. In June, she went to
Father Kleinsorge for advice about how to get along, and in
early August, she was still considering the two alternatives he
suggested—taking work as a domestic for some of the Allied
occupation forces, or borrowing from her relatives enough
money, about five hundred yen, or a bit more than thirty
dollars, to repair her rusty sewing machine and resume the
work of a seamstress.

When Mr. Tanimoto returned from Shikoku, he draped a tent
he owned over the roof of the badly damaged house he had
rented in Ushida. The roof still leaked, but he conducted ser-

vices in the damp living room. He began thinking about raising money to restore his church in the city. He became quite
friendly with Father Kleinsorge and saw the Jesuits often. He
envied them their Church's wealth; they seemed to be able to
do anything they wanted. He had nothing to work with except his own energy, and that was not what it had been.

The Society of Jesus had been the first institution to build a
relatively permanent shanty in the ruins of Hiroshima. That
had been while Father Kleinsorge was in the hospital. As soon
as he got back, he began living in the shack, and he and another priest, Father Laderman, who had joined him in the
mission, arranged for the purchase of three of the standard-
ized "barracks," which the city was selling at seven thousand
yen apiece. They put two together, end to end, and made a
pretty chapel of them; they ate in the third. When materials
were available, they commissioned a contractor to build a
three-story mission house exactly like the one that had been
destroyed in the fire. In the compound, carpenters cut timbers, gouged mortises, shaped tenons, whittled scores of
wooden pegs and bored holes for them, until all the parts for
the house were in a neat pile; then, in three days, they put the
whole thing together, like an Oriental puzzle, without any
nails at all. Father Kleinsorge was finding it hard, as Dr. Fujii
had suggested he would, to be cautious and to take his naps.
He went out every day on foot to call on Japanese Catholics
and prospective converts. As the months went by, he grew
more and more tired. In June, he read an article in the Hiroshima *Chugoku* warning survivors against working too hard—
but what could he do? By July, he was worn out, and early in
August, almost exactly on the anniversary of the bombing, he
went back to the Catholic International Hospital, in Tokyo,
for a month's rest.

Whether or not Father Kleinsorge's answers to Miss Sasaki's
questions about life were final and absolute truths, she
seemed quickly to draw physical strength from them. Dr.
Sasaki noticed it and congratulated Father Kleinsorge. By
April 15th, her temperature and white count were normal and
the infection in the wound was beginning to clear up. On

the twentieth, there was almost no pus, and for the first time she jerked along a corridor on crutches. Five days later, the wound had begun to heal, and on the last day of the month she was discharged.

During the early summer, she prepared herself for conversion to Catholicism. In that period she had ups and downs. Her depressions were deep. She knew she would always be a cripple. Her fiancé never came to see her. There was nothing for her to do except read and look out, from her house on a hillside in Koi, across the ruins of the city where her parents and brother died. She was nervous, and any sudden noise made her put her hands quickly to her throat. Her leg still hurt; she rubbed it often and patted it, as if to console it.

It took six months for the Red Cross Hospital, and even longer for Dr. Sasaki, to get back to normal. Until the city restored electric power, the hospital had to limp along with the aid of a Japanese Army generator in its back yard. Operating tables, X-ray machines, dentist chairs, everything complicated and essential came in a trickle of charity from other cities. In Japan, face is important even to institutions, and long before the Red Cross Hospital was back to par on basic medical equipment, its directors put up a new yellow brick veneer façade, so the hospital became the handsomest building in Hiroshima—from the street. For the first four months, Dr. Sasaki was the only surgeon on the staff and he almost never left the building; then, gradually, he began to take an interest in his own life again. He got married in March. He gained back some of the weight he lost, but his appetite remained only fair; before the bombing, he used to eat four rice balls at every meal, but a year after it he could manage only two. He felt tired all the time. "But I have to realize," he said, "that the whole community is tired."

A year after the bomb was dropped, Miss Sasaki was a cripple; Mrs. Nakamura was destitute; Father Kleinsorge was back in the hospital; Dr. Sasaki was not capable of the work he once could do; Dr. Fujii had lost the thirty-room hospital it took him many years to acquire, and had no prospects of rebuilding it; Mr. Tanimoto's church had been ruined and he no longer had his exceptional vitality. The lives of these six people, who were among the luckiest in Hiroshima, would never be the same. What they thought of their experiences and of the use of the atomic bomb was, of course, not unanimous. One feeling they did seem to share, however, was a curious kind of elated community spirit, something like that of the Londoners after their blitz—a pride in the way they and their fellow-survivors had stood up to a dreadful ordeal. Just before the anniversary, Mr. Tanimoto wrote in a letter to an American some words which expressed this feeling: "What a heartbreaking scene this was the first night! About midnight I landed on the riverbank. So many injured people lied on the ground that I made my way by striding over them. Repeating 'Excuse me,' I forwarded and carried a tub of water with me and gave a cup of water to each one of them. They raised their upper bodies slowly and accepted a cup of water with a bow and drunk quietly and, spilling any remnant, gave back a cup with hearty expression of their thankfulness, and said, 'I couldn't help my sister, who was buried under the house, because I had to take care of my mother who got a deep wound on her eye and our house soon set fire and we hardly escaped. Look, I lost my home, my family, and at last my-self bitterly injured. But now I have gotted my mind to dedicate what I have and to complete the war for our country's sake.' Thus they pledged to me, even women and children did the same. Being entirely tired I lied down on the ground among them, but couldn't sleep at all. Next morning I found many men and women dead, whom I gave water last night. But, to my great surprise, I never heard any one cried in disorder, even though they suffered in great agony. They died in silence, with no grudge, setting their teeth to bear it. All for the country!

"Dr. Y. Hiraiwa, professor of Hiroshima University of Literature and Science, and one of my church members, was buried by the bomb under the two storied house with his son, a student of Tokyo University. Both of them could not move an inch under tremendously heavy pressure. And the house already caught fire. His son said, 'Father, we can do nothing except make our mind up to consecrate our lives for the country. Let us give *Banzai* to our Emperor.' Then the father followed after his son, '*Tenno-heika, Banzai, Banzai, Banzai!*' In the result, Dr. Hiraiwa said, 'Strange to say, I felt calm and bright and peaceful spirit in my heart, when I chanted *Banzai* to Tenno.' Afterward his son got out and digged down and pulled out his father and thus they were saved. In thinking of their experience of that time Dr. Hiraiwa repeated, 'What a fortunate that we are Japanese! It was my first time I ever tasted such a beautiful spirit when I decided to die for our Emperor.'

"Miss Kayoko Nobutoki, a student of girl's high school, Hiroshima Jazabuin, and a daughter of my church member, was taking rest with her friends beside the heavy fence of the Buddhist Temple. At the moment the atomic bomb was dropped, the fence fell upon them. They could not move a bit under such a heavy fence and then smoke entered into even a crack and choked their breath. One of the girls begun to sing *Kimi ga yo*, national anthem, and others followed in chorus and died. Meanwhile one of them found a crack and struggled hard to get out. When she was taken in the Red Cross Hospital she told how her friends died, tracing back in her memory to singing in chorus our national anthem. They were just 13 years old.

"Yes, people of Hiroshima died manly in the atomic bombing, believing that it was for Emperor's sake."

A surprising number of the people of Hiroshima remained more or less indifferent about the ethics of using the bomb. Possibly they were too terrified by it to want to think about it at all. Not many of them even bothered to find out much about what it was like. Mrs. Nakamura's conception of it—and awe of it—was typical. "The atom bomb," she would say when asked about it, "is the size of a matchbox. The heat of it is six thousand times that of the sun. It exploded in the air. There is some radium in it. I don't know just how it works, but when the radium is put together, it explodes." As for the use of the bomb, she would say, "It was war and we had to expect it." And then she would add, *"Shikata ga nai,"* a Japanese expression as common as, and corresponding to, the Russian word *"nichevo"*: "It can't be helped. Oh, well. Too bad." Dr. Fujii said approximately the same thing about the use of the bomb to Father Kleinsorge one evening, in German: "*Da ist nichts zu machen.* There's nothing to be done about it."

Many citizens of Hiroshima, however, continued to feel a hatred for Americans which nothing could possibly erase. "I see," Dr. Sasaki once said, "that they are holding a trial for war criminals in Tokyo just now. I think they ought to try the men who decided to use the bomb and they should hang them all."

Father Kleinsorge and the other German Jesuit priests, who, as foreigners, could be expected to take a relatively detached view, often discussed the ethics of using the bomb. One of them, Father Siemes, who was out at Nagatsuka at the time of the attack, wrote in a report to the Holy See in Rome, "Some of us consider the bomb in the same category as poison gas and were against its use on a civilian population. Others were of the opinion that in total war, as carried on in Japan, there was no difference between civilians and soldiers, and that the bomb itself was an effective force tending to end the bloodshed, warning Japan to surrender and thus to avoid total destruction. It seems logical that he who supports total war in principal cannot complain of a war against civilians. The crux of the matter is whether total war in its present form is justifiable, even when it serves a just purpose. Does it not have material and spiritual evil as its consequences which far exceed whatever good might result? When will our moralists give us a clear answer to this question?"

It would be impossible to say what horrors were embedded in the minds of the children who lived through the day of the bombing in Hiroshima. On the surface their recollections, months after the disaster, were of an exhilarating adventure. Toshio Nakamura, who was ten at the time of the bombing, was soon able to talk freely, even gaily, about the experience, and a few weeks before the anniversary he wrote the following matter-of-fact essay for his teacher at Nobori-cho Primary School: "The day before the bomb, I went for a swim. In the morning, I was eating peanuts. I saw a light. I was knocked to little sister's sleeping place. When we were saved, I could only see as far as the tram. My mother and I started to pack our things. The neighbors were walking around burned and bleeding. Hataya-*san* told me to run away with her. I said I

wanted to wait for my mother. We went to the park. A
whirlwind came. At night a gas tank burned and I saw the
reflection in the river. We stayed in the park one night. Next
day I went to Taiko Bridge and met my girl friends Kikuki
and Murakami. They were looking for their mothers. But
Kikuki's mother was wounded and Murakami's mother, alas,
was dead."

*The New Yorker*, August 31, 1946

CHRONOLOGY

MAPS

BIOGRAPHICAL NOTES

NOTE ON THE TEXTS

NOTES

GLOSSARY

INDEX

# Chronology, 1933 –1945

Adolf Hitler, leader since 1921 of the National Socialist German Workers' (Nazi) Party, is named chancellor of Germany by President Paul von Hindenburg on January 30, heading cabinet with only two other Nazi members. (Appointment is result of agreement between Hitler and small group of right-wing politicians and military leaders, who hope that Nazis will provide popular support for an authoritarian government dominated by traditional conservatives and the army.) Hitler dissolves Reichstag (parliament), in which Nazis hold almost 34 percent of the seats, and calls for new election. Using emergency decree powers of the 1919 Weimar constitution and exploiting their control of the Prussian state police, Nazis begin campaign of violence and intimidation directed against Communists and Social Democrats. Following destruction of Reichstag chamber by arson on February 27, emergency decree is issued suspending all civil liberties and allowing indefinite detention without trial. In election on March 5, Nazis win 44 percent of Reichstag seats. On March 23 Reichstag approves, 441–94, enabling act that allows Hitler unilaterally to alter the constitution and enact legislation (dissenting votes are from Social Democrats; all of the Communist deputies have been arrested). Nazis begin purging civil service and educational institutions of Jews and political opponents and take control of trade unions, civil organizations, and local and state governments throughout Germany. Decree issued July 14 makes Nazis only legal party in Germany. Germany withdraws from League of Nations and Geneva Disarmament Conference on October 14. Hitler continues policy, begun by military in early 1920s, of clandestinely circumventing 1919 Versailles Peace Treaty, which limited German army to 100,000 men and prohibited it from possessing tanks or aircraft.

Tensions increase between Hitler and leadership of the SA ("Storm Detachment," Nazi party paramilitary force), who seek greater share of power and more radical social and economic change. With support from the army, Hitler has SA leaders and several other political opponents shot without trial, June 30 – July 2. Hindenburg dies on August 1 and Hitler is proclaimed Führer ("Leader") of Germany; military and civil service personnel swear personal oath of allegiance to him on August 2. Purge of SA makes the SS ("Protection Detachment," originally Hitler's Nazi party bodyguard) the main instrument of terror in Germany (in 1936 SS is given control of all German police).

859

1935 Hitler reintroduces military conscription on March 16 and announces that Germany will no longer honor military restrictions of Versailles Treaty. Britain and Germany conclude naval pact on June 18 that allows Germany to contravene Versailles Treaty by building surface ships over 10,000 tons and U-boats (submarines). "Nuremberg laws" enacted in September deprive German Jews of their remaining citizenship rights and make marriages between Jews and non-Jews a criminal offense.

Italy, ruled by Fascist dictator Benito Mussolini since 1922, invades Ethiopia on October 3. League of Nations votes limited economic sanctions against Italy in October but does not impose oil embargo.

1936 Ultranationalist Japanese army officers stage coup attempt in Tokyo, February 26, that is quickly suppressed by army high command. Incident weakens civilian government in Japan and strengthens influence of generals favoring further expansion in China (Japanese had seized Manchuria in 1931 and part of northeast China in 1933).

Hitler reoccupies German Rhineland, an area demilitarized under the Versailles Treaty, on March 7; France and Britain take no action.

Italian army completes conquest of Ethiopia on May 6. League of Nations votes July 4 to lift sanctions against Italy.

Civil war begins in Spain on July 17 with army rebellion against elected left-wing Republican government. Italy and Germany move quickly to support insurgents with arms, transport, and troops (at their peak Italian forces in Spain number 50,000; German forces reach 10,000, including strong air force contingent that gains valuable experience). Soviet Union begins supplying arms and military specialists to the Republican government in autumn, and directs Communist parties to organize International Brigades of foreign volunteers. Britain, France, and the United States adopt policy of nonintervention.

1937 Eight prominent generals are executed in Moscow on June 12 on false charges of treason as Josef Stalin, general secretary of the Soviet Communist party since 1922, begins purge of Soviet military (by late 1938 over 80 percent of the senior commanders in the Soviet army will have been shot or imprisoned; victims include many key proponents of modern mechanized warfare).

Fighting breaks out near Peking on July 7 between Chinese troops and Japanese legation garrison, and by the end of July Japanese troops control the Peking-Tientsin region. Chinese Nationalist leader Chiang Kai-shek orders attack on Japanese zone in Shanghai on August 14, leading to full-scale Sino-Japanese war.

Japanese army breaks through Chinese lines at Shanghai in November and enters Nanking, Chinese Nationalist capital, on December 13; its capture is followed by weeks of widespread killing, rape, and looting in which at least 40,000 Chinese die.

1938    German army occupies Austria without opposition on March 12, and on March 13 Germany annexes Austria in violation of the Versailles Treaty. Britain and France take no action. Hitler begins planning invasion of Czechoslovakia and launches propaganda campaign protesting alleged persecution of Germans in the Sudetenland (border regions of Bohemia and Moravia, which contain frontier fortifications essential to Czech defense). Neville Chamberlain, Conservative prime minister of Great Britain since May 1937 and leading proponent of conciliatory "appeasement" policy toward Germany, presses Czech government to make concessions to Sudeten Germans while declaring that Britain and France will fight Germany if it attacks Czechoslovakia (France has treaty of alliance with Czechoslovakia; Soviet Union is committed to assisting Czechoslovakia once France takes military action). Hitler escalates threats against Czechoslovakia in September. Chamberlain goes to Germany twice to negotiate with Hitler, while French and Soviet governments are unable to agree on response to crisis. French army and British navy begin partial mobilization, September 24–27, as German military prepares to attack Czechoslovakia on September 30. Chamberlain, French premier Édouard Daladier, Mussolini, and Hitler meet in Munich, September 29–30, and agree that Czechoslovakia will cede Sudetenland to Germany; Hitler and Chamberlain also sign declaration of Anglo-German friendship. Chamberlain returns to England and declares that agreement will bring "peace in our time." German army enters Sudetenland on October 1. Britain and Germany accelerate rearmament efforts, and Hitler plans invasion of remainder of Czechoslovakia.

After five-month battle, Japanese capture Wuhan in central China on October 25; by end of year Sino-Japanese war approaches stalemate as Japanese consolidate their conquests.

Nazi party carries out pogrom throughout Germany, November 9–10, in which 91 German Jews are killed; in its aftermath, 26,000 Jews are sent to concentration camps, and expropriation of Jewish property is intensified (pogrom becomes known as "Kristallnacht," from the broken glass of Jewish-owned shop windows).

1939    German army occupies Czechoslovakia on March 15 in violation of Munich Pact. Bohemia and Moravia become German protectorate, Slovakia a German satellite state; Hungary annexes

Ruthenia. Under threat of attack, Lithuania cedes city of Memel to Germany on March 23. Spanish civil war ends March 29 with victory of insurgent Nationalist regime led by General Francisco Franco. Chamberlain abandons appeasement policy after seizure of Czechoslovakia, and on March 31 declares that Britain and France will defend Poland against aggression.

Apr.–May    Hitler orders preparations for attack on Poland completed by September 1. Italy occupies Albania on April 7. Germany and Italy sign military alliance on May 22. Soviet and Japanese troops clash in disputed Khalkhin Gol region along Mongolian-Manchurian border in late May; both sides send reinforcements, and fighting continues for three months.

June–Aug.    Britain, France, and the Soviet Union are unable to agree on terms for an alliance. Soviet offensive in late August drives Japanese from Khalkhin Gol region (cease-fire is declared September 16; Soviet victory will contribute to Japanese decision not to attack Soviet Union in summer 1941). Germany and Soviet Union sign nonaggression pact on August 23 containing secret protocol partitioning Poland and establishing spheres of influence in eastern Europe.

Sept.    Germany invades Poland September 1. Italy declares neutrality despite alliance with Germany. Britain, Australia, New Zealand, and France declare war on Germany September 3 (South Africa and Canada declare war by September 10). Winston Churchill, severest critic of Chamberlain appeasement policy, joins British cabinet as First Lord of the Admiralty. Britain begins naval blockade of Germany. President Franklin D. Roosevelt signs American neutrality proclamation on September 5 after expressing sympathy for Allied cause in radio address. Luftwaffe (German air force) achieves air superiority over Poland, and German army advances rapidly despite determined Polish resistance. Soviets invade eastern Poland on September 17. Warsaw falls to Germans September 27, and fighting in Poland ends October 6. (New Polish government is formed in exile; its air, land, and naval forces will fight with Allies until end of the war.) SS units in Poland begin committing widespread atrocities. Allies do not attack into western Germany, fearing that assault against frontier fortifications would be repulsed with heavy losses and hoping that blockade will eventually cause German economic collapse. Numerically weaker German navy does not attempt to break blockade, but begins attacking British commerce (although Germans begin war with less than 30 U-boats capable of operating in the Atlantic, Allies will lose over 2 million tons of merchant shipping to U-boats, surface ships, mines, and aircraft by end of June 1940; Germans lose 24 U-boats in first ten months of war). Hitler orders planning for attack in western Europe.

General George C. Marshall, new U.S. Army Chief of Staff, begins planning expansion and modernization of the army, which has less than 200,000 men on active service (German army has mobilized over 2,700,000).

Oct.          Hitler orders killing of mentally and physically handicapped Germans (over 100,000 such persons will be systematically murdered before killings are suspended in August 1941). Soviets press Finnish government to make territorial concessions. British code-breakers continue work begun by Poles in 1930s on Enigma machine used by German armed forces to cipher radio messages (by late May 1940 British are able to break some Luftwaffe Enigma ciphers on daily basis).

Nov.–Dec.     U.S. neutrality law is modified on November 4 to allow Britain and France to purchase munitions and transport them in their own shipping. Soviet Union invades Finland November 30. Initial Soviet attacks are unsuccessful due to poor training, tactics, and leadership, and Finnish superiority at winter warfare.

1940          Reinforced and reorganized Soviet forces launch successful offensive against Finns in February. Finland signs armistice, March 13, yielding border territory to Soviets. Paul Reynaud succeeds Daladier as premier of France on March 21.

April         Germans invade Denmark and Norway (both neutral countries) April 9, beginning campaign designed to obtain northern naval bases and safeguard shipments of Swedish iron ore along Norwegian coast. Denmark is occupied without resistance. Attacks by sea and air against Norwegian ports and airfields achieve surprise, but despite initial confusion and loss of Oslo, Norwegian forces resist. British navy and air force attack German ships, and British troops begin landing in Norway April 14 (later joined by French and Polish forces). Germans win air superiority and Allies are unable to prevent German capture of key objectives.

Germans begin confining Polish Jews in ghettos.

May           British and French troops are evacuated from central Norway in early May; fighting continues in the north. After bitter parliamentary debate over Norwegian campaign, Chamberlain resigns May 10 and is replaced as prime minister by Churchill, who forms coalition government with opposition Labour party. Germans invade Holland, Belgium, and Luxembourg (all neutral countries) on May 10 and launch heavy air attacks against France. British and French send strong forces into Belgium and Holland, where they take up defensive positions. Allies fail to detect movement of concentrated German armor through the Ardennes, and Germans break through French positions along the Meuse River at Sedan on May 13. Dutch army capitulates,

May 15, after heavy German bombing of Rotterdam. German armored formations rapidly advance across northeastern France with close support from the Luftwaffe, which has achieved air superiority. French army, which has dispersed most of its tanks along the front in small units, is unable to mount effective counterattacks. Germans reach English Channel near Abbeville on May 20, completing encirclement of British and French armies in Belgium. After attempts to break encirclement fail, British begin evacuating troops from Dunkirk on May 27. Belgian army capitulates May 28 as Germans continue attacks on trapped Allied forces (Belgian and Dutch governments have gone into exile in Britain).

June          Dunkirk evacuation ends June 4 after approximately 225,000 British and 110,000 French troops are rescued; all of their heavy weapons and equipment are abandoned. Germans launch new offensive June 5 and break through French defensive line along Somme and Aisne rivers. Allies evacuate remaining troops from northern Norway June 8, and Norwegian government-in-exile orders its army to cease fighting on June 9. Italy declares war on France and Britain June 10. German army enters Paris on June 14. New French government headed by Marshal Philippe Pétain asks for armistice on June 17. Brigadier General Charles de Gaulle flies to England and organizes Free French movement. Armistice between France and Germany is signed June 22. Germans occupy northern France and Atlantic coast; Pétain establishes collaborationist regime (known as "Vichy," after its capital) with authority over unoccupied southern zone, North Africa, and other French colonies overseas.

Soviets occupy Lithuania on June 15 and force Romania to cede Bessarabia and northern Bukovina on June 27 (Soviet annexation of Lithuania, Latvia, and Estonia is completed by August 3, 1940).

Churchill government moves toward full mobilization of British society and economy for prolonged war and maximum military production, while Hitler directs that German economy continue to give high priority to production of goods for civilian consumption; German war production also suffers from confused planning and expectation that war will not be prolonged. (In 1940–41 Britain produces 6,200 tanks and self-propelled guns and 35,000 military aircraft, while Germany manufactures 5,400 tanks and self-propelled guns and 22,000 military aircraft.)

U.S. Congress approves major expansion of armed forces in response to German victories, but public opinion remains divided over extent to which U.S. should aid Britain. American arms production increases rapidly to fill orders from Britain and U.S. military.

July        British demand on July 3 that French fleet based at Mers-el-Kebir in Algeria take immediate action to ensure that its ships will not fall under German control. When French commander obeys order from Vichy to reject ultimatum, British ships open fire, destroying or damaging three battleships and killing over 1,200 French sailors. British and Italians begin prolonged naval struggle for control of Mediterranean.

Heavy air fighting begins between Luftwaffe and Royal Air Force (RAF) in early July as Germans attack Channel ports and convoys. Germans begin planning invasion of England; weakness of German navy, increased by serious losses in Norwegian campaign, makes achievement of air superiority over southern England essential. RAF and Luftwaffe fighter planes are roughly equal in number and performance, and British fighter production is higher; although Luftwaffe has more trained pilots, their fighters have limited range that allows them to escort bombers only over southern England. Revolutionary RAF air defense system allows commanders to control interception of enemy formations using information from radar (invented in Britain in 1935 and still secret in 1940) and ground observers.

Germans use naval and air bases along French coast to renew offensive against British commerce in the Atlantic, sinking over 5 million tons between July 1940 and June 1941 while losing only 20 U-boats. Loss of merchant shipping poses serious threat to British ability to wage war.

British form commando units for conducting coastal raids and begin working with exile governments to organize and supply resistance movements in occupied Europe (resistance movements will engage in espionage, sabotage, propaganda, and occasionally partisan warfare; Germans respond with indiscriminate reprisals).

In late July Hitler directs planning to begin for invasion of Soviet Union in 1941, intending to deprive Britain of possible ally and fulfill long-standing ambition of conquering "living space" (*Lebensraum*) for Germany in the east. Soviets continue supplying large amounts of raw materials to Germany while consolidating control over newly acquired territory.

Konoye Fumimaro becomes prime minister of Japan on July 17. New cabinet, which includes General Tojo Hideki as war minister, decides to seek alliance with Germany and Italy, isolate Nationalist China from foreign supplies, and pursue aggressive policy against vulnerable French and Dutch colonies in Southeast Asia in order to secure sources of oil, rubber, tin, and other raw materials.

Aug.        Luftwaffe begins offensive against RAF fighter airfields and air defense headquarters on August 13. Although German aircraft losses are higher than British, by end of August damage to airfields and attrition of fighter pilots places severe strain on RAF.

Sept.    In attempt to damage British morale and draw out remaining RAF fighters, Luftwaffe begins heavy bombing of London on September 7; switch in targets gives respite to RAF airfields. Battle of Britain reaches climax on September 15, when British destroy 60 aircraft while losing 26. Hitler indefinitely postpones invasion on September 17.

Under executive agreement concluded September 2, U.S. sends 50 old destroyers to Britain in return for bases in British territories in the Western Hemisphere (British are in severe need of escort vessels for convoys). Roosevelt signs act on September 16 establishing first peacetime draft in American history; law requires draftees to serve for only one year.

Italian army in Libya invades Egypt on September 13 and advances 60 miles before halting.

Under Japanese pressure, Vichy French agree on September 22 to allow Japan to station troops and aircraft in northern Indochina. U.S. responds with embargo of iron and steel scrap exports to Japan. Germany, Italy, and Japan sign Tripartite Pact, designed to deter the U.S. from entering the war in Europe or Asia, on September 27.

Oct.–Nov.    Germans gradually end daylight raids and begin intensive night bombing of London and other cities in campaign ("The Blitz") that continues into May 1941. Luftwaffe loses over 1,700 aircraft in Battle of Britain, July 10–October 31, 1940, the RAF over 900. RAF engages in limited night bombing of Germany. Hitler and Franco meet on October 23 and are unable to agree on terms for Spain to enter the war against Britain. Italy invades Greece October 28. Greek army repels attack and advances into Albania by the end of 1940. British carrier aircraft destroy or damage three Italian battleships in night raid on Taranto harbor, November 11–12.

Roosevelt is reelected for unprecedented third term on November 5.

Dec.    British and Indian troops in Egypt begin successful offensive against Italians on December 9 (Indian, Australian, New Zealand, South African, and Canadian troops comprise major portion of forces under British command throughout campaigns in the Mediterranean).

Hitler issues directive on December 18 for German invasion of Soviet Union in late spring 1941, with objective of capturing Leningrad, Moscow, and Kiev by early autumn. Encouraged by Stalin's 1937–38 purge of the army and poor Soviet performance in Finnish war, German high command expects to destroy

Soviet army during summer in series of encirclement battles near frontier.

1941       British begin series of offensives against Italians in Ethiopia and Somalia on January 19 (last Italian garrison in Ethiopia surrenders November 28, 1941).

British advance in North Africa stops at El Agheila in Libya on February 9 after capturing 130,000 Italian prisoners in two months; British, Indian, and Australian troops in campaign never total more than about 30,000. German forces land in Libya as British send troops and aircraft from North Africa to Greece.

In response to worsening British financial crisis, Roosevelt administration proposes Lend-Lease bill, which authorizes U.S. government to purchase war materials and then "lend" or "lease" them to Allied nations. House of Representatives passes bill by 260–165 vote on February 8.

March     After Senate passes Lend-Lease by 60–31, Roosevelt signs bill into law on March 11 (most Lend-Lease aid is never repaid in any form).

British sink three Italian cruisers and two destroyers off Greece in Battle of Cape Matapan, March 28–29, and achieve ascendancy over Italian navy in the Mediterranean. Germans and Italians (Axis) launch offensive in Libya on March 31 and drive British back to Egyptian border.

April      Coup in Iraq brings pro-German government to power (new regime is ousted by Allied military intervention, May 30, as British act to protect Persian Gulf oil fields). Germans invade Yugoslavia and Greece April 6. Yugoslavia surrenders April 17 and is partitioned into German, Italian, Hungarian, and Bulgarian zones; Germans also establish Serbian and Croatian puppet regimes. (Two rival resistance movements, the Serbian nationalist Chetniks and the Partisans, formed by Communist leader Tito, begin fighting Axis forces and each other in 1941.) Germans achieve air superiority in Greece and advance rapidly. British begin evacuating troops April 24. Germans capture Athens April 27, and country is occupied by Germans, Italians, and Bulgarians.

Stalin receives warnings of impending German attack from Soviet, British, and American sources, but dismisses them as British "provocations" designed to involve Soviets in war with Germany.

Roosevelt orders U.S. navy on April 10 to patrol into mid-Atlantic and report sightings of German ships to Allies.

U.S. and Japanese diplomats begin informal talks in Washington. Japan and Soviet Union sign neutrality pact on April 13. Roosevelt signs executive order on April 15 permitting pilots to resign from the U.S. armed forces and volunteer for combat service in China (American Volunteer Group, later known as the

"Flying Tigers," begins operations in late December 1941 and becomes part of U.S. army air forces in summer 1942).

May     Intensive bombing of Britain ends as Luftwaffe redeploys to the eastern front; British civilian deaths from bombing exceed 40,000.

Germans begin airborne invasion of Crete on May 20 and win battle for island June 1 after intense fighting. British are able to evacuate most of their troops despite heavy German air attacks. (German aircraft and U-boats inflict serious losses on British navy in Mediterranean in 1941–42.)

Sinking of German battleship *Bismarck* by the Royal Navy on May 27 ends Atlantic commerce raiding by large surface ships (in 1942 all large German warships are withdrawn to Germany or Norway, where they operate against convoys to Soviet Union with little success; limited raiding by armed merchant ships continues until autumn 1943).

U.S. begins sending Lend-Lease supplies to Nationalist China.

June    British invade Vichy-controlled Syria and Lebanon on June 8 (Vichy forces surrender July 11).

Germans invade Soviet Union on June 22, attacking with 3 million men (Soviet army has about 5 million men overall, with 3 million serving in western districts). Attack achieves complete surprise. Britain and United States pledge aid to Soviets. Romania, Italy, Hungary, Slovakia, and Finland declare war on Soviet Union. Luftwaffe destroys 4,000 Soviet aircraft in first week of fighting and wins control of air. German armor advances rapidly and Soviets suffer huge losses of men and matériel in series of encirclements.

Special SS and police units (*Einsatzgruppen*) begin systematically murdering Jewish population in conquered Soviet territory with assistance of German army and local collaborators; over 500,000 Jews are killed by December 1941. (Although no written orders survive, evidence strongly indicates that by spring 1941 Hitler had directed SS leaders to plan and carry out extermination of European Jews.) Hitler also orders mass murder of Roma and Sinti (Gypsies), which results in at least 250,000 deaths by 1945, and merciless treatment of Soviet prisoners; by early 1942 over two-thirds of the 3 million Soviet soldiers captured in 1941 have been shot, or have died from hunger, disease, and exposure.

British break Enigma machine cipher used by German navy and begin reading U-boat radio signals. Tracking of U-boat movements allows Royal Navy to engage in evasive convoy routing, and U-boat sinkings, July–December 1941, fall to about 700,000 tons, while U-boat losses in this period rise to 23 as number and effectiveness of British and Canadian escort vessels increase.

Japanese government debates whether to join attack on Soviet Union.

July–Aug. Germans capture Smolensk, 400 miles east of frontier and 250 miles west of Moscow, on July 16. Supply difficulties, mechanical wear on vehicles, heavy casualties, and fierce Soviet resistance begin to slow German advance. Hitler orders halt in attack on Moscow in August and shifts armored forces from central front to offensives against Leningrad and the Ukraine. Soviets begin organizing partisan warfare behind German lines.

U.S. troops land in Iceland in July, relieving British forces for use elsewhere (British occupied island in May 1940). Churchill and Roosevelt meet off Newfoundland, August 9–12, to discuss strategy (first of their 12 wartime conferences). U.S. House of Representatives votes 203–202 to extend required service of draftees beyond one year; vote allows expansion of armed forces to continue.

British and Soviets occupy Iran on August 25 and begin opening overland supply route into Soviet Union; British also send convoys to Russian Arctic ports of Murmansk and Archangel, despite increasingly heavy losses to U-boat and aircraft attack. (U.S. later opens major shipping route across North Pacific to Siberia, and supplies most of the aid sent to Soviets, including extremely valuable railroad and telephone equipment, large amounts of food, and over 400,000 trucks.)

Japanese government formally decides on July 2 to remain neutral in German-Soviet war unless the Soviet Union collapses, to occupy southern Indochina, and to prepare for war with Britain and the United States. Vichy French sign agreement on July 21 giving Japanese military control of southern Indochina, including air and naval bases that can be used to attack Malaya, the Dutch East Indies, and the Philippines. Roosevelt responds on July 26 by freezing Japanese assets in the U.S. (implementation of policy results in total embargo of oil exports to Japan, although Roosevelt intended only to sharply reduce them; U.S. is the source of 80 percent of Japanese oil imports).

Sept. Germans begin siege of Leningrad (some supplies continue to reach city across Lake Lagoda). Kiev falls to Germans, September 19, during encirclement battle in which they capture over 500,000 prisoners.

Following U-boat attack on U.S. destroyer, September 4, Roosevelt orders navy to escort convoys between the U.S. and Iceland and to destroy Axis naval vessels operating in this zone.

As negotiations in Washington continue, Japanese leadership decides on September 3 to go to war with the United States unless the U.S. accepts Japanese domination of China and Southeast Asia.

Oct.        Germans begin attack on Moscow October 2 and capture over
            600,000 prisoners before advance is halted October 30 by au-
            tumn rain and mud. Soviet defense is strengthened by increasing
            production of T-34 tanks (until 1943 T-34 is superior to all Ger-
            man tanks, and is equal to new German models introduced in
            1943). Relocation of factories to Urals region allows Soviet arms
            production to increase in 1942 despite German occupation of
            many key industrial centers.
                Roosevelt orders intensification of U.S. research into atomic
            weapons on October 9 after receiving British report concluding
            that atomic bomb could be built within three years.
                U-boat sinks U.S. destroyer on convoy duty in Atlantic,
            October 31, killing 115 men.
                Konoye resigns as Japanese prime minister on October 16 and
            is succeeded by Tojo. Navy staff approves, October 20, proposal
            by fleet commander Admiral Yamamoto Isoroku to begin war
            with surprise air attack against U.S. naval base at Pearl Harbor in
            Hawaii (Yamamoto had begun planning for attack in December
            1940).

Nov.        Attack on Moscow resumes November 15 after ground freezes.
            Germans continue offensive in blizzards and subzero tempera-
            tures despite lack of winter clothing and equipment and reach
            within 15 miles of Moscow by end of November.
                British begin successful offensive into Libya on November 18.
                Japanese government formally decides on November 5 to
            begin war in early December. War plan calls for conquering the
            Philippines, Malaya, Dutch East Indies, Burma, and the Ameri-
            can islands in the western Pacific within six months, creating an
            extended defensive perimeter; Japanese hope that the U.S. will
            negotiate peace rather than fight a long and costly war. Task
            force of six aircraft carriers and 24 supporting ships sails from
            northern Japan on November 26 and begins crossing Pacific,
            avoiding normal shipping routes and maintaining complete radio
            silence.

Dec.        Soviets surprise Germans by launching major counteroffen-
            sive around Moscow on December 5, using recently mobilized
            reservists and troops brought from Siberia during autumn. Ger-
            mans are driven back and their central front is threatened with
            disintegration.
                Deciphered Japanese diplomatic messages alert Roosevelt and
            his senior advisers that Japanese have decided to go to war, but
            do not indicate that Pearl Harbor will be attacked. Administra-
            tion anticipates that hostilities will begin in Malaya and East
            Indies, and army and navy commanders in Hawaii fail to act on
            general warnings of war and do not detect approaching task
            force. Japanese carriers approach to within 200 miles of Oahu on

morning of December 7 and launch 350 aircraft in two waves. At 7:55 A.M. (Honolulu time) attack on Pearl Harbor and nearby airfields begins, achieving complete surprise. Attack sinks or damages eight battleships, three cruisers, three destroyers, and four auxiliary vessels, destroys 188 aircraft, and kills 2,335 servicemen. (Two battleships and one auxiliary vessel are permanently lost; all of the other ships are eventually repaired and see service during the war.) Japanese lose only 29 aircraft, but fail to launch second strike against oil storage tanks and repair facilities, allowing Pearl Harbor to continue serving as fleet base. All three U.S. carriers in the Pacific are at sea and escape damage (Japan has total of 10 carriers, the U.S. seven).

Japanese begin offensive across Southeast Asia, attacking Hong Kong, occupying Thailand, landing in northern Malaya, and bombing the Philippines on December 8 (December 7 in U.S.). In the Philippines more than 100 U.S. aircraft are destroyed on the ground nine hours after General Douglas MacArthur and other commanders learn of Pearl Harbor attack. United States, Britain, and Commonwealth nations declare war on Japan on December 8. Japanese capture Guam and land advance forces on main Philippine island of Luzon on December 10. Sinking of British battleship and battle cruiser by aircraft off Malaya on December 10 gives Japanese control of South China Sea, and long range and superior performance of their Zero fighters give Japanese control of the air in Malaya and over Luzon. Attempted landing on Wake Island is repulsed by U.S. marines on December 11.

Germany and Italy declare war on the United States on December 11 and the U.S. immediately responds with its own declarations. Hitler assumes direct operational control of German army, dismisses many senior commanders, and forbids general retreat on eastern front.

Roosevelt and Churchill begin conference in Washington, December 22, which confirms strategy, agreed upon in earlier Anglo-American consultations, of defeating Germany before Japan (Germany is considered by both American and British leaders to be the more dangerous enemy).

Main Japanese force of 43,000 men lands on Luzon in the Philippines on December 22. Japanese capture Wake Island on December 23. About 15,000 American and 65,000 Filipino troops on Luzon retreat to Bataan peninsula, where they suffer from severe shortages of food and medicine. British garrison surrenders at Hong Kong on December 25. U.S. submarines begin operations in Pacific, but achieve little success at first due to poor tactics, inexperienced leadership, defective torpedoes, and doctrine that emphasizes attacks on well-defended warships.

1942   Japanese forces begin offensive on Bataan, January 9, land in Dutch East Indies, January 11, advance into southern Burma, January 15, and seize Rabaul on New Britain on January 23. British, Indian, and Australian forces retreat from southern Malaya to Singapore on January 31, ending campaign in which 35,000 Japanese with superior training, equipment, and leadership defeat 60,000 Allied troops.

Stalin orders general offensive along entire front against advice of senior army commanders, who favor concentrating Soviet forces to achieve destruction of Germans outside of Moscow. Resulting dispersion of reserves, heavy losses since June 1941, and strength of German defensive positions prevent Soviets from winning decisive victory (Soviets will drive Germans back 80 miles from Moscow but fail to relieve Leningrad or regain major ground on southern front before thaw in April brings reduction in fighting).

Germans and Italians end their retreat in Libya at El Algheila. Reinforcement of Luftwaffe in Mediterranean allows more Axis supply ships to reach North Africa. Axis counterattack on January 21 reaches Gazala on February 7 before halting.

U-boats open offensive along U.S. Atlantic coast in January (later extended to Gulf of Mexico and Caribbean). Refusal of U.S. navy to organize coastal convoys until late spring and delay in instituting coastal blackout results in heavy losses, especially of tankers.

SS leaders meet with other German officials in Berlin district of Wannsee on January 20 to coordinate plans for deportation and murder of European Jews. *Einsatzgruppen* continue mass killings in eastern Europe in 1942, while from December 1941 to November 1942 SS establishes killing centers in Poland at Chelmno, Belzec, Auschwitz-Birkenau, Sobibor, Treblinka, and Majdanek, where Jews are brought by train from throughout Europe to be gassed. Genocide campaign eventually involves thousands of German officials and European collaborators and continues until the end of the war.

Feb.–Mar.   New Enigma cipher, introduced February 1, ends British reading of U-boat signals, while German navy begins breaking British code used to control convoy movements. Germans sink over 3 million tons of shipping, January–June 1942, while losing only 21 U-boats.

RAF abandons attempts to bomb precise targets at night and begins "area bombing" offensive designed to break morale of German industrial workers by destroying their housing (British will not have sufficient aircraft to begin sustained bombing offensive until 1943).

Germans begin economic mobilization for prolonged war and,

despite Allied bombing, are able to increase weapons production in 1942–44 by reducing civilian production, improving their economic planning and administration, and exploiting slave labor from occupied countries. (In 1942–44 Germany produces 37,000 tanks and self-propelled guns, while Britain manufactures 20,000; the Soviet Union, 77,000; and the U.S., 72,000. Germany produces 80,000 military aircraft in 1942–44, while Japan manufactures 53,500; Britain, 76,000; the Soviet Union, 100,000; and the U.S., 230,000.)

Japanese halt offensive on Bataan, February 8, and wait for reinforcements after suffering heavy losses in combat and from disease. Strength of Japanese air and naval forces in Pacific prevents any U.S. attempt to relieve or evacuate Philippines. Japanese attack Singapore on February 8. Singapore garrison surrenders on February 15 in worst British defeat of the war (Japanese capture 130,000 prisoners in Malaya and Singapore). Dutch, British, Australian, and U.S. navies lose five cruisers and six destroyers in surface actions in East Indies, February 27–March 1. Japanese capture Rangoon on March 8 and continue their advance into Burma, severing Allied supply route into China. MacArthur leaves the Philippines. Last Allied forces on Java surrender, March 12, completing Japanese conquest of Dutch East Indies.

Roosevelt signs executive order on February 19 that results by September 1942 in internment without trial or hearing of over 120,000 Japanese-Americans and Japanese resident aliens living on the West Coast. (Japanese-Americans are eventually permitted to join the military, and over 17,000 serve in the infantry in Europe and in front-line intelligence units in Asia and the Pacific.)

April      Japanese launch new offensive on Bataan on April 3. Campaign ends April 9 with surrender of 12,000 U.S. and 63,000 Filipino troops, who are forced to make 65-mile "Death March" on which thousands are murdered or die from disease. (Less than 60 percent of the 20,000 Americans captured in the Philippines survive the war.) Japanese carriers raid into the Indian Ocean in early April, bombing Ceylon and sinking a British light carrier and two cruisers. In raid designed to raise American morale, 16 twin-engine B-25 bombers take off from aircraft carrier 650 miles from Japan on April 18 and bomb Tokyo and four other cities before flying on to China. Raid causes very little damage, but shames Japanese commanders and results in final approval of proposal by Yamamoto to capture Midway Island and draw U.S. carriers into decisive battle. U.S. navy learns from Japanese radio signals of planned landing at Port Moresby in southeastern New Guinea, first in series of operations designed to sever

U.S.–Australia supply routes. Admiral Chester Nimitz, commander of U.S. Pacific fleet, sends two carriers to Coral Sea to block invasion.

May           Japanese capture of Corregidor on May 6 ends major resistance in the Philippines (Filipino guerrillas will fight throughout Japanese occupation). In Battle of the Coral Sea, May 7–8, U.S. navy turns back Port Moresby invasion force, losing one carrier and two smaller ships while sinking a Japanese light carrier and inflicting damage and aircraft losses that prevent two other Japanese carriers from participating in subsequent Midway operation. Battle is first in naval history fought between opposing carrier forces, and in which opposing ships never come into sight of one another. Japanese complete conquest of Burma in mid-May. U.S. navy codebreakers provide detailed information concerning Midway operation and simultaneous diversionary attack on Aleutian Islands. Nimitz commits the three remaining carriers in Pacific fleet to battle in hopes of taking Japanese by surprise (Yamamoto anticipates that U.S. carriers will be in harbor when Midway invasion begins).

British invade Vichy-controlled island of Madagascar on May 5 to prevent its possible use as naval base by Axis (campaign continues until Vichy forces surrender on November 5, 1942).

Soviet offensive against Kharkov in eastern Ukraine is defeated, May 12–29, with loss of over 200,000 prisoners.

Axis begins new offensive in Libya on May 26.

June          In Battle of Midway, June 3–6, U.S. carrier aircraft sink four Japanese carriers and one cruiser, while the U.S. loses one carrier and one destroyer to air and submarine attack. Japanese navy also loses many of its most experienced pilots, and abandons planned invasion of Midway. Victory allows U.S. to take the initiative in the Pacific war.

Japanese occupy Kiska and Attu, uninhabited islands at western end of the Aleutians, June 6–7.

Roosevelt authorizes full-scale U.S. effort to build atomic weapons on June 17.

Germans capture 30,000 Allied prisoners in Libyan port of Tobruk on June 21 and then advance into Egypt.

Germans launch general offensive in southern Russia and eastern Ukraine on June 28 with objective of capturing Caucasian oil fields (Germans no longer have enough men, vehicles, or draft horses to attack along entire front as in 1941; though heavy fighting will occur on central and northern fronts in 1942, neither side will gain or lose much territory).

July          British halt Axis advance in Egypt near El Alamein, only 60 miles from Alexandria, in heavy fighting July 1–22. Defense is aided by recent breaking of German army Enigma ciphers. (Allies will intermittently gain valuable intelligence from German army signals for remainder of war.)

German attack in southern Russia rapidly gains ground, but Soviets are generally able to retreat and avoid major encirclements. Hitler issues directive on July 23 calling for simultaneous advances southward into the Caucasus and eastward toward Stalingrad, industrial and transportation center on Volga River; order results in serious overextension of German forces.

U-boats end American coastal offensive and return in strength to Atlantic convoy routes, sinking over 3 million tons of shipping, July–December 1942; although Germans lose 65 U-boats in this period, increased production replaces these losses and allows Germany to begin 1943 with over 200 operational U-boats. Allied convoys lose most heavily in "air gap," mid-Atlantic region beyond the range of land-based air patrols (U-boats have limited underwater speed and endurance; to effectively pursue convoys, they must cruise on the surface and risk air attack). Although new American construction promises to eventually replace losses, rate of sinking threatens ability of Allies to move men and supplies overseas and launch offensives against the Axis.

U.S. transport aircraft based in northeastern India begin flying supplies across mountains ("The Hump") into China.

Japanese land at Buna on northern coast of eastern New Guinea (Papua), July 21, and begin overland advance toward Port Moresby. Americans prepare for landing on Guadalcanal, first stage of planned counteroffensive in the Solomon Islands and New Guinea with ultimate objective of capturing Rabaul, key Japanese naval and air base in the southwest Pacific.

Aug.  Marines land on Guadalcanal and nearby islands of Tulagi and Gavutu, August 7, and capture partially constructed airfield on northern Guadalcanal; surviving Japanese retreat inland. Night attack by Japanese cruiser force early on August 9 sinks one Australian and three U.S. cruisers in Battle of Savo Island. (For most of Guadalcanal campaign superior training, tactics, equipment, and torpedoes give Japanese navy advantage in night surface engagements.) Allied transport ships are withdrawn on August 9 before they are fully unloaded, leaving 17,000 marines onshore short of supplies and equipment. Marines establish defensive perimeter around airfield (Henderson Field) and complete its construction. Japanese begin landing reinforcements on Guadalcanal. First aircraft land at Henderson Field on August 20. U.S. achieves control of air during day, but Japanese navy is able to land supplies and troops and bombard American positions at night. Japanese lose one light carrier in Battle of the Eastern Solomons on August 24. In Papua Japanese continue advance across Owen Stanley mountains toward Port Moresby, and on

August 25 land troops at Milne Bay on eastern end of New Guinea.

Germans advance into northern Caucasus. Allied raid against French port of Dieppe on August 19 is repulsed with loss of over 3,000 men killed or captured, almost all of them Canadian; disaster causes Allied planners to avoid direct assaults on well-defended ports in future amphibious landings.

Renewed Axis offensive in Egypt is defeated in battle of Alam Halfa, August 30–September 5. British receive emergency shipment of American tanks and prepare for major counteroffensive in Egypt.

Sept.     Germans reach outskirts of Stalingrad in early September. Stalin agrees to proposal by generals Georgi Zhukov and Alexander Vasilevsky to hold city with minimum of forces possible while building large reserves of men, tanks, and artillery for counteroffensive against German flanks in open country outside Stalingrad. House-to-house fighting begins in city.

Australian defenders repulse Milne Bay landing in New Guinea, and surviving Japanese are evacuated on September 7. Major Japanese attack on Henderson Field on Guadalcanal is defeated in heavy fighting, September 12–14. Air and sea engagements in Solomons continue as both sides struggle to send men and supplies to Guadalcanal. Australians halt Japanese advance 30 miles from Port Moresby, September 16, then take the offensive (both sides in Papua fighting suffer from extreme terrain and climate conditions).

Oct.–Nov.   British offensive at El Alamein begins October 23 and achieves decisive victory. Axis forces begin retreating toward Libya on November 4. U.S. and British forces land in Morocco and Algeria on November 8. Fighting between Allied and Vichy French troops ends November 11. Germans occupy southern France and begin moving troops and aircraft into Tunisia. British troops enter Tunisia November 16 and encounter strong German resistance. Vichy French navy scuttles remainder of its Mediterranean fleet to prevent its falling under German control.

Soviet positions in Stalingrad are reduced by mid-November to series of strongholds in ruins along Volga. Soviet counteroffensive outside Stalingrad begins November 19, and on November 23 Soviets complete encirclement of 250,000 German troops. Hitler forbids trapped German forces from attempting to break out of encirclement.

Two Japanese battleships bombard Henderson Field early on October 14, destroying about half the aircraft on Guadalcanal. Japanese land several thousand reinforcements and attack Henderson Field perimeter, October 23–26, but are repulsed in intense fighting and lose over 2,000 dead. U.S. loses aircraft carrier in Battle of Santa Cruz Islands, October 26; Japanese have two carriers damaged, and suffer severe aircraft losses (U.S. now has only two carriers in Pacific, both of which are undergoing repair for battle damage). Australians advance over Owen Stanley mountains in Papua.

In series of air attacks, submarine attacks, and two night surface engagements fought November 13-15 and later known as Naval Battle of Guadalcanal, U.S. loses two cruisers and seven destroyers while sinking two Japanese battleships, one cruiser, and three destroyers, and destroying large convoy carrying reinforcements and supplies. Increasing numbers of Japanese troops on Guadalcanal die from hunger and disease as U.S. gains control of waters around island.

Australians force Japanese in Papua to retreat into fortified Buna-Gona coastal area. American troops are flown into improvised landing strips and join attack on Buna-Gona position.

Dec.    German offensive designed to break into Stalingrad encirclement fails. Soviets launch new offensive on December 16 that threatens to reach Rostov-on-Don and cut off German forces in the Caucasus.

Tunisian fighting stalemates as winter rains make road movement extremely difficult. Axis forces continue retreat across Libya.

British break U-boat Enigma cipher system introduced in February 1942 and begin intermittently reading U-boat signals (Enigma cipher keys change daily; some keys are never broken, while others are broken only after considerable delay).

First self-sustaining nuclear chain reaction is achieved on December 2 at University of Chicago.

U.S. forces on Guadalcanal begin series of attacks against Japanese positions on jungle-covered ridges overlooking Henderson Field. Allies suffer high casualties in offensive against Buna-Gona in Papua, but use air attacks to keep supplies from reaching Japanese defenders. Concerned by Allied gains in Papua, Japanese command decides on December 26 to evacuate Guadalcanal.

British and Indian troops begin limited offensive in Burma in Arakan region along coast.

1943    Germans begin retreating from Caucasus. Soviets continue offensives in southern Russia and, in northwestern Russia, open narrow land corridor into Leningrad on January 18.

Roosevelt announces and Churchill endorses demand for "unconditional surrender" of Germany, Italy, and Japan at close of their conference in Casablanca, January 24. American bombers based in England attack Germany for first time on January 27. (American air strategy calls for daylight precision bombing of key industrial targets by aircraft flying beyond the range of fighter escort; U.S. commanders believe that close-formation flying and heavy defensive armament will sufficiently protect bombers against fighter attack.)

Americans begin major offensive on Guadalcanal. Allies complete capture of Buna-Gona position on January 22, ending six-month campaign in Papua costing about 3,000 U.S. and Australian and 7,000 Japanese lives.

Feb.–Mar.    Last German troops in Stalingrad surrender on February 2. Soviets capture Kharkov February 16 as their advance threatens destruction of entire German southern front. Germans open counteroffensive against overextended Soviet forces on February 20, and recapture Kharkov March 14. Front stabilizes as thaw in late March brings lull in fighting.

British forces advance from Libya into southeastern Tunisia. Germans begin counteroffensive against U.S. troops in Tunisia, February 14, and capture Kasserine Pass before being halted by British and American forces on February 22. British drive Axis forces from Mareth Line, defensive position in southeastern Tunisia, March 20–28.

RAF begins sustained night area bombing offensive against Germany on March 5, repeatedly attacking cities in the Ruhr and elsewhere with hundreds of bombers; by July 1943 campaign exceeds intensity of 1940–41 "Blitz" of Britain.

U-boats sink nearly 1.2 million tons of shipping, January–March 1943; Allies sink 40 U-boats, but grow increasingly concerned about safety of North Atlantic convoy routes.

Japanese complete evacuation of Guadalcanal on February 8, ending air, sea, and land campaign in which 7,000 Americans and 30,000 Japanese die (over 4,700 U.S. deaths are at sea). Allies begin logistical preparations for further operations in New Guinea and the Solomons with eventual objective of capturing Rabaul. (All Allied plans for amphibious operations are constrained by worldwide shortages of shipping and landing craft, and operations in the Pacific are generally given lower priority than those in Europe in accordance with "Germany First" strategy.) Losses at Midway, Guadalcanal, and Papua force Japanese to go on defensive throughout Pacific. In Battle of the Bismarck Sea, March 2–4, U.S. and Australian aircraft destroy convoy bringing reinforcements to Lae in eastern New Guinea, killing over 3,000 Japanese troops at sea. American air strength in Southwest Pacific increases as U.S. begins to produce land-based fighter aircraft equal in performance to the Japanese Zero.

Japanese begin series of counterattacks in Burma against Allied advance in the Arakan.

April Germans begin planning offensive to destroy Soviet forces in large salient around Kursk. Soviets anticipate attack and begin building anti-tank defenses and accumulating armored reserves.

Axis forces retreat into northern Tunisia as Allied air attacks sharply reduce supplies reaching them from across the Mediterranean.

Jewish resistance organizations in Warsaw ghetto begin uprising on April 19 as SS prepares to send remaining inhabitants to Treblinka extermination camp.

Secret scientific laboratory at Los Alamos, New Mexico, begins work on design and manufacture of fission atomic weapons (construction of industrial facility for separating uranium-235 from uranium ore began in November 1942 at Oak Ridge, Tennessee; in August 1943 construction begins at Hanford, Washington, for reactor and processing plant for production of plutonium-239).

May–June Allies break through Axis lines in northern Tunisia after heavy fighting, May 6–7. North African campaign ends May 13 with capture of 125,000 German and 115,000 Italian troops.

Fighting in Warsaw ends May 15. Ghetto is destroyed by SS, and 56,000 Jews are killed either in Warsaw or at Treblinka; several thousand survivors hide among Polish population.

Allies gain decisive advantage in Battle of the Atlantic as increasing numbers of long-range land-based aircraft and small escort aircraft carriers close mid-Atlantic "air gap." Improved airborne and ship radar, growing number of escort vessels with high-frequency direction-finding equipment (used to locate U-boats making radio transmissions), improved tactics and weapons, and increasing success in reading U-boat ciphers also contribute to sinking of 15 U-boats in April 1943 and 41 in May. On May 24 German navy orders U-boats to withdraw from main North Atlantic convoy routes. Allies adopt secure cipher for convoy signals in June.

Roosevelt, Churchill, and their staffs meet in Washington in May and set May 1, 1944, as date (D-Day) for cross-Channel invasion of France and opening of major land campaign against Germans in northwest Europe.

U.S. forces land on Attu in Aleutians on May 11 and kill last defenders on May 30 as Japanese garrison fights until it is annihilated; over 2,300 Japanese and 600 Americans die in battle (Japanese will evacuate Kiska in July).

British and Indian troops in Burma retreat from Arakan.

Allies launch major offensive in Southwest Pacific on June 30, with U.S. and Australian troops attacking in New Guinea and U.S. forces landing on New Georgia in the Solomons.

July Germans launch offensive against Kursk salient July 5, beginning largest tank battle of the war. British and Americans invade

Sicily July 10. Germans are unable to break through Soviet defenses and suffer heavy tank losses. Concerned about possible Italian collapse, Hitler orders Kursk offensive abandoned on July 13 and begins shifting troops to Italy. Mussolini is overthrown by coup in Rome, July 25, and new Italian government begins secret talks with Allies on surrender. (New regime imprisons Mussolini, but he is freed by Germans on September 12 and establishes a fascist government in northern Italy.)

RAF night raid on Hamburg on July 28 kills 40,000 civilians when unusually dense concentration of incendiary bombs create intense fires.

Aug.        Soviets begin series of major offensives on southern and central fronts on August 3 and capture Kharkov on August 23.

Allies enter Messina August 17, ending Sicilian campaign; most German troops escape to southern Italy.

American bombers attack Regensburg and Schweinfurt, August 17, in their deepest raid yet into Germany, losing 60 out of 376 aircraft. RAF continues area offensive against German cities.

Anglo-American chiefs of staff approve choice of Caen-Bayeux area of Normandy for invasion (landing area is later extended westward onto shore of Cotentin peninsula).

Americans capture Munda airfield, key objective on New Georgia, on August 5 after heavy fighting. U.S. destroyers sink three Japanese destroyers bringing reinforcements to New Georgia on August 6 as effective use of radar gives U.S. navy increasing advantage in night surface engagements. Japanese resistance on New Georgia ends in late August.

Sept.       British troops cross Straits of Messina on September 3 and land in southern Italy. Italian surrender is announced September 8. U.S. and British forces land at Salerno on September 9. Germans occupy Italy and launch counterattacks at Salerno, September 12–16, that threaten beachhead before they are repulsed with aid of heavy naval gunfire. Allied advance northward is slowed by mountainous terrain, poor roads, and extensive German demolitions.

Soviets capture Smolensk September 25 and begin establishing bridgeheads along western bank of Dnieper River. Recovery of agricultural and industrial resources of eastern Ukraine eases strain on Soviet economy.

U-boats return to North Atlantic convoy routes, hoping to regain initiative by using new acoustic homing torpedoes against escorts, but Allies quickly adopt effective countermeasures. Sinkings by U-boats, April–December 1943, total 1.4 million tons, while Allies sink 197 U-boats in this period.

U.S. and Australian forces land in New Guinea near Lae, September 4, and capture village on September 16. Allies continue offensive westward along northern New Guinea coast in series of overland advances and amphibious landings. U.S. submarine operations become increasingly effective as reliability of American torpedoes improves and more submarines are equipped with search radar. Submarine campaign now concentrates on destruction of merchant ships transporting oil and raw materials from Southeast Asia to Japan, and is aided by intelligence derived from decoded Japanese signals. Japanese lose 2.8 million tons of shipping from December 1941 to December 1943, almost 80 percent sunk by submarines; in this period 22 U.S. submarines are lost on Pacific patrols. (Japanese use their submarines for attacks on warships and for transporting supplies to isolated island garrisons, and lose 130 during the war.)

Oct.  Allies enter Naples October 1 and attack across Volturno River in mid-October. New Italian government declares war on Germany October 13.

Soviets attack across Dnieper into western Ukraine, preventing the Germans from using the river as winter defensive line. (Summer and autumn Soviet offensives in 1943 are aided by growing strength of their air force in close support of ground operations, and by increasing mobility given to their army by American trucks; most of German army still relies upon horse-drawn transport.)

U.S. loses 148 bombers over Germany in seven days, including 60 out of 291 sent October 14 on second raid against Schweinfurt ball-bearing plants. Losses force suspension of raids beyond range of fighter escort, which extends only over northwestern Germany.

Allies begin series of intensive air attacks on Rabaul; new plan calls for Rabaul to be heavily bombed and blockaded, but rejects land assault as unnecessary and highly costly.

Nov.–Dec.  Germans reinforce troops in France and begin strengthening coastal fortifications in anticipation of Allied invasion in 1944 (majority of German army will continue to fight Soviets for remainder of war).

Soviets capture Kiev November 6. Series of Soviet offensives in south during winter result in heavy German casualties and recovery by early 1944 of almost all Ukrainian territory lost in 1941.

In Italy, Allies attack across Sangro River in late November and reach Garigliano River in December. Heavy infantry casualties, difficult terrain, bad weather, and skillful defense slow Allied advance as Germans fight to hold southern Italy for as long as possible. (Hitler fears that Allies will use central and northern Italy to invade the Balkans, depriving Germany of important raw materials.)

RAF attacks Berlin November 18, beginning unsuccessful attempt to repeat devastation caused in Hamburg; British lose over 500 bombers in 16 raids through late March 1944.

Roosevelt, Churchill, and Stalin meet in Teheran, November 28–December 1. Stalin promises to enter war against Japan after defeat of Germany, and Roosevelt and Churchill agree in principle to major shifts in Polish borders (Poland eventually loses 70,000 square miles of its pre-war territory to the Soviet Union and is compensated with 40,000 square miles of eastern Germany, from which several million Germans are expelled in 1945–46). General Dwight Eisenhower is appointed as supreme allied commander for invasion of France with orders to "undertake operations aimed at the heart of Germany" and the destruction of its armed forces.

U.S. troops land on November 1 on Bougainville in the Solomons, where they establish defensive perimeter and begin constructing airfield. Japanese concentrate aircraft and warships at Rabaul to oppose Bougainville landing, but abandon counter-offensive after damaging raids by U.S. carrier aircraft in early November (in early 1944 Japanese withdraw remaining aircraft from Rabaul).

Growing number of U.S. aircraft carriers and support ships allows launching of series of offensives against Japanese-held Gilbert, Marshall, and Caroline island chains in central Pacific. (In 1942–45, Japanese bring into service 14 carriers of all sizes, many of them inadequate conversions of existing ships, while the U.S. commissions 17 large fleet carriers, nine light carriers, and 77 small escort carriers.) American forces land on Tarawa and Makin atolls in the Gilberts on November 20. Battle on Tarawa ends on November 23 after 1,000 Americans and 4,800 Japanese are killed. Fighting on Makin ends on November 23 with destruction of smaller Japanese garrison. U.S. marines land on Cape Gloucester at western end of New Britain on December 26.

1944        Soviet offensive, January 14–27, drives Germans away from Leningrad and brings final end to siege in which 800,000–1,000,000 Soviet civilians died of starvation and disease.

Allies launch major offensive against Gustav Line, main German defensive position south of Rome, on January 17. British and American troops land at Anzio, 30 miles south of Rome and 60 miles behind Gustav Line, on January 22. Germans send troops to contain beachhead as Allied forces consolidate their position near the coast. Heavy fighting continues along Gustav Line, especially in mountains around Cassino, town commanding main highway to Rome.

Marines capture airfield on Cape Gloucester and repulse Japanese counterattacks. After preliminary carrier raids and shore bombardment, U.S. forces begin landing on Kwajalein atoll in the Marshalls on January 31.

Feb. – Mar.  Attacks by British, Indian, and New Zealand troops, February 15–18 and March 15–23, fail to drive Germans from Cassino. German counteroffensive at Anzio is repulsed in intense fighting, February 16–18, but Allies are unable to subsequently advance from beachhead.

Increasing numbers of P-51B long-range fighter aircraft allow U.S. to resume daylight raids deep into Germany in series of raids against aircraft factories, February 20–25 ("Big Week"). Escorted U.S. bombers attack Berlin on March 6 as daylight air battle continues over Germany with heavy losses on both sides. RAF suspends deep raids into Germany and begins major bombing campaign against French and Belgian railway system in preparation for invasion.

Using dummy landing craft, false radio signals, and their complete control of the German espionage network in Britain, Allies begin successful deception operation designed to lead Germans to suspect invasion will occur not in Normandy but in the Pas de Calais, northeastern region of France that is closer to Germany.

Fighting on Kwajalein ends February 4. U.S. launches highly successful carrier raid against Truk, major Japanese air and naval base in the Carolines (after further raids against Truk in April, Carolines are bypassed for remainder of war). Landings begin on Eniwetok atoll in the Marshalls, February 17, and fighting continues until February 23. U.S. casualties in Marshalls are lower than on Tarawa; Japanese garrisons are almost completely annihilated.

British and Indian troops advance in Burma in renewed offensive in the Arakan. Japanese counterattack and succeed in encircling several Allied positions, but surrounded troops receive supplies by parachute drop and hold their positions (in previous jungle battles in Southeast Asia, Allied troops usually retreated when the Japanese launched infiltration attacks against their supply lines). Small American infantry force joins U.S.-trained and -equipped Chinese troops in offensive in northern Burma intended to increase flow of supplies into China.

U.S. troops land in Admiralty Islands north of New Britain on February 29, and Japanese resistance on islands ends March 18. Japanese counteroffensive on Bougainville in March is defeated in heavy fighting. Securing of bases on Bougainville, New Britain, and Admiralties completes the containment of Japanese at Rabaul. (Australian troops relieve U.S. forces on New Britain and Bougainville in autumn 1944, and fighting continues on both islands until the end of the war, when over 90,000 Japanese troops surrender.)

Japanese launch major offensive into northeastern India on March 8 with objective of capturing Allied bases at Imphal and Kohima. British and Indian troops withdraw into perimeter around Imphal airfields as siege begins on March 29.

April    Soviets approach Hungarian border and cross into northern Romania before end of their spring offensive.

British garrison at Kohima is besieged, April 5–18, but is supplied by parachute drops during intense close-range battle. Heavy fighting continues at Kohima, Imphal, and in Arakan throughout spring.

Japanese begin series of major offensives in central and southern China on April 17 that continue into autumn and inflict severe losses on Nationalist Chinese forces.

U.S. forces land at Aitape and Hollandia in northern New Guinea on April 22, bypassing Japanese position at Wewak in westward advance designed to secure bases for invasion of the Philippines.

May      Allies launch major offensive in Italy against Gustav Line on May 11. French and North African troops break through and force German withdrawal. Polish troops capture monastery at Cassino, May 18. Allies break out of Anzio beachhead, May 23, but are unable to trap retreating Germans, who begin pulling back in stages to Gothic Line, defensive position extending across northern Italy from Pisa to Rimini.

Allies win air superiority over western Europe as Luftwaffe is crippled by heavy losses in battles with U.S. fighters over Germany and increasing shortages of fuel and adequately trained pilots. U.S. begins bombing synthetic oil plants.

Heavy fighting continues in northwestern New Guinea as U.S. forces begin offensive in Wakde-Sarmi area, May 17, and land on Biak island, May 27, where they meet strong resistance from Japanese dug into hillside caves and bunkers (fighting continues on Biak until end of July).

U.S. and Chinese troops capture Myitkyina airfield in northern Burma on May 17 and begin battle for nearby town.

June     Allies enter Rome June 4. Eisenhower postpones D-Day, which had been rescheduled for June 5, because of adverse weather forecast, then decides to invade on June 6. British and American parachute and glider troops begin airborne assault on Normandy during night of June 5–6 and secure key positions on western and eastern flanks of invasion area. American, British, and Canadian troops begin landing on five Normandy beaches on morning of June 6 in largest amphibious operation in history. Resistance is heaviest on Omaha Beach, where U.S. infantry suffers heavy casualties before capturing high ground overlooking shore. German commanders are surprised by timing and location of invasion and respond slowly. By night of June 6 Allies have landed over 150,000 men at cost of about 10,000 men killed, wounded, or captured. Initial German counterattacks fail, and individual beachheads are joined into single continuous front by June 12. Allied control of air and sea allows rapid buildup of men and matériel in Normandy, while German reinforcements are delayed by Allied air attack, sabotage and ambushes by the French resistance, and belief by German commanders that Allies will launch second invasion in the Pas de Calais. Germans concentrate majority of their armored forces at eastern end of front to defend Caen from British and Canadian attacks. (Open country southeast of Caen is suitable for rapid armored advance; Germans hope to keep Allies confined in hedgerow country near coast, well-suited to their defensive tactics.)

Germans begin attacking London with V-1 unmanned jet aircraft on June 13.

Soviets concentrate massive numbers of men, tanks, artillery, and aircraft in Belorussia and on June 22 launch offensive that destroys center of German eastern front (Soviet deception plan has led Germans to send their reserves to northern Ukraine in anticipation of a renewed attack there).

British and Canadians continue attacks in Caen sector. Americans capture port of Cherbourg June 27.

U.S. troops invade Saipan in the Marianas on June 15, beginning campaign designed to secure bases for long-range bombing of Japan. Japanese navy responds in hopes of winning decisive victory, leading to first carrier engagement in Pacific since October 1942. In Battle of the Philippine Sea, June 19–20, Japanese lose three carriers (two of which are sunk by U.S. submarines) and over 400 aircraft; U.S. loses about 50 aircraft in combat. (U.S. navy fighter pilots are now better trained than Japanese, and fly new Hellcat fighters superior to the Zero; effectiveness of anti-aircraft fire from U.S. ships is significantly increased by use of radar proximity fuses. Increasing shortage of fuel prevents Japanese from adequately training pilots to replace those lost in Philippine Sea.) Heavy fighting continues on Saipan, where Japanese defenders make extensive use of caves in jungle-covered hills.

U.S. begins bombing Japan from Chinese airfields on June 15, but is unable to mount major attacks due to supply difficulties in China.

Allied forces in India end siege of Imphal on June 22.

July      Soviets capture Minsk in Belorussia on July 3 and begin offensive into the Baltic states. By mid-July German losses in Belorussia total 350,000 men, mostly killed or captured. Soviets launch offensive in northern Ukraine and advance into Poland.

Americans capture key crossroads at St. Lô in western Normandy on July 18 after weeks of costly fighting. British offensive southeast of Caen, July 18–20, fails to break through but causes further attrition of German armor.

Hitler is slightly wounded when bomb planted by anti-Nazi military officers explodes at his East Prussian headquarters on July 20. Coup attempt in Berlin fails when his survival becomes known (over 200 people are executed for involvement in the plot). Americans launch major offensive west of St. Lô on July 25 that breaks through German lines and allows U.S. armor to reach open country.

Soviets establish bridgeheads across Vistula River and begin fighting in eastern suburbs of Warsaw.

Fighting ends on Saipan on July 9. Over 8,000 Japanese civilians living on the island commit suicide rather than surrender. Tojo resigns on July 18 and is replaced as prime minister by General Koiso Kuniaki. Marianas campaign continues with landings on Guam, July 21, and Tinian, July 24.

Japanese abandon Imphal offensive on July 9 and retreat through mountains into Burma; 30,000–50,000 Japanese die in Imphal-Kohima battles, many from hunger and disease. British prepare for offensive into Burma at end of monsoon season.

U.S. forces reach northwestern end of New Guinea on July 30. (Fighting continues in New Guinea until end of war, especially between Australians and Japanese in Aitape-Wewak area.)

Aug.  Polish Home Army, anti-communist resistance movement, begins uprising against Germans in Warsaw on August 1. Soviets obstruct Western attempts to parachute aid to insurgents. Soviet offensive in Poland is slowed by shortage of supplies and increasing German resistance.

U.S. forces advance rapidly into Brittany and northeastern France as British and Canadians attack south from Caen. German counteroffensive intended to cut off American advance is defeated, August 7–10. U.S. and French troops land in southern France west of Cannes on August 15. Refusal of Hitler to authorize retreat in Normandy results in severe German losses of men and equipment in "pocket" near Falaise, closed by U.S., Canadian, and Polish troops, August 19–21. Paris is liberated by French troops on August 25 as Germans retreat across France. Losses in Normandy campaign in men killed, wounded, or captured are 450,000 for Germans and over 200,000 for Allies.

Soviets launch offensive into Romania August 20. New Romanian government signs armistice with Soviets August 23, then declares war on Hungary and Germany. Germans lose almost 200,000 men killed or captured in collapse of Romanian front.

Allies begin offensive along Adriatic coast of Italy against Gothic Line on August 25.

U-boats are forced to leave French Atlantic ports and retreat to Norwegian and German bases. Use of *Schnorchel* underwater breathing apparatus allows increasing number of U-boats to recharge their batteries without surfacing, but their effectiveness is severely limited by slow underwater speed. German development of new class of U-boats capable of high underwater speeds worries Allies, but production difficulties and Allied bombing prevents them from becoming operational before the end of the war. U-boats sink 1 million tons of shipping, January 1944 – May 1945; Allies sink 393 U-boats (27,500 U-boat crewmen are killed, 1939 – 45).

Effective Japanese resistance ends on Tinian and Guam in early August; over 5,000 Americans and about 50,000 Japanese are killed in Marianas campaign, mostly on Saipan.

Allied forces capture town of Myitkyina on August 3 as engineers work on Ledo Road, new overland route from India through north Burma into China.

Sept.            Finland signs armistice with Soviet Union on September 4. Bulgaria declares war on Germany September 8 as Soviet army enters the country.

British troops liberate Brussels, September 3, and Antwerp on September 4. Germans begin attacking London with V-2 ballistic missiles on September 8. U.S. forces advancing from northern and southern France meet near Dijon and American patrols cross German frontier near Aachen, September 11. Allied advance is slowed by difficulty in bringing gasoline and other supplies forward from Normandy and the Mediterranean coast (Germans still control Scheldt estuary leading to Antwerp and have left garrisons in many Channel and Brittany ports). Hitler begins planning late autumn counteroffensive in the Ardennes designed to split the Allied front and recapture Antwerp. American and British airborne troops land near Dutch towns of Eindhoven, Nijmegen, and Arnhem on September 17 as British armored forces attack northward in operation designed to seize bridges across Waal, Maas, and lower Rhine rivers. Attack is halted south of Rhine, and on September 26 surviving British airborne troops at Arnhem are either evacuated across river or taken prisoner; total Allied casualties in operation are over 17,000 men killed, wounded, or captured.

Attacks on Gothic Line continue on both Adriatic and Mediterranean sides of the Apennines.

Loss of Romanian oil fields and continued U.S. bombing of synthetic oil plants causes fuel shortage that cripples Luftwaffe training and operations and severely affects motorized forces of German army.

Soviets attack into Hungary in late September.

Americans begin campaign in Palau Islands with landings on

Peleliu, September 15, and Anguar, September 17. Resistance on Peleliu is unexpectedly intense, and U.S. troops begin protracted struggle to kill Japanese defenders fighting from fortified caves in steep coral ridges.

Oct.

Warsaw uprising ends October 2; over 200,000 Poles are killed during revolt and the city is almost completely destroyed. Soviet advance into Romania and Bulgaria forces Germans to begin evacuating Greece, Albania, and southern Yugoslavia.

Canadian troops begin offensive to clear Scheldt estuary on October 6. Germans begin bombarding Antwerp with V-1s and V-2s on October 13 (attacks are extended to other Belgian cities during winter; V-weapons kill over 12,000 people in England and Belgium by spring 1945 and cause considerable destruction, but are too inaccurate to be militarily effective).

Luftwaffe begins limited operational use of Me-262 jet fighter, with top speed 100 miles per hour faster than American P-51B, but is unable to regain control of the air because of difficulty of mass-producing jet engines, crippling lack of fuel, severe shortage of trained pilots, and overwhelming Allied numerical superiority. German war production begins to decline as intensive bombing of transportation system disrupts the movement of coal and other industrial materials.

Soviets reach Baltic coast of Lithuania on October 9. German coup installs fascist puppet regime in Hungary on October 16, preventing Hungarian armistice with Soviets. Soviet troops and Titoist Partisans capture Belgrade on October 20. U.S. troops capture Aachen, first German city to fall to Allies, on October 21. Continuing Allied attacks in Holland, Aachen region, Lorraine, and Alsace gain ground slowly in face of determined German resistance, bad weather, difficult terrain, and shortages of supplies and infantry replacements. Germans build armored reserves for Ardennes counteroffensive. Heavy rain and flooded rivers make Allied operations in Italy increasingly difficult.

U.S. troops begin invasion of Philippines with landing on island of Leyte on October 20. Japanese navy commits most of its remaining ships to battle in attempt to destroy supply ships for invasion force. In the Battle of Leyte Gulf, complex series of air, submarine, and night and day surface engagements fought around northern and central Philippine islands, October 23–27, Japanese lose four carriers, three battleships, nine cruisers, and nine destroyers; U.S. losses are one light carrier, two escort carriers, and three destroyers (battle is largest naval engagement in history). Defeat leaves Japanese incapable of mounting major naval operations. An escort carrier sunk on October 25 is victim of first mass suicide attack ("kamikaze") by Japanese aircraft. Suicide attacks against ships continue as Japanese attempt to break American morale; kamikaze tactics also allow minimally trained pilots to cause greater damage than they would in conventional attacks.

Nov.     Roosevelt is reelected for fourth term on November 6. Scheldt estuary is cleared of German troops on November 8 (minesweeping delays arrival of first supply ships in Antwerp until November 28). Major American offensive launched near Aachen on November 16 reaches Roer River by end of November but is unable to advance further.

Heavy fighting continues on Leyte as Japanese reinforce island with troops from Luzon. Japanese resistance ends on Peleliu in late November; over 1,200 Americans and 11,000 Japanese are killed in Palaus, mostly on Peleliu. U.S. begins bombing Japan from bases in the Marianas on November 24, attacking industrial targets in daylight from high altitude, although high winds and dense clouds over targets make accurate bombing extremely difficult.

Japanese begin consolidating gains from 1944 offensives in southern China (in 1945 some conquered territory is abandoned in order to free troops for use elsewhere).

Dec.     Winter halts major Allied offensive operations in Italy. Germans attack thinly held American front in the Ardennes on December 16. After initial surprise and confusion, U.S. commanders begin sending reinforcements and planning counterattacks. Bad weather prevents air attacks on advancing Germans. Outnumbered American troops delay or prevent German capture of key road junctions, and offensive quickly falls behind schedule. German advance is halted east of the Meuse River on December 24 and U.S. counteroffensive against southern flank of German salient ("the Bulge") begins December 25. Allied fighter-bombers attack as weather improves.

British, Indian, and African troops begin advancing across Chindwin River in northern Burma. U.S. troops in Philippines land on island of Mindoro on December 15. Major Japanese resistance on Leyte ends on December 31.

Japanese merchant fleet is crippled by loss of 3.9 million tons of shipping in 1944 (U.S. submarines sink 70 percent of total tonnage, with carrier aircraft destroying most of remainder). Land-based aircraft begin using bases on Mindoro for attacks on shipping in South China Sea.

1945     Germans launch counteroffensive against Americans in Alsace on January 1 that threatens Strasbourg before it is halted in late January. By January 16 heavy fighting has regained Allies almost all ground lost in December; Ardennes battle costs U.S. 19,000 men killed, 47,000 wounded, and 15,000 captured; Germans lose 80,000–100,000 men killed, wounded, or captured.

Soviets launch offensive in Poland January 12, attacking out of Vistula bridgeheads with overwhelming superiority in men and weapons, and capture Warsaw January 17 (German forces in Poland have been weakened by priority given by Hitler to Ardennes offensive and defense of Hungarian oil fields). German front disintegrates, and millions of refugees flee as Soviet troops advance into eastern Germany, where they commit widespread murder and rape against civilian population. Soviets reach Oder River, 50 miles east of Berlin, on January 31.

U.S. invasion force sailing from Leyte to Luzon comes under heavy kamikaze attack. Troops begin landing at Lingayen Gulf on January 9. Japanese do not defend invasion beaches and withdraw into Luzon mountains. American forces encounter increasing resistance as they advance inland.

British forces in Burma begin series of crossings of Irrawaddy River. U.S. and Chinese troops open Ledo Road into China.

Feb.          Roosevelt, Churchill, and Stalin meet at Yalta in the Crimea, February 4–11, and reach agreements on occupation of Germany, organization of the United Nations, terms for Soviet entry into war against Japan, and holding of free elections in Poland (Soviets will fail to honor agreement on Poland).

Allies begin series of attacks into the German Rhineland on February 8. Soviet advance on Berlin is halted along Oder by supply difficulties and concern about remaining German forces in East Prussia and Silesia; Soviets shift forces to complete conquest of both regions. German resistance in Budapest ends February 13 after seven-week battle in city (intense fighting continues in Hungary until early April). RAF bombing of Dresden on February 13–14 kills approximately 60,000 civilians and destroys much of city. Allies advance toward Rhine in heavy fighting.

U.S. troops reach northern suburbs of Manila on February 3, then begin house-to-house battle for city. American carrier aircraft attack Japan on February 16 in first in series of raids. U.S. troops land on Palawan as operations begin to free central and southern Philippines from Japanese.

Marines land on Iwo Jima, volcanic island 760 miles south of Tokyo, on February 19 in attack aimed at capturing airfields for use as refueling and emergency landing strips by bombers based in the Marianas. Island is defended by over 21,000 Japanese fighting from extensive network of tunnels, bunkers, and caves. Marines capture summit of Mount Suribachi at southern end of Iwo Jima on February 23 (photograph of second flag raising on Suribachi becomes famous). Intense fighting continues as marines slowly advance northward.

British and Indian troops in Burma continue offensive across

Irrawaddy, receiving supplies by air and successfully using tanks in open country east of the river.

March    Americans capture bridge across Rhine at Remagen on March 7. Allies make series of assault crossings of the Rhine, March 22–24. Heavy losses in Ardennes and Rhineland battles leave Germans incapable of mounting continuous defense east of the Rhine, and U.S. troops begin rapid advance across northern Germany.

Battle for Manila ends on March 3 after most of the city is destroyed; about 1,000 Americans and 20,000 Japanese die in the fighting, while as many as 100,000 Filipino civilians are killed by artillery fire or are massacred by Japanese troops. Fighting continues in Luzon mountains.

U.S. abandons high-altitude daylight precision bombing of Japan and begins low-altitude night area attacks. In first major raid using new tactics, 334 B-29 bombers attack Tokyo with napalm on night of March 9–10, killing at least 84,000 civilians. (Incendiary bombing of Japanese cities continues until end of war, killing over 180,000 people and causing immense devastation.)

Major fighting on Iwo Jima ends on March 26 as marines overrun Japanese positions on northern end of the island. Battle costs lives of over 6,800 Americans and 20,000 Japanese.

Allies capture Meiktila, key Burmese transportation center, March 3, and successfully defend it against counterattacks.

April    U.S. forces encircle over 300,000 German troops in the Ruhr on April 1 and advance rapidly across northern Germany toward the Elbe River. Allies open spring offensive in Italy on April 9. American troops reach the Elbe near Magdeburg, about 60 miles west of Berlin, on April 11. Roosevelt dies of cerebral hemorrhage on April 12, and Vice-President Harry S. Truman becomes president. Eisenhower halts advance toward Berlin and directs Allied commanders to concentrate instead on destruction of remaining German forces west of the Elbe, an objective he considers to be of greater military importance. Soviets launch massive offensive across Oder and Neisse rivers toward Berlin on April 16. U.S. and Soviet troops meet on Elbe at Torgau, east of Leipzig, on April 25, cutting Germany in half. Soviets begin assault on center of Berlin on April 26. Mussolini is summarily shot by Italian partisans near Milan on April 28 as Allies advance rapidly northward. Hitler appoints Admiral Karl Dönitz, commander of the German navy, as his successor, then commits suicide in his Berlin bunker on April 30, with attacking Soviet troops only a quarter of a mile away.

U.S. forces invade Okinawa, densely populated island 350 miles southwest of Japan, on April 1 in largest amphibious operation of Pacific war. Japanese do not defend landing beaches, concentrating troops instead in caves, bunkers, and tunnels dug into series of steep ridges on southern end of island. U.S. troops quickly capture airfields in center of island and begin advancing north and south. Prime Minister Koiso resigns on April 5 and is succeeded by retired admiral Suzuki Kantaro. Japanese begin series of mass air attacks against Okinawa invasion fleet, using both conventional and kamikaze tactics. Major Japanese resistance in northern Okinawa ends in late April, but intense fighting continues in south.

Allied forces in central Burma begin mechanized advance southward toward Rangoon.

May     German forces in Italy surrender, May 2. (Losses of men killed, wounded, or captured in Italian campaign are 312,000 for the Allies, 435,000 for the Germans.) Berlin garrison surrenders on May 2. British troops reach the Baltic and U.S. forces advance into Bavaria and Austria as organized German resistance on the western front collapses. U.S. troops reach Mauthausen, last in series of concentration camps liberated by Americans in spring 1945, on May 5. After their offer to surrender only in the west is summarily rejected, representatives of German high command sign unconditional surrender on all fronts at Reims, France, on May 7, effective May 8; at Soviet insistence, surrender is again signed in Berlin on May 9.

Australian troops land in Borneo on May 1, beginning campaign that continues until the end of the war. Indian troops occupy Rangoon on May 3 before monsoon brings halt to major Allied operations in Southeast Asia.

Intense kamikaze raids continue on U.S. and British ships off Okinawa, with especially heavy attacks directed at destroyers and other escort vessels serving as radar pickets. U.S. army troops and marines attack Shuri Line, main defensive position in southern Okinawa, despite heavy rain, thick mud, and most intense Japanese artillery fire of Pacific war. Loss of key hill positions forces Japanese withdrawal from Shuri Line in late May.

June     Major fighting on Okinawa ends on June 21 after final Japanese defensive line is overrun. Americans lose 7,600 dead in land fighting; 4,900 men are killed in Okinawa naval campaign, mostly by kamikazes. Over 100,000 Japanese and Okinawan soldiers and between 70,000 and 150,000 Okinawan civilians are killed. U.S. invasion of Kyushu, southernmost of Japanese home islands, is scheduled for November 1, 1945.

July     Blockade of Japan intensifies as U.S. bombers lay thousands of mines in ports and straits of Japanese home islands, drastically reducing coastal shipping essential to Japanese economy. Continued U.S. air and submarine attacks reduce Japanese merchant fleet to one-sixth of its 1941 size and effectively end importation of oil, food, and raw materials into Japan. (During Pacific war U.S. submarines also sink eight Japanese carriers and one battleship; 52 boats and 3,500 men are lost in wartime submarine operations.)

Liberation of Philippines is proclaimed on July 5, but U.S. and Filipino troops continue fighting on Luzon and Mindanao until end of war, when over 110,000 surviving Japanese surrender. U.S. loses 14,000 men killed in Philippines land fighting, October 1944–August 1945, while over 300,000 Japanese either are killed or die from starvation and disease. (Philippines campaign engages more U.S. troops than any other operation in Pacific war.)

Japanese begin diplomatic effort to enlist Soviets in mediating end to the Pacific war. U.S. learns from reading coded messages between Tokyo and Japanese ambassador in Moscow that Japanese government considers unconditional surrender unacceptable, but is unable to agree on acceptable peace terms.

Los Alamos scientists test implosion design for atomic bomb using plutonium in desert 60 miles northwest of Alamogordo, New Mexico, on July 16, detonating device with explosive force equivalent to 18,000 tons of TNT. (Design for "gun assembly" bomb using uranium-235 is judged not to require explosive testing.) At conference in Potsdam, Germany, Stalin promises Truman that Soviet Union will enter war against Japan on August 15. Truman and senior advisers agree to use atomic bombs if Japanese reject ultimatum demanding their surrender, and order is transmitted on July 25. United States, Britain, and China issue Potsdam Declaration on July 26, calling for unconditional surrender of Japanese armed forces and warning that the "alternative for Japan is prompt and utter destruction." Declaration does not mention Japanese emperor, but promises eventual establishment of a "peacefully inclined and responsible" Japanese government "in accordance with the freely expressed will of the Japanese people." Japanese government rejects Potsdam ultimatum on July 28.

Aug.

B-29 flying from Tinian drops uranium bomb over Hiroshima on August 6. Weapon explodes 1,900 feet above city at 8:16 A.M. with force equivalent to about 13,000 tons of TNT, killing at least 80,000 people. Soviet Union declares war on Japan on August 8 and launches massive invasion of Manchuria on August 9. Plutonium bomb is dropped by B-29 over Nagasaki on August 9, and explodes 1,650 feet above city at 11:02 A.M. with force equivalent to 22,000 tons of TNT, killing at least 35,000 people (hills shield part of Nagasaki from blast and heat of bomb). Japanese supreme council divides over issue of surrender, with prime minister, foreign minister, and navy minister favoring immediate acceptance of Potsdam Declaration on condition that the Allies preserve the sovereignty of the emperor; army minister and army and navy chiefs of staff advocate continuing the war in hopes of obtaining better terms. Emperor Hirohito makes unprecedented intervention on August 10 by expressing support for immediate conditional acceptance of Potsdam Declaration. Conditional surrender offer is communicated to Allies on August 10 as U.S. continues large-scale conventional air attacks on Japan. American reply on August 11 states that the authority of the Emperor "to rule the state" after the surrender "shall be subject" to the decisions of the Allied occupation commander. Hirohito decides on August 14 to accept terms of U.S. reply. Truman announces Japanese surrender on August 14. Coup attempt by army officers in Tokyo fails to prevent unprecedented radio broadcast by Emperor on August 15 announcing surrender to Japanese people.

Sept.  Surrender is formally signed onboard American battleship in Tokyo Bay on September 2.

Over 293,000 Americans died in battle, from battle wounds, or as prisoners of war from 1941 to 1945, while another 115,000 Americans died from non-combat causes while serving in the armed forces during World War II. Over 107,000 died in battle in the war against Japan, and over 185,000 were killed in the war against Italy and Germany, mostly in the 1944–45 campaign in northwest Europe. Battle deaths by service were approximately 180,000 in the army, 55,000 in the army air forces, 38,000 in the navy, and 20,000 in the marines.

Britain lost 400,000 dead in the war, including over 60,000 civilians killed by air attacks and over 30,000 merchant seamen killed by enemy action. Canada lost over 39,000 military dead; India, 36,000; Australia, 27,000; and New Zealand, over 11,000. France lost about 200,000 military and at least 400,000 civilian dead, and there were more than 300,000 military and civilian dead in Italy. Over 1 million people died in Yugoslavia. Japan lost at least 1,500,000 military and 400,000 civilian dead in 1941–45, as well as 185,000 soldiers killed in China, 1937–41. Germany lost at least 3,300,000 military dead; over 500,000 German civilians were killed in air raids and another 1 million civilians died during the Soviet conquest of eastern Germany in 1945. At least 5,400,000 people died in Poland, almost all of them as the result of German atrocities. About 3 million of the Polish dead were Jews, and throughout Europe at least 5,750,000 Jews were murdered. Chinese deaths from 1937 to 1945 are estimated at between 10 and 15 million, mostly from famine. The Soviet Union lost at least 20 million military and civilian dead, and perhaps as many as 27 million. It is estimated that between 50 and 60 million people died in World War II.

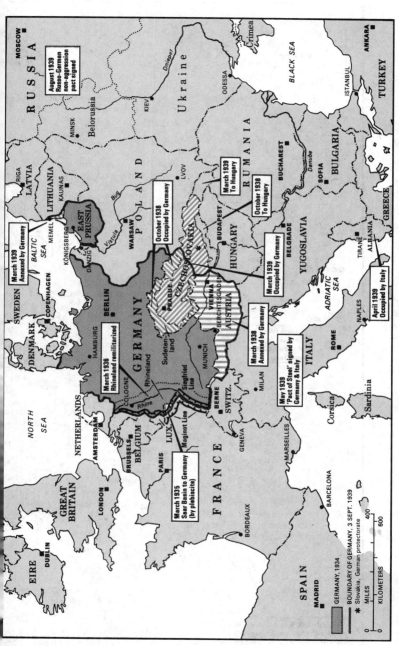

Europe, 1934–39

ARCTIC OCEAN

REYKJAVIK ICELAND

NAR

TRONDHEIM

BERGEN    OSLO

STOCKH

**9 April 1940 Germany invades Norway & Denmark**

**3 Sept 1939 Britain & France declare war on Germany**

ATLANTIC

NORTH SEA

EDINBURGH

**1 Sept 1939 Germany inva Poland**

DENMARK
COPENHAGEN

GREAT

EIRE
DUBLIN

LIVERPOOL

BRITAIN

DANZIG

OCEAN

NETH.

HAMBURG

AMSTERDAM

BERLIN

LONDON

DUNKIRK    BRUSSELS    COLOGNE

BELG.    Rhine    GERMANY

**10 May 1940 Germany invades the Low Countries and France**

4 June 1940

PARIS    LUX.    PRAGUE

Danube

FRANCE

MUNICH    VIENNA

HU

VICHY    BERNE    SWITZ.

Bay of
Biscay

**25 June 1940**
BORDEAUX
(Vichy France)

MILAN    BELG

MARSEILLES    TURIN    VENICE    YUGO

FLORENCE    Adriatic Sea

LISBON    MADRID

**10 June 1940 Italy declares war on Britain and France**

ROME

A

SPAIN    NAPLES

Sardinia

PORTUGAL

GIBRALTAR (Br)    PALERMO

SP.MOR.    Sicily    **28
Ita
Gre**

CASABLANCA    ORAN    ALGIERS    TUNIS    MALTA (Br)

MOROCCO
(Fr)

ALGERIA
(Fr)

TUNISIA
(Fr)

TRIPOLI

SIRTE

**Ceded Rumanian territories:**
**1. Bessarabia & N. Bukovina to Russia, June 1940**
**2. S. Dobruja to Bulgaria, August 1940**
**3. Transylvania to Hungary, September 1940**

LI
(Ita

The War in Europe,
1939-40

**Barents Sea**

MURMANSK

*White Sea*

ARCHANGEL

**AXIS PARTNERS: 1939**

GERMANY
ITALY
GERMAN SATELLITE
GERMAN OCCUPIED, 27 SEPT 1939
GERMAN OCCUPIED, 23 JUNE 1940
GERMAN FRONT LINES AT DATES SHOWN

| 0 | MILES | 500 |
|---|---|---|
| 0 | KILOMETERS | 800 |

Ceded to Russia, 1940

**30 Nov 1939-1 March 1940
Russo-Finnish War**

*L. Ladoga*

LENINGRAD

**June 1940
Annexed by Russia**

R U S S I A

MOSCOW

SMOLENSK

VORONEZH

*Volga*

NAS

MINSK

**17 Sept 1939
Russia invades
Poland**

KHARKOV

STALINGRAD

KIEV

*Dnieper*

ROSTOV

*Don*

*Caspian
Sea*

V

ODESSA

1

SEVASTOPOL

TIFLIS

MANIA

AREST

*BLACK SEA*

nube

2

IRAN

ULGARIA

FIA

ISTANBUL

ANKARA

T U R K E Y

CE

IRAQ
(Br)

ATHENS

SYRIA
(Fr)

Dodecanese
(Italian)

Cyprus
(Br)

DAMASCUS

Crete

N       S   E   A

PALESTINE
(Br)

AMMAN
TRANSJORDAN
(Br)

JERUSALEM

TOBRUK

ALEXANDRIA

*Suez
Canal*

SAUDI
ARABIA

ZI

CAIRO

*Nile*

E G Y P T
(Br protectorate)

The War in Europe
and North Africa,
1941-42

GERMAN OCCUPIED, 1 JAN 1941
ALLIED WITH AXIS
GERMAN OCCUPIED,
1 JAN – 29 MAY 1941
22 JUNE 1941 – 19 NOV 1942
GERMAN FRONT LINES
— 16 JULY 1941
— 5 DECEMBER 1941
— END-APRIL 1942
— 19 NOVEMBER 1942

0        MILES        500
0      KILOMETERS     800

**15 Sept 1941
Siege of Leningrad
begins**

**5/6 Dec 1941-end April 1942
Russian counteroffensive
on Moscow axis**

**19 Nov 1942
High-tide of German expansion,
Russian counteroffensive begins**

rents Sea

MANSK

*White Sea*

ARCHANGEL

PETROZAVODSK

*L. Ladoga*

LENINGRAD

DEMYANSK

MOSCOW

R U S S I A

*Volga*

TULA

SMOLENSK

VORONEZH

MINSK

KHARKOV

STALINGRAD

KIEV

*Dnieper*

*Don*

Caspian
Sea

ZAPOROZHYE

ROSTOV

ODESSA

GROZNY

NOVOROSSIISK

NIA
ST

SEVASTOPOL

TIFLIS

ARIA

BLACK SEA

IRAN

ISTANBUL

ANKARA

T U R K E Y

HENS

Dodecanese
(Italian)

rete

SYRIA
(Free French)

IRAQ
(Br)

Cyprus
(Br)

DAMASCUS

S E A

PALESTINE
(Br)
JERUSALEM

AMMAN
TRANSJORDAN
(Br)

n Army
ss the desert

ALEXANDRIA

*Suez
Canal*

SAUDI
ARABIA

EL ALAMEIN

*Nile*

CAIRO

**23 Oct-4 Nov 1942
Battle of El Alamein**

E G Y P T

ARCTIC OCEAN

ICELAND
REYKJAVIK

NARVI

N
O
R
W
A
Y

TRONDHEIM

S
W
E
D
E
N

BERGEN
OSLO
STOCKHO

ATLANTIC

NORTH
SEA

DENMARK COPENHAGEN

Baltic

DANZIG

OCEAN

EDINBURGH

EIRE
DUBLIN

GREAT
LIVERPOOL
BRITAIN

NETH.

HAMBURG

BERLIN

**6 June 1944**
**D-day: Allied forces**
**land in Normandy**

AMSTERDAM
LONDON

CHERBOURG

BRUSSELS BELG.

COLOGNE

GERMANY

PRAGUE

CAEN

PARIS LUX.

Rhine

SLOV

FRANCE

MUNICH VIENNA

Danube

HUN

Bay of
Biscay

VICHY

BERNE
SWITZ.

MILAN

BORDEAUX

TURIN VENICE

MARSEILLES

FLORENCE

BELGR
YUGO

**15 Aug 1944**
**Landings in**
**St Tropez area**

Corsica

**22 Jan 1944**
**Landings at Anzio**

**27 Jan-18 May**
**Battles for Cas**

ROME
CASSINO

LISBON

MADRID

SPAIN

PORTUGAL

**Sept 1943**
**Landings at Reggio (3rd)**
**and Salerno (9th)**

ANZIO
NAPLES
SALERNO

AL

**8 Sept 194**
**Italy surre**

PALERMO

REGGIO

Sicily

GIBRALTAR (Br)
SP.MOR.

M
E
D
I
T
E
R
R
A

**10 July 19**
**Allied forc**
**land in Si**

CASABLANCA

ORAN

ALGIERS

BÔNE

TUNIS

C.Bon

MALTA

MOROCCO
(Free Fr)

ALGERIA
(Free French)

KASSERINE

TUNISIA
(Free Fr)

**11 May 1943**
**Axis forces in N.**
**Africa surrender**

MARETH

TRIPOLI

SIRTE

L I B

The War in Europe, and North Africa, 1943-44

**Barents Sea**

LIBERATED/OCCUPIED BY ALLIES
23 JUNE –15 DECEMBER 1944 *
15 DECEMBER 1944 – 7 MAY 1945

ALLIED FRONT LINES
—————— 25 AUGUST 1944
– – – – – – 15 DECEMBER 1944
–·–·–·–· 21 MARCH 1945
–··–··–·· 7 MAY 1945

* German forces withdrew from Greece, Albania
and Yugoslavia in face of partisan attacks

0          MILES          500
0          KILOMETERS          800

MURMANSK

White Sea

ARCHANGEL

L.Ladoga

LENINGRAD

PSKOV

MOSCOW

R U S S I A

...AS

SMOLENSK

MINSK

VORONEZH

Volga

KHARKOV

STALINGRAD

KIEV          Dnieper

Don

Caspian
Sea

ROSTOV

ODESSA

SEVASTOPOL

TIFLIS

...ANIA

25 Aug 1944
Rumania and
8 Dec 1944
Bulgaria declare
war on Germany

BLACK SEA

...REST

...ube

...GARIA

IRAN

...IA

ISTANBUL          ANKARA

T U R K E Y

...CE

SYRIA          IRAQ
(Free Fr)          (Br)

...ATHENS

Cyprus
(Br)

DAMASCUS

Dodecanese

Crete

...N          S   E   A

PALESTINE
(Br)          AMMAN

JERUSALEM          TRANSJORDAN
(Br)

TOBRUK          ALEXANDRIA

Suez
Canal

SAUDI
ARABIA

EL ALAMEIN          Nile          CAIRO

E G Y P T
(Br prot)

Japanese Expansion, 1931-41

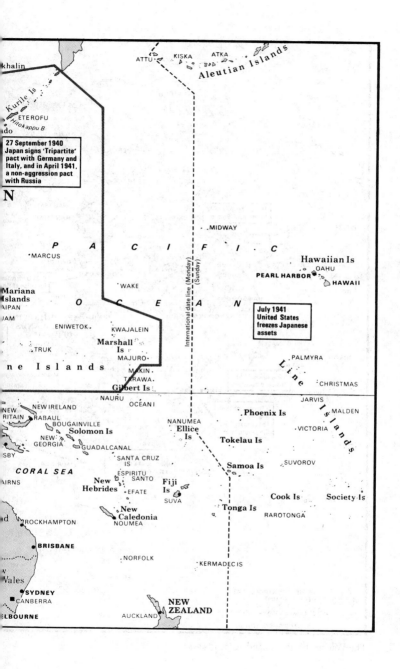

khalin

ETEROFU
Hitokappu B
do

**27 September 1940**
**Japan signs 'Tripartite'**
**pact with Germany and**
**Italy, and in April 1941,**
**a non-aggression pact**
**with Russia**

N

ATTU · KISKA · ATKA
Aleutian Islands

P       A       C       I       F       I       C
·MARCUS
·MIDWAY

**Hawaiian Is**
OAHU
**PEARL HARBOR** ·
**HAWAII**

WAKE

**Mariana**
**Islands**
AIPAN                    O                 C              E          A          N
JAM              ENIWETOK·        KWAJALEIN

**July 1941**
**United States**
**freezes Japanese**
**assets**

·TRUK            **Marshall**
**Is**
MAJURO·
ne  Islands                      ·PALMYRA

MAKIN·                                              Line
TARAWA·                                            ·CHRISTMAS
**Gilbert Is**
NAURU·                                          JARVIS·
NEW IRELAND        OCEAN I                                    ·MALDEN
NEW
RITAIN ▲RABAUL                    NANUMEA         · **Phoenix Is**
BOUGAINVILLE              **Ellice**                       ·VICTORIA
NEW·  **Solomon Is**        **Is**·
GEORGIA  △GUADALCANAL                  **Tokelau Is**
SBY               SANTA CRUZ                                ·SUVOROV
IS
**CORAL SEA**      ESPIRITU                 **Samoa Is**
AIRNS              SANTO    **Fiji**
**New** ᗿ  SANTO  **Is** ᗧ
**Hebrides** ·EFATE   ᗧ                          **Cook Is**      **Society Is**
SUVA
**New**                **Tonga Is**       RAROTONGA
ROCKHAMPTON    **Caledonia**
NOUMEA

●**BRISBANE**

·NORFOLK           ·KERMADEC IS

·Vales
●**SYDNEY**
●CANBERRA                                **NEW**
LBOURNE              AUCKLAND   **ZEALAND**

International date line (Monday)
(Sunday)

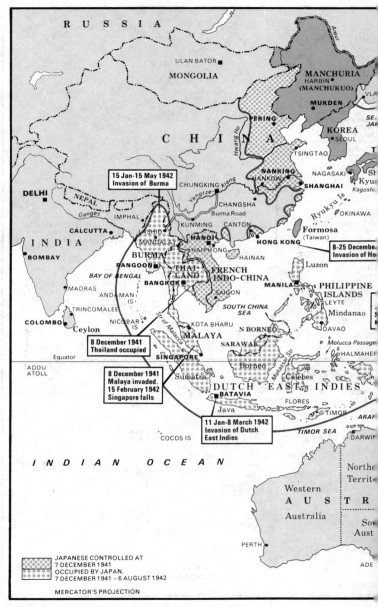

The War in the Pacific and Asia, 1941-42

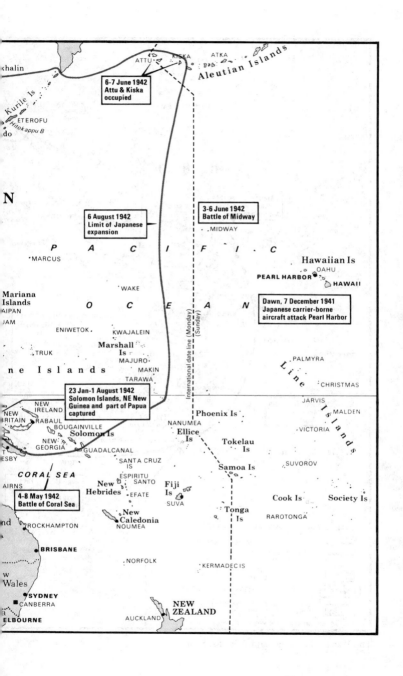

**6-7 June 1942**
Attu & Kiska
occupied

Aleutian Islands

**3-6 June 1942**
Battle of Midway

**6 August 1942**
Limit of Japanese
expansion

· MIDWAY

*P        A        C        I        F        I        C*

· MARCUS

*O        C        E        A        N*

Hawaiian Is
· OAHU
PEARL HARBOR ·
· HAWAII

**Dawn, 7 December 1941**
Japanese carrier-borne
aircraft attack Pearl Harbor

· WAKE

Mariana
Islands
AIPAN

JAM

ENIWETOK       · KWAJALEIN

· TRUK           **Marshall
                   Is**
                   · MAJURO

ne  Islands        · MAKIN
                    TARAWA

International date line (Monday)
(Sunday)

· PALMYRA

*Line*

· CHRISTMAS

JARVIS

**23 Jan-1 August 1942**
Solomon Islands, NE New
Guinea and part of Papua
captured

NEW
IRELAND

NEW
RITAIN  · RABAUL
· BOUGAINVILLE
**Solomon Is**
NEW
GEORGIA
· GUADALCANAL

ESBY

*CORAL SEA*

AIRNS

**4-8 May 1942**
Battle of Coral Sea

nd  · ROCKHAMPTON

· BRISBANE

· SANTA CRUZ
     IS

· ESPIRITU
   SANTO
**New     · EFATE
Hebrides**

**New
Caledonia**
NOUMEA

Phoenix Is

NANUMEA
**Ellice
Is**

Fiji
Is
SUVA

Tokelau
Is

**Samoa Is**

Cook Is

· MALDEN

· VICTORIA

*Islands*

· SUVOROV

Society Is

RAROTONGA

· NORFOLK

· KERMADEC IS

· Tonga
   Is

w
Wales

· SYDNEY
· CANBERRA

ELBOURNE

AUCKLAND

**NEW
ZEALAND**

The War in the Pacific and Asia, 1942-44

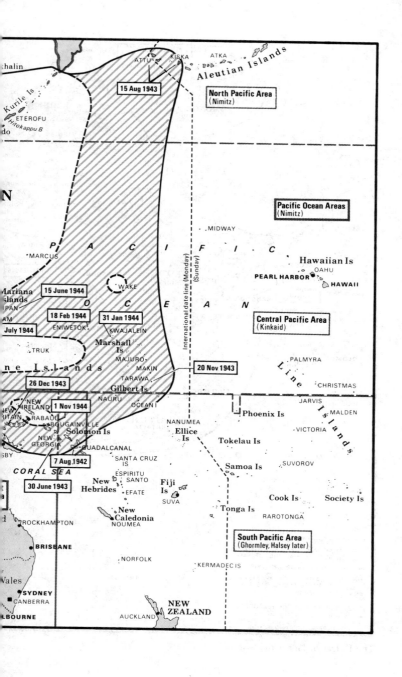

halin

ATKA

Kurile Is
ETEROFU
Hitokappu B
do

ATTU KISKA
**Aleutian Islands**

**15 Aug 1943**

**North Pacific Area**
(Nimitz)

N

**Pacific Ocean Areas**
(Nimitz)

P A C I F I C

MIDWAY

MARCUS

Mariana
slands
PAN
AM
July 1944

**15 June 1944**

O

WAKE

**Hawaiian Is**
OAHU
PEARL HARBOR
HAWAII

**18 Feb 1944**    **31 Jan 1944**

ENIWETOK

C

E

A

N

KWAJALEIN

**Marshall
Is**

TRUK

MAJURO
MAKIN
TARAWA

**Central Pacific Area**
(Kinkaid)

ne  I s l a n d s

**26 Dec 1943**

Gilbert Is
NAURU
OCEAN I

**20 Nov 1943**

PALMYRA

Line  Islands

CHRISTMAS

NEW
IRELAND
RITAIN
RABAUL
BOUGAINVILLE
Solomon Is
NEW
GEORGIA
GUADALCANAL
SBY

**1 Nov 1944**

JARVIS
**Phoenix Is**    MALDEN

NANUMEA
Ellice
Is

VICTORIA

Tokelau Is

**7 Aug 1942**
*CORAL SEA*

**30 June 1943**

SANTA CRUZ
IS
ESPIRITU
SANTO
New   EFATE
Hebrides

Fiji
Is
SUVA

Samoa Is

SUVOROV

Cook Is    Society Is

a

ROCKHAMPTON

BRISBANE

New
Caledonia
NOUMEA

Tonga Is

RAROTONGA

**South Pacific Area**
(Ghormley, Halsey later)

Vales

SYDNEY
CANBERRA
LBOURNE

NORFOLK

KERMADEC IS

**NEW
ZEALAND**
AUCKLAND

International date line (Monday)
(Sunday)

The Defeat of Japan, 1944-45

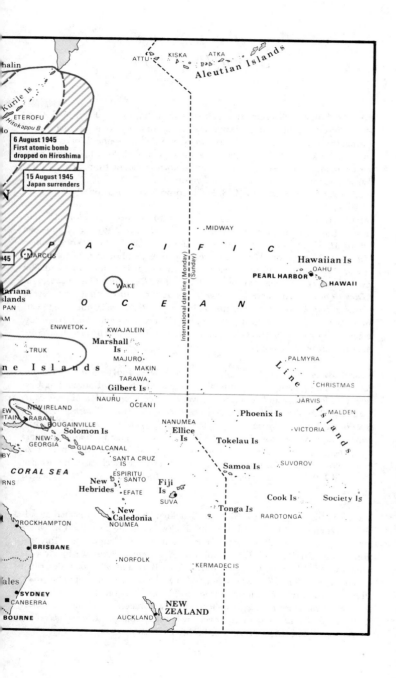

ATTU KISKA ATKA
Aleutian Islands

Sahalin

Kurile Is
ETEROFU
Hitokappu B

**6 August 1945**
**First atomic bomb**
**dropped on Hiroshima**

**15 August 1945**
**Japan surrenders**

· MIDWAY

1945  MARCUS

P        A        C        I        F        I        ·        C

WAKE

Hawaiian Is
OAHU
**PEARL HARBOR**  ⌂**HAWAII**

ariana
slands
PAN
AM

O        C        E        A        N

ENIWETOK·        KWAJALEIN

**Marshall**
**Is**
MAJURO·
MAKIN
·TRUK
TARAWA
**Gilbert Is**
NAURU        OCEAN I

PALMYRA
CHRISTMAS

L i n e   I s l a n d s

ne  Islands

JARVIS

NEW IRELAND
TAIN RABAUL
BOUGAINVILLE
**Solomon Is**
NEW
GEORGIA   GUADALCANAL
SANTA CRUZ
IS
ESPIRITU
**New**   SANTO
**Hebrides**  ·EFATE

**Phoenix Is**        ·MALDEN
NANUMEA
**Ellice**           ·VICTORIA
**Is**
**Tokelau Is**

SUVOROV

CORAL SEA

RNS

Fiji
Is
SUVA

**Samoa Is**

**Cook Is**        Society Is

**New**
**Caledonia**
NOUMEA

·**Tonga Is**
RAROTONGA

ROCKHAMPTON

·NORFOLK

·KERMADEC IS

**BRISBANE**

ales
**SYDNEY**
CANBERRA

**BOURNE**

AUCKLAND

**NEW**
**ZEALAND**

International date line (Monday)
(Sunday)

# Biographical Notes

**PHELPS ADAMS** (December 14, 1902–January 13, 1991)  Born in Boston, Massachusetts. Educated at University of Colorado, Columbia School of Journalism, London School of Economics, and the Sorbonne. Worked briefly for New York *Herald* before joining staff of New York *Sun*, becoming a reporter in 1926 and serving as Washington correspondent from 1928 to 1950. War correspondent aboard U.S.S. *Enterprise*, April–May 1945. Worked as public relations executive for U.S. Steel Corporation, 1950–67.

**JAMES AGEE** (November 27, 1909–May 15, 1955)  Born in Knoxville, Tennessee. Educated at Harvard. Staff writer for *Fortune*, 1932–37. Published *Permit Me Voyage* (1934), a poetry collection, and *Let Us Now Praise Famous Men* (1941), report on Alabama sharecroppers with photographs by Walker Evans. Wrote book and film reviews and feature articles for *Time* and film reviews for *The Nation*. Wrote screenplays for *The Quiet One* (1949), *The African Queen* (1951), and *The Night of the Hunter* (1955); published novella *The Morning Watch* (1951). His novel *A Death in the Family*, published posthumously in 1957, won the Pulitzer Prize. Film reviews and screenplays collected in *Agee on Film* (1958–60), and correspondence in *The Letters of James Agee to Father Flye* (1962).

**SUSAN B. ANTHONY II** (July 26, 1916–July 8, 1991)  Born in Easton, Pennsylvania (great-niece of suffragist Susan B. Anthony). Educated at University of Rochester and American University. Reporter for *Washington Star*, 1942–43. Published *Out of the Kitchen—Into the War: Women's Winning Role in the Nation's Drama* in 1943, followed by *Women During the War and After* (1945). Wrote for *Key West Citizen* (1950–53) and *Jamaica Gleaner* (1956–60). In later years, active in organizing alcoholism treatment programs; converted to Roman Catholicism and served as Eucharistic minister in Deerfield Beach, Florida. Her autobiography, *The Ghost in My Life*, appeared in 1971.

**JACK BELDEN** (1910–89)  Born in Brooklyn, New York. Educated at Adelphi Academy and Colgate University. Following graduation lived in China for ten years, eventually becoming correspondent for United Press, International News Service, and *Time*; published *New Fourth Army* (1938). Accompanied General Joseph Stilwell on retreat from Burma in May 1942, described in *Retreat with Stilwell* (1942). Wounded at Salerno, Italy, in September 1943; after months of rehabilitation, returned to Europe to cover the final phases of the war. *Still Time to Die*, a collection of war pieces, published in 1944. Returned to China in 1946 to cover civil war; published *China Shakes the World* (1949). Spent last decades of his life in Paris.

WALTER BERNSTEIN (August 20, 1919–  )  Born in Brooklyn, New York. Educated at Dartmouth. Wrote for *The New Yorker* and *Yank*, publishing accounts of army training camps and later covering the war in Italy; in Yugoslavia in early 1944 met and interviewed Tito. In Hollywood, worked on screenplay of *Kiss the Blood Off My Hands* (1948); active in writing scripts for live television; blacklisted during 1950s. Later screenwriting credits include *That Kind of Woman* (1959), *Heller in Pink Tights* (1960), *Paris Blues* (1961), *Fail Safe* (1964), *The Train* (1964), *The Money Trap* (1966), *The Molly Maguires* (1970), *The Front* (1976), *Semi-Tough* (1977), *Yanks* (1978), and *The House on Carroll Street* (1988).

HOMER BIGART (October 25, 1907–April 16, 1991)  Born in Hawley, Pennsylvania. Educated Carnegie Institute of Technology and New York University. Began to work for New York *Herald Tribune* as copyboy in 1929; became reporter in 1933. Traveled to Europe as war correspondent in 1942, moving to Pacific theater in autumn 1944. Won Pulitzer Prize in 1950 for coverage of Korean War (in Korea, intense professional rivalry with fellow *Tribune* correspondent Marguerite Higgins became famous among journalists). Left *Tribune* for *The New York Times* in 1955. In later years covered the Middle East, the trial of Nazi war criminal Adolf Eichmann, and the Vietnam War. Writings collected posthumously in *Forward Positions: The War Correspondence of Homer Bigart* (1992).

HOWARD BRODIE (November 28, 1915–  )  Born in Oakland, California. Educated at Art Institute of San Francisco, Art Students League, New York, and University of Ghana (Accra). Staff artist for *Life*, *Yank*, *Collier's*, Associated Press, and (from 1969 to 1989) for CBS News. As sketch artist, covered World War II, the Korean War, the Vietnam War, and many important trials and public hearings, including those of Jack Ruby, James Earl Ray, Sirhan Sirhan, Lt. William Calley, Charles Manson, the Chicago Seven, and the Watergate conspirators. A portfolio of his art, *Howard Brodie's War Drawings*, was published in 1963.

JOHN H. CRIDER (February 26, 1906–July 7, 1966)  Born in Mount Vernon, New York. Educated at Columbia School of Journalism. After graduation worked for *The New York Times*. Worked briefly as economic correspondent for *Time* in 1942 before rejoining the *Times*. Published *The Bureaucrat* (1944). In 1946, appointed editor-in-chief of *Boston Herald*; received Pulitzer Prize in 1949 for economic reporting. Dismissed in 1951 after internal dispute over his editorial attacks on Senator Robert A. Taft. Later worked for CBS, *Life*, and *Barron's Weekly*, as diplomatic correspondent in London for International News Service, for Committee for Economic Development, and for Morgan Guaranty Trust Company (1964–66).

ED CUNNINGHAM (1913–84)  Staff correspondent for *Yank*, 1942–45; served in China-Burma-India theater under General Joseph Stilwell, also in

Middle East and North Africa; covered Ardennes battle, 1944–45. Later worked as editor for *Pic* and *Liberty* magazines, and as promotion director for Celanese Corporation. Author of *Your Career: How to Choose a Profession and How to Prepare For It* (1949) and *Guide to Earning a Living* (1955).

**BILL DAVIDSON** (March 4, 1918–   )  Born in Jersey City, New Jersey. Educated at New York University. Correspondent for *Yank*; later worked as writer and editor for *Collier's* (1946–56), *Look* (1956–61), and *The Saturday Evening Post* (1961–69). From 1971 he was a contributing editor to *TV Guide*. Books include *The Real and the Unreal* (1961), *The Crickets All Look Alike* (1962), *Indict and Convict: The Inside Story of a Prosecutor and His Staff in Action* (1971), *Cut Off: Behind Enemy Lines in the Battle of the Bulge with Two Small Children, Ernest Hemingway, and Other Misanthropes* (1972), *Spencer Tracy: Tragic Idol* (1987), and *Jane Fonda: An Intimate Biography* (1990); co-authored autobiographies of Sid Caesar and Danny Thomas.

**PEGGY HULL DEUELL** (December 30, 1889–June 19, 1967)  Born Henrietta Eleanor Goodnough in Bennington, Kansas. Worked from age 16 at Junction City (Kansas) *Sentinel* (1905–8), then at *Denver Republican, Honolulu Evening Bulletin, Minneapolis Tribune,* and *Cleveland Plain Dealer* (for whom she covered U.S. army expedition against Pancho Villa in 1916). Married to reporter George C. Hull, 1910–14. Reported on American training camps in France during World War I for *El Paso Morning-Times* and *Chicago Tribune*; forced to return to U.S. because of lack of accreditation as war correspondent. Traveled to Siberia in 1918 to cover American military intervention in Russia for Newspaper Enterprise Association. Between the wars lived at various times in Paris, Shanghai, and New York, working as freelance reporter; covered Japanese attack on Shanghai in 1932 for *New York Daily News*; married to *Daily News* managing editor Harvey Vail Dueull, 1933–39. Traveled in 1943 to Pacific theater for *Cleveland Plain Dealer*. Retired to Carmel Valley, California, after the war.

**JANET FLANNER** (March 13, 1892–November 7, 1978)  Born in Indianapolis, Indiana. Studied for two years at University of Chicago (dismissed for exerting "rebellious influence"). Served as film critic for *Indianapolis Star*; active in support of woman suffrage; worked at girls' reformatory in Pennsylvania. Settled in Paris in 1922, living for 18 years at Hotel Saint-Germain-des-Pres; under pen name "Genêt," became Paris correspondent of *The New Yorker* from its founding in 1925. *The Cubical City*, a novel, appeared in 1926. Returned to U.S. in October 1939. *New Yorker* pieces collected in *An American in Paris* (1940) and *Pétain: The Old Man of France* (1944); translated two novels by Colette, *Chéri* (1929) and *Claudine at School* (1930). Returned to Paris in November 1944; went to Germany, reporting from Cologne and Buchenwald. Continued "Letter from Paris" for *The New Yorker* for 30 years. Writings collected in *Men and Monuments* (1957), *Paris Journal: 1944–1965* (1965), *Paris Journal: 1965–1971* (1971), *Paris Was Yesterday, 1925–1930* (1971), and

*London Was Yesterday, 1934–1939* (1975), along with the posthumous volumes *Janet Flanner's World: Uncollected Writings, 1932–1975* (1979) and *Darlinghissima: Letters to a Friend* (1985). Died in New York.

MARTHA GELLHORN (November 1908–  ) Born in St. Louis, Missouri. Educated at Bryn Mawr. Worked in New York for *The New Republic* and in Albany as a reporter for *Times Union*. Traveled in Europe and around the U.S. in early 1930s, often with French writer Bertrand de Jouvenel. First novel, *What Mad Pursuit*, published 1934. Worked as field investigator for Federal Emergency Relief Administration; dined at White House with the Roosevelts, forming lifelong friendship with Eleanor Roosevelt. *The Trouble I've Seen*, collection of short stories based on relief work, published 1936. On trip to Key West in December 1936 met Ernest Hemingway and traveled with him in Spain, March–May 1937; worked in field hospitals and visited Loyalist fronts; account of fighting published in *Collier's*, to which she became a regular contributor. Returned three more times to Spain in 1938, and also reported from England and Czechoslovakia. Lived with Hemingway in Cuba for much of 1939–40, writing novel *A Stricken Field* (1940) and story collection *The Heart of Another* (1941). Covered Soviet-Finnish War, November–December 1939. Married Hemingway in November 1940, and traveled to Asia in February 1941, spending several months in China with him and traveling on alone to Java and Singapore. Covered war in Europe, October 1943–February 1944 and May 1944–May 1945. Published novel *Liana* (1944). Marriage to Hemingway ended in 1945. Collaborated with Virginia Cowles on play *Love Goes to Press* (1946), comedy about war correspondents. Reported on Indonesian rebellion against the Dutch and on Nuremberg war crimes trials. In 1947 launched attack on House Un-American Activities Committee. Published novels *The Wine of Astonishment* (1948; republished as *Point of No Return*), *His Own Man* (1961), and *The Lowest Trees Have Tops* (1967), story collections *The Honeyed Peace* (1953), *Two by Two* (1958), *Pretty Tales for Tired People* (1965), and *The Weather in Africa* (1981), and memoir *Travels with Myself and Another* (1978). Married to T. S. Matthews, 1954–63. Settled in England. War reporting collected in *The Face of War* (1959; revised edition, 1987). Reported on Eastern Europe and the Middle East; traveled to Vietnam as correspondent for *The Guardian* in 1966, and to Israel in 1967 during Six-Day War; reported on El Salvador and Nicaragua during 1980s.

BRENDAN GILL (October 4, 1914–  ) Born in Hartford, Connecticut. Educated at Yale. Contributor to *The New Yorker* since 1936, writing frequently on film and theater. During World War II wrote on aspects of the American home front. In later years active in campaign to preserve urban landmarks in New York City. Books include *The Trouble of One House* (1950), *The Day the Money Stopped* (1957), *Tallulah* (1972), *Ways of Loving* (1974), *Here at The New Yorker* (1978), *A Fair Land to Build In* (1984), *Many Masks: A Life of Frank Lloyd Wright* (1987), and *A New York Life* (1990).

PHILIP HAMBURGER (July 2, 1914–    ) Born 1914, in Wheeling, West Virginia. Educated at Johns Hopkins and Columbia School of Journalism. Staff member of *The New Yorker* from 1939, writing profiles and contributing to regular features, including "Talk of the Town" and "Notes for a Gazetteer." During leave of absence, 1941–43, worked for Office of Facts and Figures and Office of War Information. Books include *The Oblong Blur and Other Odysseys* (1949), *J.P. Marquand, Esq.* (1952), *Mayor Watching and Other Pleasures* (1958), *Our Man Stanley* (1963), *An American Notebook* (1965), and *Curious World: A New Yorker at Large* (1987).

ERNEST HEMINGWAY (July 21, 1899–July 2, 1961) Born in Oak Park, Illinois. Reporter for *Kansas City Star*. Served as ambulance driver with Italian army in World War I and was severely wounded. Traveled to France in 1921 as foreign correspondent for *Toronto Star*. First collection of stories, *In Our Time*, appeared in 1925, followed by novels *The Torrents of Spring* and *The Sun Also Rises* in 1926. Returned to U.S. in 1928, settling in Key West in 1930. Subsequent volumes of fiction include *Men Without Women* (1927), *A Farewell to Arms* (1929), *Winner Take Nothing* (1933), and *To Have and Have Not* (1937); also published *Death in the Afternoon* (1932), a study of bullfighting, and *The Green Hills of Africa* (1935), an account of big-game hunting. Traveled to Spain with Martha Gellhorn, covering Spanish Civil War as correspondent for North American Newspaper Alliance, 1936–37, an experience that formed the basis for *For Whom the Bell Tolls* (1940). With Gellhorn (who became his third wife in 1940), settled in Cuba, 1939–40; traveled with her to China as correspondent for *PM*. Went to London in May 1944 as war correspondent for *Collier's*, filing stories on D-Day invasion, liberation of Paris, and entry of American forces into Germany. Became subject of Army inquiry for carrying weapons and other violations of Geneva Convention rules for war correspondents, but was able to avoid censure. Married former war correspondent Mary Welsh in 1946. In postwar period published *Across the River and Into the Trees* (1950), a novel incorporating many of his World War II experiences, and *The Old Man and the Sea* (1952).

JOHN HERSEY (June 17, 1914–March 24, 1993) Born in Tientsin, China, son of American missionaries; spent first ten years of life in China. Educated at Yale and Cambridge. Worked for Sinclair Lewis as secretary in 1937. Began to work for *Time* in 1937; traveled to Asia as correspondent in 1939; went to England in 1942 to cover war. Covered Southwest Pacific and Italy for *Time* and *Life*, and published three nonfiction books about the war: *Men on Bataan* (1942), *Into the Valley* (1943), and *Hiroshima* (1946). His novel *A Bell for Adano*, about American occupation of Sicily, won Pulitzer Prize for 1944. Master of Pierson College at Yale, 1965–70. Later novels include *The Wall* (1950), *The Marmot Drive* (1953), *A Single Pebble* (1956), *The War Lover* (1959), *The Child Buyer* (1960), *Too Far to Walk* (1966), *Under the Eye of the Storm* (1967), and *The Call* (1985); also published nonfiction including *The Algiers Motel Incident* (1968), *Letter to the Alumni* (1970), and *The President* (1975).

MARGUERITE HIGGINS (September 3, 1920–January 3, 1966) Born in Hong Kong; grew up in Oakland, California. Educated at University of California and Columbia School of Journalism. Correspondent for New York *Herald Tribune* from 1942. Went to France as war correspondent in early 1945; traveled into southern Germany in April, and was present at liberation of Dachau and Buchenwald. Served as head of *Tribune*'s Berlin bureau, 1945–50; appointed head of Tokyo bureau in 1950. During Korean War, covered battle of Inchon, winning Pulitzer Prize in 1951; reporting collected in *War in Korea* (1951). In 1954 covered French defeat in Vietnam. Published *News Is a Singular Thing*, a memoir, and *Red Plush and Black Bread*, an account of the Soviet Union, in 1955. Left *Tribune* in 1963 to write for New York *Newsday*. With Peter Lisagor wrote *Overtime in Heaven: Adventures in the Foreign Service* (1964). Traveled ten times to Vietnam between 1953 and 1965, and collected writings on the war in *Saigon Summary* (1964) and *Our Vietnam Nightmare* (1965). In Vietnam contracted leishmaniasis, a rare tropical disease, and died in Washington, D.C.

RICHARD C. HOTTELET (September 22, 1917–  ) Born in Brooklyn, New York. Educated at Brooklyn College and Friedrich-Wilhelms Universität, Berlin. Foreign correspondent for United Press, 1938–42; imprisoned by the Gestapo, March–July 1941, on charges of spying. Following release, worked in London for Office of War Information, 1942–44. Was a broadcaster for CBS, 1944–56, and a CBS correspondent in New York from 1956.

VIRGINIA IRWIN (June 29, 1908–August 19, 1980) Born in Quincy, Illinois. Educated at Lindenwood College (St. Charles, Missouri) and Gem City Business College (Quincy, Illinois). Began working for St. Louis *Post-Dispatch* in 1932, becoming feature writer for the paper's magazine supplement. After outbreak of World War II, focused on home front, including 11-part series on women in war industries; denied assignment as war correspondent, went to Europe to work for Red Cross. Received accreditation from War Department just before D-Day, and arrived in France in July 1944; covered war in France, Belgium, Holland, Luxemburg, and Germany. In late April 1945, without official permission, drove to Berlin with Boston *Traveler* correspondent Andrew Tully, witnessing final days of fighting; military authorities delayed publication of story and stripped her of credentials as war correspondent. Worked at New York bureau of *Post-Dispatch*, 1946–60.

EDWARD KENNEDY (1905–63) Born in Brooklyn, New York. Studied architecture at Carnegie Tech. Worked for Cannonsburg (Pennsylvania) *Daily Notes* and on newspapers in New York, New Jersey, and Washington, D.C. Became staff member of Paris edition of *Herald Tribune* in 1931. Subsequently returned to U.S. and worked for *Newark Ledger*. Joined Associated Press in 1932; assigned to Paris bureau, 1934. Covered Spanish Civil War and developments in Balkans and Middle East. Accompanied General Archibald Wavell to Crete in 1940; was only American to cover British capture of

Tobruk; subsequently reported on Italian campaign, including Anzio. After breaking a pledge to delay reporting the German surrender for 24 hours, stripped of credentials as war correspondent and dismissed by Associated Press. Became managing editor of Santa Barbara (California) *Press* in 1946, and in 1949 joined *Monterey Peninsula Herald*.

HELEN KIRKPATRICK (1909–   ) Born in Rochester, New York. Educated at Smith College and University of Geneva. Worked for Foreign Policy Association in Geneva as editor and writer for *Geneva Research Bulletin*. Wrote for British publications including *Manchester Guardian, London News Chronicle, London Daily Telegraph*; edited *Whitehall News*; foreign correspondent in Geneva for New York *Herald Tribune*. Published *This Terrible Peace* (1938) and *Under the British Umbrella: What the English Are and How They Go to War* (1939). Foreign correspondent for *Chicago Daily News* in London, 1939-44. Traveled with Free French forces; covered Normandy advance and liberation of Paris, then became *Daily News* Paris bureau chief before going into Germany in April 1945. In 1946 became foreign correspondent for New York *Post*. As head of information division of Economical Cooperation Administration in Paris, 1949–51, involved in implementation of Marshall Plan. Later served as adviser to Dean Acheson in State Department's European Affairs Bureau and as assistant to the president of Smith College, 1953–55.

WILLIAM L. LAURENCE (March 7, 1888–March 19, 1977) Born in Salantai, Lithuania, son of Lipman and Sarah Siew. Came to U.S. in 1905, adopting name Laurence; studied at Harvard and Boston University. Became U.S. citizen in 1913; after serving in World War I studied at University of Besançon in France. Wrote for New York *World* from 1926, and in 1930 moved to *The New York Times*, specializing in science reporting. Won Pulitzer Prize for 1936. In front-page story published in the *Times* in May 1940, predicted development of atomic energy. Attached to the Manhattan Project, witnessed secret Alamogordo atomic test explosion on July 16, 1945, and accompanied bombing mission over Nagasaki, winning a second Pulitzer Prize in 1946. Science editor of the *Times*, 1956–64. Author of *Dawn Over Zero: The Story of the Atomic Bomb* (1946), *The Hell Bomb* (1951), and *Men and Atoms* (1959). Died in Majorca.

W. H. LAWRENCE (1916–72) Born William H. Lawrence in Lincoln, Nebraska. Began newspaper work while still in high school; briefly attended University of Nebraska. After working for *Lincoln Star, Omaha World-Herald*, and Associated Press, joined United Press in Chicago in 1936. Worked as labor reporter, covering General Motors strike of 1936–37, before transferring to Washington bureau. Joined *The New York Times* in 1941. Stationed in Moscow in 1943; visited site of Babi Yar massacre in Kiev and Majdanek extermination camp near Lublin, Poland. Subsequently covered war on Guam and Okinawa and flew on B-29 raids over Japan. Reported postwar developments in Eastern Europe and Latin America, and covered the Korean

War. Served as Washington correspondent of the *Times* until 1961, when he joined ABC as White House correspondent. Died of heart attack while covering New Hampshire presidential primary. A memoir, *Six Presidents, Too Many Wars*, published posthumously in 1972.

TOM LEA (July 11, 1907–  ) Born in El Paso, Texas. Studied at Art Institute of Chicago. Worked as mural painter and commercial artist in Chicago (1926–33), New Mexico (1933–35), and El Paso from 1936. War correspondent for *Life*, 1941–46; combat experiences recounted in *A Grizzly from the Coral Sea* (1944) and *Peleliu Landing* (1945). Author of *The Brave Bulls* (1949), *The Wonderful Country* (1952), *The King Ranch* (1957), *The Primal Yoke* (1960), *The Hands of Cantu* (1964), *A Picture Gallery* (1968), *In the Crucible of the Sun* (1974), and *The Southwest: It's Where I Live* (1992).

A. J. LIEBLING (October 18, 1904–December 21, 1963) Born Abbott Joseph Liebling in New York City. Educated at Dartmouth and Columbia School of Journalism. Worked for *The New York Times* as copyreader, 1925–26, and briefly for Providence (R.I.) *Journal* as reporter. Sailed to Europe in summer 1926; studied French medieval literature at Sorbonne. Returned to Providence in autumn 1927, continuing to write for *Journal*. Moved to New York and wrote for New York *World*, 1930–31, and *World-Telegram*, 1931–35. Married Ann Quinn in 1934, despite knowing that she was schizophrenic (in the course of their marriage she was hospitalized many times). Joined staff of *The New Yorker* in 1935; early pieces collected in *Back Where I Came From* (1938) and *The Telephone Booth Indian* (1942). Flew to Europe in October 1939 to cover war; remained in Paris until June 10, 1940; returned to U.S. by way of Lisbon. Flew to Britain in July 1941 to cover war; after briefly returning to U.S. in early 1942, sailed to Algeria in November. Followed war on Tunisian front, January–May 1943. Early war pieces collected in *The Road Back to Paris* (1944). Covered D-Day invasion and afterwards spent two months in Normandy and Brittany, June–August, before returning to U.S. Began writing column "The Wayward Press" in 1945. Collected material from French resistance newspapers for *La République du Silence* (1946). Criticized House Un-American Activities Committee and became friend of Alger Hiss. Divorced from Ann Quinn; married Lucille Spectorsky in 1949; following dissolution of second marriage, married novelist Jean Stafford in 1959. Later books include *The Wayward Pressman* (1947), *Mink and Red Herring: The Wayward Pressman's Casebook* (1949), *Chicago: The Second City* (1952), *The Honest Rainmaker: The Life and Times of Colonel John R. Stingo* (1953), *The Sweet Science* (1956), *Normandy Revisited* (1958), *The Press* (1961), *The Earl of Louisiana* (1961), and *Between Meals: An Appetite for Paris* (1962). Wartime articles collected posthumously in *Mollie & Other War Pieces* (1964).

ANNE O'HARE MCCORMICK (May 16, 1880–May 29, 1954) Born Elizabeth O'Hare in Wakefield, Yorkshire, England; family moved to U.S. shortly after her birth, settling in Columbus, Ohio. Graduated St. Mary of the

Springs Academy in Columbus. After father deserted family, moved with mother and siblings to Cleveland. Became associate editor of religious publication *Catholic Universe Bulletin*. Married Francis McCormick in 1910 and traveled with him frequently to Europe; contributed articles and poetry to many periodicals; became regular correspondent for *The New York Times* in 1922, contributing column "In Europe" (later "Abroad"). As freelancer covering rise of fascism in Italy, did important early interview with Mussolini; met with many other world leaders including Stalin, Hitler, and Churchill. Wrote study of Soviet Union, *The Hammer and the Scythe* (1928). Became first woman member of *Times* editorial staff in 1936; won Pulitzer Prize the following year. During World War II served on Advisory Committee on Post-War Foreign Policy; was a delegate to UNESCO conferences in 1946 and 1948. Journalism collected in *The World at Home* (1956) and *Vatican Journal, 1921–1954* (1957).

JOHN P. MARQUAND   (November 10, 1893–July 16, 1960)   Born in Wilmington, Delaware. Educated at Harvard. Worked as reporter for *Boston Daily Evening Transcript*, 1914–16. Served in France in World War I as artillery officer, April–November 1918. After the war worked briefly for New York *Tribune* and as advertising copywriter for J. Walter Thompson agency. Contributed short fiction regularly to *Ladies' Home Journal*, *The Saturday Evening Post*, and other popular magazines. His early novels included *The Unspeakable Gentleman* (1922), *The Black Cargo* (1925), *Warning Hill* (1930), *Ming Yellow* (1930), and series of novels about Japanese detective Mr. Moto. Won Pulitzer Prize in 1937 for *The Late George Apley*. During World War II served as intelligence director for secret biological warfare project at Camp Detrick, Maryland. Later works include *Wickford Point* (1939), *H. M. Pulham, Esq.* (1941), *So Little Time* (1943), *B. F.'s Daughter* (1946), *Point of No Return* (1949), *Sincerely, Willis Wayde* (1955), *Women and Thomas Harrow* (1958), *Life at Happy Knoll* (1957), and *Timothy Dexter Revisited* (1960). Journalism and other writings collected in *Thirty Years* (1954).

BILL MAULDIN   (October 29, 1921–   )   Born in Mountain Park, New Mexico. Attended high school in Phoenix, Arizona; studied at Chicago Academy of Fine Arts. Served with 45th Infantry Division and as staff cartoonist for *Stars and Stripes*, 1940–45; participated in campaigns in Italy and France. Cartoons collected in *Star Spangled Banter* (1941), *Sicily Sketch Book* (1943), *Mud, Mules and Mountains* (1943), and *This Damn Tree Leaks* (1945); won Pulitzer Prize as cartoonist in 1945. *Up Front*, collection of cartoons with linking text, became a bestseller in 1945. After the war, cartoonist for St. Louis *Post-Dispatch* until 1962, and thereafter for *Chicago Sun-Times*. Appeared as actor in films *Teresa* (1950) and *The Red Badge of Courage* (1950). Received second Pulitzer Prize in 1959. Later publications include *Back Home* (1945), *A Sort of a Saga* (1949), *Bill Mauldin's Army* (1951), *Bill Mauldin in Korea* (1952), *What's Got Your Back Up?* (1961), *I've Decided I Want My Seat Back* (1965), *Mud and Guts* (1978), and *Let's*

*Declare Ourselves Winners and Get the Hell Out* (1985); *The Brass Ring*, an autobiography, appeared in 1971.

LEE MILLER (April 23, 1907–July 27, 1977)  Born Elizabeth Miller in Poughkeepsie, New York. Studied at theater school in Paris, 1925–26. In 1927 met Condé Nast and became model for *Vogue*; worked as model for photographers including Edward Steichen and Arnold Genthe. Studied at Art Students League in New York. Returned to France in 1929 and lived with Surrealist artist and photographer Man Ray; established her own photography studio; starred in Jean Cocteau's film *Le Sang d'un poète* (*The Blood of a Poet*, 1930). Opened studio in New York in 1932 and took portraits of many artists and celebrities including Virgil Thompson, Joseph Cornell, and Gertrude Lawrence. Married wealthy Egyptian Aziz Eloui in 1934; lived with him for three years in Cairo and Alexandria. Returned to Paris in summer of 1937; met Roland Penrose, English painter and writer, and traveled with him throughout Europe. Settled with Penrose in London after outbreak of war in 1939. Joined staff of *Vogue*; in addition to fashion photography, took pictures of London Blitz and British war effort; photographs collected in *Grim Glory: Pictures of Britain Under Fire* (1940) and *Wrens in Camera* (1942). In June 1944 traveled to Normandy as war correspondent for *Vogue*; was present at siege of St. Malo and liberation of Paris; covered fighting in Luxemburg and Alsace and advance of Allies into Germany. Married Ronald Penrose in 1947. Photographs included in exhibit *The Family of Man* in 1955.

MACK MORRISS (November 11, 1919–February 18, 1976)  Born in Baltimore, Maryland; lifelong resident of Elizabethton, Tennessee. Staff writer for *Yank*, May 1942–July 1945; covered campaigns on Guadalcanal and New Georgia in the Solomons, Siegfried Line and Huertgen Forest in the European theater, and was among first American correspondents to enter Berlin after its fall in May 1945 in defiance of ban by Allied authorities. After the war worked briefly for *Life* and as freelance writer, 1946–51; published war novel *The Proving Ground* (1951). Editor, Elizabethton *Star*, 1951–55; newscaster and later manager of radio station WBEJ, 1956–76. Mayor of Elizabethton, 1966–69.

EDWARD R. MURROW (April 25, 1908–April 27, 1965)  Born Egbert Roscoe Murrow in Greensboro, North Carolina. Educated at Washington State College. President of National Student Federation of America (1930–31); as assistant director of Institute of International Education, 1932–34, participated in resettlement of German scholars fleeing Nazism. Became director of talks and educational programs for CBS in 1935, and in 1937 became head of CBS European bureau in London; assembled staff that eventually included William L. Shirer, Howard K. Smith, Charles Collingwood, Larry Lesueur, Richard C. Hottelet, and Cecil Brown. Became well known for broadcasts during London Blitz; broadcasts collected in *This Is London*

(1941). Continued to report on war from Europe and North Africa. Became CBS vice-president for news programs in 1946. Produced radio program *Hear It Now*, which moved to television as *See It Now* (1951–58); also developed interview program *Person-to-Person* (1953–59). Critical television report on Senator Joseph McCarthy in 1954 played significant role in undermining McCarthy's influence. Became head of U.S. Information Agency in 1961, resigning in 1964 due to illness.

CARL MYDANS  (May 20, 1907–   )   Born in Boston, Massachusetts. Educated at Boston University. Photographer for Farm Security Administration in 1935; subsequently on staff of *Life* (1936–72). Married Shelley Smith in 1938, collaborating with her on coverage of events in Europe and Asia; interned with her by Japanese in January 1942 for 22 months, first in the Philippines and later in Shanghai; repatriated in December 1943 on *Gripsholm*. Covered war in Italy and France; joined MacArthur's forces for invasion of Luzon in January 1945. After the war, served as *Time-Life* bureau chief in Tokyo. Author of *More Than Meets the Eye* (1959) and *The Violent Peace* (with Shelley Mydans, 1968). Photographic work collected in *China: A Visual Adventure* (1979) and *Carl Mydans: Photo-Journalist* (1985).

SHELLEY MYDANS  (May 20, 1915–   )   Born Shelley Smith in Palo Alto, California. Reporter for *Literary Digest*. Became researcher for newly founded *Life* in 1936; married *Life* photographer Carl Mydans in 1938. With him, traveled to Europe to cover war; at end of 1940 the Mydans went to China to cover Sino-Japanese War. While in the Philippines to report on war preparations in Asia, trapped in Manila during Japanese invasion. Interned in January 1942 with other Americans for eight months in Manila, then transferred to prison camp in Shanghai; repatriated in December 1943. Published novel *The Open City* (1945), based on internment experience. Filed stories from Guam before rejoining Carl in Philippines before Japanese surrender. After war worked as *Time* broadcaster and correspondent in Tokyo. Author with Carl Mydans of *The Violent Peace* (1968); also wrote historical novels *Thomas* (1965) and *Vermilion Bridge* (1980).

MINÉ OKUBO  (June 27, 1912–   )   Born in Riverdale, California. Educated at Riverside Junior College and University of California at Berkeley. Received art fellowship and traveled in Europe, 1938–39. Worked as artist for Federal Arts Program; received prizes and exhibited work in San Francisco in 1940 and 1941. Interned in 1942 at Tanforan Relocation Camp in San Bruno, California; transferred later to Central Utah Relocation Camp, Topaz, Utah; helped found literary magazine *Trek* with other internees. Released from camp in March 1944 to accept job offer from *Fortune* in New York to illustrate special issue on Japan; remained in New York, working as illustrator and freelance graphic artist. Participated in 1945 in exhibit of drawings and paintings of Japanese relocation camps; published *Citizen 13660*, memoir of internment camps, in 1946. Testified in 1981 before government commission on wartime relocation. Major retrospectives of her work were held in Oakland in 1974, in New York in 1985, and in Boston in 1993.

**S. J. PERELMAN** (February 1, 1904–October 17, 1979) Born Sidney Joseph Perelman in Brooklyn, New York. Educated at Brown University. Published *Dawn Ginsbergh's Revenge* (1929) and *Parlor, Bedlam and Bath* (1930, with Quentin Reynolds). Contributed regularly to *The New Yorker* from 1931. Writings collected in *Strictly from Hunger* (1937), *Look Who's Talking* (1940), *The Dream Department* (1943), *Crazy Like a Fox* (1944), *Keep It Crisp* (1946), *Acres and Pains* (1946), *Westward Ha!* (1948), *Listen to the Mocking Bird* (1949), *The Swiss Family Perelman* (1950), *The Ill-Tempered Clavichord* (1953), *The Road to Miltown* (1957), *The Rising Gorge* (1961), *Chicken Inspector No. 23* (1966), *Baby, It's Cold Inside* (1970), *Vinegar Puss* (1975), and *Eastward Ha!* (1977). Also wrote film scripts and stage plays including *One Touch of Venus* (1943, with Ogden Nash) and *The Beauty Part* (1962).

**ERNIE PYLE** (August 3, 1900–April 18, 1945) Born Ernest Taylor Pyle on farm near Dana, Indiana. Attended Indiana University but did not complete journalism degree. Worked briefly in early 1923 as reporter for a local paper, *The La Porte Herald*, then joined the Scripps-Howard *Washington Daily News*. In 1926, with wife, Geraldine Siebolds, traveled around the U.S.; worked for a short time in New York for the *Evening World* before returning to *Washington Daily News* in 1927 as telegraph editor. Wrote aviation column and became aviation editor for Scripps-Howard chain, 1928–32. Managing editor of *Daily News*, 1932–35. In 1935 began six-day-a-week human interest column based on regular travels across U.S. and to Alaska, Hawaii, and Central and South America (prewar columns collected posthumously in *Home Country*, 1947). Went to England in November 1940 for three-month stay; columns collected in *Ernie Pyle in England* (1941). Divorced in July 1942; Geraldine committed to sanitarium shortly afterward for six-month stay. Flew to England in June 1942 to cover training of American troops. Accompanied Allied troops to Algeria in November 1942; went to Tunisian front in January 1943. Remarried to Geraldine by proxy in March 1943. Covered Tunisian war with 1st Infantry Division until campaign's end in mid-May; Tunisian dispatches collected in *Here Is Your War* (1943). Covered Sicilian campaign (July–August 1943) and returned to U.S. in September; Geraldine hospitalized again at end of visit. Returned to Italy in November; at Anzio in March 1944, narrowly escaped death from a German bomb. Won Pulitzer Prize for 1943. Went to France immediately after D-Day invasion. Featured in *Time* cover story in July. Caught in accidental bombing of U.S. troops by American aircraft in Normandy on July 25, 1944. *Brave Men*, another compilation of columns, published 1944. Returned to U.S. in September and was hailed by press and public. Geraldine made suicide attempt during visit. Involved in discussions with makers of *The Story of G.I. Joe*, film based on his columns. In January 1945 sailed to Hawaii to cover Pacific theater; boarded aircraft carrier U.S.S. *Cabot*, sailing to Marianas and then proceeding to Okinawa with 1st Marine Division. Killed by Japanese sniper on Ie Shima, small island near Okinawa. Final columns collected in *Last Chapter* (1946).

ERIC SEVAREID   (November 26, 1912–July 9, 1992)   Born Arnold Eric Sevareid in Velva, North Dakota. Educated at University of Minnesota. Made 2,200-mile canoe journey from Minneapolis to Hudson Bay in 1930 (recounted experience in 1935 book *Canoeing with the Cree*). Worked as copyboy and later as reporter for Minneapolis newspapers (1931–36). Studied at London School of Economics. Reporter and city editor for Paris edition of *Herald Tribune* (1938–39) and night editor for United Press in Paris (1939). Became European correspondent for CBS in August 1939. Accompanied French army and air force in France and Belgium, 1939–40; later covered China-Burma-India theater, Italian campaign, and activities of Yugoslav partisans; landed with American forces in southern France and later crossed the Rhine with them into Germany. National correspondent for CBS, including regular commentaries on *CBS Evening News*, until he retired in 1977. Books include *Not So Wild a Dream* (1946), *In One Ear: 107 Snapshots of Men and Events* (1952), *Small Sounds in the Night* (1956), *This Is Eric Sevareid* (1964), *Politics and the Press* (1967), and *Edward R. Murrow* (1979).

IRWIN SHAW   (February 27, 1913–May 16, 1984)   Born in Brooklyn, New York. Educated at Brooklyn College. Became known at an early age for his short stories (collected in *Sailor Off the Bremen*, 1939, and *Welcome to the City*, 1941) and for plays including *Bury the Dead* (1936), *Siege* (1937), and *The Gentle People* (1939). In World War II, stationed in North Africa, Middle East, and western Europe; contributed to *Stars and Stripes* and *Yank*; assigned to Signal Corps film unit headed by director George Stevens. War novel *The Young Lions* (1948) was followed by many others including *The Troubled Air* (1951), *Lucy Crown* (1956), *Two Weeks in Another Town* (1960), *Rich Man, Poor Man* (1970), *Evening in Byzantium* (1973), *Nightwork* (1975), *The Top of the Hill* (1979), and *Acceptable Losses* (1981), along with further story collections including *Tip on a Dead Jockey* (1957) and *God Was Here But He Left Early* (1973).

ROBERT SHERROD   (February 8, 1909–February 14, 1994)   Born Thomas County, Georgia. Educated University of Georgia. Worked as reporter for *Atlanta Constitution*, Palm Beach (Fla.) *Daily News*, and other newspapers (1929–35). Correspondent and editor for *Time* and *Life* (1935–52). Began covering U.S. military in mid-1941; traveled with first convoys for Australia in February 1942, and covered Marine landings on Tarawa, Saipan, and Iwo Jima. Far East correspondent (1952–55) and editor (1955–64) at *The Saturday Evening Post*; vice-president of Curtis Publishing (1965–66). Author of *Tarawa: The Story of a Battle* (1944), *On to Westward: War in the Central Pacific* (1945), and *History of Marine Corps Aviation in World War II* (1952); contributed to *Life's Picture History of World War II* (1950) and *Apollo Expeditions to the Moon* (1975).

**I. F. STONE** (December 24, 1907–June 18, 1989)   Born Isidor Feinstein Stone in Philadelphia, Pennsylvania. Educated at University of Pennsylvania. Published *The Progress* in Haddonfield, New Jersey, in 1922. Worked as reporter in New Jersey and Philadelphia (1923–33) and for New York *Post* (1933–39). Associate editor (1938–40) and Washington editor (1940–46) of *The Nation*. Between 1942 and 1952 he was a reporter and columnist for various New York papers including *PM*, the *Star*, and the *Daily Compass*. Published *I. F. Stone's Bi-Weekly* (later *I. F. Stone's Weekly*) in Washington, D.C., 1953–71. Author of *The Court Disposes* (1937), *Business as Usual* (1941), *Underground to Palestine* (1946), *This Is Israel* (1948), *The Hidden History of the Korean War* (1952), *The Truman Era* (1953), *The Haunted Fifties* (1964), *In a Time of Torment* (1967), *The Killings at Kent State: How Murder Went Unpunished* (1970), *Polemics and Prophecies* (1971), *The Best of I. F. Stone's Weekly* (1973), and *The Trial of Socrates* (1988). Writings collected in six volumes as *A Nonconformist History of Our Times*, including volume devoted to World War II period, *The War Years, 1939–1945* (1988).

**VINCENT TUBBS** (September 25, 1915–February 1989)   Born in Dallas, Texas. Educated at Morehouse College and Atlanta University. Editor and publisher of *Macon Broadcast*, 1940–41; news editor, *Norfolk Journal and Guide*, 1942–43. From 1943 to 1947 he was foreign and war correspondent for *Baltimore Afro-American*, and was an editor of the paper until 1954. Subsequently worked as editor for *Ebony* (1954–55) and *Jet* (1955–59), before establishing successful career in Hollywood as film publicist. Elected president of Hollywood Publicists' Guild in 1967; press director for community relations at Warner Brothers, 1971–80.

**WILLIAM WALTON** (1909–94)   Born in Jacksonville, Illinois. Educated at Illinois College and University of Wisconsin. Worked for Associated Press in Chicago and New York from 1935 to 1940. Covered war news for *PM* (1940–42) and for *Time* and *Life* (1942–46); parachuted into Normandy at beginning of D-Day invasion, June 1944. Washington editor of *The New Republic*, 1946–49. Later worked as painter and freelance writer; served as chairman of Fine Arts Commission, 1963–71. Author of *The Evidence of Washington* (1968) and editor of *A Civil War Courtship: The Letters of Edwin Weller From Antietam to Atlanta* (1980).

**E. B. WHITE** (July 11, 1899–October 1, 1985)   Born Elwyn Brooks White in Mount Vernon, New York. Educated at Cornell University. Worked from 1921 as reporter and editor for the *Cornell Sun*, the United Press, and the *Seattle Times*; also worked as advertising copywriter. Became contributor and editor at *The New Yorker*, largely responsible for " Talk of the Town." Wrote monthly column "One Man's Meat" for *Harper's Magazine*, 1938–43. Lived with his wife Katharine on farm in Maine from 1938. Books include *Is Sex Necessary?* (with James Thurber, 1929), *Every Day Is Saturday* (1934), *The Fox of Peapack* (1938), *Quo Vadimus?* (1939), *One Man's Meat* (1942), *Stuart*

*Little* (1945), *The Wild Flag* (1946), *Here Is New York* (1949), *Charlotte's Web* (1952), *The Second Tree from the Corner* (1953), *The Points of My Compass* (1962), and *The Trumpet of the Swan* (1970); co-edited *A Subtreasury of American Humor* (1941). Awarded Presidential Medal of Freedom in 1963 and Pulitzer Prize special citation in 1978.

EVAN WYLIE (December 9, 1916– ) Born Evan McLeod Wylie in Dunellen, New Jersey. Educated University of Virginia. Staff editor for *Newsweek*, 1941–42. Staff writer for *Yank*, 1944–45. After war, contributed frequently to periodicals including *The Saturday Evening Post*, *Holiday*, *Collier's*, *Life*, and *The Reader's Digest*. Co-authored *Movin' On Up* (1966), autobiography of Mahalia Jackson; other books include *The Nine Months* (1971), a novel, and *A Guide to Voluntary Sterilization: The New Birth Control* (1972). With Jack Ruge, wrote play later adapted into film *Joe Butterfly* (1957); also wrote screenplays and television scripts. Contributing editor to *Yankee* since 1980.

# *Note on the Texts*

This volume collects newspaper and magazine articles, transcripts of radio broadcasts, and excerpts from books by American writers and reporters written between 1944 and 1946, and dealing with events connected with World War II and its aftermath in the period between February 1944 and August 1946. The texts chosen are the first published versions.

The following is a list of the sources of the texts included in this volume, listed alphabetically by author. For untitled pieces and book excerpts, a phrase selected from the text has been enclosed in quotation marks and used as a title. (In the case of articles from *Yank* and some newspapers, variant versions may exist in different editions.)

Phelps Adams. Attack on Carrier Bunker Hill: *The New York Sun*, June 28, 1945.

James Agee. "These Terrible Records of War": *The Nation*, March 24, 1945. "A Soldier Died Today": *Time*, April 23, 1945.

Susan B. Anthony II. Working at the Navy Yard: *The New Republic*, May 1, 1944.

Jack Belden. Retreat in Belgium: *Time*, January 1, 1945.

Walter Bernstein. Search for a Battle: *The New Yorker*, September 23, 1944.

Homer Bigart. Cassino, Once Thriving, Is Turned Into a Scene of Unrelieved Grimness: New York *Herald Tribune*, May 20, 1944. Japan Signs, Second World War Is Ended: New York *Herald Tribune*, September 2, 1945. A Month After the Atom Bomb: Hiroshima Still Can't Believe It: New York *Herald Tribune*, September 5, 1945.

Howard Brodie. Jump-Off: *Yank*, March 11, 1945 (Continental Edition); drawings from *Yank*, April 13, 1945.

John H. Crider. U.S. Board Bares Atrocity Details Told by Witnesses at Polish Camps: *The New York Times*, November 26, 1944.

Ed Cunningham. The Battle of the Bulge: *Yank*, March 2, 1945.

Bill Davidson. "Rommel—Count Your Men": *Yank*, September 29, 1944.

Peggy Hull Deuell. Death of Carrier Described: *Cleveland Plain Dealer*, December 7, 1944.

Janet Flanner (Genêt). Letter from Cologne: *The New Yorker*, March 31, 1945. "Let Us Weep For This Man" (originally published as "Letter from Paris"): *The New Yorker*, April 28, 1945. "A Sad Homecoming" (originally published as "Letter from Paris"): *The New Yorker*, May 5, 1945.

*Fortune*. Issei, Nisei, Kibei: *Fortune*, April 1944. Drawings by Miné Okubo.

Martha Gellhorn. The First Hospital Ship (originally published as "The Wounded Come Home"): *Collier's*, August 5, 1944. The Gothic Line (originally published as "Cracking the Gothic Line"): *Collier's*, October 28,

1944. The Battle of the Bulge: Gellhorn, *The Face of War* (New York: Simon & Schuster, 1959). Das Deutsches Volk (originally published as "We Were Never Nazis"): *Collier's*, May 26, 1945. The Russians (originally published as "The Russians' Invisible Wall"): *Collier's*, June 30, 1945. Dachau (originally published as "Dachau: Experimental Murder"): *Collier's*, June 23, 1945.

Brendan Gill. Young Man Behind Plexiglass: *The New Yorker*, August 12, 1944.

Philip Hamburger. Letter from Rome: *The New Yorker*, May 19, 1945.

Ernest Hemingway. How We Came to Paris: *Collier's*, October 7, 1944.

John Hersey. Hiroshima: *The New Yorker*, August 31, 1946.

Marguerite Higgins. Freed Captives Fill Roads That Lead to France: New York *Herald Tribune*, April 3, 1945. 33,000 Dachau Captives Freed by 7th Army: New York *Herald Tribune*, May 1, 1945.

Richard C. Hottelet. Big Jump into Germany: *Collier's*, May 5, 1945.

Virginia Irwin. "A Giant Whirlpool of Destruction": St. Louis *Post-Dispatch*, May 9, May 10, and May 11, 1945.

Edward Kennedy. The War in Europe Is Ended!: *The New York Times*, May 8, 1945.

Helen Kirkpatrick. Daily News Writer Sees Man Slain at Her Side in Hail of Lead: *The Chicago Daily News*, August 26, 1944.

William L. Laurence. Atomic Bombing of Nagasaki Told By Flight Member: *The New York Times*, September 9, 1945.

W. H. Lawrence. Nazi Mass Killing Laid Bare in Camp: *The New York Times*, August 30, 1944.

Tom Lea. Peleliu Landing: Lea, *Peleliu Landing* (El Paso: Carl Hertzog, 1945).

A. J. Liebling. Notes from the Kidnap House: *The New Yorker*, April 22, 1944. Cross-Channel Trip: *The New Yorker*, July 1, July 8, and July 15, 1944. The A.P. Surrender: *The New Yorker*, May 19, 1945.

Anne O'Hare McCormick. The Italian Ordeal Surprises Members of Congress: *The New York Times*, December 23, 1944.

John P. Marquand. Iwo Jima Before H-Hour: *Harper's Magazine*, May 1945.

Bill Mauldin. *Up Front*: Mauldin, *Up Front* (New York: Henry Holt and Company, 1945).

Mack Morriss. My Old Outfit: *Yank*, December 1, 1944. War in the Huertgen Forest: *Yank*, January 5, 1945.

Lee Miller. U.S.A. Tent Hospital: *Vogue*, Summer 1944. Photographs by Lee Miller. The Siege of St. Malo: *Vogue*, October 1944. Photographs by Lee Miller.

Edward R. Murrow. "For Most of It I Have No Words": Edward Bliss, Jr. (ed.), *In Search of Light: The Broadcasts of Edward R. Murrow, 1938–1961* (New York: Alfred A. Knopf, 1967), pp. 90–95.

Carl Mydans. "My God! It's Carl Mydans!": *Life*, February 19, 1945.

Shelley Mydans. Guam Holdouts Give Up: *Life*, July 9, 1945.

S. J. Perelman. Take Two Parts Sand, One Part Girl, and Stir: *The New Yorker*, July 8, 1944.

Ernie Pyle. "Those Lulls That Sometimes Come in War": Scripps-Howard wire copy, February 16, 1944. "The Night Was Full of Distant Warfare": Scripps-Howard, February 23, 1944. "A Certain Fundamental Appreciation for the Ridiculous": Scripps-Howard, February 24, 1944. "The Trail Was Never Straight": Scripps-Howard. February 25, 1944. "A Life of Flying in Combat": Scripps-Howard, April 14, 1944. "Their Hunger Most Surely Was Genuine": Scripps-Howard, March 22, 1944. "Nobody Is Wholly Safe": Scripps-Howard, March 28, 1944. "You Just Lie in Your Foxhole": Scripps-Howard, April 1, 1944. "A Look I Dread To See": Scripps-Howard, April 5, 1944. "And Yet We Got On": Scripps-Howard, June 12, 1944. "The Wreckage Was Vast and Startling": Scripps-Howard, June 16, 1944. "This Long Thin Line of Personal Anguish": Scripps-Howard, June 17, 1944. "They Weren't Heroic Figures": Scripps-Howard, July 13, 1944. "A Small Assembly Plant": Scripps-Howard, July 27, 1944. "The Heavy Ordnance Company": Scripps-Howard, August 1, 1944. "The Great Attack": Scripps-Howard, August 7, 1944. "A Ghastly Relentlessness": Scripps-Howard, August 8, 1944. "The Universe Became Filled with a Gigantic Rattling": August 9, 1944. "Anybody Makes Mistakes": Scripps-Howard, August 10, 1944. "This Weird Hedgerow Fighting": Scripps-Howard, August 11, 1944. "Each One Is a Separate Little War": Scripps-Howard, August 12, 1944. "Nothing Left Behind But the Remains": Scripps-Howard, August 21, 1944. "Wounded and Trapped": Scripps-Howard, August 22, 1944. A Last Word: Pyle, *Brave Men* (New York: Henry Holt and Company, 1944), pp. 464–466.

Eric Sevareid. The Price We Pay in Italy: *The Nation*, December 9, 1944.

Irwin Shaw. Morts pour la Patrie: *The New Yorker*, August 25, 1945.

Robert Sherrod. Gone to Earth: *Time*, July 17, 1944. The Nature of the Enemy: *Time*, August 7, 1944. The First Three Days: *Life*, March 5, 1945.

I. F. Stone. For the Jews—Life or Death?: *The Nation*, June 10, 1944.

Rupert Trimmingham and others. Democracy?: *Yank*, April 28, June 9, and July 28, 1944.

Vincent Tubbs. No Picturesque Battle Scenes in SWP War: *Baltimore Afro-American*, February 12, 1944. Homesick Joe in Pacific: *Baltimore Afro-American*, February 26, 1944. Men Can't Sleep; They Talk, Dream of Home: *Baltimore Afro-American*, March 18, 1944. Girls Thrill New Caledonia G.I.s: *Baltimore Afro-American*, May 6, 1944. 93rd Div. Patrol Kills 20 Japs, Escapes 3 Ambushes: *Baltimore Afro-American*, June 3, 1944.

William Walton. Now the Germans Are the Refugees: *Life*, November 6, 1944.

E. B. White. Beautiful Upon a Hill: *The New Yorker*, May 12, 1945.

Evan Wylie. Ernie Pyle: *Yank*, May 18, 1945.


This volume presents the texts listed here without change except for the correction of typographical errors, but it does not attempt to reproduce features of their typographic design. The following is a list of typographical errors corrected, cited by page and line number: 16.10, tatoo; 16.29, up walked; 18.2, of science; 35.33, smoke ahead; 74.34, up of; 76.26, troup; 77.11, shreaked; 148.35, in in; 197.33, Welch of Watts; 198.12, expect; 201.7, do with; 202.10, stonewall; 205.4, irresistible; 224.35, reconnaisance; 235.31, guns; 623.26, stook; 264.13, reverbrated; 499.14, out; 564.6, Two hundred; 603.14, her.'; 639.22, pea; 643.25, richocheted; 644.11, lazily; 657.5, superstitution; 661.1, dialague; 669.29, imposisble; 712.10, Capt.; 714.29, Guards—Maj.; 738.21, FUSAC; 764.26, 764.33, Seeney; 766.25, Denny.

# ACKNOWLEDGMENTS

Great care has been taken to trace all owners of copyright material included in this book. If any have been inadvertently omitted or overlooked, acknowledgment will gladly be made in future printings.

James Agee. "These Terrible Records of War": Reprinted with permission; © The Nation Company, Inc. "A Soldier Died Today": © 1945 Time Inc.; reprinted by permission.

Susan B. Anthony II. Working at the Navy Yard: Originally appeared in *The New Republic*.

Jack Belden. Retreat in Belgium: © 1945 Time Inc.; reprinted by permission.

Walter Bernstein. Search for a Battle: Published in *Keep Your Head Down* by Walter Bernstein. Copyright © 1945. Used by permission of Viking-Penguin, a divison of Penguin Books, USA, Inc. Originally published in *The New Yorker*.

Homer Bigart. Cassino, Once Thriving, Is Turned Into a Scene of Unrelieved Grimness: From the New York *Herald Tribune*, May 20, 1944. © 1944, New York Herald Tribune Inc.; all rights reserved; reprinted by permission. Japan Signs, Second World War Is Ended: From the New York *Herald Tribune*, September 2, 1945. © 1945, New York Herald Tribune Inc.; all rights reserved; reprinted by permission. A Month After the Atom Bomb: Hiroshima Still Can't Believe It: From the New York *Herald Tribune*, September 5, 1945. © 1945, New York Herald Tribune Inc.; all rights reserved; reprinted by permission.

John H. Crider. U.S. Board Bares Atrocity Details Told by Witnesses at Polish Camps: Copyright © 1944 by The New York Times Company; reprinted by permission.

Peggy Hull Deuell. Death of Carrier Described: Reprinted by permission of *The Cleveland Plain Dealer*.

Janet Flanner (Genêt). Letter from Cologne: First published in *The New Yorker*, March 31, 1945. Reprinted by permission of William Murray. "Let Us Weep For This Man": First published in *The New Yorker*, April 28, 1945. Reprinted by permission of William Murray. "A Sad Homecoming": First published in *The New Yorker*, May 5, 1945. Reprinted by permission of William Murray.

*Fortune*. Issei, Nisei, Kibei: © 1944 Time, Inc. All rights reserved. Drawings reproduced by permission of Miné Okubo.

Martha Gellhorn. The First Hospital Ship; The Gothic Line; The Battle of the Bulge; Das Deutsches Volk; The Russians; Dachau: From *The Face of War*, copyright © 1988, reprinted by permission of Grove/Atlantic, Inc.

Brendan Gill. Young Man Behind Plexiglass: From *The New Yorker Book of War Pieces* (Schocken Books). © 1944, 1972 The New Yorker Magazine, Inc. All rights reserved.

Philip Hamburger. Letter from Rome: From *The New Yorker Book of War Pieces* (Schocken Books). © 1945, 1973 The New Yorker Magazine, Inc. All rights reserved.

Ernest Hemingway. How We Came to Paris: Reprinted by permission of Charles Scribner's Sons, an imprint of Macmillan Publishing Company, from *By-Line: Ernest Hemingway*, edited by William White. Copyright © 1944, © by Mary Hemingway. Originally appeared in *Collier's* magazine.

John Hersey. Hiroshima: Reprinted by arrangement with Alfred A. Knopf, Inc.

Marguerite Higgins. Freed Captives Fill Roads That Lead to France: From the New York *Herald Tribune*, April 3, 1945. © 1945, New York Herald Tribune, Inc.; all rights reserved; reprinted by permission. 33,000 Dachau Captives Freed by 7th Army: From the New York *Herald Tribune*, May 1, 1945. © 1945, New York Herald Tribune, Inc.; all rights reserved; reprinted by permission.

Richard C. Hottelet. Big Jump into Germany: Reprinted by permission of the author.

Virginia Irwin. "A Giant Whirlpool of Destruction": Reprinted with the permission of St. Louis *Post-Dispatch*, © 1945.

Edward Kennedy. The War in Europe Is Ended!: Copyright © 1945 by The New York Times Company; reprinted by permission.

Helen Kirkpatrick. Daily News Writer Sees Man Slain at Her Side in Hail of Lead: Reprinted by permission of the author.

William L. Laurence. Atomic Bombing of Nagasaki Told By Flight Member: Copyright © 1945 by The New York Times Company; reprinted by permission.

W. H. Lawrence. Nazi Mass Killing Laid Bare in Camp: Copyright © 1944 by The New York Times Company; reprinted by permission.

Tom Lea. Peleliu Landing: Reprinted by permission of the author and The Still Point Press. Drawings reprinted by permission of the Harry Ransom Humanities Research Center of The University of Texas at Austin.

A. J. Liebling. Notes from the Kidnap House: *The New Yorker*, April 22, 1944. © 1964 by Jean Stafford, renewed in 1992 by Norma Stonehill. Cross-Channel Trip: *The New Yorker*, July 1, July 8, and July 15, 1944. © 1964 by Jean Stafford, renewed in 1992 by Norma Stonehill. The A.P. Surrender: *The New Yorker*, May 19, 1945. © copyright 1945 by A. J. Liebling, copyright renewed 1973 by Jean Stafford.

Anne O'Hare McCormick. The Italian Ordeal Surprises Members of Congress: Copyright © 1944 by The New York Times Company; reprinted by permission.

John P. Marquand. Iwo Jima Before H-Hour: From *Thirty Years* by John P. Marquand. Copyright © 1954 by John P. Marquand; copyright renewed 1982 by John P. Marquand, Jr., and Christina Welch. By permission of Little, Brown & Co.

Bill Mauldin. *Up Front*: Published by arrangement with W. W. Norton Co., Inc.

Lee Miller. U.S.A. Tent Hospital: Reprinted by permission of The Ebury Press from *Lee Miller's War* (1992); originally published in *Vogue*. The Siege of St. Malo: Reprinted by permission of The Ebury Press from *Lee Miller's War* (1992); originally published in *Vogue*.

Edward R. Murrow. "For Most of It I Have No Words": Edward Bliss, Jr. (ed.), *In Search of Light: The Broadcasts of Edward R. Murrow, 1938–1961*. © by Edward R. Murrow; copyright renewed 1969 by Janet H. B. Murrow and Charles Casey Murrow. First published by CBS in *Talks* 9:1 (1944).

Carl Mydans. "My God! It's Carl Mydans!": Copyright 1945 Time, Inc.; originally published in *Life*; reprinted with permission.

Shelley Mydans. Guam Holdouts Give Up: Copyright 1945 Time, Inc.; originally published in *Life*; reprinted with permission.

S. J. Perelman. Take Two Parts Sand, One Part Girl, and Stir: Reprinted by permission of Harold Ober Associates, Inc. Copyright 1944 by S. J. Perelman. Copyright renewed 1971 by S. J. Perelman. First published in *The New Yorker*.

Ernie Pyle. All Ernie Pyle pieces reprinted by permission of the Scripps-Howard Fund. The assistance of Weil Journalism Library, Indiana University, is gratefully acknowledged.

Eric Sevareid. The Price We Pay in Italy: Reprinted with permission from *The Nation* magazine. © The Nation Company, Inc.

Irwin Shaw. Morts pour la Patrie: Reprinted with permission. © Irwin Shaw.

Robert Sherrod. Gone to Earth: © 1944 Time, Inc. Reprinted by permission. The Nature of the Enemy: © 1944 Time, Inc. Reprinted by permission. The First Three Days: © 1945 Time, Inc. Reprinted by permission.

I. F. Stone. For the Jews—Life or Death?: Reprinted with permission from *The Nation* magazine. © The Nation Company, Inc.

Vincent Tubbs. All Vincent Tubbs pieces reprinted by permission of the Afro-American Newspapers Archives and Research Center.

E. B. White. Beautiful Upon a Hill: Reprinted by permission; © 1945, 1973 The New Yorker Magazine, Inc. All rights reserved.

# Notes

In the notes below, the reference numbers denote page and line of this volume (the line count includes headings and captions). No note is made for information that can be found in common desk-reference books such as *Webster's Collegiate* and *Webster's Biographical* dictionaries. Footnotes and bracketed editorial notes within the text were in the originals. For historical background see Chronology in this volume. For weapons and military terms not identified in the Notes, see Glossary in this volume. For further historical background and references to other studies on the war, see Gerhard L. Weinberg, *A World at Arms: A Global History of World War II* (Cambridge: Cambridge University Press, 1994). For further background on wartime journalists and journalism, see Frederick S. Voss, *Reporting the War: The Journalistic Coverage of World War II* (Washington, D.C.: Smithsonian Institution Press for the National Portrait Gallery, 1994), and *Ernie's War: The Best of Ernie Pyle's World War II Dispatches,* ed. David Nichols (New York: Touchstone, 1987). For more detailed maps, see *The Times Atlas of the Second World War,* ed. John Keegan (New York: Harper & Row, 1989), and Richard Natkiel, *Atlas of World War II* (New York: Military Press, 1985).

1.6–7    "X" company]  Company E, 168th Infantry Regiment, 34th Infantry Division, not identified for security reasons in Pyle's original column.

1.20    * * *]  These asterisks, and all others in pieces by Pyle printed in this volume, appear in the copy originally submitted to Scripps-Howard.

2.26    Cassino]  See Chronology, January 1944.

7.39    Ben Robertson]  Correspondent for *PM,* left-wing New York City tabloid newspaper, and author of *I Saw England.*

11.6    CAPE GLOUCESTER]  At the western end of New Britain Island.

11.27–28    Enoc Waters . . . Defender]  War correspondent for the *Chicago Defender,* an African-American newspaper. In 1957 Waters became editor of Associated Negro Press news service and later published *American Diary: A Personal History of the Black Press* (1987).

14.37–38    belt . . . stitches]  In Japanese, *senninbari.* See also page 527.18–23 in this volume.

15.37–38    General Rupertus]  Major General William H. Rupertus, commander of the First Marine Division.

21.12    Salerno]  See Chronology, September 1943.

36.35–36      Sergt. Buck Eversole]   Platoon sergeant Frank "Buck" Eversole of Company E, 168th Infantry (see note 1.6–7) was the subject of two of Pyle's columns, February 21–22, 1944, in which he was described as "the kind of man you instinctively feel safer with than with other people" and as a "senior partner now in the institution of death." Eversole survived the war.

40.24      D-day]   The Allies landed at Anzio on January 22, 1944 ("D-day" was a term used by military planners to designate the day an operation would begin).

47.5–6      Japanese . . . Bataan]   See Chronology, April 1942. William Dyess, an air force officer who had survived the Bataan "Death March," escaped from the Philippines to Australia in 1943 and provided the U.S. government with its first eyewitness account of the Bataan atrocities. The government made information based on his report public on January 28, 1944.

48.37      Terminal Island]   In 1942 a Japanese community of some 2,100 fishermen, of whom 800 were aliens, lived on Terminal Island, where ten fish canneries were located.

49.5–6      Attorney General Warren]   Earl Warren (1891–1974), later Chief Justice of the U.S. Supreme Court, 1953–69.

50.31–32      Japanese . . . Santa Barbara]   The shelling was aimed at an oil-field west of Santa Barbara, California, and caused no significant damage.

54.2      Dies Committee]   The House Committee to Investigate Un-American Activities, founded in 1938 and chaired by Martin Dies Jr. (1901–72), Democratic Representative from Texas.

60.36      combat unit]   The 442nd Regimental Combat Team, a reinforced infantry regiment, fought in Italy and France in 1944–45. It became the most decorated unit of its size in the U.S. army.

63.38      *Gripsholm*]   Swedish vessel used in the exchange of Japanese interned in the U.S. and Americans interned by the Japanese.

66.38      all-Japanese-American battalion]   The 100th Battalion, drawn from Nisei members of the Hawaii National Guard, began fighting in Italy in the autumn of 1943. It became part of the 442nd Regimental Combat Team in the summer of 1944.

67.25–27      cases . . . higher courts]   In *Korematsu* v. *United States,* decided on December 18, 1944, the U.S. Supreme Court upheld by a 6 to 3 vote the conviction of a Japanese-American citizen for violating the 1942 military order excluding people of Japanese ancestry from the Pacific Coast. The majority opinion, written by Justice Hugo Black, accepted "the finding of the military authorities" that military necessity made it "impossible to bring about an immediate segregation of the disloyal from the loyal. . . . " Justice Frank Murphy, in dissent, described the decision as a "legalization of racism."

67.38 Hickam Field] Air base near Pearl Harbor, attacked on December 7, 1941.

68.17 Stimson . . . Knox] Henry Lewis Stimson, secretary of war, 1940–45; Frank Knox, secretary of the navy, 1940–44.

71.20 Adolf Hitler line] Heavily fortified defensive position about nine miles behind the Gustav Line. The Germans began falling back from Cassino to the Hitler Line on May 17, 1944. On May 23 Canadian troops broke through the Hitler Line west of Cassino as the Allies continued their offensive toward Rome.

72.30–31 100th . . . Hawaiians] See note 66.38.

76.23 "Cabin . . . "Bataan,"] *Cabin in the Sky* (1943), musical directed by Vincente Minnelli and starring Eddie Anderson and Ethel Waters; *Bataan* (1943), directed by Tay Garnett and starring Robert Taylor.

78.30 Langston Hughes's "Freedom Road,"] Song co-written in 1942 by Hughes and Emerson Harper, and first sung publicly by Kenneth Spencer at Cafe Society in New York.

80.26–27 Pierre Cot] Cot was a Radical Socialist who served as Air Minister under Léon Blum.

81.4 arrest . . . Riom trial] Léon Blum was arrested by the Vichy government on September 15, 1940, and was informed on October 8 by a special court sitting at Riom that he would be tried, along with several other leaders of the Third Republic, on charges of having failed to adequately prepare France for war. On October 16, 1941, Pétain used special powers given to him by the Vichy constitution to declare Blum, Daladier, Reynaud, and Gamelin guilty of the charges and condemned them to life imprisonment. Despite Pétain's judgment, the Riom court began its public proceedings on February 19, 1942, with foreign journalists, including Americans, in attendance. Blum and Daladier mounted a vigorous defense, and the trial was suspended on April 14, 1942. On March 31, 1943, the Germans deported Blum to Buchenwald. He was liberated by American troops on May 4, 1945.

81.36 Smuts' speech last November] Field Marshal Jan Christiaan Smuts (1870–1950), prime minister of South Africa, had said that since France was no longer a great power, its only choice was to join the British Commonwealth.

82.15 Ribar] Ivan Ribar (1881–1968) presided over the meetings of the Anti-Fascist Council of National Liberation of Yugoslavia, which met in Partisan-controlled territory in November 1942 and November 1943. At its second meeting, the Council proclaimed an end to the monarchy and named Tito president of a provisional Yugoslav government. Ribar's son, Ivo-Lola Ribar (1916–43), a leading Yugoslav Communist, Partisan leader, and close Tito associate, was killed in a German air attack shortly before the November 1943 Council session.

83.9    Kolchak government]   Britain, France, and the United States supplied aid to Admiral Aleksandr Kolchak (1873–1920), "supreme ruler" of the anti-Bolshevik regime established in Omsk, Siberia, in November 1918. The Red Army captured Omsk in November 1919, and Kolchak fled to Irkutsk, where he was shot by the Bolsheviks on February 7, 1920.

83.30    AMG]    Allied Military Government, also known as AMGOT.

83.36    Arthur Krock]    Krock (1886–1974) was Washington bureau chief of *The New York Times*, 1932–53.

86.5    Beveridge Plan]    Economist Sir William Beveridge (1879–1963) chaired the committee appointed by the British government in June 1941 to review existing social insurance programs. Its report, *Social Insurance and Allied Services,* published on December 1, 1942, proposed the creation of a comprehensive social insurance system that would guarantee every individual a minimum income. Many of its provisions, including the creation of a national health service, were implemented by the Labour government in 1945–51.

86.9–10    Stalin's decree . . . Third International]    Stalin dissolved the Communist International (Comintern), also known as the Third International, on May 5, 1943.

86.11–12    Confédération . . . Travail]    The General Confederation of Labor, founded as an organization of trade unions in 1895, became the national representative of labor movements in France after joining with the national federation of labor exchanges in 1902.

88.5    Schutzstaffel]    Literally, "Protection Detachment"; the SS, which trained French collaborators to fight on the eastern front as well as against the resistance in France.

88.6    Lorraine cross]    The cross of Lorraine was adopted as the symbol of the Free French movement.

88.33    *Winterhilfe*]    Winter Relief, fund administered by the Nazi party ostensibly for assisting the poor.

98.2    Nanking infamy]    See Chronology, 1937.

101.8–9    "free ports" . . . Samuel Grafton]    In his syndicated column for April 5, 1944, Grafton proposed creating "free ports for refugees," where European Jews could be sheltered without the host country incurring any obligation to accept them as permanent immigrants. In June 1944 President Roosevelt agreed to create an "Emergency Refugee Shelter" in the U.S., and in August 1,000 Jewish refugees were admitted into the country from southern Italy and housed at Fort Oswego, New York.

101.21–22    "deadline" . . . Hungary]    The press had reported that Budapest Jews had been ordered to move into ghettoes by June 1, 1944.

101.23–24      Bulgaria . . . puppet regime]   The report of a change in government in Bulgaria was incorrect. In early 1943 over 11,000 Jews were deported from Bulgarian-occupied areas of Greece and Yugoslavia to extermination camps in Poland, but plans to deport the 50,000 Jews living in Bulgaria were abandoned because of adverse public opinion, including the opposition of the Orthodox Church hierarchy.

102.29      White Paper]   British government policy statement, issued in May 1939, that restricted Jewish immigration to Palestine over the next five years to 75,000 people.

106.2      British port]   When Liebling prepared "Cross-Channel Trip" for publication in his collection *Mollie & Other War Pieces* (1964), he identified the port as Weymouth in a footnote.

106.39      Sheepshead Bay]   In Brooklyn, New York.

107.21–23      C.O. . . . over]   In a footnote in *Mollie* Liebling identified the officer as Eugene Carusi.

109.17      Off to Buffalo]   "Shuffle Off to Buffalo," by Al Dubin and Harry Warren, dance number from the movie musical *Forty Second Street* (1932).

109.18      shaking . . . pants]   In the text printed in *Mollie,* this reads: "making in my pants."

109.37      The beach]   Omaha Beach.

112.5–6      Allen . . . El Guettar]   Major General Terry Allen commanded the 1st Infantry Division in Tunisia. On March 23, 1943, the 1st Division repulsed a counterattack by the veteran 10th Panzer Division at El Guettar. Liebling witnessed the battle and described it in a profile of Allen published in *The New Yorker* and in the final chapter of his book *The Road Back to Paris* (1944).

112.23      'Knight Without Armor.']   Novel (1933) by James Hilton.

112.29      Pangloss]   Candide's tutor, who holds, despite the terrible misadventures that befall him and his companions, that all is for the best in the best of all possible worlds.

118.26      World's . . . Club]   "Club" featured in a long-running advertising campaign for Aqua Velva shaving cream; its putative members included Sir Cedric Hardwicke, Douglas Fairbanks, Jr., George Biddle, Rear Admiral Yates Stirling, Jr., and Major George Fielding Eliot.

122.6–7      Captain Horatio Hornblower]   Fictional naval commander in a series of novels by C. S. Forester (1899–1966) set during the Napoleonic wars.

125.6      eyeglasses . . . lenses]   In a footnote in *Mollie,* Liebling wrote: "This was me. It seemed more reserved at the time to do it this way—a news story in which the writer said *he* was bathed in blood would have made me distrust it, if I had been a reader."

127.3    dry tail]    In the text printed in *Mollie,* this reads: "dry ass."

128.9    shaking . . . pants]    See note 109.18.

128.16    swamped . . . wave]    In *Mollie* Liebling noted: "These were amphibious tanks, with inflated canvas 'jackets,' and they were self-propelled. The censor allowed no reference to them, since they were a novelty. Of 32 headed for our beach, 28 flooded out. Only the weather was to blame."

128.33    got bitched up]    In the text printed in *Mollie,* this reads: "fucked up."

129.39–40    damaged . . . it]    In the text printed in *Mollie,* this reads: "sank a ship near it, a transport called the Susan B. Anthony."

130.4–5    an arrow."]    In the text printed in *Mollie,* this was followed by: "Susan B. put her nose in the air and slipped backward calmly, like a lady lowering herself into an armchair. In twenty minutes she was gone. It looked as if all her crew got off."

134.8    good . . . mine]    In the text printed in *Mollie,* this reads: "Commander Carusi" (see note 107.21–23). Liebling added in a footnote: "Carusi says that he was lying outside the dugout awaiting evacuation next morning, when one medical corpsman said to another, 'No use taking that white-haired old sonofabitch. He won't make it.' It made Gene so sore he *ordered* them to take him. They got him back to England and he survived."

135.3–6    de Gaulle . . . London.]    Broadcast to the French people on June 18, 1940, after the new Pétain government asked the Germans for an armistice.

137.1    Field Division]    An infantry division capable of undertaking mobile operations, so-called to distinguish it from lower-quality "static" divisions intended solely for manning coastal fortifications.

138.38    *Oberstleutnant*]    Lieutenant colonel.

139.13    my favorite outfit]    Identified by Liebling in a footnote in *Mollie* as "16th Regiment, First Division."

139.26    Todt organization]    German construction organization that built major fortifications, named for Fritz Todt (1891–1942), Reich minister for armaments 1940–42.

141.33–34    Nelson's . . . duty."]    Sent at the Battle of Trafalgar, October 21, 1805.

145.24    permitted . . . units]    Identified by Pyle in his collection *Brave Men* (1944) as "the First and Twenty-ninth Divisions."

166.10–11    Earl Wilson's column]    "It Happened One Night" ran in the New York *Post,* 1942–83.

167.8		darb] A lulu; a honey; a beaut.

173.5		last charge] In the early morning of July 7, 1944, about 3,000 Japanese soldiers and sailors attacked American positions on Saipan. After the attack was repulsed, many of the surviving Japanese killed themselves with hand grenades.

174.35–36		torpedoes] Bangalore torpedoes, tubes filled with explosive and used for demolishing enemy obstacles and fortifications.

181.5		wooden bullets] While there is no record of wooden bullets being used by the Germans in World War II, wood was used in the manufacture of German hand grenades and anti-personnel mines; in addition, soldiers were sometimes wounded by wood splinters created by shells exploding in woods, orchards, or hedgerows.

181.36		Wangensteen] Owen Wangensteen (1898–1981), chief of surgery at the University of Minnesota (1930–67).

184.29		P-Planes] Pilotless planes. See V-1 in Glossary.

186.38		Reichswehr] Name for the German armed forces, 1919–35; from 1935 to 1945 they were known as the Wehrmacht.

194.11		the city] In his collection *Brave Men* (1944), Pyle identified the city as Cherbourg and the formation he was with as the Ninth Infantry Division.

201.29		great attack] Made by three American infantry divisions across the St. Lô–Périers road on July 25, 1944.

202.1		our regiment] Pyle was with the 12th Infantry Regiment.

210.32–33		killed . . . American troops] The "short" bombing on July 25, 1944, killed 111 Americans and wounded 490. Among the dead was Lieutenant General Lesley McNair, the highest-ranking American officer killed in action during the war. McNair, who from 1942 to 1944 directed the organization and training of U.S. army ground forces, had gone to Normandy to observe the troops in action.

219.26		live or not] Flight Lieutenant Robert G. F. Lee, who had been shot down five days before his rescue, survived his wounds.

228.20		haircutting] In many liberated French towns, women accused of having had intimate relations with German soldiers were forced to have their heads shaved.

228.40		CIC] Counter-Intelligence Corps.

231.38		*digue*] Embankment.

237.2		oil bombs] Napalm.

242.5		General Leclerc] Commander of the 2nd French Armored Division. Captain Vicomte Jacques-Philippe de Hautecloque escaped to England in 1940 and joined the Free French, adopting the nom de guerre Leclerc to protect his wife and children in France. In early 1941 Leclerc led a column from Fort Lamy in Chad across 1,000 miles of the Sahara to Kufra, an oasis in southeastern Libya, where he captured the Italian garrison, raised the tricolor, and led his officers in swearing an oath that they would fight until all of France had been liberated. After conducting further operations against the Italians in southern Libya, Leclerc and his troops joined the British in Tunisia. In 1943 Leclerc was chosen by de Gaulle to organize and train the 2nd Armored Division. The division landed in Normandy on August 1, 1944, entered Paris on August 25, and fought in France and Germany until the end of the war. Leclerc was killed in an airplane crash in 1947 and was posthumously promoted to marshal of France.

242.11　　Colonel B]　Colonel David Bruce (1898–1977) of the Office of Strategic Services, the American intelligence and special operations organization. Bruce was London chief of the OSS and directed its European operations. He later served as U.S. ambassador to France (1948–49), West Germany (1957–58), and Great Britain (1961–69).

256.40　　O.D.s]　Olive drab uniforms.

263.12　　Koenig . . . Juin]　General Marie Pierre Joseph Koenig (1898–1970) commanded the French Forces of the Interior and became military governor of Paris after its liberation. The prolonged defense of Bir Hakeim, Libya, from May 27 to June 11, 1942, by Free French forces under his command helped restore French military prestige in Britain and the U.S. General Alphonse Juin (1888–1967) commanded the French army in North Africa under Vichy from 1940 to 1942, then joined the Allies after they landed in Morocco and Algeria in November 1942. In December 1943 he assumed command of the French Expeditionary Corps in Italy and played a major role in the breaking of the Gustav Line in May 1944.

264.38–39　　the militia]　The *Milice,* formed by Vichy in 1943, fought the French resistance and assisted the SS in arresting and deporting Jews.

267.7–8　　River Rouge]　Site of a large Ford automotive assembly line near Detroit, Michigan.

267.9　　1,500,000]　It is now estimated that between 200,000 and 360,000 people died at Majdanek.

268.27　　I am . . . believe]　Lawrence had previously expressed skepticism about allegations of German atrocities. After visiting Babi Yar, the ravine near Kiev where the Germans had murdered over 30,000 Jews, Lawrence had written in *The New York Times* on November 29, 1943, that "it is impossible for this correspondent to judge the truth or falsity of the story told to us" by Soviet authorities concerning the massacre.

268.31–32　　Polish . . . Liberation]　Communist-dominated Polish provisional government established by the Soviets in Lublin on July 22, 1944, in opposition to the Polish government-in-exile in London.

296.2 V-mail] Printed correspondence forms that were microfilmed, sent across the Atlantic, and then enlarged and delivered.

300.15–16 vote . . . Congress.] A Roosevelt administration proposal to provide soldiers with federal absentee ballots for the 1944 election was resisted by both Republicans and southern Democrats. The Senate passed a bill that kept absentee balloting under the control of the states, but it was modified by the House to allow states to permit use of a federal ballot, and to enable soldiers denied a state ballot to request a federal one. Despite the defeat of the administration proposal, over four million soldiers and sailors voted in the 1944 election.

301.4 attempted . . . Hitler] See Chronology, July 1944.

313.10 Ghoum] American term for Moroccan mountain troops fighting with the French army.

316.6 Venafro] In Italy, about 12 miles east of Cassino.

318.3 "Lili Marlene"] German song (1938) about a woman waiting for a soldier, with words by Hans Leip and music by Norbert Schultze.

322.33 Schicklgruber] Original family name of Alois Hitler, Adolf Hitler's father. It was used to refer disparagingly to Adolf Hitler.

348.32 "Li'l Abner"] Comic strip (1934–77) by Al Capp.

354.1–2 volkswagen] German military vehicle, similar to the American jeep, manufactured by the Volkswagen company.

360.9 "screaming meemie"] See *Nebelwerfer* in Glossary.

366.8 phosphorus] White phosphorus, an incendiary weapon.

379.9 blurp gun] See machine pistol in Glossary.

414.6–7 CIC . . . PWD] The Counter Intelligence Corps, Allied Military Government, Allied Control Commission, and Psychological Warfare Division.

416.6 glider bombs] Radio-controlled glide bombs, first used successfully by the Germans in September 1943.

416.11 "Anzio Express,"] "Anzio Express" and "Anzio Annie" were Allied names for two long-range German artillery guns, mounted on railroad cars, that were used to shell the beachhead. The guns fired a 564-pound shell 280 mm. in diameter and had a maximum range of over 38 miles.

424.11 American-Canadian division] The 1st Special Service Force, a special operations unit with a strength of about 2,500 men.

445.5 General Maitland Wilson] Sir Henry Maitland Wilson (1881–1964), Supreme Allied Commander in the Mediterranean from January to November 1944.

464.30     potato-masher grenade] Grenade with cylindrical explosive charge attached to a wooden throwing stick.

476.32–33     League of Nations . . . Ethiopian grab] See Chronology, 1935–36.

477.2     Senator Nye] Gerald P. Nye, Republican of North Dakota, was a leading isolationist.

477.34–35     André Kostelanetz] Russian born American conductor (1901–80) known for his arrangements of light music.

479.18     Fred Perry] British tennis player Frederick J. Perry (1909–95) was the champion at Wimbledon, 1934–36, and held the U.S. Open title, 1933–34 and 1936.

484.23     Stalag Luft] German prisoner-of-war camp administered by the Luftwaffe.

487.33     Eaker and Doolittle] The Eighth Air Force, whose four-engine bombers raided Germany from bases in England, was commanded by Major General Ira Eaker from December 1942 to January 1944, and by Lieutenant General James Doolittle from January 1944 to May 1945.

490.3     *Gothic Line*] German defensive position traversing northern Italy from Pisa to Rimini.

490.29     Hitler line] See note 71.20.

491.40     Desert Air Force] RAF command specializing in close support of ground operations, originally formed during the North African campaign.

493.6     Siegfried Line] Allied name for the German "West Wall," fortifications along the western German frontier.

496.18     sadism . . . Kesselring] Field Marshal Albert Kesselring (1885–1960), commander of German forces in Italy, issued orders in June and July 1944 calling for "severe measures" to be taken in reprisal for Italian partisan attacks, including public hangings, the burning of villages, and the shooting of ten Italians for every German soldier killed. Hundreds of Italian civilians, including women and children, were killed by German troops during the retreat to the Gothic Line. Kesselring was sentenced to death for war crimes by a British court in 1947, but his sentence was commuted to life imprisonment, and he was released from prison in 1952.

497.28–29     Soon . . . Lombardy plain] German resistance and bad weather prevented the Allies from breaking into the plain until April 1945.

498.9     *Peleliu Island*] See Chronology, September and November 1944.

498.27     kingposts] Short masts used to support cargo booms.

516.27     the Fifth] The Fifth Marine Regiment.

520.4    *Banzai*]  Japanese war cry, from *Tenno heika banzai*: "May the Son of Heaven live ten thousand years!" (The emperor was called "Son of Heaven.")

537.6–7    Maastricht . . . two days before]  Maastricht was liberated by the U.S. First Army on September 14, 1944.

537.18–22    "I'll Never . . . Dorsey's arrangement]  Song (1940) by Ruth Lowe, recorded by Tommy Dorsey's orchestra and its lead singer, Frank Sinatra.

537.26    Fort]  B-17; see Glossary.

537.36–37    "Or you might . . . long funny ears."]  From "Swinging on a Star," words by Johnny Burke and music by Jimmy Van Heusen, sung by Bing Crosby in *Going My Way* (1944).

540.21    Schofield Barracks]  Army base on Oahu in Hawaii.

541.38    four days]  August 7–10, 1944.

543.13    cavalry]  Motorized troops normally attached to division headquarters and used for reconnaissance.

543.28–29    Screaming Minnies]  See *Nebelwerfer* in Glossary.

548.7    second . . . Philippine Sea]  Also known as the Battle of Leyte Gulf; see Chronology, October 1944.

548.27    day . . . death]  The *Princeton* was sunk on October 24, 1944.

553.10    Birkenau]  The camp at Birkenau (Brzezinka), also known as Auschwitz II, was located a mile west of the main Auschwitz camp. Construction of the Birkenau camp began in October 1941.

553.11    horrors of Lublin]  See pp. 267–72 in this volume.

553.13    Lublin 1,500,000]  See note 267.9.

553.14    1,500,000 to 1,765,000]  It is now estimated that 1,100,000 people died at Auschwitz-Birkenau between June 1940, when Auschwitz was established as a concentration camp for Polish political prisoners, and January 27, 1945, when the Soviet army liberated Auschwitz-Birkenau. About 90 percent of the victims were Jews from throughout occupied Europe. The gassing of Jews at Auschwitz-Birkenau began in February 1942 and continued until late November 1944, when Himmler ordered the SS to dismantle and destroy the gas chambers and crematoria.

554.6    two . . . Jews]  Walter Rosenberg and Alfred Wetzler, who both survived the war (Rosenberg subsequently adopted the name Rudolf Vrba, which was the name on the false identity papers he used in Slovakia after his escape from the camp). Their 30-page report, based on information collected by dozens of Auschwitz prisoners, was sent to Jaromir Kopecky, the diplomatic representative in Switzerland of the Czechoslovak government-in-exile, in May 1944, and summaries of the report were given to Allied governments by early July. The full text reached the War Refugee Board in the United States in mid-October 1944.

554.8    Polish major] Jerzy Tabeau, a Polish medical student who escaped from Birkenau on November 19, 1943. His account of the camp was circulated by the Polish resistance as "The Report of a Polish Major." Tabeau joined a partisan unit of the Polish Socialist Party and survived the war.

554.9–10    Bergson . . . Liberation] Peter H. Bergson was the pseudonym of Hillel Kook, the leader of a group of young Jews who came to the United States from Palestine in 1939–40 to raise money for the militant underground group Irgun Zvai Leumi. In July 1943 Bergson helped organize the Emergency Committee to Save the Jewish People of Europe, which vigorously criticized the Roosevelt administration for its failure to help Jewish refugees. The Hebrew Committee of National Liberation, founded in May 1944, was intended to serve as a government-in-exile for the Jews of Palestine.

559.14–15    brother of Léon Blum] René Blum, former director of the Ballet de Monte Carlo, was arrested by the Gestapo in December 1941 and deported to Auschwitz in September 1942.

560.3    HUERTGEN FOREST] American name for forested area in Germany southeast of Aachen and west of the Roer River. U.S. troops first entered the forest on September 14, 1944, and heavy fighting continued in the region until early December. Over 23,000 Americans were killed, wounded, or captured in the Huertgen Forest, and another 8,000 became casualties from trench foot, exposure, and combat exhaustion. The area was finally cleared of German forces in February 1945.

560.15    Grosshau] Captured by the 4th Infantry Division on November 30, 1944.

560.29    New Georgia] See Chronology, June and August 1943.

562.20–21    Fourth . . . divisions] One regiment of the 4th Division, the 12th Infantry, began fighting in the Huertgen Forest on November 6, 1944. The 8th and 22nd Infantry Regiments began their attack on November 16, and the entire division was relieved between December 3 and 11, after having achieved a maximum advance of over three miles. During the Huertgen battle the 4th Infantry Division lost over 4,000 men killed, wounded, or captured, and suffered another 2,000 casualties from combat exhaustion, trench foot, and other "nonbattle" causes. The 1st, 8th, 9th, and 28th Infantry Divisions also fought in the Huertgen Forest, September–December 1944.

563.23    primacord] Detonating cord.

564.14    assault guns] Turretless tanks, used to provide close artillery support for infantry.

567.11–12    attempt . . . Rapido River]   The attack, made across the narrow but deep and fast-flowing river between January 20 and 22, 1944, failed
to secure a foothold on the opposite bank. Casualties in the 36th Infantry
Division were reported as 143 men killed, 663 wounded, and 875 missing (it is
believed that about 500 of the missing men were captured by the Germans).
After the war, the Veterans Association of the 36th Division publicly criticized
General Mark Clark, commander of the U.S. Fifth Army at the time, for
having ordered the assault.

568.35–36    Hermann Göring divisions]   The Hermann Göring division
was a panzer grenadier (motorized infantry) formation manned mainly by
Luftwaffe personnel.

574.5    Von Rundstedt's Breakthrough]   Field Marshal Gerd von Rundstedt (1875–1953), commander-in-chief of the German army in the West from
September 1944 to March 1945, was widely credited in the Allied press with
responsibility for the Ardennes offensive. Postwar investigation established
that the offensive was actually conceived by Hitler, who insisted upon its
execution despite Von Rundstedt's opposition.

574.6–7    Elsenborn . . . Bastogne]   By holding Elsenborn Ridge, at the
northern end of the Ardennes front, in intense fighting from December 18 to
21, 1944, U.S. troops blocked three roads crucial to the main German attack
toward the Meuse River near Liège. Despite being surrounded from December 21 to 26, American troops also held Bastogne, a key road junction in the
southern Ardennes, and disrupted German attempts to reach the Meuse
River near Dinant.

574.27–28    Bullingen . . . Stavelot]   The 2nd Infantry Division was
heavily engaged near Büllingen as part of the battle to hold the Elsenborn
Ridge. The 30th Infantry Division recaptured Stavelot, 20 miles southeast of
Liège, on December 18, 1944, and defended it against German counterattacks, December 19–20.

575.3–4    Hotton]   The town, about 25 miles south of Liège, was attacked
on December 21, 1944.

576.19    M4 tank]   See Sherman tank in Glossary.

580.34–35    150 American prisoners . . . 43]   Subsequent investigation determined that 86 American soldiers were killed in the massacre at the
Baugnez crossroads near Malmédy. Troops of the 1st SS Panzer Division
killed at least 150 American prisoners and 138 Belgian civilians during the
Ardennes offensive.

583.16–17    SS Panzer . . . Malmedy]   In 1946 the U.S. army tried 73
officers and men of the Waffen SS, almost all of them from the 1st SS Panzer
Division, for their role in the killing of American prisoners and Belgian civilians in the Ardennes. All of the defendants were found guilty, and 43 were
sentenced to death, 22 to life imprisonment, and eight to prison terms of
between 10 and 20 years. A public campaign to overturn the verdicts was

launched in Germany and the United States, with critics of the trial, including Senator Joseph McCarthy, claiming that army investigators had used violence and coercion to exact false confessions. All of the death sentences were eventually commuted, and all of the defendants were released from prison by the end of 1956.

584.21     six-by-sixes]    Six-wheeled trucks with six-wheel drive.

586.30     Belgian village]    Cheneux, recaptured by troops of the 82nd Airborne division, December 20–21, 1944.

591.12–13     eight-day push]    In January 1945.

597.28     robombs]    See V-1 in Glossary.

612.9–12     Frank Hewlett . . . Virginia]    The Hewletts were reunited during the liberation of the camp.

631.20     alligators]    See LVT in Glossary.

634.18–19     Vice Admiral Richmond Kelly Turner]    Turner (1885–1961) was amphibious forces commander during the landings on Guadalcanal, New Georgia, the Gilberts, the Marshalls, and the Marianas.

637.35–38     They died . . . body.]    This passage also appeared in a story by Sherrod about Iwo Jima printed in *Time* on March 5, 1945. In the *Time* version, Sherrod added: "Only the legs were easy to identify—Japanese if wrapped in khaki puttees, American if covered by canvas leggings."

643.23     T/Sgt]    Technical Sergeant.

643.28     S/Sgt]    Staff Sergeant.

649.35     Arnhem]    See Chronology, September 1944.

660.18–19     "The Crazy Ray."]    English title of Clair's experimental short film *Paris qui dort* (1923).

662.28     First Army's . . . city.]    Cologne was captured by U.S. troops March 5–7, 1945.

667.35     French Armed Elite Guard]    A Waffen SS division composed of French volunteers, the "Charlemagne," was formed in late 1944. It was virtually annihilated fighting on the eastern front in 1945.

671.13     *Schweinhunde*]    Swine dogs.

675.30     Oradour]    Troops of the 2nd SS Panzer Division murdered 642 people in Oradour-sur-Glane, about ten miles northwest of Limoges, on June 10, 1944. After shooting the men of the village inside several barns and garages, the SS set the church on fire and then shot at the women and children as they tried to escape. The massacre was committed in reprisal for recent attacks made by the French resistance in the region.

680.14     Whitman's great threnody]    "When Lilacs Last in the Dooryard Bloom'd" (1865–66), on the death of President Lincoln.

686.5 D-Day] Okinawa was invaded on April 1, 1945; American troops landed on Ie Shima on April 16.

689.30 *"C'est. . . l'humanité."*] "It is painful for the whole human race."

690.10–11 *"Monsieur Truman. . . 1948"*] "Mr. Truman will be president until 1948."

691.1 *la liberté d'aimer"*] "The liberty to love."

694.18 *"on. . . nommer."*] "Cannot be named."

697.30 Nuremberg law] See Chronology, 1935.

699.38–39 still in Ravensbrück] About 17,000 prisoners were sent on a forced march westward from the camp on April 15, 1945, during which hundreds of prisoners were shot or died from exhaustion. The Soviet army liberated Ravensbrück on April 30.

712.10–11 Capt. . . . Erween] War correspondents accredited with the U.S. army wore military uniform.

717.21 "Sonny Boy."] Al Jolson's theme song, written by Jolson, B. G. DeSylva, Lew Brown, and Ray Henderson, was first featured in the film musical *The Singing Fool* (1928).

718.40 Grover Whalen] New York city police commissioner, known for his role in organizing public ceremonies, including homecoming parades after World War I.

722.8–15 Blum . . . Jacob] Blum and the other special prisoners were liberated in the Italian Tyrol by American troops on May 4, 1945. Yakov Stalin, who had been captured in 1941 while serving in the Soviet army, was not among them; it is believed that he died in a German concentration camp in 1943.

723.1 French general] General Charles Delestraint, who had commanded the Gaullist resistance organization *Armée Secrète* until his arrest on June 9, 1943.

726.35 pyramidon] A white crystalline solid used as an anti-pyretic and analgesic.

733.12 SHAEF] Supreme Headquarters Allied Expeditionary Force, the supreme Allied command for western Europe, headed by Eisenhower.

734.27 Shubert pass] Revocable reviewer's pass provided by the Shubert theaters in New York City.

736.25 Dieppe] See Chronology, August 1942.

745.5–6 Committee of National Liberation] A coalition of anti-fascist, anti-monarchial political parties, including the Communists, that was formed in Milan in September 1943. The CNL opposed both the Germans and the government established by Marshal Badoglio after the overthrow of Mussolini.

746.17 Clara Petacci, Pavolini, Starace] Petacci was Mussolini's mistress. Alessandro Pavolini (b. 1903) held important posts in Mussolini's government and became secretary general of the Fascist party in September 1943. Achille Starace (b. 1889) was secretary general of the Fascist party, 1932–39, and chief of staff of the Fascist militia, 1939–41.

748.1 Toscanini] Arturo Toscanini (1867–1957), an anti-fascist émigré, was a former chief conductor at La Scala.

749.23 Stassen] Harold Stassen, former governor of Minnesota and member of the U.S. delegation to the conference.

750.13 weekend with Argentina and Poland] The United States supported the admission to the Conference of Argentina, which had declared war on Germany and Japan on March 27, 1945, but opposed the participation of the Communist-dominated Polish provisional government. Despite Soviet support for immediate Polish participation, the Conference voted to delay admission of a Polish delegation until the provisional government was recognized by all four of the powers (Britain, China, the Soviet Union, and the United States) that had sponsored the San Francisco Conference. On July 5, 1945, Britain and the U.S. recognized the new Polish government, and Poland became a participating member of the United Nations.

751.7–8 triplets . . . Argentina] Despite continuing opposition by the Soviet Union, which denounced the Argentine government as pro-fascist, the Conference had voted to admit Argentina. The Conference had also voted to admit the Soviet republics of Belorussia and Ukraine as members of the United Nations.

752.6 Sol Bloom] Bloom, a Democrat from New York City, was chairman of the House Foreign Affairs Committee.

754.7–8 Admiral Mitscher] Mitscher (1887–1947) commanded Task Force 58, the fast carrier task force of the Pacific fleet, from January to November 1944 and February to May 1945.

754.24 Franklin] The *Franklin* was hit by two bombs off the Japanese coast on March 19, 1945, while preparing to launch an air strike; 724 men were killed.

760.14 Yamato] The *Yamato* was sunk by American carrier aircraft on April 7, 1945, while sailing toward Okinawa. *Yamato* and its sister ship, *Musashi,* were the largest battleships ever built. (*Musashi* was sunk by U.S. carrier aircraft on October 24, 1944, during the Battle of Leyte Gulf.)

763.29–30 different . . . Hiroshima] See Chronology, July–August 1945.

764.11 Dumbos and Superdumbos] Seaplanes used for rescue missions.

764.28 The Great Artiste] Sweeney had flown *The Great Artiste* as the instrument plane on the Hiroshima mission. Piloted by Captain Frederick Bock, *The Great Artiste* was also used as the instrument plane on the Nagasaki mission, and was the aircraft on which Laurence flew. Sweeney flew the Nagasaki mission in a B-29 named *Bock's Car,* which carried the atomic bomb.

766.23 Cheshire . . . pilot] Cheshire had flown 100 missions as a bomber pilot in the war against Germany and been awarded the Victoria Cross. As commander of the elite 617 Squadron in 1944, he had pioneered the use of low-level target marking in both day and night precision bombing attacks.

766.25 William G. Penney] Penney later directed the development of the British atomic bomb. The first British bomb, exploded off the Australian coast in October 1952, was a plutonium implosion design very similar to that of the Nagasaki weapon.

766.28 "Y-Site"] The laboratory at Los Alamos, New Mexico.

770.5−6 primary . . . secondary] The primary target for the mission was the industrial city of Kokura, but when the bombardier on *Bock's Car* was unable to locate his visual aiming point through the smoke and haze obscuring the city, Ashworth, the Manhattan Project "weaponeer" in charge of arming the bomb, and Sweeney decided to fly to the secondary target, Nagasaki.

813.3 Grummans] Manufacturer of U.S. naval aircraft, including the F6F Hellcat fighter and the TBF Avenger bomber.

821.24 Grand Slam] A 22,000 pound bomb, used in March and April 1945 to destroy German railway viaducts and bridges.

834.4−5 Hirohito . . . Tenno] In Japan the reigning emperor was referred to as Tenno or Tenno Heika (Son of Heaven) rather than by his personal name.

840.23 torii] A simple gateway at the entrance to the grounds of a Shinto shrine.

848.25 *Cryptomeria japonica*] Japanese cedar.

# Glossary of Military Terms

*Notes on U.S. Army organization appear at the end of the Glossary*

Amphtrack]  Amphibious tractor. See LVT.

AT]  Anti-tank.

A-20]  Twin-engine U.S. bomber. The "Havoc" had a three-man crew and a top speed of over 300 mph and was armed with at least seven machine guns; different versions carried between 2,000 and 4,000 pounds of bombs.

Bailey bridge]  Bridge made from prefabricated steel segments, which could be rapidly assembled by combat engineers.

Bazooka]  American tube-shaped, shoulder-fired rocket launcher, designed as a close-range anti-tank weapon and also used by the infantry against concrete fortifications. The launcher was 54 inches long and fired a 3.5 pound projectile 2.36 inches (60 mm.) in diameter with an effective range of 100 yards. Although the projectile was usually incapable of penetrating the frontal armor of German tanks, it was often effective when used against their thinner side and rear armor, or their tracks. Americans also referred to German shoulder-fired anti-tank weapons, such as the widely used *Panzerfaust* ("tank fist") as "bazookas." The *Panzerfaust* fired a 3.5 pound projectile 150 mm. in diameter that was capable of penetrating the frontal armor of Allied tanks; it had an effective range of 30 meters (later extended to 60 meters). Both the bazooka and *Panzerfaust* projectiles used specially shaped explosive charges to create a focused high-speed stream of incandescent metallic particles.

Bofors]  Rapid-firing 40 mm. anti-aircraft gun, effective against airplanes flying below 11,000 feet.

Browning automatic rifle]  American rifle capable of full automatic fire, used as a light machine gun by army and marine infantry. It fired a .30 caliber bullet (i.e., a bullet 30/100 of an inch in diameter), was fed from a 20-round magazine, had an effective range of over 600 yards, and weighed 19 pounds.

Butterfly bomb]  Small German anti-personnel bomb.

B-17]  Four-engine U.S. heavy bomber. The "Flying Fortress" had a ten-man crew, a cruising speed of about 215 mph, was armed with 13 machine guns, and normally carried 4,000–6,000 pounds of bombs.

B-26]  Twin-engine U.S. medium bomber. The "Marauder" had a six-man crew, a top speed of about 280 mph, carried 4,000 pounds of bombs, and was armed with up to 12 machine guns.

B-29]  Four-engine U.S. heavy bomber, used in the Pacific and Asia in

1944–45. The "Superfortress" had an 11-man crew, a cruising speed of 290 mph, and normally carried 12,000 pounds of bombs (20,000 pounds was the maximum load). It was armed with ten machine guns and a rapid-firing 20 mm. cannon, although in 1945 many B-29s had their machine-gun turrets removed to increase speed and bomb load.

Carbine] A short rifle. The American M-1 carbine was a semiautomatic weapon with a 15-round magazine; it fired a .30 caliber bullet, had an effective range of 300 yards, and weighed six pounds.

C-46] Twin-engine American transport aircraft. Introduced into service in 1944, it was larger than the C-47.

C-47] Twin-engine American transport aircraft, the military version of the DC-3 passenger plane.

C ration] American canned field rations that could be eaten hot or cold.

DE] Destroyer escort, a small (1,100–1,450 tons displacement) U.S. naval vessel intended primarily for anti-submarine and anti-aircraft duty.

D ration] American emergency field ration consisting of a fortified chocolate bar.

Duck] Six-wheeled American amphibious truck equipped with a propeller and rudder that could carry 25 men or 5,000 pounds of cargo. Also known as the DUKW, after the code name under which it was developed.

E-boat] Allied name for small, fast German torpedo boat.

88] German artillery gun firing shells or armor-piercing solid shot 88 mm. in diameter. Originally produced as an anti-aircraft gun, its high velocity and flat trajectory made it an extremely effective anti-tank gun, and it was also used as field artillery, often firing shells fused to burst in the air above Allied troops. As an anti-tank gun, it was effective at ranges up to 2,000 yards; as artillery, it could fire a 20-pound shell almost ten miles (17,500 yards).

F6F] See Hellcat.

Focke-Wulf 190] Single-engine, single-seat German fighter that entered service in late 1941. The FW-190 had a top speed of 395 mph (increased to 408 mph in some 1943 models) and was armed with four 20 mm. rapid-fire cannon and two machine guns.

Fortress] See B-17.

4.2 mortar] U.S. mortar that fired a 24-pound shell 4.2 inches in diameter, with a maximum range of over 2.5 miles (4,500 yards).

F.F.I.] *Forces Françaises de l'Intérieur*, name given in spring 1944 to all armed members of the French resistance under the control of the de Gaulle government (the Communist-led *Francs-Tireurs et Partisans* were officially under the command of the F.F.I. leadership, but often acted independently).

Garand]　See M-1 rifle.

G-1, G-2, G-3, G-4]　U.S. army terms for staff sections at division, corps, army, or army group level, used to refer to both the section itself and to the staff officer who headed it. G-1 was personnel and administration; G-2, intelligence; G-3, operations and training; G-4, supply and maintenance.

Hellcat]　Single-engine, single-seat U.S. naval fighter. Developed in response to the Japanese Zero, it entered carrier service in September 1943. The "Hellcat" had a top speed of 375 mph and was armed with six machine guns.

Higgins boat]　See LCVP.

Howitzer]　An artillery gun capable of being elevated past 45°.

Judy]　American code name for single-engine Japanese dive bomber that entered service in 1943. It had a two-man crew, a top speed of 343 mph, carried 1,100 pounds of bombs, and was armed with three machine guns.

Knee mortar]　Allied name for small Japanese mortar. It weighed ten pounds, fired a 1.75 pound shell 50 mm. in diameter, and had a range of 700 yards.

K ration]　American canned and packaged field rations, usually eaten cold in forward areas.

LCIL]　Landing Craft Infantry, Large. The LCIL was a sea-going vessel that could land 200 men directly onto a beach.

LCM]　Landing Craft, Mechanized. The LCM was 50 feet long and could carry 60 men, six jeeps, or two DUKW trucks. Over 8,600 were built during the war.

LCVP]　Landing Craft, Vehicle and Personnel, designed by New Orleans boatbuilder Andrew J. Higgins. The LCVP was 36 feet long and could carry 36 men or a 2.5 ton truck. Over 23,000 were made during the war.

LST]　Landing Ship Tank, sea-going vessel capable of unloading 18 tanks or 500 tons of cargo directly onto a beach.

LVT]　Landing Vehicle, Tracked. American amphibious tractor that used specially shaped tracks to travel through water and over land. It could carry up to 20 men or two tons of cargo.

LVTA]　An LVT armed with a turret-mounted 75 mm. howitzer, used to provide close fire support in amphibious landings.

Liberty ship]　Mass-produced American ship capable of carrying over 10,000 tons of cargo. Over 2,700 Liberty ships were launched between 1941 and 1945.

Luger] German semiautomatic pistol.

M-1 rifle] Standard U.S. infantry rifle of World War II, often called the "Garand" after its inventor, John C. Garand. A semiautomatic weapon, it fired a .30 caliber bullet, held eight rounds in its magazine, had an effective range of 550 yards, and weighed over nine pounds.

Machine pistol] German submachine gun. The widely-used MP 40 fired a 9 mm. bullet, had a 32-round magazine, weighed about 10 pounds, and had an effective range of over 100 yards. (Submachine guns fire pistol ammunition, hence the German term *Maschinen Pistole.*)

Mark IV tank] German medium tank. It weighed 25 tons, had a five-man crew, a maximum speed of 25 mph, armor 80 mm. thick in the front and 30 mm. thick on the side, and was armed with a high-velocity 75 mm. gun. Almost 9,000 were produced between 1942 and 1945.

Mark V tank] German medium tank. The "Panther" weighed 45 tons, had a five-man crew, a maximum speed of 29 mph, and was armed with a high-velocity 75 mm. gun. Its front armor, 80 mm. thick, was sloped to deflect shot; the side armor was 40 mm. thick. Approximately 5,500 were produced between 1943 and 1945.

Mark VI tank] German heavy tank that entered service in late 1942. The "Tiger" weighed 56 tons, had a five-man crew, a maximum speed of 25 mph, armor 100 mm. thick on the front and turret and 60 mm. thick on the side, and was armed with a high-velocity 88 mm. gun. Highly effective in defensive fighting, the Tiger lacked mobility and mechanical reliability. Only 1,350 were made.

ME-109] Messerschmitt Bf 109, single-engine, single-seat German fighter. The Bf 109G, the main Luftwaffe fighter from 1942 to 1945, had a top speed of 403 mph and was armed with one (sometimes three) 20 mm. cannon and two machine guns.

MLR] Main line of resistance.

Mustang] See P-51.

*Nambu*] American term for Japanese 6.5 mm. and 7.7 mm. light machine guns.

*Nebelwerfer*] Literally, "smoke thrower"; German multi-barreled rocket launcher. The most common version was a six-barreled weapon that fired a 75-pound rocket 150 mm. in diameter. It had a range of over four miles (7,300 yards). Allied troops called the *Nebelwerfer* the "screaming meemie" from the sound its rockets (which were fitted with sirens) made in flight.

Norden bomb sight] American bomb sight that was linked to the aircraft autopilot, allowing the bombardier to control the plane's course during the final approach to the target.

'03 rifle] U.S. bolt-action rifle, also known as the Springfield Model 1903. It fired a .30 caliber bullet, held five rounds in its clip, weighed nine pounds, and had an effective range of over 600 yards.

Oerlikon] Rapid-firing 20 mm. anti-aircraft gun used against low-flying aircraft.

105] Standard American field artillery gun of World War II. It fired a 33-pound shell 105 mm. in diameter and had a maximum range of almost seven miles (12,200 yards).

155] American artillery gun firing a 95-pound shell 155 mm. in diameter. The 155 mm. howitzer had a range of over nine miles (16,000 yards); a longer-range gun, called the "Long Tom," could fire the same shell over 14.5 miles (25,700 yards).

Panzer grenadier] German motorized infantry. Panzer grenadier divisions, and the panzer grenadier regiments in panzer (armored) divisions, were equipped with sufficient trucks and half-tracks to move the formation's personnel, weapons, and equipment. (Most German infantry divisions relied on horse-drawn transport and artillery, and their men had to march cross-country when rail transport was unavailable.)

P-38] Twin-engine, single-seat U.S. fighter with distinctive twin-boomed airframe. The "Lightning" entered service in late 1942, had a top speed of 395 mph, and was armed with a 20 mm. cannon and four machine guns. P-38s achieved their greatest success in aerial combat against the Japanese, and were also used as photo-reconnaissance and fighter-bomber aircraft.

P-47] Single-engine, single-seat U.S. fighter and fighter-bomber. Introduced into service in 1943, the "Thunderbolt" had a maximum speed of 406 mph (increased to 429 mph in 1944 models) and was armed with eight machine guns. Used as a fighter-bomber, it could carry eight air-to-ground rockets or 2,000 pounds of bombs.

P-51] Single-engine, single-seat U.S. fighter with the range to escort bombers deep into Germany while flying from British bases. The P-51B "Mustang" entered service in late 1943, had a maximum speed of 445 mph, and was armed with six machine guns.

Rifle grenade] Grenade fired from the muzzle of a rifle, using a special attachment and blank propellant cartridge.

S-1, S-2, S-3, S-4] U.S. army terms for staff sections at battalion or regimental level, used to refer to both the section itself and to the staff officer who headed it. See G-1, etc.

S mine] German anti-personnel mine containing over 300 ball bearings packed around an explosive charge, usually connected to a trip wire. When triggered, a propellant charge would lift the mine several feet into the air, where it would then explode.

SS] Schutzstaffel ("Protection Detachment"). Originally Hitler's Nazi party bodyguard, after 1933 the SS became the main instrument of state terror in Germany, with control over the police, the security service, and the concentration camps. The SS also had its own military force, known after 1940 as the Waffen (Armed) SS. Numbering 28,000 men at the start of the war, by 1944 the Waffen SS had over 500,000 men in its ranks and included seven well-equipped panzer (armored) divisions.

75 mm. howitzer] American field artillery gun that could be broken down into sections for easier transport. It fired a 14.6 pound shell 75 mm. in diameter and had a range of over 5.5 miles (9,750 yards).

Sherman tank] American medium tank. About 49,000 Shermans were manufactured between 1942 and 1945, and it became the standard tank used by the western Allies. The Sherman weighed 33 tons, had a five-man crew, a maximum speed of 25 mph, armor ranging in thickness from 25 to 75 mm., and was armed with a 75 mm. gun. While the Sherman proved to be a highly mobile and mechanically reliable tank and had a higher rate of fire and faster turret traverse than German tanks, its frontal armor provided inadequate protection against high-velocity German 75 mm. and 88 mm. armor-piercing shot, while its 75 mm. gun proved incapable of penetrating the frontal armor of the German "Panther" and "Tiger" under almost all combat conditions. In late 1944 a new Sherman model entered service equipped with a high-velocity 76 mm. gun, but many of the earlier models remained in service until the end of the war in Europe.

Shoe mine] *Schü* mine (from *Schützenmine*, "rifleman's mine"), German anti-personnel mine with explosive charge of about seven ounces. The explosive was placed inside a wooden box instead of a metal casing to prevent detection by metal mine detectors.

Spandau] Allied name for 7.92 mm. light machine guns used by German infantry.

Tank destroyer] American armored vehicle, built on a tank chassis but with an open turret and thin armor. The M-10 tank destroyer, introduced in 1942, was armed with a high-velocity anti-tank gun that fired 15-pound armor-piercing solid shot 76.2 mm. in diameter. Introduced into service in late 1944, the M-36 tank destroyer was armed with a high-velocity 90 mm. anti-tank gun.

TBF] Single-engine U.S. torpedo bomber that entered carrier service in 1942. The "Avenger" had a crew of three, a top speed of 257 mph, and was armed with up to five machine guns. It could carry either one torpedo or 2,000 pounds of bombs; some aircraft were equipped to fire air-to-ground rockets.

TD] Tank destroyer.

Teller mine] German anti-tank mine containing 9 to 12 pounds of high explosives.

Thompson submachine gun] American submachine gun. It fired a .45 caliber bullet, had a 20-round magazine, an effective range of 100 yards, and weighed 12 pounds.

Thunderbolt] See P-47.

Tiger tank] See Mark VI tank.

Time-fire] Artillery shells fused to explode in the air in order to disperse fragments over a wider area.

Typhoon] Single-engine, single-seat British fighter, used primarily as a fighter-bomber. Introduced into service in 1942, it had a top speed of 395 mph (increased to 412 mph in later models) and was armed with four rapid-firing 20 mm. cannon. It could carry eight air-to-ground rockets or 2,000 pounds of bombs.

T-4] Rank of sergeant in the U.S. army technical services.

T-5] Rank of corporal in the U.S. army technical services.

V-1] Unmanned German jet aircraft used to bombard Britain and Belgium in 1944-45. The V-1 (*Vergeltungswaffe*, "reprisal weapon") was guided by a gyroscope, had a speed of 350 mph, and carried 1,870 pounds of explosive in its warhead. About 40 per cent of the V-1s launched were destroyed by Allied fighters or anti-aircraft fire. (The V-2, also used by the Germans in 1944-45, was a liquid-fueled ballistic missile with a 2,000 pound warhead. It traveled at supersonic speeds and could not be intercepted.)

Wehrmacht] Name for the German armed forces, 1935-45.

Zero] Single-engine, single-seat Japanese naval fighter. Highly maneuverable, it had a maximum speed of 316 mph (increased to 336 mph in 1942 models and 358 mph in 1944) and was armed with two 20 mm. cannon and two machine guns.


## U.S. ARMY ORGANIZATION

*Unit and formation strengths given below are those established by the U.S. Army for its infantry in 1943; equivalent units and formations in the U.S. Marines were similar in size.*

Platoon] Unit of about 40 men, commanded by a second lieutenant.

Company] Unit made up of three rifle platoons, one weapons platoon, and other troops, with 193 men at full strength; usually commanded by a captain.

Battalion] Unit made up of three rifle companies, one weapons company, and a headquarters company, with 871 men at full strength; usually commanded by a lieutenant colonel.

Regiment] Formation made up of three battalions plus supporting troops, including artillery. It had 3,118 men at full strength and was commanded by a colonel.

Division] Formation made up of three regiments plus supporting troops, including artillery and combat engineers. It had 14,253 men at full strength and was commanded by a major general. The U.S. Army raised 89 divisions during World War II (67 infantry, 16 armored, five airborne, and one cavalry), and the Marine Corps raised six.

# Index

CATALOGING INFORMATION

Reporting World War II.
     p.   cm. — (The library of America ; 77–78)
   Contents:  1. American journalism, 1938–1944 — 2. American
journalism, 1944–1946.
  1. Journalism—United States—History—20th century.  2. World
War, 1939–1945—Press coverage—United States.  I. Title: Reporting
World War Two.  II. Title:  Reporting World War 2.  III. Series.

PN4867.R47    1995      94–45463
071'.3—dc20
ISBN 1–883011–05–1 (V. 2)

# THE LIBRARY OF AMERICA SERIES

*This book is set in 10 point Linotron Galliard,*
*a face designed for photocomposition by Matthew Carter*
*and based on the sixteenth-century face Granjon. The paper is*
*acid-free Ecusta Nyalite and meets the requirements for permanence*
*of the American National Standards Institute. The binding*
*material is Brillianta, a woven rayon cloth made by*
*Van Heek-Scholco Textielfabrieken, Holland.*
*The composition is by The Clarinda*
*Company. Printing and binding by*
*R. R. Donnelley & Sons Company.*
*Designed by Bruce Campbell.*